T0418290

# MILESTONE DOCUMENTS
## OF THE SUPREME COURT

Exploring the Cases
That Shaped America

# MILESTONE DOCUMENTS OF THE SUPREME COURT

Exploring the Cases
That Shaped America

Volume 1: 1803–1908

Paul Finkelman

Editor in Chief

Schlager

Dallas, Texas

**Milestone Documents of the Supreme Court: Exploring the Cases That Shaped America**

Schlager Group Inc.

10228 E. Northwest HWY, STE 1151
Dallas, TX 75238
USA
(888) 416-5727
info@schlagergroup.com


You can find Schlager Group online at https://www.schlagergroup.com

For Schlager Group:
Vice President, Editorial: Sarah Robertson
Vice President, Operations and Strategy: Benjamin Painter
Founder and President: Neil Schlager


Printed in the United States of America 10 9 8 7 6 5 4 3 2 1
Print ISBN: 9781935306863
eBook: 9781935306870

Library of Congress Control Number: 2023934505

# CONTENTS

## Volume 3: 1972–2022

# READER'S GUIDE

## Overview

*Milestone Documents of the Supreme Court* covers both iconic and controversial decisions from the early republic to the present day. From early decisions that outlined the roles and powers of the three branches of government to contemporary cases about LGBTQ rights and reproductive rights, this set pairs each Court decision with in-depth commentary and analysis by a team of legal scholars and historians. The set includes 81 cases.

## Organization

The set is organized chronologically in three volumes:

- Volume 1: 1803–1908
- Volume 2: 1915–1971
- Volume 3: 1972–2022

Within each volume, entries likewise are arranged chronologically by year.

## Entry Format

Each entry in Milestone Documents of the Supreme Court follows the same structure using the same standardized headings. The entries are divided into three main sections: Fact Box, Commentary and Analysis, and Document Text. Following is the full list of entry headings:

- The **Fact Box** includes the basic facts of the case: the year it was delivered, the author of the majority opinion (and in some cases, concurrences and/or dissents), the vote, the formal citation, and a statement summarizing the significance of the case.
- **Overview** gives a brief summary of the document and its importance in history.
- **Context** places the document in its historical framework.
- **About the Author** presents a brief biographical profile of the person or persons who wrote the opinion(s) in the case.
- **Explanation and Analysis of the Document** consists of a detailed examination of the Court's opinion, generally in section-by-section or paragraph-by-paragraph format.
- **Questions for Further Study** proposes study questions for students.
- **Further Reading** lists books, articles, and websites for further research.
- **Document Text** includes the full or abridged text of the majority opinion and, in some cases, important concurrences and/or dissents. Abridgements of the text are indicated by ellipses.
- **Glossary** defines important, difficult, or unusual terms in the document text.

Each entry features the byline of the scholar who wrote the commentary.

## Features

At the end of Volume 3, readers will find a cumulative Index.

## Questions

We welcome questions and comments about the set. Readers may direct any such questions to the following address:

## The Editor

Schlager Group Inc.
10228 E. Northwest HWY
Suite 1151
Dallas, TX 75238
info@schlagergroup.com

# CONTRIBUTORS

## Editor in Chief

Paul Finkelman
Robert E. and Susan T. Rydell Visiting Professor, Gustavus Adolphus College, and the President William McKinley Distinguished Professor, Emeritus at Albany Law School

## Contributors

David Gray Adler
Alturas Institute

Richard L. Aynes
University of Akron

W. Lewis Burke
University of South Carolina School of Law

Michael Martin Carver
Bowling Green State University

Henry L. Chambers, Jr.
University of Richmond School of Law

Michael Chang
University of California – Berkeley

Stephen Clark
Albany Law School

Thomas H. Cox
Sam Houston State University

Leigh Dyer
Independent Scholar

Ryan Fontanella
St. Philip's College

Raymond Pierre Hylton
Virginia Union University

Tom Lansford
University of Southern Mississippi

Karen Linkletter
Management as a Liberal Art Research Institute

Bryant Macfarlane
Kansas State University

Scott A. Merriman
Troy University

Michael J. O'Neal
Independent Scholar

Alicia R. Ouellette
Albany Law School

Lisa Paddock
Independent Scholar

Jonathan Rees
Colorado State University—Pueblo

Anthony Santoro
Sogang University

Kenneth R. Shepherd
Henry Ford College

David Simonelli
Youngstown State University

Brooks D. Simpson
Arizona State University

Randy Wagner
Independent Scholar

Peter Wallenstein
Virginia Tech University

R. Owen Williams
Independent Scholar

Charles L. Zelden
Nova Southeastern University

# INTRODUCTION

At the beginning of the American Revolution, Thomas Paine wrote what might be the most important book in American history, *Common Sense.* In it he explained in common language, and with great insight, why law is central to American culture: "Let a day be solemnly set apart for proclaiming the Charter; let it be brought forth placed on the Divine Law, the Word of God; let a crown be placed thereon, by which the World may know, that so far as we approve of monarchy, that in America THE LAW IS KING. For as in absolute governments the King is Law, so in free Countries the law ought to be king; and there ought to be no other."

A half-century later, in *Democracy in America,* his classic book observing American society and culture, the French scholar Alexis de Tocqueville observed: "In America there are no nobles or literary men, and the people are apt to mistrust the wealthy; lawyers consequently form the highest political class and the most cultivated portion of society. . . . If I were asked where I place the American aristocracy, I should reply without hesitation that it is not among the rich, who are united by no common tie, but that it occupies the judicial bench and bar." He concluded that "The courts of justice are the only possible medium between the central power and the administrative bodies; they alone can compel the elected functionary to obey, without violating the rights of the elector." Because of the nature of the Constitution, de Tocqueville observed, "Few laws can escape the searching analysis of the judicial power for any length of time, for there are few which are not prejudicial to some private interest or other." But he thought this was central to the success of the nation, concluding: "The peace, the prosperity, and the very existence of the Union are vested in the hands of the seven judges (which was then the size of the Supreme Court). Without their active co-operation the Constitution would be a dead letter: . . . Their power is enormous, but it is clothed in the authority of public opinion. They are the all-powerful guardians of a people which respects law, but they would be impotent against popular neglect or popular contempt."

Indeed, it seems that sooner or later almost every major political, social, and economic issue in the United States ends up at the doorstep of the Supreme Court. That Court cannot always solve these issues—for example, the Court's attempt to settle the national debate over slavery led to the disastrous decision in *Dred Scott v. Sandford* (1857), which settled nothing and indirectly, at least, helped push the nation closer to civil war. Sometimes the Court simply gets it wrong, and individuals or whole communities suffer. In *Frank v. Mangum* (1915), for example, the Court refused to require that a state give a criminal defendant a fair trial, In the end the defendant, Leo Frank (who was clearly innocent of any crime), was sentenced to life in prison but then lynched by a carefully planned attack on the state penitentiary. A different decision might have led to his being freed before this could happen. On the other hand, sometimes the Court has been able to cut through social conflict to solve something the political institutions were incapable of dealing with. In *Brown v. Board of Education* (1954) the Court unanimously concluded that segregation in schools was unconstitutional. Thirteen years later the Court asserted, in *Loving v. Virginia* (1967), that state prohibitions on interracial marriage were also unconstitutional. It would be hard to find any responsible public officials or citizens who would reverse these outcomes, and in the end, many of the strongest supporters of racial segregation came to praise these decisions for cutting the gordian knot of legalized racism in the American South.

Similarly, in *Baker v. Carr* (1962), the Court required states to have legislative districts that were as close as possible to being equal in size. At the time many states had districts that were mockeries of democracy. For example, in Vermont one legislative district had only 238 people, while another had about 33,000 people. California had one state senate district with about six million people in it, while another district had about 14,000 people. But the existing state legislatures would never have redistricted on their own, because some legislators would have lost their seats, and overrepresented rural districts would have lost power to cities and suburbs with greater populations. Chief Justice Earl Warren considered this to be the most important decision of his career, because it made America more democratic and made fair representation a reality. Today almost all state legislative districts are nearly identical in size, making all votes in the state "equal."

The Court issued its very first opinion on August 3, 1791. *West v. Barnes* was a relatively insignificant dispute over land between citizens of Massachusetts and Rhode Island. Since then, the Supreme Court has decided thousands of cases and also declined to hear even more cases. Most are not major cases, although they were usually important to the parties. In these volumes we have chosen the most iconic, important cases in the Court's history. They cover the development of American political institutions; issues of slavery, race, and the rights of minorities; the fundamental liberties of the American people; and political disputes between states, between states and the national government, and disagreements between one branch of the government and another. There are cases on freedom of religion, freedom of speech and the press, and the struggle to provide fair trials for accused criminals. The cases here show the slow movement in America for legal and social equality for women, African Americans, Asian Americans, Hispanic Americans, and other minorities. The rights of people to live their private lives, in private, has been before the Court on such issues as birth control, pregnancy, marriage, and private relationships between adults. There are big cases involving national leaders, from Secretary of State James Madison to Presidents Richard M. Nixon, Bill Clinton, and George W. Bush.

Could there be other cases in this set? Surely there could be others. As the Editor in Chief, I had to make tough and painful decisions of what *not* to include. But I believe that these cases provide a powerful lesson in American constitutional law and constitutionalism. They demonstrate how Americans have turned to the courts for personal justice, economic opportunity, access to the political process, and protection of minorities and those who are without political power. Today many of the decisions in the cases appear abhorrent. They have been overturned by the court of history, by constitutional amendments, state and federal laws, and subsequent Supreme Court decisions. Readers will notice that in many cases, we've chosen to include dissents along with the majority opinion in a case. Very often, the dissents are more important than the opinion of the Court, because the dissents have pointed to the future, and for more fair justice and law.

—Paul Finkelman, Robert E. and Susan T. Rydell Visiting Professor, Gustavus Adolphus College, and the President William McKinley Distinguished Professor, Emeritus at Albany Law School

# MILESTONE DOCUMENTS OF THE SUPREME COURT

Exploring the Cases
That Shaped America

# MARBURY V. MADISON

| | |
|---|---|
| **DATE**<br>1803 | **CITATION**<br>5 U.S. 137 |
| **AUTHOR**<br>John Marshall | **SIGNIFICANCE**<br>Declared an act of Congress unconstitutional, fully empowering the third branch of government and establishing the principle of judicial review |
| **VOTE**<br>4-0 | |

## Overview

*Marbury v. Madison* was the first significant decision handed down by the U.S. Supreme Court after John Marshall was sworn in as its chief justice in 1801. In *Marbury*, for the first time, the Supreme Court declared an act of Congress unconstitutional; it would not do so again until *Dred Scott v. Sandford* struck down the Missouri Compromise in 1857. *Marbury* was not the Court's first exercise of judicial review—the power to determine the constitutionality of legislative and administrative acts—but by declaring the Court the final arbiter of constitutional questions, this seminal decision fully empowered the third branch of government, making the concept of federal checks and balances a reality.

Chief Justice William Rehnquist once described *Marbury* as "the most famous case ever decided by the United States Supreme Court." It is not surprising that the late chief justice, who headed one of the most activist Courts in the nation's history—one that overturned a notably high number of federal statutes—should hold *Marbury* in such high regard. But Rehnquist is hardly alone in his admiration for this decision, which governments around the world consider a blueprint for drafting constitutions and formatting the role of judicial systems. With *Marbury*, the judiciary became something more than an institution—it became political.

## Context

The significance of *Marbury*—like that of its author, Marshall—is bound up with that of Marshall's second cousin and primary rival, Thomas Jefferson. By the time of the fourth presidential election in 1800, the previously dominant Federalist Party, of which Marshall was a leading member, was in disarray. The High Federalists, a party fraction dominated by Alexander Hamilton, actively undermined the reelection of John Adams, their party's nominee. The Republicans nominated Thomas Jefferson and Aaron Burr, and they won the election handily, garnering seventy-three electoral votes to the Federalists' sixty-five.

Naming the next president, however, proved far more difficult. Electoral rules of the day dictated that the runner-up be declared vice president, irrespective of party affiliation. Republican solidarity resulted in a tie between Jefferson and Burr, and by constitutional

**Marshall's famous line inscribed on the wall of the U.S. Supreme Court Building**
(Wikimedia Commons)

fiat the election was thrown into the House of Representatives. The House—dominated by Federalists—supported Burr, believing him to be more malleable than Jefferson, an impression that Burr encouraged. Nonetheless, Jefferson was declared the winner after the thirty-sixth ballot and took the presidential oath of office one month after Marshall was sworn in as chief justice.

In the final days of the Adams administration, the Federalists, attempting to pack the federal judiciary with party loyalists, passed two laws: the 1801 Judiciary Act, which the Republicans later repealed, and a law creating a number of justice of the peace positions in the District of Columbia. Adams made his appointments to these positions on March 2, 1801, two days before Jefferson's inauguration, and the appointees were confirmed the following day. Some of the appointees' commissions, however, were not delivered before midnight of March 3, when the Jefferson administration took over, and Jefferson ordered these commissions held back. One of the affected appointees was William

Marbury, who then petitioned the Supreme Court for a writ of mandamus requiring the secretary of state, James Madison, to surrender his commission.

## About the Author

Born on the northwestern frontier of Virginia, John Marshall was the eldest of fifteen children. Marshall's formal education lasted only two years. His education came mainly from his father, who not only schooled his son in *Blackstone's Commentaries on the Laws of England* but also introduced him to politics. The senior Marshall, who served in the Virginia House of Burgesses, also acted as George Washington's assistant surveyor. Father and son enlisted together after war broke out between England and its American colonies in 1776. Serving first with the Culpepper Minute Men and then in the Continental Army, John Marshall was with George Washington at Valley Forge during the long, cold winter of 1777 to 1778. This experience of watching his fellow soldiers freeze owing to congressional impotence and inaction ostensibly fostered Marshall's lifelong commitment to a strong central government.

After the war, Marshall attended law lectures at the College of William and Mary in Williamsburg before being admitted to the bar. He set up his law practice in Richmond, where he devoted his time to defending Virginia debtors attempting to avoid prewar obligations to British debtors, eventually arguing one such case—*Ware v. Hylton* (1796)—before the U.S. Supreme Court. This was his only appearance before the Court as an attorney. Marshall became involved in state and local politics, serving several terms in the Virginia House of Delegates. Marshall's passionate advocacy for a federal constitution at the Virginia ratifying conventional led Washington to offer him a commission as the first United States attorney for the District of Columbia. Marshall declined this offer, as he did offers to serve as minister to France and associate justice of the U.S. Supreme Court.

Marshall's reasons for refusing such honors seem to have been primarily financial. Marshall, who was married and had ten children to support, was deeply in debt owing to land speculation. Financial considerations also weighed heavily in his decision to accept a commission to write the five volumes of *The Life of George Washington*, which appeared between 1805 and 1807. In the interim he did accept a government appointment as special envoy to France, a job that promised significant financial rewards. His mission was aborted by the infamous XYZ Affair, during which the French demanded a bribe as a condition to negotiating an end to naval hostilities with the United States. But Marshall's services, including a published response to the blackmailers, earned him $20,000 and public acclaim. Shortly afterward, at Washington's urging Marshall ran for and won a seat in the U.S. House of Representatives, where he successfully defended the Adams administration from Republican attacks. In 1800 the grateful president made Marshall his secretary of state. During the final days of the Adams administration, Marshall served both in this capacity and as chief justice of the Supreme Court.

Thus Marshall began his tenure on the Court under a cloud—one that darkened a month later when his arch antagonist Jefferson took office, making Marshall the first justice to serve under a president from the opposing political party. For Jefferson and his followers, the chief justice was himself one of the spurious "midnight judges." It was not long, however, before Marshall established his authority—as well as the Court's authority—by writing the majority opinion in *Marbury*. Any justice in Marshall's position today would be obliged to recuse him-or herself because of a potential conflict of interest, but Marshall, exercising his considerable powers of logic and diplomacy, managed to craft a decision that at once made the Supreme Court the ultimate arbiter of the constitutionality of legislation and launched his career as the "Great Chief Justice."

Marshall dominated the Court as no other chief justice has. His forceful but engaging personality helped him unite his brother justices, and his enormous capacity for work consolidated his power by allowing him to write the majority of his Court's opinions. Later, as Republicans came to outnumber Federalists on the high bench, Marshall still managed to make most Court decisions unanimous. In *McCulloch v. Maryland* (1819), the case that best illustrates the power of judicial review, the Court unanimously upheld Congress's right to charter a national bank, despite the Republican claim that the Constitution did not grant Congress this right and that the Tenth Amendment reserved all unenumerated powers for the states. Ever the Federalist, Marshall famously countered this argument by saying, "We must never forget that it is a *constitution* we are expounding . . . intended to endure for ages to come, and consequently, to be adapted to the various *crises* of human affairs" (McCulloch v. Maryland, http://www.landmarkcases.org/mcculloch/home.html).

During the final decade of Marshall's tenure, the Court—like the nation as a whole—confronted the steadily increasing power of the states' rights movement. The movement, long championed by Jeffersonian Republicans, reached a kind of apogee under the newly formed Democratic-Republican Party and its standard-bearer Andrew Jackson. Marshall suffered his first significant defeat when the seventh president of the United States refused to honor the chief justice's opinion for the Court in *Worcester v. Georgia* (1832), upholding the sovereignty of the Cherokee Nation: Jackson is reported to have greeted news of *Worcester* by saying, "Well, John Marshall has made his decision; now let him enforce it" (Breyer, http://www.supremecourtus.gov/publicinfo/speeches/sp_05-23-03.html). Having spent three decades enhancing the power of the Court, Marshall seems to have met his match. He hoped to outlast Jackson, believing that Jackson's successor might return some balance to the Court, but Marshall did not succeed. On July 6, 1835, grieving his wife's death and suffering from a liver ailment, he succumbed to injuries incurred in a stage coach accident and became the first chief justice to die while still on the bench.

## Explanation and Analysis of the Document

Marshall's opinion for the Court opens with a brief recital of the legal history of the case. During its previous term, the Court had handed down a ruling requiring Secretary of State James Madison to "show cause" or offer evidence as to why the Court should not issue a writ of mandamus compelling him to deliver the commission making William Marbury a justice of the peace for the District of Columbia. Because Madison had failed to produce such evidence, Marbury made a motion for the Court to issue a writ forcing Madison's hand. Because of what Marshall calls "the peculiar delicacy" and "novelty" of the facts surrounding Marbury's case as well as the "real difficulty" of the legal issues they present, the Court is obliged to consider the following issues: Does Marbury have a right to the commission he demands to receive? If Marbury is entitled to his commission, and if his right to receive it has been violated, do the laws of the United States provide him with a legal remedy? If such a remedy exists in law, is the correct method of achieving its execution a writ of mandamus issued by the Supreme Court?

Marshall then considers each issue in turn. First, he declares that once the president has signed a federal commission, an appointment has been made, and the commission becomes "complete" when the secretary of state fixes the paper memorializing the commission with the seal of the United States. Because both these preconditions have been met, withholding the commission from its intended recipient (Marbury) constitutes a violation of a right legally conferred upon him. Marshall next considers the second issue, declaring that the "very essence of civil liberty" is the right of everyone to be protected from harm by the laws of the land. Marshall then cites as support for this proposition a truism that dates from the foundation of the republic—the United States is a government of laws, not men. That is, the law applies equally to every citizen of this country, regardless of who he or she is and regardless of his or her station in life. A republic, unlike a monarchy, exists only because its inhabitants have consented to be governed by representatives they themselves select. By such reasoning, Marshall underscores the significance of Marbury's case, making his right to his commission representative of the rights of all Americans to be treated equally under the law.

Marshall next parses the law as it applies to the facts of Marbury's case. Marbury's commission as a justice of the peace is a product of the constitutional grant of certain discretionary powers to the president, who is permitted to appoint individuals to help him perform his constitutionally mandated duties. These officers, who act on his order and who carry the weight of his authority, are of his own choosing; in selecting them the president is answerable to the people only in political terms (for example, during elections) and to his own conscience. Offices such as the one Marbury claims as his own are decidedly political appointments, and those who occupy them do so at the behest of the president. They are not elected and therefore are accountable to the people only indirectly through the leader they have chosen.

Marshall's next rhetorical tack is almost a sleight of hand: He compares political appointees chosen by the president and acting as the president's surrogates ("their acts are his acts") with government officials acting at the behest of the legislature. We are meant to understand that the first is William Marbury, while the second is the other party to this case, James Madison. The problem with this analysis is that, as secretary of state, Madison arguably occupies the same space Marbury occupies as a presidential political appointee. Marshall does not let such niceties stand in his way. When a government officer is charged with carrying out acts that the rights of others depend on, such an officer is acting under cover of law and, Marshall claims, is, therefore, answerable to the law, not just to the president. This logic extends, the chief justice says, even to "political or confidential agents of the executive" when they are charged—by law—with fulfilling responsibilities that the rights of others depend on. Because Marbury was legally entitled to his commission, he was deprived of his rights when Madison refused to deliver it. Therefore, Marshall asserts, William Marbury has a legal right to receive something that properly belongs to him.

So far, his decision is good. Marshall, however, has painted himself into a corner. If Marbury, the plaintiff in this case, has a legal right to his commission, then the implication is that the defendant, Madison, can be legally obligated to deliver it. We are now swimming in murky waters, for Madison unquestionably is himself a political appointee acting on behalf of the president. How can the judiciary constitutionally force the administrative branch to carry out what is at bottom a political act? To answer this unstated question, Marshall next considers two things: (1) the power of the Supreme Court and (2) the nature of the writ for which Marbury has applied.

Marshall handily dismisses the question of Marbury's chosen instrument: The case for a writ of mandamus is "plain." The other question, however, goes to the heart of the matter and is far more complex. Marshall proceeds cautiously. The judiciary is granted original jurisdiction in cases involving federal officials by law—specifically, by section 13 of the Judiciary Act of 1789—and is given the right to issue writs of mandamus against such officials. Because a writ of mandamus is the appropriate vehicle for carrying out the law in this case, if the Court cannot issue such a writ under the present circumstances, the only logical conclusion is that the empowering legislation is unconstitutional. But Marshall says wait: The Constitution vests the whole judicial power in one Supreme Court and in lower courts created by Congress. Because this power carries with it the responsibility to adjudicate all cases arising under the laws of the United States, the Court clearly has jurisdiction over the current case. The Constitution also grants the Court original jurisdiction "in all cases affecting ambassadors, other public ministers and consuls, and those in which a state shall be a party. In all other cases, the supreme court shall have appellate jurisdiction." But in directly accepting Marbury's case rather than referring it to a lower court, the Supreme Court is exercising original jurisdiction.

Madison's attorneys argued that the constitutional grant of original jurisdiction is too general and unspecific to be taken literally. They argued that the framers of the Constitution intended Congress to be responsible for assigning original jurisdiction in cases involving parties others than those spelled out in Article III. Marshall counters that this argument is a tautology; if the framers intended for Congress to assign original jurisdiction to one federal court or another, most of the language creating the Court is unnecessary. Looked at

this way, the constitutional distribution of jurisdiction is "form without substance." Next, Marshall plays his trump card: "It cannot be presumed that any clause in the constitution is intended to be without effect; and therefore such construction is inadmissible, unless the words require it." If Madison's argument carries the day, it renders parts of the nation's foundation document meaningless. Plainly, such a proposition is untenable—and besides, this interpretation goes against the plain meaning of the words in the document.

Article III of the Constitution organizes the judiciary into one Supreme Court and as many lower courts as the legislature deems necessary. It goes on to enumerate the respective powers of these two types of courts, specifying which types of cases can come before the Supreme Court directly and stating that in all other cases the Court will have appellate jurisdiction or the power to review decisions of lower courts. If the Supreme Court were to issue a writ of mandamus, either it would be exercising its original jurisdiction, or such an action would be necessary to the exercise of its appellate jurisdiction. A mandamus can be issued to a lower court, but if the Supreme Court did so in this instance, ordering Madison, a political officer, to deliver Marbury's commission, it would be exercising original jurisdiction. Because section 13 the Judiciary Act of 1789 authorizes the Court to perform this act, Marshall is obliged to conclude that at least this aspect of the legislation establishing the U.S. court system is unconstitutional.

The Court is left with the question of whether it can actually exercise jurisdiction in the case before it, given that the grant of such jurisdiction is constitutionally suspect. Marshall rather blithely dismisses this issue: "The question, whether an act, repugnant to the constitution, can become the law of the land, is a question deeply interesting to the United States; but, happily, not of an intricacy proportioned to its interest." Arguably, he is within his rights in doing so. Marbury brought his case under section 13 of the 1789 Judiciary Act, invoking the Court's original jurisdiction. If the Court is unable, in this case, to exercise original jurisdiction, it need not decide Marbury's case on its merits. Instead, as the chief justice asserts, "It seems only necessary to recognise certain principles, supposed to have been long and well established, to decide it."

Citing the right of a people to formulate rules it proposes to live by, Marshall endorses the supremacy of the Constitution, which, he says, should be a singular endeavor. In the United States the foundation document both sets up discrete branches of government and spells out limitations on each of them. Restrictions the framers of the Constitution placed on the legislature, for example, were not intended to be flexible. If they were, the very idea that informs our country would be negated: "The distinction between a government with limited and unlimited powers is abolished, if those limits do not confine the persons on whom they are imposed, and if acts prohibited and acts allowed are of equal obligation." Marshall follows this observation with a statement that goes to the heart of the larger issues at stake in *Marbury*: "It is a proposition too plain to be contested, that the constitution controls any legislative act repugnant to it; or, that the legislature may alter the constitution by an ordinary act." Either the Constitution is paramount, superior law inhospitable to amendment, or it is on a par with ordinary legislation and changeable at will. Governments with written constitutions must assume the former and, as a result, must also declare laws at odds with their constitutions null and void.

But is a court bound to follow a law even if it is unconstitutional? This question provokes Marshall to issue one of the most resonant statements in Supreme Court history: "It is emphatically the province and duty of the judicial department to say what the law is." Thus the concept of judicial review was elevated to the status of law. The Supreme Court, since its earliest days, had been working toward this idea, which is rooted in English common law but only implicit in the U.S. Constitution. For Marshall, judicial review was a matter of first principles as well as common sense. If a rule is applied to a given case, it is the judiciary's job to interpret that rule. If two laws conflict, it is up to the judiciary to decide the proper operation of each. And if a law appears to be at odds with the Constitution, as in the present case, only a court can decide which law governs. "This is of the very essence of judicial duty."

Marshall states that those who argue that ordinary legislation trumps the Constitution undermine the very foundation of all written constitutions. With rising Federalist feeling, he declares that to do so gives the legislature license to do what is expressly forbidden by the Constitution and lends it the kind of power and omnipotence the Constitution was designed to proscribe. Because in America written constitutions are so revered, bowing to the changeable dictates of legislation

would not be brooked. But while Marshall takes away from the legislative branch with one hand, he gives to the judiciary with the other. The Constitution extends the right to decide all cases arising under it to the judicial branch. He asks rhetorically whether it was the intention of the framers that, in deciding such cases, the judiciary should interpret the Constitution—the very document that grants this branch its power. He flatly answers, "This is too extravagant to be maintained," and then he provides a number of examples to illustrate the absurdity of rulings made in the absence of judicial examination of constitutional precepts. As evidence of the judiciary's significance to the constitutional scheme of governance, Marshall also cites a number of passages seemingly addressed specifically to the courts such as "No person . . . shall be convicted of treason unless on the testimony of two witnesses to the same overt act, or on confession in open court." Evidence like this, he says, proves that the framers intended the Constitution to be as binding on the judicial branch as it is upon the legislature and other "departments."

Marshall concludes the opinion of the Court with what seems almost an afterthought: "The rule must be discharged." In the end, William Marbury's petition was rejected, but not on the ground that the judiciary had no power over the executive branch, which had occasioned the case by refusing to deliver Marbury's commission. Instead of ceding power to the presidency by simply dismissing Marbury's application, or trampling on the executive branch by demanding that Madison deliver the plaintiff's commission, Marshall skillfully expanded the authority of the judiciary, making it a truly coequal branch of the governing structure. The federal government may be based on a system of checks and balances, but after *Marbury*, the Court would always control the scales of justice.

## Impact

Although the doctrine of judicial review was always a part of the American legal tradition, *Marbury* placed it squarely at the heart of U.S. governance. Had Marshall not challenged the authority of the legislative branch with such skill, another fifty years might have passed before the Court disputed the constitutionality of a federal statute. After such a long period of judicial inaction, this attempt to overturn legally sanctioned slavery might not have succeeded. In addition to reinforcing judicial independence, Marshall's opinion shored up the principle of separation of powers, which helps maintain America's identity as a nation of laws, not men. There is some indication that Marshall played a role in directing William Marbury's actions in filing his petition with the Supreme Court rather than with a lower court, where his chances of success were clearly better, but Marbury did not lose his suit because of who he was—or even because of his political affiliation.

Chief Justice Marshall never again ruled against the constitutionality of a piece of legislation, and *Marbury* itself was not cited as legal precedent for judicial review until 1887. Another eight years would pass before the case would be employed as a tool for striking down an act of Congress. In the present day, however, judicial review has come into its own as activist Courts overturn laws on a regular basis. On the other hand, the precedent Marshall set in *Marbury* of protecting the Court by avoiding a confrontation with Jefferson has been revisited on numerous occasions, with the Court deferring to executive authority, especially in time of war or other national emergency. Lacking either an army or the power to impose taxes, the Court is left with a mere concept as a means of enforcing its decisions—but without *Marbury v. Madison*, it would not have even that much.

## Questions for Further Study

1. Given that judicial review grants the right to say what the law is to unelected judges, can this principle ever be reconciled with democratic ideals?

2. How can judicial review be considered central to constitutional interpretation when our founding document does not even acknowledge the concept?

3. Why do you think the Supreme Court has resorted to judicial review so frequently in modern times?v

## Further Reading

### *Books*

Brookhiser, Richard. *John Marshall: The Man Who Made the Supreme Court.* New York: Basic Books, 2018.

Kahn, Paul W. *The Reign of Law: Marbury v. Madison and the Construction of America*, new ed. New Haven: Yale University Press, 2002.

Nelson, William E. *Marbury v. Madison: The Origins and Legacy of Judicial Review*, 2nd ed. Lawrence: University Press of Kansas, 2018.

Paddock, Lisa. *Facts about the Supreme Court of the United States.* New York: H. W. Wilson, 1996.

Paul, Joel Richard. *Without Precedent: Chief Justice John Marshall and His Times.* New York: Riverhead Books, 2018.

Schwartz, Bernard. *A History of the Supreme Court.* New York: Oxford University Press, 1993.

Tushnet, Mark, ed. *Arguing Marbury v. Madison.* Palo Alto, CA: Stanford University Press, 2005.

Warren, Charles. *The Supreme Court in United States History.* 3 vols. Boston: Little, Brown, 1924.

**<u>Further Reading</u>**

**<u>*Articles*</u>**

Bamzai, Aditya. "*Marbury v. Madison* and the Concept of Judicial Deference." *Missouri Law Review* 81, no. 4 (Fall 2016): 1057–73.

Bartels, Brandon L., and Christopher D. Johnston. "On the Ideological Foundations of Supreme Court Legitimacy in the American Public." *American Journal of Political Science* 57, no. 1 (January 2013): 184–99.

**<u>*Websites*</u>**

Breyer, Stephen. "Boston College Law School Commencement Remarks, May 23, 2003." Supreme Court of the United States website. http://www.supremecourtus.gov/publicinfo/speeches/sp_05-23-03.html.

"*Marbury v. Madison* (1803)." Landmark Supreme Court Cases website. http://www.landmarkcases.org/marbury/home.html.

"*McCulloch v. Maryland* (1819)." Landmark Supreme Court Cases website. http://www.landmarkcases.org/mcculloch/home.html.

Rehnquist, William H. "Remarks of the Chief Justice William H. Rehnquist: Federal Judges Association, May 8, 2001." Supreme Court of the United States website. http://www.supremecourtus.gov/publicinfo/speeches/sp_05-08-01.html.

—Commentary by Lisa Paddock

# MARBURY V. MADISON

## Document Text

AT the December term 1801, William Marbury, Dennis Ramsay, Robert Townsend Hooe, and William Harper, by their counsel severally moved the court for a rule to James Madison, secretary of state of the United States, to show cause why a mandamus should not issue commanding him to cause to be delivered to them respectively their several commissions as justices of the peace in the district of Columbia.

This motion was supported by affidavits of the following facts: that notice of this motion had been given to Mr. Madison; that Mr. Adams, the late president of the United States, nominated the applicants to the senate for their advice and consent to be appointed justices of the peace of the district of Columbia; that the senate advised and consented to the appointments; that commissions in due form were signed by the said president appointing them justices, &c. and that the seal of the United States was in due form affixed to the said commissions by the secretary of state; that the applicants have requested Mr. Madison to deliver them their said commissions, who has not complied with that request; and that their said commissions are withheld from them; that the applicants have made application to Mr. Madison as secretary of state of the United States at his office, for information whether the commissions were signed and sealed as aforesaid; that explicit and satisfactory information has not been given in answer to that inquiry, either by the secretary of state, or any officer in the department of state; that application has been made to the secretary of the senate for a certificate of the nomination of the applicants, and of the advice

and consent of the senate, who has declined giving such a certificate; whereupon a rule was made to show cause on the fourth day of this term. This rule having been duly served—Mr. Jacob Wagner and Mr. Daniel Brent, who had been summoned to attend the court, and were required to give evidence, objected to be sworn, alleging that they were clerks in the department of state, and not bound to disclose any facts relating to the business or transactions of the office.

The court ordered the witnesses to be sworn, and their answers taken in writing; but informed them that when the questions were asked they might state their objections to answering each particular question, if they had any.

Mr. Lincoln, who had been the acting secretary of state, when the circumstances stated in the affidavits occurred, was called upon to give testimony. He objected to answering. The questions were put in writing.

The court said there was nothing confidential required to be disclosed. If there had been, he was not obliged to answer it, and if he thought any thing was communicated to him confidentially he was not bound to disclose, nor was he obliged to state any thing which would criminate himself.

The questions argued by the counsel for the relators were, 1. Whether the supreme court can award the writ of mandamus in any case. 2. Whether it will lie to a secretary of state, in any case whatever. 3. Whether in the present case the court may award a mandamus to James Madison, secretary of state.

## Mr. Chief Justice MARSHALL delivered the opinion of the Court

At the last term, on the affidavits then read and filed with the clerk, a rule was granted in this case, requiring the secretary of state to show cause why a mandamus should not issue, directing him to deliver to William Marbury his commission as a justice of the peace for the county of Washington, in the district of Columbia.

No cause has been shown, and the present motion is for a mandamus. The peculiar delicacy of this case, the novelty of some of its circumstances, and the real difficulty attending the points which occur in it, require a complete exposition of the principles on which the opinion to be given by the court is founded.

These principles have been, on the side of the applicant, very ably argued at the bar. In rendering the opinion of the court, there will be some departure in form, though not in substance, from the points stated in that argument.

In the order in which the court has viewed this subject, the following questions have been considered and decided.

1. Has the applicant a right to the commission he demands?

2. If he has a right, and that right has been violated, do the laws of his country afford him a remedy?

3. If they do afford him a remedy, is it a mandamus issuing from this court?

The first object of inquiry is,

1. Has the applicant a right to the commission he demands?

His right originates in an act of congress passed in February 1801, concerning the district of Columbia.

After dividing the district into two counties, the eleventh section of this law enacts, "that there shall be appointed in and for each of the said counties, such number of discreet persons to be justices of the peace as the president of the United States shall, from time to time, think expedient, to continue in office for five years." It appears from the affidavits, that in compliance with this law, a commission for William Marbury as a justice of peace for the county of Washington was signed by John Adams, then president of the United States; after which the seal of the United States was affixed to it; but the commission has never reached the person for whom it was made out.

In order to determine whether he is entitled to this commission, it becomes necessary to inquire whether he has been appointed to the office. For if he has been appointed, the law continues him in office for five years, and he is entitled to the possession of those evidences of office, which, being completed, became his property.

The second section of the second article of the constitution declares, "the president shall nominate, and, by and with the advice and consent of the senate, shall appoint ambassadors, other public ministers and consuls, and all other officers of the United States, whose appointments are not otherwise provided for."

The third section declares, that "he shall commission all the officers of the United States."

An act of congress directs the secretary of state to keep the seal of the United States, "to make out and record, and affix the said seal to all civil commissions to officers of the United States to be appointed by the president, by and with the consent of the senate, or by the president alone; provided that the said seal shall not be affixed to any commission before the same shall have been signed by the president of the United States."

These are the clauses of the constitution and laws of the United States, which affect this part of the case. They seem to contemplate three distinct operations:

1. The nomination. This is the sole act of the president, and is completely voluntary.

2. The appointment. This is also the act of the president, and is also a voluntary act, though it can only be performed by and with the advice and consent of the senate.

3. The commission. To grant a commission to a person appointed, might perhaps be deemed a duty enjoined by the constitution. "He shall," says that instrument, "commission all the officers of the United States."

The acts of appointing to office, and commissioning the person appointed, can scarcely be considered as one and the same; since the power to perform them is given in two separate and distinct sections of the constitution. The distinction between the appointment and the commission will be rendered more apparent by adverting to that provision in the second section of the second article of the constitution, which authorises congress "to vest by law the appointment of such inferior officers as they think proper, in the president alone, in the courts of law, or in the heads of departments;" thus contemplating cases where the law may direct the president to commission an officer appointed by the courts or by the heads of departments. In such a case, to issue a commission would be apparently a duty distinct from the appointment, the performance of which perhaps, could not legally be refused.

Although that clause of the constitution which requires the president to commission all the officers of the United States, may never have been applied to officers appointed otherwise than by himself, yet it would be difficult to deny the legislative power to apply it to such cases. Of consequence the constitutional distinction between the appointment to an office and the commission of an officer who has been appointed, remains the same as if in practice the president had commissioned officers appointed by an authority other than his own.

It follows too, from the existence of this distinction, that, if an appointment was to be evidenced by any public act other than the commission, the performance of such public act would create the officer; and if he was not removable at the will of the president, would either give him a right to his commission, or enable him to perform the duties without it.

These observations are premised solely for the purpose of rendering more intelligible those which apply more directly to the particular case under consideration. This is an appointment made by the president, by and with the advice and consent of the senate, and is evidenced by no act but the commission itself. In such a case therefore the commission and the appointment seem inseparable; it being almost impossible to show an appointment otherwise than by proving the existence of a commission: still the commission is not necessarily the appointment; though conclusive evidence of it.

But at what stage does it amount to this conclusive evidence?

The answer to this question seems an obvious one. The appointment being the sole act of the president, must be completely evidenced, when it is shown that he has done every thing to be performed by him.

Should the commission, instead of being evidence of an appointment, even be considered as constituting the appointment itself; still it would be made when the last act to be done by the president was performed, or, at furthest, when the commission was complete.

The last act to be done by the president, is the signature of the commission. He has then acted on the advice and consent of the senate to his own nomination. The time for deliberation has then passed. He has decided. His judgment, on the advice and consent of the senate concurring with his nomination, has been made, and the officer is appointed. This appointment is evidenced by an open, unequivocal act; and being the last act required from the person making it, necessarily excludes the idea of its being, so far as it respects the appointment, an inchoate and incomplete transaction.

Some point of time must be taken when the power of the executive over an officer, not removable at his will, must cease. That point of time must be when the constitutional power of appointment has been exercised. And this power has been exercised when the last act, required from the person possessing the power, has been performed. This last act is the signature of the commission. This idea seems to have prevailed with the legislature, when the act passed converting the department of foreign affairs into the department of state. By that act it is enacted, that the secretary of state shall keep the seal of the United States, "and shall make out and record, and shall affix the said seal to all civil commissions to officers of the United States, to be appointed by the president:" "provided that the said seal shall not be affixed to any commission, before the same shall have been signed by the president of the United States; nor to any other instrument or act, without the special warrant of the president therefor."

The signature is a warrant for affixing the great seal to the commission; and the great seal is only to be affixed to an instrument which is complete. It attests, by an act supposed to be of public notoriety, the verity of the presidential signature.

It is never to be affixed till the commission is signed, because the signature, which gives force and effect to the commission, is conclusive evidence that the appointment is made.

The commission being signed, the subsequent duty of the secretary of state is prescribed by law, and not to be guided by the will of the president. He is to affix the seal of the United States to the commission, and is to record it.

This is not a proceeding which may be varied, if the judgment of the executive shall suggest one more eligible, but is a precise course accurately marked out by law, and is to be strictly pursued. It is the duty of the secretary of state to conform to the law, and in this he is an officer of the United States, bound to obey the laws. He acts, in this respect, as has been very properly stated at the bar, under the authority of law, and not by the instructions of the president. It is a ministerial act which the law enjoins on a particular officer for a particular purpose.

If it should be supposed, that the solemnity of affixing the seal, is necessary not only to the validity of the commission, but even to the completion of an appointment, still when the seal is affixed the appointment is made, and the commission is valid. No other solemnity is required by law; no other act is to be performed on the part of government. All that the executive can do to invest the person with his office, is done; and unless the appointment be then made, the executive cannot make one without the co-operation of others.

After searching anxiously for the principles on which a contrary opinion may be supported, none have been found which appear of sufficient force to maintain the opposite doctrine.

Such as the imagination of the court could suggest, have been very deliberately examined, and after allowing them all the weight which it appears possible to give them, they do not shake the opinion which has been formed.

In considering this question, it has been conjectured that the commission may have been assimilated to a deed, to the validity of which, delivery is essential.

This idea is founded on the supposition that the commission is not merely evidence of an appointment, but is itself the actual appointment; a supposition by no means unquestionable. But for the purpose of examining this objection fairly, let it be conceded, that the principle, claimed for its support, is established.

The appointment being, under the constitution, to be made by the president personally, the delivery of the deed of appointment, if necessary to its completion, must be made by the president also. It is not necessary that the livery should be made personally to the grantee of the office: it never is so made. The law would seem to contemplate that it should be made to the secretary of state, since it directs the secretary to affix the seal to the commission after it shall have been signed by the president. If then the act of livery be necessary to give validity to the commission, it has been delivered when executed and given to the secretary for the purpose of being sealed, recorded, and transmitted to the party.

But in all cases of letters patent, certain solemnities are required by law, which solemnities are the evidences of the validity of the instrument. A formal delivery to the person is not among them. In cases of commissions, the sign manual of the president, and the seal of the United States, are those solemnities. This objection therefore does not touch the case.

It has also occurred as possible, and barely possible, that the transmission of the commission, and the acceptance thereof, might be deemed necessary to complete the right of the plaintiff.

The transmission of the commission is a practice directed by convenience, but not by law. It cannot therefore be necessary to constitute the appointment which must precede it, and which is the mere act of the president. If the executive required that every person appointed to an office, should himself take means to procure his commission, the appointment would not be the less valid on that account. The appointment is the sole act of the president; the transmission of the commission is the sole act of the officer to whom that duty is assigned, and may be accelerated or retarded by circumstances which can have no influence on the appointment. A commission is transmitted to a person already appointed; not to a person to be appointed or not, as the letter enclosing the commission should happen to get into the post-office and reach him in safety, or to miscarry.

It may have some tendency to elucidate this point, to inquire, whether the possession of the original commission be indispensably necessary to authorize a person, appointed to any office, to perform the duties of that office. If it was necessary, then a loss of the commission would lose the office. Not only negligence, but accident or fraud, fire or theft, might deprive an individual of his office. In such a case, I presume it could not be doubted, but that a copy from the record of the office of the secretary of state, would be, to every intent and purpose, equal to the original. The act of congress has expressly made it so. To give that copy validity, it would not be necessary to prove that the original had been transmitted and afterwards lost. The copy would be complete evidence that the original had existed, and that the appointment had been made, but not that the original had been transmitted. If indeed it should appear that the original had been mislaid in the office of state, that circumstance would not affect the operation of the copy. When all the requisites have been performed which authorize a recording officer to record any instrument whatever, and the order for that purpose has been given, the instrument is in law considered as recorded, although the manual labour of inserting it in a book kept for that purpose may not have been performed.

In the case of commissions, the law orders the secretary of state to record them. When therefore they are signed and sealed, the order for their being recorded is given; and whether inserted in the book or not, they are in law recorded.

A copy of this record is declared equal to the original, and the fees to be paid by a person requiring a copy are ascertained by law. Can a keeper of a public record erase therefrom a commission which has been recorded? Or can he refuse a copy thereof to a person demanding it on the terms prescribed by law?

Such a copy would, equally with the original, authorize the justice of peace to proceed in the performance of his duty, because it would, equally with the original, attest his appointment.

If the transmission of a commission be not considered as necessary to give validity to an appointment; still less is its acceptance. The appointment is the sole act of the president; the acceptance is the sole act of the officer, and is, in plain common sense, posterior to the appointment. As he may resign, so may he refuse to accept: but neither the one nor the other is capable of rendering the appointment a nonentity.

That this is the understanding of the government, is apparent from the whole tenor of its conduct.

A commission bears date, and the salary of the officer commences from his appointment; not from the transmission or acceptance of his commission. When a person, appointed to any office, refuses to accept that office, the successor is nominated in the place of the person who has declined to accept, and not in the place of the person who had been previously in office and had created the original vacancy.

It is therefore decidedly the opinion of the court, that when a commission has been signed by the president, the appointment is made; and that the commission is complete when the seal of the United States has been affixed to it by the secretary of state.

Where an officer is removable at the will of the executive, the circumstance which completes his appointment is of no concern; because the act is at any time revocable; and the commission may be arrested, if still in the office. But when the officer is not removable at the will of the executive, the appointment is not revocable and cannot be annulled. It has conferred legal rights which cannot be resumed.

The discretion of the executive is to be exercised until the appointment has been made. But having once made the appointment, his power over the office is terminated in all cases, where by law the officer is not removable by him. The right to the office is then in the person appointed, and he has the absolute, unconditional power of accepting or rejecting it.

Mr. Marbury, then, since his commission was signed by the president and sealed by the secretary of state, was appointed; and as the law creating the office gave the officer a right to hold for five years independent of the executive, the appointment was not revocable; but vested in the officer legal rights which are protected by the laws of his country.

To withhold the commission, therefore, is an act deemed by the court not warranted by law, but violative of a vested legal right.

This brings us to the second inquiry; which is,

2. If he has a right, and that right has been violated, do the laws of his country afford him a remedy? The very essence of civil liberty certainly consists in the right of every individual to claim the protection of the laws, whenever he receives an injury. One of the first duties of government is to afford that protection. In Great Britain the king himself is sued in the respectful form of a petition, and he never fails to comply with the judgment of his court.

In the third volume of his Commentaries, page 23, Blackstone states two cases in which a remedy is afforded by mere operation of law.

"In all other cases," he says, "it is a general and indisputable rule, that where there is a legal right, there is also a legal remedy by suit or action at law whenever that right is invaded."

And afterwards, page 109 of the same volume, he says, "I am next to consider such injuries as are cognizable by the courts of common law. And herein I shall for the present only remark, that all possible injuries whatsoever, that did not fall within the exclusive cognizance of either the ecclesiastical, military, or maritime tribunals, are, for that very reason, within the cognizance of the common law courts of justice; for it is a settled and invariable principle in the laws of England, that every right, when withheld, must have a remedy, and every injury its proper redress."

The government of the United States has been emphatically termed a government of laws, and not of men. It will certainly cease to deserve this high appellation, if the laws furnish no remedy for the violation of a vested legal right.

If this obloquy is to be cast on the jurisprudence of our country, it must arise from the peculiar character of the case.

It behoves us then to inquire whether there be in its composition any ingredient which shall exempt from legal investigation, or exclude the injured party from legal redress. In pursuing this inquiry the first question which presents itself, is, whether this can be arranged with that class of cases which come under the description of damnum absque injuria—a loss without an injury.

This description of cases never has been considered, and it is believed never can be considered as comprehending offices of trust, of honour or of profit. The office of justice of peace in the district of Columbia is such an office; it is therefore worthy of the attention and guardianship of the laws. It has received that attention and guardianship. It has been created by special act of congress, and has been secured, so far as the laws can give security to the person appointed to fill it, for five years. It is not then on account of the worthlessness of the thing pursued, that the injured party can be alleged to be without remedy.

Is it in the nature of the transaction? Is the act of delivering or withholding a commission to be considered as a mere political act belonging to the executive department alone, for the performance of which entire confidence is placed by our constitution in the supreme executive; and for any misconduct respecting which, the injured individual has no remedy.

That there may be such cases is not to be questioned; but that every act of duty to be performed in any of the great departments of government constitutes such a case, is not to be admitted.

By the act concerning invalids, passed in June 1794, the secretary at war is ordered to place on the pension list all persons whose names are contained in a report previously made by him to congress. If he should refuse to do so, would the wounded veteran be without remedy? Is it to be contended that where the law in precise terms directs the performance of an act in which an individual is interested, the law is incapable of securing obedience to its mandate? Is it on account of the character of the person against whom the complaint is made? Is it to be contended that the heads of departments are not amenable to the laws of their country?

Whatever the practice on particular occasions may be, the theory of this principle will certainly never be maintained. No act of the legislature confers so extraordinary a privilege, nor can it derive countenance from the doctrines of the common law. After stating that personal injury from the king to a subject is presumed to be impossible, Blackstone, Vol. III. p. 255, says, "but injuries to the rights of property can scarcely be committed by the crown without the intervention of its officers: for whom, the law, in matters of right, entertains no respect or delicacy;

but furnishes various methods of detecting the errors and misconduct of those agents by whom the king has been deceived and induced to do a temporary injustice."

By the act passed in 1796, authorizing the sale of the lands above the mouth of Kentucky river, the purchaser, on paying his purchase money, becomes completely entitled to the property purchased; and on producing to the secretary of state the receipt of the treasurer upon a certificate required by the law, the president of the United States is authorized to grant him a patent. It is further enacted that all patents shall be countersigned by the secretary of state, and recorded in his office. If the secretary of state should choose to withhold this patent; or the patent being lost, should refuse a copy of it; can it be imagined that the law furnishes to the injured person no remedy?

It is not believed that any person whatever would attempt to maintain such a proposition.

It follows then that the question, whether the legality of an act of the head of a department be examinable in a court of justice or not, must always depend on the nature of that act.

If some acts be examinable, and others not, there must be some rule of law to guide the court in the exercise of its jurisdiction.

In some instances there may be difficulty in applying the rule to particular cases; but there cannot, it is believed, be much difficulty in laying down the rule.

By the constitution of the United States, the president is invested with certain important political powers, in the exercise of which he is to use his own discretion, and is accountable only to his country in his political character, and to his own conscience. To aid him in the performance of these duties, he is authorized to appoint certain officers, who act by his authority and in conformity with his orders.

In such cases, their acts are his acts; and whatever opinion may be entertained of the manner in which executive discretion may be used, still there exists, and can exist, no power to control that discretion. The subjects are political. They respect the nation, not individual rights, and being entrusted to the executive, the decision of the executive is conclusive. The application of this remark will be perceived by adverting to the act of congress for establishing the department of foreign affairs. This officer, as his duties were prescribed by that act, is to conform precisely to the will of the president. He is the mere organ by whom that will is communicated. The acts of such an officer, as an officer, can never be examinable by the courts.

But when the legislature proceeds to impose on that officer other duties; when he is directed peremptorily to perform certain acts; when the rights of individuals are dependent on the performance of those acts; he is so far the officer of the law; is amenable to the laws for his conduct; and cannot at his discretion sport away the vested rights of others.

The conclusion from this reasoning is, that where the heads of departments are the political or confidential agents of the executive, merely to execute the will of the president, or rather to act in cases in which the executive possesses a constitutional or legal discretion, nothing can be more perfectly clear than that their acts are only politically examinable. But where a specific duty is assigned by law, and individual rights depend upon the performance of that duty, it seems equally clear that the individual who considers himself injured has a right to resort to the laws of his country for a remedy.

If this be the rule, let us inquire how it applies to the case under the consideration of the court. The power of nominating to the senate, and the power of appointing the person nominated, are political powers, to be exercised by the president according to his own discretion. When he has made an appointment, he has exercised his whole power, and his discretion has been completely applied to the case. If, by law, the officer be removable at the will of the president, then a new appointment may be immediately made, and the rights of the officer are terminated. But as a fact which has existed cannot be made never to have existed, the appointment cannot be annihilated; and consequently if the officer is by law not removable at the will of the president, the rights he has acquired are protected by the law, and are not resumable by the president. They cannot be extinguished by executive authority, and he has the privilege of asserting them in like manner as if they had been derived from any other source.

The question whether a right has vested or not, is, in its nature, judicial, and must be tried by the judicial authority, If, for example, Mr. Marbury had taken the oaths of a magistrate, and proceeded to act as one; in consequence of which a suit had been instituted against him, in which his defence had depended on his being a magistrate; the validity of his appointment must have been determined by judicial authority.

So, if he conceives that by virtue of his appointment he has a legal right either to the commission which has been made out for him or to a copy of that commission, it is equally a question examinable in a court, and the decision of the court upon it must depend on the opinion entertained of his appointment.

That question has been discussed, and the opinion is, that the latest point of time which can be taken as that at which the appointment was complete, and evidenced, was when, after the signature of the president, the seal of the United States was affixed to the commission.

It is then the opinion of the court,

1. That by signing the commission of Mr. Marbury, the president of the United States appointed him a justice of peace for the county of Washington in the district of Columbia; and that the seal of the United States, affixed thereto by the secretary of state, is conclusive testimony of the verity of the signature, and of the completion of the appointment; and that the appointment conferred on him a legal right to the office for the space of five years.

2. That, having this legal title to the office, he has a consequent right to the commission; a refusal to deliver which is a plain violation of that right, for which the laws of his country afford him a remedy.

It remains to be inquired whether,

3. He is entitled to the remedy for which he applies. This depends on,

1. The nature of the writ applied for. And,

2. The power of this court.

1. The nature of the writ.

Blackstone, in the third volume of his Commentaries, page 110, defines a mandamus to be, "a command issu-

ing in the king"s name from the court of king"s bench, and directed to any person, corporation, or inferior court of judicature within the king"s dominions, requiring them to do some particular thing therein specified which appertains to their office and duty, and which the court of king"s bench has previously determined, or at least supposes, to be consonant to right and justice."

Lord Mansfield, in 3 Burrows, 1266, in the case of The King v. Baker et al. states with much precision and explicitness the cases in which this writ may be used.

"Whenever," says that very able judge, "there is a right to execute an office, perform a service, or exercise a franchise (more especially if it be in a matter of public concern or attended with profit), and a person is kept out of possession, or dispossessed of such right, and has no other specific legal remedy, this court ought to assist by mandamus, upon reasons of justice, as the writ expresses, and upon reasons of public policy, to preserve peace, order and good government." In the same case he says, "this writ ought to be used upon all occasions where the law has established no specific remedy, and where in justice and good government there ought to be one."

In addition to the authorities now particularly cited, many others were relied on at the bar, which show how far the practice has conformed to the general doctrines that have been just quoted.

This writ, if awarded, would be directed to an officer of government, and its mandate to him would be, to use the words of Blackstone, "to do a particular thing therein specified, which appertains to his office and duty, and which the court has previously determined or at least supposes to be consonant to right and justice." Or, in the words of Lord Mansfield, the applicant, in this case, has a right to execute an office of public concern, and is kept out of possession of that right.

These circumstances certainly concur in this case.

Still, to render the mandamus a proper remedy, the officer to whom it is to be directed, must be one to whom, on legal principles, such writ may be directed; and the person applying for it must be without any other specific and legal remedy.

1. With respect to the officer to whom it would be directed. The intimate political relation, subsisting between the president of the United States and the heads

of departments, necessarily renders any legal investigation of the acts of one of those high officers peculiarly irksome, as well as delicate; and excites some hesitation with respect to the propriety of entering into such investigation. Impressions are often received without much reflection or examination; and it is not wonderful that in such a case as this, the assertion, by an individual, of his legal claims in a court of justice, to which claims it is the duty of that court to attend, should at first view be considered by some, as an attempt to intrude into the cabinet, and to intermeddle with the prerogatives of the executive.

It is scarcely necessary for the court to disclaim all pretensions to such a jurisdiction. An extravagance, so absurd and excessive, could not have been entertained for a moment. The province of the court is, solely, to decide on the rights of individuals, not to inquire how the executive, or executive officers, perform duties in which they have a discretion. Questions, in their nature political, or which are, by the constitution and laws, submitted to the executive, can never be made in this court.

But, if this be not such a question; if so far from being an intrusion into the secrets of the cabinet, it respects a paper, which, according to law, is upon record, and to a copy of which the law gives a right, on the payment of ten cents; if it be no intermeddling with a subject, over which the executive can be considered as having exercised any control; what is there in the exalted station of the officer, which shall bar a citizen from asserting, in a court of justice, his legal rights, or shall forbid a court to listen to the claim; or to issue a mandamus, directing the performance of a duty, not depending on executive discretion, but on particular acts of congress and the general principles of law?

If one of the heads of departments commits any illegal act, under colour of his office, by which an individual sustains an injury, it cannot be pretended that his office alone exempts him from being sued in the ordinary mode of proceeding, and being compelled to obey the judgment of the law. How then can his office exempt him from this particular mode of deciding on the legality of his conduct, if the case be such a case as would, were any other individual the party complained of, authorize the process?

It is not by the office of the person to whom the writ is directed, but the nature of the thing to be done, that the propriety or impropriety of issuing a mandamus is to be determined. Where the head of a department acts in a case in which executive discretion is to be exercised; in which he is the mere organ of executive will; it is again repeated, that any application to a court to control, in any respect, his conduct, would be rejected without hesitation.

But where he is directed by law to do a certain act affecting the absolute rights of individuals, in the performance of which he is not placed under the particular direction of the president, and the performance of which the president cannot lawfully forbid, and therefore is never presumed to have forbidden; as for example, to record a commission, or a patent for land, which has received all the legal solemnities; or to give a copy of such record; in such cases, it is not perceived on what ground the courts of the country are further excused from the duty of giving judgment, that right to be done to an injured individual, than if the same services were to be performed by a person not the head of a department.

This opinion seems not now for the first time to be taken up in this country.

It must be well recollected that in 1792 an act passed, directing the secretary at war to place on the pension list such disabled officers and soldiers as should be reported to him by the circuit courts, which act, so far as the duty was imposed on the courts, was deemed unconstitutional; but some of the judges, thinking that the law might be executed by them in the character of commissioners, proceeded to act and to report in that character.

This law being deemed unconstitutional at the circuits, was repealed, and a different system was established; but the question whether those persons, who had been reported by the judges, as commissioners, were entitled, in consequence of that report, to be placed on the pension list, was a legal question, properly determinable in the courts, although the act of placing such persons on the list was to be performed by the head of a department.

That this question might be properly settled, congress passed an act in February 1793, making it the duty of the secretary of war, in conjunction with the attorney general, to take such measures as might be necessary to obtain an adjudication of the supreme court of the United States on the validity of any such rights, claimed under the act aforesaid.

After the passage of this act, a mandamus was moved for, to be directed to the secretary at war, commanding him to place on the pension list a person stating himself to be on the report of the judges.

There is, therefore, much reason to believe, that this mode of trying the legal right of the complainant, was deemed by the head of a department, and by the highest law officer of the United States, the most proper which could be selected for the purpose.

When the subject was brought before the court the decision was, not, that a mandamus would not lie to the head of a department, directing him to perform an act, enjoined by law, in the performance of which an individual had a vested interest; but that a mandamus ought not to issue in that case—the decision necessarily to be made if the report of the commissioners did not confer on the applicant a legal right.

The judgment in that case is understood to have decided the merits of all claims of that description; and the persons, on the report of the commissioners, found it necessary to pursue the mode prescribed by the law subsequent to that which had been deemed unconstitutional, in order to place themselves on the pension list.

The doctrine, therefore, now advanced is by no means a novel one.

It is true that the mandamus, now moved for, is not for the performance of an act expressly enjoined by statute.

It is to deliver a commission; on which subjects the acts of congress are silent. This difference is not considered as affecting the case. It has already been stated that the applicant has, to that commission, a vested legal right, of which the executive cannot deprive him. He has been appointed to an office, from which he is not removable at the will of the executive; and being so appointed, he has a right to the commission which the secretary has received from the president for his use. The act of congress does not indeed order the secretary of state to send it to him, but it is placed in his hands for the person entitled to it; and cannot be more lawfully withheld by him, than by another person.

It was at first doubted whether the action of detinue was not a specific legal remedy for the commission which has been withheld from Mr. Marbury; in which

case a mandamus would be improper. But this doubt has yielded to the consideration that the judgment in detinue is for the thing itself, or its value. The value of a public office not to be sold, is incapable of being ascertained; and the applicant has a right to the office itself, or to nothing. He will obtain the office by obtaining the commission, or a copy of it from the record.

This, then, is a plain case of a mandamus, either to deliver the commission, or a copy of it from the record; and it only remains to be inquired,

Whether it can issue from this court.

The act to establish the judicial courts of the United States authorizes the supreme court "to issue writs of mandamus, in cases warranted by the principles and usages of law, to any courts appointed, or persons holding office, under the authority of the United States."

The secretary of state, being a person, holding an office under the authority of the United States, is precisely within the letter of the description; and if this court is not authorized to issue a writ of mandamus to such an officer, it must be because the law is unconstitutional, and therefore absolutely incapable of conferring the authority, and assigning the duties which its words purport to confer and assign.

The constitution vests the whole judicial power of the United States in one supreme court, and such inferior courts as congress shall, from time to time, ordain and establish. This power is expressly extended to all cases arising under the laws of the United States; and consequently, in some form, may be exercised over the present case; because the right claimed is given by a law of the United States.

In the distribution of this power it is declared that "the supreme court shall have original jurisdiction in all cases affecting ambassadors, other public ministers and consuls, and those in which a state shall be a party. In all other cases, the supreme court shall have appellate jurisdiction."

It has been insisted at the bar, that as the original grant of jurisdiction to the supreme and inferior courts is general, and the clause, assigning original jurisdiction to the supreme court, contains no negative or restrictive words; the power remains to the legislature to assign original jurisdiction to that court in other cases than those specified in the article which has been recited; provided those cases belong to the judicial power of the United States.

If it had been intended to leave it in the discretion of the legislature to apportion the judicial power between the supreme and inferior courts according to the will of that body, it would certainly have been useless to have proceeded further than to have defined the judicial power, and the tribunals in which it should be vested. The subsequent part of the section is mere surplusage, is entirely without meaning, if such is to be the construction. If congress remains at liberty to give this court appellate jurisdiction, where the constitution has declared their jurisdiction shall be original; and original jurisdiction where the constitution has declared it shall be appellate; the distribution of jurisdiction made in the constitution, is form without substance.

Affirmative words are often, in their operation, negative of other objects than those affirmed; and in this case, a negative or exclusive sense must be given to them or they have no operation at all.

It cannot be presumed that any clause in the constitution is intended to be without effect; and therefore such construction is inadmissible, unless the words require it. If the solicitude of the convention, respecting our peace with foreign powers, induced a provision that the supreme court should take original jurisdiction in cases which might be supposed to affect them; yet the clause would have proceeded no further than to provide for such cases, if no further restriction on the powers of congress had been intended. That they should have appellate jurisdiction in all other cases, with such exceptions as congress might make, is no restriction; unless the words be deemed exclusive of original jurisdiction.

When an instrument organizing fundamentally a judicial system, divides it into one supreme, and so many inferior courts as the legislature may ordain and establish; then enumerates its powers, and proceeds so far to distribute them, as to define the jurisdiction of the supreme court by declaring the cases in which it shall take original jurisdiction, and that in others it shall take appellate jurisdiction, the plain import of the words seems to be, that in one class of cases its jurisdiction is original, and not appellate; in the other

it is appellate, and not original. If any other construction would render the clause inoperative, that is an additional reason for rejecting such other construction, and for adhering to the obvious meaning.

To enable this court then to issue a mandamus, it must be shown to be an exercise of appellate jurisdiction, or to be necessary to enable them to exercise appellate jurisdiction.

It has been stated at the bar that the appellate jurisdiction may be exercised in a variety of forms, and that if it be the will of the legislature that a mandamus should be used for that purpose, that will must be obeyed. This is true; yet the jurisdiction must be appellate, not original.

It is the essential criterion of appellate jurisdiction, that it revises and corrects the proceedings in a cause already instituted, and does not create that case. Although, therefore, a mandamus may be directed to courts, yet to issue such a writ to an officer for the delivery of a paper, is in effect the same as to sustain an original action for that paper, and therefore seems not to belong to appellate, but to original jurisdiction. Neither is it necessary in such a case as this, to enable the court to exercise its appellate jurisdiction.

The authority, therefore, given to the supreme court, by the act establishing the judicial courts of the United States, to issue writs of mandamus to public officers, appears not to be warranted by the constitution; and it becomes necessary to inquire whether a jurisdiction, so conferred, can be exercised.

The question, whether an act, repugnant to the constitution, can become the law of the land, is a question deeply interesting to the United States; but, happily, not of an intricacy proportioned to its interest. It seems only necessary to recognise certain principles, supposed to have been long and well established, to decide it.

That the people have an original right to establish, for their future government, such principles as, in their opinion, shall most conduce to their own happiness, is the basis on which the whole American fabric has been erected. The exercise of this original right is a very great exertion; nor can it nor ought it to be frequently repeated. The principles, therefore, so established are deemed fundamental. And as the authority, from which they proceed, is supreme, and can seldom act, they are designed to be permanent.

This original and supreme will organizes the government, and assigns to different departments their respective powers. It may either stop here; or establish certain limits not to be transcended by those departments.

The government of the United States is of the latter description. The powers of the legislature are defined and limited; and that those limits may not be mistaken or forgotten, the constitution is written. To what purpose are powers limited, and to what purpose is that limitation committed to writing; if these limits may, at any time, be passed by those intended to be restrained? The distinction between a government with limited and unlimited powers is abolished, if those limits do not confine the persons on whom they are imposed, and if acts prohibited and acts allowed are of equal obligation. It is a proposition too plain to be contested, that the constitution controls any legislative act repugnant to it; or, that the legislature may alter the constitution by an ordinary act.

Between these alternatives there is no middle ground. The constitution is either a superior, paramount law, unchangeable by ordinary means, or it is on a level with ordinary legislative acts, and like other acts, is alterable when the legislature shall please to alter it.

If the former part of the alternative be true, then a legislative act contrary to the constitution is not law: if the latter part be true, then written constitutions are absurd attempts, on the part of the people, to limit a power in its own nature illimitable.

Certainly all those who have framed written constitutions contemplate them as forming the fundamental and paramount law of the nation, and consequently the theory of every such government must be, that an act of the legislature repugnant to the constitution is void.

This theory is essentially attached to a written constitution, and is consequently to be considered by this court as one of the fundamental principles of our society. It is not therefore to be lost sight of in the further consideration of this subject.

If an act of the legislature, repugnant to the constitution, is void, does it, notwithstanding its invalidity, bind the courts and oblige them to give it effect? Or, in other words, though it be not law, does it constitute a rule as operative as if it was a law? This would be to overthrow in fact what was established in theory; and would seem, at first view, an absurdity too gross

to be insisted on. It shall, however, receive a more attentive consideration.

It is emphatically the province and duty of the judicial department to say what the law is. Those who apply the rule to particular cases, must of necessity expound and interpret that rule. If two laws conflict with each other, the courts must decide on the operation of each. So if a law be in opposition to the constitution: if both the law and the constitution apply to a particular case, so that the court must either decide that case conformably to the law, disregarding the constitution; or conformably to the constitution, disregarding the law: the court must determine which of these conflicting rules governs the case. This is of the very essence of judicial duty.

If then the courts are to regard the constitution; and he constitution is superior to any ordinary act of the legislature; the constitution, and not such ordinary act, must govern the case to which they both apply.

Those then who controvert the principle that the constitution is to be considered, in court, as a paramount law, are reduced to the necessity of maintaining that courts must close their eyes on the constitution, and see only the law.

This doctrine would subvert the very foundation of all written constitutions. It would declare that an act, which, according to the principles and theory of our government, is entirely void, is yet, in practice, completely obligatory. It would declare, that if the legislature shall do what is expressly forbidden, such act, notwithstanding the express prohibition, is in reality effectual. It would be giving to the legislature a practical and real omnipotence with the same breath which professes to restrict their powers within narrow limits. It is prescribing limits, and declaring that those limits may be passed at pleasure.

That it thus reduces to nothing what we have deemed the greatest improvement on political institutions—a written constitution, would of itself be sufficient, in America where written constitutions have been viewed with so much reverence, for rejecting the construction. But the peculiar expressions of the constitution of the United States furnish additional arguments in favour of its rejection.

The judicial power of the United States is extended to all cases arising under the constitution. Could it be the intention of those who gave this power, to say that, in using it, the constitution should not be looked into? That a case arising under the constitution should be decided without examining the instrument under which it arises?

This is too extravagant to be maintained.

In some cases then, the constitution must be looked into by the judges. And if they can open it at all, what part of it are they forbidden to read, or to obey?

There are many other parts of the constitution which serve to illustrate this subject.

It is declared that "no tax or duty shall be laid on articles exported from any state." Suppose a duty on the export of cotton, of tobacco, or of flour; and a suit instituted to recover it. Ought judgment to be rendered in such a case? ought the judges to close their eyes on the constitution, and only see the law.

The constitution declares that "no bill of attainder or ex post facto law shall be passed."

If, however, such a bill should be passed and a person should be prosecuted under it, must the court condemn to death those victims whom the constitution endeavours to preserve?

"No person," says the constitution, "shall be convicted of treason unless on the testimony of two witnesses to the same overt act, or on confession in open court."

Here the language of the constitution is addressed especially to the courts. It prescribes, directly for them, a rule of evidence not to be departed from. If the legislature should change that rule, and declare one witness, or a confession out of court, sufficient for conviction, must the constitutional principle yield to the legislative act?

From these and many other selections which might be made, it is apparent, that the framers of the constitution contemplated that instrument as a rule for the government of courts, as well as of the legislature.

Why otherwise does it direct the judges to take an oath to support it? This oath certainly applies, in an especial manner, to their conduct in their official character. How immoral to impose it on them, if they were to be used as the instruments, and the knowing instruments, for violating what they swear to support!

The oath of office, too, imposed by the legislature, is completely demonstrative of the legislative opinion on this subject. It is in these words: "I do solemnly swear that I will administer justice without respect to persons, and do equal right to the poor and to the rich; and that I will faithfully and impartially discharge all the duties incumbent on me as according to the best of my abilities and understanding, agreeably to the constitution and laws of the United States."

Why does a judge swear to discharge his duties agreeably to the constitution of the United States, if that constitution forms no rule for his government? if it is closed upon him and cannot be inspected by him.

If such be the real state of things, this is worse than solemn mockery. To prescribe, or to take this oath, becomes equally a crime.

It is also not entirely unworthy of observation, that in declaring what shall be the supreme law of the land, the constitution itself is first mentioned; and not the laws of the United States generally, but those only which shall be made in pursuance of the constitution, have that rank.

Thus, the particular phraseology of the constitution of the United States confirms and strengthens the principle, supposed to be essential to all written constitutions, that a law repugnant to the constitution is void, and that courts, as well as other departments, are bound by that instrument.

The rule must be discharged.

## Glossary

**jurisdiction:** the power to hear and decide cases

**writ:** a court order mandating performance of a specified act

**writ of mandamus:** a court order compelling a government official to perform some necessary duty

# Martin v. Hunter's Lessee

| DATE | CITATION |
|------|----------|
| 1816 | 14 U.S. 304 |
| **AUTHOR** | **SIGNIFICANCE** |
| Joseph Story | Asserted for first time the Supreme Court's authority to hear appeals of state supreme court cases involving the constitutionality of federal laws or treaties |
| **VOTE** | |
| 6-0 | |

## Overview

*Martin v. Hunter's Lessee* (1816), a landmark U.S. Supreme Court decision in the development of federal-state relations, asserted for the first time the Supreme Court's authority under Section 25 of the federal Judiciary Act of 1789 to hear appellate state supreme court cases involving the constitutionality of federal laws or treaties. *Martin*'s origins lay in 300,000 acres of land in Virginia's "Northern Neck" region, which Charles II of England had granted to the Fairfax family in 1649. In 1776, when the American colonies declared independence from Britain, many colonists—including Thomas Fairfax, the sixth Lord Fairfax—remained loyal to Britain. From 1779 to 1785, however, Virginia's legislature passed several acts confiscating Loyalist-owned lands. When Fairfax died in 1781, he willed his property to his nephew, Denny Martin. The following year, however, Virginia legislators passed an act arguing that Martin, a foreign national, could not inherit property in the Old Dominion. Virginia took formal possession of the Fairfax estate and granted it to private citizens, such as David Hunter, who received 788 acres. To complicate matters, John Marshall, who would become chief justice of the United States, suc-

cessfully represented Martin's land claims in *Hite v. Fairfax* (1786). The Fairfax litigation may have led Martin to sell 160,000 acres to a Virginia land speculators cartel that included John and James Marshall.

In 1800 Martin died and willed his land to his brother, Thomas Martin. When Thomas Martin attempted to take the property, Hunter sued him in Virginia court in *Hunter v. Fairfax's Devisee* (1810). When the Court of Appeals of Virginia upheld Hunter's claim, Martin appealed the decision on a writ of error to the U.S. Supreme Court. As chief justice, Marshall recused himself owing to his financial interests in the Fairfax lands. In *Fairfax's Devisee v. Hunter's Lessee* (1813), Justice Joseph Story ruled that English common law, international precedents, the Treaty of Paris (1783), and the Jay Treaty (1794) gave Martin title to the land. Story remanded the case to the Virginia courts, ordering them to recognize Martin's claims. In *Hunter v. Martin* (1815), however, the Court of Appeals of Virginia chief justice Spencer Roane declared that Section 25 of the Judiciary Act of 1789 unconstitutionally violated state sovereignty. Martin repealed the case to the Supreme Court, and in *Martin v. Hunter's Lessee* (1816),

**Joseph Story**
(Library of Congress)

Story argued that the American people, not the states, created the Constitution, Congress, and federal judiciary and that only impartial federal courts could hear cases involving international law. Under the Judiciary Act of 1789, the Supreme Court had the authority to hear state cases involving international treaties. The Constitution's supremacy clause likewise compelled state judges to abide by federal rulings. Martin, therefore, remained the land's owner. Although it was a defining moment in Story's judicial career, *Martin v. Hunter's Lessee* was an unpopular decision and a victory for noncitizens' property rights. Land speculators, such as Martin and Marshall, secured fortunes of the expansive estates, while Roane decried the decision as an example of a "consolidationist" Supreme Court increasing the federal government's power at the expense of the states.

## Context

In the seventeenth century, English monarchs such as James I and Charles I granted large North American land tracts to loyal political supporters like the Fairfax family. Well-established social patterns of pa-

ternalism and deference allowed large, landholding families to wield considerable power over the landless masses in colonial Virginia. But increasing tensions over taxation between the British government and the American colonies led to the 1775 outbreak of the American Revolution, with many of the colonies divided between Patriot and Loyalist camps. Many Loyalists like Lord Fairfax escaped the conflict to Canada or Britain. In 1779 Thomas Jefferson, a leading advocate of independence, became Virginia's wartime governor. Under his administration, the state legislature passed a series of acts confiscating abandoned Loyalist land. These confiscation acts were often upheld by state courts that were eager to pay down Virginia's war debts and strike a blow against the unpopular Tories.

In 1781, at the end of the Revolutionary War, Loyalist land claims remained unresolved. In the Treaty of Paris, American delegates pledged to honor prewar debts owed to British creditors, encourage state legislatures to honor British and Loyalist land claims, and prevent future confiscation of Loyalist property. The government created by the Articles of Confederation attempted to enforce these treaty provisions but met stubborn resistance from the states. In the 1780s Federalists such as Alexander Hamilton and James Madison promoted a stronger central government to protect property rights and international treaty obligations. Following the creation and partial ratification of the U.S. Constitution in 1787, the Federalist administrations of George Washington and John Adams cultivated stronger diplomatic and economic ties with Britain. When Britain declared war on France after the French Revolution, President Washington dispatched Chief Justice John Jay to Britain to negotiate a secret treaty declaring American neutrality in the conflict. When Congress ratified the unpopular Jay Treaty in 1796, it agreed to recognize the property rights of British subjects on American soil.

When Jefferson assumed office in March 1801, he immediately announced a new direction in federal power, lowering taxes, slashing federal spending, and reducing the U.S. military. Jefferson heavily criticized the "midnight appointments" of his predecessor and experimented with impeaching federal judicial appointees. When Republicans failed to impeach U.S. Supreme Court Justice Samuel Chase, Jefferson appointed the Republicans Joseph Story and William

Johnson to the Court. Ironically, Story became Marshall's closest friend and collaborator, and Johnson frequently made more nationalistic decisions than Marshall did. Anti-British sentiment remained high during the Jeffersonian period. In 1807 the HMS *Leopard*, a British warship, fired on the USS *Chesapeake* off the Virginia coast, prompting Jefferson to issue embargo acts against Britain and France. Frequent British impressment of American sailors worsened diplomatic relations between the two nations. Under these circumstances, many Americans felt lingering hostility toward those who had remained loyal to the British government during the Revolutionary War and considered the forfeiture of their lands as a fair prize of war.

Anti-British sentiment was particularly high in Virginia, where Roane and Thomas Ritchie, editor of the *Richmond Enquirer*, formed a political machine called the "Richmond Junto," which controlled Republican politics in the Old Dominion. Roane, Ritchie, and Jefferson watched with concern as the federal government and the Marshall Court became more powerful after the War of 1812. Roane decided to use the issue of Loyalist lands to express his views on federal-state relations in *Fairfax's Devisee v. Hunter's Lessee* (1813). The public anticipated the U.S. Supreme Court's decision in *Martin v. Hunter's Lessee* in the spring of 1816 with great interest.

## About the Author

Joseph Story was born on September 18, 1779, in Marblehead, Massachusetts. His parents were ardent Unitarians and Patriots during the Revolutionary War. His father was a leading member of the Sons of Liberty, participated in the Boston Tea Party, and was a Continental army physician. Story excelled academically at Marblehead Academy and Harvard University and graduated in 1798, second in his class. The prominent Massachusetts attorneys Samuel Sewall and Samuel Putnam trained Story as a legal specialist in maritime and admiralty cases.

During his private law career in Salem, Massachusetts, Story became a Jeffersonian Republican. He was elected to the Massachusetts House of Representatives in 1805. Four years later the Massachusetts governor appointed Story to complete a con-

gressional term left vacant by the death of Jacob Crowinshield. Story broke party ranks to speak against Jefferson's embargo acts, earning him the president's lifelong dislike. Story resumed his law practice in 1809 and successfully argued *Fletcher v. Peck* before the U.S. Supreme Court in 1810. Story became speaker of the Massachusetts House of Representatives the following year. In November 1811 President James Madison nominated Story as a U.S. Supreme Court justice. On February 3, 1812, Story became the High Court's youngest justice at age thirty-two, and he served for thirty-two years. For much of his early career, he worked closely with the chief justice, John Marshall, to uphold a broad interpretation of the Constitution and a strong federal government that could keep state powers in check. Story tried unsuccessfully to promote a national common law system that would have provided uniform precedents and punishments for federal criminal and civil cases.

Story received a major opportunity to expound his nationalistic theories in 1813 in *Fairfax's Devisee v. Hunter's Lessee*. The case ultimately dealt with the U.S. Supreme Court's appellate jurisdiction for cases involving federal law or treaties under Section 25 of the Judiciary Act of 1789. Story reversed the decision of the Court of Appeals of Virginia and ordered Hunter to return the land to Martin. When the Virginia court refused to comply with the decision, Martin again appealed the case to the Supreme Court. Story's subsequent decision in *Martin v. Hunter's Lessee* provided an endorsement of federalism that would become a landmark constitutional decision.

Story often clashed over Federalist issues with Johnson, his Jefferson-appointed colleague. Johnson, born in South Carolina in 1771, sprang from working-class roots. He attended Princeton, became an attorney, and served three terms as a Republican congressman, serving briefly as Speaker of the House of Representatives. In 1802 Jefferson appointed Johnson to the Supreme Court, primarily to counterbalance Marshall's nationalist tendencies. Johnson, however, proved to be an independent figure, defying his nationalist-minded colleagues, such as Marshall and Story, as well as Jefferson on several occasions. In *Martin v. Hunter's Lessee*, Johnson concurred with Story's validation of Section 25 of the Judiciary Act of 1789, but he did so from different constitutional grounds.

## Explanation and Analysis of the Document

### Syllabus

The case includes a syllabus of the facts and background events of *Martin v. Hunter's Lessee*. The syllabus discusses the writ of error that brings the case before the Court, and it quotes Roane's *Hunter v. Martin* decision that "so much of the 25th section of the act of Congress to establish the judicial courts of the United States, as extends the appellate jurisdiction of the Supreme Court to this Court, is not in pursuance of the Constitution of the United States." The syllabus chronicles the original state court case launched in April 1791 by Hunter against Martin and lists the facts of the case.

### Story's Opinion of the Court

In Story's *Martin v. Hunter's Lessee* decision, he cites Roane's *Hunter v. Martin* decision and acknowledges the current case's complexity. He notes that the "people of the United States," not the states, created the Constitution. The American people have the right to regulate and limit state powers under the Constitution. The Tenth Amendment to the Constitution reveals that states remain sovereign except in those areas where the framers granted power to the federal government. Story then argues that although the federal government can claim only powers granted under the Constitution, such powers should be reasonably, not strictly, construed. The framers created a Constitution "to endure through a long lapse of ages," with Congress creating laws to carry out constitutional goals during changing social circumstances. Article III of the Constitution created the Supreme Court, empowered Congress to create lower federal courts, and set jurisdictional boundaries for all federal courts. The American people empower these courts through the Constitution to act on individuals and states.

Article III obligates Congress to establish federal courts and staff them with tenured judges. Without a federal court system, the federal government cannot carry out its powers expressly granted under the Constitution, such as punishing crimes committed against the United States or hearing court cases that involved two states. In order to create such a federal court system, Congress must be allowed to vest the entire judicial power of the federal government in the federal court system. Story admits that what types of inferior courts Congress is obligated to create is a difficult question. He maintains that under Article III, Congress must create some inferior federal courts, which could serve as courts of original jurisdiction for cases involving constitutional issues, federal laws, treaties, and so on. The Constitution does not specify what courts to create, however, so Congress has discretion to organize such tribunals.

Story makes these general points before turning to a more specific discussion of which cases the Supreme Court wields jurisdiction over. He insists that under Article III, Section 2, the Supreme Court wields appellate jurisdiction over "all cases" involving the Constitution, federal laws, and treaties. Story also admits, however, that the Constitution grants the Supreme Court jurisdiction over "controversies to which the United States shall be a party." Thus the Constitution gives the Supreme Court automatic jurisdiction over national security issues, such as federal laws and treaties, but leaves it to Congress to grant the Supreme Court the power to hear other types of cases that might become more important to national interests over time. Story, making this distinction, nevertheless remarks that, regardless of whether federal court jurisdiction is granted by the Constitution or Congress, such authority can be wielded only by federal, not state, courts. Furthermore, it could be fully exercised where such federal jurisdiction existed.

Story argues that as the Constitution does not specifically limit the ability of Congress to grant the Supreme Court appellate jurisdiction, Congress could give the Court appellate jurisdiction over types of cases not specifically mentioned by the Constitution, including cases originating in state courts. Ultimately, "it is the case, then, and not the court, that gives the jurisdiction." Congress has merely to show that the Supreme Court deserves such power through clear and necessary implication. Story reasons that if federal appellate power applied only to federal but not to state courts, then the federal courts could not carry out their enumerated jurisdiction over cases specifically mentioned in the Constitution. If Congress creates no lower federal courts, then, of course, the Supreme Court would have appellate powers over state courts—in those areas in which the Constitution grants the Supreme Court such power.

Story states that the framers had foreseen that cases involving national issues might arise in state courts. They accordingly created Article VI of the Constitution, which made the Constitution, federal laws, and treaties "the supreme law of the land" and which bound state court judges to obey these precedents. Without the supremacy clause, state courts could rule on matters such as issuing paper money or ex post facto laws, which are powers the Constitution grants to Congress. For these reasons, federal appellate power must obviously extend to state court cases.

Story dismisses criticisms that federal appellate jurisdiction over state cases goes against the spirit of the Constitution and impairs states' rights. He points to the fact that the Constitution limits state power in a number of areas, such as senatorial and presidential elections. State judges are likewise bound by their oaths and the supremacy clause to uphold the Constitution and federal law. In response to the charge that federal courts might abuse their power to revise federal or state law, Story responds, "From the very nature of things, the absolute right of decision, in the last resort, must rest somewhere—wherever it may be vested, it is susceptible of abuse." It is simply a matter of common and legal sense that appellate courts, rather than courts of original jurisdiction, should be given the right to make final determinations in such cases.

Story likewise argues that giving the federal courts appellate powers was perfectly in keeping with American constitutional traditions. Under the Articles of Confederation, Congress had been granted the power to establish courts to rule on state prizes cases. Far from being a threat to states' rights, such a measure had been seen as important to public safety and national security. The fact that the Constitution, which called for a much stronger central government, gives jurisdiction of prizes cases to the federal courts reveals that federal appellate jurisdiction is in no way an aberration in American jurisprudence.

In addition to arguments that federal appellate powers are unconstitutional, Story contends with charges that such a system is impractical as well. After all, state judges would obey their oaths and uphold federal laws in all state cases, regardless of federal jurisdiction. In a similar fashion, Congress could remove all cases from state to federal court before they were decided at the local level. Story admits that state and federal judges

are quite similar in "learning, integrity, and wisdom." The American people, however, have created the Constitution to remove important cases involving national security from local concerns and temptations, so that they might be resolved by an impartial tribunal that spoke for the entire country. Federal appellate jurisdiction would likewise help regulate and harmonize state court cases into a manageable whole. A federal appeals process would also protect the rights of defendants who have lost cases in state court and who would otherwise have no rights to appeal.

Story admits that the Constitution does not grant any branch of the federal government the express power to remove cases from state to federal court. Yet such a power is a necessary one for the federal courts to have. Since the Constitution does not prohibit Congress from exercising such power, it could allow federal courts to take charge of state court cases at any time in their deliberations. Under these circumstances, it is perfectly appropriate for a federal court to review a state court case on a writ of error. Furthermore, if state courts could refuse to obey such writs, the resulting legal chaos would undermine private rights and public safety. Under these circumstances, Section 25 of the federal Judiciary Act of 1789 is "supported by the letter and spirit of the Constitution."

Although Story grounds his defense of federal appellate power on the Constitution, he shows how his decision also makes sense within a historical context. He points out as a matter of historical fact that both Federalists and Antifederalists had widely accepted the fact that if the Constitution were adopted, it would grant appellate jurisdiction over state courts. In a similar fashion, many of these same Federalists had gone on to serve in the first Congress and had helped to create the Judiciary Act of 1789. Until the current controversy, Story notes, state courts had frequently acquiesced when the Supreme Court reviewed their cases. Such compliance places federal appellate power "upon a foundation of authority which cannot be shaken without delivering over the subject to perpetual and irremediable doubts."

Having defended the rights of federal courts to hear state court cases on appeal, Story examines whether the current controversy is admissible in federal court under Section 25 of the Judiciary Act of 1789. Stripped of jargon, Section 25 states that state supreme court decisions involving federal law, constitutional issues, or federal treaties could be appealed to the U.S. Supreme Court on a writ of error. As the Court of Appeals of Virginia declares the Supreme Court's decision in *Fairfax's Devisee v. Hunter's Lessee* null and void, the matter pertains perfectly to the guidelines for a writ of error under Section 25, in which state supreme court cases that conflict with federal law could be appealed to the U.S. Supreme Court.

Despite this reasoning, Story argues that without the Virginia court's unwillingness to support a Supreme Court decision, Martin still has a right to have his case heard in federal court. Story admits that the case is centered on private land claims contested by two Virginia citizens under state law. Martin's inheritance of Virginia land hinges upon the validity of Denny Martin's land claims under the provisions of the Treaty of Paris and the Jay Treaty. The Court of Appeals of Virginia has considered Martin's land claims in relation to these treaties and rejects them to rule in favor of Hunter. Thus the Supreme Court could examine the same legal matters and rule in favor of Martin.

Story addresses the question of whether the Supreme Court could rule only on the matter of federal treaties and not state land titles. He responds that Congress grants the Supreme Court the latitude to consider all legal points in a case when determining its outcome. The Supreme Court could also consider the Jay Treaty, which upholds Loyalist property rights, even though the treaty was created only after the Hunter-Fairfax controversy had begun. Story asserts that when Congress had ratified the Jay Treaty, it became the supreme law of the land and attached itself to the case.

Story rejects the remaining arguments against Martin's land claims as merely procedural rather than substantive in nature. The writ of error has been properly submitted from the Virginia Court of Errors and is therefore eligible for review by the Supreme Court. Even though the judge issuing the writ of error had not followed procedure and taken a bond, the writ had still been issued in good faith and was therefore valid. Story also declines to discuss whether the Supreme Court could legally issue a writ of mandamus to the Court of Appeals of Virginia, as the matter is not necessary to solve the case before the Court. He thus concludes his opinion by stating that it is "the opinion of the whole Court that the judgment of the Court of Appeals of

Virginia, rendered on the mandate in this cause, be reversed, and the judgment of the District Court, held at Winchester, be, and the same is hereby, affirmed."

### *Johnson's Separate Opinion*

In his concurring opinion, commenting on Story's decision not to determine whether federal courts could issue writs of mandamus to state courts, Johnson states that the Supreme Court is correspondingly supreme in its jurisdiction but not willing to force the state courts to comply with its decisions. Against such a backdrop, Johnson stresses his agreement with Story's decision, "but not altogether in the reasoning or opinion of my brother who delivered it." Given the natural tendency for people to disagree, Johnson feels a need to defend his concurring opinion on his own terms.

Johnson states that he wishes to express his opinion because he views "this question as one of the most momentous importance; as one which may affect, in its consequences, the permanence of the American Union." The important case represents a collision between federal law and the laws of one of the most powerful states in the Union. Johnson warns that the federal government must carry out its constitutionally mandated powers or cease to exist. On the other hand, to subordinate states' rights to federal interests would destroy democratic government in the United States. Although Johnson admires the Old Dominion's pluck for standing up for its rights, he criticizes the Court of Appeals of Virginia for taking such an extreme position. The legal issue at hand is whether the Virginia court was bound to obey the Supreme Court's orders in *Fairfax's Devisee v. Hunter's Lessee*. Instead, Roane and his colleagues had provoked a larger confrontation over whether the Supreme Court has jurisdiction over state courts at all.

Johnson maintains that Virginia's stance is an alarming one. If Virginia could challenge Supreme Court decisions, then what could prevent other states from doing likewise? Although the Supreme Court is no more infallible than the state courts, it has a tradition of respect and comity with the state courts. Furthermore, the Supreme Court represents every state in the Union, and thus one can count on it to be more magnanimous, especially when the public interest is at stake.

To further promote the Supreme Court's virtue, Johnson places the blame for the current conflict squarely on the shoulders of the Virginia courts. He points out that Roane had acquiesced to the Supreme Court's writ of error in the original case of *Fairfax's Devisee v. Hunter's Lessee*. The Supreme Court, therefore, believes that the Court of Appeals of Virginia would abide by its decision, regardless of how the Court rules. Had Roane refused to comply with the initial writ and raised jurisdictional issues at that point, at least the Supreme Court would have been aware of the crisis. In such a case, the Supreme Court would not have issued an order demanding that the Court of Appeals of Virginia comply with the *Fairfax* decision, and the matter could have been amicably disposed of in Circuit Court. The Founders anticipated that state courts might refuse to obey federal court decisions and thus gave the federal courts the power to compel them to obey. But federal courts could use their discretion in exercising such powers with the hope that comity might prevent crises between the states and federal government. By its rash actions, writes Johnson, Virginia forces the Supreme Court to take an adversarial position; the current situation is Virginia's own making.

Johnson begins his opinion by stating that, even though the Treaty of Paris and the Jay Treaty were not central to the land issues in *Fairfax's Devisee v. Hunter's Lessee*, any part of the case that calls into question the validity of these treaties makes it applicable for review by the Supreme Court. To declare that the Supreme Court could rule on the constitutionality of federal treaties but on not state land laws would mean that the Court could render a hypothetical decision in favor of Martin but have no means of actually enforcing it. Rather than view the case as a matter of federal courts invading the state legal system, Johnson argues that the more proper question is "whether the State tribunals can constitutionally exercise jurisdiction in any of the cases to which the judicial power of the United States extends." Johnson admits that the Constitution is vague as to whether state courts could act in federal matters if Congress or the federal courts refused to do so. Johnson sees the Constitution as a "tripartite" contract between the people, states, and federal government. Under the terms of this agreement, each party surrenders part of its powers for the greater good, particularly the right to mete out justice. In addition, the framers wrote the Constitution in plain, obvious language that empowers the federal government to fully exercise the powers it was given in the areas assigned to it by the Constitution, such as the power to extend federal appellate power over certain controversies or cases. Just as individuals could renounce rights created for their benefit, so too state courts could act in areas in which Congress declines to rule. The federal government could curtail such state power at any time.

The central issue remains whether federal courts have appellate power over state courts, and Johnson admits that he is undecided. He merely maintains that Congress at no point makes a systematic attempt to turn the state courts into inferior courts. Certainly, instances in which states could arrest, imprison, and sentence to death foreign ministers or federal agents exist. Under such circumstances, federal appellate power is necessary to preserve both justice and the Union. If ever the federal courts should attempt to force state courts to adopt federal law, then the Supreme Court would have to deal with the matter as it arose. For the moment, however, it is merely enough to show that Congress has the authority to grant the Supreme Court the right to hear state supreme court cases in civil matters. Congress, in passing the Judiciary Act of 1789, had allowed states to retain a great deal of their sovereignty. Congress gave plaintiffs and defendants the ability to appeal their cases in both state and federal court. State court justices can issue or decline to issue writs of error to the Supreme Court. Cases under review require that both parties appear and explain their legal arguments to a new court. In any event, the Supreme Court seeks to hear cases based on their merits and not on whether they come from a state or federal court in particular.

Johnson reasons that Congress gave federal courts appellate power over state cases for two specific reasons. First, a federal appeals process gives defendants full rights to appeal their state cases, a right they would not enjoy under state law. Second, even if Congress grants federal courts original jurisdiction over all cases involving the Constitution and federal laws, there would still be entire classes of cases beyond the reach of federal jurisdiction. This could lead to endless confusion throughout the nation as different courts handed down conflicting decisions, with no means of regulation.

Johnson concludes that he believes his opinions are not merely constitutional but also practical and that they jeopardize neither the survival of the Union nor the dignity of the states. State courts should not fear federal power simply because the federal courts provide another forum to hear their cases. With a common commitment to justice and comity, the federal and state courts could work together, without the need for compulsion, which neither Congress nor the Supreme Court attempts nor plans to attempt.

## Impact

*Martin v. Hunter's Lessee* received mixed reviews from the American public. Northern newspapers generally supported it but gave the case clinical summaries rather than ringing endorsements. On the other hand, southern papers voiced concerns about an increase in federal power over the states. The Richmond Junto's official party organ, the *Richmond Enquirer*, printed a verbatim copy of Johnson's opinion but not that of Story. Many contemporaries believed that even though Marshall had recused himself from the case, he and Story had informally colluded to craft a nationalistic decision that upheld both the right of the Supreme Court to review state court cases and Marshall's Virginia land claims.

Story's success in defending federal power in Martin inspired the Marshall Court to further expand its authority over state courts in areas like banking, contracts, lottery tickets, and interstate commerce. Yet following the election of Andrew Jackson as president in 1828, the Supreme Court began to moderate its nationalistic approach. The Civil War sparked a revolution in federal-state relations. Union victory solidified federal control over the states and led to the creation of the Fourteenth Amendment, which made the Bill of Rights binding on the states. Following the Great Depression in 1929 and the New Deal of the 1930s, the Supreme Court gradually began to allow the federal government direct control over traditionally state-granted affairs.

### Questions for Further Study

1. Given the sheer size of the Fairfax estates, why did neither David Hunter nor Thomas Martin seek an out-of-court resolution? Why did both men fight so hard to win title over a relatively meager 788 acres of land when America enjoyed a booming frontier?

2. Why did Spencer Roane wait until relatively late in the judicial proceedings to declare a U.S. Supreme Court decision unconstitutional? Why not simply refuse to allow the Supreme Court the ability to review the case in the first place?

3. Why did the Virginia Court of Appeals attempt to turn a matter involving land claims into a wider dispute over the right of federal courts to hear state cases?

4. In contrast, why did the Supreme Court decline to issue a writ of mandamus to force the Virginia court to appeal with its initial decision in 1813?

## Further Reading

### *Books*

Beeman, Richard. *The Old Dominion and the New Nation, 1788–1801.* Lexington: University Press of Kentucky, 1972.

Currie, David P. *The Constitution in the Supreme Court: The First Hundred Years, 1789–1888.* Chicago: University of Chicago Press, 1985.

Henkin, Louis. *Foreign Affairs and the United States Constitution.* New York: Oxford University Press, 1996.

Hoffer, Peter Charles, Williamjames Hull Hoffer, and N.E.H. Hull. *The Supreme Court: An Essential History,* 2nd ed. Lawrence: University Press of Kansas, 2018.

Horwitz, Morton J. *The Transformation of American Law, 1780–1860.* Cambridge, MA: Harvard University Press, 1977.

Johnson, Herbert A. *The Chief Justiceship of John Marshall, 1801–1835.* Columbia: University of South Carolina Press, 1997.

Lennox, John. *Joseph Story: A Story of Love, Hate, Slavery, Power, and Forgiveness.* Wheaton, IL: Crossway, 2019.

Marcus, Maeva, ed. *Origins of the Federal Judiciary: Essays on the Judiciary Act of 1789.* New York: Oxford University Press, 1992.

Middlekauff, Robert. *The Glorious Cause: The American Revolution, 1763–1789.* New York: Oxford University Press, 1985.

Newmeyer, R. Kent. *Supreme Court Justice Joseph Story: Statesman of the Old Republic.* Chapel Hill: University of North Carolina Press, 1985.

Robarge, David S. *A Chief Justice's Progress: John Marshall From Revolutionary Virginia to the Supreme Court.* Westport, CT: Greenwood Press, 2000.

Roeber, A. G. *Faithful Magistrates and Republican Lawyers: Creators of Virginia Legal Culture, 1680–1810.* Chapel Hill: University of North Carolina Press, 1981.

White, G. Edward. *The Marshall Court and Cultural Change, 1815–1835.* New York: Oxford University Press, 1991.

### *Websites*

"Martin v. Hunter's Lessee." Cornell University Law School website. Accessed April 12, 2023. http://www.law.cornell.edu/supct/html/historics/USSC_CR_0014_0304_ZS.html.

"Martin v. Hunter's Lessee." U.S. Supreme Court Media Oyez website. Accessed April 12, 2023. http://www.oyez.org/cases/1792-1850/1816/1816_0/.

"The Thomas Jefferson Papers." The Library of Congress "American Memory" website. Accessed April 12, 2023. http://memory.loc.gov/ammem/collections/jefferson_papers/index.html.

—Commentary by Thomas H. Cox

# MARTIN V. HUNTER'S LESSEE

## Document Text

### STORY, J., delivered the opinion of the Court

This is a writ of error from the Court of Appeals of Virginia founded upon the refusal of that Court to obey the mandate of this Court requiring the judgment rendered in this very cause, at February Term, 1813, to be carried into due execution. The following is the judgment of the Court of Appeals rendered on the mandate:

> The Court is unanimously of opinion, that the appellate power of the Supreme Court of the United States does not extend to this Court, under a sound construction of the Constitution of the United States; that so much of the 25th section of the act of Congress to establish the judicial courts of the United States, as extends the appellate jurisdiction of the Supreme Court to this Court, is not in pursuance of the Constitution of the United States; that the writ of error in this cause was improvidently allowed under the authority of that act; that the proceedings thereon in the Supreme Court were coram non judice in relation to this Court, and that obedience to its mandate be declined by the Court.

The questions involved in this judgment are of great importance and delicacy. Perhaps it is not too much to affirm that, upon their right decision rest some of the most solid principles which have hitherto been supposed to sustain and protect the Constitution itself. The great respectability, too, of the Court whose decisions we are called upon to review, and the entire deference which we entertain for the learning and ability of that Court, add much to the difficulty of the task which has so unwelcomely fallen upon us. It is, however, a source of consolation, that we have had the assistance of most able and learned arguments to aid our inquiries; and that the opinion which is now to be pronounced has been weighed with every solicitude to come to a correct result, and matured after solemn deliberation.

Before proceeding to the principal questions, it may not be unfit to dispose of some preliminary considerations which have grown out of the arguments at the bar.

The Constitution of the United States was ordained and established not by the States in their sovereign capacities, but emphatically, as the preamble of the Constitution declares, by "the people of the United States." There can be no doubt that it was competent to the people to invest the general government with all the powers which they might deem proper and necessary, to extend or restrain these powers according to their own good pleasure, and to give them a paramount and supreme authority. As little doubt can there be that the people had a right to prohibit to the States the exercise of any powers which were, in their judgment, incompatible with the objects of the general compact, to make the powers of the State governments, in given cases, subordinate to those of the nation, or to reserve to themselves those sovereign authorities which they might not choose to delegate to either. The Constitution was not, therefore, necessarily carved out of existing State sovereignties, nor a surrender of powers already existing in State institutions, for the powers of the States depend upon their own Constitutions, and the people of every State had the right to modify and restrain them according to their own views of the policy or principle. On the other hand, it is perfectly clear that the sovereign powers vested in the State governments by their respective Constitutions remained unaltered and unimpaired except so far as they were granted to the Government of the United States.

These deductions do not rest upon general reasoning, plain and obvious as they seem to be. They have been positively recognised by one of the articles in amendment of the Constitution, which declares that

> The powers not delegated to the United States by the Constitution, nor prohibited by it to the States, are reserved to the States respectively, or to the people.

The government, then, of the United States can claim no powers which are not granted to it by the Constitution, and the powers actually granted, must be such as are expressly given, or given by necessary implication. On the other hand, this instrument, like every other grant, is to have a reasonable construction, according to the import of its terms, and where a power is expressly given in general terms, it is not to be restrained to particular cases unless that construction grow out of the context expressly or by necessary implication. The words are to be taken in their natural and obvious sense, and not in a sense unreasonably restricted or enlarged.

The Constitution unavoidably deals in general language. It did not suit the purposes of the people, in framing this great charter of our liberties, to provide for minute specifications of its powers or to declare the means by which those powers should be carried into execution. It was foreseen that this would be a perilous and difficult, if not an impracticable, task. The instrument was not intended to provide merely for the exigencies of a few years, but was to endure through a long lapse of ages, the events of which were locked up in the inscrutable purposes of Providence. It could not be foreseen what new changes and modifications of power might be indispensable to effectuate the general objects of the charter, and restrictions and specifications which at the present might seem salutary might in the end prove the overthrow of the system itself. Hence its powers are expressed in general terms, leaving to the legislature from time to time to adopt its own means to effectuate legitimate objects and to

mould and model the exercise of its powers as its own wisdom and the public interests, should require.

With these principles in view, principles in respect to which no difference of opinion ought to be indulged, let us now proceed to the interpretation of the Constitution so far as regards the great points in controversy.

The third article of the Constitution is that which must principally attract our attention. The 1st. section declares,

> The judicial power of the United States shall be vested in one Supreme Court, and in such other inferior Courts as the Congress may, from time to time, ordain and establish.

The 2d section declares, that

> The judicial power shall extend to all cases in law or equity, arising under this Constitution, the laws of the United States, and the treaties made, or which shall be made, under their authority; to all cases affecting ambassadors, other public ministers and consuls; to all cases of admiralty and maritime jurisdiction; to controversies to which the United States shall be a party; to controversies between two or more States; between a State and citizens of another State; between citizens of different States; between citizens of the same State, claiming lands under the grants of different States; and between a State or the citizens thereof, and foreign States, citizens, or subjects.

It then proceeds to declare, that

> in all cases affecting ambassadors, other public ministers and consuls, and those in which a State shall be a party, the Supreme Court shall have original jurisdiction. In all the other cases before mentioned, the Supreme Court shall have appellate jurisdiction both as to law and fact, with such exceptions and under such regulations, as the Congress shall make.

Such is the language of the article creating and defining the judicial power of the United States. It is the voice of the whole American people solemnly declared, in establishing one great department of that Government which was, in many respects, national, and in all, supreme. It is a part of the very same instrument which was to act not merely upon individuals, but upon States, and to deprive them altogether of the exercise of some powers of sovereignty and to restrain and regulate them in the exercise of others.

Let this article be carefully weighed and considered. The language of the article throughout is manifestly designed to be mandatory upon the Legislature. Its obligatory force is so imperative, that Congress could not, without a violation of its duty, have refused to carry it into operation. The judicial power of the United States shall be vested (not may be vested) in one Supreme Court, and in such inferior Courts as Congress may, from time to time, ordain and establish. Could Congress have lawfully refused to create a Supreme Court, or to vest in it the constitutional jurisdiction?

> The judges, both of the supreme and inferior courts, shall hold their offices during good behaviour, and shall, at stated times, receive, for their services, a compensation which shall not be diminished during their continuance in office.

Could Congress create or limit any other tenure of the judicial office? Could they refuse to pay at stated times the stipulated salary, or diminish it during the continuance in office? But one answer can be given to these questions: it must be in the negative. The object of the Constitution was to establish three great departments of Government—the legislative, the executive, and the judicial departments. The first was to pass laws, the second to approve and execute them, and the third to expound and enforce them. Without the latter, it would be impossible to carry into effect some of the express provisions of the Constitution. How, otherwise, could crimes against the United States be tried and punished? How could causes between two States be heard and determined? The judicial power must, therefore, be vested in some court by Congress; and to suppose that it was not an obligation binding on them, but might, at their pleasure, be omitted or declined, is to suppose that, under the sanction of the Constitution, they might defeat the Constitution itself, a construction which would lead to such a result cannot be sound.

The same expression, "shall be vested," occurs in other parts of the Constitution in defining the powers of the other coordinate branches of the Government. The first article declares that "all legislative powers herein granted shall be vested in a Congress of the United States." Will it be contended that the legislative power is not absolutely vested? that the words merely refer to some future act, and mean only that the legislative power may hereafter be vested? The second article declares that "the executive power shall be vested in a President of the United States of America." Could Congress vest it in any other person, or is it to await their good pleasure whether it is to vest at all? It is apparent that such a construction, in either case, would be utterly inadmissible. Why, then, is it entitled to a better support in reference to the judicial department?

If, then, it is a duty of Congress to vest the judicial power of the United States, it is a duty to vest the whole judicial power. The language, if imperative as to one part, is imperative as to all. If it were otherwise, this anomaly would exist, that Congress might successively refuse to vest the jurisdiction in any one class of cases enumerated in the Constitution, and thereby defeat the jurisdiction as to all, for the Constitution has not singled out any class on which Congress are bound to act in preference to others.

The next consideration is as to the Courts in which the judicial power shall be vested. It is manifest that a Supreme Court must be established; but whether it be equally obligatory to establish inferior Courts is a question of some difficulty. If Congress may lawfully omit to establish inferior Courts, it might follow that, in some of the enumerated cases, the judicial power could nowhere exist. The Supreme Court can have original jurisdiction in two classes of cases only, *viz.*, in cases affecting ambassadors, other public ministers and consuls, and in cases in which a State is a party. Congress cannot vest any portion of the judicial power of the United States except in Courts ordained and established by itself, and if, in any of the cases enumerated in the Constitution, the State courts did not then possess jurisdiction, the appellate jurisdiction of the Supreme Court (admitting that it could act on State courts) could not reach those cases, and, consequently, the injunction of the Constitution that the judicial power "shall be vested," would be disobeyed. It would seem therefore to follow that Congress are bound to create some inferior Courts in which to vest all that jurisdiction which, under the Constitution, is exclusively vested in the United States, and of which the Supreme Court cannot take original cognizance. They might establish one or more inferior Courts; they might parcel out the jurisdiction among such Courts, from time to time, at their own pleasure. But the whole judicial power of the United States should be at all times vested, either in an original or appellate form, in some Courts created under its authority.

This construction will be fortified by an attentive examination of the second section of the third article. The words are "the judicial power shall extend," &c. Much minute and elaborate criticism has been employed upon these words. It has been argued that they are equivalent to the words "may extend," and that "extend" means to widen to new cases not before within the scope of the power. For the reason which have been already stated, we are of opinion that the words are used in an imperative sense. They import an absolute grant of judicial power. They cannot have a relative signification applicable to powers already granted, for the American people had not made any previous grant. The Constitution was for a new Government, organized with new substantive powers, and not a mere supplementary charter to a Government already existing. The Confederation was a compact between States, and its structure and powers were wholly unlike those of the National Government. The Constitution was an act of the people of the United States to supersede the Confederation, and not to be ingrafted on it, as a stock through which it was to receive life and nourishment.

If, indeed, the relative signification could be fixed upon the term "extend," it could not (as we shall hereafter see) subserve the purposes of the argument in support of which it has been adduced. This imperative sense of the words "shall extend" is strengthened by the context. It is declared that, "in all cases affecting ambassadors, &c., that the Supreme Court shall have original jurisdiction." Could Congress withhold original jurisdiction in these cases from the Supreme Court? The clause proceeds—

> in all the other cases before mentioned, the Supreme Court shall have appellate jurisdiction, both as to law and fact, with such exceptions, and under such regulations, as the Congress shall make.

The very exception here shows that the framers of the Constitution used the words in an imperative sense. What necessity could there exist for this exception if the preceding words were not used in that sense? Without such exception, Congress would, by the preceding words, have possessed a complete power to regulate the appellate jurisdiction, if the language were only equivalent to the words "may have" appellate jurisdiction. It is apparent, then, that the exception was intended as a limitation upon the preceding words, to enable Congress to regulate and restrain the appellate power, as the public interests might, from time to time, require.

Other clauses in the Constitution might be brought in aid of this construction, but a minute examination of them cannot be necessary, and would occupy too much time. It will be found that whenever a particular object is to be effected, the language of the Constitution is always imperative, and cannot be disregarded without violating the first principles of public duty. On the other hand, the legislative powers are given in language which implies discretion, as, from the nature of legislative power, such a discretion must ever be exercised.

It being, then, established that the language of this clause is imperative, the next question is as to the cases to which it shall apply. The answer is found in the Constitution itself. The judicial power shall extend to all the cases enumerated in the Constitution. As the mode is not limited, it may extend to all such cases, in any form, in which judicial power may be exercised. It may therefore extend to them in the shape of original or appellate jurisdiction, or both, for there is nothing in the nature of the cases which binds to the exercise of the one in preference to the other.

In what cases (if any) is this judicial power exclusive, or exclusive at the election of Congress? It will be observed that there are two classes of cases enumerated in the Constitution between which a distinction seems to be drawn. The first class includes cases arising under the Constitution, laws, and treaties of the United States, cases affecting ambassadors, other public ministers and consuls, and cases of admiralty and maritime jurisdiction. In this class, the expression is, and that the judicial power shall extend to all cases; but in the subsequent part of the clause which embraces all the other cases of national cognizance, and forms the second class, the word "all" is dropped, seemingly *ex industria*. Here the judicial authority is to extend to controversies (not to all controversies) to which the United States shall be a party, &c. From this difference of phraseology, perhaps, a difference of constitutional intention may, with propriety, be inferred. It is hardly to be presumed that the variation in the language could have been accidental. It must have been the result of some determinate reason, and it is not very difficult to find a reason sufficient to support the apparent change of intention. In respect to the first class, it may well have been the intention of the framers of the Constitution imperatively to extend the judicial power either in an original or appellate form to all cases, and in the latter class to leave it to Congress to qualify the jurisdiction, original or appellate, in such manner as public policy might dictate.

The vital importance of all the cases enumerated in the first class to the national sovereignty might warrant such a distinction. In the first place, as to cases arriving under the Constitution, laws, and treaties of the United States. Here the State courts could not ordinarily possess a direct jurisdiction. The jurisdiction over such cases could not exist in the State courts previous to the adoption of the Constitution, and it could not afterwards be directly conferred on them, for the Constitution expressly requires the judicial power to be vested in courts ordained and established by the United States. This class of cases would embrace civil as well as criminal jurisdiction, and affect not only our internal policy, but our foreign relations. It would therefore be perilous to restrain it in any manner whatsoever, inasmuch as it might hazard the national safety. The same remarks may be urged as to cases affecting ambassadors, other public ministers, and consuls, who are emphatically placed under the guardianship of the law of nations, and as to cases of admiralty and maritime jurisdiction, the admiralty jurisdiction embraces all questions of prize and salvage, in the correct adjudication of which foreign nations are deeply interested; it embraces also maritime torts, contracts, and offences, in which the principles of the law and comity of nations often form an essential inquiry. All these cases, then, enter into the national policy, affect the national rights, and may compromit the national sovereignty. The original or appellate jurisdiction ought not therefore to be restrained, but should be commensurate with the mischiefs intended to be remedied, and, of course, should extend to all cases whatsoever.

A different policy might well be adopted in reference to the second class of cases, for although it might be fit that the judicial power should extend to all controversies to which the United States should be a party, yet this power night not have been imperatively given, least it should imply a right to take cognizance of original suits brought against the United States as defendants in their own Courts. It might not have been deemed proper to submit the sovereignty of the United States, against their own will to judicial cognizance, either to enforce rights or to prevent wrongs; and as to the other cases of the second class, they might well be left to be exercised under the exceptions and regulations which Congress might, in their wisdom, choose to apply. It is also worthy of remark that Congress seem, in a good degree, in the establishment of the present judicial system, to have adopted this distinction. In the first class of cases, the jurisdiction is not limited except by the subject matter; in the second, it is made materially to depend upon the value in controversy.

We do not, however, profess to place any implicit reliance upon the distinction which has here been stated and endeavoured to be illustrated. It has the rather been brought into view in deference to the legislative opinion, which has so long acted upon, and enforced this distinction. But there is, certainly, vast weight in the argument which has been urged that the Constitution is imperative upon Congress to vest all the judicial power of the United States, in the shape of original jurisdiction, in the Supreme and inferior courts created under its own authority. At all events, whether the one construction or the other prevail, it is manifest that the judicial power of the United States is unavoidably, in some cases, exclusive of all State authority, and in all others, may be made so at the election of Congress. No part of the criminal jurisdiction of the United States can, consistently with the Constitution, be delegated to State tribunals. The admiralty and maritime jurisdiction is of the same exclusive cognizance, and it can only be in those cases where, previous to the Constitution, State tribunals possessed jurisdiction independent of national authority that they can now constitutionally exercise a concurrent jurisdiction. Congress, throughout the Judicial Act, and particularly in the 9th, 11th, and 13th sections, have legislated upon the supposition that, in all the cases to which the judicial powers of the United States extended, they might rightfully vest exclusive jurisdiction in their own Courts.

But even admitting that the language of the Constitution is not mandatory, and that Congress may constitutionally omit to vest the judicial power in Courts of the United

States, it cannot be denied that, when it is vested, it may be exercised to the utmost constitutional extent.

This leads us to the consideration of the great question as to the nature and extent of the appellate jurisdiction of the United States. We have already seen that appellate jurisdiction is given by the Constitution to the Supreme Court in all cases where it has not original jurisdiction, subject, however, to such exceptions and regulations as Congress may prescribe. It is therefore capable of embracing every case enumerated in the Constitution which is not exclusively to be decided by way of original jurisdiction. But the exercise of appellate jurisdiction is far from being limited by the terms of the Constitution to the Supreme Court. There can be no doubt that Congress may create a succession of inferior tribunals, in each of which it may vest appellate as well as original jurisdiction. The judicial power is delegated by the Constitution in the most general terms, and may therefore be exercised by Congress under every variety of form of appellate or original jurisdiction. And as there is nothing in the Constitution which restrains or limits this power, it must therefore, in all other cases, subsist in the utmost latitude of which, in its own nature, it is susceptible.

As, then, by the terms of the Constitution, the appellate jurisdiction is not limited as to the Supreme Court, and as to this Court it may be exercised in all other cases than those of which it has original cognizance, what is there to restrain its exercise over State tribunals in the enumerated cases? The appellate power is not limited by the terms of the third article to any particular Courts. The words are, "the judicial power (which includes appellate power) shall extend to all cases," &c., and "in all other cases before mentioned, the Supreme Court shall have appellate jurisdiction." It is the case, then, and not the court, that gives the jurisdiction. If the judicial power extends to the case, it will be in vain to search in the letter of the Constitution for any qualification as to the tribunal where it depends. It is incumbent, then, upon those who assert such a qualification to show its existence by necessary implication. If the text be clear and distinct, no restriction upon its plain and obvious import ought to be admitted, unless the inference be irresistible.

If the Constitution meant to limit the appellate jurisdiction to cases pending in the Courts of the United States, it would necessarily follow that the jurisdiction

of these Courts would, in all the cases enumerated in the Constitution, be exclusive of State tribunals. How otherwise could the jurisdiction extend to all cases arising under the Constitution, laws, and treaties of the United States, or to all cases of admiralty and maritime jurisdiction? If some of these cases might be entertained by State tribunals, and no appellate jurisdiction as to them should exist, then the appellate power would not extend to all, but to some, cases. If State tribunals might exercise concurrent jurisdiction over all or some of the other classes of cases in the Constitution without control, then the appellate jurisdiction of the United States might, as to such cases, have no real existence, contrary to the manifest intent of the Constitution. Under such circumstances, to give effect to the judicial power, it must be construed to be exclusive, and this not only when the *casus foederis* should arise directly, but when it should arise incidentally in cases pending in State courts. This construction would abridge the jurisdiction of such Court far more than has been ever contemplated in any act of Congress.

On the other hand, if, as has been contended, a discretion be vested in Congress to establish or not to establish inferior Courts, at their own pleasure, and Congress should not establish such Courts, the appellate jurisdiction of the Supreme Court would have nothing to act upon unless it could act upon cases pending in the State courts. Under such circumstances it must be held that the appellate power would extend to State courts, for the Constitution is peremptory that it shall extend to certain enumerated cases, which cases could exist in no other Courts. Any other construction, upon this supposition, would involve this strange contradiction that a discretionary power vested in Congress, and which they might rightfully omit to exercise, would defeat the absolute injunctions of the Constitution in relation to the whole appellate power.

But it is plain that the framers of the Constitution did contemplate that cases within the judicial cognizance of the United States not only might, but would, arise in the State courts in the exercise of their ordinary jurisdiction. With this view, the sixth article declares, that

> This Constitution, and the laws of the United States which shall be made in pursuance thereof, and all treaties made, or which shall be made, under the authority of the United States, shall be the supreme law of the land,

and the judges in every State shall be bound thereby, anything in the Constitution or laws of any State to the contrary notwithstanding.

It is obvious that this obligation is imperative upon the State judges in their official, and not merely in their private, capacities. From the very nature of their judicial duties, they would be called upon to pronounce the law applicable to the case in judgment. They were not to decide merely according to the laws or Constitution of the State, but according to the Constitution, laws and treaties of the United States—"the supreme law of the land."

A moment's consideration will show us the necessity and propriety of this provision in cases where the jurisdiction of the State courts is unquestionable. Suppose a contract for the payment of money is made between citizens of the same State, and performance thereof is sought in the courts of that State; no person can doubt that the jurisdiction completely and exclusively attaches, in the first instance, to such courts. Suppose at the trial the defendant sets up in his defence a tender under a State law making paper money a good tender, or a State law impairing the obligation of such contract, which law, if binding, would defeat the suit. The Constitution of the United States has declared that no State shall make any thing but gold or silver coin a tender in payment of debts, or pass a law impairing the obligation of contracts. If Congress shall not have passed a law providing for the removal of such a suit to the courts of the United States, must not the State court proceed to hear and determine it? Can a mere plea in defence be, of itself, a bar to further proceedings, so as to prohibit an inquiry into its truth or legal propriety when no other tribunal exists to whom judicial cognizance of such cases is confided? Suppose an indictment for a crime in a State court, and the defendant should allege in his defence that the crime was created by an *ex post facto* act of the State, must not the State court, in the exercise of a jurisdiction which has already rightfully attached, have a right to pronounce on the validity and sufficiency of the defence? It would be extremely difficult, upon any legal principles, to give a negative answer to these inquiries. Innumerable instances of the same sort might be stated in illustration of the position, and unless the State courts could sustain jurisdiction in such cases, this clause of the sixth article would be without meaning or effect, and public mischiefs of a most enormous magnitude would inevitably ensue.

It must therefore be conceded that the Constitution not only contemplated, but meant to provide for, cases within the scope of the judicial power of the United States which might yet depend before State tribunals. It was foreseen that, in the exercise of their ordinary jurisdiction, State courts would incidentally take cognizance of cases arising under the Constitution, the laws, and treaties of the United States. Yet to all these cases the judicial power, by the very terms of the Constitution, is to extend. It cannot extend by original jurisdiction if that was already rightfully and exclusively attached in the State courts, which (as has been already shown) may occur; it must therefore extend by appellate jurisdiction, or not at all. It would seem to follow that the appellate power of the United States must, in such cases, extend to State tribunals; and if in such cases, there is no reason why it should not equally attach upon all others within the purview of the Constitution.

It has been argued that such an appellate jurisdiction over State courts is inconsistent with the genius of our Governments, and the spirit of the Constitution. That the latter was never designed to act upon State sovereignties, but only upon the people, and that, if the power exists, it will materially impair the sovereignty of the States, and the independence of their courts. We cannot yield to the force of this reasoning; it assumes principles which we cannot admit, and draws conclusions to which we do not yield our assent.

It is a mistake that the Constitution was not designed to operate upon States in their corporate capacities. It is crowded with provisions which restrain or annul the sovereignty of the States in some of the highest branches of their prerogatives. The tenth section of the first article contains a long list of disabilities and prohibitions imposed upon the States. Surely, when such essential portions of State sovereignty are taken away or prohibited to be exercised, it cannot be correctly asserted that the Constitution does not act upon the States. The language of the Constitution is also imperative upon the States as to the performance of many duties. It is imperative upon the State legislatures to make laws prescribing the time, places, and manner of holding elections for senators and representatives, and for electors of President and Vice-President. And in these as well as some other cases, Congress have a right to revise, amend, or supersede the laws which may be passed by State legislatures. When therefore the States are stripped of some of the highest attributes of sovereignty, and the same are given to the United States; when the legislatures of the States are, in some respects, under the control of Congress, and in every case are, under the Constitution, bound by the paramount authority of the United States, it is certainly difficult to support the argument that the appellate power over the decisions of State courts is contrary to the genius of our institutions. The courts of the United States can, without question, revise the proceedings of the executive and legislative authorities of the States, and if they are found to be contrary to the Constitution, may declare them to be of no legal validity. Surely the exercise of the same right over judicial tribunals is not a higher or more dangerous act of sovereign power.

Nor can such a right be deemed to impair the independence of State judges. It is assuming the very ground in controversy to assert that they possess an absolute independence of the United States. In respect to the powers granted to the United States, they are not independent; they are expressly bound to obedience by the letter of the Constitution, and if they should unintentionally transcend their authority or misconstrue the Constitution, there is no more reason for giving their judgments an absolute and irresistible force than for giving it to the acts of the other coordinate departments of State sovereignty.

The argument urged from the possibility of the abuse of the revising power is equally unsatisfactory. It is always a doubtful course to argue against the use or existence of a power from the possibility of its abuse. It is still more diffi ult by such an argument to ingraft upon a general power a restriction which is not to be found in the terms in which it is given. From the very nature of things, the absolute right of decision, in the last resort, must rest somewhere—wherever it may be vested, it is susceptible of abuse. In all questions of jurisdiction, the inferior or appellate court must pronounce the final judgment; and common sense, as well as legal reasoning, has conferred it upon the latter.

It has been further argued against the existence of this appellate power that it would form a novelty in our judicial institutions. This is certainly a mistake. In the Articles of Confederation, an instrument framed with infinitely more deference to State rights and State jealousies, a power was given to Congress to establish "courts for revising and determining, finally, appeals in all cases of captures." It is remarkable that

no power was given to entertain original jurisdiction in such cases, and consequently the appellate power (although not so expressed in terms) was altogether to be exercised in revising the decisions of State tribunals. This was, undoubtedly, so far a surrender of State sovereignty, but it never was supposed to be a power fraught with public danger or destructive of the independence of State judges. On the contrary, it was supposed to be a power indispensable to the public safety, inasmuch as our national rights might otherwise be compromitted and our national peace been dangered. Under the present Constitution, the prize jurisdiction is confined to the courts of the United States, and a power to revise the decisions of State courts, if they should assert jurisdiction over prize causes, cannot be less important or less useful than it was under the Confederation.

In this connexion, we are led again to the construction of the words of the Constitution, "the judicial power shall extend," &c. If, as has been contended at the bar, the term "extend" have a relative signification, and mean to widen an existing power, it will then follow, that, as the confederation gave an appellate power over State tribunals, the Constitution enlarged or widened that appellate power to all the other cases in which jurisdiction is given to the Courts of the United States. It is not presumed that the learned counsel would choose to adopt such a conclusion.

It is further argued that no great public mischief can result from a construction which shall limit the appellate power of the United States to cases in their own Courts, first because State judges are bound by an oath to support the Constitution of the United States, and must be presumed to be men of learning and integrity, and secondly because Congress must have an unquestionable right to remove all cases within the scope of the judicial power from the State courts to the courts of the United States at any time before final judgment, though not after final judgment. As to the first reason—admitting that the judges of the State courts are, and always will be, of as much learning, integrity, and wisdom as those of the courts of the United States (which we very cheerfully admit), it does not aid the argument. It is manifest that the Constitution has proceeded upon a theory of its own, and given or withheld powers according to the judgment of the American people, by whom it was adopted. We can only construe its powers, and cannot inquire into the policy or principles which induced the grant of them. The Constitution has presumed (whether rightly or wrongly we do not inquire) that State attachments, State prejudices, State jealousies, and State interests might sometimes obstruct or control, or be supposed to obstruct or control, the regular administration of justice. Hence, in controversies between States, between citizens of different States, between citizens claiming grants under different States, between a State and its citizens, or foreigners, and between citizens and foreigners, it enables the parties, under the authority of Congress, to have the controversies heard, tried, and determined before the national tribunals. No other reason than that which has been stated can be assigned why some, at least, of those cases should not have been left to the cognizance of the State courts. In respect to the other enumerated cases—the cases arising under the Constitution, laws, and treaties of the United States, cases affecting ambassadors and other public ministers, and cases of admiralty and maritime jurisdiction—reasons of a higher and more extensive nature, touching the safety, peace, and sovereignty of the nation, might well justify a grant of exclusive jurisdiction.

This is not all. A motive of another kind, perfectly compatible with the most sincere respect for State tribunals, might induce the grant of appellate power over their decisions. That motive is the importance, and even necessity, of uniformity of decisions throughout the whole United States upon all subjects within the purview of the Constitution. Judges of equal learning and integrity in different States might differently interpret a statute or a treaty of the United States, or even the Constitution itself; if there were no revising authority to control these jarring and discordant judgments and harmonize them into uniformity, the laws, the treaties, and the Constitution of the United States would be different in different States, and might perhaps never have precisely the same construction, obligation, or efficacy in any two States. The public mischiefs that would attend such a State of things would be truly deplorable, and it cannot be believed that they could have escaped the enlightened convention which formed the Constitution. What, indeed, might then have been only prophecy has now become fact, and the appellate jurisdiction must continue to be the only adequate remedy for such evils.

There is an additional consideration, which is entitled to great weight. The Constitution of the United States was designed for the common and equal benefit of all the people of the United States. The judicial power was granted for the same benign and salutary purposes. It was not to be exercised exclusively for the benefit of parties who might be plaintiffs, and would elect the national forum, but also for the protection of defendants who might be entitled to try their rights, or assert their privileges, before the same forum. Yet, if the construction contended for be correct, it will follow that, as the plaintiff may always elect the State court, the defendant may be deprived of all the security which the Constitution intended in aid of his rights. Such a State of things can in no respect be considered as giving equal rights. To obviate this difficulty, we are referred to the power which it is admitted Congress possess to remove suits from State courts to the national Courts, and this forms the second ground upon which the argument we are considering has been attempted to be sustained.

This power of removal is not to be found in express terms in any part of the Constitution; if it be given, it is only given by implication, as a power necessary and proper to carry into effect some express power. The power of removal is certainly not, in strictness of language; it presupposes an exercise of original jurisdiction to have attached elsewhere. The existence of this power of removal is familiar in courts acting according to the course of the common law in criminal as well as civil cases, and it is exercised before as well as after judgment. But this is always deemed in both cases an exercise of appellate, and not of original, jurisdiction. If, then, the right of removal be included in the appellate jurisdiction, it is only because it is one mode of exercising that power, and as Congress is not limited by the Constitution to any particular mode or time of exercising it, it may authorize a removal either before or after judgment. The time, the process, and the manner must be subject to its absolute legislative control. A writ of error is indeed but a process which removes the record of one court to the possession of another court, and enables the latter to inspect the proceedings, and give such judgment as its own opinion of the law and justice of the case may warrant. There is nothing in the nature of the process which forbids it from being applied by the legislature to interlocutory as well as final judgments. And if the right of removal from State courts exist before judgment, because it is included in the appellate power, it must for the same reason exist after judgment. And if the appellate power by the Constitution does not include cases pending in State courts, the right of removal, which is but a mode of exercising that power, cannot be applied to them. Precisely the same objections therefore exist as to the right of removal before judgment as after, and both must stand or fall together. Nor, indeed, would the force of the arguments on either side materially vary if the right of removal were an exercise of original jurisdiction. It would equally trench upon the jurisdiction and independence of State tribunals.

The remedy, too, of removal of suits would be utterly inadequate to the purposes of the Constitution if it could act only on the parties, and not upon the State courts. In respect to criminal prosecutions, the difficulty seems admitted to be insurmountable; and in respect to civil suits, there would, in many cases, be rights without corresponding remedies. If State courts should deny the constitutionality of the authority to remove suits from their cognizance, in what manner could they be compelled to relinquish the jurisdiction? In respect to criminal cases, there would at once be an end of all control, and the state decisions would be paramount to the Constitution; and though, in civil suits, the courts of the United States might act upon the parties, yet the State courts might act in the same way, and this conflict of jurisdictions would not only jeopardise private rights, but bring into imminent peril the public interests.

On the whole, the Court are of opinion that the appellate power of the United States does extend to cases pending in the State courts, and that the 25th section of the judiciary act, which authorizes the exercise of this jurisdiction in the specified cases by a writ of error, is supported by the letter and spirit of the Constitution. We find no clause in that instrument which limits this power, and we dare not interpose a limitation where the people have not been disposed to create one.

Strong as this conclusion stands upon the general language of the Constitution, it may still derive support from other sources. It is an historical fact that this exposition of the Constitution, extending its appellate power to State courts, was, previous to its adoption, uniformly and publicly avowed by its friends and admitted by its enemies as the basis of their respective reasonings, both in and out of the State conventions. It is an historical fact that, at the time when the Judicia-

ry Act was submitted to the deliberations of the first Congress, composed, as it was, not only of men of great learning and ability but of men who had acted a principal part in framing, supporting, or opposing that Constitution, the same exposition was explicitly declared and admitted by the friends and by the opponents of that system. It is an historical fact that the Supreme Court of the United States have, from time to time, sustained this appellate jurisdiction in a great variety of cases brought from the tribunals of many of the most important States in the Union, and that no State tribunal has ever breathed a judicial doubt on the subject, or declined to obey the mandate of the Supreme Court until the present occasion. This weight of contemporaneous exposition by all parties, this acquiescence of enlightened State courts, and these judicial decisions of the Supreme Court through so long a period do, as we think, place the doctrine upon a foundation of authority which cannot be shaken without delivering over the subject to perpetual and irremediable doubts.

The next question which has been argued is whether the case at bar be within the purview of the 25th section of the Judiciary Act, so that this Court may rightfully sustain the present writ of error. This section, stripped of passages unimportant in this inquiry, enacts, in substance, that a final judgment or decree in any suit in the highest court of law or equity of a State, where is drawn in question the validity of a treaty or statute of, or an authority excised under, the United States, and the decision is against their validity, or where is drawn in question the validity of a statute of, or an authority exercised under, any State, on the ground of their being repugnant to the Constitution, treaties, or laws, of the United States, and the decision is in favour of such their validity, or of the Constitution, or of a treaty or statute of, or commission held under, the United States, and the decision is against the title, right, privilege, or exemption specially set up or claimed by either party under such clause of the said Constitution, treaty, statute, or commission, may be reexamined and reversed or affirmed in the Supreme Court of the United States upon a writ of error in the same manner, and under the same regulations, and the writ shall have the same effect, as if the judgment or decree complained of had been rendered or passed in a Circuit Court, and the proceeding upon the reversal shall also be the same, except that the Supreme Court, instead of remanding the cause for a final decision, as before provided, may, at their discretion, if the cause shall have been once remanded before, proceed to a final decision of the same and award execution. But no other error shall be assigned or regarded as a ground of reversal in any such case as aforesaid, than such as appears upon the face of the record, and immediately respects the before-mentioned question of validity or construction of the said Constitution, treaties, statutes, commissions, or authorities in dispute.

That the present writ of error is founded upon a judgment of the Court below which drew in question and denied the validity of a statute of the United States is incontrovertible, for it is apparent upon the face of the record. That this judgment is final upon the rights of the parties is equally true, for if well founded, the former judgment of that court was of conclusive authority, and the former judgment of this Court utterly void. The decision was therefore equivalent to a perpetual stay of proceedings upon the mandate, and a perpetual denial of all the rights acquired under it. The case, then, falls directly within the terms of the Act. It is a final judgment in a suit in a State court denying the validity of a statute of the United States, and unless a distinction can be made between proceedings under a mandate and proceedings in an original suit, a writ of error is the proper remedy to revise that judgment. In our opinion, no legal distinction exists between the cases.

In causes remanded to the Circuit Courts, if the mandate be not correctly executed, a writ of error or appeal has always been supposed to be a proper remedy, and has been recognized as such in the former decisions of this Court. The statute gives the same effect to writs of error from the judgments of State courts as of the Circuit Courts, and in its terms provides for proceedings where the same cause may be a second time brought up on writ of error before the Supreme Court. There is no limitation or description of the cases to which the second writ of error may be applied, and it ought therefore to be coextensive with the cases which fall within the mischiefs of the statute. It will hardly be denied that this cause stands in that predicament; and if so, then the appellate jurisdiction of this Court has rightfully attached.

But it is contended, that the former judgment of this Court was rendered upon a case not within the purview of this section of the Judicial Act, and that, as it was pronounced by an incompetent jurisdiction, it was utterly void, and cannot be a sufficient foundation to sustain any subsequent proceedings. To this argument several answers may be given. In the first place, it is not admitted that, upon this writ of error, the former record is before us. The error now assigned is not in the former proceedings, but in the judgment rendered upon the mandate issued after the former judgment. The question now litigated is not upon the construction of a treaty, but upon the constitutionality of a statute of the United States, which is clearly within our jurisdiction. In the next place, in ordinary cases a second writ of error has never been supposed to draw in question the propriety of the first judgment, and it is difficult to perceive how such a proceeding could be sustained upon principle. A final judgment of this Court is supposed to be conclusive upon the rights which it decides, and no statute has provided any process by which this Court can revise its own judgments. In several cases which have been formerly adjudged in this Court, the same point was argued by counsel, and expressly overruled. It was solemnly held that a final judgment of this Court was conclusive upon the parties, and could not be reexamined.

In this case, however, from motives of a public nature, we are entirely willing to wave all objections and to go back and reexamine the question of jurisdiction as it stood upon the record formerly in judgment. We have great confidence that our jurisdiction will, on a careful examination, stand confirmed as well upon principle as authority. It will be recollected that the action was an ejectment for a parcel of land in the Northern Neck, formerly belonging to Lord Fairfax. The original plaintiff claimed the land under a patent granted to him by the State of Virginia in 1789, under a title supposed to be vested in that State by escheat or forfeiture. The original defendant claimed the land as devisee under the will of Lord Fairfax. The parties agreed to a special statement of facts in the nature of a special verdict, upon which the District Court of Winchester, in 1793, gave a general judgment for the defendant, which judgment was afterwards reversed in 1810 by the Court of Appeals, and a general judgment was rendered for the plaintiff; and from this last judgment a writ of error was brought to the Supreme Court. The statement of facts contained a regular deduction of the title of Lord Fairfax until his death, in 1781, and also the title of his devisee. It also contained a regular deduction of the title of the plaintiff, under the State of Virginia, and further referred to the treaty of peace of 1783, and to the acts of Virginia respecting the lands of Lord Fairfax, and the supposed escheat or forfeiture thereof, as component parts of the case. No facts disconnected with the titles thus set up by the parties were alleged on either side. It is apparent from this summary explanation that the title thus set up by the plaintiff might be open to other objections; but the title of the defendant was perfect and complete if it was protected by the treaty of 1783. If therefore this Court had authority to examine into the whole record, and to decide upon the legal validity of the title of the defendant, as well as its application to the treaty of peace, it would be a case within the express purview of the 25th section of the Act, for there was nothing in the record upon which the Court below could have decided but upon the title as connected with the treaty; and if the title was otherwise good, its sufficiency must have depended altogether upon its protection under the treaty. Under such circumstances it was strictly a suit where was drawn in question the construction of a treaty, and the decision was against the title specially set up or claimed by the defendant. It would fall, then, within the very terms of the Act.

The objection urged at the bar is that this Court cannot inquire into the title, but simply into the correctness of the construction put upon the treaty by the Court of Appeals, and that their judgment is not reexaminable here unless it appear on the face of the record that some construction was put upon the treaty. If therefore that court might have decided the case upon the invalidity of the title (and, *non constat*, that they did not) independent of the treaty, there is an end of the appellate jurisdiction of this Court. In support of this objection, much stress is laid upon the last clause of the section, which declares that no other cause shall be regarded as a ground of reversal than such as appears on the face of the record and immediately respects the construction of the treaty, &c., in dispute.

If this be the true construction of the section, it will be wholly inadequate for the purposes which it professes to have in view, and may be evaded at pleasure. But we see no reason for adopting this narrow construction; and there are the strongest reasons against it founded upon the words as well as the intent of the legislature. What is the case for which the body of the section provides a remedy by writ of error? The answer must be in the words of the section, a suit where is drawn in

question the construction of a treaty, and the decision is against the title set up by the party. It is therefore the decision against the title set up with reference to the treaty, and not the mere abstract construction of the treaty itself, upon which the statute intends to found the appellate jurisdiction. How, indeed, can it be possible to decide whether a title be within the protection of a treaty until it is ascertained what that title is, and whether it have a legal validity? From the very necessity of the case, there must be a preliminary inquiry into the existence and structure of the title before the Court can construe the treaty in reference to that title. If the Court below should decide, that the title was bad, and therefore not protected by the treaty, must not this Court have a power to decide the title to be good, and therefore protected by the treaty? Is not the treaty, in both instances, equally construed, and the title of the party, in reference to the treaty, equally ascertained and decided? Nor does the clause relied on in the objection impugn this construction. It requires that the error upon which the Appellate Court is to decide shall appear on the face of the record, and immediately respect the questions before mentioned in the section. One of the questions is as to the construction of a treaty upon a title specially set up by a party, and every error that immediately respects that question must, of course, be within the cognizance, of the Court. The title set up in this case is apparent upon the face of the record, and immediately respects the decision of that question; any error therefore in respect to that title must be reexaminable, or the case could never be presented to the Court.

The restraining clause was manifestly intended for a very different purpose. It was foreseen that the parties might claim under various titles, and might assert various defences altogether independent of each other. The Court might admit or reject evidence applicable to one particular title, and not to all, and, in such cases, it was the intention of Congress to limit what would otherwise have unquestionably attached to the Court, the right of revising all the points involved in the cause. It therefore restrains this right to such errors as respect the questions specified in the section; and, in this view, it has an appropriate sense, consistent with the preceding clauses. We are therefore satisfied that, upon principle, the case was rightfully before us, and if the point were perfectly new, we should not hesitate to assert the jurisdiction.

But the point has been already decided by this Court upon solemn argument. In *Smith v. The State of Maryland*, 6 Cranch 286, precisely the same objection was taken by counsel, and overruled by the unanimous opinion of the Court. That case was, in some respects, stronger than the present; for the court below decided expressly that the party had no title, and therefore the treaty could not operate upon it. This Court entered into an examination of that question, and, being of the same opinion, affirmed the judgment. There cannot, then, be an authority which could more completely govern the present question.

It has been asserted at the bar that, in point of fact, the Court of Appeals did not decide either upon the treaty or the title apparent upon the record, but upon a compromise made under an act of the legislature of Virginia. If it be true (as we are informed) that this was a private act, to take effect only upon a certain condition, *viz.*, the execution of a deed of release of certain lands, which was matter *in pais*, it is somewhat difficult to understand how the Court could take judicial cognizance of the act or of the performance of the condition, unless spread upon the record. At all events, we are bound to consider that the Court did decide upon the facts actually before them. The treaty of peace was not necessary to have been stated, for it was the supreme law of the land, of which all Courts must take notice. And at the time of the decision in the Court of Appeals and in this Court, another treaty had intervened, which attached itself to the title in controversy and, of course, must have been the supreme law to govern the decision if it should be found applicable to the case. It was in this view that this Court did not deem it necessary to rest its former decision upon the treaty of peace, believing that the title of the defendant was, at all events, perfect under the treaty of 1794.

The remaining questions respect more the practice than the principles of this Court. The forms of process and the modes of proceeding in the exercise of jurisdiction are, with few exceptions, left by the Legislature to be regulated and changed as this Court may, in its discretion, deem expedient. By a rule of this Court, the return of a copy of a record of the proper court, under the seal of that court, annexed to the writ of error, is declared to be "a sufficient compliance with the mandate of the writ." The record in this case is duly certified by the clerk of the Court of Appeals and annexed to the writ of error. The objection therefore which has been urged to the sufficiency of the return cannot prevail.

Another objection is that it does not appear that the judge who granted the writ of error did, upon issuing the citation, take the bond required by the 22d section of the Judiciary Act.

We consider that provision as merely directory to the judge; and that an omission does not avoid the writ of error. If any party be prejudiced by the omission, this Court can grant him summary relief by imposing such terms on the other party as, under all the circumstances, may be legal and proper. But there is nothing in the record by which we can judicially know whether a bond has been taken or not, for the statute does not require the bond to be returned to this Court, and it might with equal propriety be lodged in the Court below, who would ordinarily execute the judgment to be rendered on the writ. And the presumption of law is, until the contrary appears, that every judge who signs a citation has obeyed the injunctions of the Act.

We have thus gone over all the principal questions in the cause, and we deliver our judgment with entire confidence that it is consistent with the Constitution and laws of the land.

We have not thought it incumbent on us to give any opinion upon the question, whether this Court have authority to issue a writ of mandamus to the Court of Appeals to enforce the former judgments, as we do not think it necessarily involved in the decision of this cause.

It is the opinion of the whole Court that the judgment of the Court of Appeals of Virginia, rendered on the mandate in this cause, be reversed, and the judgment of the District Court, held at Winchester, be, and the same is hereby, affirmed.

## *J. Johnson*

It will be observed in this case that the Court disavows all intention to decide on the right to issue compulsory process to the State courts, thus leaving us, in my opinion, where the Constitution and laws place us— supreme over persons and cases as far as our judicial powers extend, but not asserting any compulsory control over the State tribunals.

In this view I acquiesce in their opinion, but not altogether in the reasoning or opinion of my brother who delivered it. Few minds are accustomed to the same habit of thinking, and our conclusions are most satisfactory to ourselves when arrived at in our own way.

I have another reason for expressing my opinion on this occasion. I view this question as one of the most momentous importance; as one which may affect, in its consequences, the permanence of the American Union. It presents an instance of collision between the judicial powers of the Union, and one of the greatest States in the Union, on a point the most delicate and difficult to be adjusted. On the one hand, the General Government must cease to exist whenever it loses the power of protecting itself in the exercise of its constitutional powers. Force, which acts upon the physical powers of man, or judicial process, which addresses itself to his moral principles or his fears, are the only means to which governments can resort in the exercise of their authority. The former is happily unknown to the genius of our Constitution except as far as it shall be sanctioned by the latter, but let the latter be obstructed in its progress by an opposition which it cannot overcome or put by, and the resort must be to the former, or government is no more.

On the other hand, so firmly am I persuaded that the American people can no longer enjoy the blessings of a free government whenever the State sovereignties shall be prostrated at the feet of the General Government, nor the proud consciousness of equality and security any longer than the independence of judicial power shall be maintained consecrated and intangible, that I could borrow the language of a celebrated orator and exclaim, "I rejoice that Virginia has resisted."

Yet here I must claim the privilege of expressing my regret, that the opposition of the high and truly respected tribunal of that State had not been marked with a little more moderation. The only point necessary to be decided in the case then before them was "whether they were bound to obey the mandate emanating from this Court?" But, in the judgment entered on their minutes, they have affirmed that the case was, in this Court, *coram non judice*, or, in other words, that this Court had not jurisdiction over it.

This is assuming a truly alarming latitude of judicial power. Where is it to end? It is an acknowledged principle of, I believe, every Court in the world that not only the decisions, but everything done under the judicial process of courts not having jurisdiction are, *ipso facto*, void. Are, then, the judgments of this Court to be reviewed in every court of the Union? and is every recovery of money, every change of property, that has taken place under our process to be considered as null, void, and tortious?

We pretend not to more infallibility than other courts composed of the same frail materials which compose this. It would be the height of affectation to close our minds upon the recollection that we have been extracted from the same seminaries in which originated the learned men who preside over the State tribunals. But there is one claim which we can with confidence assert in our own name upon those tribunals—the profound, uniform, and unaffected respect which this Court has always exhibited for State decisions give us strong pretensions to judicial comity. And another claim I may assert, in the name of the American people; in this Court, every State in the Union is represented; we are constituted by the voice of the Union, and when decisions take place which nothing but a spirit to give ground and harmonize can reconcile, ours is the superior claim upon the comity of the State tribunals. It is the nature of the human mind to press a favourite hypothesis too far, but magnanimity will always be ready to sacrifice the pride of opinion to public welfare.

In the case before us, the collision has been, on our part, wholly unsolicited. The exercise of this appellate jurisdiction over the State decisions has long been acquiesced in, and when the writ of error in this case was allowed by the President of the Court of Appeals of Virginia, we were sanctioned in supposing that we were to meet with the same acquiescence there. Had that Court refused to grant the writ in the first instance, or had the question of jurisdiction, or on the mode of exercising jurisdiction, been made here originally, we should have been put on our guard, and might have so modelled the process of the Court as to strip it of the offensive form of a mandate. In this case it might have been brought down to what probably the 25th section of the Judiciary Act meant it should be, to-wit, an alternative judgment either that the State court may finally proceed at its option to carry into effect the judgment of this Court or, if it declined doing so, that then this Court would proceed itself to execute it. The language, sense, and operation of the 25th section on this subject merit particular attention. In the preceding section, which has relation to causes brought up by writ of error from the Circuit Courts of the United States, this Court is instructed not to issue executions, but to send a special mandate to the Circuit Court to award execution thereupon. In case of the Circuit Court's refusal to obey such mandate, there could be no doubt as to the ulterior measures; compulsory process might, unquestionably, be resorted to. Nor, indeed, was there any reason to suppose that they ever would refuse, and therefore there is no provision made for authorizing this Court to execute its own judgment in cases of that description. But not so in cases brought up from the State courts; the framers of that law plainly foresaw that the State courts might refuse, and not being willing to leave ground for the implication that compulsory process must be resorted to, because no specific provision was made, they have provided the means, by authorizing this Court, in case of reversal of the State decision, to execute its own judgment. In case of reversal, only was this necessary, for, in case of affirmance, this collision could not arise. It is true that the words of this section are that this Court may, in their discretion, proceed to execute its own judgment. But these words were very properly put in, that it might not be made imperative upon this Court to proceed indiscriminately in this way, as it could only be necessary in case of the refusal of the State courts, and this idea is fully confirmed by the words of the 13th section, which restrict this Court in issuing the writ of mandamus, so as to confine it expressly to those Courts which are constituted by the United States.

In this point of view, the Legislature is completely vindicated from all intention to violate the independence of the State judiciaries. Nor can this Court, with any more correctness, have imputed to it similar intentions. The form of the mandate issued in this case is that known to appellate tribunals, and used in the ordinary cases of writs of error from the courts of the United States. It will, perhaps, not be too much, in such cases, to expect of those who are conversant in the forms, fictions, and technicality of the law not to give the process of courts too literal a construction. They should be considered with a view to the ends they are intended to answer and the law and practice in which they originate. In this view, the mandate was no more than a mode of submitting to that court the option which the 25th section holds out to them.

Had the decision of the Court of Virginia been confined to the point of their legal obligation to carry the judgment of this Court into effect, I should have thought it unnecessary to make any further observations in this cause. But we are called upon to vindicate our general revising power, and its due exercise in this particular case.

Here, that I may not be charged with arguing upon a hypothetical case, it is necessary to ascertain what the real question is which this Court is now called to decide on.

In doing this, it is necessary to do what, although, in the abstract, of very questionable propriety, appears to be generally acquiesced in, to-wit, to review the case as it originally came up to this Court on the former writ of error. The cause, then, came up upon a case stated between the parties, and under the practice of that State, having the effect of a special verdict. The case stated brings into view the treaty of peace with Great Britain, and then proceeds to present the various laws of Virginia and the facts upon which the parties found their respective titles. It then presents no particular question, but refers generally to the law arising out of the case. The original decision was obtained prior to the Treaty of 1794, but before the case was adjudicated in this Court, the Treaty of 1794 had been concluded.

The difficulties of the case arise under the construction of the 25th section above alluded to, which, as far as it relates to this case, is in these words:

> A final judgment or decree in any suit, in the highest Court of law or equity of a State in which a decision in the suit could be had, . . . where is drawn in question the construction of any clause of the Constitution or of a treaty, . . . and the decision is against the title set up or claimed by either party under such clause, may be reexamined and reversed, or affirmed. . . . But no other error shall be assigned or regarded as a ground of reversal in any such case as aforesaid than such as appears on the face of the record and immediately respects the before-mentioned questions of validity or construction of the said treaties,

&c.

The first point decided under this state of the case was that, the judgment being a part of the record, if that judgment was not such as, upon that case, it ought to have been, it was an error apparent on the face of the record. But it was contended that the case there stated presented a number of points upon which the decision below may have been founded, and that it did not therefore necessarily appear to have been an error immediately respecting a question on the construction of a treaty. But the Court held that, as the reference was general to the law arising out of the case, if one question arose which called for the construction of a treaty, and the decision negatived the right set up under it, this Court will reverse that decision, and that it is the duty of the party who would avoid the inconvenience of this principle so to mould the case as to obviate the ambiguity. And under this point arises the question whether this Court can inquire into the title of the party, or whether they are so restricted in their judicial powers as to be confined to decide on the operation of a treaty upon a title previously ascertained to exist.

If there is any one point in the case on which an opinion may be given with confidence, it is this, whether we consider the letter of the statute, or the spirit, intent, or meaning, of the Constitution and of the legislature, as expressed in the 27th section, it is equally clear that the title is the primary object to which the attention of the Court is called in every such case. The words are, "and the decision be against the title," so set up, not against the construction of the treaty contended for by the party setting up the title. And how could it be otherwise? The title may exist notwithstanding the decision of the State courts to the contrary, and, in that case, the party is entitled to the benefits intended to be secured by the treaty. The decision to his prejudice may have been the result of those very errors, partialities, or defects in State jurisprudence against which the Constitution intended to protect the individual. And if the contrary doctrine be assumed, what is the consequence? This Court may then be called upon to decide on a mere hypothetical case—to give a construction to a treaty without first deciding whether there was any interest on which that treaty, whatever be its proper construction, would operate. This difficulty was felt and weighed in the case of *Smith and the State of Maryland*, and that decision was founded upon the idea that this Court was not thus restricted.

But another difficulty presented itself: the Treaty of 1794 had become the supreme law of the land since the judgment rendered in the Court below. The defendant, who was at that time an alien, had now become

confirmed in his rights under that treaty. This would have been no objection to the correctness of the original judgment. Were we, then, at liberty to notice that treaty in rendering the judgment of this Court?

Having dissented from the opinion of this Court in the original case on the question of title, this difficulty did not present itself in my way in the view I then took of the case. But the majority of this Court determined that, as a public law, the treaty was a part of the law of every case depending in this Court; that, as such, it was not necessary that it should be spread upon the record, and that it was obligatory upon this Court, in rendering judgment upon this writ of error, notwithstanding the original judgment may have been otherwise unimpeachable. And to this opinion I yielded my hearty consent, for it cannot be maintained that this Court is bound to give a judgment unlawful at the time of rendering it, in consideration that the same judgment would have been lawful at any prior time. What judgment can now be lawfully rendered between the parties is the question to which the attention of the Court is called. And if the law which sanctioned the original judgment expire pending an appeal, this Court has repeatedly reversed the judgment below, although rendered whilst the law existed. So, too, if the plaintiff in error die pending suit, and his land descend on an alien, it cannot be contended that this Court will maintain the suit in right of the judgment in favour of his ancestor, notwithstanding his present disability.

It must here be recollected that this is an action of ejectment. If the term formally declared upon expires pending the action, the Court will permit the plaintiff to amend by extending the term—why? Because, although the right may have been in him at the commencement of the suit, it has ceased before judgment, and, without this amendment, he could not have judgment. But suppose the suit were really instituted to obtain possession of a leasehold, and the lease expire before judgment, would the Court permit the party to amend in opposition to the right of the case? On the contrary, if the term formally declared on were more extensive than the lease in which the legal title was founded, could they give judgment for more than costs? It must be recollected that, under this judgment, a writ of restitution is the fruit of the law. This, in its very nature, has relation to, and must be founded upon, a present existing right at the time of judgment. And whatever be the cause which takes this right away, the remedy must, in the reason and nature of things, fall with it.

When all these incidental points are disposed of, we find the question finally reduced to this—does the judicial power of the United States extend to the revision of decisions of State courts in cases arising under treaties? But in order to generalize the question and present it in the true form in which it presents itself in this case, we will inquire whether the Constitution sanctions the exercise of a revising power over the decisions of State tribunals in those cases to which the judicial power of the United States extends?

And here it appears to me that the great difficulty is on the other side. That the real doubt is whether the State tribunals can constitutionally exercise jurisdiction in any of the cases to which the judicial power of the United States extends.

Some cession of judicial power is contemplated by the third article of the Constitution; that which is ceded can no longer be retained. In one of the Circuit Courts of the United States, it has been decided (with what correctness I will not say) that the cession of a power to pass an uniform act of bankruptcy, although not acted on by the United States, deprives the States of the power of passing laws to that effect. With regard to the admiralty and maritime jurisdiction, it would be difficult to prove that the States could resume it if the United States should abolish the Courts vested with that jurisdiction; yet it is blended with the other cases of jurisdiction in the second section of the third article, and ceded in the same words. But it is contended that the second section of the third article contains no express cession of jurisdiction; that it only vests a power in Congress to assume jurisdiction to the extent therein expressed. And under this head arose the discussion on the construction proper to be given to that article.

On this part of the case, I shall not pause long. The rules of construction, where the nature of the instrument is ascertained, are familiar to every one. To me, the Constitution appears, in every line of it, to be a contract which, in legal language, may be denominated tripartite. The parties are the people, the States, and the United States. It is returning in a circle to contend that it professes to be the exclusive act of the people, for what have the people done but to form this compact? That the States are recognised as parties to it is

evident from various passages, and particularly that in which the United States guaranty to each State a republican form of Government.

The security and happiness of the whole was the object, and, to prevent dissention and collision, each surrendered those powers which might make them dangerous to each other. Well aware of the sensitive irritability of sovereign States, where their wills or interests clash, they placed themselves, with regard to each other, on the footing of sovereigns upon the ocean, where power is mutually conceded to act upon the individual, but the national vessel must remain unviolated. And to remove all ground for jealousy and complaint, they relinquish the privilege of being any longer the exclusive arbiters of their own justice where the rights of others come in question or the great interests of the whole may be affected by those feelings, partialities, or prejudices, which they meant to put down forever.

Nor shall I enter into a minute discussion on the meaning of the language of this section. I have seldom found much good result from hypercritical severity in examining the distinct force of words. Language is essentially defective in precision, more so than those are aware of who are not in the habit of subjecting it to philological analysis. In the case before us, for instance, a rigid construction might be made which would annihilate the powers intended to be ceded. The words are, "shall extend to;" now that which extends to does not necessarily include in, so that the circle may enlarge until it reaches the objects that limit it, and yet not take them in. But the plain and obvious sense and meaning of the word "shall," in this sentence, is in the future sense, and has nothing imperative in it. The language of the framers of the Constitution is "We are about forming a General Government—when that Government is formed, its powers shall extend," &c. I therefore see nothing imperative in this clause, and certainly it would have been very unnecessary to use the word in that sense; for, as there was no controlling power constituted, it would only, if used in an imperative sense, have imposed a moral obligation to act. But the same result arises from using it in a future sense, and the Constitution everywhere assumes as a postulate that wherever power is given, it will be used, or at least used as far as the interests of the American people require it, if not from the natural proneness of man to the exercise of power, at least from a sense of duty and the obligation of an oath.

Nor can I see any difference in the effect of the words used in this section, as to the scope of the jurisdiction of the United States' courts over the cases of the first and second description comprised in that section. "Shall extend to controversies," appears to me as comprehensive in effect as "shall extend to all cases." For if the judicial power extend "to controversies between citizen and alien," &c., to what controversies of that description does it not extend? If no case can be pointed out which is excepted, it then extends to all controversies.

But I will assume the construction as a sound one that the cession of power to the General Government means no more than that they may assume the exercise of it whenever they think it advisable. It is clear that Congress have hitherto acted under that impression, and my own opinion is in favour of its correctness. But does it not then follow that the jurisdiction of the State court, within the range ceded to the General Government, is permitted, and may be withdrawn whenever Congress think proper to do so? As it is a principle that everyone may renounce a right introduced for his benefit, we will admit that, as Congress have not assumed such jurisdiction, the State courts may constitutionally exercise jurisdiction in such cases. Yet surely the general power to withdraw the exercise of it includes in it the right to modify, limit, and restrain that exercise.

This is my domain, put not your foot upon it; if you do, you are subject to my laws; I have a right to exclude you altogether; I have, then, a right to prescribe the terms of your admission to a participation. As long as you conform to my laws, participate in peace, but I reserve to myself the right of judging how far your acts are conformable to my laws.

Analogy, then, to the ordinary exercise of sovereign authority would sustain the exercise of this controlling or revising power.

But it is argued that a power to assume jurisdiction to the constitutional extent does not necessarily carry with it a right to exercise appellate power over the State tribunals.

This is a momentous questions, and one on which I shall reserve myself uncommitted for each particular case as it shall occur. It is enough, at present, to have shown that Congress has not asserted, and this Court has not attempted, to exercise that kind of authority *in personam* over the State courts which would place them in the relation of an inferior responsible body without their own acquiescence. And I have too much confidence in the State tribunals to believe that a case ever will occur in which it will be necessary for the General Government to assume a controlling power over these tribunals. But is it difficult to suppose a case which will call loudly for some remedy or restraint? Suppose a foreign minister or an officer acting regularly under authority from the United States, seized today, tried tomorrow, and hurried the next day to execution. Such cases may occur, and have occurred, in other countries. The angry vindictive passions of men have too often made their way into judicial tribunals, and we cannot hope forever to escape their baleful influence. In the case supposed, there ought to be a power somewhere to restrain or punish, or the Union must be dissolved. At present, the uncontrollable exercise of criminal jurisdiction is most securely confided to the State tribunals. The Courts of the United States are vested with no power to scrutinize into the proceedings of the State courts in criminal cases; on the contrary, the General Government has, in more than one instance, exhibited their confidence by a wish to vest them with the execution of their own penal law. And extreme, indeed, I flatter myself, must be the case in which the General Government could ever be induced to assert this right. If ever such a case should occur, it will be time enough to decide upon their constitutional power to do so.

But we know that, by the 3d article of the Constitution, judicial power, to a certain extent, is vested in the General Government, and that, by the same instrument, power is given to pass all laws necessary to carry into effect the provisions of the Constitution. At present, it is only necessary to vindicate the laws which they have passed affecting civil cases pending in State tribunals.

In legislating on this subject, Congress, in the true spirit of the Constitution, have proposed to secure to everyone the full benefit of the Constitution without forcing any one necessarily into the courts of the United States. With this view, in one class of cases, they have not taken away absolutely from the State courts all the cases to which their judicial power extends, but left it to the plaintiff to bring his action there originally if he choose, or to the defendant to force the plaintiff into the courts of the United States where they have jurisdiction, and the former has instituted his suit in the State courts. In this case, they have not made it legal for the defendant to plead to the jurisdiction, the effect of which would be to put an end to the plaintiff's suit and oblige him, probably at great risk or expense, to institute a new action; but the Act has given him a right to obtain an order for a removal, on a petition to the State court, upon which the cause, with all its existing advantages, is transferred to the Circuit Court of the United States. This, I presume, can be subject to no objection, as the Legislature has an unquestionable right to make the ground of removal a ground of plea to the jurisdiction, and the Court must then do no more than it is now called upon to do, to-wit, give an order or a judgment, or call it what we will, in favour of that defendant. And so far from asserting the inferiority of the State tribunal, this act is rather that of a superior, inasmuch as the Circuit Court of the United States becomes bound, by that order, to take jurisdiction of the case. This method, so much more unlikely to affect official delicacy than that which is resorted to in the other class of cases, might perhaps have been more happily applied to all the cases which the Legislature thought it advisable to remove from the State courts. But the other class of cases, in which the present is included, was proposed to be provided for in a different manner. And here, again, the Legislature of the Union evince their confidence in the State tribunals, for they do not attempt to give original cognizance to their own Circuit Courts of such cases, or to remove them by petition and order; but still believing that their decisions will be generally satisfactory, a writ of error is not given immediately as a question within the jurisdiction of the United States shall occur, but only in case the decision shall finally, in the Court of the last resort, be against the title set up under the Constitution, treaty, &c.

In this act I can see nothing which amounts to an assertion of the inferiority or dependence of the State tribunals. The presiding judge of the State court is himself authorized to issue the writ of error, if he will, and thus give jurisdiction to the Supreme Court; and if he thinks proper to decline it, no compulsory process is provided by law to oblige him. The party who imagines himself aggrieved is then at liberty to apply to a judge of the United States, who issues the writ of error, which (whatever the form) is, in substance, no more than a mode of compelling the opposite party to appear before this Court and maintain the legality of his judgment obtained before the state tribunal. An exemplification of a record is the common property of every one who chooses to apply and pay for it, and thus the

case and the parties are brought before us; and so far is the court itself from being brought under the revising power of this Court that nothing but the case, as presented by the record and pleadings of the parties, is considered, and the opinions of the court are never resorted to unless for the purpose of assisting this Court in forming their own opinions.

The absolute necessity that there was for Congress to exercise something of a revising power over cases and parties in the State courts will appear from this consideration.

Suppose the whole extent of the judicial power of the United States vested in their own courts, yet such a provision would not answer all the ends of the Constitution, for two reasons:

1st. Although the plaintiff may, in such case, have the full benefit of the Constitution extended to him, yet the defendant would not, as the plaintiff might force him into the court of the State at his election.

2dly. Supposing it possible so to legislate as to give the courts of the United States original jurisdiction in all cases arising under the Constitution, laws, &c., in the words of the 2d section of the 3d article (a point on which I have some doubt, and which in time might perhaps, under some *quo minus* fiction or a willing construction, greatly accumulate the jurisdiction of those Courts), yet a very large class of cases would remain unprovided for. Incidental questions would often arise, and as a Court of competent jurisdiction in the principal case must decide all such questions, whatever laws they arise under, endless might be the diversity of decisions throughout the Union upon the Constitution, treaties, and laws of the United States, a subject on which the tranquillity of the Union, internally and externally, may materially depend.

I should feel the more hesitation in adopting the opinions which I express in this case were I not firmly convinced that they are practical, and may be acted upon without compromitting the harmony of the Union or bringing humility upon the State tribunals. God forbid that the judicial power in these States should ever for a moment, even in its humblest departments, feel a doubt of its own independence. Whilst adjudicating on a subject which the laws of the country assign finally to the revising power of another tribunal, it can feel no such doubt. An anxiety to do justice is ever relieved by the knowledge that what we do is not final between the parties. And no sense of dependence can be felt from the knowledge that the parties, not the Court, may be summoned before another tribunal. With this view, by means of laws, avoiding judgments obtained in the State courts in cases over which Congress has constitutionally assumed jurisdiction, and inflicting penalties on parties who shall contumaciously persist in infringing the constitutional rights of others—under a liberal extension of the writ of injunction and the habeas corpus *ad subjiciendum*, I flatter myself that the full extent of the constitutional revising power may be secured to the United States, and the benefits of it to the individual, without ever resorting to compulsory or restrictive process upon the State tribunals; a right which, I repeat again, Congress has not asserted, nor has this Court asserted, nor does there appear any necessity for asserting.

The remaining points in the case being mere questions of practice, I shall make no remarks upon them.

Judgment affirmed.

---

## Glossary

**appellate jurisdiction:** the right of a court to hear cases previously heard by other, lower courts

**comity:** legal reciprocity shown between different governments or jurisdictions

*coram non judice*: a legal term used to describe a legal proceeding without proper venue or jurisdiction

**devisee:** a person who inherits land through a will

**ejectment:** a common law term to describe the recovery of land ("real property")

**escheat:** the right of a state to take property that has no legal heirs or claimants

*ex industria*: by industry or labor

*ex post facto*: operating retroactively

**General Government:** the federal government of the United States

*in pais*: performed out of court

*non constat*: a legal term meaning "it is not certain"; refers to information that is hard to argue in court

**original jurisdiction:** the right of a court to hear a case for the first time

*quo minus*: a writ sworn out by a debtor, claiming that he has been injured by his or her creditor and is thus unable to pay his or her debt

**right of removal:** the right to transfer a case from one court to another

**vested:** granted or endowed; said of a right that, when granted, cannot be taken away

**vide:** see

**viz:** namely

**writ of error:** a writ from an appellate court to a court of original jurisdiction for a record of the case in question, so that the case may be reviewed for possible legal errors

# TRUSTEES OF DARTMOUTH COLLEGE V. WOODWARD

| | |
|---|---|
| **DATE**<br>1819 | **CITATION**<br>17 U.S. 518 |
| **AUTHOR**<br>John Marshall | **SIGNIFICANCE**<br>Held that the contract clause of the U.S. Constitution prohibited states from violating transactions involving individual property rights with private or public corporations |
| **VOTE**<br>5-1 | |

## Overview

 Argued March 10–12, 1818, and decided on February 25, 1819, the case of *Trustees of Dartmouth College v. Woodward* was brought about when a leadership vacancy within the trustees and president of the private Dartmouth College allowed the Legislature of New Hampshire to attempt to convert the college to a public university. The legislature argued that the charter of the school, granted by King George III in 1769, was not a legally binding document after the American Revolution severed the political relations between the government and its citizens. The legislature passed an amendment to the charter that transferred control of the school to officials appointed by the governor. The original trustees filed suit, arguing that the transfer violated the corporate rights, the state constitution, and the U.S. Constitution. A state court ruled the legislature's action valid because the American Revolution had rendered the college a public corporation. As such, it was subject to state legislation. The future secretary of state Daniel Webster argued the case in the U.S. Supreme Court, and the Court reversed the decision of the state court. Gabriel Duvall dissented from the majority but declined to write a separate opinion.

## Context

Dartmouth College is one of the nine colonial colleges chartered before the American Revolution. It was founded by Congregationalist minister Eleazar Wheelock to convert and train Native Americans to serve as missionaries to their people. After the success of his earlier effort at Moor's Indian Charity School, Wheelock wanted to move to a location closer to Native American tribes and expand the school into a college. It was chartered in 1769 after the royal governor of New Hampshire provided the land and charter in the name of George III. The charter created a self-perpetuating board of trustees to oversee its operations, and the trustees would appoint a president to lead the college's daily operations. The charter outlined that Dartmouth College existed "for the education and instruction of Youth of the Indian Tribes in this Land in reading, writing & all parts of Learning which shall appear necessary and expedient for civilizing & christianizing Children of Pagans as well as in all liberal Arts and Sciences and also of English Youth and any others." Eleazer Wheelock was appointed the first president of Dartmouth and would serve in this position until his death in April 1779. The trustees appointed Wheelock's son John to succeed his father as president.

After the American Revolution, the college, like nearly every other higher-learning institution, experienced a slump that lasted for several years, threatening its continued operation. Although the college was a private religious institution, the State of New Hampshire stepped in and provided funds several times to keep the college operating. During this time, the trustees, primarily Federalists in their political alignment, continued to emphasize the religious mission of the college over its educational functions. However, by 1815 the tumultuous relationship between several trustees and John Wheelock had reached a boiling point, and Wheelock was fired.

The Democratic-Republicans who controlled the legislature of New Hampshire in 1815 were ideologically opposed to religious authority in social or political affairs and firmly believed in the rights of the people over the rights of the elite. An earlier U.S. Supreme Court decision, *Fletcher v. Peck* (1810), had argued that states could not violate contracts for the transfer of private property, even if such transfers were established through illegal actions such as bribery. However, the legislature understood the situation in New Hampshire to be a different matter, one that rested on the police power clause of the Constitution. The New Hampshire legislature saw education as a public good subject to legislative authority. The leadership fallout at Dartmouth College was seen as an opportunity to transfer the school from a private religious college to a secular public university, a structure that more closely aligned with the political outlook of the Democratic-Republicans. One of Wheelock's supporters on the board of trustees was the secretary and treasurer, William Woodward. Woodward had control of the college's charter, seal, and records and worked with the legislature to alter the school's charter. The act not only reinstated Wheelock but directed the governor to appoint all leadership positions, added more seats to the board of trustees, and created a state board with oversight and veto authority over the school's trustees. The amendment also transferred the property and other holdings of Dartmouth College to the state, effectively transferring the school from a private to a public institution.

The original board of trustees immediately filed suit, and an injunction allowed the original board to operate Dartmouth until the judiciary resolved the matter. The trustees hired Dartmouth alumnus Daniel Webster to represent them in their suit against Woodward, arguing that through him, the legislature had violated their rights as a private corporation in a breach of common

***Dartmouth alumnus Daniel Webster argued the case.***
(Otto Bettman)

contract law, the state constitution, and the Constitution of the United States. The New Hampshire court ruled that the legislature's actions were entirely valid partly because the charter had been a contract between King George III and Eleazer Wheelock, both of whom no longer held any reasonable claim to the institution. The court also declared that by accepting public funds, the college ceased being a private institution. As a public institution, the religious mission of the college was in direct violation of the doctrine of separation of church and state. The U.S. Supreme Court reversed the state court's decision, holding that the state had violated the private property rights of the private corporation, and restored the control of the original board of trustees, unseating Wheelock and Woodward.

## About the Author

John Marshall was born in Germantown, Virginia, in 1755 to Thomas Marshall, a surveyor and land agent, and Mary Randolph Keith, a second cousin of Thomas Jefferson. Marshall was the eldest of fifteen children. He grew up in a two-room log cabin and had only one year of formal education but was a voracious reader. John and Thomas Marshall joined the 3rd Virginia Regiment, participating in several battles, including the Battle of Brandywine Creek and the transformative winter at Valley Forge. Marshall was furloughed from service in 1780 and began studying law under George Wythe at the College of William and Mary. The same year, John Marshall was admitted to the Virginia Bar. He would briefly return to service in Continental Army before being elected to the Council of State of the Virginia House of Delegates in 1782.

Marshall would continue to serve as an influential state councilman while taking on new responsibilities as the recorder of the Richmond courts and building a private law practice. After witnessing the failures of the Articles of Confederation in Shay's Rebellion, Marshall became a fierce proponent of constitutional ratification, working alongside James Madison in the Virginia Ratifying Convention of 1788. Marshall declined the nomination of George Washington to assume the duties of the U.S. attorney for Virginia and the U.S. attorney general, choosing instead to pursue the private practice of law.

In 1797 Marshall served on a three-member commission to France that would later become known as the XYZ Affair, leading to the undeclared quasi-war with France. Marshall supported many actions during this time but spoke against the Alien and Sedition Acts as unnecessary and corrosively divisive acts on American society. In 1789 his efforts during the XYZ Affair, along with the support of Patrick Henry, won Marshall the seat as congressman of Virginia's 13th District. Marshall would turn down the nomination of John Adams to the U.S. Supreme Court, instead seeking to represent the people of Virginia in Congress. By 1800, his actions in Congress led to President Adams nominating him briefly for secretary of war before withdrawing the nomination and instead nominating Marshall for secretary of state. Marshall accepted the nomination and took office in June 1800. He would be instrumental in ending the quasi-war and ongoing clashes with Britain and Spain and enforcing maritime rights through North Africa among the Barbary States.

In January 1801 President John Adams, after the loss of several justices, appointed Marshall to the U.S. Supreme Court as chief justice, believing Marshall could heal divisions and propel the Court to a position of prominence in the federal government. Marshall was confirmed later that month and assumed the office of chief justice on February 4, 1801. Marshall did not disappoint.

In the years preceding the Marshall Court, the U.S. Supreme Court had made only 63 decisions, none of which had struck down a state or federal law. Marshall's 34-year tenure as chief justice would produce more than 1,000 decisions—about half of which were authored by Marshall himself—and establish the U.S. Supreme Court as an influential actor in shaping the federal government. The Marshall Court would strike down federal law only once, in *Marbury v. Madison* (1803). However, this ruling would assume the powers of the Court to check the actions of the president, Congress, the states, and lower courts in interpreting the U.S. Constitution. The Marshall Court would generally enforce strong governmental powers. Marshall would die in Philadelphia on July 6, 1835, the last of the founding generation.

## Explanation and Analysis of the Document

Chief Justice Marshall begins his opinion by bluntly stating that the contracts clause of the U.S. Constitution declares that no state shall make any law impairing the obligations of contracts. The American Revolution did not dissolve these rights. As such, the actions of the New Hampshire legislature were unconstitutional and rendered void. Marshall then pauses his opinion and begins to outline the case by citing the charter's language at length to point out that the charter provided the trustees of Dartmouth College particular rights to be exercised "in all courts forever hereafter." The charter grants the trustees the ability "for the use of said Dartmouth College, to have, get, acquire, purchase, receive, hold, possess and enjoy, tenements, hereditaments, jurisdictions, and franchises, for themselves and their successors." Marshall outlines that this includes the buildings, land, and the right to "have, accept and receive any rents, profits, annuities, gifts, legacies, donations or bequests of any kind whatsoever" for the support and operation of Dartmouth College.

Marshall then cites "An Act to amend the charter, and enlarge and improve the corporation of Dartmouth

College" at equal length. This act clearly states the legislature's interpretation that "knowledge and learning generally diffused through a community, are essential to the preservation of a free government," which, in the legislative opinion, were "more extensively useful" in the form of a public university. In this transformation, the legislature directed that the new board of trustees "and their successors in that capacity" would "forever have hold, use, exercise and enjoy all the powers, authorities, rights, property, liberties, privileges and immunities which have hitherto been possessed, enjoyed and used by the Trustees of Dartmouth College" with several exceptions. One of those was the assumption of all property by the state. This also created the requirement of the president of Dartmouth University for an annual report on the operations and status of funds to the governor of New Hampshire. Marshall continues by citing the decision of the New Hampshire Superior Court that such actions were "not repugnant to the Constitution of the United States."

Then Marshall concludes that the Superior Court of New Hampshire had ruled in error. Marshall argues that "a corporation is established for purposes of general charity, or for education generally, does not, *per se*, make it a public corporation, liable to the control of the legislature." The charter did not create, as the legislature had interpreted, a "civil institution to be employed in the administration of government," which would require the restructuring of the mission and control of the school according to the doctrine of separation of church and state. Marshall continues that the funds initially raised by Eleazar Wheelock and continued to be submitted by contributors freely giving assets for the mission outlined in the charter for Dartmouth established property in the trust of twelve trustees appointed according to the bylaws of the charter in perpetuity. Marshall argues that the act of the legislature of New Hampshire violates the contract clause of the U.S. Constitution in directing the transfer and retention of property rights against the will of the legally defined owner—the corporation overseen by the Board of Trustees. By establishing a corporation, Wheelock had created "an artificial being, invisible,

intangible, and existing only in contemplation of the law." This being, according to Marshall, held "a perpetual succession of individuals" with the rights secured by the Constitution as "one immortal being."

Marshall argues that "no person can be compelled to be a member of such a corporation against his will" and that the creation of the new organization was done intentionally to disenfranchise the legal rights, privileges, and immunities to private property of free citizens guilty of no offense. "Their object and effect," according to Marshall, "is, to take away from one, rights, property and franchises, and to grant them to another. This is not the exercise of legislative power. To justify the taking away of vested rights, there must be a forfeiture; to adjudge upon and declare which, is the proper province of the judiciary. Attainder and confiscation are acts of sovereign power, not acts of legislation." Marshall concludes his opinion with the observation that Dartmouth College "is no more a state instrument than a natural person exercising the same powers would be."

## Impact

Though *Dartmouth v. Woodward* was not the first case in which Chief Justice Marshall struck down a state effort to transfer property rights citing the sanctity of the contract clause of the Constitution, it would become the most influential in creating the recognition of private corporations as legal entities. Though later decisions such as *Terrett v. Taylor* (1815), *Pennsylvania College Cases* (1871), *Shields v. Ohio* (1877), *Miller v. State* (1881), and *Greenwood v. Fright Company* (1888) held that states did have the right to vacate or alter private contracts, these decisions required that such actions be reasonable and not cause undue harm to the members of the corporation. *Dartmouth v. Woodward* would establish limits on the states to interfere with private corporations and commercial enterprises. This then motivated more corporations to be formed, which resulted in a significant rise in the establishment of American businesses.

## Questions for Further Study

1. Despite the decision in *Dartmouth v. Woodward*, was the state legislature of New Hampshire acting in good faith in directing the transfer of Dartmouth from a private to a public institution? Why or why not?

2. How might Native Americans following this case have argued that it provided them with a case against the American government?

3. Most decisions that altered the judgment rendered in *Dartmouth v. Woodward* came after the American Civil War. Why would so many cases follow this event?

4. Did John Marshall's past life experiences have an impact on shaping this decision? If so, which ones, and how? If not, why not?

5. Justice Duvall was the only justice to dissent, but he chose not to write an opinion. What does this suggest about how strongly Justice Duvall felt about the decision and his dissent?

## Further Reading

### *Books*

Calloway, Colin. *The Indian History of an American Institution: Native Americans and Dartmouth.* Lebanon: Dartmouth College Press, 2010.

Lamoreaux, Naomi, and William Novak, eds. *Corporations and American Democracy.* Cambridge: Harvard University Press, 2017.

Newmyer, Kent. *John Marshall and the Heroic Age of the Supreme Court.* Baton Rouge: Louisiana State University Press, 2001.

Winkler, Adam. *We the Corporations: How American Businesses Won their Civil Rights.* New York: Liveright, 2018.

### *Websites*

Bomboy, Scott. "Daniel Webster's Unique Supreme Court Legacy." National Constitution Center. Accessed January 18, 2023, https://constitutioncenter.org/blog/daniel-websters-unique-supreme-court-legacy.

"Judicial Nationalism." Digital History. 2021. Accessed January 18, 2023, http://www.digitalhistory.uh.edu/disp_textbook.cfm?smtID=2&psid=3528.

Vile, John R. "Dartmouth College v. Woodward (1819)." First Amendment Encyclopedia. 2009. Accessed January 18, 2023, http://www.mtsu.edu/first-amendment/article/729/dartmouth-college-v-woodward.

—Commentary by Bryant Macfarlane

# TRUSTEES OF DARTMOUTH COLLEGE V. WOODWARD

## Document Text

### *Mr. Chief Justice MARSHALL delivered the opinion of the Court*

This is an action of trover, brought by the Trustees of Dartmouth College against William H. Woodward, in the State court of New Hampshire, for the book of records, corporate seal, and other corporate property, to which the plaintiffs allege themselves to be entitled.

A special verdict, after setting out the rights of the parties, finds for the defendant, if certain acts of the Legislature of New Hampshire, passed on the 27th of June, and on the 18th of December 1816, be valid, and binding on the Trustees, without their assent, and not repugnant to the Constitution of the United States; otherwise, it finds for the plaintiffs.

The Superior Court of judicature of New Hampshire rendered a judgment upon this verdict for the defendant, which judgment has been brought before this court by writ of error. The single question now to be considered is do the acts to which the verdict refers violate the Constitution of the United States?

This court can be insensible neither to the magnitude nor delicacy of this question. The validity of a legislative act is to be examined; and the opinion of the highest law tribunal of a State is to be revised—an opinion which carries with it intrinsic evidence of the diligence, of the ability, and the integrity, with which it was formed. On more than one occasion, this Court has expressed the cautious circumspection with which it approaches the consideration of such questions, and has declared that in no doubtful case would it pro-

nounce a legislative act to be contrary to the Constitution. But the American people have said in the Constitution of the United States that "no State shall pass any bill of attainder, *ex post facto law,* or law impairing the obligation of contracts." In the same instrument, they have also said, "that the judicial power shall extend to all cases in law and equity arising under the Constitution." On the judges of this Court, then, is imposed the high and solemn duty of protecting, from even legislative violation, those contracts which the Constitution of our country has placed beyond legislative control; and however irksome the task may be, this is a duty from which we dare not shrink.

The title of the plaintiffs originates in a charter dated the 13th day of December, in the year 1769, incorporating twelve persons therein mentioned, by the name of "The Trustees of Dartmouth College," granting to them and their successors the usual corporate privileges and powers, and authorizing the Trustees, who are to govern the college, to fill up all vacancies which may be created in their own body.

The defendant claims under three acts of the Legislature of New Hampshire, the most material of which was passed on the 27th of June, 1816, and is entitled "An act to amend the charter, and enlarge and improve the corporation of Dartmouth College." Among other alterations in the charter, this act increases the number of Trustees to twenty-one, gives the appointment of the additional members to the executive of the State, and creates a Board of Overseers with power to inspect and control the most important acts of the Trustees. This Board consists of twenty-five persons. The President of the Senate, the speaker of the house of representatives, of New Hampshire, and the Governor and Lieutenant Governor of Vermont, for the time being, are to be members *ex officio*. The Board is to be completed by the Governor and Council of New Hampshire, who are also empowered to fill all vacancies which may occur. The acts of the 18th and 26th of December are supplemental to that of the 27th of June, and are principally intended to carry that act into effect. The majority of the Trustees of the college have refused to accept this amended charter, and have brought this suit for the corporate property, which is in possession of a person holding by virtue of the acts which have been stated.

It can require no argument to prove that the circumstances of this case constitute a contract. An application is made to the Crown for a charter to incorporate a religious and literary institution. In the application, it is stated that large contributions have been made for the object, which will be conferred on the corporation as soon as it shall be created. The charter is granted, and on its faith the property is conveyed. Surely, in this transaction, every ingredient of a complete and legitimate contract is to be found. The points for consideration are, 1. Is this contract protected by the Constitution of the United States? 2. Is it impaired by the acts under which the defendant holds?

1. On the first point, it has been argued that the word "contract," in its broadest sense, would comprehend the political relations between the government and its citizens, would extend to offices held within a State, for State purposes, and to many of those laws concerning civil institutions, which must change with circumstances and be modified by ordinary legislation, which deeply concern the public, and which, to preserve good government, the public judgment must control. That even marriage is a contract, and its obligations are affected by the laws respecting divorces. That the clause in the Constitution, if construed in its greatest latitude, would prohibit these laws. Taken in its broad, unlimited sense, the clause would be an unprofitable and vexatious interference with the internal concerns of a State, would unnecessarily and unwisely embarrass its legislation, and render immutable those civil institutions, which are established for purposes of internal government, and which, to subserve those purposes, ought to vary with varying circumstances. That, as the framers of the Constitution could never have intended to insert in that instrument a provision so unnecessary, so mischievous, and so repugnant to its general spirit, the term "contract" must be understood in a more limited sense. That it must be understood as intended to guard against a power of at least doubtful utility, the abuse of which had been extensively felt, and to restrain the legislature in future from violating the right to property. That, anterior to the formation of the Constitution, a course of legislation had prevailed in many, if not in all, of the States, which weakened the confidence of man in man, and embarrassed all transactions between individuals, by dispensing with a faithful performance of engagements. To correct this mischief by restraining the power which produced it, the State legislatures were forbidden "to pass any law impairing the obligation of contracts," that is, of contracts respecting property, under which some individual could claim a right to something beneficial to himself, and that, since the clause in the Constitution must in construction receive some limitation, it may be confined, and ought to be confined, to cases of this description, to cases within the mischief it was intended to remedy.

The general correctness of these observations cannot be controverted. That the framers of the Constitution did not intend to restrain the States in the regulation of their civil institutions, adopted for internal government, and that the instrument they have given us is not to be so construed, may be admitted. The provision of the Constitution never has been understood to embrace other contracts than those which respect property, or some object of value, and confer rights which may be asserted in a court of justice. It never has been understood to restrict the general right of the legislature to legislate on the subject of divorces. Those acts enable some tribunals not to impair a marriage contract, but to liberate one of the parties, because it has been broken by the other. When any State legislature shall pass an act annulling all marriage contracts, or allowing either party to annul it, without the consent of the other, it will be time enough to inquire, whether such an act be constitutional.

The parties in this case differ less on general principles, less on the true construction of the Constitution in the abstract, than on the application of those principles to this case and on the true construction of the charter of 1769. This is the point on which the cause essentially depends. If the act of incorporation be a grant of political power, if it create a civil institution, to be employed in the administration of the government, or if the funds of the college be public property, or if the State of New Hampshire, as a government, be alone interested in its transactions, the subject is one in which the legislature of the State may act according to its own judgment, unrestrained by any limitation of its power imposed by the Constitution of the United States.

But if this be a private eleemosynary institution, endowed with a capacity to take property for objects unconnected with government, whose funds are bestowed by individuals on the faith of the charter; if the donors have stipulated for the future disposition and management of those funds in the manner prescribed by themselves, there may be more difficulty in the case, although neither the persons who have made these stipulations, nor those for whose benefit they were made should be parties to the cause. Those who are no longer interested in the property may yet retain such an interest in the preservation of their own arrangements as to have a right to insist that those arrangements shall be held sacred. Or, if they have themselves disappeared, it becomes a subject of serious and anxious inquiry whether those whom they have legally empowered to represent them forever may not assert all the rights which they possessed while in being; whether, if they be without personal representatives who may feel injured by a violation of the compact, the Trustees be not so completely their representatives in the eye of the law as to stand in their place not only as respects the government of the College, but also as respects the maintenance of the College charter. It becomes then the duty of the Court, most seriously to examine this charter and to ascertain its true character.

From the instrument itself, it appears that, about the year 1754, the Rev. Eleazer Wheelock established, at his own expense and on his own estate, a charity school for the instruction of Indians in the Christian religion. The success of this institution inspired him with the design of soliciting contributions in England for carrying on and extending his undertaking. n this pious work, he employed the Rev. Nathaniel Whitaker, who, by virtue of a power of attorney from Dr. Wheelock, appointed the Earl of Dartmouth and others Trustees of the money which had been and should be contributed, which appointment Dr. Wheelock confirmed by a deed of trust authorizing the Trustees to fix on a site for the College. They determined to establish the school on Connecticut River in the western part of New Hampshire, that situation

being supposed favorable for carrying on the original design among the Indians and also for promoting learning among the English, and the proprietors in the neighborhood having made large offers of land on condition that the College should there be placed. Dr. Wheelock then applied to the Crown for an act of incorporation, and represented the expediency of appointing those whom he had, by his last will, named as Trustees in America to be members of the proposed corporation. "In consideration of the premises," "for the education and instruction of the youth of the Indian tribes," &c., "and also of English youth, and any others," the charter was granted, and the Trustees of Dartmouth College were, by that name, created a body corporate, with power, *for the use of the said College,* to acquire real and personal property, and to pay the President, tutors and other officers of the College, such salaries as they shall allow.

The charter proceeds to appoint Eleazer Wheelock, "the founder of said College," President thereof, with power, by his last will, to appoint a successor, who is to continue in office until disapproved by the Trustees. In case of vacancy, the Trustees may appoint a President, and in case of the ceasing of a President, the senior professor or tutor, being one of the Trustees, shall exercise the office until an appointment shall be made. The Trustees have power to appoint and displace professors, tutors and other officers, and to supply any vacancies which may be created in their own body by death, resignation, removal or disability, and also to make orders, ordinances and laws for the government of the College, the same not being repugnant to the laws of Great Britain or of New Hampshire, and not excluding any person on account of his speculative sentiments in religion, or his being of a religious profession different from that of the Trustees. This charter was accepted, and the property, both real and personal, which had been contributed for the benefit of the College was conveyed to, and vested in, the corporate body.

From this brief review of the most essential parts of the charter, it is apparent that the funds of the College consisted entirely of private donations. It is, perhaps, not very important who were the donors. The probability is that the Earl of Dartmouth, and the other Trustees in England, were, in fact, the largest contributors. Yet the legal conclusion from the facts recited in the charter would probably be that Dr. Wheelock was the founder of the College. The origin of the institution was undoubtedly the Indian charity school established by Dr. Wheelock at his own expense. It was at his instance and to enlarge this school that contributions were solicited in England. The person soliciting these contributions was his agent, and the Trustees who received the money were appointed by, and act under, his authority. It is not too much to say that the funds were obtained by him in trust, to be applied by him to the purposes of his enlarged school. The charter of incorporation was granted at his instance. The persons named by him in his last will as the Trustees of his charity school compose a part of the corporation, and he is declared to be the founder of the College, and its President for life. Were the inquiry material, we should feel some hesitation in saying that Dr. Wheelock was not, in law, to be considered as the founder, 1 Bl.Com. 481, of this institution, and as possessing all the rights appertaining to that character. But be this as it may, Dartmouth College is really endowed by private individuals, who have bestowed their funds for the propagation of the Christian religion among the Indians and for the promotion of piety and learning generally. From these funds the salaries of the tutors are drawn, and these salaries lessen the expense of education to the students. It is then an eleemosynary (1 Bl. Com. 471), and so far as respects its funds, a private corporation.

Do its objects stamp on it a different character? Are the Trustees and professors public officers, invested with any portion of political power, partaking in any degree in the administration of civil government, and performing duties which flow from the sovereign authority? That education is an object of national concern, and a proper subject of legislation, all admit. That there may be an institution, founded by government and placed entirely under its immediate control, the officers of which would be public officers, amenable exclusively to government, none will deny. But is Dartmouth College such an institution? Is education altogether in the hands of government? Does every teacher of youth become a public officer, and do donations for the purpose of education necessarily become public property so far that the will of the legislature, not the will of the donor, becomes the law of the donation? These questions are of serious moment to society, and deserve to be well considered.

Doctor Wheelock, as the keeper of his charity school, instructing the Indians in the art of reading, and in our holy religion, sustaining them at his own expense and on the voluntary contributions of the charitable,

could scarcely be considered as a public officer exercising any portion of those duties which belong to government, nor could the legislature have supposed that his private funds, or those given by others, were subject to legislative management because they were applied to the purposes of education. When, afterwards, his school was enlarged and the liberal contributions made in England and in America enabled him to extend his care to the education of the youth of his own country, no change was wrought in his own character or in the nature of his duties. Had he employed assistant tutors with the funds contributed by others, or had the Trustees in England established a school, with Dr. Wheelock at its head, and paid salaries to him and his assistants, they would still have been private tutors, and the fact that they were employed in the education of youth could not have converted them into public officers, concerned in the administration of public duties, or have given the legislature a right to interfere in the management of the fund. The Trustees, in whose care that fund was placed by the contributors, would have been permitted to execute their trust uncontrolled by legislative authority.

Whence, then, can be derived the idea that Dartmouth College has become a public institution, and its Trustees public officers, exercising powers conferred by the public for public objects? Not from the source whence its funds were drawn, for its foundation is purely private and eleemosynary; not from the application of those funds, for money may be given for education, and the persons receiving it do not, by being employed in the education of youth, become members of the civil government. Is it from the act of incorporation? Let this subject be considered.

A corporation is an artificial being, invisible, intangible, and existing only in contemplation of law. Being the mere creature of law, it possesses only those properties which the charter of its creation confers upon it either expressly or as incidental to its very existence. These are such as are supposed best calculated to effect the object for which it was created. Among the most important are immortality, and, if the expression may be allowed, individuality—properties by which a perpetual succession of many persons are considered as the same, and may act as a single individual. They enable a corporation to manage its own affairs and to hold property without the perplexing intricacies, the hazardous and endless necessity, of perpetual conveyances for the purpose of transmitting it from hand to hand. It is chiefly for the purpose of clothing bodies of men, in succession, with these qualities and capacities that corporations were invented, and are in use. By these means, a perpetual succession of individuals are capable of acting for the promotion of the particular object like one immortal being. But this being does not share in the civil government of the country, unless that be the purpose for which it was created. Its immortality no more confers on it political power, or a political character, than immortality would confer such power or character on a natural person. It is no more a state instrument than a natural person exercising the same powers would be. If, then, a natural person, employed by individuals in the education of youth or for the government of a seminary in which youth is educated would not become a public officer or be considered as a member of the civil government, how is it that this artificial being, created by law for the purpose of being employed by the same individuals, for the same purposes, should become a part of the civil government of the country? Is it because its existence, its capacities, its powers, are given by law? Because the government has given it the power to take and to hold property, in a particular form, and for particular purposes, has the government a consequent right substantially to change that form, or to vary the purposes to which the property is to be applied? This principle has never been asserted or recognised, and is supported by no authority. Can it derive aid from reason?

The objects for which a corporation is created are universally such as the government wishes to promote. They are deemed beneficial to the country, and this benefit constitutes the consideration, and in most cases, the sole consideration of the grant. In most eleemosynary institutions, the object would be difficult, perhaps unattainable, without the aid of a charter of incorporation. Charitable or public-spirited individuals, desirous of making permanent appropriations for charitable or other useful purposes, find it impossible to effect their design securely and certainly without an incorporating act. They apply to the government, state their beneficent object, and offer to advance the money necessary for its accomplishment, provided the government will confer on the instrument which is to execute their designs the capacity to execute them. The proposition is considered and approved. The benefit to the public is considered as an ample compen-

sation for the faculty it confers, and the corporation is created. If the advantages to the public constitute a full compensation for the faculty it gives, there can be no reason for exacting a further compensation by claiming a right to exercise over this artificial being, a power which changes its nature and touches the fund for the security and application of which it was created. There can be no reason for implying in a charter, given for a valuable consideration, a power which is not only not expressed, but is in direct contradiction to its express stipulations.

From the fact, then, that a charter of incorporation has been granted, nothing can be inferred which changes the character of the institution or transfers to the government any new power over it. The character of civil institutions does not grow out of their incorporation, but out of the manner in which they are formed and the objects for which they are created. The right to change them is not founded on their being incorporated, but on their being the instruments of government, created for its purposes. The same institutions, created for the same objects, though not incorporated, would be public institutions, and, of course, be controllable by the legislature. The incorporating act neither gives nor prevents this control. Neither, in reason, can the incorporating act change the character of a private eleemosynary institution.

We are next led to the inquiry for whose benefit the property given to Dartmouth College was secured? The counsel for the defendant have insisted that the beneficial interest is in the people of New Hampshire. The charter, after reciting the preliminary measures which had been taken, and the application for an act of incorporation, proceeds thus:

"Know ye, therefore that we, considering the premises, and being willing to encourage the laudable and charitable design of spreading Christian knowledge among the savages of our American wilderness, and also that the best means of education be established in our province of New Hampshire, for the benefit of said province, do, of our special grace,"

&c. Do these expressions bestow on New Hampshire any exclusive right to the property of the College, any exclusive interest in the labors of the professors? Or do they merely indicate a willingness that New Hampshire should enjoy those advantages which result to all from the establishment of a seminary of learning in the neighborhood? On this point, we think it impossible to entertain a serious doubt. The words themselves, unexplained by the context, indicate that the "benefit intended for the province" is that which is derived from "establishing the best means of education therein," that is, from establishing in the province, Dartmouth College, as constituted by the charter. But, if these words, considered alone, could admit of doubt, that doubt is completely removed, by an inspection of the entire instrument.

The particular interests of New Hampshire never entered into the mind of the donors; never constituted a motive for their donation. The propagation of the Christian religion among the savages and the dissemination of useful knowledge among the youth of the country were the avowed and the sole objects of their contributions. In these, New Hampshire would participate, but nothing particular or exclusive was intended for her. Even the site of the College was selected not for the sake of New Hampshire, but because it was "most subservient to the great ends in view" and because liberal donations of land were offered by the proprietors on condition that the institution should be there established. The real advantages from the location of the College are perhaps not less considerable to those on the west than to those on the east side of Connecticut River. The clause which constitutes the incorporation and expresses the objects for which it was made declares those objects to be the instruction of the Indians "and also of English youth, and any others." So that the objects of the contributors and the incorporating act were the same—the promotion of Christianity and of education generally, not the interests of New Hampshire particularly.

From this review of the charter, it appears that Dartmouth College is an eleemosynary institution incorporated for the purpose of perpetuating the application of the bounty of the donors to the specified objects of that bounty; that its Trustees or Governors were originally named by the founder and invested with the power of perpetuating themselves; that they are not public officers, nor is it a civil institution, participating in the administration of government, but a charity school or a seminary of education incorporated for the preservation of its property and the perpetual application of that property to the objects of its creation.

Yet a question remains to be considered of more real difficulty, on which more doubt has been entertained than on all that have been discussed. The founders of the College, at least, those whose contributions were in money, have parted with the property bestowed upon it, and their representatives have no interest in that property. The donors of land are equally without interest so long as the corporation shall exist. Could they be found, they are unaffected by any alteration in its Constitution, and probably regardless of its form, or even of its existence. The students are fluctuating, and no individual among our youth has a vested interest in the institution which can be asserted in a Court of justice. Neither the founders of the College nor the youth for whose benefit it was founded complain of the alteration made in its charter, or think themselves injured by it. The Trustees alone complain, and the Trustees have no beneficial interest to be protected. Can this be such a contract as the Constitution intended to withdraw from the power of State legislation? Contracts the parties to which have a vested beneficial interest, and those only, it has been said, are the objects about which the Constitution is solicitous, and to which its protection is extended.

The Court has bestowed on this argument the most deliberate consideration, and the result will be stated. Dr. Wheelock, acting for himself and for those who, at his solicitation, had made contributions to his school, applied for this charter, as the instrument which should enable him, and them, to perpetuate their beneficent intention. It was granted. An artificial, immortal being was created by the Crown, capable of receiving and distributing forever, according to the will of the donors, the donations which should be made to it. On this being the contributions which had been collected were immediately bestowed. These gifts were made not indeed to make a profit for the donors or their posterity, but for something, in their opinion, of inestimable value—for something which they deemed a full equivalent for the money with which it was purchased. The consideration for which they stipulated is the perpetual application of the fund to its object in the mode prescribed by themselves. Their descendants may take no interest in the preservation of this consideration. But, in this respect, their descendants are not their representatives; they are represented by the corporation. The corporation is the assignee of their rights, stands in their place, and distributes their bounty as they would themselves have distributed it had they been immortal. So, with respect to the students who are to derive learning from this source, the corporation is a Trustee for them also. Their potential rights, which, taken distributively, are imperceptible, amount collectively to a most important interest. These are, in the aggregate, to be exercised, asserted and protected by the corporation. They were as completely out of the donors, at the instant of their being vested in the corporation, and as incapable of being asserted by the students as at present.

According to the theory of the British Constitution, their Parliament is omnipotent. To annul corporate rights might give a shock to public opinion, which that government has chosen to avoid, but its power is not questioned. Had parliament, immediately after the emanation of this charter and the execution of those conveyances which followed it, annulled the instrument, so that the living donors would have witnessed the disappointment of their hopes, the perfidy of the transaction would have been universally acknowledged. Yet then, as now, the donors would have no interest in the property; then, as now, those who might be students would have had no rights to be violated; then, as now, it might be said that the Trustees, in whom the rights of all were combined, possessed no private, individual, beneficial interests in the property confided to their protection. Yet the contract would, at that time, have been deemed sacred by all. What has since occurred to strip it of its inviolability? Circumstances have not changed it. In reason, in justice, and in law, it is now what is was in 1769.

This is plainly a contract to which the donors, the Trustees, and the Crown (to whose rights and obligations New Hampshire succeeds) were the original parties. It is a contract made on a valuable consideration. It is a contract for the security and disposition of property. It is a contract on the faith of which real and personal estate has been conveyed to the corporation. It is, then, a contract within the letter of the Constitution, and within its spirit also, unless the fact that the property is invested by the donors in Trustees for the promotion of religion and education, for the benefit of persons who are perpetually changing, though the objects remain the same, shall create a particular exception taking this case out of the prohibition contained in the Constitution.

It is more than possible that the preservation of rights of this description was not particularly in the view of the framers of the Constitution when the clause under consideration was introduced into that instrument. It is probable that interferences of more frequent occurrence, to which the temptation was stronger, and of which the mischief was more extensive, constituted the great motive for imposing this restriction on the State legislatures. But although a particular and a rare case may not, in itself, be of sufficient magnitude to induce a rule, yet it must be governed by the rule, when established, unless some plain and strong reason for excluding it can be given. It is not enough to say that this particular case was not in the mind of the convention when the article was framed, nor of the American people when it was adopted. It is necessary to go further and to say that, had this particular case been suggested, the language would have been so varied as to exclude it, or it would have been made a special exception. The case, being within the words of the rule, must be within its operation likewise, unless there be something in the literal construction so obviously absurd or mischievous or repugnant to the general spirit of the instrument as to justify those who expound the Constitution in making it an exception.

On what safe and intelligible ground can this exception stand? There is no expression in the Constitution, no sentiment delivered by its contemporaneous expounders, which would justify us in making it. In the absence of all authority of this kind, is there in the nature and reason of the case itself that which would sustain a construction of the Constitution not warranted by its words? Are contracts of this description of a character to excite so little interest that we must exclude them from the provisions of the Constitution as being unworthy of the attention of those who framed the instrument? Or does public policy so imperiously demand their remaining exposed to legislative alteration as to compel us, or rather permit us, to say that these words, which were introduced to give stability to contracts and which in their plain import comprehend this contract, must yet be so construed as to exclude it?

Almost all eleemosynary corporations, those which are created for the promotion of religion, of charity, or of education, are of the same character. The law of this case is the law of all. In every literary or charitable institution, unless the objects of the bounty be themselves incorporated, the whole legal interest is in Trustees, and can be asserted only by them. The donors, or claimants of the bounty, if they can appear in Court at all, can appear only to complain of the Trustees. In all other situations, they are identified with, and personated by, the Trustees, and their rights are to be defended and maintained by them. Religion, charity and education are, in the law of England, legatees or donees, capable of receiving bequests or donations in this form. They appear in court, and claim or defend by the corporation. Are they of so little estimation in the United States that contracts for their benefit must be excluded from the protection of words which in their natural import include them? Or do such contracts so necessarily require new modeling by the authority of the legislature that the ordinary rules of construction must be disregarded in order to leave them exposed to legislative alteration?

All feel that these objects are not deemed unimportant in the United States. The interest which this case has excited proves that they are not. The framers of the Constitution did not deem them unworthy of its care and protection. They have, though in a different mode, manifested their respect for science by reserving to the government of the Union the power

"to promote the progress of science and useful arts by securing for limited times, to authors and inventors, the exclusive right to their respective writings and discoveries."

They have so far withdrawn science and the useful arts from the action of the State governments. Why then should they be supposed so regardless of contracts made for the advancement of literature as to intend to exclude them from provisions, made for the security of ordinary contracts between man and man? No reason for making this supposition is perceived.

If the insignificance of the object does not require that we should exclude contracts respecting it from the protection of the Constitution, neither, as we conceive, is the policy of leaving them subject to legislative alteration so apparent as to require a forced construction of that instrument in order to effect it. These eleemosynary institutions do not fill the place which would otherwise be occupied by government, but that which would otherwise remain vacant. They are complete acquisitions to literature. They are donations to education, donations, which any government must be disposed rather to encourage than to discountenance. It requires no

very critical examination of the human mind to enable us to determine that one great inducement to these gifts is the conviction felt by the giver that the disposition he makes of them is immutable. It is probable that no man ever was, and that no man ever will be, the founder of a college, believing at the time that an act of incorporation constitutes no security for the institution, believing that it is immediately to be deemed a public institution, whose funds are to be governed and applied not by the will of the donor, but by the will of the legislature. All such gifts are made in the pleasing, perhaps, delusive, hope that the charity will flow forever in the channel which the givers have marked out for it. If every man finds in his own bosom strong evidence of the universality of this sentiment, there can be but little reason to imagine that the framers of our Constitution were strangers to it, and that, feeling the necessity and policy of giving permanence and security to contracts, of withdrawing them from the influence of legislative bodies, whose fluctuating policy, and repeated interferences, produced the most perplexing and injurious embarrassments, they still deemed it necessary to leave these contracts subject to those interferences. The motives for such an exception must be very powerful to justify the construction which makes it.

The motives suggested at the bar grow out of the original appointment of the Trustees, which is supposed to have been in a spirit hostile to the genius of our government, and the presumption that, if allowed to continue themselves, they now are, and must remain forever, what they originally were. Hence is inferred the necessity of applying to this corporation, and to other similar corporations, the correcting and improving hand of the legislature.

It has been urged repeatedly, and certainly with a degree of earnestness which attracted attention that the Trustees, deriving their power from a regal source, must, necessarily, partake of the spirit of their origin, and that their first principles, unimproved by that resplendent light which has been shed around them, must continue to govern the College and to guide the students. Before we inquire into the influence which this argument ought to have on the constitutional question, it may not be amiss to examine the fact on which it rests. The first Trustees were undoubtedly named in the charter by the Crown, but at whose suggestion were they named? By whom were they selected? The charter informs us. Dr. Wheelock had represented "that, for many weighty reasons, it would be expedient that the gentlemen whom he had already nominated in his last will to be Trustees in America should be of the corporation now proposed."

When afterwards the Trustees are named in the charter, can it be doubted that the persons mentioned by Dr. Wheelock in his will were appointed? Some were probably added by the Crown, with the approbation of Dr. Wheelock. Among these is the doctor himself. If any others were appointed at the instance of the Crown, they are the Governor, three members of the Council, and the Speaker of the House of Representatives of the Colony of New Hampshire. The stations filled by these persons ought to rescue them from any other imputation than too great a dependence on the Crown. If, in the revolution that followed, they acted under the influence of this sentiment, they must have ceased to be Trustees; if they took part with their countrymen, the imputation which suspicion might excite would no longer attach to them. The original Trustees, then, or most of them, were named by Dr. Wheelock, and those who were added to his nomination, most probably with his approbation, were among the most eminent and respectable individuals in New Hampshire.

The only evidence which we possess of the character of Dr. Wheelock is furnished by this charter. The judicious means employed for the accomplishment of his object, and the success which attended his endeavors, would lead to the opinion that he united a sound understanding to that humanity and benevolence which suggested his undertaking. It surely cannot be assumed that his Trustees were selected without judgment. With as little probability can it be assumed that, while the light of science and of liberal principles pervades the whole community, these originally benighted Trustees remain in utter darkness, incapable of participating in the general improvement; that while the human race is rapidly advancing, they are stationary. Reasoning *a priori*, we should believe that learned and intelligent men, selected by its patrons for the government of a literary institution, would select learned and intelligent men for their successors, men as well fitted for the government of a College as those who might be chosen by other means. Should this reasoning ever prove erroneous in a particular case, public opinion, as has been stated at the bar, would correct the institution. The mere possibility of the contrary would not justify a construction of the Constitution which should exclude these contracts from the protection of a provision whose terms comprehend them.

The opinion of the Court, after mature deliberation, is that this is a contract the obligation of which cannot be impaired without violating the Constitution of the United States. This opinion appears to us to be equally supported by reason and by the former decisions of this Court.

2. We next proceed to the inquiry whether its obligation has been impaired by those acts of the Legislature of New Hampshire to which the special verdict refers. From the review of this charter which has been taken, it appears that the whole power of governing the College, of appointing and removing tutors, of fixing their salaries, of directing the course of study to be pursued by the students, and of filling up vacancies created in their own body, was vested in the Trustees. On the part of the Crown, it was expressly stipulated that this corporation thus constituted should continue forever, and that the number of Trustees should forever consist of twelve, and no more. By this contract, the Crown was bound, and could have made no violent alteration in its essential terms without impairing its obligation.

By the revolution, the duties as well as the powers, of government devolved on the people of New Hampshire. It is admitted that among the latter was comprehended the transcendent power of Parliament, as well as that of the executive department. It is too clear to require the support of argument that all contracts and rights respecting property, remained unchanged by the revolution. The obligations, then, which were created by the charter to Dartmouth College were the same in the new that they had been in the old government. The power of the government was also the same. A repeal of this charter at any time prior to the adoption of the present Constitution of the United States would have been an extraordinary and unprecedented act of power, but one which could have been contested only by the restrictions upon the legislature, to be found in the constitution of the State. But the Constitution of the United States has imposed this additional limitation—that the legislature of a State shall pass no act "impairing the obligation of contracts."

It has been already stated that the act "to amend the charter, and enlarge and improve the corporation of Dartmouth College" increases the number of Trustees to twenty-one, gives the appointment of the additional members to the executive of the State, and creates a Board of Overseers, to consist of twenty-five persons, of whom twenty-one are also appointed by the Executive of New Hampshire, who have power to inspect and control the most important acts of the Trustees.

On the effect of this law, two opinions cannot be entertained. Between acting directly and acting through the agency of Trustees and Overseers, no essential difference is perceived. The whole power of governing the College is transferred from Trustees, appointed according to the will of the founder, expressed in the charter, to the Executive of New Hampshire. The management and application of the funds of this eleemosynary institution, which are placed by the donors in the hands of Trustees named in the charter, and empowered to perpetuate themselves, are placed by this act under the control of the government of the State. The will of the State is substituted for the will of the donors in every essential operation of the College. This is not an immaterial change. The founders of the College contracted not merely for the perpetual application of the funds which they gave, to the objects for which those funds were given; they contracted also to secure that application by the constitution of the corporation.

They contracted for a system which should, so far as human foresight can provide, retain forever the government of the literary institution they had formed in the hands of persons approved by themselves. This system is totally changed. The charter of 1769 exists no longer. It is reorganized, and reorganized in such a manner as to convert a literary institution, moulded according to the will of its founders, and placed under the control of private literary men, into a machine entirely subservient to the will of government. This may be for the advantage of this College in particular, and may be for the advantage of literature in general, but it is not according to the will of the donors, and is subversive of that contract on the faith of which their property was given.

In the view which has been taken of this interesting case, the Court has confined itself to the rights possessed by the Trustees as the assignees and representatives of the donors and founders, for the benefit of religion and literature. Yet it is not clear that the Trustees ought to be considered as destitute of such beneficial interest in themselves as the law may respect. In addition to their

being the legal owners of the property, and to their having a freehold right in the powers confided to them, the charter itself countenances the idea that Trustees may also be tutors, with salaries. The first President was one of the original Trustees, and the charter provides that. in case of vacancy in that office,

"the senior professor or tutor, *being one of the Trustees,* shall exercise the office of President, until the Trustees shall make choice of, and appoint a President."

According to the tenor of the charter, then, the Trustees might, without impropriety, appoint a President and other professors from their own body. This is a power not entirely unconnected with an interest. Even if the proposition of the counsel for the defendant were sustained, if it were admitted that those contracts only are protected by the Constitution, a beneficial interest in which is vested in the party, who appears in Court to assert that interest, yet it is by no means clear that the Trustees of Dartmouth College have no beneficial interest in themselves. But the Court has deemed it unnecessary to investigate this particular point, being of opinion on general principles that, in these private eleemosynary institutions, the body corporate, as possessing the whole legal and equitable interest and completely representing the donors for the purpose of executing the trust, has rights which are protected by the Constitution.

It results from this opinion that the acts of the Legislature of New Hampshire which are stated in the special verdict found in this cause are repugnant to the Constitution of the United States, and that the judgment on this special verdict ought to have been for the plaintiffs. The judgment of the State Court must, therefore, be reversed.

### *Mr. Justice STORY*

This is a cause of great importance, and as the very learned discussions as well here as in the State Court show, of no inconsiderable difficulty. There are two questions to which the appellate jurisdiction of this Court properly applies:

1. Whether the original charter of Dartmouth College is a contract within the prohibitory clause of the Constitution of the United States, which declares that no State shall pass any "law impairing the obligation of contracts?" 2. If so, whether the legislative acts of New

Hampshire of the 27th of June, and of the 18th and 27th of December, 1816, or any of them, impair the obligations of that charter?

It will be necessary, however, before we proceed to discuss these questions, to institute an inquiry into the nature, rights and duties of aggregate corporations at common law, that we may apply the principles drawn from this source to the exposition of this charter, which was granted emphatically with reference to that law.

An aggregate corporation, at common law, is a collection of individuals, united into one collective body under a special name and possessing certain immunities, privileges and capacities in its collective character which do not belong to the natural persons composing it. Among other things, it possesses the capacity of perpetual succession, and of acting by the collected vote or will of its component members, and of suing and being sued in all things touching its corporate rights and duties. It is, in short, an artificial person, existing in contemplation of law and endowed with certain powers and franchises which, though they must be exercised through the medium of its natural members, are yet considered as subsisting in the corporation itself as distinctly as if it were a real personage. Hence, such a corporation may sue and be sued by its own members, and may contract with them in the same manner as with any strangers. 1 Bl.Com. 469, 475, 1 Kyd on Corp. 13, 69, 189, 1 Wooddes. 471, &c. A great variety of these corporations exist in every country governed by the common law, in some of which, the corporate existence is perpetuated by new elections, made from time to time, and in others by a continual accession of new members, without any corporate act. Some of these corporations are, from the particular purposes to which they are devoted, denominated spiritual, and some lay, and the latter are again divided into civil and eleemosynary corporations. It is unnecessary, in this place, to enter into any examination of civil corporations. Eleemosynary corporations are such as are constituted for the perpetual distribution of the free alms and bounty of the founder in such manner as he has directed, and in this class are ranked hospitals for the relief of poor and impotent persons, and Colleges for the promotion of learning and piety and the support of persons engaged in literary pursuits. 1 Bl.Com. 469, 470, 471, 482; 1 Kyd on Corp. 25; 1 Wooddes. 474; *Attorney General v. Whorwood,* 1 Ves. 534; *St. John's College v. Todington,* 1 Bl.Rep. 84, S.C. 1 Burr. 200; *Philips v. Bury,* 1 Ld. Raym. 5, S.C. 2 T.R. 346; *Porter's Case,* 1 Co. 22, b. 23.

Another division of corporations is into public and private. Public corporations are generally esteemed such as exist for public political purposes only, such as towns, cities, parishes and counties, and in many respects they are so, although they involve some private interests; but, strictly speaking, public corporations are such only as are founded by the government for public purposes, where the whole interests belong also to the government. If, therefore, the foundation be private, though under the charter of the government, the corporation is private, however extensive the uses may be to which it is devoted, either by the bounty of the founder, or the nature and objects of the institution. For instance, a bank created by the government for its own uses, whose stock is exclusively owned by the government, is, in the strictest sense, public corporation. So an hospital created and endowed by the government for general charity. But a bank whose stock is owned by private persons is a private corporation, although it is erected by the government and its objects and operations partake of a public nature. The same doctrine may be affirmed of insurance, canal, bridge and turnpike companies. In all these cases, the uses may, in a certain sense, be called public, but the corporations are private—as much so, indeed, as if the franchises were vested in a single person.

This reasoning applies in its full force to eleemosynary corporations. An hospital founded by a private benefactor is, in point of law, a private corporation although dedicated by its charter to general charity. So a College, founded and endowed in the same manner, although, being for the promotion of learning and piety, it may extend its charity to scholars from every class in the community, and thus acquire the character of a public institution. This is the unequivocal doctrine of the authorities, and cannot be shaken but by undermining the most solid foundations of the common law. *Philips v. Bury,* 1 Lord Raym. 5, 9, S. C. 2 T.R. 346.

It was, indeed, supposed at the argument that if the uses of an eleemosynary corporation be for general charity, this alone would constitute it a public corporation. But the law is certainly not so. To be sure, in a certain sense, every charity which is extensive in its reach may be called a public charity, in contradistinction to a charity embracing but a few definite objects. In this sense, the language was unquestionably used by Lord Hardwicke in the case cited at the argument, *Attorney General v. Pearce,* 2 Atk. 87, 1 Bac.Abr. tit. Charitable

Uses, E, 589; and in this sense, a private corporation may well enough be denominated a public charity. So it would be if the endowment, instead of being vested in a corporation, were assigned to a private trustee; yet, in such a case, no one would imagine that the trust ceased to be private, or the funds became public property. That the mere act of incorporation will not change the charity from a private to a public one is most distinctly asserted in the authorities. Lord Hardwicke, in the case already alluded to, says

"the charter of the Crown cannot make a charity more or less public, but only more permanent than it would otherwise be; but it is the extensiveness which will constitute it a public one. A devise to the poor of the parish is a public charity. Where testators leave it to the discretion of a trustee to choose out the objects, though each particular object may be said to be private, yet, in the extensiveness of the benefit accruing from them, they may properly be called public charities. A sum to be disposed of by A.B. and his executors, at their discretion, among poor housekeepers, is of this kind."

The charity, then, may, in this sense, be public although it may be administered by private trustees; and for the same reason, it may thus be public though administered by a private corporation. The fact, then that the charity is public affords no proof that the corporation is also public; and consequently, the argument, so far as it is built on this foundation, falls to the ground. If, indeed, the argument were correct, it would follow that almost every hospital and college would be a public corporation, a doctrine utterly irreconcilable with the whole current of decisions since the time of Lord Coke. *Case of Sutton's Hospital,* 10 Co. 23.

When, then, the argument assumes that, because the charity is public, the corporation is public, it manifestly confounds the popular with the strictly legal sense of the terms. And if it stopped here, it would not be very material to correct the error. But it is on this foundation that a superstructure is erected which is to compel a surrender of the cause. When the corporation is said, at the bar, to be public, it is not merely meant that the whole community may be the proper objects of the bounty, but that the government have the sole right, as trustees of the public interests, to regulate, control and direct the corporation and its funds and its franchises at its own good will and pleasure. Now such an authority does not exist in the govern-

ment except where the corporation, is, in the strictest sense, public—that is, where its whole interests and franchises are the exclusive property and domain of the government itself. If it had been otherwise, courts of law would have been spared many laborious adjudications in respect to eleemosynary corporations, and the visitatorial powers over them, from the time of Lord Holt down to the present day. *Rex v. Bury,* 1 Lord Raym. 5; S. C. Comb. 265; Holt 715; 1 Show. 360; 4 Mod. 106; Skin. 447; and Lord Holt's opinion from his own MS., in 2 T.R. 346. Nay, more, private Trustees for charitable purposes would have been liable to have the property confided to their care taken away from them, without any assent or default on their part, and the administration submitted not to the control of law and equity, but to the arbitrary discretion of the government. Yet who ever thought before that the munificent gifts of private donors for general charity became instantaneously the property of the government, and that the Trustees appointed by the donors, whether corporate or unincorporated, might be compelled to yield up their rights to whomsoever the government might appoint to administer them? If we were to establish such a principle, it would extinguish all future eleemosynary endowments, and we should find as little of public policy as we now find of law to sustain it.

An eleemosynary corporation, then, upon a private foundation, being a private corporation, it is next to be considered what is deemed a foundation, and who is the founder. This cannot be stated with more brevity and exactness than in the language of the elegant commentator upon the laws of England:

"The founder of all corporations [says Sir William Blackstone], in the strictest and original sense, is the King alone, for he only can incorporate a society, and in civil corporations, such as mayor, commonalty, &c., where there are no possessions or endowments given to the body, there is no other founder but the King; but in eleemosynary foundations, such as Colleges and hospitals, where there is an endowment of lands, the law distinguishes and makes two species of foundation, the one *fundatio incipiens,* or the incorporation, in which sense the King is the general founder of all Colleges and hospitals, the other *fundatio perficiens,* or the dotation of it, in which sense the first gift of the revenues is the foundation, and he who gives them is, in the law, the founder; and it is in this last sense we generally call a man the founder of a college or hospital."

1 Bl.Com. 480, 10 Co. 33.

To all eleemosynary corporations, a visitatorial power attaches as a necessary incident, for these corporations being composed of individuals, subject to human infirmities, are liable as well as private persons to deviate from the end of their institution. The law, therefore, has provided that there shall somewhere exist a power to visit, inquire into, and correct all irregularities and abuses in such corporations, and to compel the original purposes of the charity to be faithfully fulfilled. 1 Bl.Com. 480. The nature and extent of this visitatorial power has been expounded with admirable fulness and accuracy by Lord Holt in one of his most celebrated judgments. *Phillips v. Bury,* 1 Lord Raym. 5, S. C. 2 T.R. 346. And of common right, by the dotation, the founder and his heirs are the legal visitors, unless the founder has appointed and assigned another person to be visitor. For the founder may, if he please, at the time of the endowment, part with his visitatorial power, and the person to whom it is assigned will, in that case, possess it in exclusion of the founder's heirs. 1 Bl.Com. 482. This visitatorial power is therefore an hereditament founded in property, and valuable, in intendment of law, and stands upon the maxim that he who gives his property has a right to regulate it in future. It includes also the legal right of patronage, for as Lord Holt justly observes, "patronage and visitation are necessary consequents one upon another." No technical terms are necessary to assign or vest the visitatorial power; it is sufficient if, from the nature of the duties to be performed by particular persons under the charter it can be inferred that the founder meant to part with it in their favor; and he may divide it among various persons, or subject it to any modifications or control, by the fundamental statutes of the corporation. But where the appointment is given in general terms, the whole power vests in the appointee. *Eden v. Foster,* 2 P.Wms. 325; *Attorney General v. Middleton,* 2 Ves. 327; *St. Johns College v. Todington,* 1 Bl.Rep. 84., S. C. 2 Burr. 200; *Attorney General v. Clare College,* 3 Atk. 662; S. C. 1 Ves. 78. In the construction of charters, too, it is a general rule that if the objects of the charity are incorporated, as for instance the master and fellows of a college or the master and poor of a hospital, the visitatorial power, in the absence of any special appointment, silently vests in the founder and his heirs. But where Trustees or Governors are incorporated to manage the charity, the visitatorial power is deemed

to belong to them in their corporate character. *Philips v. Bury,* 1 Lord Raym. 5; S. C. 2 T.R. 346; *Green v. Rutherforth,* 1 Ves. 472; *Attorney General v. Middleton,* 2 Ves. 327; *Case of Sutton Hospital,* 10 Co. 23, 31.

When a private eleemosynary corporation is thus created by the charter of the Crown, it is subject to no other control on the part of the Crown than what is expressly or implicitly reserved by the charter itself. Unless a power be reserved for this purpose, the Crown cannot, in virtue of its prerogative, without the consent of the corporation, alter or amend the charter or divest the corporation of any of its franchises, or add to them, or add to, or diminish the number of the trustees, or remove any of the members, or change or control the administration of the charity, or compel the corporation to receive a new charter. This is the uniform language of the authorities, and forms one of the most stubborn and well settled doctrines of the common law. *See Rex v. Pasmore,* 3 T.R. 199, and the cases there cited.

But an eleemosynary, like every other corporation, is subject to the general law of the land. It may forfeit its corporate franchises by misuser or nonuser of them. I t is subject to the controlling authority of its legal visitor, who, unless restrained by the terms of the charter, may amend and repeal its statutes, remove its officers, correct abuses, and generally superintend the management of the trusts. Where, indeed, the visitatorial power is vested in the Trustees of the charity in virtue of their incorporation, there can be no amotion of them from their corporate capacity. But they are not, therefore, placed beyond the reach of the law. As managers of the revenues of the corporation, they are subject to the general superintending power of the court of chancery, not as itself possessing a visitatorial power, or a right to control the charity, but as possessing a general jurisdiction, in all cases of an abuse of trust, to redress grievances and suppress frauds. And where a corporation is a mere trustee of a charity, a court of equity will go yet further, and though it cannot appoint or remove a corporator, it will, yet, in a case of gross fraud or abuse of trust, take away the trust from the corporation and vest it in other hands. *Mayor, &c. of Coventry v. Attorney General,* 7 Bro.Parl.Cases 235; *Attorney General v. Earl of Clarendon,* 17 Ves. 491, 499.

Thus much it has been thought proper to premise respecting the nature, rights, and duties of eleemosynary corporations growing out of the common law. We may now proceed to an examination of the original charter of Dartmouth College.

It begins by a recital, among other things that the Rev. Eleazer Wheelock, of Lebanon, in Connecticut, about the year 1754, at his own expense, on his own estate, set on foot an Indian charity school, and, by the assistance of other persons, educated a number of the children of the Indians, and employed them as missionaries and schoolmasters among the savage tribes; that the design became reputable among the Indians, so that more desired the education of their children at the school than the contributions in the American colonies would support; that the said Wheelock thought it expedient to endeavor to procure contributions in England, and requested the Rev. Nathaniel Whitaker to go to England as his attorney to solicit contribution, and also solicited the Earl of Dartmouth and others to receive the contributions and become trustees thereof, which they cheerfully agreed to; and he constituted them trustees accordingly, by a power of attorney, and they testified their acceptance by a sealed instrument, *that the said Wheelock also authorized the Trustees to fix and determine upon the place for the said school,* and, to enable them understandingly to give the preference, laid before them the several offers of the governments in America inviting the settlement of the school among them; that a large number of the proprietors of lands in the western parts of New Hampshire, to aid the design, and *considering that the same school might be enlarged and improved to promote learning among the English,* and to supply the churches there with an orthodox ministry, promised large tracts of land for the uses aforesaid, *provided the school should be settled in the western part of said province;* that the trustees thereupon gave a preference to the western part of said province, brk:

lying on Connecticut River, as a situation most convenient for said school; *that the said Wheelock further represented the necessity for a legal incorporation, in order to the safety and wellbeing of said seminary, and its being capable of the tenure and disposal of lands and bequests for the use of the same;* that in the infancy of said institution, *certain gentlemen whom he had already nominated in his last will* (which he had transmitted to the Trustees in England) *to be Trustees in America should be the corporation now proposed, and lastly that there were already large contributions for said school*

*in the hands of the Trustees in England,* and further success might be expected, for which reason the said Wheelock desired they might be invested with all that power therein which could consist with their distance from the same. The charter, after these recitals, declares that the King, *considering the premises,* and being willing to encourage the charitable design, and that the best means of education might be established in New Hampshire for the benefit thereof, does, of his *special grace, certain knowledge* and *mere motion,* ordain and grant that there be a College erected in New Hampshire by the name of Dartmouth College, for the education and instruction of youth of the Indian tribes *and also of English youth and others;* that *the Trustees of said College shall be a corporation forever, by the name of the Trustees of Dartmouth College;* that the then Governor of New Hampshire, the said Wheelock, and ten other persons, specially named in the charter, shall be Trustees of the said College, and that *the whole number of Trustees shall forever thereafter consist of twelve, and no more,* that the said corporation shall have power to sue and to be sued by their corporate name, and to acquire and hold for *the use of the said Dartmouth College,* lands, tenements, hereditaments and franchises; to receive, purchase and build any houses for *the use of said College,* in such town in the western part of New Hampshire, as the Trustees, or a major part of them, shall, by a written instrument, agree on, and to receive, accept and dispose of any lands, goods, chattels, rents, gifts, legacies, &c., not exceeding the yearly value of six thousand pounds. It further declares that the Trustees, or a major part of them, regularly convened (*for which purpose seven shall form a quorum*), shall have authority to appoint and remove the professors, tutors and other officers of the College, and to pay them, and also such *missionaries* and *schoolmasters as shall be employed by the Trustees for instructing the Indians,* salaries and allowances, as well as other corporate expenses, out of the corporate funds. It further declares that, the *said Trustees,* as often as one or more of the Trustees shall die, or by removal or otherwise, shall, according to their judgment, become unfit or incapable to serve the interests of the College, shall have power to *elect and appoint other Trustees* in their stead, so that when the whole number shall be complete of *twelve Trustees, eight* shall be resident freeholders of New Hampshire, and seven of the whole number laymen. It further declares that the Trustees shall have power, from time to time, to make and establish rules, ordinances and laws for the government of the College not repugnant to the laws of the land, and to confer collegiate degrees. It further appoints the said Wheelock, whom it denominates "the founder of the College," to be President of the College, with authority to appoint his successor, who shall be President, until disapproved of by the Trustees. It then concludes with a direction that it shall be the duty of the President to transmit to the Trustees in England, so long as they should perpetuate their Board, and as there should be Indian natives remaining to be proper objects of the bounty, an annual account of all the disbursements from the donations in England, and of the general plans and prosperity of the institution.

Such are the most material clauses of the charter. It is observable, in the first place, that no endowment whatever is given by the Crown, and no power is reserved to the Crown or government in any manner to alter, amend or control the charter. It is also apparent from the very terms of the charter that Dr. Wheelock is recognised as the founder of the College, and that the charter is granted upon his application, and that the Trustees were in fact nominated by him. In the next place, it is apparent that the objects of the institution are purely charitable, for the distribution of the private contributions of private benefactors. The charity was, in the sense already explained, a public charity—that is, for the general promotion of learning and piety—but in this respect it was just as much public before as after the incorporation. The only effect of the charter was to give permanency to the design by enlarging the sphere of its action and granting a perpetuity of corporate powers and franchises, the better to secure the administration of the benevolent donations. As founder, too, Dr. Wheelock and his heirs would have been completely clothed with the visitatorial power; but the whole government and control, as well of the officers as of the revenues of the College, being with his consent assigned to the Trustees in then corporate character, the visitatorial power, which is included in this authority, rightfully devolved on the Trustees. As managers of the property and revenues of the corporation, they were amenable to the jurisdiction of the judicial tribunals of the State; but as visitors, their discretion was limited only by the charter, and liable to no supervision or control, at least unless it was fraudulently misapplied.

From this summary examination it follows that Dartmouth College was, under its original charter, a private eleemosynary corporation, endowed with the usual privileges and franchises of such corporations, and among others, with a legal perpetuity, and was exclusively under the government and control of twelve Trustees, who were to be elected and appointed, from time to time by the existing Board as vacancies or removals should occur.

We are now led to the consideration of the first question in the cause—whether this charter is a contract within the clause of the Constitution prohibiting the States from passing any law impairing the obligation of contracts. In the case of *Fletcher v. Peck*, 6 Cranch 87, 10 U. S. 136, this Court laid down its exposition of the word "contract" in this clause in the following manner:

"A contract is a compact between two or more persons, and is either executory or executed. An executory contract is one in which a party binds himself to do or not to do a particular thing. A contract executed is one in which the object of the contract is performed, and this, says Blackstone, differs in nothing from a grant. A contract executed, as well as one that is executory, contains obligations binding on the parties. A grant, in its own nature, amounts to an extinguishment of the right of the grantor, and implies a contract not to reassert that right. A party is always estopped by his own grant."

This language is perfectly unambiguous, and was used in reference to a grant of land by the Governor of a State under a legislative act. It determines in the most unequivocal manner that the grant of a State is a contract, within the clause of the Constitution now in question, and that it implies a contract not to reassume the rights granted; *a fortiori* the doctrine applies to a charter or grant from the King.

But it is objected that the charter of Dartmouth College is not a contract contemplated by the Constitution, because no valuable consideration passed to the King as an equivalent for the grant, it purporting to be granted *ex mero motu*, and further that no contracts merely voluntary are within the prohibitory clause. It must be admitted that mere executory contracts cannot be enforced at law unless there be a valuable consideration to sustain them, and the Constitution certainly did not mean to create any new obligations or give any new efficacy to nude pacts. But it must, on the other hand, be also admitted that the Constitution did intend to preserve all the obligatory force of contracts which they have by the general principles of law. Now when a contract has once passed, *bona fide*, into grant, neither the King nor any private person who may be the grantor can recall the grant of the property, although the conveyance may have been purely voluntary. A gift, completely executed, is irrevocable. The property conveyed by it becomes, as against the donor, the absolutet property of the donee, and no subsequent change of intention of the donor can change the rights of the donee. 2 Bl.Com. 441, Jenk.Cent. 104. And a gift by the Crown of incorporeal hereditaments, such as corporate franchises, when executed, comes completely within the principle, and is, in the strictest sense of the terms, a grant. 2 Bl.Com. 317, 346; Shep.Touch. ch. 12, p. 227. Was it ever imagined that land voluntarily granted to any person by a State was liable to be resumed at its own good pleasure? Such a pretension would, under any circumstances, be truly alarming, but in a country like ours, where thousands of land titles had their origin in gratuitous grants of the States, it would go far to shake the foundations of the best settled estates. And a grant of franchises is not, in point of principle, distinguishable from a grant of any other property. If, therefore, this charter were a pure donation, when the grant was complete and accepted by the grantees, it involved a contract that the grantees should hold, and the grantor should not reassume the grant, as much as if it had been founded on the most valuable consideration.

But it is not admitted that this charter was not granted for what the law deems a valuable consideration. For this purpose, it matters not how trifling the consideration may be—a pepper-corn is as good as a thousand dollars. Nor is it necessary that the consideration should be a benefit to the grantor. It is sufficient if it import damage or loss, or forbearance of benefit, or any act done or to be done, on the part of the grantee. It is unnecessary to State cases; they are familiar to the mind of every lawyer. *Pillans v. Van Mierop*, per Yates, J., 3 Burr. 1663; *Forth v. Stanton*, 1 Saund. 211; Williams' note 2, and the cases there cited.

With these principles in view, let us now examine the terms of this charter. It purports, indeed, on its face, to be granted "of the special grace, certain knowledge and *mere motion*" of the King, but these words were introduced for a very different purpose from that now contended for. It is a general rule of the common law (the reverse of that applied in ordinary cases) that a grant of the King, at the suit of the grantee, is to be construed most beneficially for the King and most strictly against the grantee. Wherefore it is usual to insert in the King's grants a clause that they are made not at the *suit of the grantee*, but of the special grace, certain knowledge and mere motion of the King, and then they receive a more liberal construction. This is the true object of the clause in question, as we are informed by the most accurate authorities. 2 Bl.Com. 347; Finch's Law 100; 10 Rep. 112; 1 Shep.Abridg. 136; Bull.N.P. 136. But the charter also, on its face, purports to be granted in consideration *of the premises* in the introductory recitals.

Now among these recitals it appears that Dr. Wheelock had founded a charity school at his own expense, on his own estate; that divers contributions had been made in the colonies by others for its support; that new contributions had been made, and were making, in England, for this purpose, and were in the hands of Trustees appointed by Dr. Wheelock to act in his behalf; that Dr. Wheelock had consented to have the school established at such other place as the Trustees should select; that offers had been made by several of the governments in America, inviting the establishment of the school among them; that offers of land had also been made by divers proprietors of lands in the western parts of New Hampshire if the school should be established there; that the Trustees had finally consented to establish it in New Hampshire; and that Dr. Wheelock represented that, to effectuate the purposes of all parties, an incorporation was necessary. Can it be truly said that these recitals contain no legal consideration of benefit to the Crown, or of forbearance of benefit on the other side? Is there not an implied contract by Dr. Wheelock, if a charter is granted, that the school shall be removed from his estate to New Hampshire?; and that he will relinquish all his control over the funds collected and to be collected in England under his auspices and subject to his authority?; that he will yield up the management of his charity school to the Trustees of the College?; that he will relinquish all the offers made by other American governments and devote his patronage to this institution? It will scarcely be denied that he gave up the right any longer to maintain the charity school already established on his own estate, and that the funds collected for its use and subject to his management were yielded up by him as an endowment of the College. The very language of the charter supposes him to be the legal owner of the funds of the charity school, and, in virtue of this endowment, declares him the founder of the College. It matters not whether the funds were great or small; Dr. Wheelock had procured them by his own influence, and they were under his control, to be applied to the support of his charity school, and when he relinquished this control, he relinquished a right founded in property acquired by his labors. Besides, Dr. Wheelock impliedly agreed to devote his future services to the College, when erected, by becoming President thereof at a period when sacrifices must necessarily be made to accomplish the great design in view. If, indeed, a pepper-corn be, in the eye of the law, of sufficient value to found a contract, as upon a valuable consideration, are these implied agreements, and these relinquishments of right and benefit, to be deemed wholly worthless? It has never been doubted that an agreement not to exercise a trade in a particular place was a sufficient consideration to sustain a contract for the payment of money; *a fortiori,* the relinquishment of property which a person holds, or controls the use of, as a trust, is a sufficient consideration, for it is parting with a legal right. Even a right of patronage (*jus patronatus*) is of great value in intendment of law. Nobody doubts that an advowson is a valuable hereditament, and yet, in fact, it is but a mere trust, or right of nomination to a benefice, which cannot be legally sold to the intended incumbent. 2 Bl.Com. 22; Christian's note.

In respect to Dr. Wheelock, then, if a consideration be necessary to support the charter as a contract, it is to be found in the implied stipulations on his part in the charter itself. He relinquished valuable rights and undertook a laborious office in consideration of the grant of the incorporation.

This is not all. A charter may be granted upon an executory, as well as an executed or present, consideration. When it is granted to persons who have not made application for it, until their acceptance thereof, the grant is yet *in fieri.* Upon the acceptance, there is an implied contract on the part of the grantees, in consideration of the charter, that they will perform the duties, and exercise the authorities conferred by it. This was the doctrine asserted by the late learned Mr. Justice Buller in a modern case. *Rex v. Pasmore,* 3 T.R. 199, 239, 246. He there said,

"I do not know how to reason on this point better than in the manner urged by one of the relator's counsel, who considered the grant of incorporation to be a compact between the Crown and a certain number of the subjects, the latter of whom undertake, in consideration of the privileges which are bestowed, to exert themselves for the good government of the place,"

(*i.e.,* the place incorporated). It will not be pretended that if a charter be granted for a bank, and the stockholders pay in their own funds, the charter is to be deemed a grant without consideration, and therefore, revocable at the pleasure of the grantor. Yet here, the funds are to be managed and the services performed exclusively for the use and benefit of the stockholders themselves. And where the grantees are mere trustees to perform services without reward, exclusively for the benefit of others, for public charity, can it be reasonably argued that these services are less valuable to the government than if performed for the private emolument of the Trustees themselves? In respect then to the Trustees also, there was a valuable consideration for the charter, the consideration of services agreed to be rendered by them in execution of a charity, from which they could receive no private remuneration.

There is yet another view of this part of the case which deserves the most weighty consideration. The corporation was expressly created for the purpose of distributing in perpetuity the charitable donations of private benefactors. By the terms of the charter, the Trustees, and their successors, in their corporate capacity, were to receive, hold and exclusively manage all the funds so contributed. The Crown, then, upon the face of the charter, pledged its faith that the donations of private benefactors should be perpetually devoted to their original purposes, without any interference on its own part, and should be forever administered by the Trustees of the corporation, unless its corporate franchises should be taken away by due process of law. From the very nature of the case, therefore, there was an implied contract on the part of the Crown with every benefactor that, if he would give his money, it should be deemed a charity protected by the charter, and be administered by the corporation according to the general law of the land. As soon, then, as a donation was made to the corporation, there was an implied contract, springing up and founded on a valuable consideration that the Crown would not revoke or alter the charter or change its administration without the consent of the corporation. There was also an implied contract between the corporation itself and every benefactor, upon a like consideration, that it would administer his bounty according to the terms and for the objects stipulated in the charter.

In every view of the case, if a consideration were necessary (which I utterly deny) to make the charter a valid contract, a valuable consideration did exist as to the founder, the Trustees, and the benefactors. And upon the soundest legal principles, the charter may be properly deemed, according to the various aspects in which it is viewed, as a several contract with each of these parties in virtue of the foundation or the endowment of the College, or the acceptance of the charter, or the donations to the charity.

And here we might pause; but there is yet remaining another view of the subject which cannot consistently be passed over without notice. It seems to be assumed by the argument of the defendant's counsel that there is no contract whatsoever, in virtue of the charter, between the Crown and the corporation itself. But it deserves consideration whether this assumption can be sustained upon a solid foundation.

If this had been a new charter, granted to an existing corporation, or a grant of lands to an existing corporation, there could not have been a doubt that the grant would have been an executed contract with the corporation— as much so as if it had been to any private person. But it is supposed that as this corporation was not then in existence, but was created, and its franchises bestowed, *uno flatu;* the charter cannot be construed a contract, because there was no person *in rerum natura* with whom it might be made. Is this, however, a just and legal view of the subject? If the corporation had no existence so as to become a contracting party, neither had it for the purpose of receiving a grant of the franchises. The truth is that there may be a priority of operation of things in the same grant, and the law distinguishes and gives such priority, wherever it is necessary to effectuate the objects of the grant. *Case of Sutton's Hospital,* 10 Co. 23; *Buckland v. Fowcher,* cited 10 Co. 27, 28, and recognised in *Attorney General v. Bowyer,* 3 Ves.Jun. 714, 726, 727, S. P. Highmore on Mortm. 200, &c. From the nature of things, the artificial person called a corporation must be created before it can be capable of taking anything. When, therefore, a charter is granted and it brings the corporation into existence without any act of the natural persons who compose it, and gives

such corporation any privileges, franchises or property, the law deems the corporation to be first brought into existence, and then clothes it with the granted liberties and property. When, on the other hand, the corporation is to be brought into existence by some future acts of the corporators, the franchises remain in abeyance until such acts are done, and, when the corporation is brought into life, the franchises instantaneously attach to it. There may be, in intendment of law, a priority of time, even in an instant, for this purpose. And if the corporation have an existence before the grant of its other franchises attaches, what more difficulty is there in deeming the grant of these franchises a contract with it than if granted by another instrument at a subsequent period?

It behooves those also who hold that a grant to a corporation not then in existence is incapable of being deemed a contract on that account to consider whether they do not, at the same time, establish that the grant itself is a nullity for precisely the same reason. Yet such a doctrine would strike us all, as pregnant with absurdity, since it would prove that an act of incorporation could never confer any authorities or rights or property on the corporation it created. It may be admitted that two parties are necessary to form a perfect contract, but it is denied that it is necessary that the assent of both parties must be at the same time. If the legislature were voluntarily to grant land in fee to the first child of A. to be hereafter born, as soon as such child should be born, the estate would vest in it. Would it be contended that such grant, when it took effect, was revocable, and not an executed contract, upon the acceptance of the estate? The same question might be asked in a case of a gratuitous grant by the King or the legislature to A. for life, and afterwards, to the heirs of B., who is then living. Take the case of a bank, incorporated for a limited period upon the express condition that it shall pay out of its corporate funds a certain sum as the consideration for the charter, and, after the corporation is organized, a payment duly made of the sum out of the corporate funds; will it be contended that there is not a subsisting contract between the government and the corporation, by the matters thus arising *ex post facto,* that the charter shall not be revoked, during the stipulated period? Suppose, an act declaring that all persons, who should thereafter pay into the public treasury a stipulated sum should be tenants in common of certain lands belonging to the State, in certain proportions; if a person, afterwards born, pays the stipulated sum into the treasury, is it less a contract with him than it would be with a person *in esse* at the time the act passed? We must admit that there may be future springing contracts in respect to persons not now *in esse* or we shall involve ourselves in inextricable difficulties. And if there may be, in respect to natural persons, why not also in respect to artificial persons, created by the law for the very purpose of being clothed with corporate powers? I am unable to distinguish between the case of a grant of land or of franchises to an existing corporation and a like grant to a corporation brought into life for the very purpose of receiving the grant. As soon as it is *in esse* and the franchises and property become vested and executed in it, the grant is just as much an executed contract as if its prior existence had been established for a century.

Supposing, however that in either of the views which have been suggested the charter of Dartmouth College is to be deemed a contract; we are yet met with several objections of another nature. It is, in the first place, contended that it is not a contract, within the prohibitory clause of the Constitution, because that clause was never intended to apply to mere contracts of civil institution, such as the contract of marriage, or to grants of power to State officers, or to contracts relative to their offices, or to grants of trust to be exercised for purposes merely public, where the grantees take no beneficial interest.

It is admitted that the State legislatures have power to enlarge, repeal and limit the authorities of public officers, in their official capacities, in all cases where the constitutions of the States respectively do not prohibit them; and this, among others, for the very reason that there is no express or implied contract that they shall always, during their continuance in office, exercise such authorities. They are to exercise them only during the good pleasure of the legislature. But when the legislature makes a contract with a public officer, as in the case of a stipulated salary for his services during a limited period, this, during the limited period, is just as much a contract within the purview of the constitutional prohibition as a like contract would be between two private citizens. Will it be contended that the legislature of a State can diminish the salary of a judge holding his office during good behavior? Such an authority has never yet been asserted, to our knowledge. It may also be admitted that corporations for mere

public government, such as towns, cities and counties, may in many respects be subject to legislative control. But it will hardly be contended that, even in respect to such corporations, the legislative power is so transcendent that it may, at its will, take away the private property of the corporation or change the uses of its private funds, acquired under the public faith. Can the legislature confiscate to its own use the private funds which a municipal corporation holds under its charter without any default or consent of the corporators? If a municipal corporation be capable of holding devises and legacies to charitable uses (as may municipal corporations are), does the legislature, under our forms of limited government, possess the authority to seize upon those funds and appropriate them to other uses at its own arbitrary pleasure, against the will of the donors and donees? From the very nature of our governments, the public faith is pledged the other way, and that pledge constitutes a valid compact, and that compact is subject only to judicial inquiry, construction and abrogation. This Court have already had occasion, in other causes, to express their opinion on this subject, and there is not the slightest inclination to retract it. *Terrett v. Taylor,* 9 Cranch 43; *Town of Pawlet v. Clark,* 9 Cranch 292.

As to the case of the contract of marriage, which the argument supposes not to be within the reach of the prohibitory clause, because it is matter of civil institution, I profess not to feel the weight of the reason assigned for the exception. In a legal sense, all contracts recognised as valid in any country may be properly said to be matters of civil institution, since they obtain their obligation and construction *jure loci contractus.* Titles to land constituting part of the public domain, acquired by grants under the provisions of existing laws by private persons, are certainly contracts of civil institution. Yet no one ever supposed that, when acquired *bona fide,* they were not beyond the reach of legislative revocation. And so, certainly, is the established doctrine of this Court. *Terret v. Taylor,* 9 Cranch 43; *Town of Pawlet v. Clark,* 9 Cranch 292. A *general* law regulating divorces from the contract of marriage, like a law regulating remedies in other cases of breaches of contracts, is not necessarily a law impairing *the obligation of such a contract. Holmes v. Lansing,* 3 Johns.Cas. 73. It may be the only effectual mode of enforcing the obligations of the contract on both sides. A law punishing a breach of a contract, by imposing a forfeiture of the rights acquired under it, or dissolving it because the mutual obligations were no longer observed, is in no correct sense a law impairing the obligations of the contract. Could a law, compelling a specific performance, by giving a new remedy, be justly deemed an excess of legislative power? Thus far the contract of marriage has been considered with reference to general laws regulating divorces upon breaches of that contract. But if the argument means to assert that the legislative power to dissolve such a contract, without *any breach on either side, against the wishes of the parties,* and without any judicial inquiry to ascertain a breach, I certainly am not prepared to admit such a power, or that its exercise would not entrench upon the prohibition of the Constitution. If, under the faith of existing laws, a contract of marriage be duly solemnized, or a marriage settlement be made (and marriage is always in law a valuable consideration for a contract), it is not easy to perceive why a dissolution of its obligations, without any default or assent of the parties, may not as well fall within the prohibition as any other contract for a valuable consideration. A man has just as good a right to his wife as to *the property* acquired under a marriage contract. He has a legal right to her society and her fortune, and to divest such right, without his default and against his will, would be as flagrant a violation of the principles of justice as the confiscation of his own estate. I leave this case, however, to be settled when it shall arise. I have gone into it because it was urged with great earnestness upon us, and required a reply. It is sufficient now to say that, as at present advised, the argument derived from this source does not press my mind with any new and insurmountable difficulty.

In respect also to grants and contracts, it would be far too narrow a construction of the Constitution to limit the prohibitory clause to such only where the parties take for their own private benefit. A grant to a private Trustee, for the benefit of a particular *cestui que trust* or for any special, private or public charity cannot be the less a contract because the Trustee takes nothing for his own benefit. A grant of the next presentation to a church is still a contract, although it limit the grantee to a mere right of nomination or patronage. 2 Bl.Com. 21. The fallacy of the argument consists in assuming the very ground in controversy. It is not admitted that a contract with a Trustee is, in its own nature, revocable, whether it be for special or general purposes,

for public charity or particular beneficence. A private donation vested in a trustee for objects of a general nature does not thereby become a public trust which the government may, at its pleasure, take from the Trustee, and administer in its own way. The truth is that the government has no power to revoke a grant, *even of its own funds,* when given to a private person, or a corporation, for special uses It cannot recall its own endowments, granted to any hospital or College, or city or town, for the use of such corporations. The only authority remaining to the government is judicial, to ascertain the validity of the grant, to enforce its proper uses, to suppress frauds, and, if the uses are charitable, to secure their regular administration, through the means of equitable tribunals, in cases where there would otherwise be a failure of justice.

Another objection growing out of and connected with that which we have been considering is that no grants are within the constitutional prohibition except such as respect *property* in the strict sense of the term, that is to say, beneficial interests in lands, tenements and hereditaments, &c., which may be sold by the grantees for their own benefit, and that grants of franchises, immunities and authorities not valuable to the parties, *as property,* are excluded from its purview. No authority has been cited to sustain this distinction, and no reason is perceived to justify its adoption. There are many rights, franchises and authorities which are valuable in contemplation of law where no beneficial interest can accrue to the possessor. A grant of the next presentation to a church, limited to the grantee alone, has been already mentioned. A power of appointment, reserved in a marriage settlement, either to a party or a stranger, to appoint uses in favor of third persons, without compensation, is another instance.

A grant of lands to a Trustee, to raise portions or pay debts is, in law, a valuable grant, and conveys a legal estate. Even a power given by will to executors to sell an estate for payment of debts is, by the better opinions and authority, coupled with a trust, and capable of survivorship. Many dignities and offices existing at common law are merely honorary, and without profit, and sometimes are onerous. Yet a grant of them has never been supposed the less a contract on that account. In respect to franchises, whether corporate or not, which include a pernancy of profits, such as a right of fishery, or to hold a ferry, a market or a fair, or to erect a turnpike, bank or bridge, there is no pretence to say that grants of them are not within the Constitution. Yet they may, in point of fact, be of no exchangeable value to the owners. They may be worthless in the market. The truth, however, is that all incorporeal hereditaments, whether they be immunities, dignities, offices or franchises, or other rights, are deemed valuable in law. The owners have a legal estate and property in them, and legal remedies to support and recover them, in case of any injury, obstruction or disseisin of them. Whenever they are the subjects of a contract or grant, they are just as much within the reach of the Constitution as any other grant.

Nor is there any solid reason why a contract for the exercise of a mere authority should not be just as much guarded as a contract for the use and dominion of property. Mere naked powers which are to be exercised for the exclusive benefit of the grantor are revocable by him *for that very reason*. But it is otherwise where a power is to be exercised in aid of a right vested in the *grantee*. We all know that a power of attorney, forming a part of a security upon the assignment of a chose in action, is not revocable by the grantor. For it then sounds in contract, and is coupled with an interest. *Walsh v. Whitcomb,* 2 Esp. 565; *Bergen v. Bennett,* 1 Caines' Cases in Error 1, 15; *Raymond v. Squire,* 11 Johns. 47. So, if an estate be conveyed in trust for the grantor, the estate is irrevocable in the grantee, although he can take no beneficial interest for himself. Many of the best settled estates stand upon conveyances of this nature, and there can be no doubt that such grants are contracts within the prohibition in question.

In respect to *corporate franchises,* they are, properly speaking, legal estates, vested in the corporation itself, as soon as it is *in esse*. They are not mere naked powers granted to the corporation, but powers coupled with an interest. The property of the corporation rests upon the possession of its franchises, and whatever may be thought as to the corporators, it cannot be denied that the corporation itself has a legal interest in them. It may sue and be sued for them. Nay, more, this very right is one of its ordinary franchises. "It is likewise a franchise," says Mr. Justice Blackstone,

"for a number of persons to be incorporated and subsist as a body politic, with power to maintain perpetual succession, and do other corporate acts, and each individual member of such corporation is also said to have a franchise or freedom."

2 Bl.Com. 37; 1 Kyd on Corp. 14, 16. In order to get rid of the legal difficulty of these franchises being considered as valuable hereditaments or property, the counsel for the defendant are driven to contend that the corporators or Trustees are mere agents of the corporation, in whom no beneficial interest subsists, and so nothing but a naked power is touched by removing them from the trust, and then to hold the corporation itself a mere ideal being, capable indeed of holding property or franchises, but having no interest in them which can be the subject of contract. Neither of these positions is admissible. The former has been already sufficiently considered, and the latter may be disposed of in a few words. The corporators are not mere agents, but have vested rights in their character as corporators. The right to be a freeman of a corporation is a valuable temporal right. It is a right of voting and acting in the corporate concerns, which the law recognises and enforces, and for a violation of which it provides a remedy. It is founded on the same basis as the right of voting in public elections; it is as sacred a right, and whatever might have been the prevalence of former doubts, since the time of Lord Holt, such a right has always been deemed a valuable franchise or privilege. *Ashby v. White,* 2 Lord Raym. 938; 1 Kyd on Corp. 16.

This reasoning, which has been thus far urged applies with full force to the case of Dartmouth College. The franchises granted by the charter were vested in the Trustees, in their corporate character. The lands and other property, subsequently acquired, were held by them in the same manner. They were the private demesnes of the corporation, held by it not, as the argument supposes, for the use and benefit of the people of New Hampshire, but, as the charter itself declares, "for the use of Dartmouth College." There were not, and in the nature of things, could not be, any other *cestui que use* entitled to claim those funds. They were, indeed, to be devoted to the promotion of piety and learning, not at large, but in that *College* and the establishments connected with it; and the mode in which the charity was to be applied, and the objects of it, were left solely to the Trustees, who were the legal Governors and administrators of it. No particular person in New Hampshire possessed a vested right in the bounty, nor could he force himself upon the Trustees as a proper object. The legislature itself could not deprive the Trustees of the corporate funds, nor annul their discretion in the application of them, nor distribute them among its its own favorites. Could the Legislature of New Hampshire have seized the land given by the State of Vermont to the corporation and appropriated it to uses distinct from those intended by the charity, against the will of the Trustees? This question cannot be answered in the affirmative until it is established that the legislature may lawfully take the property of A. and give it to B., and if it could not take away or restrain the corporate *funds*, upon what pretence can it take away or restrain the corporate *franchises?* Without the franchises, the funds could not be used for corporate purposes, but without the funds, the possession of the franchises might still be of inestimable value to the College, and to the cause of religion and learning.

Thus far, the rights of the corporation itself in respect to its property and franchises have been more immediately considered. But there are other rights and privileges, belonging to the Trustees collectively and severally, which are deserving of notice. They are intrusted with the exclusive power to manage the funds, to choose the officers, and to regulate the corporate concerns according to their own discretion. The *jus patronatus* is vested in them. The visitatorial power, in its most enlarged extent, also belongs to them. When this power devolves upon the founder of a charity, it is an hereditament, descendible in perpetuity to his heirs, and in default of heirs, it escheats to the government. *Rex v. St. Catherine's Hall,* 4 T.R. 233. It is a valuable right, founded in property, as much so as the right of patronage in any other case. It is a right which partakes of a judicial nature. May not the founder as justly contract for the possession of this right, in return for his endowment, as for any other equivalent? and if, instead of holding it as an hereditament, he assigns it in perpetuity to the Trustees of the corporation, is it less a valuable hereditament in their hands? The right is not merely a collective right in all the Trustees, each of them also has a franchise in it. Lord Holt says,

"it is agreeable to reason and the rules of law that a franchise should be vested in the corporation aggregate, and yet the benefit redound to the particular members and be enjoyed by them in their private capacities. Where the privilege of election is used by particular persons, it is a particular right vested in each particular man."

*Ashby v. White,* 2 Lord Raym. 938, 952; *Attorney General v. Dixie,* 13 Ves. 519. Each of the Trustees had a right to vote in all elections. If obstructed in the exercise of it, the law furnished him with an adequate recompense in damages. If ousted unlawfully from his office, the law would, by a mandamus, compel a restoration.

It is attempted, however, to establish that the Trustees have no interest in the corporate franchises, because it is said that they may be witnesses in a suit brought against the corporation. The case cited at the bar certainly goes the length of asserting that, in a suit brought against a charitable corporation for a recompence for services performed for the corporation, the Governors, constituting the corporation (but whether intrusted with its funds or not by the act of incorporation does not appear), are competent witnesses against the plaintiff. *Weller v. Governor of the Foundling Hospital,* 1 Peake's N.P.Rep. 153. But assuming this case to have been rightly decided (as to which, upon the authorities, there may be room to doubt), the corporators being technically parties to the record, *Attorney General v. City of London,* 3 Bro.Ch.C. 171; S. C. 1 Ves.Jun. 243; *Burton v. Hinde,* 5 T.R. 174, *Nason v. Thatcher,* 7 Mass.Rep. 398; Phillips on Evid. 42, 52, 57 and notes; 1 Kyd on Corp. 304, &c.; Highmore on Mortm. 514, it does not establish that, in a suit for the corporate property vested in the Trustees in their corporate capacity, the Trustees are competent witnesses. At all events, it does not establish that, in a suit for the corporate franchises to be exercised by the Trustees, or to enforce their visitatorial power, the Trustees would be competent witnesses. On a mandamus to restore a Trustee to his corporate or visitatorial power, it will not be contended that the Trustee is himself a competent witness to establish his own rights or the corporate rights. Yet why not, if the law deems that a Trustee has no interest in the franchise? The test of interest assumed in the argument proves nothing in this case. It is not enough to establish that the Trustees are sometimes competent witnesses; it is necessary to show that they are always so in respect to the corporate franchises and their own. It will not be pretended that, in a suit for damages for obstruction in the exercise of his official powers, a Trustee is a disinterested witness. Such an obstruction is not a *damnum absque injuria.* Each Trustee has a vested right, and legal interest, in his office, and it cannot be divested but by due course of law. The illustration, therefore, lends no new force to the argument, for it does not establish that, when their own rights are in controversy, the Trustees have no legal interest in their offices.

The principal objections having been thus answered, satisfactorily, at least, to my own mind, it remains only to declare that my opinion, after the most mature deliberation, is that the charter of Dartmouth College, granted in 1969, is a contract within the purview of the constitutional prohibition.

I might now proceed to the discussion of the second question, but it is necessary previously to dispose of a doctrine which has been very seriously urged at the bar, *viz.*, that the charter of Dartmouth College was dissolved at the Revolution, and is therefore a mere nullity. A case before Lord Thurlow has been cited in support of this doctrine. *Attorney General v. City of London*, 3 Bro.Ch.C. 171; S. C. 1 Ves.Jun. 243. The principal question in that case was whether the corporation of William & Mary College, in Virginia (which had received its charter from King William and Queen Mary) should still be permitted to administer the charity under Mr. Boyle's will, no interest having passed to the College under the will, but it acting as an agent or trustee under a decree in chancery, or whether a new scheme for the administration of the charity should be laid before the Court. Lord Thurlow directed a new scheme because the College, belonging to an independent government, was no longer within the reach of the Court. And he very unnecessarily added that he could not now consider the College as a corporation, or, as another report, 1 Ves.Jun. 243, states, that he could not take notice of it, as a corporation, it not having proved its existence, as a corporation, at all. If, by this, Lord Thurlow meant to declare that all charters acquired in America from the Crown, were destroyed by the Revolution, his doctrine is not law, and if it had been true, it would equally apply to all other grants from the Crown, which would be monstrous. It is a principle of the common law which has been recognised as well in this as in other Courts that the division of an empire works no forfeiture of previously vested rights of property. And this maxim is equally consonant with the common sense of mankind and the maxims of eternal justice. *Terrett v. Taylor*, 9 Cranch 43, 13 U. S. 50; *Kelly v. Harrison*, 5 Johns.Cas. 29; *Jackson v. Lunn*, 3 Johns.Cas.. 109; *Calvin's Case*, 7 Co. 27. This objection therefore may be safely dismissed without further comment.

The remaining inquiry is whether the acts of the Legislature of New Hampshire now in question, or any of them, impair the obligations of the charter of Dartmouth College. The attempt certainly is to force upon the corporation a new charter, against the will of the corporators. Nothing seems better settled at the common law than the doctrine that the Crown cannot force upon a private corporation a new charter, or compel the old members to give up their own franchises, or to admit new members into the corporation. *Rex v. Vice-Chancellor of Cambridge,* 3 Burr. 1656; *Rex v. Pasmore*, 3 T.R. 240; 1 Kyd on Corp. 65; *Rex v. Larwood,* Comb. 316. Neither can the Crown compel a man to become a member of such corporation against his will. *Rex v. Dr. Askew,* 4 Burr. 2200. As little has it been supposed that, under our limited governments, the legislature possessed such transcendent authority. On one occasion, a very able court held that the State legislature had no authority to compel a person to become a member of a mere private corporation, created for the promotion of a private enterprise, because every man had a right to refuse a grant. *Ellis v. Marshall,* 2 Mass.Rep. 269. On another occasion, the same learned Court declared that they were all satisfied that the rights legally vested in a corporation cannot be controlled or destroyed by any subsequent statute unless *a power for that purpose be reserved to the legislature in the act of incorporation. Wales v. Stetson,* 2 Mass.Rep. 143, 146. These principles are so consonant with justice, sound policy, and legal reasoning that it is difficult to resist the impression of their perfect correctness. The application of them, however, does not, from our limited authority, properly belong to the appellate jurisdiction of this Court in this case.

A very summary examination of the acts of New Hampshire will abundantly show that, in many material respects, they change the charter of Dartmouth College. The Act of the 27th of June, 1816, declares that the corporation known by the name of the Trustees of Dartmouth College shall be called the Trustees of Dartmouth University. That the whole number of Trustees shall be *twenty-one*, a majority of whom shall form a quorum, that they and their successors shall hold, use, and enjoy forever all the powers, authorities, rights, property, liberties, privileges and immunities, heretofore held, &c., by the Trustees of Dartmouth College, except where the act otherwise provides; that they shall also have power to determine the times and places of their meetings, and manner of notifying the same; to organize Colleges in the University; to establish an institute and elect fellows and members thereof; to appoint and displace officers and determine their duties and compensation; to delegate the power of supplying vacancies in any of the offices of the University for a limited term; to pass ordinances for the government of the students; to prescribe the course of education; and to arrange, invest and employ the funds of the University. The act then provides for the appointment of a Board of twenty-five overseers, fifteen of whom shall form a quorum, of whom five are to be such *ex officio,* and the residue of the Overseers, as well as the new Trustees, are to be appointed by the Governor and Council. The Board of Overseers are, among other things, to have power, "to *inspect* and *confirm,* or *disapprove* and *negative,* such votes and proceedings of the Board of Trustees as shall relate to the appointment and removal of President, professors, and other permanent officers of the University, and determine their salaries; to the establishment of Colleges and professorships, and the erection of new College buildings." The act then provides that the President and professors shall be *nominated* by the *Trustees,* and *appointed* by the *Overseers,* and shall be liable to be suspended and removed in the same manner, and that *each of the two Boards of Trustees and Overseers shall have power to suspend and remove any member of their respective Boards.* The Supplementary Act of the 18th of December, 1816, declares that *nine* Trustees shall form a quorum, and that *six* votes at least shall be necessary for the passage of any act or resolution. The Act of the 26th of December, 1816, contains other provisions not very material to the question before us.

From this short analysis, it is apparent that, in substance, a new corporation is created, including the old corporators, with new powers, and subject to a new control, or that the old corporation is newly organized and enlarged, and placed under an authority hitherto unknown to it. The Board of Trustees are increased from twelve to twenty-one. The College becomes a University. The property vested in the old Trustees is transferred to the new Board of Trustees, in their corporate capacities. The quorum is no longer *seven,* but *nine.* The old Trustees have no longer the sole right to perpetuate their succession by electing other Trustees, but the *nine* new Trustees are, in the first instance, to be appointed by the Governor and Council, and the new Board are then to elect other Trustees from time to time, as vacancies occur. The new Board, too, have the power to suspend or remove any member,

so that a *minority* of the old Board, cooperating with the new Trustees, possess the unlimited power to remove the *majority* of the *old* Board. The powers, too, of the corporation are varied. It has authority to organize new Colleges in "the University, and to establish an institute, and elect fellows and members thereof." A Board of Overseers is created (a board utterly unknown to the old charter), and is invested with a general supervision and negative upon all the most important acts and proceedings of the Trustees. And to give complete effect to this new authority, instead of the right to appoint, the trustees are, in future, only to nominate, and the Overseers are to approve, the President and professors of the University.

If these are not essential changes, impairing the rights and authorities of the Trustees and vitally affecting the interests and organization of Dartmouth College under its old charter, it is difficult to conceive what acts, short of an unconditional repeal of the charter, could have that effect. If a grant of land or franchises be made to A., in trust for special purposes, can the grant be revoked, and a new grant thereof be made to A., B. and C., in trust for the same purposes, without violating the obligation of the first grant? If property be vested by grant in A. and B., for the use of a College, or an hospital, of private foundation, is not the obligation of that grant impaired when the estate is taken from their exclusive management and vested in them in common with ten other persons? If a power of appointment be given to A. and B., is it no violation of their right to annul the appointment unless it be assented to by five other persons, and then confirmed by a distinct body? If a bank or insurance company, by the terms of its charter, be under the management of directors, elected by the stockholders, would not the rights acquired by the charter be impaired if the legislature should take the right of election from the stockholders and appoint directors unconnected with the corporation? These questions carry their own answers along with them. The common sense of mankind will teach us that all these cases would be direct infringements of the legal obligations of the grants to which they refer, and yet they are, with no essential distinction, the same as the case now at the bar.

In my judgment, it is perfectly clear that any act of a legislature which takes away any powers or franchises vested by its charter in a private corporation, or its corporate officers, or which restrains or controls the legitimate exercise of them, or transfers them to other persons without its assent is a violation of the obligations of that charter. If the legislature mean to claim such an authority, it must be reserved in the grant. The charter of Dartmouth College contains no such reservation, and I am therefore bound to declare that the acts of the Legislature of New Hampshire now in question do impair the obligations of that charter, and are consequently unconstitutional and void.

In pronouncing this judgment, it has not for one moment escaped me how delicate, difficult, and ungracious is the task devolved upon us. The predicament in which this Court stands in relation to the nation at large is full of perplexities and embarrassments. It is called to decide on causes between citizens of different States, between a State and its citizens, and between different States. It stands, therefore in the midst of jealousies and rivalries of conflicting parties with the most momentous interests confided to its care. Under such circumstances, it never can have a motive to do more than its duty, and I trust it will always be found to possess firmness enough to do that.

Under these impressions, I have pondered on the case before us with the most anxious deliberation. I entertain great respect for the Legislature whose acts are in question. I entertain no less respect for the enlightened tribunal whose decision we are called upon to review. In the examination, I have endeavored to keep my steps *super antiquas vias* of the law, under the guidance of authority and principle. It is not for judges to listen to the voice of persuasive eloquence or popular appeal. We have nothing to do, but to pronounce the law as we find it, and, having done this, our justification must be left to the impartial judgment of our country.

## Glossary

**eleemosynary:** supported by charity

**ex post facto law:** a retroactive law; a law that imposes a punishment for an action that was not illegal when it was done

**trover:** a lawsuit to recover damages or the value of property that has been wrongfully used by someone else

# MCCULLOCH V. MARYLAND

| DATE | CITATION |
|---|---|
| 1819 | 17 U.S. 316 |
| **AUTHOR** | **SIGNIFICANCE** |
| John Marshall | Affirmed the power of Congress to incorporate a national bank, defining the scope of Congress's legislative authorities and embracing a broad view of national power |
| **VOTE** | |
| 7-0 | |

## Overview

Federalism, the division of sovereign power between national and state governments, creates perpetual tension over the degree of power possessed by each level of government. Innovating such a division in 1787, the framers of the U.S. Constitution could offer only an impressionistic blueprint. Granting the new national government power with regard to several broadly worded subjects, the framers left the details—and thus the precise division of power—to future development. How much power did those grants actually bestow on the national government of the United States? Chief Justice John Marshall's 1819 opinion in *McCulloch v. Maryland* was the foundational Supreme Court decision that initiated the process of answering that question, which very much remains relevant in modern times.

## Context

The scope of the national government's power became one of the most controversial political issues in the years following the ratification of the Constitution.

On one side, such members of the founding generation as Thomas Jefferson and James Madison pressed for constitutional interpretations that would seriously constrain the power of the national government and, as a result, enhance the power of the states. Against them, arguing for interpretations that would enhance national power at the expense of the states, were such figures as Alexander Hamilton, John Adams, and, though trying to remain above the fray, George Washington himself. Although slavery and race would later define debates about "states' rights" and have too often been ignored as a subtext of this early controversy, the disagreement was about far more. Broader matters of individual liberty, self-government, unity, and even national security were thought to be at stake. The competing conceptions of federalism became a major impetus behind the rise of political parties in this era, with Jeffersonian Republicans favoring a weaker national government and Hamiltonian Federalists a stronger one.

In this clash over federalism, the national government's incorporation of a bank became an early flashpoint. Hamilton, as Washington's secretary of the treasury, proposed a national bank in 1790 as a way to spur economic investment, support national debt management, facilitate federal tax collection, and, less officially, give monied interests a stake in the success of the national government. Congress approved the bank bill and sent it to Washington for his signature. Jefferson, then Washington's secretary of state, vigorously opposed the incorporation of a bank as exceeding the constitutional powers of the national government. Washington, however, agreed with Hamilton's defense of the bank's constitutionality and signed the bill, creating the First Bank of the United States.

After the electoral revolution of 1800, when Jefferson and his Republicans ousted Federalists from Congress and the presidency, political polarization over federalism diminished. As president, Jefferson exercised broader powers than he previously would have conceded to the national government, such as with his conclusion of the Louisiana Purchase, while Federalists, no longer in control, became less vigorous advocates for broad national power once it was wielded by their opponents. When the expiration of the First Bank in 1811 contributed to financial woes, which the War of 1812 only exacerbated, Madison, having succeeded Jefferson as president, signed a bill to incorporate the Second Bank of the United States on April 10, 1816. Even though as a House member Madison had strenuously opposed Hamilton's original bill as unconstitutional, he waived those earlier objections based on the general acceptance of the First Bank's constitutionality during the ensuing years. By then, nationalism was ascendant in the United States, as it coincidentally was in Europe as well.

Within three years, however, the Second Bank was publicly reviled, though not principally because of objections related to federalism. The bank's loose lending practices during an economic boom gave way in the depression that followed to policies of strict recapture. Maryland and other states then moved against the bank by taxing its operation; two states even banned its operation altogether. At the same time, word was emerging that James McCulloch, the chief agent of the Baltimore branch, and some unscrupulous conspirators had bilked the bank out of $1 million. Opposition to national power had diminished, but opposition to the Second Bank itself was great, and Congress seriously debated abolishing it. It was in this atmosphere that the Supreme Court decided the *McCulloch* case, in which the Court affirmed Congress's power to incor-

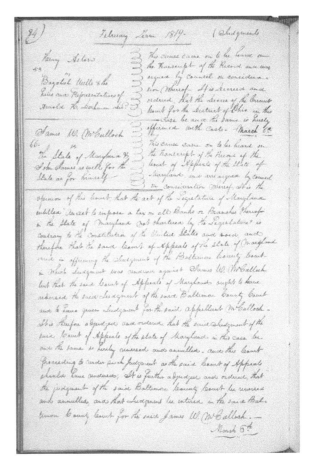

**McCulloch v. Maryland**
(National Archives and Records Administration)

porate a national bank and struck down Maryland's attempt to tax it.

## About the Author

Despite cultural similarities to Jefferson and Madison, John Marshall was a consummate Federalist and a strong supporter of national power. Born in 1755 in Virginia to a successful and locally prominent family, Marshall became a lawyer and served as state politician, diplomat, and secretary of state before becoming chief justice of the United States on February 4, 1801. Appointed by President Adams, a Federalist, in the waning days of his administration, Marshall and other judicial appointees would remain the only source of Federalist power after the imminent Jeffersonian takeover of the presidency and Congress. Marshall did not disappoint. By the time he died in 1835 after serving as the Supreme Court's chief justice for nearly thirty-five years, Marshall had greatly expanded the reputation and influence of the Court and had penned landmark legal opinions that laid the foundations for dramatic expansions in the scope of the national government that would occur over the ensuing two centuries. Jeffersonians may have won the elections of 1800, but owing to Marshall's commanding Federalist presence on the Court, they ultimately lost the struggle to give federalism a strongly decentralized bent.

At least two factors that distinguished Marshall from his Virginia contemporaries may help to explain his regionally dissident opinion in favor of national power. First, Marshall saw extensive action as a first lieutenant during the Revolutionary War, including enduring the harsh winter at Valley Forge. He witnessed the problems of supply and support that plagued the Continental army owing to the weak national government and selfish recalcitrance among the states in the era before the Constitution. Second, neither Marshall nor his family ever engaged in large-scale agricultural production, although they held significant land. As a result, Marshall, who never owned more than a handful of slaves, was less invested in the slavery-dependent plantation economy of the South. Indeed, his writings, particularly in later years, disclose a disdain for slavery. From his position on the Court, he ruled that slaves were people, not property, and his will bestowed freedom upon his longtime personal servant.

## Explanation and Analysis of the Document

Paragraphs 1–10 are background materials that precede Marshall's actual opinion, which begins at paragraph 11. Paragraph 1 indicates that the Supreme Court took the case by issuing a writ of error to Maryland's highest court. Paragraph 2 is a "statement of the case," a summary of proceedings to date. On behalf of Maryland, John James, a state treasurer, sued James McCulloch, the chief agent of the Second Bank's Baltimore branch, to recover unpaid taxes that the bank allegedly owed the state. A county court ruled for Maryland based on an agreed-upon "statement of facts," a procedure that avoided a trial. On appeal, Maryland's highest court upheld the county court's judgment.

Paragraphs 3–5 reproduce the statement of facts, as confirmed by both parties to the case. Paragraph 3 cites the federal statute that established the Second

Bank and the Maryland statute that taxed the bank. The Second Bank was organized in Philadelphia and, without Maryland's authorization, established a Baltimore branch. The branch engaged in certain transactions with George Williams, a shady business partner of McCulloch. The bank did not pay the Maryland tax even though the state did nothing to obstruct payment. Paragraph 4 identifies the case's primary question—whether Maryland's tax is constitutional—and specifies the remedies sought by each side. Paragraph 5 notes that the parties preserve their appeals and agree to be bound by the statement of facts.

Paragraphs 6–10 reproduce the Maryland tax statute. As paragraph 8 discloses, the statute taxed the transactions of any bank lacking a state charter. As paragraph 9 discloses, the statute imposed penalties on bank employees.

### Chief Justice John Marshall's Opinion for the Court

Paragraph 11 marks the start of Marshall's opinion, which was unanimously joined by the associate justices. In paragraph 12 Marshall explains that Maryland ("the defendant") challenges the constitutionality of the federal law incorporating the Second Bank and that McCulloch ("the plaintiff") challenges the constitutionality of Maryland's tax. The Supreme Court, Marshall observes, bears the "awful responsibility" of adjudicating this dispute, which may have significant ramifications for federalism.

### Power of Congress to Charter a Bank

In paragraph 13 Marshall turns to the first main issue: the power of Congress to charter a bank. In paragraphs 14–17 Marshall explains why judicial review should be restrained. In paragraph 14 he cites long-standing congressional and judicial acquiescence as a reason to presume the Second Bank constitutional. He concedes in paragraph 15 that the Court could halt an obvious constitutional violation ("a bold and daring usurpation") but also that the historical acquiescence cautions against it. The acquiescence is held to particularly matter when only federalism, not civil liberties, is at stake.

In paragraph 16 Marshall adverts to the extensive political debate over the bank's constitutionality. He makes tacit reference to James Madison's opposition to the original bill in Congress, Thomas Jefferson's opposition to it inside George Washington's cabinet, Washington's decision to approve the original bill, and Madison's subsequent change of opinion after the original act lapsed. Given this background, a court would be hard pressed to view the bank as obviously unconstitutional, although Marshall adds in paragraph 17 that the constitutionality of the Second Bank does not necessarily depend on this background.

In paragraphs 18–22 Marshall rejects a compact theory of federalism, which would view the Constitution as emanating from the states, not the people. He acknowledges in paragraph 19 that state legislatures chose the delegates to the Constitutional Convention of 1787 and that the Constitution was ratified on a state-by-state basis. He reasons, however, that the document was ratified not by state legislatures but by the people in representative conventions, the closest mechanism to statewide direct democracy in the eighteenth century. In paragraph 20 Marshall quotes from the Constitution's preamble and identifies the people, not the states, as the foundational source of the Constitution's authority. Implicitly referencing the Declaration of Independence, Marshall reasons in paragraph 21 that even though the people had already delegated their sovereign power to state governments, they could reclaim it and re-delegate it to a new system of government. In paragraph 22 Marshall emphasizes the federal government's popular basis, anticipating Abraham Lincoln's Gettysburg Address.

In paragraph 23 Marshall acknowledges that Congress possesses only limited powers as enumerated in the Constitution (principally in Article I, Section 8). He calls the point so obvious that the Constitution's "enlightened friends"—the authors of the Federalist Papers—devoted more time than necessary to establishing the proposition. But the difficult question, Marshall says, is identifying the scope of those powers.

In paragraphs 24–26 Marshall establishes that federal laws take precedence over state laws. In paragraph 25 he offers a functional justification: In a collective, the whole must bind the parts. In paragraphs 25 and 26 he adds a textual justification—the "supremacy" clause of the Constitution (Article VI, Clause 2), which expressly declares federal law supreme.

In paragraph 27—a critical passage—Marshall introduces the doctrine of "implied powers." Even though the chartering of a bank or other corporation is not an enumerated power, this doctrine establishes how Congress might nevertheless have that power as adjunct to its enumerated powers. Marshall offers a comparative textual justification for this doctrine. While the Articles of Confederation, the forerunner of the Constitution, reserved to the states all powers that were not "expressly delegated" to the Confederation Congress (Article II), the parallel provision of the Constitution itself (Amendment X) omits the word "expressly," thus allowing the inference that Congress possesses some powers that are not specifically enumerated. Marshall then reinforces his view by considering the very nature of a constitution, which he characterizes as a concise document that contains only "great outlines," not implementation details. Marshall alludes to this conception when he famously announces here that "it is a constitution we are expounding."

In paragraph 28 Marshall introduces a critical distinction between means and ends. He holds that Congress does not have the power to charter a bank merely because that power is lesser than the great enumerated powers. Rather, Congress has power to charter a bank because, in Marshall's view, that power is not an end in itself but merely a means to an end. The enumerated powers, he reasons, address ends, not means, so one would not expect to find the power to charter a bank—a mere means—among the enumerated powers. Further, the framers of the Constitution could not have intended to grant Congress "ample powers" without "ample means" for executing them. Surely, Marshall says, the power of Congress to raise and spend revenue (Article I, Section 8, Clause 1) includes as an implied power the means of transporting revenue from the place it was raised to the place it will be spent.

In paragraphs 29–31 Marshall requires Maryland to explain how the power to charter a bank is different from any other means that Congress might use in executing its enumerated powers. Although Maryland holds that the power is a sovereign one, Marshall states that the same is true of other means, such as physically transporting federal revenue. In paragraph 32 Marshall notes that the question is not whether chartering a bank is a sovereign power but, rather, which sovereign possesses the power in a system where sovereignty is split. Marshall then rejects Maryland's argument that the chartering of banks is a state power because states had that power first. The argument is untenable because it would not apply to any state admitted to the Union after the ratification of the Constitution. Marshall then reiterates that the chartering of a bank is an apt means to a legitimate federal end and is thus an implicit adjunct to Congress's enumerated powers.

In paragraph 33 Marshall turns from implied powers to the Constitution's "necessary and proper" clause (Article I, Section 8, Clause 18), which explicitly empowers Congress to enact all laws that are "necessary and proper" for executing its enumerated powers. In paragraph 34 Marshall accuses Maryland of arguing that the clause is not, as written, a grant of power but a restriction on Congress's choice of means. In paragraphs 35–36 Marshall digresses to reject Maryland's argument that the clause merely ensures that Congress can enact laws. Marshall notes that that power is already obvious from other provisions.

In paragraph 37 Marshall introduces Maryland's principal argument: that the word *necessary* means "indispensably necessary," such that the clause in question empowers Congress to make only those laws that are indispensable to the execution of its enumerated powers, limiting Congress to only those means that are the "most direct and simple." In paragraph 38 Marshall reasons that *necessary* need not be interpreted as "indispensable," as it can have less strong senses. The Constitution itself elsewhere uses a related phrase with a qualifying word, "absolutely necessary" (Article I, Section 10), to convey the sense of "indispensable." Marshall reasons that such ambiguous words as *necessary* should thus be interpreted in light of "the subject, the context, [and] the intention of the person using them." Marshall then considers each of those three matters in turn.

In paragraph 39 Marshall first discusses the "necessary and proper" clause's subject, which he describes as facilitation of the execution of Congress's "great powers." Interpreting the word *necessary* to limit Congress's choice of means would contradict that function. Marshall again invokes the nature of a constitution, which is "to endure for ages to come" and be "adapted to the various *crises* of human affairs." Limiting Congress's choice of means in achieving its designated ends would unduly tie the hands of future generations. This limitation would make the Constitution function more like a legal code, as if the framers had intended to preemptively micromanage "exigencies which, if foreseen at all, must have been seen dimly, and which can be

best provided for as they occur." Marshall then cites statutory oaths of office as being not indispensably necessary to the execution of Congress's powers while still being something that Congress surely can require.

In paragraphs 40–43 Marshall analogizes the incorporation of a bank to the enactment of criminal restrictions. He observes in paragraph 40 that the power to punish people is not an enumerated power and that Congress could execute its enumerated powers without creating any criminal restrictions. Although Congress could set up a postal system and federal courts without criminalizing interference with their operations, Marshall states in paragraph 41 that such criminal restrictions are nevertheless useful. The power to punish, Marshall reasons in paragraph 42, is a means for executing Congress's enumerated powers and is within Congress's power even if merely conducive, but not actually indispensable, to its execution of enumerated powers. If *necessary* should not be interpreted to mean "indispensable" with respect to the creation of criminal restrictions, Marshall asks in paragraph 43, why should it be read that way with respect to the incorporation of a bank?

In paragraph 44 Marshall considers the specific context in which the word *necessary* appears in the clause in question. He explains that qualifying the word by pairing it with the phrase *and proper* would not make sense if *necessary* already meant "indispensable."

In paragraphs 45–47 Marshall further considers the intentions of the framers. He rejects Maryland's restrictive interpretation of "necessary" in paragraph 45 because it would effectively function as a limitation on Congress's power, given that broader power could be inferred even without the "necessary and proper" clause. The restriction of Congress's power could not have been the intent because, as Marshall observes in paragraph 46, the clause is placed among the grants of power to Congress (Article I, Section 8), not among the restrictions on the power of Congress (Article I, Section 9). Moreover, he argues in paragraph 47 that the clause indeed reads like a grant of power, yet if the framers had had any incentive to conceal a provision's true purpose, the incentive would have been to conceal grants of power, not to conceal restrictions on power.

In paragraph 48 Marshall concludes that the "necessary and proper" clause does not restrict the discretion of Congress to choose the appropriate means for executing its enumerated powers. If nothing else, he holds, the clause removes any doubt about the power of Congress to legislate.

In paragraph 49 Marshall articulates the enduring standard for determining whether a law is within Congress's power: "Let the end be legitimate, let it be within the scope of the constitution, and all means which are appropriate, which are plainly adapted to that end, which are not prohibited, but consist with the letter and spirit of the constitution, are constitutional."

In paragraphs 50–52 Marshall reasons that chartering a bank is an appropriate means for achieving congressional ends. In paragraph 50 he reiterates that the creation of a corporation is not an end in itself but is merely a means for achieving other ends. As such, there is no reason to suppose that it would be enumerated in the Constitution as a distinct power of Congress. In paragraph 51 Marshall analogizes a corporation to a territorial government, which he says is universally regarded as an appropriate, corporate means for exercising Congress's power to regulate federal territory. In paragraph 52 Marshall reasons that if Congress may create one kind of corporate entity, a territorial legislature, it may create other kinds, including banks, where doing so is an appropriate adjunct to the execution of its enumerated powers. Experts agree, he adds, that a bank is a useful took. Even James Madison (among the era's "statesmen of the first class"), who initially opposed the bank, eventually approved of it. Marshall points out that the erstwhile Confederation Congress also felt a need to create a bank, even though doing so might well have exceeded its powers under the Articles of Confederation.

In paragraph 53 Marshall explains that the extent to which a federal law is necessary is a matter for Congress, not the judiciary, to determine. In paragraph 54 he rejects the argument that the existence of banks chartered by the states deprives Congress of the power to charter banks. In paragraphs 55–57, Marshall at last concludes that the Second Bank of the United States is constitutional.

### *Maryland's Power to Tax the Bank*

In paragraph 58 Marshall turns to the second main issue: the power of the state of Maryland to tax the Second Bank. In paragraphs 59–65 Marshall explains that the supremacy of federal law implicitly restricts the power of states to tax whenever an exercise of that pow-

er is incompatible with federal law, echoing his opinion in *Marbury v. Madison* (1803) at the end of paragraph 59. In paragraphs 60–61 he alludes to the Constitution's "supremacy" clause (Article VI, Clause 2), reasoning that the power to destroy something is incompatible with the power to create and preserve it. After complimenting the attorneys in paragraph 62, Marshall turns Maryland's key argument back onto the state in paragraphs 63–64. Referring to the Constitution's explicit restriction on state import and export taxes (Article I, Section 10), he rejects the negative inference that all other state taxes must be permissible. Instead, Marshall views the provision as textual confirmation that the power of states to tax must sometimes yield to the supremacy of federal law. The question, then, is whether a particular state tax would "defeat the legitimate operations" of the federal government.

Before addressing that issue, Marshall digresses in paragraphs 66–72 in order to offer an alternative line of reasoning based on democratic theory and state sovereignty. His overall point here is that states might not have the power to tax any federal entity at all. Reminiscent of the "no taxation without representation" credo of the American Revolution, Marshall observes in paragraphs 66–67 that a legislator's interest in reelection is the "only security" against "erroneous and oppressive taxation." But this security is lacking, he reasons, when a state taxes a federal entity. The people of other states, who have an equal financial interest in the federal entity, have no democratic check on the legislators of the taxing state. Marshall concedes in paragraph 68–69 that a state may tax foreign goods when present in the state, despite the similar absence of a democratic check. That concession prompts him to refocus the inquiry on the scope of state sovereignty in paragraphs 70–71. Although a state may tax things over which it has sovereignty, including foreign goods when present in the state, a state has no sovereignty over federal entities because those entities owe their existence to the people of the entire nation, not to the state. Marshall concludes in paragraph 72 that, in this view, there is no need to ask whether the Constitution deprives states of any power to tax federal entities because that power was never part of their sovereign powers anyway.

In paragraphs 73–75 Marshall rejects Maryland's appeal to self-restraint. Noting famously in paragraph 74 that "the power to tax involves the power to destroy," Marshall specifically rejects Maryland's argument that the security of federal operations must rest solely on confidence that states will voluntarily refrain from using their taxing power to destroy those operations. In paragraph 75 Marshall relies again on democratic theory. Only Congress, he reasons, can be trusted to control federal operations because only Congress represents all of the people. In contrast, the people of other states have no electoral check on the Maryland legislature if it decides to tax federal operations.

In paragraphs 76–78 Marshall extrapolates from Maryland's argument to show that, taken to its logical conclusion, the argument would effectively subordinate the federal government to the individual states. If states may tax a federally chartered bank, Marshall reasons in paragraph 77, they may also tax any other federal operation, such as federal courts. In paragraph 78 Marshall dismisses as inconsequential Maryland's disavowal of any present intention to tax anything other than federal property within its borders. If states could tax federal operations, he adds, they could even regulate federal operations using state powers other than taxation. At its core, Marshall concludes, Maryland's view would subvert the principle of federal supremacy that is expressly established in the supremacy clause.

In paragraphs 79–80 Marshall rejects Maryland's appeal to the Federalist Papers. Maryland cited Federalist Paper no. 33, in which Alexander Hamilton argues that the "necessary and proper" clause does not empower Congress to prohibit state taxes. Quoting Federalist no. 31, Marshall responds by limiting Hamilton's argument to the context in which he made it: a discussion over whether Congress could directly outlaw state taxes in general. Marshall explains in paragraph 80 that Hamilton was not considering the possibility that states might try to tax federal operations.

In paragraphs 81–83 Marshall returns to democratic theory to reject Maryland's argument that if Congress can tax a state-chartered bank, then states must be able to tax a federally chartered bank. In paragraph 82 Marshall denies this asserted reflexivity with another tacit appeal to the Revolutionary-era credo of "no taxation without representation." If Congress taxes state-chartered banks, people of the states are represented in Congress and are taxing themselves. On the other hand, if one state taxes a federally chartered bank, affecting the interests of everyone in the nation, people in other states have no representation in the taxing state's legislature and thus no electoral check on its taxing

decision. In paragraph 83 Marshall suggests, in the alternative, that even if Maryland's equation of the two situations were accurate, he would deny either government the power to tax the other; he still would not grant Maryland the power to tax a federal operation.

Marshall finally announces in paragraphs 84–86 the conclusion that Maryland's tax is an unconstitutional interference with a federal operation. Significantly, however, he qualifies the Court's opinion in paragraph 86. He leaves open the possibility that Maryland might be able to tax the bank's real estate and shareholders, as long as such taxes apply on a nondiscriminatory basis to all real estate and shareholders, not just to the Second Bank of the United States.

In paragraph 87 Marshall renders judgment. Holding the Maryland courts to have erred, Marshall orders the county court to rule for McCulloch.

## Impact

In the present as in the past, Supreme Court decisions are apt to be immediately judged by the public based not on the legal principles established but on the specific outcomes in the cases at hand. The particular issue of state taxation of the Second Bank was in fact short lived, becoming wholly moot when the bank's charter expired in 1836.

Despite the diminished polarization concerning federalism and the prevailing acceptance that the bank was constitutional, Marshall's opinion nevertheless generated some intense reactions on federalism grounds. Spencer Roane, a judge of the Virginia Court of Appeals, published a series of popular essays attacking the decision for adopting a broadly nationalistic conception of federalism that, in his view, threatened the continued viability of the states. Criticism of *McCulloch* on that basis was sufficiently serious, in fact, to induce Marshall himself to take the highly unusual step of defending his own opinion in his own series of popular essays, which he published under a pseudonym. Still, polarization over federalism had diminished enough by 1819 that *McCulloch* survived the contemporaneous attacks.

In the modern era, no one reads *McCulloch* in order to figure out whether Congress has the power to incorporate a bank. Rather, *McCulloch* remains one of the most significant Supreme Court decisions of all time because of its embrace of a broad view of national power. While relatively unexploited during the remainder of the nineteenth century, that view allowed for a breathtaking expansion of the federal government in the twentieth century, particularly during and after the Great Depression of the 1930s. *McCulloch* underlay famous Court decisions upholding the power of Congress to tell a lone farmer in Ohio how much wheat he could grow for his own personal use, to prohibit a local restaurant from maintaining a "whites only" policy, and to criminalize one person's simple possession of marijuana.

Some two centuries of experience have largely confirmed the fears of *McCulloch*'s critics. Indeed, national power has expanded beyond anything Marshall himself could have imagined. At the same time, however, into the twenty-first century the United States not only remained intact and resisted tyranny but also developed into one of the world's wealthiest, most advanced, and most powerful countries. A different *McCulloch*, one adopting a stingier view of national power, would have produced a United States that would be unrecognizable today, if still united at all.

---

## Questions for Further Study

1. A traditional ideal holds that judges should set aside their own political preferences and interpret the Constitution as neutrally as humanly possible. Is Marshall's opinion in *McCulloch* persuasive as a neutral interpretation of the Constitution, or does it seem driven by his own Federalist preferences for a strong national government?

2. Marshall reasons in paragraph 28 that a government given "ample powers" must also have "ample means" for executing those powers, and he repeatedly stresses that the choice of means should be left to the discretion of Congress. A fundamental principle in the law of the European Union, however, is "subsidiarity." This principle postulates that a governmental function should be performed by the lowest level of government that can effectively and efficiently perform it. Compare and contrast the rationale under subsidiarity for transferring a power to a higher level of government and Marshall's rationale for recognizing an implied power in the national government. Would subsidiarity accord with Marshall's rejection of the argument, in paragraph 54, that Congress lacks the power to incorporate a bank because state-incorporated banks are more than adequate to serve Congress's needs? If not, which rationale is superior? Why?

3. The framers of the Constitution were influenced by the eighteenth-century French philosopher Montesquieu, who advocated a form of federalism in Volume 1, Book 9 of his work *The Spirit of Laws*. What would Montesquieu have thought of the result in *McCulloch* and of Marshall's justifications for his conclusions?

4. Unlike the U.S. Constitution, the Constitution Act of Canada grants enumerated powers not only to the Parliament of Canada (section 91) but also to the provincial legislatures (section 92). If, as in *McCulloch*, it was unclear whether a particular power could be exercised by Parliament or by a provincial legislature, how would the Supreme Court of Canada resolve the dispute under the Constitution Act? Compare and contrast its probable approach with Marshall's approach in *McCulloch*.

5. In paragraph 86 of the *McCulloch* opinion, Marshall leaves open the question of whether Maryland could subject the Second Bank of the United States to the same property taxes that it imposes on all other property in Maryland. In light of the rationales that Marshall offers in striking down the tax at issue in *McCulloch*, how should this open question have been answered if Maryland had subsequently tried to subject the bank to its ordinary property tax laws? How would you resolve any contradictions that might arise among the rationales that Marshall offers if applied to such a situation?

---

## Further Reading

### Books

Black, Charles L., Jr. *Structure and Relationship in Constitutional Law.* Woodbridge, CT: Ox Bow Press, 1985.

Dangerfield, George. *The Awakening of American Nationalism, 1815–1828.* New York: Harper & Row, 1965.

Ellis, Richard E. *Aggressive Nationalism: McCulloch v. Maryland and the Foundation of Federal Authority in the Young Republic.* Oxford, UK: Oxford University Press, 2007.

Ely, John Hart. *Democracy and Distrust: A Theory of Judicial Review.* Cambridge, MA: Harvard University Press, 1980.

Killenbeck, Mark R. *M'Culloch v. Maryland: Securing a Nation.* Lawrence: University Press of Kansas, 2006.

Schwartz, David S. *The Spirit of the Constitution: John Marshall and the 200-Year Odyssey of McCulloch v. Maryland.* New York: Oxford University Press, 2019.

Shapiro, David L. *Federalism: A Dialogue.* Evanston, IL: Northwestern University Press, 1995.

Simon, James F. *What Kind of Nation: Thomas Jefferson, John Marshall, and the Epic Struggle to Create a United States.* New York: Simon & Schuster, 2002.

Smith, Jean Edward. J*ohn Marshall: Definer of a Nation.* New York: H. Holt, 1996.

White, G. Edward. *The Marshall Court and Cultural Change, 1815–35.* New York: Macmillan, 1988.

### Articles

Amar, Akhil Reed. "Intratextualism." *Harvard Law Review* 112, no. 4 (February 1999): 747–827.

Barnett, Randy E. "The Original Meaning of the Necessary and Proper Clause." *University of Pennsylvania Journal of Constitutional Law* 6 (2003): 183–221.

Beck, J. Randy. "The New Jurisprudence of the Necessary and Proper Clause." *University of Illinois Law Review* 2002 (2002): 581–649.

Clark, Stephen. "Progressive Federalism? A Gay Liberationist Perspective." Albany Law Review 66 (2003): 719–757.

Currie, David P. "The Constitution in the Supreme Court: State and Congressional Powers, 1801–1835." *University of Chicago Law Review* 49, no. 4 (1982): 887–975.

Finkelman, Paul. "The Constitution and the Intentions of the Framers: The Limits of Historical Analysis." *University of Pittsburgh Law Review* 50 (1989): 349–398.

Frankfurter, Felix. "John Marshall and the Judicial Function." *Harvard Law Review* 69, no. 2 (December 1955): 217–238.

Kurland, Philip B. "Curia Regis: Some Comments on the Divine Right of Kings and Courts 'To Say What the Law Is.'" *Arizona Law Review* 23 (1981): 581–597.

## Further Reading

### Articles

Lawson, Gary, and Patricia B. Granger. "The 'Proper' Scope of Federal Power: A Jurisdictional Interpretation of the Sweeping Clause." *Duke Law Journal* 43, no. 2 (November 1993): 267–336.

Ray, Clyde. "John Marshall, McCulloch v. Maryland, and the Concept of Constitutional Sovereignty." *Perspectives on Political Science* 47, no. 2 (2018): 65-77.

Rubin, Edward, and Malcolm Feeley. "Federalism: Some Notes on a National Neurosis." *UCLA Law Review* 41 (April 1994): 903–952.

Schwartz, David S. "Misreading McCulloch v. Maryland." *Pennsylvania Journal of Constitutional Law* 18 (2015): 1–94.

Wechsler, Herbert. "The Political Safeguards of Federalism: The Role of the States in the Composition and Selection of the National Government." *Columbia Law Review* 54 (1954): 543–560.

### Websites

"McCulloch v. Maryland (1819)." Landmark Supreme Court Cases website. Accessed April 12, 2023. http://www.landmarkcases.org/mcculloch/home.html.

"McCulloch v. Maryland (1819)." National Archives "Our Documents" website. Accessed April 12, 2023. http://www.ourdocuments.gov/doc.php?flash=true&doc=21.

"McCulloch v. Maryland (1977)." Internet Archive website. Accessed April 12, 2023. http://www.archive.org/details/gov.ntis.AVA02154VNB1.

—Commentary by Stephen Clark

# MCCULLOCH V. MARYLAND

## Document Text

### Syllabus

This was an action of debt, brought by the defendant in error, John James, who sued as well for himself as for the State of Maryland, in the County Court of Baltimore County, in the said State, against the plaintiff in error, McCulloch, to recover certain penalties, under the act of the legislature of Maryland, hereafter mentioned. Judgment being rendered against the plaintiff in error, upon the following statement of facts, agreed and submitted to the Court by the parties, was affirmed by the Court of Appeals of the State of Maryland, the highest Court of law of said State, and the cause was brought, by writ of error, to this Court.

It is admitted by the parties in this cause, by their counsel, that there was passed, on the 10th day of April 1816, by the Congress of the United States, an act, entitled, "an act to incorporate the subscribers to the Bank of the United States;" and that there was passed on the 11th day of February 1818, by the general assembly of Maryland, an act, entitled, "an act to impose a tax on all Banks, or branches thereof, in the State of Maryland, *not chartered by the legislature*," which said acts are made part of this statement, and it is agreed, may be read from the statute books in which they are respectively printed. It is further admitted, that the President, Directors and Company of the Bank of the United States, incorporated by the act of Congress aforesaid, did organize themselves, and go into full operation, in the city of Philadelphia, in the State of Pennsylvania, in pursuance of the said act, and that they did on the ___ day of _____ 1817, establish a branch of the said Bank, or an office of discount and deposit, in the

city of Baltimore, in the State of Maryland, which has, from that time, until the first day of May 1818, ever since transacted and carried on business as a Bank, or office of discount and deposit, and as a branch of the said Bank of the United States, by issuing Bank notes and discounting promissory notes, and performing other operations hhe constitution of the United States and composing one of the States of the Union. It is further admitted, that James William McCulloch, the defendant below, being the cashier of the said branch, or office of discount and deposit, did, on the several days set forth in the declaration in this cause, issue the said respective Bank notes therein described, from the said branch or office, to a certain George Williams, in the city of Baltimore, in part payment of a promissory note of the said Williams, discounted by the said branch or office, which said respective Bank notes were not, nor was either of them, so issued, on stamped paper, in the manner prescribed by the act of assembly aforesaid. It is further admitted, that the said President, Directors and Company of the Bank of the United States, and the said branch, or office of discount and deposit, have not, nor has either of them, paid in advance, or otherwise, the sum of fifteen thousand dollars, to the treasurer of the Western Shore, for the use of the State of Maryland, before the issuing of the said notes, or any of them, nor since those periods. And it is further admitted, that the treasurer of the Western Shore of Maryland, under the direction of the governor and council of the said State, was ready, and offered to deliver to the said President, Directors and Company of the said Bank, and to the said branch, or office of discount and deposit, stamped paper of the kind and denomination required and described in the said act of assembly.

The question submitted to the Court for their decision in this case, is, as to the validity of the said act of the general assembly of Maryland, on the ground of its being repugnant to the constitution of the United States, and the act of Congress aforesaid, or to one of them. Upon the foregoing statement of facts, and the pleadings in this cause (all errors in which are hereby agreed to be mutually released), if the Court should be of opinion, that the plaintiffs are entitled to recover, then judgment, it is agreed, shall be entered for the plaintiffs for twenty-five hundred dollars, and costs of suit. But if the Court should be of opinion, that the plaintiffs are not entitled to recover upon the statement and pleadings aforesaid, then judgment of non pros shall be entered, with costs to the defendant.

It is agreed, that either party may appeal from the decision of the County Court, to the Court of Appeals, and from the decision of the Court of Appeals to the Supreme Court of the United States, according to the modes and usages of law, and have the same benefit of this statement of facts, in the same manner as could be had, if a jury had been sworn and empanelled in this cause, and a special verdict had been found, or these facts had appeared and been stated in an exception taken to the opinion of the Court, and the Court's direction to the jury thereon.

Copy of the act of the Legislature of the State of Maryland, referred to in the preceding statement.

*An Act to impose a Tax on all Banks or Branches thereof, in the State of Maryland, not chartered by the Legislature.*

*Be it enacted by the General Assembly of Maryland*, that if any Bank has established, or shall, without authority from the State first had and obtained, establish any branch, office of discount and deposit, or office of pay and receipt in any part of this State, it shall not be lawful for the said branch, office of discount and deposit, or office of pay and receipt, to issue notes, in any manner, of any other denomination than five, ten, twenty, fifty, one hundred, five hundred and one thousand dollars, and no note shall be issued, except upon stamped paper of the following denominations; that is to say,

every five dollar note shall be upon a stamp of ten cents; every ten dollar note, upon a stamp of twenty cents; every twenty dollar note, upon a stamp of thirty cents; every fifty dollar note, upon a stamp of fifty cents; every one hundred dollar note, upon a stamp of one dollar; every five hundred dollar note, upon a stamp of ten dollars; and every thousand dollar note, upon a stamp of twenty dollars; which paper shall be furnished by the treasurer of the Western Shore, under the direction of the governor and council, to be paid for upon delivery; *Provided always*, that any institution of the above description may relieve itself from the operation of the provisions aforesaid, by paying annually, in advance, to the treasurer of the Western Shore, for the use of State, the sum of fifteen thousand dollars.

*And be it enacted*, that the President, Cashier, each of the Directors and Officers of every institution established, or to be established as aforesaid, offending against the provisions aforesaid, shall forfeit a sum of five hundred dollars for each and every offence, and every person having any agency in circulating any note aforesaid, not stamped as aforesaid directed, shall forfeit a sum not exceeding one hundred dollars every penalty aforesaid, to be recovered by indictment, or action of debt, in the County Court of the county where the offence shall be committed, one-half to the informer, and the other half to the use of the State.

*And be it enacted*, that this act shall be in full force and effect from and after the first day of May next.

### Mr. Chief Justice MARSHALL delivered the opinion of the Court

In the case now to be determined, the defendant, a sovereign State, denies the obligation of a law enacted by the legislature of the Union, and the plaintiff, on his part, contests the validity of an act which has been passed by the legislature of that State. The constitution of our country, in its most interesting and vital parts, is to be considered; the conflicting powers of the government of the Union and of its members, as marked in that constitution, are to be discussed; and an opinion given, which may essentially influence the great operations of the government. No tribunal can approach such a question without a deep sense of its importance, and of the awful responsibility involved in its decision. But it must be decided peacefully, or remain a source of hostile legislation, perhaps, of hostility of a still more serious nature; and if it is to be so decided, by this tribunal alone can the decision be made. On the Supreme Court of the United States has the constitution of our country devolved this important duty.

The first question made in the cause is, has Congress power to incorporate a bank?

It has been truly said, that this can scarcely be considered as an open question, entirely unprejudiced by the former proceedings of the nation respecting it. The principle now contested was introduced at a very early period of our history, has been recognised by many successive legislatures, and has been acted upon by the judicial department, in cases of peculiar delicacy, as a law of undoubted obligation.

It will not be denied, that a bold and daring usurpation might be resisted, after an acquiescence still longer and more complete than this. But it is conceived, that a doubtful question, one on which human reason may pause, and the human judgment be suspended, in the decision of which the great principles of liberty are not concerned, but the respective powers of those who are equally the representatives of the people, are to be adjusted; if not put at rest by the practice of the government, ought to receive a considerable impression from that practice. An exposition of the constitution, deliberately established by legislative acts, on the faith of which an immense property has been advanced, ought not to be lightly disregarded.

The power now contested was exercised by the first Congress elected under the present constitution. The bill for incorporating the Bank of the United States did not steal upon an unsuspecting legislature, and pass unobserved. Its principle was completely understood, and was opposed with equal zeal and ability. After being resisted, first, in the fair and open field of debate, and afterwards, in the executive cabinet, with as much persevering talent as any measure has ever experienced, and being supported by arguments which convinced minds as pure and as intelligent as this country can boast, it became a law. The original act was permitted to expire; but a short experience of the embarrassments to which the refusal to revive it exposed the government, convinced those who were most prejudiced against the measure of its necessity, and induced the passage of the present law. It would require no ordinary share of intrepidity, to assert that a measure adopted under these circumstances, was a bold and plain usurpation, to which the constitution gave no countenance.

These observations belong to the cause; but they are not made under the impression, that, were the question entirely new, the law would be found irreconcilable with the constitution.

In discussing this question, the counsel for the State of Maryland have deemed it of some importance, in the construction of the constitution, to consider that instrument, not as emanating from the people, but as the act of sovereign and independent States. The powers of the general government, it has been said, are delegated by the States, who alone are truly sovereign; and must be exercised in subordination to the States, who alone possess supreme dominion.

It would be difficult to sustain this proposition. The convention which framed the constitution was indeed elected by the State legislatures. But the instrument, when it came from their hands, was a mere proposal, without obligation, or pretensions to it. It was reported to the then existing Congress of the United States, with a request that it might "be submitted to a convention of delegates, chosen in each State by the people thereof, under the recommendation of its legislature, for their assent and ratification." This mode of proceeding was adopted; and by the convention, by Congress, and by the State legislatures, the instrument was submitted to the people. They acted upon it in the only manner in which they can act safely, effectively and wisely, on such a subject, by assembling in convention. It is true, they assembled in their several States—and where else should they have assembled? No political dreamer was ever wild enough to think of breaking down the lines which separate the States, and of compounding the American people into one common mass. Of consequence, when they act, they act in their States. But the measures they adopt do not, on that account, cease to be the measures of the people themselves, or become the measures of the State governments.

From these conventions, the constitution derives its whole authority. The government proceeds directly from the people; is "ordained and established," in the name of the people; and is declared to be ordained, "in order to form a more perfect union, establish justice, insure domestic tranquillity, and secure the blessings of liberty to themselves and to their posterity." The assent of the States, in their sovereign capacity, is implied, in calling a convention, and thus submitting that instrument to the people. But the people were at perfect liberty to accept or reject it; and their act was final. It required not the affirmance, and could not be negatived, by the State governments. The constitution, when thus adopted, was of complete obligation, and bound the State sovereignties.

It has been said, that the people had already surrendered all their powers to the State sovereignties, and had nothing more to give. But, surely, the question whether they may resume and modify the powers granted to government, does not remain to be settled in this country. Much more might the legitimacy of the general government be doubted, had it been created by the States. The powers delegated to the State sovereignties were to be exercised by themselves, not by a distinct and independent sovereignty, created by themselves. To the formation of a league, such as was the confederation, the State sovereignties were certainly competent. But when, "in order to form a more perfect union," it was deemed necessary to change this alliance into an effective government, possessing great and sovereign powers, and acting directly on the people, the necessity of referring it to the people, and of deriving its powers directly from them, was felt and acknowledged by all.

The government of the Union, then (whatever may be the influence of this fact on the case), is, emphatically and truly, a government of the people. In form, and in substance, it emanates from them. Its powers are granted by them, and are to be exercised directly on them, and for their benefit.

This government is acknowledged by all, to be one of enumerated powers. The principle, that it can exercise only the powers granted to it, would seem too apparent, to have required to be enforced by all those arguments, which its enlightened friends, while it was depending before the people, found it necessary to urge; that principle is now universally admitted. But the question respecting the extent of the powers actually granted, is perpetually arising, and will probably continue to arise, so long as our system shall exist.

In discussing these questions, the conflicting powers of the general and State governments must be brought into view, and the supremacy of their respective laws, when they are in opposition, must be settled.

If any one proposition could command the universal assent of mankind, we might expect it would be this—that the government of the Union, though limited in its powers, is supreme within its sphere of action. This would seem to result, necessarily, from its nature. It is the government of all; its powers are delegated by all; it represents all, and acts for all. Though any one State may be willing to control its operations, no State is willing to allow others to control them. The nation, on those subjects on which it can act, must necessarily bind its component parts. But this question is not left to mere reason: the people have, in express terms, decided it, by saying, "this constitution, and the laws of the United States, which shall be made in pursuance thereof," "shall be the supreme law of the land," and by requiring that the members of the State legislatures, and the officers of the executive and judicial departments of the States, shall take the oath of fidelity to it.

The government of the United States, then, though limited in its powers, is supreme; and its laws, when made in pursuance of the constitution, form the supreme law of the land, "anything in the constitution or laws of any State to the contrary notwithstanding."

Among the enumerated powers, we do not find that of establishing a bank or creating a corporation. But there is no phrase in the instrument which, like the articles of confederation, excludes incidental or implied powers; and which requires that everything granted shall be expressly and minutely described. Even the 10th amendment, which was framed for the purpose of quieting the excessive jealousies which had been excited, omits the word "expressly," and declares only, that the powers "not delegated to the United States, nor prohibited to the States, are reserved to the States or to the people;" thus leaving the question, whether the particular power which may become the subject of contest, has been delegated to the one government, or prohibited to the other, to depend on a fair construction of the whole instrument. The men who drew and adopted this amendment had experienced the embarrassments resulting from the insertion of this word in the articles of confederation, and probably omitted it, to avoid those embarrassments. A constitution, to contain an accurate detail of all the subdivisions of which its great powers will admit, and of all the means by which they may be carried into execution, would partake of the prolixity of a legal code, and could scarcely be embraced by the human mind. It would, probably, never be understood by the public. Its nature, therefore, requires, that only its great outlines should be marked, its important objects designated, and the minor ingredients which compose those objects, be deduced from the nature of the objects themselves. That this idea was entertained by the framers of the American constitution, is not only to be inferred from the nature of the instrument, but from the language. Why else were some of the limitations, found in the 9th section of the 1st article, introduced? It is also, in some degree, warranted, by their having omitted to use any restrictive term which might prevent its receiving a fair and just interpretation. In considering this question, then, we must never forget that it is a constitution we are expounding.

Although, among the enumerated powers of government, we do not find the word "bank" or "incorporation," we find the great powers, to lay and collect taxes; to borrow money; to regulate commerce; to declare and conduct a war; and to raise and support armies and navies. The sword and the purse, all the external relations, and no inconsiderable portion of the industry of the nation, are entrusted to its government. It can never be pretended, that these vast powers draw after them others of inferior importance, merely because they are inferior. Such an idea can never be advanced. But it may with great reason be contended, that a government, entrusted with such ample powers, on the due execution of which the happiness and prosperity of the nation so vitally depends, must also be entrusted with ample means for their execution. The power being given, it is the interest of the nation to facilitate its execution. It can never be their interest, and cannot be presumed to have been their intention, to clog and embarrass its execution, by withholding the most appropriate means. Throughout this vast republic, from the St. Croix to the Gulph of Mexico, from the Atlantic to the Pacific, revenue is to be collected and expended, armies are to be marched and supported. The exigencies of the nation may require, that the treasure raised in the north should be transported to the south, that raised in the east, conveyed to the west, or that this order should be reversed. Is that construction of the constitution to be preferred, which would render these operations difficult, hazardous and expensive? Can we

adopt that construction (unless the words imperiously require it), which would impute to the framers of that instrument, when granting these powers for the public good, the intention of impeding their exercise, by withholding a choice of means? If, indeed, such be the mandate of the constitution, we have only to obey; but that instrument does not profess to enumerate the means by which the powers it confers may be executed; nor does it prohibit the creation of a corporation, if the existence of such a being be essential, to the beneficial exercise of those powers. It is, then, the subject of fair inquiry, how far such means may be employed.

It is not denied, that the powers given to the government imply the ordinary means of execution. That, for example, of raising revenue, and applying it to national purposes, is admitted to imply the power of conveying money from place to place, as the exigencies of the nation may require, and of employing the usual means of conveyance. But it is denied, that the government has its choice of means; or, that it may employ the most convenient means, if, to employ them, it be necessary to erect a corporation.

On what foundation does this argument rest? On this alone: the power of creating a corporation, is one appertaining to sovereignty, and is not expressly conferred on Congress. This is true. But all legislative powers appertain to sovereignty. The original power of giving the law on any subject whatever, is a sovereign power; and if the government of the Union is restrained from creating a corporation, as a means for performing its functions, on the single reason that the creation of a corporation is an act of sovereignty; if the sufficiency of this reason be acknowledged, there would be some difficulty in sustaining the authority of Congress to pass other laws for the accomplishment of the same objects.

The government which has a right to do an act, and has imposed on it, the duty of performing that act, must, according to the dictates of reason, be allowed to select the means; and those who contend that it may not select any appropriate means, that one particular mode of effecting the object is excepted, take upon themselves the burden of establishing that exception.

The creation of a corporation, it is said, appertains to sovereignty. This is admitted. But to what portion of sovereignty does it appertain? Does it belong to one more than to another? In America, the powers of sovereignty are divided between the government of the Union, and those of the States. They are each sovereign, with respect to the objects committed to it, and neither sovereign, with respect to the objects committed to the other. We cannot comprehend that train of reasoning, which would maintain, that the extent of power granted by the people is to be ascertained, not by the nature and terms of the grant, but by its date. Some State constitutions were formed *before*, some *since* that of the United States. We cannot believe, that their relation to each other is in any degree dependent upon this circumstance. Their respective powers must, we think, be precisely the same, as if they had been formed at the same time. Had they been formed at the same time, and had the people conferred on the general government the power contained in the constitution, and on the States the whole residuum of power, would it have been asserted, that the government of the Union was not sovereign, with respect to those objects which were entrusted to it, in relation to which its laws were declared to be supreme? If this could not have been asserted, we cannot well comprehend the process of reasoning which maintains, that a power appertaining to sovereignty cannot be connected with that vast portion of it which is granted to the general government, so far as it is calculated to subserve the legitimate objects of that government. The power of creating a corporation, though appertaining to sovereignty, is not, like the power of making war, or levying taxes, or of regulating commerce, a great substantive and independent power, which cannot be implied as incidental to other powers, or used as a means of executing them. It is never the end for which other powers are exercised, but a means by which other objects are accomplished. No contributions are made to charity, for the sake of an incorporation, but a corporation is created to administer the charity; no seminary of learning is instituted, in order to be incorporated, but the corporate character is conferred to subserve the purposes of education. No city was ever built, with the sole object of being incorporated, but is incorporated as affording the best means of being well governed. The power of creating a corporation is never used for its own sake, but for the purpose of effecting something else. No sufficient reason is, therefore, perceived, why it may not pass as incidental to those powers which are expressly given, if it be a direct mode of executing them.

But the constitution of the United States has not left the right of Congress to employ the necessary means, for the execution of the powers conferred on the government, to general reasoning. To its enumeration of powers is added, that of making "all laws which shall be necessary and proper, for carrying into execution the foregoing powers, and all other powers vested by this constitution, in the government of the United States, or in any department thereof."

The counsel for the State of Maryland have urged various arguments, to prove that this clause, though, in terms, a grant of power, is not so, in effect; but is really restrictive of the general right, which might otherwise be implied, of selecting means for executing the enumerated powers.

In support of this proposition, they have found it necessary to contend, that this clause was inserted for the purpose of conferring on Congress the power of making laws. That, without it, doubts might be entertained, whether Congress could exercise its powers in the form of legislation.

But could this be the object for which it was inserted? A government is created by the people, having legislative, executive and judicial powers. Its legislative powers are vested in a Congress, which is to consist of a Senate and House of Representatives. Each house may determine the rule of its proceedings; and it is declared, that every bill which shall have passed both houses, shall, before it becomes a law, be presented to the President of the United States. The 7th section describes the course of proceedings, by which a bill shall become a law; and, then, the 8th section enumerates the powers of Congress. Could it be necessary to say, that a legislature should exercise legislative powers, in the shape of legislation? After allowing each house to prescribe its own course of proceeding, after describing the manner in which a bill should become a law, would it have entered into the mind of a single member of the convention, that an express power to make laws was necessary, to enable the legislature to make them? That a legislature, endowed with legislative powers, can legislate, is a proposition too self-evident to have been questioned.

But the argument on which most reliance is placed, is drawn from that peculiar language of this clause. Congress is not empowered by it to make all laws, which may have relation to the powers conferred on the government, but such only as may be "*necessary and proper*" for carrying them into execution. The word "*necessary*" is considered as controlling the whole sentence, and as limiting the right to pass laws for the execution of the granted powers, to such as are indispensable, and without which the power would be nugatory. That it excludes the choice of means, and leaves to Congress, in each case, that only which is most direct and simple.

Is it true, that this is the sense in which the word "necessary" is always used? Does it always import an absolute physical necessity, so strong, that one thing to which another may be termed necessary, cannot exist without that other? We think it does not. If reference be had to its use, in the common affairs of the world, or in approved authors, we find that it frequently imports no more than that one thing is convenient, or useful, or essential to another. To employ the means necessary to an end, is generally understood as employing any means calculated to produce the end, and not as being confined to those single means, without which the end would be entirely unattainable. Such is the character of human language, that no word conveys to the mind, in all situations, one single definite idea; and nothing is more common than to use words in a figurative sense. Almost all compositions contain words, which, taken in a their rigorous sense, would convey a meaning different from that which is obviously intended. It is essential to just construction, that many words which import something excessive, should be understood in a more mitigated sense—in that sense which common usage justifies. The word "necessary" is of this description. It has not a fixed character, peculiar to itself. It admits of all degrees of comparison; and is often connected with other words, which increase or diminish the impression the mind receives of the urgency it imports. A thing may be necessary, very necessary, absolutely or indispensably necessary. To no mind would the same idea be conveyed by these several phrases. The comment on the word is well illustrated by the passage cited at the bar, from the 10th section of the 1st article of the constitution. It is, we think, impossible to compare the sentence which prohibits a State from laying "imposts, or duties on imports or exports, except what may be *absolutely* necessary for executing its inspection laws," with that which authorizes Congress "to make all laws which shall be necessary and proper for carrying into execution" the powers of the general government, without feeling a conviction, that the convention understood itself to change materially the meaning of the word "necessary," by prefixing the word "absolutely." This word, then, like others, is used in various senses; and, in its construction, the subject, the context, the intention of the person using them, are all to be taken into view.

Let this be done in the case under consideration. The subject is the execution of those great powers on which the welfare of a nation essentially depends. It must have been the intention of those who gave these powers, to insure, so far as human prudence could insure, their beneficial execution. This could not be done, by confiding the choice of means to such narrow limits as not to leave it in the power of Congress to adopt any which might be appropriate, and which were conducive to the end. This provision is made in a constitution, intended to endure for ages to come, and consequently, to be adapted to the various *crises* of human affairs. To have prescribed the means by which government should, in all future time, execute its powers, would have been to change, entirely, the character of the instrument, and give it the properties of a legal code. It would have been an unwise attempt to provide, by immutable rules, for exigencies which, if foreseen at all, must have been seen dimly, and which can be best provided for as they occur. To have declared, that the best means shall not be used, but those alone, without which the power given would be nugatory, would have been to deprive the legislature of the capacity to avail itself of experience, to exercise its reason, and to accommodate its legislation to circumstances. If we apply this principle of construction to any of the powers of the government, we shall find it so pernicious in its operation that we shall be compelled to discard it. The powers vested in Congress may certainly be carried into execution, without prescribing an oath of office. The power to exact this security for the faithful performance of duty, is not given, nor is it indispensably necessary. The different departments may be established; taxes may be imposed and collected; armies and navies may be raised and maintained; and money may be borrowed, without requiring an oath of office. It might be argued, with as much plausibility as other incidental powers have been assailed, that the convention was not unmindful of this subject. The oath which might be exacted—that of fidelity to the constitution—is prescribed, and no other can be required. Yet, he would be charged with insanity, who should contend, that the legislature might not superadd, to the oath directed by the constitution, such other oath of office as its wisdom might suggest.

So, with respect to the whole penal code of the United States: whence arises the power to punish, in cases not prescribed by the constitution? All admit, that the government may, legitimately, punish any violation of its laws; and yet, this is not among the enumerated powers of Congress. The right to enforce the observance of law, by punishing its infraction, might be denied, with the more plausibility, because it is expressly given in some cases. Congress is empowered "to provide for the punishment of counterfeiting the securities and current coin of the United States," and "to define and punish piracies and felonies committed on the high seas, and offences against the law of nations." The several powers of Congress may exist, in a very imperfect State, to be sure, but they may exist and be carried into execution, although no punishment should be inflicted, in cases where the right to punish is not expressly given.

Take, for example, the power "to establish post-offices and post-roads." This power is executed, by the single act of making the establishment. But, from this has been inferred the power and duty of carrying the mail along the post-road, from one post-office to another. And from this implied power, has again been inferred the right to punish those who steal letters from the post-office, or rob the mail. It may be said, with some plausibility, that the right to carry the mail, and to punish those who rob it, is not indispensably necessary to the establishment of a post-office and post-road. This right is indeed essential to the beneficial exercise of the power, but not indispensably necessary to its existence. So, of the punishment of the crimes of stealing or falsifying a record or process of a Court of the United States, or of perjury in such Court. To punish these offences, is certainly conducive to the due administration of justice. But courts may exist, and may decide the causes brought before them, though such crimes escape punishment.

The baneful influence of this narrow construction on all the operations of the government, and the absolute impracticability of maintaining it, without rendering the government incompetent to its great objects, might be illustrated by numerous examples drawn from the constitution, and from our laws. The good

sense of the public has pronounced, without hesitation, that the power of punishment appertains to sovereignty, and may be exercised, whenever the sovereign has a right to act, as incidental to his constitutional powers. It is a means for carrying into execution all sovereign powers, and may be used, although not indispensably necessary. It is a right incidental to the power, and conducive to its beneficial exercise.

If this limited construction of the word "necessary" must be abandoned, in order to punish, whence is derived the rule which would reinstate it, when the government would carry its powers into execution, by means not vindictive in their nature? If the word "necessary" means "needful," "requisite," "essential," "conducive to," in order to let in the power of punishment for the infraction of law; why is it not equally comprehensive, when required to authorize the use of means which facilitate the execution of the powers of government, without the infliction of punishment?

In ascertaining the sense in which the word "necessary" is used in this clause of the constitution, we may derive some aid from that with which it is associated. Congress shall have power "to make all laws which shall be necessary and *proper* to carry into execution" the powers of the government. If the word "necessary" was used in that strict and rigorous sense for which the counsel for the State of Maryland contend, it would be an extraordinary departure from the usual course of the human mind, as exhibited in composition, to add a word, the only possible effect of which is, to qualify that strict and rigorous meaning; to present to the mind the idea of some choice of means of legislation, not strained and compressed within the narrow limits for which gentlemen contend.

But the argument which most conclusively demonstrates the error of the construction contended for by the counsel for the State of Maryland, is founded on the intention of the convention, as manifested in the whole clause. To waste time and argument in proving that, without it, Congress might carry its powers into execution, would be not much less idle, than to hold a lighted taper to the sun. As little can it be required to prove, that in the absence of this clause, Congress would have some choice of means. That it might employ those which, in its judgment, would most advantageously effect the object to be accomplished. That any means adapted to the end, any means which tended directly to the execution of the constitutional powers of the government, were in themselves constitutional. This clause, as construed by the State of Maryland, would abridge, and almost annihilate, this useful and necessary right of the legislature to select its means. That this could not be intended, is, we should think, had it not been already controverted, too apparent for controversy. We think so for the following reasons:

1st. The clause is placed among the powers of Congress, not among the limitations on those powers.

2nd. Its terms purport to enlarge, not to diminish the powers vested in the government. It purports to be an additional power, not a restriction on those already granted. No reason has been, or can be assigned, for thus concealing an intention to narrow the discretion of the national legislature, under words which purport to enlarge it. The framers of the constitution wished its adoption, and well knew that it would be endangered by its strength, not by its weakness. Had they been capable of using language which would convey to the eye one idea, and, after deep reflection, impress on the mind, another, they would rather have disguised the grant of power, than its limitation. If, then, their intention had been, by this clause, to restrain the free use of means which might otherwise have been implied, that intention would have been inserted in another place, and would have been expressed in terms resembling these. "In carrying into execution the foregoing powers, and all others," &c., "no laws shall be passed but such as are necessary and proper." Had the intention been to make this clause restrictive, it would unquestionably have been so in form as well as in effect.

The result of the most careful and attentive consideration bestowed upon this clause is, that if it does not enlarge, it cannot be construed to restrain the powers of Congress, or to impair the right of the legislature to exercise its best judgment in the selection of measures to carry into execution the constitutional powers of the government. If no other motive for its insertion can be suggested, a sufficient one is found in the desire to remove all doubts respecting the right to legislate on that vast mass of incidental powers which must be involved in the constitution, if that instrument be not a splendid bauble.

We admit, as all must admit, that the powers of the government are limited, and that its limits are not to be transcended. But we think the sound construction of the constitution must allow to the national legislature that discretion, with respect to the means by which the powers it confers are to be carried into execution, which will enable that body to perform the high duties assigned to it, in the manner most beneficial to the people. Let the end be legitimate, let it be within the scope of the constitution, and all means which are appropriate, which are plainly adapted to that end, which are not prohibited, but consist with the letter and spirit of the constitution, are constitutional.

That a corporation must be considered as a means not less usual, not of higher dignity, not more requiring a particular specification than other means, has been sufficiently proved. If we look to the origin of corporations, to the manner in which they have been framed in that government from which we have derived most of our legal principles and ideas, or to the uses to which they have been applied, we find no reason to suppose, that a constitution, omitting, and wisely omitting, to enumerate all the means for carrying into execution the great powers vested in government, ought to have specified this. Had it been intended to grant this power, as one which should be distinct and independent, to be exercised in any case whatever, it would have found a place among the enumerated powers of the government. But being considered merely as a means, to be employed only for the purpose of carrying into execution the given powers, there could be no motive for particularly mentioning it.

The propriety of this remark would seem to be generally acknowledged, by the universal acquiescence in the construction which has been uniformly put on the 3rd section of the 4th article of the constitution. The power to "make all needful rules and regulations respecting the territory or other property belonging to the United States," is not more comprehensive, than the power "to make all laws which shall be necessary and proper for carrying into execution" the powers of the government. Yet all admit the constitutionality of a territorial government, which is a corporate body.

If a corporation may be employed, indiscriminately with other means, to carry into execution the powers of the government, no particular reason can be assigned for excluding the use of a bank, if required for its fiscal operations. To use one, must be within the discretion of Congress, if it be an appropriate mode of executing the powers of government. That it is a convenient, a useful, and essential instrument in the prosecution of its fiscal operations, is not now a subject of controversy. All those who have been concerned in the administration of our finances, have concurred in representing its importance and necessity; and so strongly have they been felt, that statesmen of the first class, whose previous opinions against it had been confirmed by every circumstance which can fix the human judgment, have yielded those opinions to the exigencies of the nation. Under the confederation, Congress, justifying the measure by its necessity, transcended, perhaps, its powers, to obtain the advantage of a bank; and our own legislation attests the universal conviction of the utility of this measure. The time has passed away, when it can be necessary to enter into any discussion, in order to prove the importance of this instrument, as a means to effect the legitimate objects of the government.

But, were its necessity less apparent, none can deny its being an appropriate measure; and if it is, the decree of its necessity, as has been very justly observed, is to be discussed in another place. Should Congress, in the execution of its powers, adopt measures which are prohibited by the constitution; or should Congress, under the pretext of executing its powers, pass laws for the accomplishment of objects not entrusted to the government; it would become the painful duty of this tribunal, should a case requiring such a decision come before it, to say, that such an act was not the law of the land. But where the law is not prohibited, and is really calculated to effect any of the objects entrusted to the government, to undertake here to inquire into the decree of its necessity, would be to pass the line which circumscribes the judicial department, and to tread on legislative ground. This Court disclaims all pretensions to such a power.

After this declaration, it can scarcely be necessary to say, that the existence of State banks can have no possible influence on the question. No trace is to be found in the constitution, of an intention to create a dependence of the government of the Union on those of the States, for the execution of the great powers assigned to it. Its means are adequate to its ends; and on those means alone was it expected to rely for the accomplishment of its ends. To impose on it the necessity of resorting to means which it cannot control, which another government may furnish or withhold,

would render its course precarious, the result of its measures uncertain, and create a dependence on other governments, which might disappoint its most important designs, and is incompatible with the language of the constitution. But were it otherwise, the choice of means implies a right to choose a national bank in preference to State banks, and Congress alone can make the election.

After the most deliberate consideration, it is the unanimous and decided opinion of this Court, that the act to incorporate the Bank of the United States is a law made in pursuance of the constitution, and is a part of the supreme law of the land.

The branches, proceeding from the same stock, and being conducive to the complete accomplishment of the object, are equally constitutional. It would have been unwise, to locate them in the charter, and it would be unnecessarily inconvenient, to employ the legislative power in making those subordinate arrangements. The great duties of the bank are prescribed; those duties require branches; and the bank itself may, we think, be safely trusted with the selection of places where those branches shall be fixed; reserving always to the government the right to require that a branch shall be located where it may be deemed necessary.

It being the opinion of the Court, that the act incorporating the bank is constitutional; and that the power of establishing a branch in the State of Maryland might be properly exercised by the bank itself, we proceed to inquire—

2. Whether the State of Maryland may, without violating the constitution, tax that branch?

That the power of taxation is one of vital importance; that it is retained by the States; that it is not abridged by the grant of a similar power to the government of the Union; that it is to be concurrently exercised by the two governments—are truths which have never been denied. But such is the paramount character of the constitution, that its capacity to withdraw any subject from the action of even this power, is admitted. The States are expressly forbidden to lay any duties on imports or exports, except what may be absolutely necessary for executing their inspection laws. If the obligation of this prohibition must be conceded—if it may restrain a State from the exercise of its taxing power on imports and exports—the same paramount character would seem to restrain, as it certainly may restrain, a State from such other exercise of this power, as is in its nature incompatible with, and repugnant to, the constitutional laws of the Union. A law, absolutely repugnant to another, as entirely repeals that other as if express terms of repeal were used.

On this ground, the counsel for the bank place its claim to be exempted from the power of a State to tax its operations. There is no express provision for the case, but the claim has been sustained on a principle which so entirely pervades the constitution, is so intermixed with the materials which compose it, so interwoven with its web, so blended with its texture, as to be incapable of being separated from it, without rending it into shreds.

This great principle is, that the constitution and the laws made in pursuance thereof are supreme; that they control the constitution and laws of the respective States, and cannot be controlled by them. From this, which may be almost termed an axiom, other propositions are deduced as corollaries, on the truth or error of which, and on their application to this case, the cause has been supposed to depend. These are, 1st. That a power to create implies a power to preserve: 2nd. That a power to destroy, if wielded by a different hand, is hostile to, and incompatible with these powers to create and to preserve: 3d. That where this repugnancy exists, that authority which is supreme must control, not yield to that over which it is supreme.

These propositions, as abstract truths, would, perhaps, never be controverted. Their application to this case, however, has been denied; and both in maintaining the affirmative and the negative, a splendor of eloquence, and strength of argument, seldom, if ever, surpassed, have been displayed.

The power of Congress to create, and of course, to continue, the bank, was the subject of the preceding part of this opinion; and is no longer to be considered as questionable.

That the power of taxing it by the States may be exercised so as to destroy it, is too obvious to be denied. But taxation is said to be an absolute power, which acknowledges no other limits than those expressly prescribed in the constitution, and like sovereign power of

every other description, is entrusted to the discretion of those who use it. But the very terms of this argument admit, that the sovereignty of the State, in the article of taxation itself, is subordinate to, and may be controlled by the constitution of the United States. How far it has been controlled by that instrument, must be a question of construction. In making this construction, no principle, not declared, can be admissible, which would defeat the legitimate operations of a supreme government. It is of the very essence of supremacy, to remove all obstacles to its action within its own sphere, and so to modify every power vested in subordinate governments, as to exempt its own operations from their own influence. This effect need not be stated in terms. It is so involved in the declaration of supremacy, so necessarily implied in it, that the expression of it could not make it more certain. We must, therefore, keep it in view, while construing the constitution.

The argument on the part of the State of Maryland, is, not that the States may directly resist a law of Congress, but that they may exercise their acknowledged powers upon it, and that the constitution leaves them this right, in the confidence that they will not abuse it.

Before we proceed to examine this argument, and to subject it to test of the constitution, we must be permitted to bestow a few considerations on the nature and extent of this original right of taxation, which is acknowledged to remain with the States. It is admitted, that the power of taxing the people and their property, is essential to the very existence of government, and may be legitimately exercised on the objects to which it is applicable, to the utmost extent to which the government may choose to carry it. The only security against the abuse of this power, is found in the structure of the government itself. In imposing a tax, the legislature acts upon its constituents. This is, in general, a sufficient security against erroneous and oppressive taxation.

The people of a State, therefore, give to their government a right of taxing themselves and their property, and as the exigencies of government cannot be limited, they prescribe no limits to the exercise of this right, resting confidently on the interest of the legislator, and on the influence of the constituent over their representative, to guard them against its abuse. But the means employed by the government of the Union have no such security, nor is the right of a State to tax them sustained by the same theory. Those means are not given by the people of a particular State, not given by the constituents of the legislature, which claim the right to tax them, but by the people of all the States. They are given by all, for the benefit of all—and upon theory, should be subjected to that government only which belongs to all.

It may be objected to this definition, that the power of taxation is not confined to the people and property of a State. It may be exercised upon every object brought within its jurisdiction.

This is true. But to what source do we trace this right? It is obvious, that it is an incident of sovereignty, and is co-extensive with that to which it is an incident. All subjects over which the sovereign power of a State extends, are objects of taxation; but those over which it does not extend, are, upon the soundest principles, exempt from taxation. This proposition may almost be pronounced self-evident.

The sovereignty of a State extends to everything which exists by its own authority, or is introduced by its permission; but does it extend to those means which are employed by Congress to carry into execution powers conferred on that body by the people of the United States? We think it demonstrable, that it does not. Those powers are not given by the people of a single State. They are given by the people of the United States, to a government whose laws, made in pursuance of the constitution, are declared to be supreme. Consequently, the people of a single State cannot confer a sovereignty which will extend over them.

If we measure the power of taxation residing in a State, by the extent of sovereignty which the people of a single State possess, and can confer on its government, we have an intelligible standard, applicable to every case to which the power may be applied. We have a principle which leaves the power of taxing the people and property of a State unimpaired; which leaves to a State the command of all its resources, and which places beyond its reach, all those powers which are conferred by the people of the United States on the government of the Union, and all those means which are given for the purpose of carrying those powers into execution. We have a principle which is safe for the States, and safe for the Union. We are relieved, as we ought to be, from clashing sovereignty; from interfering powers; from a

repugnancy between a right in one government to pull down, what there is an acknowledged right in another to build up; from the incompatibility of a right in one government to destroy, what there is a right in another to preserve. We are not driven to the perplexing inquiry, so unfit for the judicial department, what degree of taxation is the legitimate use, and what degree may amount to the abuse of the power. The attempt to use it on the means employed by the government of the Union, in pursuance of the constitution, is itself an abuse, because it is the usurpation of a power which the people of a single State cannot give.

We find, then, on just theory, a total failure of this original right to tax the means employed by the government of the Union, for the execution of its powers. The right never existed, and the question whether it has been surrendered, cannot arise.

But, waiving this theory for the present, let us resume the inquiry, whether this power can be exercised by the respective States, consistently with a fair construction of the constitution?

That the power to tax involves the power to destroy; that the power to destroy may defeat and render useless the power to create; that there is a plain repugnance in conferring on one government a power to control the constitutional measures of another, which other, with respect to those very measures, is declared to be supreme over that which exerts the control, are propositions not to be denied. But all inconsistencies are to be reconciled by the magic of the word CONFIDENCE. Taxation, it is said, does not necessarily and unavoidably destroy. To carry it to the excess of destruction, would be an abuse, to presume which, would banish that confidence which is essential to all government.

But is this a case of confidence? Would the people of any one State trust those of another with a power to control the most insignificant operations of their State government? We know they would not. Why, then, should we suppose, that the people of any one State should be willing to trust those of another with a power to control the operations of a government to which they have confided their most important and most valuable interests? In the legislature of the Union alone, are all represented. The legislature of the Union alone, therefore, can be trusted by the people with the power of controlling measures which concern all, in the confidence that it will not be abused. This, then, is not a case of confidence, and we must consider it is as it really is.

If we apply the principle for which the State of Maryland contends, to the constitution, generally, we shall find it capable of changing totally the character of that instrument. We shall find it capable of arresting all the measures of the government, and of prostrating it at the foot of the States. The American people have declared their constitution and the laws made in pursuance thereof, to be supreme; but this principle would transfer the supremacy, in fact, to the States.

If the States may tax one instrument, employed by the government in the execution of its powers, they may tax any and every other instrument. They may tax the mail; they may tax the mint; they may tax patent-rights; they may tax the papers of the custom-house; they may tax judicial process; they may tax all the means employed by the government, to an excess which would defeat all the ends of government. This was not intended by the American people. They did not design to make their government dependent on the States.

Gentlemen say, they do not claim the right to extend State taxation to these objects. They limit their pretensions to property. But on what principle, is this distinction made? Those who make it have furnished no reason for it, and the principle for which they contend denies it. They contend, that the power of taxation has no other limit than is found in the 10th section of the 1st article of the constitution; that, with respect to everything else, the power of the States is supreme, and admits of no control. If this be true, the distinction between property and other subjects to which the power of taxation is applicable, is merely arbitrary, and can never be sustained. This is not all. If the controlling power of the States be established; if their supremacy as to taxation be acknowledged; what is to restrain their exercising control in any shape they may please to give it? Their sovereignty is not confined to taxation; that is not the only mode in which it might be displayed. The question is, in truth, a question of supremacy; and if the right of the States to tax the means employed by the general government be conceded, the declaration that the constitution, and the laws made in pursuance thereof, shall be the supreme law of the land, is empty and unmeaning declamation.

In the course of the argument, the *Federalist* has been quoted; and the opinions expressed by the authors of that work have been justly supposed to be entitled to great respect in expounding the constitution. No tribute can be paid to them which exceeds their merit; but in applying their opinions to the cases which may arise in the progress of our government, a right to judge of their correctness must be retained; and to understand the argument, we must examine the proposition it maintains, and the objections against which it is directed. The subject of those numbers, from which passages have been cited, is the unlimited power of taxation which is vested in the general government. The objection to this unlimited power, which the argument seeks to remove, is stated with fullness and clearness. It is, "that an indefinite power of taxation in the latter (the government of the Union) might, and probably would, in time, deprive the former (the government of the States) of the means of providing for their own necessities; and would subject them entirely to the mercy of the national legislature. As the laws of the Union are to become the supreme law of the land; as it is to have power to pass all laws that may be necessary for carrying into execution the authorities with which it is proposed to vest it; the national government might, at any time, abolish the taxes imposed for State objects, upon the pretence of an interference with its own. It might allege a necessity for doing this, in order to give efficacy to the national revenues; and thus, all the resources of taxation might, by degrees, become the subjects of federal monopoly, to the entire exclusion and destruction of the State governments."

The objections to the constitution which are noticed in these numbers, were to the undefined power of the government to tax, not to the incidental privilege of exempting its own measures from State taxation. The consequences apprehended from this undefined power were, that it would absorb all the objects of taxation, "to the exclusion and destruction of the State governments." The arguments of the *Federalist* are intended to prove the fallacy of these apprehensions; not to prove that the government was incapable of executing any of its powers, without exposing the means it employed to the embarrassments of State taxation. Arguments urged against these objections, and these apprehensions, are to be understood as relating to the points they mean to prove. Had the authors of those excellent essays been asked, whether they contended for that construction of the constitution, which would place within the reach of the States those measures which the government might adopt for the execution of its powers; no man, who has read their instructive pages, will hesitate to admit, that their answer must have been in the negative.

It has also been insisted, that, as the power of taxation in the general and State governments is acknowledged to be concurrent, every argument which would sustain the right of the general government to tax banks chartered by the States, will equally sustain the right of the States to tax banks chartered by the general government.

But the two cases are not on the same reason. The people of all the States have created the general government, and have conferred upon it the general power of taxation. The people of all the States, and the States themselves, are represented in Congress, and, by their representatives, exercise this power. When they tax the chartered institutions of the States, they tax their constituents; and these taxes must be uniform. But when a State taxes the operations of the government of the United States, it acts upon institutions created, not by their own constituents, but by people over whom they claim no control. It acts upon the measures of a government created by others as well as themselves, for the benefit of others in common with themselves. The difference is that which always exists, and always must exist, between the action of the whole on a part, and the action of a part on the whole—between the laws of a government declared to be supreme, and those of a government which, when in opposition to those laws, is not supreme.

But if the full application of this argument could be admitted, it might bring into question the right of Congress to tax the State banks, and could not prove the rights of the States to tax the Bank of the United States.

The Court has bestowed on this subject its most deliberate consideration. The result is a conviction that the States have no power, by taxation or otherwise, to retard, impede, burden, or in any manner control, the operations of the constitutional laws enacted by Congress to carry into execution the powers vested in the general government. This is, we think, the unavoidable consequence of that supremacy which the constitution has declared.

We are unanimously of opinion, that the law passed by the legislature of Maryland, imposing a tax on the Bank of the United States, is unconstitutional and void.

This opinion does not deprive the States of any resources which they originally possessed. It does not extend to a tax paid by the real property of the bank, in common with the other real property within the State, nor to a tax imposed on the interest which the citizens of Maryland may hold in this institution, in common with other property of the same description throughout the State. But this is a tax on the operations of the bank, and is, consequently, a tax on the operation of an instrument employed by the government of the Union to carry its powers into execution. Such a tax must be unconstitutional.

JUDGMENT. This cause came on to be heard, on the transcript of the record of the Court of Appeals of the State of Maryland, and was argued by counsel: on consideration whereof, it is the opinion of this Court, that the act of the legislature of Maryland is contrary to the constitution of the United States, and void; and therefore, that the said Court of Appeals of the State of Maryland erred, in affirming the judgment of the Baltimore County Court, in which judgment was rendered against James W. McCulloch; but that the said Court of Appeals of Maryland ought to have reversed the said judgment of the said Baltimore County Court, and ought to have given judgment for the said appellant, McCulloch: It is, therefore, adjudged and ordered, that the said judgment of the said Court of Appeals of the State of Maryland in this case, be, and the same hereby is, reversed and annulled. And this Court, proceeding to render such judgment as the said Court of Appeals should have rendered; it is further adjudged and ordered, that the judgment of the said Baltimore County Court be reversed and annulled, and that judgment be entered in the said Baltimore County Court for the said James W. McCulloch.

## Glossary

**action of debt:** a type of lawsuit seeking to obtain something owed

**defendant in error:** a litigant who has won in the lower court and is opposing an appeal

**enumerated powers:** governmental powers that are explicitly listed in the text of the Constitution as having been bestowed upon Congress

**implied powers:** governmental powers that are not explicitly listed in the text of the Constitution as having been bestowed upon Congress but that can be inferred as adjuncts to Congress's enumerated powers

**judgment of non pros:** short for "judgment of *non prosequitur*," a judgment rendered against a plaintiff who has failed to litigate his or her case

**legal code:** a systematic consolidation of all the enacted laws of a jurisdiction

**plaintiff in error:** a litigant who has lost in the lower court and has appealed

**prolixity:** state of being excessively detailed or tedious

**writ of error:** a written court order requiring a lower court to send a case up to an appellate court for a review of the lower court's ruling

# COHENS V. VIRGINIA

| DATE | CITATION |
|------|----------|
| 1821 | 19 U.S. 264 |

| AUTHOR | SIGNIFICANCE |
|--------|--------------|
| Chief Justice John Marshall | Upheld the power of the U.S. Supreme Court to review a state court criminal case if it involves a federal statute, a federal right, or a clause under the U.S. Constitution |

| VOTE | |
|------|--|
| 6-0 | |

## Overview

 Philip and Mendes Cohen were natives of Richmond, Virginia, but their family moved to Baltimore around 1808. In 1812 their eldest brother, Jacob I. Cohen, founded Cohen's Lottery and Exchange Office and employed his five brothers to work in the business. All three brothers served in a volunteer militia company during the War of 1812 and participated in the Battle of Baltimore. After the war, Philip and Mendes moved to Norfolk to operate a branch of the family business on the wharf in Norfolk, Virginia, where, among other things, they sold tickets for the National Lottery in the District of Columbia. An act of Congress authorized the National Lottery to raise money to build a City Hall in Washington, D.C. At the time, lotteries were a common method for states, municipalities, and approved charitable entities to raise funds. After January 1, 1820, Virginia prohibited the sale of tickets for "foreign"—that is, out-of-state—lotteries. The Cohens were charged under this law for selling such tickets, and they were fined $100 plus court costs of a bit over $30. They appealed their conviction to the Supreme Court on two grounds.

First, they argued that the Virginia law violated the commerce clause of the Constitution (Article I, Section 8, Clause 3), which provides that Congress has the power "To regulate Commerce with foreign Nations, and among the several States, and with the Indian Tribes." Under this clause a state was generally not allowed to prohibit the sale of goods produced in one state that were taken into another state and sold there. Such a regulation of interstate commerce was solely in the discretion of Congress. The Cohens argued that lottery tickets were products that were transported and sold as part of interstate commerce. While lottery tickets were a special kind of commerce, not a normal "product," they were popular throughout the United States, and lottery tickets from one state were often legally sold in another state. Virginia argued that a lottery ticket was a special kind of product, akin to liquor, for example, which states could regulate or prohibit.

Second, the Cohens argued that even if states could ban "foreign" lottery tickets (that is tickets from other states or other countries), the Virginia law could not apply to the National Lottery because it was created by an act of Congress, and federal law was superior to

**1818 portrait of Mendes Cohen**
(Joseph Wood)

state law. Here they relied on the supremacy clause of the U.S. Constitution (Article VI, Clause 2), which states: "This Constitution, and the Laws of the United States which shall be made in Pursuance thereof; and all Treaties made, or which shall be made, under the Authority of the United States shall be the supreme Law of the Land, and the Judges in every state shall be bound thereby, any Thing in the Constitution or Laws of any State to the Contrary notwithstanding." Put in simple language, this meant that no state could overrule a federal law by a state statute or a provision of a state constitution. Thus, since Congress created these lottery tickets, Virginia could not overrule the federal law by banning their sale in its borders.

The case was important, not because of the actual amount of money at issue but because Virginia denied the Supreme Court had the power to hear the case. The Supreme Court rejected this claim by Virginia, issuing a major opinion on the power of the Supreme Court to hear appeals from state courts where a federal law or a right under the U.S. Constitution was at issue. Virginia's political leaders were furious that the Court took the case and emphatically maintained its right to hear it. However, in the end the Court sided with Virginia, holding that prohibiting the sale of out-of-state lottery tickets did not violate the commerce clause and also

concluding that the federal law creating the National Lottery in the District of Columbia was really the equivalent of a local law, applying only to the national capital, and thus Virginia's refusal to allow the District of Columbia tickets to be sold in the state did not violate the supremacy clause.

There were two parts to the case. Virginia first challenged the jurisdiction of the Court itself. Virginia argued that the U.S. Supreme Court lacked the legal authority (or power) to hear an appeal from state criminal conviction. Virginia's argument was that the U.S. Constitution has no effect on Virginia's criminal jurisprudence. Generally speaking, this was a correct reading of the Constitution at the time. The Bill of Rights, for example, limited the actions of the federal government, but not those of the states. It did not impact state laws or court decisions until after the ratification of the Fourteenth Amendment in 1868 and mostly after a number of Supreme Court decisions in the twentieth century. But, in a powerful and emphatic opinion, Chief Justice Marshall rejected Virginia's argument, based in part on the supremacy clause of the Constitution. Marshall argued that the Court was not challenging the right of Virginia to maintain its criminal laws, but if the law itself violated federal law or a specific clause of the U.S. Constitution, as it applied to a federal statute, then the Supreme Court had to have jurisdiction. Many political leaders in Virginia were furious about this opinion, arguing it undermined the power of the states to regulate local issues and local economic policy. After deciding that the Court did in fact have jurisdiction (the power to hear the case), the Supreme Court heard arguments on the substance of the case. Two days later the Court sided with Virginia, asserting that the law creating the lottery in Washington, D.C., did not require that other places allow the sale of the Washington, D.C., lottery tickets. Thus, the state of Virginia won the case, and the Cohen brothers paid their fine. However, many of Virginia's political leaders remained angry and hostile to Marshall (who was from Virginia himself) because of he did not support their states' rights position.

## Context

There are two contexts to this case. The first concerns lotteries and the national economy; the second concerns the meaning and interpretation of the U.S. Constitution.

In the early national period, most state and local revenue came from taxes on land, excise taxes, and taxes on personal property, such as carriages, farm equipment, and enslaved humans. The federal government was mostly funded by taxes on imported goods, some excise taxes through the sale of public land in the West, and some government services such as licensing fees, court costs, and the post office. At this time, there were no income taxes or sales taxes at the local, state, or national level.

Governments and tax revenues were small, and lotteries were a common and important way for governments at the local and state levels to raise money for public works projects. The nation's capital was particularly stressed for revenue because it was small and had to rely on appropriations from Congress, which were not always sufficient. Thus, Washington, D.C., with permission from Congress in the form of a federal statute, operated various lotteries, known as the National Lottery. The first lottery was in 1793, and even President Washington bought a ticket. There were other District of Columbia lotteries in 1812 and 1820. As the political scientist and legal scholar Mark Graber notes in his 1995 article "The Passive-Aggressive Virtues," the "original states found lotteries a less painful device than taxation for extracting necessary revenue from a reluctant citizenry." The National Lottery created in 1820 was to raise money for building a city hall in the national capital. Without a lottery, the federal government would have had to use tax money to construct this building.

Sales of lottery tickets were popular, and entrepreneurs like the Cohen brothers brought the tickets to consumers who lived far from Washington, D.C. Virginia prohibited the sale of out-of-state lottery tickets in part because they were popular and thus successfully competed with the sale of tickets within Virginia. The Virginia law was a classic example of a state using its legislature to favor a local business (the sale of local Virginia lottery tickets) at the expense of an out-of-state business (the National Lottery). In an economy where lottery tickets were important for the revenue they raised for the local and state governments, this was a serious issue. The Virginia law may have enhanced the state's economy, but it threatened not only the Cohens' business but the economic welfare of the nation's capital.

The second and more important issue was the power of the Supreme Court. In the decade leading up to this case, the Supreme Court under John Marshall had issued a number of opinions that angered states' rights politicians, particularly in Virginia. The key cases in this context were *Martin v. Hunter's Lessee* (1816), *McCulloch v. Maryland* (1819), and *Dartmouth College v. Woodward* (1819).

In *Martin v. Hunter's Lessee*, a unanimous Supreme Court reaffirmed an earlier decision that had overturned actions by Virginia involving some 300,000 acres of land that had once been owned by Thomas, Lord Fairfax, the colonial governor of the Virginia colony. When the American Revolution began, Lord Fairfax remained in Virginia and never supported or opposed the Revolution. He died peacefully in 1781, bequeathing his huge quantity of land to his nephew, Rev. Denny Martin, who changed his name to Denny Fairfax to inherit the land. Denny Fairfax lived in England. After the Revolution, Virginia, which was now independent from England, seized the land because, under traditional common law, aliens could not inherit property in the state. However, the Treaty of Paris (1783), ending the Revolution, prohibited the confiscation of land owned by citizens of Great Britain. This was reaffirmed by the Jay Treaty in 1794. Thus, Denny Fairfax had a strong legal claim to his inheritance. In 1789, ignoring the requirements of the 1783 Treaty with Great Britain, Virginia sold 788 acres of the Fairfax land to David Hunter, who rented it out to someone else (known in the case as "Hunter's lessee"). In 1793, while an attorney and politician in Virginia, John Marshall and other investors purchased 160,000 acres of Fairfax lands from Denny Fairfax. This included the land Virginia had sold to Hunter.

The ownership of this land was litigated in the Virginia courts and in federal courts. Rev. Denny Fairfax died in 1800, and the claim to the land passed to his brother, General Philip Martin, who was also a British citizen. In 1810 Virginia's highest court ruled that the state had properly confiscated the land and that the treaties with Great Britain in 1783 and 1794 could not affect Virginia law. This was a direct rejection of the supremacy clause of the Constitution, which provides that "all Treaties made, or which shall be made under the Authority of the United States shall be the supreme Law of the Land." In *Fairfax's Devisee v. Hunter's Lessee* (1813), the United States Supreme Court ordered the Virginia court to give title to Philip Martin and others, including John Marshall, who had purchased some of the land. In 1815 the Virginia Court of Appeals unanimously refused to comply, arguing that the U.S. Supreme Court had no power to overrule the Virginia courts. The Virginia court articulated a strong states' rights position that the federal courts could not overrule state courts on matters of state law. This led to *Martin v. Hunter's Lessee* (1816). Chief Justice Marshall did not take part in the two cases before the Supreme Court because he was one of the people who claimed to legally own the land. Writing for the Supreme Court, Justice Joseph Story lectured the Virginia court on its obligations to comply with a Supreme Court decision. Virginia did so, but the case led to great anger among Virginia politicians.

In *McCulloch v. Maryland* (1819) Chief Justice Marshall wrote a major opinion—many argue his most important opinion—upholding the power of Congress to establish the Bank of the United States. In doing so he overturned a Maryland law designed to tax the bank out of existence. He based his decision on the implied powers of Congress in the Constitution, asserting, "Let the end be legitimate, let it be within the scope of the constitution, and all means which are appropriate, which are plainly adapted to that end, which are not prohibited, but consist with the letter and spirit of the constitution, are constitutional." He argued that the essence of the "necessary and proper" clause of Article I of the Constitution gave Congress "implied powers" necessary to run the country that were not enumerated in the Constitution because the clause was "made in a constitution, intended to endure for ages to come, and consequently, to be adapted to the various *crises* of human affairs. To have prescribed the means by which government should, in all future time, execute its powers, would have been to change, entirely, the character of the instrument, and give it the properties of a legal code."

In the same term, in *Dartmouth College v. Woodward* (1819), Marshall struck down a New Hampshire law that allowed the state to take over the private college. Marshall said that this violated the clause in the Constitution that prohibited the states from "impairing the Obligation of Contracts," because the original charter to create the college was in fact a contract. The state legislature had tried to unilaterally amend the charter of Dartmouth College to change it from a private college to a public university. The Court prevented this. On the same grounds, in *Sturgis v. Crowninshield* (1819), Marshall struck down the application of a New York bankruptcy law to debts incurred before the passage of the law. He asserted that this law would violate the contract between the parties, which went into effect before the bankruptcy law had been passed.

Taken together, these cases led political leaders and public officials, especially in Virginia, to fear that the national government would soon have the power to swallow up the powers of the states. Marshall's nationalistic jurisprudence led to a growing states' rights backlash over the power of the federal government, and particularly the Supreme Court. This set the stage for *Cohens v. Virginia*.

## About the Author

The author of this opinion was John Marshall, the longest serving chief justice (so far) in the history of the U.S. Supreme Court. Many scholars also believe he is the most important and influential justice in the history of the Court. He came from a middle-class family in what was then Virginia's sparsely populated frontier. Growing up, he was the "poor cousin" of his relatives in many important Virginia families, including the political powerful and wealthy Randolphs and Jeffersons. Marshall served as captain under George Washington in the Revolution and during the war became a committed and strong nationalist. He lacked a college education but briefly studied law at the College of William and Mary near the end of the war and quickly became one of the most successful lawyers in Virginia. Illustrative of his rising status and clear abilities, he married Mary "Polly" Ambler, with the blessings of her father, Jaquelin Ambler, who was a powerful and wealthy political leader and the state treasurer for Virginia. They had a long and apparently happy marriage, but it was also a union that helped Marshall's career. In 1788 he was a leading supporter of the U.S. Constitution at the Virginia ratifying convention. He served in the Virginia legislature, as a diplomat in France, as a member of Congress, and as secretary of state under President John Adams, who nominated him to be chief justice at the very end of his term in office. He assumed that role in 1801 and remined until 1835. He wrote 58 percent of all the opinions delivered while he was on the Court. This included 508 majority opinions, twenty-five concurrences, and a mere six dissents. He dominated the Court for the first two decades as chief justice, but in the last eight years he was less powerful as new justices, with different views of law and constitutional interpretation, came on the Court. Nearly 200 years after his death, his opinions are still cited. Indeed, five of the ten Supreme Court decisions most cited by the Court itself are Marshall opinions.

Almost all of Marshall's opinions were directed at strengthening the national government, empowering Congress, making the Supreme Court a full co-equal branch of the government, supporting a growing commercial economy, protecting private property, and protecting slavery. Many of his opinions on economic development and those articulating an expansive understanding of the Constitution and the power of the national government are considered among the most important in U.S. history. He was fearless in challenging the goals of his nemesis (and distant cousin), Thomas Jefferson, when Jefferson tried to arbitrarily use the law to persecute his political enemies. He became very wealthy through the purchase of land and humans, owning nearly 200 enslaved people when he died. He served in the Virginia state constitutional convention and as the leader of the Virginia branch of the American Colonization Society, an organization devoted to removing all free Blacks from the United States. He also wrote three opinions that devastated the rights of Native Americans, holding that they did not own the land they lived on, that the U.S. government could take their land by treaty, purchase, or through military force, and that they could not defend their rights in federal court.

## Explanation and Analysis of the Document

*Cohens v. Virginia* takes up nearly 200 papers in United States Reports, which indicates its importance at the time it was delivered. The report included massive arguments by the attorneys, who were among the best in the nation. The Cohens hired Senator William Pinkney of Maryland, who had previously been a diplomat and the attorney general of the United States under James Madison. He was considered to be the foremost lawyer in the nation, arguing an astounding eighty-four cases before the Supreme Court before his untimely death at age fifty-eight in 1822. In 1819 he successfully defended the constitutionality of the Bank of the Unit-

ed States in *McCulloch v. Maryland*. Joining him was David B. Ogden, another prominent lawyer and a congressman from New York. Representing Virginia were Congressman Philip Barbour, who would later serve on the U.S. Supreme Court, and Congressman Alexander Smyth. Later in the case Daniel Webster, another major Supreme Court litigator, would argue the case for Virginia, and Attorney General William Wirt would support the Cohens.

The Court first heard arguments on whether it had jurisdiction. Arguments in the case began on February 18, 1821, and lasted some days. The printed report of the case includes eighty-five pages of arguments from the lawyers. Essentially, the lawyers for Virginia, Barbour and Smyth, argued that the U.S. Supreme Court had no power to overturn a state criminal conviction. Ogden and Pinkney argued that the issue was not the crime or the conviction but whether the law under which the Cohens were convicted violated the U.S. Constitution.

After extensive argument, Marshall quickly wrote a very long opinion, which he gave on March 3. In print it is fifty-five pages long, which at the time made it one of the longest in the history of the Court. Marshall produced this opinion in about two weeks, writing with a quill pen. He had no clerks or secretaries. It was a masterful piece of work, touching on history, law, philosophy, and political theory. He cited foreign legal treatises, other cases, the Federalist Papers, the ideas of the Founders, and his understanding of what happened at the Constitutional Convention.

He began with a simple and clear analysis of Virginia trial court. There were no factual issues in question. The Cohens did not deny they had sold the lottery tickets that violated the Virginia law. The only question was whether, under the U.S. Constitution, that law was valid. As Marshall noted, both sides agreed: "If upon this case the Court shall be of opinion that the acts of Congress before mentioned were valid, and, on the true construction of those acts, the lottery tickets sold **by** the defendants as aforesaid, might lawfully be sold within the State of Virginia, notwithstanding the act or statute of the general assembly of Virginia prohibiting such sale, then judgment [is] to be entered for the defendants: And if the Court should be of opinion that the statute or act of the General Assembly of the State of Virginia, prohibiting such sale, is valid, notwithstanding the said acts of Congress, then judgment to be entered [is] that the defendants are guilty, and that the Commonwealth, recover against them one hundred dollars and costs." The Virginia trial court ruled the state laws were valid and fined the Cohens. Virginia further argued that the Court could not hear the case.

But Marshall disagreed. He asserted that "the authoritative language of the American people," which came from the Constitution itself, "marks, with lines too strong to be mistaken, the characteristic distinction between the government of the Union, and those of the States. The general government, though limited as to its objects, is supreme with respect to those objects. This principle is a part of the constitution, and if there be any who deny its necessity, none can deny its authority." In other words, while the powers and jurisdiction of the federal government were limited, where it had such power and jurisdiction, it was "supreme." This power had to reside with the national government and the Supreme Court, in the words of the Constitution, "in order to form a more perfect union, establish justice, ensure domestic tranquillity, provide for the common defence, promote the general welfare, and secure the blessings of liberty" to the American people.

Marshall then gave a long opinion, more like an educational lecture, on why this power rested with his Court, which was tasked with resolving "controversies between States, and between a State and individuals." He asserted that the very essence of the nation was that "The constitution gave to every person, having a claim upon a State, a right to submit his case to the Court of the nation." In earlier decisions, like McCulloch v. Maryland, Marshall has asserted the power of Congress to pass all laws which were "necessary and proper" under the Constitution. Here, however, he argued "that the judicial power of every well constituted government must be co-extensive with the legislative, and must be capable of deciding every judicial question which grows out of the constitution and laws." He argued that Virginia's position would "prostrate" the national government by preventing the courts from enforcing the valid laws of Congress if a state objected to those laws. Marshall concluded this long opinion by asserting that his Court had jurisdiction to hear the case.

This part of Marshall's opinion is what makes this case central to the history of American law. Emphat-

ically, and with no room for doubt, Marshall asserted the power of the Supreme Court to hear appeals from the state courts where a federal statute or a provision of the Constitution was in dispute. Virginia's political leaders had lost. Their states' rights arguments were shattered, and Marshall had vindicated the authority—indeed, the obligation—of his Court to decide such matters. Marshall dramatically asserted that only the American people, through the amendment process, could change the Constitution or the authority of the Supreme Court to review decisions under it.

Marshall wrote: "The people made the constitution, and the people can unmake it. It is the creature of their *will*, and lives only by their will. But this supreme and irresistible power to make or to unmake, resides only in, the whole body of the people, not in any sub-division of them. The attempt of any of the parts to exercise it is usurpation, and ought to be repelled by those to whom the people have delegated their power of repelling it."

But this was not the end of the case. On March 2, 1821, the day before he read his long opinion on why the Court had jurisdiction in the case, the Court heard arguments on the merits of the case—that is, whether the Virginia law in fact violated either the U.S. Constitution or the lottery law passed by Congress.

Ogden argued the case for the Cohen brothers, but a new lawyer, Daniel Webster, appeared for the state of Virginia. Like Pinkney, Webster was a major Supreme Court litigator, having helped win both McCulloch v. Maryland and Dartmouth College v. Woodward. He would go on to serve in the Senate and twice as secretary of state. Webster argued that the lottery law was not a "national" law but one limited to the District of Columbia. Thus, Congress could not impose the lottery on the rest of the nation. The attorney general of the United States, William Wirt, also argued this part of the case for the Cohens, asserting that the Lottery Law was designed for a "great national object," and as such no state could interfere with its operation. He argued it was no different from the law creating the Bank of the United States, which Marshall had upheld in McCulloch v. Maryland.

Three days later, on March 5, Marshall ruled on whether the Virginia law violated the federal law or the Constitution. He noted that the federal law allowed the city of Washington (which Marshall refers to as "the

Corporation" because the city was "incorporated" by Congress) to sell these tickets. But the key question was, Did the act of Congress "authorize the Corporation to force the sale of these lottery tickets in States where such sales may be prohibited by law"?

Marshall concluded that "the power granted to the Corporation of Washington" did not extend "beyond the limits of the City." The "powers granted" to sell the tickets were "local in their nature" and did not extend beyond Washington, D.C. States were therefore free to allow the sale of the lottery tickets or, as Virginia did, to prohibit them. Furthermore, citizens of Virginia were free to go to Washington, D.C., to buy the tickets or to buy them in any other state where they could be sold, but Virginia retained the right to ban their sale within Virginia. Marshall conceded that the Congress could have provided for the sale of the tickets anywhere in the country, but it had not done so.

Thus, the Supreme Court affirmed the conviction of the Cohen brothers and their fine, and the case came to an end.

## Impact

*Cohens* is the tenth most cited U.S. Supreme Court decision cited by the Court itself. It is one of five Marshall opinions in the top ten of all cases the Court has cited. It is not merely a historical artifact. The Court cited it thirty times between 2000 and 2021. All told, it has been cited in more than 2,000 federal and state opinions.

The case stands for the proposition that the Supreme Court has the power to decide *what* it has the power to decide. In affirming that the Supreme Court had the power to hear the case, Marshall declared:

> The American States, as well as the American people, have believed a close and firm Union to be essential to their liberty and to their happiness. They have been taught by experience, that this Union cannot exist without a government for the whole; and they have been taught by the same experience that this government would be a mere shadow, that must disappoint all their hopes, unless invested with large portions of that sovereignty which belongs to independent States. Under

the influence of this opinion, and thus instructed by experience, the American people, in the conventions of their respective States, adopted the present constitution.

> If it could be doubted, whether from its nature, it were not supreme in all cases where it is empowered to act, that doubt would be removed by the declaration, that "this constitution, and the laws of the United States, which shall be made in pursuance thereof, and all treaties made, or which shall be made, under the authority of the United States, shall be the supreme law of the land; and the judges in every State shall be bound thereby; any thing in the constitution or laws of any State to the contrary notwithstanding."

> This is the authoritative language of the American people; and, if gentlemen please, of the American States. It marks, with lines too strong to be mistaken, the characteristic distinction between the government of the Union, and those of the States. The general government, though limited as to its objects, is supreme with respect to those objects. This principle is a part of the constitution; and if there be any who deny its necessity, none can deny its authority.

> To this supreme government ample powers are confided; and if it were possible to doubt the great purposes for which they were so confided, the people of the United States have declared, that they are given "in order to form a more perfect union, establish justice, ensure domestic tranquillity, provide for the common defence, promote the general welfare, and secure the blessings of liberty to themselves and their posterity."

The case mostly put an end to states arguing against the jurisdiction of the Supreme Court over constitutional matters. In that sense it was part of a trilogy of cases, along with *Martin v. Hunter's Lessee* and *McCulloch v. Maryland*, that set out the powers of Congress and the Supreme Court and the supremacy of the Constitution and the Court. In *Martin*, the Court emphatically, and successfully, explained to Virginia (and by extension all other states) that no state could pass legislation to overturn a treaty. In *McCulloch*, Marshall made clear that no state could attempt to destroy a federal agency (in this case the Bank of the United States) if the law creating the agency was constitutional. In both cases, the states lost on both their legal theories and on the substance of the case. In *Cohens*, the Court made clear that it had the power to hear any case involving a federal statute or the Constitution, and the states could not ignore the Court when it believed it had jurisdiction to hear the case. But, unlike *Martin* and *McCulloch*, the state of Virginia actually won the case.

Many Virginia leaders hated the case, not because of the final outcome but because the Court had even heard the case. They argued that this would destroy their ability to regulate their own society. While not part of the case, the Virginia leaders feared that *Cohens* might somehow undermine slavery. John Taylor of Caroline, a Virginian politician and states' rights theorist who served three partial terms in the U.S. Senate, published *Tyranny Unmasked* in 1822 attacking Marshall's opinions in *Cohens* and *McCulloch* as well as the general direction of the Supreme Court. Spencer Roane, who sat on Virginia's highest court from 1795 until his death in 1822, continued his long-running denunciations of Marshall in new attacks after *Cohens*. Marshall's cousin Thomas Jefferson privately

denounced the decision and tried to convince Justice William Johnson (whom Jefferson had put on the Court) to undermine Marshall.

But most of these complaints went nowhere, and Marshall continued to dominate the Court throughout most of the decade. In 1824, in *Gibbons v. Ogden*, Marshall struck down a New York law that interfered with interstate commerce. This powerful nationalist decision was very popular, and there were no complaints from any state's rights political leaders. Marshall, in effect, had "won."

Inside the Supreme Court building in Washington, D.C., is an impressive bronze statue of Chief Justice Marshall. Next to it is a plaque with quotations from various Marshall opinions. Only two opinions have two quotations: *McCulloch v. Maryland* and *Cohens*. The two quotations from *Cohens* remind us of the power of his words and of the importance of the opinion:

"A Constitution is framed for ages to come and is designed to approach immortality as nearly as human institutions can approach it. Its course cannot always be tranquil."

"The people made the Constitution, and the people can unmake it. It is the creature of their will, and lives only by their will."

## Questions for Further Study

1. This case involved a $100 fine, which in today's dollars would be about $2,500 to $3,000. The lawyers the Cohen brothers hired, especially William Pinkney, probably charged far more than the amount of the fine. Why do you think the brothers appealed rather than just paying the fine?

2. Chief Justice Marshall devoted fifty-five pages to explaining why the Court had the power to hear the case, and only seven pages, in a separate opinion, to explaining why he was upholding the decision against the Cohens. What does this tell us about the importance of the case?

3. This might seem like an odd question, but it goes to the heart of a great constitutional issue. Who "won" this case? Who are the real winners, and who are the real losers?

4. What is Chief Justice Marshall trying to accomplish with his first, fifty-five-page opinion? Is there a "subtext" to Virginia's argument that the Supreme Court has no business hearing appeals of local criminal cases? How will this fear play out in the next two centuries of American law?

5. We live in the age of Powerball lotteries, with tickets sold across the country. How might this case be considered the great-great-grandmother of the Powerball lottery?

## Further Reading

### Books

Ezell, John. *Fortune's Merry Wheel: The Lottery in America.* Cambridge: Harvard University Press, 1960.

Finkelman, Paul. *Supreme Injustice: Slavery in the Nation's Highest Court.* Cambridge: Harvard University Press, 2018.

Johnson, Herbert A. *The Chief Justice of John Marshall, 1801–1836.* Columbia: University of South Carolina Press, 1998.

Luce, W. Ray. *Cohens v. Virginia (1821): The Supreme Court and States Rights: A Reevaluation of Influences and Impacts.* New York: Garland, 1990.

Newmyer, R. Kent. *John Marshall and the Heroic Age of the Supreme Court.* Baton Rouge: Louisiana State University Press, 2001.

Urofsky, Melvin I., and Paul Finkelman. *A March of Liberty: A Constitutional History of the United States.* 2 vols. 3rd ed. New York: Oxford University Press, 2011.

White, G. Edward. *History of the Supreme Court of the United States,* Vol. 3–4: *The Marshall Court and Cultural Change, 1815–1835.* New York: Macmillan, 1988.

### Articles

Graber, Mark. "The Passive-Aggressive Virtues: Cohens v. Virginia and the Problematic Establishment of Judicial Power." *Constitutional Commentary* 12 (1995): 67, 73.

—Commentary by Paul Finkelman

# COHENS V. VIRGINIA

## Document Text

### *MR. CHIEF JUSTICE MARSHALL delivered the opinion of the Court*

This is a writ of error to a judgment rendered in the Court of Hustings for the borough of Norfolk, on an information for selling lottery tickets, contrary to an act of the Legislature of Virginia. In the State court, the defendant claimed the protection of an act of Congress. A case was agreed between the parties, which states the act of Assembly on which the prosecution was founded and the act of Congress on which the defendant relied, and concludes in these words:

"If, upon this case, the Court shall be of opinion that the acts of Congress before mentioned were valid, and, on the true construction of those acts, the lottery tickets sold by the defendants as aforesaid, might lawfully be sold within the State of Virginia, notwithstanding the act or statute of the general assembly of Virginia prohibiting such sale, then judgment to be entered for the defendants; and if the Court should be of opinion that the statute or act of the General Assembly of the State of Virginia, prohibiting such sale, is valid, notwithstanding the said acts of Congress, then judgment to be entered that the defendants are guilty, and that the Commonwealth recover against them one hundred dollars and costs."

Judgment was rendered against the defendants; and the Court in which it was rendered being the highest Court of the State in which the cause was cognizable, the record has been brought into this Court by writ of error.

The defendant in error moves to dismiss this writ, for want of jurisdiction.

In support of this motion, three points have been made, and argued with the ability which the importance of the question merits. These points are:

1st. That a State is a defendant.

2d. That no writ of error lies from this Court to a State court.

3d. The third point has been presented in different forms by the gentlemen who have argued it. The counsel who opened the cause said that the want of jurisdiction was shown by the subject matter of the case. The counsel who followed him said that jurisdiction was not given by the Judiciary Act. The Court has bestowed all its attention on the arguments of both gentlemen, and supposes that their tendency is to show that this Court has no jurisdiction of the case, or, in other words, has no right to review the judgment of the State court, because neither the Constitution nor any law of the United States has been violated by that judgment.

The questions presented to the Court by the two first points made at the bar are of great magnitude, and may be truly said vitally to affect the Union. They exclude the inquiry whether the Constitution and laws of the United States have been violated by the judgment which the plaintiffs in error seek to review; and maintain that, admitting such violation, it is not in the power of the government to apply a corrective. They maintain that the nation does not possess a department capable of restraining peaceably, and by authority of law, any attempts which may be made, by a part, against the legitimate powers of the whole, and that the government is reduced to the alternative of submitting to such attempts or of resisting them by force. They maintain that the Constitution of the United States has provided no tribunal for the final construction of itself, or of the laws or treaties of the nation, but that this power may be exercised in the last resort by the Courts of every State in the Union. That the Constitution, laws, and treaties may receive as many constructions as there are States; and that this is not a mischief, or, if a mischief, is irremediable. These abstract propositions are to be determined, for he who demands decision without permitting inquiry affirms that the decision he asks does not depend on inquiry.

If such be the Constitution, it is the duty of the Court to bow with respectful submission to its provisions. If such be not the Constitution, it is equally the duty of this Court to say so, and to perform that task which the American people have assigned to the judicial department.

1st. The first question to be considered is whether the jurisdiction of this Court is excluded by the character of the parties, one of them being a State, and the other a citizen of that State?

The second section of the third article of the Constitution defines the extent of the judicial power of the United States. Jurisdiction is given to the Courts of the Union in two classes of cases. In the first, their jurisdiction depends on the character of the cause, whoever may be the parties. This class comprehends

"all cases in law and equity arising under this Constitution, the laws of the United States, and treaties made, or which shall be made, under their authority."

This clause extends the jurisdiction of the Court to all the cases described, without making in its terms any exception whatever, and without any regard to the condition of the party. If there by any exception, it is to be implied against the express words of the article.

In the second class, the jurisdiction depends entirely on the character of the parties. In this are comprehended "controversies between two or more States, between a State and citizens of another State," "and between a State and foreign States, citizens or subjects." If these be the parties, it is entirely unimportant what may be the subject of controversy. Be it what it may, these parties have a constitutional right to come into the Courts of the Union.

The counsel for the defendant in error have stated that the cases which arise under the Constitution must grow out of those provisions which are capable of self-execution, examples of which are to be found in the 2d section of the 4th article, and in the 10th section of the 1st article.

A case which arises under a law of the United States must, we are likewise told, be a right given by some act which becomes necessary to execute the powers given in the Constitution, of which the law of naturalization is mentioned as an example.

The use intended to be made of this exposition of the first part of the section, defining the extent of the judicial power, is not clearly understood. If the intention be merely to distinguish cases arising under the Constitution from those arising under a law, for the sake of precision in the application of this argument, these propositions will not be controverted. If it be to maintain that a case arising under the Constitution, or a law, must be one in which a party comes into Court to demand something conferred on him by the Constitution or a law, we think the construction too narrow. A case in law or equity consists of the right of the one party, as well as of the other, and may truly be said to arise under the Constitution or a law of the United States whenever its correct decision depends on the construction of either. Congress seems to have intended to give its own construction of this part of the Constitution in the twenty-fifth section of the Judiciary Act, and we perceive no reason to depart from that construction.

The jurisdiction of the Court, then, being extended by the letter of the Constitution to all cases arising under it, or under the laws of the United States, it follows that those who would withdraw any case of this description from that jurisdiction, must sustain the exemption they claim on the spirit and true meaning of the Constitution, which spirit and true meaning must be so apparent as to overrule the words which its framers have employed.

The counsel for the defendant in error have undertaken to do this, and have laid down the general proposition that a sovereign independent State is not suable except by its own consent.

This general proposition will not be controverted. But its consent is not requisite in each particular case. It may be given in a general law. And if a State has surrendered any portion of its sovereignty, the question whether a liability to suit be a part of this portion depends on the instrument by which the surrender is made. If, upon a just construction of that instrument, it shall appear that the State has submitted to be sued, then it has parted with this sovereign right of judging in every case on the justice of its own pretensions, and has entrusted that power to a tribunal in whose impartiality it confides.

The American States, as well as the American people, have believed a close and firm Union to be essential to their liberty and to their happiness. They have been taught by experience that this Union cannot exist without a government for the whole, and they have been taught by the same experience that this government would be a mere shadow, that must disappoint all their hopes, unless invested with large portions of that sovereignty which belongs to independent States. Under the influence of this opinion, and thus instructed by experience, the American people, in the conventions of their respective States, adopted the present Constitution.

If it could be doubted whether, from its nature, it were not supreme in all cases where it is empowered to act, that doubt would be removed by the declaration that

"this Constitution, and the laws of the United States, which shall be made in pursuance thereof, and all treaties made, or which shall be made, under the authority of the United States, shall be the supreme law of the land; and the judges in every State shall be bound thereby; any thing in the Constitution or laws of any State to the contrary notwithstanding."

This is the authoritative language of the American people, and, if gentlemen please, of the American States. It marks, with lines too strong to be mistaken the characteristic distinction between the government of the Union and those of the States. The general government, though limited as to its objects, is supreme with respect to those objects. This principle is a part of the Constitution, and if there be any who deny its necessity, none can deny its authority.

To this supreme government ample powers are confided, and if it were possible to doubt the great purposes for which they were so confided, the people of the United States have declared that they are given

"in order to form a more perfect union, establish justice, ensure domestic tranquillity, provide for the common defence, promote the general welfare, and secure the blessings of liberty to themselves and their posterity."

With the ample powers confided to this supreme government, for these interesting purposes are connected many express and important limitations on the sovereignty of the States which are made for the same purposes. The powers of the Union, on the great subjects of war, peace, and commerce, and on many others, are in themselves limitations of the sovereignty of the States; but, in addition to these, the sovereignty of the States is surrendered in many instances where the surrender can only operate to the benefit of the people, and where, perhaps, no other power is conferred on Congress than a conservative power to maintain the principles established in the Constitution. The maintenance of these principles in their purity is certainly among the great duties of the government. One of the instruments by which this duty may be peaceably performed is the judicial department. It is authorized to decide all cases of every description arising under the Constitution or laws of the United States. From this general grant of jurisdiction, no exception is made of those cases in which a State may be a party. When we consider the situation of the government of the Union and of a State in relation to each other; the nature of our Constitution; the subordination of the State governments to that Constitution; the great purpose for which jurisdiction over all cases arising under the Constitution and laws of the United States is confided to the judicial department; are we at liberty to insert in this general grant an exception of those cases in which a State may be a party? Will the spirit of the Constitution justify this attempt to control its words? We think it will not. We think a case arising under the Constitution or laws of the United States is cognizable in the Courts of the Union whoever may be the parties to that case.

Had any doubt existed with respect to the just construction of this part of the section, that doubt would have been removed by the enumeration of those cases to which the jurisdiction of the federal Courts is extended in consequence of the character of the parties. In that enumeration, we find "controversies between two or more States, between a State and citizens of another State," "and between a State and foreign States, citizens, or subjects."

On of the express objects, then, for which the judicial department was established is the decision of controversies between States, and between a State and individuals. The mere circumstance that a State is a party gives jurisdiction to the Court. How, then, can it be contended that the very same instrument, in the very same section, should be so construed as that this same circumstance should withdraw a case from the jurisdiction of the Court where the Constitution or laws of the United States are supposed to have been violated? The Constitution gave to every person having a claim upon a State a right to submit his case to the Court of the nation. However unimportant his claim might be, however little the community might be interested in its decision, the framers of our Constitution thought it necessary for the purposes of justice to provide a tribunal as superior to influence as possible in which that claim might be decided. Can it be imagined that the same persons considered a case involving the Constitution of our country and the majesty of the laws, questions in which every American citizen must be deeply interested, as withdrawn from this tribunal, because a State is a party?

While weighing arguments drawn from the nature of government and from the general spirit of an instrument, and urged for the purpose of narrowing the construction which the words of that instrument seem to require, it is proper to place in the opposite scale those principles, drawn from the same sources, which go to sustain the words in their full operation and natural import. One of these, which has been pressed with great force by the counsel for the plaintiffs in error, is that the judicial power of every well constituted government must be coextensive with the legislative, and must be capable of deciding every judicial question which grows out of the Constitution and laws.

If any proposition may be considered as a political axiom, this, we think, may be so considered. In reasoning upon it as an abstract question, there would, probably, exist no contrariety of opinion respecting it. Every argument proving the necessity of the department proves also the propriety of giving this extent to it. We do not mean to say that the jurisdiction of the Courts of the Union should be construed to be coextensive with the legislative merely because it is fit that it should be so; but we mean to say that this fitness furnishes an argument in construing the Constitution which ought never to be overlooked, and which is most especially entitled to consideration when we are inquiring whether the words of the instrument which purport to establish this principle shall be contracted for the purpose of destroying it.

The mischievous consequences of the construction contended for on the part of Virginia are also entitled to great consideration. It would prostrate, it has been said, the government and its laws at the feet of every State in the Union. And would not this be its effect? What power of the government could be executed by its own means in any State disposed to resist its execution by a course of legislation? The laws must be executed by individuals acting within the several States. If these individuals may be exposed to penalties, and if the Courts of the Union cannot correct the judgments by which these penalties may be enforced, the course of the government may be at any time arrested by the will of one of its members. Each member will possess a veto on the will of the whole.

The answer which has been given to this argument does not deny its truth, but insists that confidence is reposed, and may be safely reposed, in the State institutions, and that, if they shall ever become so insane or so wicked as to seek the destruction of the government, they may accomplish their object by refusing to perform the functions assigned to them.

We readily concur with the counsel for the defendant in the declaration that the cases which have been put of direct legislative resistance for the purpose of opposing the acknowledged powers of the government are extreme cases, and in the hope that they will never occur, but we cannot help believing that a general conviction of the total incapacity of the government to protect itself and its laws in such cases would contribute in no inconsiderable degree to their occurrence.

Let it be admitted that the cases which have been put are extreme and improbable, yet there are gradations of opposition to the laws, far short to those cases, which might have a baneful influence on the affairs of the nation. Different States may entertain different opinions on the true construction of the constitutional powers of Congress. We know that, at one time, the assumption of the debts contracted by the several States during the war of our revolution was deemed unconstitutional by some of them. We know, too, that, at other times, certain taxes imposed by Congress have been pronounced unconstitutional. Other laws have been questioned partially, while they were supported by the great majority of the American people. We have no assurance that we shall be less divided than we have been. States may legislate in conformity to their opinions, and may enforce those opinions by penalties. It would be hazarding too much to assert that the judicatures of the States will be exempt from the prejudices by which the legislatures and people are influenced, and will constitute perfectly impartial tribunals. In many States, the judges are dependent for office and for salary on the will of the legislature. The Constitution of the United States furnishes no security against the universal adoption of this principle. When we observe the importance which that Constitution attaches to the independence of judges, we are the less inclined to suppose that it can have intended to leave these constitutional questions to tribunals where this independence may not exist, in all cases where a State shall prosecute an individual who claims the protection of an act of Congress. These prosecutions may take place even without a legislative act. A person making a seizure under an act of Congress, may be indicted as a trespasser, if force has been employed, and of this a jury may judge. How extensive may be the mischief if the first decisions in such cases should be final!

These collisions may take place in times of no extraordinary commotion. But a Constitution is framed for ages to come, and is designed to approach immortality as nearly as human institutions can approach it. Its course cannot always be tranquil. It is exposed to storms and tempests, and its framers must be unwise statesmen indeed if they have not provided it, as far as its nature will permit, with the means of self-preservation from the perils it may be destined to encounter. No government ought to be so defective in its organization as not to contain within itself the means of securing the execution of its own laws against other dangers than those which occur every day. Courts of justice are the means most usually employed, and it is reasonable to expect that a government should repose on its own Courts, rather than on others. There is certainly nothing in the circumstances under which our Constitution was formed, nothing in the history of the times, which would justify the opinion that the confidence reposed in the States was so implicit as to leave in them and their tribunals the power of resisting or defeating, in the form of law, the legitimate measures of the Union. The requisitions of Congress under the confederation were as constitutionally obligatory as the laws enacted by the present Congress. That they were habitually disregarded is a fact of universal notoriety. With the knowledge of this fact, and under its full pressure, a convention was assembled to change the system. Is it so improbable that they should confer on the judicial department the power of construing the Constitution and laws of the Union in every case, in the last resort, and of preserving them from all violation from every quarter, so far as judicial decisions can preserve them, that this improbability should essentially affect the construction of the new system? We are told, and we are truly told, that the great change which is to give efficacy to the present system is its ability to act on individuals directly, instead of acting through the instrumentality of State governments. But ought not this ability, in reason and sound policy, to be applied directly to the protection of individuals employed in the execution of the laws, as well as to their coercion. Your laws reach the individual without the aid of any other power; why may they not protect him from punishment for performing his duty in executing them?

The counsel for Virginia endeavor to obviate the force of these arguments by saying that the dangers they suggest, if not imaginary, are inevitable; that the Constitution can make no provision against them; and that, therefore, in construing that instrument, they ought to be excluded from our consideration. This state of things, they say, cannot arise until there shall be a disposition so hostile to the present political system as to produce a determination to destroy it; and, when that determination shall be produced, its effects will not be restrained by parchment stipulations. The fate of the Constitution will not then depend on judicial decisions. But, should no appeal be made to force, the States can put an end to the government by refusing to act. They have only not to elect Senators, and it expires without a struggle.

It is very true that, whenever hostility to the existing system shall become universal, it will be also irresistible. The people made the Constitution, and the people can unmake it. It is the creature of their will, and lives only by their will. But this supreme and irresistible power to make or to unmake resides only in the whole body of the people, not in any subdivision of them. The attempt of any of the parts to exercise it is usurpation, and ought to be repelled by those to whom the people have delegated their power of repelling it.

The acknowledged inability of the government, then, to sustain itself against the public will and, by force or otherwise, to control the whole nation, is no sound argument in support of its constitutional inability to preserve itself against a section of the nation acting in opposition to the general will.

It is true that, if all the States, or a majority of them, refuse to elect Senators, the legislative powers of the Union will be suspended. But if any one State shall refuse to elect them, the Senate will not, on that account, be the less capable of performing all its functions. The argument founded on this fact would seem rather to prove the subordination of the parts to the whole than the complete independence of any one of them. The framers of the Constitution were, indeed, unable to make any provisions which should protect that instrument against a general combination of the States, or of the people, for its destruction; and, conscious of this inability, they have not made the attempt. But they were able to provide against the operation of measures adopted in any one State whose tendency might be to arrest the execution of the laws, and this it was the part of true wisdom to attempt. We think they have attempted it.

It has been also urged as an additional objection to the jurisdiction of the Court that cases between a State and one of its own citizens do not come within the general scope of the Constitution, and were obviously never intended to be made cognizable in the federal Courts. The State tribunals might be suspected of partiality in cases between itself or its citizens and aliens, or the citizens of another State, but not in proceedings by a State against its own citizens. That jealousy which might exist in the first case could not exist in the last, and therefore the judicial power is not extended to the last.

This is very true, so far as jurisdiction depends on the character of the parties; and the argument would have great force if urged to prove that this Court could not establish the demand of a citizen upon his State, but is not entitled to the same force when urged to prove that this Court cannot inquire whether the Constitution or laws of the United States protect a citizen from a prosecution instituted against him by a State. If jurisdiction depended entirely on the character of the parties, and was not given where the parties have not an original right to come into Court, that part of the 2d section of the 3d article which extends the judicial power to all

cases arising under the Constitution and laws of the United States would be mere surplusage. It is to give jurisdiction where the character of the parties would not give it that this very important part of the clause was inserted. It may be true that the partiality of the State tribunals, in ordinary controversies between a State and its citizens, was not apprehended, and therefore the judicial power of the Union was not extended to such cases; but this was not the sole nor the greatest object for which this department was created. A more important, a much more interesting, object was the preservation of the Constitution and laws of the United States, so far as they can be preserved by judicial authority, and therefore the jurisdiction of the Courts of the Union was expressly extended to all cases arising under that Constitution and those laws. If the Constitution or laws may be violated by proceedings instituted by a State against its own citizens, and if that violation may be such as essentially to affect the Constitution and the laws, such as to arrest the progress of government in its constitutional course, why should these cases be excepted from that provision which expressly extends the judicial power of the Union to all cases arising under the Constitution and laws?

After bestowing on this subject the most attentive consideration, the Court can perceive no reason founded on the character of the parties for introducing an exception which the Constitution has not made, and we think that the judicial power, as originally given, extends to all cases arising under the Constitution or a law of the United States, whoever may be the parties.

It has been also contended that this jurisdiction, if given, is original, and cannot be exercised in the appellate form.

The words of the Constitution are,

"in all cases affecting ambassadors, other public ministers, and consuls, and those in which a State shall be a party, the Supreme Court shall have original jurisdiction. In all the other cases before mentioned, the Supreme Court shall have appellate jurisdiction."

This distinction between original and appellate jurisdiction, excludes, we are told, in all cases, the exercise of the one where the other is given.

The Constitution gives the Supreme Court original jurisdiction in certain enumerated cases, and gives it appellate jurisdiction in all others. Among those in which jurisdiction must be exercised in the appellate form are cases arising under the Constitution and laws of the United States. These provisions of the Constitution are equally obligatory, and are to be equally respected. If a State be a party, the jurisdiction of this Court is original; if the case arise under a Constitution or a law, the jurisdiction is appellate. But a case to which a State is a party may arise under the Constitution or a law of the United States. What rule is applicable to such a case? What, then, becomes the duty of the Court? Certainly, we think, so to construe the Constitution as to give effect to both provisions, as far as it is possible to reconcile them, and not to permit their seeming repugnancy to destroy each other. We must endeavor so to construe them as to preserve the true intent and meaning of the instrument.

In one description of cases, the jurisdiction of the Court is founded entirely on the character of the parties, and the nature of the controversy is not contemplated by the Constitution. The character of the parties is everything, the nature of the case nothing. In the other description of cases, the jurisdiction is founded entirely on the character of the case, and the parties are not contemplated by the Constitution. In these, the nature of the case is everything, the character of the parties nothing. When, then, the Constitution declares the jurisdiction, in cases where a State shall be a party, to be original, and in all cases arising under the Constitution or a law, to be appellate— the conclusion seems irresistible that its framers designed to include in the first class those cases in which jurisdiction is given because a State is a party, and to include in the second those in which jurisdiction is given because the case arises under the Constitution or a law.

This reasonable construction is rendered necessary by other considerations.

That the Constitution or a law of the United States is involved in a case, and makes a part of it, may appear in the progress of a cause in which the Courts of the Union, but for that circumstance, would have no jurisdiction, and which, of consequence, could not originate in the Supreme Court. In such a case, the jurisdiction can be exercised only in its appellate form. To deny its exercise in this form is to deny its existence, and would be to construe a clause dividing the power of the Supreme Court in such manner as in a considerable degree to defeat the power itself. All must perceive that this construction can be justified only where it is absolutely necessary. We do not think the article under consideration presents that necessity.

It is observable that, in this distributive clause, no negative words are introduced. This observation is not made for the purpose of contending that the legislature may "apportion the judicial power between the Supreme and inferior Courts according to its will." That would be, as was said by this Court in the case of *Marbury v. Madison,* to render the distributive clause "mere surplusage," to make it "form without substance." This cannot, therefore, be the true construction of the article.

But although the absence of negative words will not authorize the legislature to disregard the distribution of the power previously granted, their absence will justify a sound construction of the whole article so as to give every part its intended effect. It is admitted that "affirmative words are often, in their operation, negative of other objects than those affirmed," and that, where "a negative or exclusive sense must be given to them, or they have no operation at all" they must receive that negative or exclusive sense. But where they have full operation without it; where it would destroy some of the most important objects for which the power was created; then, we think, affirmative words ought not to be construed negatively.

The Constitution declares that, in cases where a State is a party, the Supreme Court shall have original jurisdiction, but does not say that its appellate jurisdiction shall not be exercised in cases where, from their nature, appellate jurisdiction is given, whether a State be or be not a party. It may be conceded that, where the case is of such a nature as to admit of its originating in the Supreme Court, it ought to originate there, but where, from its nature, it cannot originate in that Court, these words ought not to be so construed as to require it. There are many cases in which it would be found extremely difficult, and subversive of the spirit of the Constitution, to maintain the construction that appellate jurisdiction cannot be exercised where one of the parties might sue or be sued in this Court.

The Constitution defines the jurisdiction of the Supreme Court, but does not define that of the inferior Courts. Can it be affirmed that a State might not sue the citizen of another State in a Circuit Court? Should the Circuit Court decide for or against its jurisdiction, should it dismiss the suit or give judgment against the State, might not its decision be revised in the Supreme Court? The argument is that it could not; and the very clause which is urged to prove that the Circuit Court could give no judgment in the case is also urged to prove that its judgment is irreversible. A supervising Court, whose peculiar province it is to correct the errors of an inferior Court, has no power to correct a judgment given without jurisdiction because, in the same case, that supervising Court has original jurisdiction. Had negative words been employed, it would be difficult to give them this construction if they would admit of any other. But without negative words, this irrational construction can never be maintained.

So, too, in the same clause, the jurisdiction of the Court is declared to be original "in cases affecting ambassadors, other public ministers, and consuls." There is, perhaps, no part of the article under consideration so much required by national policy as this, unless it be that part which extends the judicial power "to all cases arising under the Constitution, laws, and treaties of the United States." It has been generally held that the State courts have a concurrent jurisdiction with the federal Courts, in cases to which the judicial power is extended, unless the jurisdiction of the federal Courts be rendered exclusive by the words of the third article. If the words, "to all cases," give exclusive jurisdiction in cases affecting foreign ministers, they may also give exclusive jurisdiction, if such be the will of Congress, in cases arising under the Constitution, laws, and treaties of the United States. Now suppose an individual were to sue a foreign minister in a State court, and that Court were to maintain its jurisdiction and render judgment against the minister— could it be contended that this Court would be incapable of revising such judgment, because the Constitution had given it original jurisdiction in the case? If this could be maintained, then a clause inserted for the purpose of excluding the jurisdiction of all other Courts than this in a particular case would have the effect of excluding the jurisdiction of this Court in that very case if the suit were to be brought in another Court and that Court were to assert jurisdiction. This tribunal, according to the argument which has been urged, could neither revise the judgment of such other Court nor suspend its proceedings, for a writ of prohibition, or any other similar writ, is in the nature of appellate process.

Foreign consuls frequently assert, in our Prize Courts, the claims of their fellow subjects. These suits are main-tained by them as consuls. The appellate power of this Court has been frequently exercised in such cases, and has never been questioned. It would be extremely mischievous to withhold its exercise. Yet the consul is a party on the record. The truth is that, where the words confer only appellate jurisdiction, original jurisdiction is most clearly not given; but where the words admit of appellate jurisdiction, the power to take cognizance of the suit originally does not necessarily negative the power to decide upon it on an appeal if it may originate in a different Court.

It is, we think, apparent that to give this distributive clause the interpretation contended for, to give to its affirmative words a negative operation, in every possible case would, in some instances, defeat the obvious intention of the article. Such an interpretation would not consist with those rules which, from time immemorial, have guided Courts in their construction of instruments brought under their consideration. It must therefore be discarded. Every part of the article must be taken into view, and that construction adopted which will consist with its words and promote its general intention. The Court may imply a negative from affirmative words where the implication promotes, not where it defeats, the intention.

If we apply this principle, the correctness of which we believe will not be controverted, to the distributive clause under consideration, the result, we think, would be this: the original jurisdiction of the Supreme Court, in cases where a State is a party, refers to those cases in which, according to the grant of power made in the preceding clause, jurisdiction might be exercised in consequence of the character of the party, and an original suit might be instituted in any of the federal Courts, not to those cases in which an original suit might not be instituted in a federal Court. Of the last description is every case between a State and its citizens, and perhaps every case in which a State is enforcing its penal laws. In such cases, therefore, the Supreme Court cannot take original jurisdiction. In every other case— that is, in every case to which the judicial power extends and in which original jurisdiction is not expressly given— that judicial power shall be exercised in the appellate, and only in the appellate, form. The original jurisdiction of this Court cannot be enlarged, but its appellate jurisdiction may be exercised in every case cognizable under the third article of the Constitution, in the federal Courts, in which original jurisdiction cannot be exercised; and the extent of this judicial power is to be measured not by giving the affirmative words of the distributive clause a negative operation in every possible case, but by giving their true meaning to the words which define its extent.

The counsel for the defendant in error urge, in opposition to this rule of construction, some dicta of the Court in the case of *Marbury v. Madison.*

It is a maxim not to be disregarded that general expressions, in every opinion, are to be taken in connection with the case in which those expressions are used. If they go beyond the case, they may be respected, but ought not to control the judgment in a subsequent suit when the very point is presented for decision. The reason of this maxim is obvious. The question actually before the Court is investigated with care, and considered in its full extent. Other principles which may serve to illustrate it are considered in their relation to the case decided, but their possible bearing on all other cases is seldom completely investigated.

In the case of *Marbury v. Madison,* the single question before the Court, so far as that case can be applied to this, was whether the legislature could give this Court original jurisdiction in a case in which the Constitution had clearly not given it, and in which no doubt respecting the construction of the article could possibly be raised. The Court decided, and we think very properly, that the legislature could not give original jurisdiction in such a case. But, in the reasoning of the Court in support of this decision, some expressions are used which go far beyond it. The counsel for Marbury had insisted on the unlimited discretion of the legislature in the apportionment of the judicial power, and it is against this argument that the reasoning of the Court is directed. They say that, if such had been the intention of the article, "it would certainly have been useless to proceed farther than to define the judicial power and the tribunals in which it should be vested." The Court says that such a construction would render the clause dividing the jurisdiction of the Court into original and appellate totally useless; that

"affirmative words are often, in their operation, negative of other objects than those which are affirmed; and, in this case [in the case of *Marbury v. Madison*], a negative or exclusive sense must be given to them or they have no operation at all."

"It cannot be presumed," adds the Court,

"that any clause in the Constitution is intended to be without effect, and therefore such a construction is inadmissible unless the words require it."

The whole reasoning of the Court proceeds upon the idea that the affirmative words of the clause giving one sort of jurisdiction must imply a negative of any other sort of jurisdiction, because otherwise the words would be totally inoperative, and this reasoning is advanced in a case to which it was strictly applicable. If, in that case, original jurisdiction could have been exercised, the clause under consideration would have been entirely useless. Having such cases only in its view, the Court lays down a principle which is generally correct, in terms much broader than the decision, and not only much broader than the reasoning with which that decision is supported, but in some instances contradictory to its principle. The reasoning sustains the negative operation of the words in that case, because otherwise the clause would have no meaning whatever, and because such operation was necessary to give effect to the intention of the article. The effort now made is to apply the conclusion to which the Court was conducted by that reasoning in the particular case to one in which the words have their full operation when understood affirmatively, and in which the negative or exclusive sense is to be so used as to defeat some of the great objects of the article.

To this construction the Court cannot give its assent. The general expressions in the case of *Marbury v. Madison* must be understood with the limitations which are given to them in this opinion— limitations which in no degree affect the decision in that case or the tenor of its reasoning.

The counsel who closed the argument put several cases for the purpose of illustration which he supposed to arise under the Constitution, and yet to be apparently without the jurisdiction of the Court.

Were a State to lay a duty on exports, to collect the money and place it in her treasury, could the citizen who paid it, he asks, maintain a suit in this Court against such State to recover back the money?

Perhaps not. Without, however, deciding such supposed case, we may say that it is entirely unlike that under consideration.

The citizen who has paid his money to his State under a law that is void is in the same situation with every other person who has paid money by mistake. The law raises an assumpsit to return the money, and it is upon that assumpsit that the action is to be maintained. To refuse to comply with this assumpsit may be no more a violation of the Constitution than to refuse to comply with any other; and as the federal Courts never had jurisdiction over contracts between a State and its citizens, they may have none over this. But let us so vary the supposed case as to give it a real resemblance to that under consideration. Suppose a citizen to refuse to pay this export duty, and a suit to be instituted for the purpose of compelling him to pay it. He pleads the Constitution of the United States in bar of the action, notwithstanding which the Court gives judgment against him. This would be a case arising under the Constitution, and would be the very case now before the Court.

We are also asked, if a State should confiscate property secured by a treaty, whether the individual could maintain an action for that property?

If the property confiscated be debts, our own experience informs us that the remedy of the creditor against his debtor remains. If it be land, which is secured by a treaty, and afterwards confiscated by a State, the argument does not assume that this title, thus secured, could be extinguished by an act of confiscation. The injured party, therefore, has his remedy against the occupant of the land for that which the treaty secures to him, not against the State for money which is not secured to him.

The case of a State which pays off its own debts with paper money no more resembles this than do those to which we have already adverted. The Courts have no jurisdiction over the contract. They cannot enforce it, nor judge of its violation. Let it be that the act discharging the debt is a mere nullity, and that it is still due. Yet the federal Courts have no cognizance of the case. But suppose a State to institute proceedings against an individual which depended on the validity of an act emitting bills of credit; suppose a State to prosecute one of its citizens for refusing paper money, who should plead the Constitution in bar of such prosecution. If his plea should be overruled, and judgment rendered against him, his case would resemble this; and, unless the jurisdiction of this Court might

be exercised over it, the Constitution would be violated, and the injured party be unable to bring his case before that tribunal to which the people of the United States have assigned all such cases.

It is most true that this Court will not take jurisdiction if it should not; but it is equally true that it must take jurisdiction if it should. The judiciary cannot, as the legislature may, avoid a measure because it approaches the confines of the Constitution. We cannot pass it by because it is doubtful. With whatever doubts, with whatever difficulties, a case may be attended, we must decide it if it be brought before us. We have no more right to decline the exercise of jurisdiction which is given than to usurp that which is not given. The one or the other would be treason to the Constitution. Questions may occur which we would gladly avoid, but we cannot avoid them. All we can do is to exercise our best judgment and conscientiously to perform our duty. In doing this on the present occasion, we find this tribunal invested with appellate jurisdiction in all cases arising under the Constitution and laws of the United States. We find no exception to this grant, and we cannot insert one.

To escape the operation of these comprehensive words, the counsel for the defendant has mentioned instances in which the Constitution might be violated without giving jurisdiction to this Court. These words, therefore, however universal in their expression, must, he contends, be limited and controlled in their construction by circumstances. One of these instances is the grant by a State of a patent of nobility. The Court, he says, cannot annul this grant. This may be very true, but by no means justifies the inference drawn from it. The article does not extend the judicial power to every violation of the Constitution which may possibly take place, but to "a case in law or equity" in which a right under such law is asserted in a Court of justice. If the question cannot be brought into a Court, then there is no case in law or equity, and no jurisdiction is given by the words of the article. But if, in any controversy depending in a Court, the cause should depend on the validity of such a law, that would be a case arising under the Constitution, to which the judicial power of the United States would extend. The same observation applies to the other instances with which the counsel who opened the cause has illustrated this argument. Although they show that there may be violations of the Constitution of which the Courts can take no cognizance, they do not show that an interpretation more restrictive than the words themselves import ought to be given to this article. They do not show that there can be "a case in law or equity," arising under the Constitution to which the judicial power does not extend.

We think, then that, as the Constitution originally stood, the appellate jurisdiction of this Court, in all cases arising under the Constitution, laws, or treaties of the United States, was not arrested by the circumstance that a State was a party.

This leads to a consideration of the Eleventh Amendment.

It is in these words:

"The judicial power of the United States shall not be construed to extend to any suit in law or equity commenced or prosecuted against one of the United States, by citizens of another State, or by citizens or subjects of any foreign State."

It is a part of our history that, at the adoption of the Constitution, all the States were greatly indebted, and the apprehension that these debts might be prosecuted in the federal Courts formed a very serious objection to that instrument. Suits were instituted, and the Court maintained its jurisdiction. The alarm was general, and, to quiet the apprehensions that were so extensively entertained, this amendment was proposed in Congress and adopted by the State legislatures. That its motive was not to maintain the sovereignty of a State from the degradation supposed to attend a compulsory appearance before the tribunal of the nation may be inferred from the terms of the amendment. It does not comprehend controversies between two or more States, or between a State and a foreign State. The jurisdiction of the Court still extends to these cases, and in these a State may still be sued. We must ascribe the amendment, then, to some other cause than the dignity of a State. There is no difficulty in finding this cause. Those who were inhibited from commencing a suit against a State, or from prosecuting one which might be commenced before the adoption of the amendment, were persons who might probably be its creditors. There was not much reason to fear that foreign or sister States would be creditors to any considerable amount, and there was reason to retain the jurisdiction of the Court in those cases, because

it might be essential to the preservation of peace. The amendment, therefore, extended to suits commenced or prosecuted by individuals, but not to those brought by States.

The first impression made on the mind by this amendment is that it was intended for those cases, and for those only, in which some demand against a State is made by an individual in the Courts of the Union. If we consider the causes to which it is to be traced, we are conducted to the same conclusion. A general interest might well be felt in leaving to a State the full power of consulting its convenience in the adjustment of its debts or of other claims upon it, but no interest could be felt in so changing the relations between the whole and its parts as to strip the government of the means of protecting, by the instrumentality of its Courts, the Constitution and laws from active violation.

The words of the amendment appear to the Court to justify and require this construction. The judicial power is not "to extend to any suit in law or equity commenced or prosecuted against one of the United States by citizens of another State, &c."

What is a suit? We understand it to be the prosecution, or pursuit, of some claim, demand, or request. In law language, it is the prosecution of some demand in a Court of justice. The remedy for every species of wrong is, says Judge Blackstone, "the being put in possession of that right whereof the party injured is deprived."

"The instruments whereby this remedy is obtained are a diversity of suits and actions, which are defined by the Mirror to be 'the lawful demand of one's right.' Or, as Bracton and Fleta express it, in the words of Justinian, 'jus prosequendi in judicio quod alicui debetur.'"

Blackstone then proceeds to describe every species of remedy by suit, and they are all cases were the party suing claims to obtain something to which he has a right.

To commence a suit is to demand something by the institution of process in a Court of justice, and to prosecute the suit is, according to the common acceptation of language, to continue that demand. By a suit commenced by an individual against a State, we should understand process sued out by that individual against the State for the purpose of establishing some claim against it by the judgment of a Court, and the prosecution of that suit is its continuance. Whatever may be the stages of its progress, the actor is still the same. Suits had been commenced in the Supreme Court against some of the States before this amendment was introduced into Congress, and others might be commenced before it should be adopted by the State legislatures, and might be depending at the time of its adoption. The object of the amendment was not only to prevent the commencement of future suits, but to arrest the prosecution of those which might be commenced when this article should form a part of the Constitution. It therefore embraces both objects, and its meaning is that the judicial power shall not be construed to extend to any suit which may be commenced, or which, if already commenced, may be prosecuted against a State by the citizen of another State. If a suit, brought in one Court and carried by legal process to a supervising Court, be a continuation of the same suit, then this suit is not commenced nor prosecuted against a State. It is clearly in its commencement the suit of a State against an individual, which suit is transferred to this Court not for the purpose of asserting any claim against the State, but for the purpose of asserting a constitutional defence against a claim made by a State.

A writ of error is defined to be a commission by which the judges of one Court are authorized to examine a record upon which a judgment was given in another Court, and, on such examination, to affirm or reverse the same according to law. If, says my Lord Coke, by the writ of error, the plaintiff may recover, or be restored to anything, it may be released by the name of an action. In Bacon's Abridgment, tit. Error, L., it is laid down that

"where, by a writ of error, the plaintiff shall recover, or be restored to any personal thing, as debt, damage, or the like, a release of all actions personal is a good plea; and when land is to be recovered or restored in a writ of error, a release of actions real is a good bar; but where, by a writ of error, the plaintiff shall not be restored to any personal or real thing, a release of all actions, real or personal, is no bar."

And for this we have the authority of Lord Coke, both in his Commentary on Littleton and in his Reports. A writ of error, then, is in the nature of a suit or action when it is to restore the party who obtains it to the possession of any thing which is withheld from him, not when its operation is entirely defensive.

This rule will apply to writs of error from the Courts of the United States, as well as to those writs in England.

Under the Judiciary Act, the effect of a writ of error is simply to bring the record into Court, and submit the judgment of the inferior tribunal to reexamination. It does not in any manner act upon the parties; it acts only on the record. It removes the record into the supervising tribunal. Where, then, a State obtains a judgment against an individual, and the Court, rendering such judgment, overrules a defence set up under the Constitution or laws of the United States, the transfer of this record into the Supreme Court, for the sole purpose of inquiring whether the judgment violates the Constitution or laws of the United States, can, with no propriety, we think, be denominated a suit commenced or prosecuted against the State whose judgment is so far reexamined. Nothing is demanded from the State. No claim against it of any description is asserted or prosecuted. The party is not to be restored to the possession of anything. Essentially, it is an appeal on a single point, and the defendant who appeals from a judgment rendered against him is never said to commence or prosecute a suit against the plaintiff who has obtained the judgment. The writ of error is given, rather than an appeal, because it is the more usual mode of removing suits at common law, and because, perhaps, it is more technically proper where a single point of law, and not the whole case, is to be reexamined. But an appeal might be given, and might be so regulated as to effect every purpose of a writ of error. The mode of removal is form, and not substance. Whether it be by writ of error or appeal, no claim is asserted, no demand is made by the original defendant; he only asserts the constitutional right to have his defence examined by that tribunal whose province it is to construe the Constitution and laws of the Union.

The only part of the proceeding which is in any manner personal is the citation. And what is the citation? It is simply notice to the opposite party that the record is transferred into another Court, where he may appear, or decline to appear, as his judgment or inclination may determine. As the party who has obtained a judgment is out of Court, and may, therefore, not know that his cause is removed, common justice requires that notice of the fact should be given him. But this notice is not a suit, nor has it the effect of process. If the party does not choose to appear, he cannot be brought into Court, nor is his failure to appear considered as a default. Judgment cannot be given against him for his nonappearance, but the judgment is to be reexamined, and reversed or affirmed, in like manner as if the party had appeared and argued his cause.

The point of view in which this writ of error, with its citation, has been considered uniformly in the Courts of the Union has been well illustrated by a reference to the course of this Court in suits instituted by the United States. The universally received opinion is that no suit can be commenced or prosecuted against the United States; that the Judiciary Act does not authorize such suits. Yet writs of error, accompanied with citations, have uniformly issued for the removal of judgments in favour of the United States into a superior Court, where they have, like those in favour of an individual, been reexamined, and affirmed or reversed. It has never been suggested that such writ of error was a suit against the United States, and, therefore, not within the jurisdiction of the appellate Court.

It is, then, the opinion of the Court that the defendant who removes a judgment rendered against him by a State court into this Court for the purpose of reexamining the question whether that judgment be in violation of the Constitution or laws of the United States does not commence or prosecute a suit against the State, whatever may be its opinion where the effect of the writ may be to restore the party to the possession of a thing which he demands.

But should we in this be mistaken, the error does not affect the case now before the Court. If this writ of error be a suit in the sense of the Eleventh Amendment, it is not a suit commenced or prosecuted "by a citizen of another State, or by a citizen or subject of any foreign State." It is not then within the Amendment, but is governed entirely by the Constitution as originally framed, and we have already seen that, in its origin, the judicial power was extended to all cases arising under the Constitution or laws of the United States, without respect to parties.

2d. The second objection to the jurisdiction of the Court is that its appellate power cannot be exercised, in any case, over the judgment of a State court.

This objection is sustained chiefly by arguments drawn from the supposed total separation of the judiciary of a State from that of the Union, and their entire independence of each other. The argument considers the federal judiciary as completely foreign to that of a State, and as being no more connected with it in any respect whatever than the court of a foreign State. If this hypothesis be just, the argument founded on it is equally so; but if the hypothesis be not supported by the Constitution, the argument fails with it.

This hypothesis is not founded on any words in the Constitution which might seem to countenance it, but on the unreasonableness of giving a contrary construction to words which seem to require it, and on the incompatibility of the application of the appellate jurisdiction to the judgments of State courts with that constitutional relation which subsists between the government of the Union and the governments of those States which compose it.

Let this unreasonableness, this total incompatibility, be examined.

That the United States form, for many and for most important purposes, a single nation has not yet been denied. In war, we are one people. In making peace, we are one people. In all commercial regulations, we are one and the same people. In many other respects, the American people are one, and the government, which is alone capable of controlling and managing their interests in all these respects, is the government of the Union. It is their government, and in that character they have no other. America has chosen to be, in many respects, and to many purposes, a nation, and for all these purposes, her government is complete; to all these objects, it is competent. The people have declared that, in the exercise of all powers given for these objects, it is supreme. It can, then, in effecting these objects, legitimately control all individuals or governments within the American territory. The Constitution and laws of a State, so far as they are repugnant to the Constitution and laws of the United States, are absolutely void. These States are constituent parts of the United States. They are members of one great empire— for some purposes sovereign, for some purposes subordinate.

In a government so constituted, is it unreasonable that the judicial power should be competent to give efficacy to the constitutional laws of the legislature? That department can decide on the validity of the Constitution or law of a State, if it be repugnant to the Constitution or to a law of the United States. Is it unreasonable that it should also be empowered to decide on the judgment of a State tribunal enforcing such unconstitutional law? Is it so very unreasonable as to furnish a justification for controlling the words of the Constitution?

We think it is not. We think that, in a government acknowledgedly supreme, with respect to objects of vital interest to the nation, there is nothing inconsistent with sound reason, nothing incompatible with the nature of government, in making all its departments supreme so far as respects those objects and so far as is necessary to their attainment. The exercise of the appellate power over those judgments of the State tribunals which may contravene the Constitution or laws of the United States is, we believe, essential to the attainment of those objects.

The propriety of entrusting the construction of the Constitution, and laws made in pursuance thereof, to the judiciary of the Union has not, we believe, as yet, been drawn into question. It seems to be a corollary from this political axiom that the federal Courts should either possess exclusive jurisdiction in such cases, or a power to revise the judgment rendered in them, by the State tribunals. If the federal and State courts have concurrent jurisdiction in all cases arising under the Constitution, laws, and treaties of the United States, and if a case of this description brought in a State court cannot be removed before judgment, nor revised after judgment, then the construction of the Constitution, laws, and treaties of the United States is not confided particularly to their judicial department, but is confided equally to that department and to the State courts, however they may be constituted. "Thirteen independent Courts," says a very celebrated statesman (and we have now more than twenty such Courts)

"of final jurisdiction over the same causes, arising upon the same laws, is a hydra in government from which nothing but contradiction and confusion can proceed."

Dismissing the unpleasant suggestion that any motives which may not be fairly avowed, or which ought not to exist, can ever influence a State or its Courts, the necessity of uniformity, as well as correctness in expounding the Constitution and laws of the United States, would itself suggest the propriety of vesting in some single tribunal the power of deciding, in the last resort, all cases in which they are involved.

We are not restrained, then, by the political relations between the general and State governments from construing the words of the Constitution defining the judicial power in their true sense. We are not bound to construe them more restrictively than they naturally import.

They give to the Supreme Court appellate jurisdiction in all cases arising under the Constitution, laws, and treaties of the United States. The words are broad enough to comprehend all cases of this description, in whatever Court they may be decided. In expounding them, we may be permitted to take into view those considerations to which Courts have always allowed great weight in the exposition of laws.

The framers of the Constitution would naturally examine the state of things existing at the time, and their work sufficiently attests that they did so. All acknowledge that they were convened for the purpose of strengthening the confederation by enlarging the powers of the government, and by giving efficacy to those which it before possessed, but could not exercise. They inform us themselves, in the instrument they presented to the American public, that one of its objects was to form a more perfect union. Under such circumstances, we certainly should not expect to find, in that instrument, a diminution of the powers of the actual government.

Previous to the adoption of the confederation, Congress established Courts which received appeals in prize causes decided in the Courts of the respective States. This power of the government to establish tribunals for these appeals was thought consistent with, and was founded on, its political relations with the States. These Courts did exercise appellate jurisdiction over those cases decided in the State courts to which the judicial power of the federal government extended.

The confederation gave to Congress the power "of establishing Courts for receiving and determining finally appeals in all cases of captures."

This power was uniformly construed to authorize those Courts to receive appeals from the sentences of State courts, and to affirm or reverse them. State tribunals are not mentioned, but this clause in the confederation necessarily comprises them. Yet the relation between the general and State governments was much weaker, much more lax, under the confederation than under the present Constitution, and the States being much more completely sovereign, their institutions were much more independent.

The Convention which framed the Constitution, on turning their attention to the judicial power, found it limited to a few objects, but exercised, with respect to some of those objects, in its appellate form, over the judgments of the State courts. They extend it, among other objects, to all cases arising under the Constitution, laws, and treaties of the United States, and, in a subsequent clause, declare that, in such cases, the Supreme Court shall exercise appellate jurisdiction. Nothing seems to be given which would justify the withdrawal of a judgment rendered in a State court on the Constitution, laws, or treaties of the United States from this appellate jurisdiction.

Great weight has always been attached, and very rightly attached, to contemporaneous exposition. No question, it is believed, has arisen to which this principle applies more unequivocally than to that now under consideration.

The opinion of the Federalist has always been considered as of great authority. It is a complete commentary on our Constitution, and is appealed to by all parties in the questions to which that instrument has given birth. Its intrinsic merit entitles it to this high rank, and the part two of its authors performed in framing the Constitution put it very much in their power to explain the views with which it was framed. These essays having been published while the Constitution was before the nation for adoption or rejection, and having been written in answer to objections founded entirely on the extent of its powers, and on its diminution of State sovereignty, are entitled to the more consideration where they frankly avow that the power objected to is given, and defend it.

In discussing the extent of the judicial power, the Federalist says,

"Here another question occurs: what relation would subsist between the national and State courts in these instances of concurrent jurisdiction? I answer that an appeal would certainly lie from the latter to the Supreme Court of the United States. The Constitution in direct terms gives an appellate jurisdiction to the Supreme Court in all the enumerated cases of federal cognizance in which it is not to have an original one, without a single expression to confine its operation to the inferior federal Courts. The objects of appeal, not the tribunals from which it is to be made, are alone contemplated. From this circumstance, and from the reason of the thing, it ought to be construed to extend to the State tribunals. Either this must be the case or the local Courts must be excluded from a concurrent jurisdiction in matters of national concern, else the judicial authority of the Union may be eluded at the pleasure of every plaintiff or prosecutor. Neither of these consequences ought, without evident necessity, to be involved; the latter would be entirely inadmissible, as it would defeat some of the most important and avowed purposes of the proposed government, and would essentially embarrass its measures. Nor do I perceive any foundation for such a supposition. Agreeably to the remark already made, the national and State systems are to be regarded as ONE WHOLE. The Courts of the latter will, of course, be natural auxiliaries to the execution of the laws of the Union, and an appeal from them will as naturally lie to that tribunal which is destined to unite and assimilate the principles of natural justice, and the rules of national decision. The evident aim of the plan of the national convention is that all the causes of the specified classes shall, for weighty public reasons, receive their original or final determination in the Courts of the Union. To confine, therefore, the general expressions which give appellate jurisdiction to the Supreme Court to appeals from the subordinate federal Courts, instead of allowing their extension to the State courts, would be to abridge the latitude of the terms, in subversion of the intent, contrary to every sound rule of interpretation."

A contemporaneous exposition of the Constitution, certainly of not less authority than that which has been just cited, is the Judiciary Act itself. We know that in the Congress which passed that Act were many eminent members of the Convention which formed the Constitution. Not a single individual, so far as is known, supposed that part of the Act which gives the Supreme Court appellate jurisdiction over the judgments of the State courts in the cases therein specified to be unauthorized by the Constitution.

While on this part of the argument, it may be also material to observe that the uniform decisions of this Court on the point now under consideration have been assented to, with a single exception, by the Courts of every State in the Union whose judgments have been revised. It has been the unwelcome duty of this tribunal to reverse the judgments of many State courts in cases in which the strongest State feelings were engaged. Judges, whose talents and character would grace any bench, to whom a disposition to submit to jurisdiction that is usurped, or to surrender their legitimate powers, will certainly not be imputed, have yielded without hesitation to the authority by which their judgments were reversed, while they perhaps disapproved the judgment of reversal.

This concurrence of statesmen, of legislators, and of judges, in the same construction of the Constitution may justly inspire some confidence in that construction.

In opposition to it, the counsel who made this point has presented in a great variety of forms the idea, already noticed, that the federal and State courts must, of necessity and from the nature of the Constitution, be in all things totally distinct and independent of each other. If this Court can correct the errors of the Court of Virginia, he says, it makes them Courts of the United States, or becomes itself a part of the judiciary of Virginia.

But it has been already shown that neither of these consequences necessarily follows. The American people may certainly give to a national tribunal a supervising power over those judgments of the State courts which may conflict with the Constitution, laws, or treaties, of the United States without converting them into federal Courts or converting the national into a State tribunal. The one Court still derives its authority from the State; the other still derives its authority from the nation.

If it shall be established, he says that this Court has appellate jurisdiction over the State courts in all cases enumerated in the 3d article of the Constitution, a complete consolidation of the States, so far as respects judicial power is produced.

But certainly the mind of the gentleman who urged this argument is too accurate not to perceive that he has carried it too far; that the premises by no means justify the conclusion. "A complete consolidation of the States, so far as respects the judicial power," would authorize the legislature to confer on the federal Courts appellate jurisdiction from the State courts in all cases

whatsoever. The distinction between such a power and that of giving appellate jurisdiction in a few specified cases in the decision of which the nation takes an interest is too obvious not to be perceived by all.

This opinion has been already drawn out to too great a length to admit of entering into a particular consideration of the various forms in which the counsel who made this point has, with much ingenuity, presented his argument to the Court. The argument in all its forms is essentially the same. It is founded not on the words of the Constitution, but on its spirit— a spirit extracted not from the words of the instrument, but from his view of the nature of our Union and of the great fundamental principles on which the fabric stands.

To this argument, in all its forms, the same answer may be given. Let the nature and objects of our Union be considered; let the great fundamental principles on which the fabric stands be examined; and we think the result must be that there is nothing so extravagantly absurd in giving to the Court of the nation the power of revising the decisions of local tribunals on questions which affect the nation as to require that words which import this power should be restricted by a forced construction. The question then must depend on the words themselves, and on their construction we shall be the more readily excused for not adding to the observations already made, because the subject was fully discussed and exhausted in the case of *Martin v. Hunter.*

3d. We come now to the third objection, which, though differently stated by the counsel, is substantially the same. One gentleman has said that the Judiciary Act does not give jurisdiction in the case.

The cause was argued in the State court, on a case agreed by the parties, which states the prosecution under a law for selling lottery tickets, which is set forth, and further states the act of Congress by which the City of Washington was authorized to establish the lottery. It then states that the lottery was regularly established by virtue of the act, and concludes with referring to the Court the questions, whether the act of Congress be valid? whether, on its just construction, it constitutes a bar to the prosecution? and, whether the act of Assembly, on which the prosecution is founded, be not itself invalid? These questions were decided against the operation of the act of Congress and in favour of the operation of the act of the State.

If the twenty-fifth section of the Judiciary Act be inspected, it will at once be perceived that it comprehends expressly the case under consideration.

But it is not upon the letter of the Act that the gentleman who stated this point in this form founds his argument. Both gentlemen concur substantially in their views of this part of the case. They deny that the act of Congress on which the plaintiff in error relies is a law of the United States; or, if a law of the United States, is within the second clause of the sixth article.

In the enumeration of the powers of Congress, which is made in the eighth section of the first article, we find that of exercising exclusive legislation over such District as shall become the seat of government. This power, like all others which are specified, is conferred on Congress as the legislature of the Union, for, strip them of that character and they would not possess it. In no other character can it be exercised. In legislating for the District, they necessarily preserve the character of the legislature of the Union, for it is in that character alone that the Constitution confers on them this power of exclusive legislation. This proposition need not be enforced.

The second clause of the sixth article declares that "This Constitution, and the laws of the United States, which shall be made in pursuance thereof, shall be the supreme law of the land."

The clause which gives exclusive jurisdiction is, unquestionably, a part of the Constitution, and, as such, binds all the United States. Those who contend that acts of Congress, made in pursuance of this power, do not, like acts made in pursuance of other powers, bind the nation ought to show some safe and clear rule which shall support this construction, and prove that an act of Congress, clothed in all the forms which attend other legislative acts and passed in virtue of a power conferred on, and exercised by Congress as the legislature of the Union, is not a law of the United States and does not bind them.

One of the gentlemen sought to illustrate his proposition that Congress, when legislating for the District, assumed a distinct character, and was reduced to a mere local legislature whose laws could possess no obligation out of the ten miles square, by a reference to the complex character of this Court. It is, they say, a Court of common law and a Court of equity. Its

character, when sitting as a Court of common law, is as distinct from its character when sitting as a Court of equity as if the powers belonging to those departments were vested in different tribunals. Though united in the same tribunal, they are never confounded with each other.

Without inquiring how far the union of different characters in one court, may be applicable, in principle, to the union in Congress of the power of exclusive legislation in some places and of limited legislation in others, it may be observed that the forms of proceedings in a court of law are so totally unlike the forms of proceedings in a court of equity that a mere inspection of the record gives decisive information of the character in which the court sits, and consequently of the extent of its powers. But if the forms of proceeding were precisely the same, and the court the same, the distinction would disappear.

Since Congress legislates in the same forms, and in the same character, in virtue of powers of equal obligation, conferred in the same instrument, when exercising its exclusive powers of legislation as well as when exercising those which are limited, we must inquire whether there be anything in the nature of this exclusive legislation which necessarily confines the operation of the laws made in virtue of this power to the place with a view to which they are made.

Connected with the power to legislate within this District is a similar power in forts, arsenals, dock yards, &c. Congress has a right to punish murder in a fort or other place within its exclusive jurisdiction, but no general right to punish murder committed within any of the States. In the act for the punishment of crimes against the United States, murder committed within a fort, or any other place or district of country under the sole and exclusive jurisdiction of the United States, is punished with death. Thus, Congress legislates in the same act under its exclusive and its limited powers.

The act proceeds to direct that the body of the criminal, after execution, may be delivered to a surgeon for dissection, and punishes any person who shall rescue such body during its conveyance from the place of execution to the surgeon to whom it is to be delivered.

Let these actual provisions of the law, or any other provisions which can be made on the subject, be considered with a view to the character in which Congress acts when exercising its powers of exclusive legislation.

If Congress is to be considered merely as a local legislature, invested, as to this object, with powers limited to the fort or other place in which the murder may be committed, if its general powers cannot come in aid of these local powers, how can the offence be tried in any other court than that of the place in which it has been committed? How can the offender be conveyed to, or tried in, any other place? How can he be executed elsewhere? How can his body be conveyed through a country under the jurisdiction of another sovereign, and the individual punished, who, within that jurisdiction, shall rescue the body.

Were any one State of the Union to pass a law for trying a criminal in a court not created by itself, in a place not within its jurisdiction, and direct the sentence to be executed without its territory, we should all perceive and acknowledge its incompetency to such a course of legislation. If Congress be not equally incompetent, it is because that body unites the powers of local legislation with those which are to operate through the Union, and may use the last in aid of the first, or because the power of exercising exclusive legislation draws after it, as an incident, the power of making that legislation effectual, and the incidental power may be exercised throughout the Union, because the principal power is given to that body as the legislature of the Union.

So, in the same act, a person who, having knowledge of the commission of murder or other felony on the high seas or within any fort, arsenal, dock yard, magazine, or other place, or district of country within the sole and exclusive jurisdiction of the United States shall conceal the same, &c., he shall be adjudged guilty of misprision of felony, and shall be adjudged to be imprisoned, &c.

It is clear that Congress cannot punish felonies generally, and, of consequence, cannot punish misprision of felony. It is equally clear that a State legislature, the State of Maryland for example, cannot punish those who, in another State, conceal a felony committed in Maryland. How, then, is it that Congress, legislating exclusively for a fort, punishes those who, out of that fort, conceal a felony committed within it?

The solution, and the only solution of the difficulty, is that the power vested in Congress, as the legislature of the United States, to legislate exclusively within any place ceded by a State, carries with it, as an incident, the right to make that power effectual. If a felon escape out of the State in which the act has been committed, the government cannot pursue him into another State and apprehend him there, but must demand him from the executive power of that other State. If Congress were to be considered merely as the local legislature for the fort or other place in which the offence might be committed, then this principle would apply to them as to other local legislatures, and the felon who should escape out of the fort or other place in which the felony may have been committed could not be apprehended by the marshal, but must be demanded from the executive of the State. But we know that the principle does not apply; and the reason is that Congress is not a local legislature, but exercises this particular power, like all its other powers, in its high character as the legislature of the Union. The American people thought it a necessary power, and they conferred it for their own benefit. Being so conferred, it carries with it all those incidental powers which are necessary to its complete and effectual execution.

Whether any particular law be designed to operate without the District or not depends on the words of that law. If it be designed so to operate, then the question, whether the power so exercised be incidental to the power of exclusive legislation, and be warranted by the Constitution, requires a consideration of that instrument. In such cases, the Constitution and the law must be compared and construed. This is the exercise of jurisdiction. It is the only exercise of it which is allowed in such a case. For the act of Congress directs that

"no other error shall be assigned or regarded as a ground or reversal, in any such case as aforesaid, than such as appears on the face of the record, and immediately respects the before mentioned questions of validity or construction of the said Constitution, treaties,"

&c.

The whole merits of this case, then, consist in the construction of the Constitution and the act of Congress.

The jurisdiction of the Court, if acknowledged, goes no farther. This we are required to do without the exercise of jurisdiction.

The counsel for the State of Virginia have, in support of this motion, urged many arguments of great weight against the application of the act of Congress to such a case as this, but those arguments go to the construction of the Constitution, or of the law, or of both, and seem, therefore, rather calculated to sustain their cause upon its merits than to prove a failure of jurisdiction in the Court.

After having bestowed upon this question the most deliberate consideration of which we are capable, the Court is unanimously of opinion that the objections to its jurisdiction are not sustained, and that the motion ought to be overruled.

*Motion denied.*

March 2d.

The cause was this day argued on the merits.

### *The opinion of the Court was delivered by MR. CHIEF JUSTICE MARSHALL*

This case was stated in the opinion given on the motion for dismissing the writ of error for want of jurisdiction in the Court. It now comes on to be decided on the question whether the Borough Court of Norfolk, in overruling the defence set up under the act of Congress, has misconstrued that act. It is in these words:

"The said Corporation shall have full power to authorize the drawing of lotteries for effecting any important improvement in the City, which the ordinary funds or revenue thereof will not accomplish: Provided that the sum to be raised in each year shall not exceed the amount of 10,000 dollars: And provided, also that the object for which the money is intended to be raised shall be first submitted to the President of the United States, and shall be approved of by him."

Two questions arise on this act.

1st. Does it purport to authorize the Corporation to force the sale of these lottery tickets in States where such sales may be prohibited by law? If it does,

2d. Is the law constitutional?

If the first question be answered in the affirmative, it will become necessary to consider the second. If it should be answered in the negative, it will be unnecessary, and consequently improper, to pursue any inquiries, which would then be merely speculative, respecting the power of Congress in the case.

In inquiring into the extent of the power granted to the Corporation of Washington, we must first examine the words of the grant. We find in them no expression which looks beyond the limits of the City. The powers granted are all of them local in their nature, and all of them such as would, in the common course of things, if not necessarily, be exercised within the city. The subject on which Congress was employed when framing this act was a local subject; it was not the establishment of a lottery, but the formation of a separate body for the management of the internal affairs of the City, for its internal government, for its police. Congress must have considered itself as delegating to this corporate body powers for these objects, and for these objects solely. In delegating these powers, therefore, it seems reasonable to suppose that the mind of the legislature was directed to the City alone, to the action of the being they were creating within the City, and not to any extraterritorial operations. In describing the powers of such a being, no words of limitation need be used. They are limited by the subject. But, if it be intended to give its acts a binding efficacy beyond the natural limits of its power, and within the jurisdiction of a distinct power, we should expect to find, in the language of the incorporating act, some words indicating such intention.

Without such words, we cannot suppose that Congress designed to give to the acts of the Corporation any other effect beyond its limits than attends every act having the sanction of local law when anything depends upon it which is to be transacted elsewhere.

If this would be the reasonable construction of corporate powers generally, it is more especially proper in a case where an attempt is made so to exercise those powers as to control and limit the penal laws of a State. This is an operation which was not, we think, in the contemplation of the legislature, while incorporating the City of Washington.

To interfere with the penal laws of a State, where they are not leveled against the legitimate powers of the Union, but have for their sole object the internal government of the country, is a very serious measure which Congress cannot be supposed to adopt lightly or inconsiderately. The motives for it must be serious and weighty. It would be taken deliberately, and the intention would be clearly and unequivocally expressed.

An act such as that under consideration ought not, we think, to be so construed as to imply this intention unless its provisions were such as to render the construction inevitable.

We do not think it essential to the corporate power in question that it should be exercised out of the City. Could the lottery be drawn in any State of the Union? Does the corporate power to authorize the drawing of a lottery imply a power to authorize its being drawn without the jurisdiction of a Corporation, in a place where it may be prohibited by law? This, we think, would scarcely be asserted. And what clear legal distinction can be taken between a power to draw a lottery in a place where it is prohibited by law and a power to establish an office for the sale of tickets in a place where it is prohibited by law? It may be urged that the place where the lottery is drawn is of no importance to the Corporation, and therefore the act need not be so construed as to give power over the place, but that the right to sell tickets throughout the United States is of importance, and therefore ought to be implied.

That the power to sell tickets in every part of the United States might facilitate their sale is not to be denied, but it does not follow that Congress designed, for the purpose of giving this increased facility, to overrule the penal laws of the several States. In the City of Washington, the great metropolis of the nation, visited by individuals from every part of the Union, tickets may be freely sold to all who are willing to purchase. Can it be affirmed that this is so limited a market that the incorporating act must be extended beyond its words, and made to conflict with the internal police of the States, unless it be construed to give a more extensive market?

It has been said that the States cannot make it unlawful to buy that which Congress has made it lawful to sell.

This proposition is not denied, and therefore the validity of a law punishing a citizen of Virginia for purchasing a ticket in the City of Washington might well be drawn into question. Such a law would be a direct attempt to counteract and defeat a measure authorized by the United States. But a law to punish the sale of lottery tickets in Virginia is of a different character. Before we can impeach its validity, we must inquire

whether Congress intended to empower this Corporation to do any act within a State which the laws of that State might prohibit.

In addition to the very important circumstance that the act contains no words indicating such intention, and that this extensive construction is not essential to the execution of the corporate power, the Court cannot resist the conviction that the intention ascribed to this act, had it existed, would have been executed by very different means from those which have been employed.

Had Congress intended to establish a lottery for those improvements in the City which are deemed national, the lottery itself would have become the subject of legislative consideration. It would be organized by law, and agents for its execution would be appointed by the President or in such other manner as the law might direct. If such agents were to act out of the District, there would be, probably, some provision made for such a state of things, and, in making such provisions, Congress would examine its power to make them. The whole subject would be under the control of the government, or of persons appointed by the government.

But in this case, no lottery is established by law, no control is exercised by the government over any which may be established. The lottery emanates from a corporate power. The Corporation may authorize or not authorize it, and may select the purposes to which the proceeds are to be applied. This Corporation is a being intended for local objects only. All its capacities are limited to the City. This, as well as every other law it is capable of making, is a by-law, and, from its nature, is only coextensive with the City. It is not probable that such an agent would be employed in the execution of a lottery established by Congress; but when it acts not as the agent for carrying into effect a lottery established by Congress, but in its own corporate capacity, from its own corporate powers, it is reasonable to suppose that its acts were intended to partake of the nature of that capacity and of those powers and, like all its other acts, be merely local in its nature.

The proceeds of these lotteries are to come in aid of the revenues of the City. These revenues are raised by laws whose operation is entirely local, and for objects which are also local, for no person will suppose that the President's house, the Capitol, the Navy Yard, or other public institution was to be benefitted by these lotteries, or was to form a charge on the City revenue. Coming in aid of the City revenue, they are of the same character with it— the mere creature of a corporate power.

The circumstances that the lottery cannot be drawn without the permission of the President, and that this resource is to be used only for important improvements, have been relied on as giving to this corporate power a more extensive operation than is given to those with which it is associated. We do not think so.

The President has no agency in the lottery. It does not originate with him, nor is the improvement to which its profits are to be applied to be selected by him. Congress has not enlarged the corporate power by restricting its exercise to cases of which the President might. approve.

We very readily admit that the act establishing the seat of government, and the act appointing commissioners to superintend the public buildings, are laws of universal obligation. We admit too that the laws of any State to defeat the loan authorized by Congress would have been void, as would have been any attempt to arrest the progress of the canal, or of any other measure which Congress may adopt. These, and all other laws relative to the District have the authority which may be claimed by other acts of the national legislature, but their extent is to be determined by those rules of construction which are applicable to all laws. The act incorporating the City of Washington is unquestionably of universal obligation; but the extent of the corporate powers conferred by that act is to be determined by those considerations which belong to the case.

Whether we consider the general character of a law incorporating a City, the objects for which such law is usually made, or the words in which this particular power is conferred, we arrive at the same result. The Corporation was merely empowered to authorize the drawing of lotteries, and the mind of Congress was not directed to any provision for the sale of the tickets beyond the limits of the Corporation. That subject does not seem to have been taken into view. It is the unanimous opinion of the Court that the law cannot be construed to embrace it.

*Judgment affirmed.*

---

### Glossary

**commerce clause:** a section of the Constitution (Article I, Section 8, Clause 3) that grants Congress the power to regulate interstate business and trade

**contravene:** contradict; violate

**the Corporation:** a reference to the city of Washington, D.C., which had been "incorporated" by Congress

**jurisdiction:** the power to hear a case

**sovereign:** independent; self-governing

**subordinate:** controlled by an authority

**tribunal:** court or judicial authority

# GIBBONS V. OGDEN

| DATE | CITATION |
|---|---|
| 1824 | 22 U.S. 1 |

| AUTHOR | SIGNIFICANCE |
|---|---|
| John Marshall; William Johnson | Addressed the issue of interstate commerce and upheld the right of Congress to regulate travel between state lines |

| VOTE | |
|---|---|
| 6-0 | |

## Overview

 The U.S. Supreme Court case *Thomas Gibbons v. Aaron Ogden* (1824), often referred to as the steamboat monopoly case, is consistently ranked by historians as one of the most important landmark decisions in American jurisprudence. *Gibbons v. Ogden* represented the first Supreme Court case to tackle the thorny issue of interstate commerce and upheld the right of Congress to regulate travel between state lines. The case originated with the development of steam travel in New York. In 1798 the state chancellor Robert R. Livingston secured a legislative monopoly on steam travel in New York waters. In 1807 Livingston and his partner, the famous inventor Robert Fulton, successfully launched their prototype *North River Steam Boat* on the Hudson River.

In 1815 Fulton and the Livingston family granted the former New Jersey governor Aaron Ogden a license under the monopoly to run steamboats from Elizabethtown, New Jersey, to New York City. In 1819 Ogden sued his former partner, the Georgia businessman Thomas Gibbons, in the New York Court of Chancery for operating steamboats in New York harbor. Gibbons coun-

tered that he possessed a federal coasting license that gave him the right to conduct business in any American port, but the New York chancellor James Kent repeatedly upheld Ogden's monopoly license. Gibbons then hired the U.S. senator Daniel Webster and the U.S. attorney general William Wirt to appeal his case to the Supreme Court. Ogden secured the services of the former New York attorneys general Thomas Addis Emmet and Thomas Oakley. After extensive deliberations, on March 2, 1824, Chief Justice John Marshall ruled that Gibbons's federal coasting license invalidated Ogden's monopoly permit. The associate justice William Johnson argued in a concurring opinion that Congress's commerce powers alone defeated the New York monopoly.

The *Gibbons v. Ogden* case interested many Americans because it involved the widely popular issue of steam travel. Gibbons, Ogden, and the legal elites involved in the case believed that steam power was vital to the commercial and social development of the young nation. Working-class Americans likewise eagerly followed stories of the case in local spapers. Although Marshall's broad decision was found favorable by the public, it ultimately failed to fully outline federal com-

**Aaron Ogden**
(Asher Brown Durand)

merce powers. *Gibbons* became a legal precedent invoked by temperance supporters, labor leaders, civil rights demonstrators, and gun-control supporters.

## Context

*Gibbons v. Ogden* occurred against a backdrop of rapid economic and social change in the young United States. Following the Revolutionary War, millions of Americans moved west across the Appalachian Mountains to settle in the ly available lands of the Midwest and Old Southwest. The American public thus became interested in er and faster forms of transportation. Steam power had already been successfully used in Great Britain to pump water out of mines and operate looms in factories. Early American inventors like John Fitch and James Rumsey hoped to build functioning steamboats that would further aid in the westward expansion of the United States.

After the War of 1812, the United States entered a full-blown "transportation revolution," involving widespread support for steam power, canals, turnpikes, and public roads. Under the leadership of the Kentucky senator Henry Clay, Congress launched a formidable array of internal improvements, dubbed the American System, designed to link the different economic sections of the nation together into a seamless whole. At the state level, the New York governor DeWitt Clinton took the lead in promoting the Erie Canal, an ambitious attempt to connect the Hudson River to the Great Lakes and thus make New York City the leading port in the fledgling nation.

Steamboat entrepreneurs like Fitch, Rumsey, and Fulton had to secure resources, patrons, and legal protection in an ad hoc manner. Given the weakness of federal patent laws, they sought state monopolies that gave them exclusive rights to steam travel at the local level. As steamboats became more widely available, competitors emerged to challenge these monopolies. This led to a series of lawsuits in state and federal courts, which became a morass of unresolved litigation. Meanwhile, the public clamored for cheaper steamboat fares and better service. The federal government in general and the Supreme Court in particular were reluctant to become involved in such an explosive issue, yet the persistence of Aaron Ogden and Thomas Gibbons in pursuing their legal conflict through the federal courts prompted the ultimate intervention of the Supreme Court in 1824.

## About the Author

John Marshall was born near Germantown, in the "northern neck" region of western Virginia, on September 24, 1755. Marshall was the eldest of fifteen children in a family of minor frontier gentry. His mother, Mary Randolph Keith, was a cousin of Thomas Jefferson's. As a member of a landholding family, Marshall learned to function in the informal political world of the frontier. In 1775 Marshall volunteered for service in the Continental army and served with distinction in several battles before surviving a brutal winter at Valley Forge. The challenges of holding the army together and negotiating with squabbling state officials for precious resources fueled Marshall's beliefs in a strong federal union and an effective central government. In 1780 Marshall briefly studied law at the College of William and Mary before returning to the army in 1781.

In 1783, at the close of the American Revolution, Marshall married Mary Willis Ambler and pursued a career as an attorney in Richmond, Virginia. Marshall's charisma and sharp legal mind helped him secure positions in the Virginia House of Delegates and in the governor's Council of State. Marshall became a staunch Federalist and enthusiastic supporter of his former military comrades George Washington and Alexander Hamilton. In 1788 Marshall served as a delegate to the Virginia ratifying convention, where he strongly urged the adoption of the U.S. Constitution. Following the creation of the fledgling federal government, Marshall turned down offers to serve as Washington's attorney general, as ambassador to France, and as an associate justice of the U.S. Supreme Court. In 1797 President John Adams appointed Marshall, Charles Pinckney, and Elbridge Gerry to serve as delegates on a diplomatic mission to France. Rejecting demands from French officials for hefty bribes in what became known as the XYZ Affair, Marshall returned to the United States to a hero's welcome. In 1798 he successfully ran for Congress, where he became a key defender of Adams's moderate brand of federalism. Two years later Marshall began a brief stint as secretary of state. In the aftermath of Adams's defeat to Thomas Jefferson in the presidential election of 1800, the incumbent president hastily nominated Marshall to serve as chief justice of the United States.

Marshall would become the longest-serving chief justice in American history, dominating the Supreme Court until his death in 1835. With the assistance of colleagues such as Joseph Story and Bushrod Washington, Marshall handed down a series of landmark decisions that upheld federal power and established the reputation of the federal judiciary as a truly coequal branch of government. In *Fletcher v. Peck* (1810), Marshall asserted that the Georgia state legislature had to recognize the validity of land claims by out-of-state speculators, even though the sale of such land involved the wholesale bribery of state legislators. Furthermore, in *Martin v. Hunter's Lessee* (1816) Marshall recognized British land claims that had been confiscated by Virginia officials during the American Revolution. In *Trustees of Dartmouth College v. Woodward* (1819) the chief justice upheld Dartmouth's state charter as a contract that could not be changed by the New Hampshire legislature.

Although Marshall strove to deliver unanimous court opinions whenever possible, he often clashed with the associate justice William Johnson over points of law. Born in South Carolina in 1771, Johnson sprang from working-class roots. He attended Princeton, became an attorney, and served three terms as a Republican congressman, briefly serving as Speaker of the House

**Thomas Gibbons**
(Wikimedia Commons)

of Representatives. In 1802 President Thomas Jefferson appointed Johnson to the Supreme Court, primarily to counterbalance the nationalist tendencies of John Marshall. Johnson, however, proved to be an independent figure, defying both Marshall and Jefferson on several occasions. For example, in *Gibbons v. Ogden*, Johnson issued a concurring opinion that argued that the commerce clause of the Constitution, the ultimate authority behind Gibbons's coasting license, invalidated the New York monopoly on its face.

## Explanation and Analysis of the Document

### *"Mr. Chief Justice Marshall Delivered the Opinion of the Court"*

Pages 186–222 of the record of *Gibbons v. Ogden* recount John Marshall's delivery of the unanimous decision in *Gibbons v. Ogden* against Aaron Ogden, delivered on March 2, 1824. Marshall begins by acknowledging that the monopoly had been supported "by names which have all the titles to consideration that virtue, intelligence, and office, can bestow," yet the Supreme Court still had the constitutional obligation to hear the case. He then upholds a broad view of the Constitution, stating that all power over interstate commerce had been given to Congress with the ratification of the Constitution. Out of necessity, the Constitution gave the federal government broad powers; to limit Congress to its enumerated powers "would cripple the government and render it unequal to the object for which it is declared to be instituted." In plain language, the Founders had granted Congress the power to "regulate commerce with foreign nations, and among the several States, and with the Indian tribes." They had understood that "commerce, undoubtedly, is traffic, but it is something more: it is intercourse." As such, Congress could regulate both the buying and selling of goods and the transportation of passengers and cargo across state lines. Since such commerce occurred "among" or "intermingled" with the states, congressional commerce power could "not stop at the external boundary line of each State, but may be introduced into the interior." Marshall concedes that states could pass safety or inspection laws based on their police powers. However, this did not give them concurrent powers over interstate commerce. Congress could recognize such state regulations and even give them the status of federal law as needed, but Congress still maintained ultimate control over interstate trade.

Marshall briefly considers whether the commerce clause by itself is enough to invalidate all attempts at concurrent state regulation. Nevertheless, the central point remains whether the New York monopoly impeded congressional authority. The Coasting Trade and Fisheries Act of 1793 gave registered vessels not only the status of American ships but also the right to travel between ports in different states. The act makes no mention of what such ships might be carrying in their holds or how they might be powered. Marshall concludes with a condemnation of states' rights activists who supported the monopoly, referring to them as "powerful and ingenious minds, taking as postulates that the powers expressly granted to the government of the Union are to be contracted by construction into the narrowest possible compass." Such individuals, Marshall warns, would "explain away the constitution

of our country and leave it a magnificent structure, indeed, to look at, but totally unfit for use." The New York steamboat monopoly, he concludes, is unconstitutional and invalid.

### "Mr. Justice Johnson"

Pages 222–239 recount Justice William Johnson's concurring opinion in *Gibbons v. Ogden*. He begins with an expression of support for Marshall's decision and then stresses the need to state his own views on the matter. Johnson eschews both broad and strict interpretations of the Constitution, stating that the "simple, classical, precise, yet comprehensive language in which it is couched leaves, at most, but very little latitude for construction." The Founders had created the Constitution to "unite this mass of wealth and power, for the protection of the humblest individual, his rights, civil and political, his interests and prosperity, are the sole end; the rest are nothing but the means." To overcome the economic rivalries of the era of the Articles of Confederation, the framers had given Congress extensive and complete control over interstate commerce. Such power obviously included the right to regulate navigation and commerce. This broad authority automatically swept away the New York monopoly, regardless of the Coasting Trade and Fisheries Act of 1793. In fact, Congress had created the coasting act to promote national trade, making any attempts at state regulation moot. To be certain, federal and state commerce powers intersected in some cases: "Wherever the powers of the respective governments are frankly exercised, with a distinct view to the ends of such powers, they may act upon the same object, or use the same means, and yet the powers be kept perfectly distinct." Ultimately, however, state power had to give way to federal authority. After concluding his defense of federal commerce powers, Johnson begs off a discussion on federal patent law.

### "Decree"

The case concludes on page 239 with John Marshall's decree of the Supreme Court. He reexamines the background of the case and his own decision, concluding that the Coasting Trade and Fisheries Act of 1793 granted Gibbons the right to trade in New York waters, state laws notwithstanding. The New York steamboat monopoly was accordingly "erroneous, and ought to be reversed, and the same is hereby reversed and annulled:

and this Court doth further DIRECT, ORDER, and DECREE that the bill of the said Aaron Ogden be dismissed, and this same is hereby dismissed accordingly."

## Impact

Public reaction to *Gibbons v. Ogden* was overwhelmingly positive. Within a month of Marshall's decision, twenty steamboats were operating in New York waters, many from other states. Middling Americans such as businessmen, merchants, artisans, and farmers quickly took advantage of the cheaper fares and better service brought by the destruction of the monopoly. Northern and western spapers cheered the *Gibbons* decision as a victory for free trade over special interests, for social progress over provincialism. Many southerners likewise reacted favorably to the decision, although some worried that the case could prove a dangerous precedent regarding federal regulation of the interstate slave trade.

Marshall's decision in *Gibbons v. Ogden* left many issues unclear, and the particular issue of state versus federal control of commerce continued to appear before the Supreme Court. By the 1830s and 1840s, as public attention shifted from economic matters to social reform, popular perceptions of the *Gibbons* case began to change. Both social elites and ordinary citizens increasingly discussed the possibility of regulating commerce to protect public "morals" as well as public safety and property rights. Legal documents and spaper accounts show that in the Court of Chief Justice Roger Taney, in cases such as *Mayor of New York v. Miln* (1837), *Groves v. Slaughter* (1841), the License Cases (1847), and the Passenger Cases (1849), state lawyers cited *Gibbons v. Ogden* to make the case for regulation in controversial issues as disparate as immigration, alcohol, and slavery within their states. In these and other cases, *Gibbons v. Ogden*, originally a decision designed to limit state authority, ironically helped mold society at the local level with the tacit approval of the federal court system. By the eve of the Civil War, *Gibbons v. Ogden* had thus helped to stimulate a national economy but had also been used as a model for a culture of social regulation.

Throughout the late nineteenth and early twentieth centuries, *Gibbons v. Ogden* continued to play a pivotal role in the ongoing controversy over commerce regulation. For instance, during the Gilded Age, the Supreme Court preserved a system of dual federalism by repeatedly citing *Gibbons v. Ogden* both to expand federal commerce power, such as in *Wabash, St. Louis & Pacific Railroad Co. v. Illinois* (1886), and to limit that authority, such as in *United States v. E. C. Knight Co.* (1895). In *Northern Securities Co. v. United States* (1904), the associate justice Harlan Stone took tentative steps to consider the motives behind state and federal trade regulation rather than simply the actual movement of goods and individuals. Following the Supreme Court decisions in *A. L. A. Schechter Poultry Corporation v. United States* (1935) and *United States v. Butler* (1936), President Franklin D. Roosevelt's court-packing scheme prompted the Court to retreat from the aspect of dual federalism limiting the national government. In language reminiscent of the state-based regulation movements of the nineteenth century, the Supreme Court increasingly broadened congressional commerce powers to encourage social reform.

Over the next sixty years the *Gibbons* decision became a precedent for cases involving segregation, such as *Heart of Atlanta Motel, Inc. v. United States* (1964), and labor issues, such as *Garcia v. San Antonio Metropolitan Transit Authority* (1985). The Rehnquist Court rejected a broad interpretation of *Gibbons v. Ogden* beginning with *United States v. Lopez* (1995), in which a federal commerce law banning handguns from school zones was struck down. This ruling sparked a reed public interest in *Gibbons v. Ogden* and how the memory of that case had changed over time. Above all, *Lopez* demonstrated the continuing relevance of the steamboat monopoly case to the ongoing debate over commerce regulation as an instrument both of economic development and of social change within a federalist framework.

## Questions for Further Study

1. Americans first began experimenting with steam power in the 1780s, and Robert Fulton produced the first practical steamboat in 1807. Nevertheless, nearly two more decades passed before the Supreme Court addressed the issues contained in *Gibbons v. Ogden*. Given the public interest in steam travel and the lucrative profits to be made from steamboat lines, why did so much time elapse before the legal conflict over steamboats reached the nation's highest court?

2. Why did litigants, attorneys, and justices involved in *Gibbons v. Ogden* center most of their arguments on factors such as federal commerce power and state monopolies instead of the rather obvious issue of federal patent rights? What about the issue of patents made it such a controversial or irrelevant topic?

3. Why did neither John Marshall nor William Johnson issue specific guidelines for federal and state commerce regulation? Could the justices' reasons have had anything to do with the explosive issue of slavery?

4. In the 1930s, New Deal attorneys argued that *Gibbons v. Ogden* foreshadowed the rise of a strong federal government with the ability to regulate not merely economic policies but also social reform across state lines. Is this a valid interpretation of Marshall's decision?

## Further Reading

### Books

Appleby, Joyce O. *Capitalism and a New Social Order: The Republican Vision of the 1790s.* New York: New York University Press, 1984.

Baxter, Maurice G. *The Steamboat Monopoly: Gibbons v. Ogden,* 1824. New York: Knopf, 1972.

Bruchey, Stuart. *Enterprise: The Dynamic Economy of a Free People.* Cambridge, MA: Harvard University Press, 1990.

Cox, Thomas H. *Gibbons v. Ogden, Law, and Society in the Early Republic.* Athens: Ohion University Press, 2009.

Currie, David P. *The Constitution in the Supreme Court: The First Hundred Years, 1789–1888.* Chicago: University of Chicago Press, 1985.

Garraty, John A., ed. *Quarrels That Have Shaped the Constitution.* New York: Perennial Library, 1987.

Gilje, Paul A., ed. *Wages of Independence: Capitalism in the Early American Republic.* Madison, WI: Madison House, 1997.

Hobson, Charles F. *The Great Chief Justice: John Marshall and the Rule of Law.* Lawrence: University Press of Kansas, 1996.

Horwitz, Morton J. *The Transformation of American Law, 1780–1860.* Cambridge, MA: Harvard University Press, 1977.

## Further Reading

### Books

Johnson, Herbert A. *The Chief Justiceship of John Marshall, 1801–1835.* Columbia: University of South Carolina Press, 1997.

Johnson, Herbert A. *Gibbons v. Ogden: John Marshall, Steamboats, and the Commerce Clause.* Lawrence: University Press of Kansas, 2010.

Kammen, Michael. *A Machine That Would Go of Itself: The Constitution in American Culture.* New Brunswick, NJ: Transaction Publishers, 2006.

Newmyer, R. Kent. *Supreme Court Justice Joseph Story: Statesman of the Old Republic.* Chapel Hill: University of North Carolina Press, 1985.

Sellers, Charles. *The Market Revolution: Jacksonian America, 1815–1846.* New York: Oxford University Press, 1991.

Stokes, Melvyn, and Stephen Conway, eds. *The Market Revolution in America: Social, Political, and Religious Expressions, 1800–1880.* Charlottesville: University Press of Virginia, 1996.

Urofsky, Melvin. "The Case of the Rival Steamboat Operator." In *Supreme Decisions: Great Constitutional Cases and Their Impact, Volume One: To 1896.* New York: Routledge, 2012.

White, G. Edward. *The Marshall Court and Cultural Change, 1815–1835.* New York: Oxford University Press, 1991.

### Articles

Primus, Richard. "The Gibbons Fallacy." *University of Pennsylvania Journal of Constitutional Law* 19, no. 3 (2017): 567–620.

### Websites

"Gibbons v. Ogden." Oyez web site. Accessed April 12, 2023. http://www.oyez.org/cases/1792-1850/1824/1824_0/.

"Gibbons v. Ogden (1824)." Landmark Supreme Court Cases website. Accessed April 12, 2023. http://www.landmarkcases.org/gibbons/home.html.

"Gibbons v. Ogden (1824)." National Archives "Our Documents" website. Accessed April 12, 2023. http://www.ourdocuments.gov/doc.php?flash=true&doc=24.

—Commentary by Thomas H. Cox

# GIBBONS V. OGDEN

## Document Text

### Mr. Chief Justice MARSHALL delivered the opinion of the Court

The appellant contends that this decree is erroneous because the laws which purport to give the exclusive privilege it sustains are repugnant to the Constitution and laws of the United States.

They are said to be repugnant:

1st. To that clause in the Constitution which authorizes Congress to regulate commerce.

2d. To that which authorizes Congress to promote the progress of science and useful arts.

The State of New York maintains the Constitutionality of these laws, and their Legislature, their Council of Revision, and their Judges, have repeatedly concurred in this opinion. It is supported by great names—by names which have all the titles to consideration that virtue, intelligence, and office can bestow. No tribunal can approach the decision of this question without feeling a just and real respect for that opinion which is sustained by such authority, but it is the province of this Court, while it respects, not to bow to it implicitly, and the Judges must exercise, in the examination of the subject, that understanding which Providence has bestowed upon them, with that independence which the people of the United States expect from this department of the government.

As preliminary to the very able discussions of the Constitution which we have heard from the bar, and as having some influence on its construction, reference has been made to the political situation of these States anterior to its formation. It has been said that they were sovereign, were completely independent, and were connected with each other only by a league. This is true. But, when these allied sovereigns converted their league into a government, when they converted their Congress of Ambassadors, deputed to deliberate on their common concerns and to recommend measures of general utility, into a Legislature, empowered to enact laws on the most interesting subjects, the whole character in which the States appear underwent a change, the extent of which must be determined by a fair consideration of the instrument by which that change was effected.

This instrument contains an enumeration of powers expressly granted by the people to their government. It has been said that these powers ought to be construed strictly. But why ought they to be so construed? Is there one sentence in the Constitution which gives countenance to this rule? In the last of the enumerated powers, that which grants expressly the means for carrying all others into execution, Congress is authorized "to make all laws which shall be necessary and proper" for the purpose. But this limitation on the means which may be used is not extended to the powers which are conferred, nor is there one sentence in the Constitution which has been pointed out by the gentlemen of the bar or which we have been able to discern that prescribes this rule. We do not, therefore, think ourselves justified in adopting it. What do gentlemen mean by a "strict construction?" If they contend only against that enlarged construction, which would extend words beyond their natural and obvious import, we might question the application of the term, but should not controvert the principle. If they contend for that narrow construction which, in support or some theory not to be found in the Constitution, would deny to the government those powers which the words of the grant, as usually understood, import, and which are consistent with the general views and objects of the instrument; for that narrow construction which would cripple the government and render it unequal to the object for which it is declared to be instituted, and to which the powers given, as fairly understood, render it competent; then we cannot perceive the propriety of this strict construction, nor adopt it as the rule by which the Constitution is to be expounded. As men whose intentions require no concealment generally employ the words which most directly and aptly express the ideas they intend to convey, the enlightened patriots who framed our Constitution, and the people who adopted it, must be understood to have employed words in their natural sense, and to have intended what they have said. If, from the imperfection of human language, there should be serious doubts respecting the extent of any given power, it is a well settled rule that the objects for which it was given, especially when those objects are expressed in the instrument itself, should have great influence in the construction. We know of no reason for excluding this rule from the present case. The grant does not convey power which might be beneficial to the grantor if retained by himself, or which can enure solely to the benefit of the grantee, but is an investment of power for the general advantage, in the hands of agents selected for that purpose, which power can never be exercised by the people themselves, but must be placed in the hands of agents or lie dormant. We know of no rule for construing the extent of such powers other than is given by the language of the instrument which confers them, taken in connexion with the purposes for which they were conferred.

The words are, "Congress shall have power to regulate commerce with foreign nations, and among the several States, and with the Indian tribes."

The subject to be regulated is commerce, and our Constitution being, as was aptly said at the bar, one of enumeration, and not of definition, to ascertain the extent of the power, it becomes necessary to settle the meaning of the word. The counsel for the appellee would limit it to traffic, to buying and selling, or the interchange of commodities, and do not admit

that it comprehends navigation. This would restrict a general term, applicable to many objects, to one of its significations. Commerce, undoubtedly, is traffic, but it is something more: it is intercourse. It describes the commercial intercourse between nations, and parts of nations, in all its branches, and is regulated by prescribing rules for carrying on that intercourse. The mind can scarcely conceive a system for regulating commerce between nations which shall exclude all laws concerning navigation, which shall be silent on the admission of the vessels of the one nation into the ports of the other, and be confined to prescribing rules for the conduct of individuals in the actual employment of buying and selling or of barter.

If commerce does not include navigation, the government of the Union has no direct power over that subject, and can make no law prescribing what shall constitute American vessels or requiring that they shall be navigated by American seamen. Yet this power has been exercised from the commencement of the government, has been exercised with the consent of all, and has been understood by all to be a commercial regulation. All America understands, and has uniformly understood, the word "commerce" to comprehend navigation. It was so understood, and must have been so understood, when the Constitution was framed. The power over commerce, including navigation, was one of the primary objects for which the people of America adopted their government, and must have been contemplated in forming it. The convention must have used the word in that sense, because all have understood it in that sense, and the attempt to restrict it comes too late.

If the opinion that "commerce," as the word is used in the Constitution, comprehends navigation also, requires any additional confirmation, that additional confirmation is, we think, furnished by the words of the instrument itself.

It is a rule of construction acknowledged by all that the exceptions from a power mark its extent, for it would be absurd, as well as useless, to except from a granted power that which was not granted—that which the words of the grant could not comprehend. If, then, there are in the Constitution plain exceptions from the power over navigation, plain inhibitions to the exercise of that power in a particular way, it is a proof that those who made these exceptions, and prescribed these inhibitions, understood the power to which they applied as being granted.

The 9th section of the 1st article declares that "no preference shall be given, by any regulation of commerce or revenue, to the ports of one State over those of another." This clause cannot be understood as applicable to those laws only which are passed for the purposes of revenue, because it is expressly applied to commercial regulations, and the most obvious preference which can be given to one port over another in regulating commerce relates to navigation. But the subsequent part of the sentence is still more explicit. It is, "nor shall vessels bound to or from one State be obliged to enter, clear, or pay duties, in another." These words have a direct reference to navigation.

The universally acknowledged power of the government to impose embargoes must also be considered as showing that all America is united in that construction which comprehends navigation in the word commerce. Gentlemen have said in argument that this is a branch of the war-making power, and that an embargo is an instrument of war, not a regulation of trade.

That it may be, and often is, used as an instrument of war cannot be denied. An embargo may be imposed for the purpose of facilitating the equipment or manning of a fleet, or for the purpose of concealing the progress of an expedition preparing to sail from a particular port. In these, and in similar cases, it is a military instrument, and partakes of the nature of war. But all embargoes are not of this description. They are sometimes resorted to without a view to war, and with a single view to commerce. In such case, an embargo is no more a war measure than a merchantman is a ship of war because both are vessels which navigate the ocean with sails and seamen.

When Congress imposed that embargo which, for a time, engaged the attention of every man in the United States, the avowed object of the law was the protection of commerce, and the avoiding of war. By its friends and its enemies, it was treated as a commercial, not as a war, measure. The persevering earnestness and zeal with which it was opposed in a part of our country which supposed its interests to be vitally affected by the act, cannot be forgotten. A want of acuteness in discovering objections to a measure to which they felt the most deep-rooted hostility will not be imputed to those who were arrayed in opposition to this. Yet they never suspected that navigation was no branch of trade, and was therefore not comprehended in the power to regulate commerce. They did, indeed, contest the constitutionality of the act, but, on a principle which admits the construction for which the appellant contends. They denied that the particular law in question was made in pursuance of the Constitution not because the power could not act directly on vessels, but because a perpetual embargo was the annihilation, and not the regulation, of commerce. In terms, they admitted the applicability of the words used in the Constitution to vessels, and that in a case which produced a degree and an extent of excitement calculated to draw forth every principle on which legitimate resistance could be sustained. No example could more strongly illustrate the universal understanding of the American people on this subject.

The word used in the Constitution, then, comprehends, and has been always understood to comprehend, navigation within its meaning, and a power to regulate navigation is as expressly granted as if that term had been added to the word "commerce."

To what commerce does this power extend? The Constitution informs us, to commerce "with foreign nations, and among thet several States, and with the Indian tribes."

It has, we believe, been universally admitted that these words comprehend every species of commercial intercourse between the United States and foreign nations. No sort of trade can be carried on between this country and any other to which this power does not extend. It has been truly said that "commerce," as the word is used in the Constitution, is a unit every part of which is indicated by the term.

If this be the admitted meaning of the word in its application to foreign nations, it must carry the same meaning throughout the sentence, and remain a unit, unless there be some plain intelligible cause which alters it.

The subject to which the power is next applied is to commerce "among the several States." The word "among" means intermingled with. A thing which is among others is intermingled with them. Commerce among the States cannot stop at the external boundary line of each State, but may be introduced into the interior.

It is not intended to say that these words comprehend that commerce which is completely internal, which is carried on between man and man in a State, or between different parts of the same State, and which does not extend to or affect other States. Such a power would be inconvenient, and is certainly unnecessary.

Comprehensive as the word "among" is, it may very properly be restricted to that commerce which concerns more States than one. The phrase is not one which would probably have been selected to indicate the completely interior traffic of a State, because it is not an apt phrase for that purpose, and the enumeration of the particular classes of commerce to which the power was to be extended would not have been made had the intention been to extend the power to every description. The enumeration presupposes something not enumerated, and that something, if we regard the language or the subject of the sentence, must be the exclusively internal commerce of a State. The genius and character of the whole government seem to be that its action is to be applied to all the external concerns of the nation, and to those internal concerns which affect the States generally, but not to those which are completely within a particular State, which do not affect other States, and with which it is not necessary to interfere for the purpose of executing some of the general powers of the government. The completely internal commerce of a State, then, may be considered as reserved for the State itself.

But, in regulating commerce with foreign nations, the power of Congress does not stop at the jurisdictional lines of the several States. It would be a very useless power if it could not pass those lines. The commerce of the United States with foreign nations is that of the whole United States. Every district has a right to participate in it. The deep streams which penetrate our country in every direction pass through the interior of almost every State in the Union, and furnish the means of exercising this right. If Congress has the power to regulate it, that power must be exercised whenever the subject exists. If it exists within the States, if a foreign voyage may commence or terminate at a port within a State, then the power of Congress may be exercised within a State.

This principle is, if possible, still more clear, when applied to commerce "among the several States." They either join each other, in which case they are separated by a mathematical line, or they are remote from each other, in which case other States lie between them. What is commerce "among" them, and how is it to be conducted? Can a trading expedition between two adjoining States, commence and terminate outside of each? And if the trading intercourse be between two States remote from each other, must it not commence in one, terminate in the other, and probably pass through a third? Commerce among the States must, of necessity, be commerce with the States. In the regulation of trade with the Indian tribes, the action of the law, especially when the Constitution was made, was chiefly within a State. The power of Congress, then, whatever it may be, must be exercised within the territorial jurisdiction of the several States. The sense of the nation on this subject is unequivocally manifested by the provisions made in the laws for transporting goods by land between Baltimore and Providence, between New York and Philadelphia, and between Philadelphia and Baltimore.

We are now arrived at the inquiry—What is this power?

It is the power to regulate, that is, to prescribe the rule by which commerce is to be governed. This power, like all others vested in Congress, is complete in itself, may be exercised to its utmost extent, and acknowledges no limitations other than are prescribed in the Constitution. These are expressed in plain terms, and do not affect the questions which arise in this case, or which have been discussed at the bar. If, as has always been understood, the sovereignty of Congress, though limited to specified objects, is plenary as to those objects, the power over commerce with foreign nations, and among the several States, is vested in Congress as absolutely as it would be in a single government, having in its Constitution the same restrictions on the exercise of the power as are found in the Constitution of the United States. The wisdom and the discretion of Congress, their identity with the people, and the influence which their constituents possess at elections are, in this, as in many other instances, as that, for example, of declaring war, the sole restraints on which they have relied, to secure them from its abuse. They are the restraints on which the people must often they solely, in all representative governments.

The power of Congress, then, comprehends navigation, within the limits of every State in the Union, so far as that navigation may be in any manner connected with "commerce with foreign nations, or among the several States, or with the Indian tribes." It may, of consequence, pass the jurisdictional line of New York and act upon the very waters to which the prohibition now under consideration applies.

But it has been urged with great earnestness that, although the power of Congress to regulate commerce with foreign nations and among the several States be coextensive with the subject itself, and have no other limits than are prescribed in the Constitution, yet the States may severally exercise the same power, within their respective jurisdictions. In support of this argument, it is said that they possessed it as an inseparable attribute of sovereignty, before the formation of the Constitution, and still retain it except so far as they have surrendered it by that instrument; that this principle results from the nature of the government, and is secured by the tenth amendment; that an affirmative grant of power is not exclusive unless in its own nature it be such that the continued exercise of it by the former possessor is inconsistent with the grant, and that this is not of that description.

The appellant, conceding these postulates except the last, contends that full power to regulate a particular subject implies the whole power, and leaves no residuum; that a grant of the whole is incompatible with the existence of a right in another to any part of it.

Both parties have appealed to the Constitution, to legislative acts, and judicial decisions, and have drawn arguments from all these sources to support and illustrate the propositions they respectively maintain.

The grant of the power to lay and collect taxes is, like the power to regulate commerce, made in general terms, and has never been understood to interfere with the exercise of the same power by the State, and hence has been drawn an argument which has been applied to the question under consideration. But the two grants are not, it is conceived, similar in their terms or their nature. Although many of the powers formerly exercised by the States are transferred to the government of the Union, yet the State governments remain, and constitute a most important part of our system. The power of taxation is indispensable to their

existence, and is a power which, in its own nature, is capable of residing in, and being exercised by, different authorities at the same time. We are accustomed to see it placed, for different purposes, in different hands. Taxation is the simple operation of taking small portions from a perpetually accumulating mass, susceptible of almost infinite division, and a power in one to take what is necessary for certain purposes is not, in its nature, incompatible with a power in another to take what is necessary for other purposes. Congress is authorized to lay and collect taxes, &c. to pay the debts and provide for the common defence and general welfare of the United States. This does not interfere with the power of the States to tax for the support of their own governments, nor is the exercise of that power by the States an exercise of any portion of the power that is granted to the United States. In imposing taxes for State purposes, they are not doing what Congress is empowered to do. Congress is not empowered to tax for those purposes which are within the exclusive province of the States. When, then, each government exercises the power of taxation, neither is exercising the power of the other. But, when a State proceeds to regulate commerce with foreign nations, or among the several States, it is exercising the very power that is granted to Congress, and is doing the very thing which Congress is authorized to do. There is no analogy, then, between the power of taxation and the power of regulating commerce.

In discussing the question whether this power is still in the States, in the case under consideration, we may dismiss from it the inquiry whether it is surrendered by the mere grant to Congress, or is retained until Congress shall exercise the power. We may dismiss that inquiry because it has been exercised, and the regulations which Congress deemed it proper to make are now in full operation. The sole question is can a State regulate commerce with foreign nations and among the States while Congress is regulating it?

The counsel for the respondent answer this question in the affirmative, and rely very much on the restrictions in the 10th section as supporting their opinion. They say very truly that limitations of a power furnish a strong argument in favour of the existence of that power, and that the section which prohibits the States from laying duties on imports or exports proves that this power might have been exercised had it not been expressly forbidden, and consequently that any other commercial regulation, not expressly forbidden, to which the original power of the State was competent may still be made.

That this restriction shows the opinion of the Convention that a State might impose duties on exports and imports, if not expressly forbidden, will be conceded, but that it follows as a consequence from this concession that a State may regulate commerce with foreign nations and among the States cannot be admitted.

We must first determine whether the act of laying "duties or imposts on imports or exports" is considered in the Constitution as a branch of the taxing power, or of the power to regulate commerce. We think it very clear that it is considered as a branch of the taxing power. It is so treated in the first clause of the 8th section: "Congress shall have power to lay and collect taxes, duties, imposts, and excises;" and, before commerce is mentioned, the rule by which the exercise of this power must be governed is declared. It is that all duties, imposts, and excises shall be uniform. In a separate clause of the enumeration, the power to regulate commerce is given, as being entirely distinct from the right to levy taxes and imposts and as being a power, not before conferred. The Constitution, then, considers these powers as substantive, and distinct from each other, and so places them in the enumeration it contains. The power of imposing duties on imports is classed with the power to levy taxes, and that seems to be its natural place. But the power to levy taxes could never be considered as abridging the right of the States on that subject, and they might, consequently, have exercised it by levying duties on imports or exports, had the Constitution contained no prohibition on this subject. This prohibition, then, is an exception from the acknowledged power of the States to levy taxes, not from the questionable power to regulate commerce.

"A duty of tonnage" is as much a tax as a duty on imports or exports, and the reason which induced the prohibition of those taxes extends to this also. This tax may be imposed by a State, with the consent of Congress, and it may be admitted that Congress cannot give a right to a State in virtue of its own powers. But a duty of tonnage being part of the power of imposing taxes, its prohibition may certainly be made to depend on Congress, without affording any implication respecting a power to regulate commerce. It is true that duties may often be, and in fact often are, imposed on

tonnage with a view to the regulation of commerce, but they may be also imposed with a view to revenue, and it was therefore a prudent precaution to prohibit the States from exercising this power. The idea that the same measure might, according to circumstances, be arranged with different classes of power was no novelty to the framers of our Constitution. Those illustrious statesmen and patriots had been, many of them, deeply engaged in the discussions which preceded the war of our revolution, and all of them were well read in those discussions. The right to regulate commerce, even by the imposition of duties, was not controverted, but the right to impose a duty for the purpose of revenue produced a war as important, perhaps, in its consequences to the human race as any the world has ever witnessed.

These restrictions, then, are on the taxing power, not on that to regulate commerce, and presuppose the existence of that which they restrain, not of that which they do not purport to restrain.

But the inspection laws are said to be regulations of commerce, and are certainly recognised in the Constitution as being passed in the exercise of a power remaining with the States.

That inspection laws may have a remote and considerable influence on commerce will not be denied, but that a power to regulate commerce is the source from which the right to pass them is derived cannot be admitted. The object of inspection laws is to improve the quality of articles produced by the labour of a country, to fit them for exportation, or, it may be, for domestic use. They act upon the subject before it becomes an article of foreign commerce or of commerce among the States, and prepare it for that purpose. They form a portion of that immense mass of legislation which embraces everything within the territory of a State not surrendered to the General Government; all which can be most advantageously exercised by the States themselves. Inspection laws, quarantine laws, health laws of every description, as well as laws for regulating the internal commerce of a State, and those which respect turnpike roads, ferries, &c., are component parts of this mass.

No direct general power over these objects is granted to Congress, and, consequently, they remain subject to State legislation. If the legislative power of the

Union can reach them, it must be for national purposes, it must be where the power is expressly given for a special purpose or is clearly incidental to some power which is expressly given. It is obvious that the government of the Union, in the exercise of its express powers—that, for example, of regulating commerce with foreign nations and among the States—may use means that may also be employed by a State in the exercise of its acknowledged powers—that, for example, of regulating commerce within the State. If Congress license vessels to sail from one port to another in the same State, the act is supposed to be necessarily incidental to the power expressly granted to Congress, and implies no claim of a direct power to regulate the purely internal commerce of a State or to act directly on its system of police. So, if a State, in passing laws on subjects acknowledged to be within its control, and with a view to those subjects, shall adopt a measure of the same character with one which Congress may adopt, it does not derive its authority from the particular power which has been granted, but from some other, which remains with the State and may be executed by the same means. All experience shows that the same measures, or measures scarcely distinguishable from each other, may flow from distinct powers, but this does not prove that the powers themselves are identical. Although the means used in their execution may sometimes approach each other so nearly as to be confounded, there are other situations in which they are sufficiently distinct to establish their individuality.

In our complex system, presenting the rare and difficult scheme of one General Government whose action extends over the whole but which possesses only certain enumerated powers, and of numerous State governments which retain and exercise all powers not delegated to the Union, contests respecting power must arise. Were it even otherwise, the measures taken by the respective governments to execute their acknowledged powers would often be of the same description, and might sometimes interfere. This, however, does not prove that the one is exercising, or has a right to exercise, the powers of the other.

The acts of Congress passed in 1796 and 1799, 2 U.S.L. 345, 3 U.S.L. 126, empowering and directing the officers of the General Government to conform to and assist in the execution of the quarantine and health laws of a State proceed, it is said, upon the idea that these laws are constitutional. It is undoubtedly true

that they do proceed upon that idea, and the constitutionality of such laws has never, so far as we are informed, been denied. But they do not imply an acknowledgment that a State may rightfully regulate commerce with foreign nations or among the States, for they do not imply that such laws are an exercise of that power, or enacted with a view to it. On the contrary, they are treated as quarantine and health laws, are so denominated in the acts of Congress, and are considered as flowing from the acknowledged power of a State to provide for the health of its citizens. But as it was apparent that some of the provisions made for this purpose and in virtue of this power might interfere with and be affected by the laws of the United States made for the regulation of commerce, Congress, in that spirit of harmony and conciliation which ought always to characterize the conduct of governments standing in the relation which that of the Union and those of the States bear to each other, has directed its officers to aid in the execution of these laws, and has, in some measure, adapted its own legislation to this object by making provisions in aid of those of the States. But, in making these provisions, the opinion is unequivocally manifested that Congress may control the State laws so far as it may be necessary to control them for the regulation of commerce. The act passed in 1803, 3 U.S.L. 529, prohibiting the importation of slaves into any State which shall itself prohibit their importation, implies, it is said, an admission that the States possessed the power to exclude or admit them, from which it is inferred that they possess the same power with respect to other articles.

If this inference were correct, if this power was exercised not under any particular clause in the Constitution, but in virtue of a general right over the subject of commerce, to exist as long as the Constitution itself, it might now be exercised. Any State might now import African slaves into its own territory. But it is obvious that the power of the States over this subject, previous to the year 1808, constitutes an exception to the power of Congress to regulate commerce, and the exception is expressed in such words, as to manifest clearly the intention to continue the preexisting right of the States to admit or exclude, for a limited period. The words are

> the migration or importation of such persons as any of the States, now existing, shall think proper to admit shall not be prohibited by the Congress prior to the year 1808.

The whole object of the exception is to preserve the power to those States which might be disposed to exercise it, and its language seems to the Court to convey this idea unequivocally. The possession of this particular power, then, during the time limited in the Constitution, cannot be admitted to prove the possession of any other similar power.

It has been said that the act of August 7, 1789, acknowledges a concurrent power in the States to regulate the conduct of pilots, and hence is inferred an admission of their concurrent right with Congress to regulate commerce with foreign nations and amongst the States. But this inference is not, we think, justified by the fact.

Although Congress cannot enable a State to legislate, Congress may adopt the provisions of a State on any subject. When the government of the Union was brought into existence, it found a system for the regulation of its pilots in full force in every State. The act which has been mentioned adopts this system, and gives it the same validity as if its provisions had been specially made by Congress. But the act, it may be said, is prospective also, and the adoption of laws to be made in future presupposes the right in the maker to legislate on the subject.

The act unquestionably manifests an intention to leave this subject entirely to the States until Congress should think proper to interpose, but the very enactment of such a law indicates an opinion that it was necessary, that the existing system would not be applicable to the state of things unless expressly applied to it by Congress. But this section is confined to pilots within the "bays, inlets, rivers, harbours, and ports of the United States," which are, of course, in whole or in part, also within the limits of some particular state. The acknowledged power of a State to regulate its police, its domestic trade, and to govern its own citizens may enable it to legislate on this subject to a considerable extent, and the adoption of its system by Congress, and the application of it to the whole subject of commerce, does not seem to the Court to imply a right in the States so to apply it of their own authority. But the adoption of the State system being temporary, being only "until further legislative provision shall be made by Congress," shows conclusively an opinion that Congress could control the whole subject, and might adopt the system of the States or provide one of its own.

A State, it is said, or even a private citizen, may construct light houses. But gentlemen must be aware that if this proves a power in a State to regulate commerce, it proves that the same power is in the citizen. States or individuals who own lands may, if not forbidden by law, erect on those lands what buildings they please, but this power is entirely distinct from that of regulating commerce, and may, we presume, be restrained if exercised so as to produce a public mischief.

These acts were cited at the bar for the purpose of showing an opinion in Congress that the States possess, concurrently with the Legislature of the Union, the power to regulate commerce with foreign nations and among the States. Upon reviewing them, we think they do not establish the proposition they were intended to prove. They show the opinion that the States retain powers enabling them to pass the laws to which allusion has been made, not that those laws proceed from the particular power which has been delegated to Congress.

It has been contended by the counsel for the appellant that, as the word "to regulate" implies in its nature full power over the thing to be regulated, it excludes necessarily the action of all others that would perform the same operation on the same thing. That regulation is designed for the entire result, applying to those parts which remain as they were, as well as to those which are altered. It produces a uniform whole which is as much disturbed and deranged by changing what the regulating power designs to leave untouched as that on which it has operated.

There is great force in this argument, and the Court is not satisfied that it has been refuted.

Since, however, in exercising the power of regulating their own purely internal affairs, whether of trading or police, the States may sometimes enact laws the validity of which depends on their interfering with, and being contrary to, an act of Congress passed in pursuance of the Constitution, the Court will enter upon the inquiry whether the laws of New York, as expounded by the highest tribunal of that State, have, in their application to this case, come into collision with an act of Congress and deprived a citizen of a right to which that act entitles him. Should this collision exist, it will be immaterial whether those laws were passed in virtue of a concurrent power "to regulate commerce with foreign nations and among the several States" or in virtue of a power to regulate their domestic trade and police. In one case and the other, the acts of New York must yield to the law of Congress, and the decision sustaining the privilege they confer against a right given by a law of the Union must be erroneous.

This opinion has been frequently expressed in this Court, and is founded as well on the nature of the government as on the words of the Constitution. In argument, however, it has been contended that, if a law passed by a State, in the exercise of its acknowledged sovereignty, comes into conflict with a law passed by Congress in pursuance of the Constitution, they affect the subject and each other like equal opposing powers.

But the framers of our Constitution foresaw this state of things, and provided for it by declaring the supremacy not only of itself, but of the laws made in pursuance of it. The nullity of any act inconsistent with the Constitution is produced by the declaration that the Constitution is the supreme law. The appropriate application of that part of the clause which confers the same supremacy on laws and treaties is to such acts of the State Legislatures as do not transcend their powers, but, though enacted in the execution of acknowledged State powers, interfere with, or are contrary to, the laws of Congress made in pursuance of the Constitution or some treaty made under the authority of the United States. In every such case, the act of Congress or the treaty is supreme, and the law of the State, though enacted in the exercise of powers not controverted, must yield to it.

In pursuing this inquiry at the bar, it has been said that the Constitution does not confer the right of intercourse between State and State. That right derives its source from those laws whose authority is acknowledged by civilized man throughout the world. This is true. The Constitution found it an existing right, and gave to Congress the power to regulate it. In the exercise of this power, Congress has passed "an act for enrolling or licensing ships or vessels to be employed in the coasting trade and fisheries, and for regulating the same." The counsel for the respondent contend that this act does not give the right to sail from port to port, but confines itself to regulating a preexisting right so far only as to confer certain privileges on enrolled and licensed vessels in its exercise.

It will at once occur that, when a Legislature attaches certain privileges and exemptions to the exercise of a right over which its control is absolute, the law must imply a power to exercise the right. The privileges are gone if the right itself be annihilated. It would be contrary to all reason, and to the course of human affairs, to say that a State is unable to strip a vessel of the particular privileges attendant on the exercise of a right, and yet may annul the right itself; that the State of New York cannot prevent an enrolled and licensed vessel, proceeding from Elizabethtown, in New Jersey, to New York, from enjoying, in her course, and on her entrance into port, all the privileges conferred by the act of Congress, but can shut her up in her own port, and prohibit altogether her entering the waters and ports of another State. To the Court, it seems very clear that the whole act on the subject of the coasting trade, according to those principles which govern the construction of statutes, implies unequivocally an authority to licensed vessels to carry on the coasting trade.

But we will proceed briefly to notice those sections which bear more directly on the subject.

The first section declares that vessels enrolled by virtue of a previous law, and certain other vessels enrolled as described in that act, and having a license in force, as is by the act required,

> and no others, shall be deemed ships or vessels of the United States, entitled to the privileges of ships or vessels employed in the coasting trade.

This section seems to the Court to contain a positive enactment that the vessels it describes shall be entitled to the privileges of ships or vessels employed in the coasting trade. These privileges cannot be separated from the trade and cannot be enjoyed unless the trade may be prosecuted. The grant of the privilege is an idle, empty form, conveying nothing, unless it convey the right to which the privilege is attached and in the exercise of which its whole value consists. To construe these words otherwise than as entitling the ships or vessels described to carry on the coasting trade would be, we think, to disregard the apparent intent of the act.

The fourth section directs the proper officer to grant to a vessel qualified to receive it, "a license for carrying on the coasting trade," and prescribes its form. After reciting the compliance of the applicant with the previous requisites of the law, the operative words of the instrument are,

> license is hereby granted for the said steamboat Bellona to be employed in carrying on the coasting trade for one year from the date hereof, and no longer.

These are not the words of the officer, they are the words of the legislature, and convey as explicitly the authority the act intended to give, and operate as effectually, as if they had been inserted in any other part of the act, than in the license itself.

The word "license" means permission or authority, and a license to do any particular thing is a permission or authority to do that thing, and if granted by a person having power to grant it, transfers to the grantee the right to do whatever it purports to authorize. It certainly transfers to him all the right which the grantor can transfer, to do what is within the terms of the license.

Would the validity or effect of such an instrument be questioned by the respondent, if executed by persons claiming regularly under the laws of New York?

The license must be understood to be what it purports to be, a legislative authority to the steamboat *Bellona* "to be employed in carrying on the coasting trade, for one year from this date."

It has been denied that these words authorize a voyage from New Jersey to New York. It is true that no ports are specified, but it is equally true that the words used are perfectly intelligible, and do confer such authority as unquestionably as if the ports had been mentioned. The coasting trade is a term well understood. The law has defined it, and all know its meaning perfectly. The act describes with great minuteness the various operations of a vessel engaged in it, and it cannot, we think, be doubted that a voyage from New Jersey to New York is one of those operations.

Notwithstanding the decided language of the license, it has also been maintained that it gives no right to trade, and that its sole purpose is to confer the American character.

The answer given to this argument that the American character is conferred by the enrollment, and not by the license, is, we think, founded too clearly in the words of the law to require the support of any additional observations. The enrollment of vessels designed for the coasting trade corresponds precisely with the registration of vessels designed for the foreign trade, and requires every circumstance which can constitute the American character. The license can be granted only to vessels already enrolled, if they be of the burthen of twenty tons and upwards, and requires no circumstance essential to the American character. The object of the license, then, cannot be to ascertain the character of the vessel, but to do what it professes to do—that is, to give permission to a vessel already proved by her enrollment to be American, to carry on the coasting trade.

But if the license be a permit to carry on the coasting trade, the respondent denies that these boats were engaged in that trade, or that the decree under consideration has restrained them from prosecuting it. The boats of the appellant were, we are told, employed in the transportation of passengers, and this is no part of that commerce which Congress may regulate.

If, as our whole course of legislation on this subject shows, the power of Congress has been universally understood in America to comprehend navigation, it is a very persuasive, if not a conclusive, argument to prove that the construction is correct, and if it be correct, no clear distinction is perceived between the power to regulate vessels employed in transporting men for hire and property for hire. The subject is transferred to Congress, and no exception to the grant can be admitted which is not proved by the words or the nature of the thing. A coasting vessel employed in the transportation of passengers is as much a portion of the American marine as one employed in the transportation of a cargo, and no reason is perceived why such vessel should be withdrawn from the regulating power of that government which has been thought best fitted for the purpose generally. The provisions of the law respecting native seamen and respecting ownership are as applicable to vessels carrying men as to vessels carrying manufactures, and no reason is perceived why the power over the subject should not be placed in the same hands. The argument urged at the bar rests on the foundation that the power of Congress does not extend to navigation as a branch of commerce, and can only be applied to that subject incidentally and occasionally. But if that foundation be removed, we must show some plain, intelligible distinction, supported by the Constitution or by reason, for discriminating between the power of Congress over vessels employed in navigating the same seas. We can perceive no such distinction.

If we refer to the Constitution, the inference to be drawn from it is rather against the distinction. The section which restrains Congress from prohibiting the migration or importation of such persons as any of the States may think proper to admit until the year 1808 has always been considered as an exception from the power to regulate commerce, and certainly seems to class migration with importation. Migration applies as appropriately to voluntary as importation does to involuntary arrivals, and, so far as an exception from a power proves its existence, this section proves that the power to regulate commerce applies equally to the regulation of vessels employed in transporting men, who pass from place to place voluntarily, and to those who pass involuntarily.

If the power reside in Congress, as a portion of the general grant to regulate commerce, then acts applying that power to vessels generally must be construed as comprehending all vessels. If none appear to be excluded by the language of the act, none can be excluded by construction. Vessels have always been employed to a greater or less extent in the transportation of passengers, and have never been supposed to be, on that account, withdrawn from the control or protection of Congress. Packets which ply along the coast, as well as those which make voyages between Europe and America, consider the transportation of passengers as an important part of their business. Yet it has never been suspected that the general laws of navigation did not apply to them.

The duty act, sections 23 and 46, contains provisions respecting passengers, and shows that vessels which transport them have the same rights, and must perform the same duties, with other vessels. They are governed by the general laws of navigation.

In the progress of things, this seems to have grown into a particular employment, and to have attracted the particular attention of government. Congress was no longer satisfied with comprehending vessels engaged

specially in this business, within those provisions which were intended for vessels generally, and, on the 2d of March, 1819, passed "an act regulating passenger ships and vessels." This wise and humane law provides for the safety and comfort of passengers, and for the communication of everything concerning them which may interest the government, to the Department of State, but makes no provision concerning the entry of the vessel or her conduct in the waters of the United States. This, we think, shows conclusively the sense of Congress (if, indeed, any evidence to that point could be required) that the preexisting regulations comprehended passenger ships among others, and, in prescribing the same duties, the Legislature must have considered them as possessing the same rights.

If, then, it were even true that the *Bellona* and the *Stoudinger* were employed exclusively in the conveyance of passengers between New York and New Jersey, it would not follow that this occupation did not constitute a part of the coasting trade of the United States, and was not protected by the license annexed to the answer. But we cannot perceive how the occupation of these vessels can be drawn into question in the case before the Court. The laws of New York, which grant the exclusive privilege set up by the respondent, take no notice of the employment of vessels, and relate only to the principle by which they are propelled. Those laws do not inquire whether vessels are engaged in transporting men or merchandise, but whether they are moved by steam or wind. If by the former, the waters of New York are closed against them, though their cargoes be dutiable goods, which the laws of the United States permit them to enter and deliver in New York. If by the latter, those waters are free to them though they should carry passengers only. In conformity with the law is the bill of the plaintiff in the State Court. The bill does not complain that the *Bellona* and the *Stoudinger* carry passengers, but that they are moved by steam. This is the injury of which he complains, and is the sole injury against the continuance of which he asks relief. The bill does not even allege specially that those vessels were employed in the transportation of passengers, but says generally that they were employed "in the transportation of passengers, or otherwise." The answer avers only that they were employed in the coasting trade, and insists on the right to carry on any trade authorized by the license. No testimony is taken, and the writ of injunction and decree restrain these licensed vessels not from carrying passengers, but from being moved through the waters of New York by steam for any purpose whatever.

The questions, then, whether the conveyance of passengers be a part of the coasting trade and whether a vessel can be protected in that occupation by a coasting license are not, and cannot be, raised in this case. The real and sole question seems to be whether a steam machine in actual use deprives a vessel of the privileges conferred by a license.

In considering this question, the first idea which presents itself is that the laws of Congress for the regulation of commerce do not look to the principle by which vessels are moved. That subject is left entirely to individual discretion, and, in that vast and complex system of legislative enactment concerning it, which embraces everything that the Legislature thought it necessary to notice, there is not, we believe, one word respecting the peculiar principle by which vessels are propelled through the water, except what may be found in a single act granting a particular privilege to steamboats. With this exception, every act, either prescribing duties or granting privileges, applies to every vessel, whether navigated by the instrumentality of wind or fire, of sails or machinery. The whole weight of proof, then, is thrown upon him who would introduce a distinction to which the words of the law give no countenance.

If a real difference could be admitted to exist between vessels carrying passengers and others, it has already been observed that there is no fact in this case which can bring up that question. And, if the occupation of steamboats be a matter of such general notoriety that the Court may be presumed to know it, although not specially informed by the record, then we deny that the transportation of passengers is their exclusive occupation. It is a matter of general history that, in our western waters, their principal employment is the transportation of merchandise, and all know that, in the waters of the Atlantic, they are frequently so employed.

But all inquiry into this subject seems to the Court to be put completely at rest by the act already mentioned, entitled, "An act for the enrolling and licensing of steamboats."

This act authorizes a steamboat employed, or intended to be employed, only in a river or bay of the United States, owned wholly or in part by an alien, resident within the United States, to be enrolled and licensed as if the same belonged to a citizen of the United States.

This act demonstrates the opinion of Congress that steamboats may be enrolled and licensed, in common with vessels using sails. They are, of course, entitled to the same privileges, and can no more be restrained from navigating waters and entering ports which are free to such vessels than if they were wafted on their voyage by the winds, instead of being propelled by the agency of fire. The one element may be as legitimately used as the other for every commercial purpose authorized by the laws of the Union, and the act of a State inhibiting the use of either to any vessel having a license under the act of Congress comes, we think, in direct collision with that act.

As this decides the cause, it is unnecessary to enter in an examination of that part of the Constitution which empowers Congress to promote the progress of science and the useful arts.

The Court is aware that, in stating the train of reasoning by which we have been conducted to this result, much time has been consumed in the attempt to demonstrate propositions which may have been thought axioms. It is felt that the tediousness inseparable from the endeavour to prove that which is already clear is imputable to a considerable part of this opinion. But it was unavoidable. The conclusion to which we have come depends on a chain of principles which it was necessary to preserve unbroken, and although some of them were thought nearly self-evident, the magnitude of the question, the weight of character belonging to those from whose judgment we dissent, and the argument at the bar demanded that we should assume nothing.

Powerful and ingenious minds, taking as postulates that the powers expressly granted to the government of the Union are to be contracted by construction into the narrowest possible compass and that the original powers of the States are retained if any possible construction will retain them may, by a course of well digested but refined and metaphysical reasoning founded on these premises, explain away the Constitution of our country and leave it a magnificent structure indeed to look at, but totally unfit for use. They may so entangle and perplex the understanding as to obscure principles which were before thought quite plain, and induce doubts where, if the mind were to pursue its own course, none would be perceived. In such a case, it is peculiarly necessary to recur to safe and fundamental principles to sustain those principles, and when sustained, to make them the tests of the arguments to be examined.

### Mr. Justice JOHNSON

The judgment entered by the Court in this cause, has my entire approbation, but, having adopted my conclusions on views of the subject materially different from those of my brethren, I feel it incumbent on me to exhibit those views. I have also another inducement: in questions of great importance and great delicacy, I feel my duty to the public best discharged by an effort to maintain my opinions in my own way.

In attempts to construe the Constitution, I have never found much benefit resulting from the inquiry whether the whole or any part of it is to be construed strictly or literally. The simple, classical, precise, yet comprehensive language in which it is couched leaves, at most, but very little latitude for construction, and when its intent and meaning is discovered, nothing remains but to execute the will of those who made it in the best manner to effect the purposes intended. The great and paramount purpose was to unite this mass of wealth and power, for the protection of the humblest individual, his rights, civil and political, his interests and prosperity, are the sole end; the rest are nothing but the means. But the principal of those means, one so essential as to approach nearer the characteristics of an end, was the independence and harmony of the States that they may the better subserve the purposes of cherishing and protecting the respective families of this great republic.

The strong sympathies, rather than the feeble government, which bound the States together during a common war dissolved on the return of peace, and the very principles which gave rise to the war of the revolution began to threaten the Confederacy with anarchy and ruin. The States had resisted a tax imposed by the parent State, and now reluctantly submitted to, or altogether rejected, the moderate demands of the Confederation. Everyone recollects the painful and threatening dis-

cussions which arose on the subject of the five percent duty. Some States rejected it altogether; others insisted on collecting it themselves; scarcely any acquiesced without reservations, which deprived it altogether of the character of a national measure; and at length, some repealed the laws by which they had signified their acquiescence.

For a century, the States had submitted, with murmurs, to the commercial restrictions imposed by the parent State; and now, finding themselves in the unlimited possession of those powers over their own commerce which they had so long been deprived of and so earnestly coveted, that selfish principle which, well controlled, is so salutary, and which, unrestricted, is so unjust and tyrannical, guided by inexperience and jealousy, began to show itself in iniquitous laws and impolitic measures from which grew up a conflict of commercial regulations destructive to the harmony of the States and fatal to their commercial interests abroad.

This was the immediate cause that led to the forming of a convention.

As early as 1778, the subject had been pressed upon the attention of Congress by a memorial from the State of New Jersey, and in 1781, we find a resolution presented to that body by one of the most enlightened men of his day, Dr. Witherspoon, affirming that

> it is indispensably necessary that the United States, in Congress assembled, should be vested with a right of superintending the commercial regulations of every State that none may take place that shall be partial or contrary to the common interests.

The resolution of Virginia, January 21, 1781, appointing her commissioners to meet commissioners from other States, expresses their purpose to be

> to take into consideration the trade of the United States, to consider how far an uniform system in their commercial regulations may be necessary to their common interests and their permanent harmony.

And Mr. Madison's resolution, which led to that measure, is introduced by a preamble entirely explicit to this point:

Whereas, the relative situation of the United States has been found, on trial, to require uniformity in their commercial regulations as the only effectual policy for obtaining, in the ports of foreign nations, a stipulation of privileges reciprocal to those enjoyed by the subjects of such nations in the ports of the United States, for preventing animosities, which cannot fail to arise among the several States, from the interference of partial and separate regulations,

&c. "therefore, resolved," &c.

The history of the times will therefore sustain the opinion that the grant of power over commerce, if intended to be commensurate with the evils existing and the purpose of remedying those evils, could be only commensurate with the power of the States over the subject. And this opinion is supported by a very remarkable evidence of the general understanding of the whole American people when the grant was made.

There was not a State in the Union in which there did not at that time exist a variety of commercial regulations; concerning which it is too much to suppose that the whole ground covered by those regulations was immediately assumed by actual legislation under the authority of the Union. But where was the existing statute on this subject that a State attempted to execute? or by what State was it ever thought necessary to repeal those statutes? By common consent, those laws dropped lifeless from their statute books for want of the sustaining power that had been relinquished to Congress.

And the plain and direct import of the words of the grant is consistent with this general understanding.

The words of the Constitution are, "Congress shall have power to regulate commerce with foreign nations, and among the several States, and with the Indian tribes."

It is not material, in my view of the subject, to inquire whether the article a or the should be prefixed to the word "power." Either or neither will produce the same result: if either, it is clear that the article "the" would be the proper one, since the next preceding grant of power is certainly exclusive, to-wit: "to borrow money on the credit of the United States." But mere verbal criticism I reject.

My opinion is founded on the application of the words of the grant to the subject of it.

The "power to regulate commerce" here meant to be granted was that power to regulate commerce which previously existed in the States. But what was that power? The States were unquestionably supreme, and each possessed that power over commerce which is acknowledged to reside in every sovereign State. The definition and limits of that power are to be sought among the features of international law, and, as it was not only admitted but insisted on by both parties in argument that, "unaffected by a state of war, by treaties, or by municipal regulations, all commerce among independent States was legitimate," there is no necessity to appeal to the oracles of the *jus commune* for the correctness of that doctrine. The law of nations, regarding man as a social animal, pronounces all commerce legitimate in a state of peace until prohibited by positive law. The power of a sovereign state over commerce therefore amounts to nothing more than a power to limit and restrain it at pleasure. And since the power to prescribe the limits to its freedom necessarily implies the power to determine what shall remain unrestrained, it follows that the power must be exclusive; it can reside but in one potentate, and hence the grant of this power carries with it the whole subject, leaving nothing for the State to act upon.

And such has been the practical construction of the act. Were every law on the subject of commerce repealed tomorrow, all commerce would be lawful, and, in practice, merchants never inquire what is permitted, but what is forbidden commerce. Of all the endless variety of branches of foreign commerce now carried on to every quarter of the world, I know of no one that is permitted by act of Congress any otherwise than by not being forbidden. No statute of the United States that I know of was ever passed to permit a commerce unless in consequence of its having been prohibited by some previous statute.

I speak not here of the treaty-making power, for that is not exercised under the grant now under consideration. I confine my observation to laws properly so called. And even where freedom of commercial intercourse is made a subject of stipulation in a treaty, it is generally with a view to the removal of some previous restriction, or the introduction of some privilege, most frequently, is identified with the return to a state of peace. But another view of the subject leads directly to the same conclusion. Power to regulate foreign commerce is given in the same words, and in the same breath, as it were, with that over the commerce of the States and with the Indian tribes. But the power to regulate foreign commerce is necessarily exclusive. The States are unknown to foreign nations, their sovereignty exists only with relation to each other and the General Government. Whatever regulations foreign commerce should be subjected to in the ports of the Union, the General Government would be held responsible for them, and all other regulations but those which Congress had imposed would be regarded by foreign nations as trespasses and violations of national faith and comity.

But the language which grants the power as to one description of commerce grants it as to all, and, in fact, if ever the exercise of a right or acquiescence in a construction could be inferred from contemporaneous and continued assent, it is that of the exclusive effect of this grant.

A right over the subject has never been pretended to in any instance except as incidental to the exercise of some other unquestionable power.

The present is an instance of the assertion of that kind, as incidental to a municipal power; that of superintending the internal concerns of a State, and particularly of extending protection and patronage, in the shape of a monopoly, to genius and enterprise.

The grant to Livingston and Fulton interferes with the freedom of intercourse, and on this principle, its constitutionality is contested.

When speaking of the power of Congress over navigation, I do not regard it as a power incidental to that of regulating commerce; I consider it as the thing itself, inseparable from it as vital motion is from vital existence.

Commerce, in its simplest signification, means an exchange of goods, but in the advancement of society, labour, transportation, intelligence, care, and various mediums of exchange become commodities, and enter into commerce, the subject, the vehicle, the agent, and their various operations become the objects of commercial regulation. Shipbuilding, the carrying trade, and propagation of seamen are such vital agents

of commercial prosperity that the nation which could not legislate over these subjects would not possess power to regulate commerce.

That such was the understanding of the framers of the Constitution is conspicuous from provisions contained in that instrument.

The first clause of the 9th section not only considers the right of controlling personal ingress or migration, as implied in the powers previously vested in Congress over commerce, but acknowledges it as a legitimate subject of revenue. And, although the leading object of this section undoubtedly was the importation of slaves, yet the words are obviously calculated to comprise persons of all descriptions, and to recognise in Congress a power to prohibit where the States permit, although they cannot permit when the States prohibit. The treaty-making power undoubtedly goes further. So the fifth clause of the same section furnishes an exposition of the sense of the Convention as to the power of Congress over navigation: "nor shall vessels bound to or from one State be obliged to enter, clear, or pay duties in another."

But it is almost labouring to prove a self-evident proposition, since the sense of mankind, the practice of the world, the contemporaneous assumption and continued exercise of the power, and universal acquiescence, have so clearly established the right of Congress over navigation, and the transportation of both men and their goods, as not only incidental to, but actually of the essence of, the power to regulate commerce. As to the transportation of passengers, and passengers in a steamboat, I consider it as having been solemnly recognised by the State of New York as a subject both of commercial regulation and of revenue. She has imposed a transit duty upon steamboat passengers arriving at Albany, and unless this be done in the exercise of her control over personal intercourse, as incident to internal commerce, I know not on what principle the individual has been subjected to this tax. The subsequent imposition upon the steamboat itself appears to be but a commutation, and operates as an indirect, instead of a direct, tax upon the same subject. The passenger pays it at last.

It is impossible, with the views which I entertain of the principle on which the commercial privileges of the people of the United States among themselves rests, to concur in the view which this Court takes of the effect of the coasting license in this cause. I do not regard it as the foundation of the right set up in behalf of the appellant. If there was any one object riding over every other in the adoption of the Constitution, it was to keep the commercial intercourse among the States free from all invidious and partial restraints. And I cannot overcome the conviction that, if the licensing act was repealed tomorrow, the rights of the appellant to a reversal of the decision complained of would be as strong as it is under this license. One half the doubts in life arise from the defects of language, and if this instrument had been called an exemption instead of a license, it would have given a better idea of its character. Licensing acts, in fact, in legislation, are universally restraining acts, as, for example, acts licensing gaming houses, retailers of spiritous liquors, &c. The act in this instance is distinctly of that character, and forms part of an extensive system the object of which is to encourage American shipping and place them on an equal footing with the shipping of other nations. Almost every commercial nation reserves to its own subjects a monopoly of its coasting trade, and a countervailing privilege in favour of American shipping is contemplated in the whole legislation of the United States on this subject. It is not to give the vessel an American character that the license is granted; that effect has been correctly attributed to the act of her enrollment. But it is to confer on her American privileges, as contradistinguished from foreign, and to preserve the government from fraud by foreigners in surreptitiously intruding themselves into the American commercial marine, as well as frauds upon the revenue in the trade coastwise, that this whole system is projected. Many duties and formalities are necessarily imposed upon the American foreign commerce which would be burdensome in the active coasting trade of the States, and can be dispensed with. A higher rate of tonnage also is imposed, and this license entitles the vessels that take it to those exemptions, but to nothing more. A common register equally entitles vessels to carry on the coasting trade, although it does not exempt them from the forms of foreign commerce or from compliance with the 16th and 17th sections of the enrolling act. And even a foreign vessel may be employed coastwise upon complying with the requisitions of the 24th section. I consider the license therefore as nothing more than what it purports to be, according to the first section of this act, conferring on the licensed vessel certain privileges in that trade not conferred on other vessels; but the abstract

right of commercial intercourse, stripped of those privileges, is common to all.

Yet there is one view in which the license may be allowed considerable influence in sustaining the decision of this Court.

It has been contended that the grants of power to the United States over any subject do not necessarily paralyze the arm of the States or deprive them of the capacity to act on the same subject. The this can be the effect only of prohibitory provisions in their own Constitutions, or in that of the General Government. The *vis vitae* of power is still existing in the States, if not extinguished by the Constitution of the United States. That, although as to all those grants of power which may be called aboriginal, with relation to the Government, brought into existence by the Constitution, they, of course, are out of the reach of State power, yet, as to all concessions of powers which previously existed in the States, it was otherwise. The practice of our Government certainly has been, on many subjects, to occupy so much only of the field opened to them as they think the public interests require. Witness the jurisdiction of the Circuit Courts, limited both as to cases and as to amount, and various other instances that might to cited. But the license furnishes a full answer to this objection, for, although one grant of power over commerce, should not be deemed a total relinquishment of power over the subject, but amounting only to a power to assume, still the power of the States must be at an end, so far as the United States have, by their legislative act, taken the subject under their immediate superintendence. So far as relates to the commerce coastwise, the act under which this license is granted contains a full expression of Congress on this subject. Vessels, from five tons upwards, carrying on the coasting trade are made the subject of regulation by that act. And this license proves that this vessel has complied with that act, and been regularly ingrafted into one class of the commercial marine of the country.

It remains, to consider the objections to this opinion, as presented by the counsel for the appellee. On those which had relation to the particular character of this boat, whether as a steamboat or a ferry boat, I have only to remark that, in both those characters, she is expressly recognised as an object of the provisions which relate to licenses.

The 12th section of the Act of 1793 has these words: "That when the master of any ship or vessel, ferry boats excepted, shall be changed," &c. And the act which exempts licensed steamboats from the provisions against alien interests shows such boats to be both objects of the licensing act and objects of that act when employed exclusively within our bays and rivers.

But the principal objections to these opinions arise,

1st. From the unavoidable action of some of the municipal powers of the States upon commercial subjects.

2d. From passages in the Constitution which are supposed to imply a concurrent power in the States in regulating commerce.

It is no objection to the existence of distinct, substantive powers that, in their application, they bear upon the same subject. The same bale of goods, the same cask of provisions, or the same ship that may be the subject of commercial regulation may also be the vehicle of disease. And the health laws that require them to be stopped and ventilated are no more intended as regulations on commerce than the laws which permit their importation are intended to innoculate the community with disease. Their different purposes mark the distinction between the powers brought into action, and while frankly exercised, they can produce no serious collision. As to laws affecting ferries, turnpike roads, and other subjects of the same class, so far from meriting the epithet of commercial regulations, they are, in fact, commercial facilities for which, by the consent of mankind, a compensation is paid upon the same principle that the whole commercial world submit to pay light money to the Danes. Inspection laws are of a more equivocal nature, and it is obvious that the Constitution has viewed that subject with much solicitude. But so far from sustaining an inference in favour of the power of the States over commerce, I cannot but think that the guarded provisions of the 10th section on this subject furnish a strong argument against that inference. It was obvious that inspection laws must combine municipal with commercial regulations, and, while the power over the subject is yielded to the States, for obvious reasons, an absolute control is given over State legislation on the subject, as far as that legislation may be exercised, so as to affect the commerce of the country. The inferences to be correctly drawn from this whole article appear to me to be altogether in favour of the exclusive grants to Congress of power over commerce, and the reverse of that which the appellee contends for.

This section contains the positive restrictions imposed by the Constitution upon State power. The first clause of it specifies those powers which the States are precluded from exercising, even though the Congress were to permit them. The second, those which the States may exercise with the consent of Congress. And here the sedulous attention to the subject of State exclusion from commercial power is strongly marked. Not satisfied with the express grant to the United States of the power over commerce, this clause negatives the exercise of that power to the States as to the only two objects which could ever tempt them to assume the exercise of that power, to-wit, the collection of a revenue from imposts and duties on imports and exports, or from a tonnage duty. As to imposts on imports or exports, such a revenue might have been aimed at directly, by express legislation, or indirectly, in the form of inspection laws, and it became necessary to guard against both. Hence, first, the consent of Congress to such imposts or duties is made necessary, and, as to inspection laws, it is limited to the minimum of expenses. Then the money so raised shall be paid into the Treasury of the United States, or may be sued for, since it is declared to be for their use. And lastly, all such laws may be modified or repealed by an act of Congress. It is impossible for a right to be more guarded. As to a tonnage duty that could be recovered in but one way, and a sum so raised, being obviously necessary for the execution of health laws and other unavoidable port expenses, it was intended that it should go into the State treasuries, and nothing more was required therefore than the consent of Congress. But this whole clause, as to these two subjects, appears to have been introduced *ex abundanti cautela*, to remove every temptation to an attempt to interfere with the powers of Congress over commerce, and to show how far Congress might consent to permit the States to exercise that power. Beyond those limits, even by the consent of Congress, they could not exercise it. And thus we have the whole effect of the clause. The inference which counsel would deduce from it is neither necessary nor consistent with the general purpose of the clause.

But instances have been insisted on with much confidence in argument in which, by municipal laws, particular regulations respecting their cargoes have been imposed upon shipping in the ports of the United

States, and one in which forfeiture was made the penalty of disobedience.

Until such laws have been tested by exceptions to their constitutionality, the argument certainly wants much of the force attributed to it; but, admitting their constitutionality, they present only the familiar case of punishment inflicted by both governments upon the same individual. He who robs the mail may also steal the horse that carries it, and would unquestionably be subject to punishment at the same time under the laws of the State in which the crime is committed and under those of the United States. And these punishments may interfere, and one render it impossible to inflict the other, and yet the two governments would be acting under powers that have no claim to identity.

It would be in vain to deny the possibility of a clashing and collision between the measures of the two governments. The line cannot be drawn with sufficient distinctness between the municipal powers of the one and the commercial powers of the other. In some points, they meet and blend so as scarcely to admit of separation. Hitherto, the only remedy has been applied which the case admits of—that of a frank and candid cooperation for the general good. Witness the laws of Congress requiring its officers to respect the inspection laws of the States and to aid in enforcing their health laws, that which surrenders to the States the superintendence of pilotage, and the many laws passed to permit a tonnage duty to be levied for the use of their ports. Other instances could be cited abundantly to prove that collision must be sought to be produced, and when it does arise, the question must be decided how far the powers of Congress are adequate to put it down. Wherever the powers of the respective governments are frankly exercised, with a distinct view to the ends of such powers, they may act upon the same object, or use the same means, and yet the powers be kept perfectly distinct. A resort to the same means therefore is no argument to prove the identity of their respective powers.

I have not touched upon the right of the States to grant patents for inventions or improvements generally, because it does not necessarily arise in this cause. It is enough for all the purposes of this decision if they cannot exercise it so as to restrain a free intercourse among the States.

DECREE. This cause came on to be heard on the transcript of the record of the Court for the Trial of Impeachments and Correction of Errors of the State of New York, and was argued by counsel. On consideration whereof, this Court is of opinion that the several licenses to the steamboats the *Stoudinger* and the *Bellona* to carry on the coasting trade, which are set up by the appellant Thomas Gibbons in his answer to the bill of the respondent, Aaron Ogden, filed in the Court of Chancery for the State of New York, which were granted under an act of Congress, passed in pursuance of the Constitution of the United States, gave full authority to those vessels to navigate the waters of the United States, by steam or otherwise, for the purpose of carrying on the coasting trade, any law of the State of New York to the contrary notwithstanding, and that so much of the several laws of the State of New York as prohibits vessels, licensed according to the laws of the United States, from navigating the waters of the State of New York by means of fire or steam is repugnant to the said Constitution, and void. This Court is therefore of opinion that the decree of the Court of New York for the Trial of Impeachments and the Correction of Errors affirming the decree of the Chancellor of that State, which perpetually enjoins the said Thomas Gibbons, the appellant, from navigating the waters of the State of New York with the steamboats the *Stoudinger* and the *Bellona* by steam or fire, is erroneous, and ought to be reversed, and the same is hereby reversed and annulled, and this Court doth further DIRECT, ORDER, and DECREE that the bill of the said Aaron Ogden be dismissed, and the same is hereby dismissed accordingly.

---

## Glossary

**chancery court:** court that specializes in constitutional issues and property disputes

**coasting license:** a license giving a vessel the right to trade in American ports

---

## Glossary

**commerce:** the buying and selling of goods and the transportation of passengers and goods

**concurrent regulation:** an area in which the jurisdictions of two governments overlap

**court of errors:** a court of appeals that reviews the decisions of other courts

**enroll:** to legally register a vessel

**injunction:** a legal writ issued by a court forbidding the undertaking of a certain action

**inspection laws:** public safety measures designed to guarantee quality of merchandise

**intercourse:** communication or trade between different individuals or groups

**monopoly:** governmental grant giving an individual the sole right over a certain activity

**police powers:** the right of a sovereign government to regulate health and morals for the public good

**quarantine laws:** laws allowing government agents to seize and hold property for public safety

# WORCESTER V. GEORGIA

| DATE | CITATION |
|---|---|
| 1832 | 31 U.S. 515 |
| **AUTHOR** | **SIGNIFICANCE** |
| John Marshall | Held that the U.S. Constitution acknowledges and recognizes Native American tribes as distinct and separate political entities that occupy their own territory over which the states have no jurisdiction |
| **VOTE** | |
| 6-1 | |

## Overview

Samuel A. Worcester was a prominent American missionary and publisher who saw the infringement of American settlement in the state of Georgia as a direct threat to the sovereignty of the Cherokee people. Worcester was one of roughly a dozen missionaries who wished to protest a Georgia law prohibiting white men from establishing residency on Cherokee land with permission from the Cherokee but without a license from the state. Worcester argued that by obeying such a law, the Cherokee had de facto surrendered their sovereignty to the state of Georgia. The missionaries established residency and began to publish a newspaper, *The Cherokee Phoenix*, that publicized their actions and advocated for the rights of the Cherokee as protected under federal law. Worcester brought two suits to the Supreme Court in 1830 and 1831, which established federal primacy over relations with Native American tribes and recognized the tribes as "domestic dependent nations." However, Georgians disagreed with the decisions and saw Worcester and his fellow missionaries as revolutionaries and ordered their arrest by militia forces in 1831. While several missionaries accepted pardons, Worcester and an-

other missionary took sentences of hard labor to put the case again before the Court. The Court again upheld the unconstitutionality of Georgia law and, in so doing, created the legal doctrine of tribal sovereignty within the United States.

## Context

As Americans marched westward after the American Revolution, white settlement continued to intrude upon Native American territory. While some encroachment was made to take lands or resources from the Cherokee, other encroachment was part of a benevolent effort to educate and attempt to acclimate tribal people into American society. One such benevolent group, the American Board of Commissioners for Foreign Missions, or American Board, was especially active in the American Southeast and, by the early 1830s, would become a significant player in the judicial fight to secure the political and civil rights of Native Americans. While several tribes chose to counter such intrusions by violence, the Cherokee Nation sought to resolve the issue through diploma-

**Samuel Worcester**
(Wikimedia Commons)

cy. However, these diplomatic actions largely failed to hold weight within Georgia. After decades of attempts by the Cherokee to demonstrate their acclimatization and compatibility with American culture, the state of Georgia continued to pursue its own right to internal control of the Cherokee within its borders.

The issue first came to the forefront of American jurisprudence in 1830 when George Corn Tassel was accused of murdering Sanders Talking Rock Ford. Both men were Cherokee, and the incident occurred well within Cherokee lands. The matter should have been resolved by Cherokee law, as the individuals and locality were all within the sovereignty of the Cherokee Nation. Failing to recognize the Cherokee as a sovereign "nation within a nation," local Georgians placed Corn Tassel on trial, where he was found guilty and sentenced to death. When an appeal to the Georgia Superior Courts was denied, Cherokee Chief John Ross and the American Board hired former U.S. Attorney General William Wirt to take Corn Tassel's case before the Supreme Court.

The Supreme Court issued a stay of execution and ordered Governor George Gilmer to produce trial records when he appeared before them in January 1831. Gilmer responded by passing a series of laws that nullified contracts with the Cherokee, required the Cherokee to make a loyalty oath to the state of Georgia, and demanded that any white person employed by the Cherokee apply for a license from the state. Gilmer also refused to observe the jurisdiction of the Supreme Court and ordered Corn Tassel to be hung on December 24, 1830. After Wirt argued the case for Corn Tassel in March of 1831, the Court ruled that because Corn Tassel was deceased, the case lacked merit, and it was dismissed.

Governor Gilmer viewed the decision as a vindication of Georgia law. He began enthusiastically enforcing the laws limiting the rights of the Cherokee and their interactions with whites within the political boundaries of Georgia. Again, Ross and the American Board hired Wirt to seek an injunction on behalf of the Cherokee. In *Cherokee Nation v. Georgia* (1831), Wirt sought an injunction arguing that Georgian law was aimed at destroying the Cherokee as a political society. Georgia argued that as a sovereign nation, the Cherokee could not bring suit to the Courts but could only seek redress through the legislature. The Court heard the case argued but determined it did not have jurisdiction over the matter and declined to issue a decision.

However, the Marshall court did issue opinions on the merits of the constitutionality of *Cherokee Nation v. Georgia*. Chief Justice John Marshall argued that the framers of the Constitution did not see Native Americans as foreign nations but as "domestic dependent nations." This meant the tribes could not bring suit as a foreign nation but had to seek redress through Congress. Justices Thompson and Story disagreed and, in their dissent, argued that if the tribes were competent enough to make treaties with the government, they were equal to any other foreign state and that the Court had jurisdiction to rule on the case. Thompson and Story argued that the actions of Georgia directly violated the powers allotted to the states concerning Native Americans in 1802. However, despite overruling such dissenting opinions, Marshall did denote that "a proper case with proper parties" should come before the Court so that the justices could develop a constitutional ruling.

The American Board and its missionaries saw Marshall's majority opinion in *Cherokee Nation v. Georgia* as an opportunity to force a decision. Samuel Worcester and eleven other missionaries discussed the opportunity and its potential ramifications and then, agreeing on a course, published a resolution in protest of the Georgia law against white men establishing residence on Cherokee lands without a permit from the state. Worcester and the missionaries argued that the law unconstitutionally limited their rights as American citizens. Worcester and the others recognized that, ideologically, obeying the Georgia law would be a de facto vacation of the Cherokee's sovereignty. Having declared their intention publicly, Governor Gilmer ordered a militia expedition to inspect the Cherokee lands to verify the illegal establishment of homes by the missionaries and arrest them.

In September 1831, eleven missionaries were placed on trial after their arrest. Having been convicted by a local court, the missionaries appealed to the Georgia Superior Courts only to have their conviction upheld. After being sentenced to four years of hard labor for their actions, nine missionaries made oaths of loyalty to the state and received pardons, but Samuel Worcester and Elizur Butler refused. The refusal of Worcester and Butler allowed the American Board to hire Wirt again to seek an injunction from the Supreme Court.

The U.S. Supreme Court heard Wirt present the case over three days in late February 1832. The case presented was without the defense of the state of Georgia. Governor Gilmer, resting on the declinations to make decisions in *Tassel v. Georgia* and *Cherokee Nation v. Georgia*, believed that the Court had no jurisdiction and sent no legal counsel to defend the state's actions. However, this time Georgia had risked much and lost. Not only did the Court hear Wirt's argument, but it decided on behalf of Worcester and Butler, issuing a writ of error to the Georgia courts to vacate the conviction and striking down the 1830 state laws enacted in response to *Tassel v. Georgia*.

## About the Author

### *The Majority Author*

Chief Justice John Marshall was born in Germantown, Virginia, in 1755 to Thomas Marshall, a surveyor and land agent, and Mary Randolph Keith, a second cousin of Thomas Jefferson. Marshall was the eldest of fif-

teen children. He grew up in a two-room log cabin and had only one year of formal education but was a voracious reader. John and Thomas Marshall joined the 3rd Virginia Regiment, participating in several battles, including the Battle of Brandywine Creek and the transformative winter at Valley Forge. Marshall was furloughed from service in 1780 and began studying law under George Wythe at the College of William and Mary. The same year, John Marshall was admitted to the Virginia Bar. He would briefly return to service in Continental Army before being elected to the Council of State of the Virginia House of Delegates in 1782.

Marshall would continue to serve as an influential state councilman while taking on new responsibilities as the recorder of the Richmond courts and building a private law practice. After witnessing the failures of the Articles of Confederation in Shay's Rebellion, Marshall became a fierce proponent of constitutional ratification, working alongside James Madison in the Virginia Ratifying Convention of 1788. Marshall declined the nomination of George Washington to assume the duties of the U.S. attorney for Virginia and the U.S. attorney general, choosing instead to pursue the private practice of law.

In 1797 Marshall served on a three-member commission to France that would later become known as the XYZ Affair, leading to the undeclared quasi-war with France. Marshall supported many actions during this time but spoke against the Alien and Sedition Acts as unnecessary and corrosively divisive acts on American society. In 1789 his efforts during the XYZ Affair, along with the support of Patrick Henry, won Marshall the seat as congressman of Virginia's 13th District. Marshall would turn down the nomination of John Adams to the U.S. Supreme Court, instead seeking to represent the people of Virginia in Congress. By 1800, his actions in Congress led to President Adams nominating him briefly for secretary of war before withdrawing the nomination and instead nominating Marshall for secretary of state. Marshall accepted the nomination and took office in June 1800. He would be instrumental in ending the quasi-war and ongoing clashes with Britain and Spain and enforcing maritime rights through North Africa among the Barbary States.

In January 1801 President John Adams, after the loss of several justices, appointed Marshall to the U.S. Supreme Court as chief justice, believing Marshall could heal divisions and propel the Court to a position of prominence in the federal government. Marshall was confirmed later that month and assumed the office of chief justice on February 4, 1801. Marshall did not disappoint.

In the years preceding the Marshall Court, the U.S. Supreme Court had made only 63 decisions, none of which had struck down a state or federal law. Marshall's 34-year tenure as chief justice would produce more than 1,000 decisions—about half of which were authored by Marshall himself—and establish the U.S. Supreme Court as an influential actor in shaping the federal government. The Marshall Court would strike down federal law only once, in *Marbury v. Madison* (1803). However, this ruling would assume the powers of the Court to check the actions of the president, Congress, the states, and lower courts in interpreting the U.S. Constitution. The Marshall Court would generally enforce strong governmental powers. Marshall would die in Philadelphia on July 6, 1835, the last of the founding generation.

### *The Dissenting Author*

Associate Justice Henry Baldwin was born January 14, 1780, in New Haven, Connecticut, to Michael Baldwin, a prosperous farmer, and Theresa Walcott. His family's wealth allowed Baldwin to attend the Hopkins School for his primary education and graduate from Yale in 1797. In 1798 he would read law under Tapping Reeve at Lichfield Law School and truly find his passion for the hands-on debate law offered. He moved to Philadelphia to clerk for Alexander Dallas, a prominent attorney who would shape Baldwin's approach to the law and help cement Baldwin's political views as a Democratic-Republican. Baldwin then moved to Pittsburgh after passing the bar in 1801, invested in iron, and formed a successful law partnership with two partners. While in Pittsburgh, Baldwin served as the publisher of the Democratic-Republican newspaper *The Tree of Liberty*. His views as publisher resulted in several duels, one of which very nearly killed him.

During the War of 1812, Baldwin served on the Pittsburgh Committee for Public Safety. Combined with his business and social prominence in Pittsburgh, Baldwin was elected to Congress in 1816, serving three terms as a staunch supporter and defender of business interests and Andrew Jackson's actions in the Seminole Wars. He also served as chairman of the House Committee on Domestic Manufactures and often clashed with John Calhoun over tariff policy. Jackson saw Baldwin as a confidant and sought Baldwin's counsel during the remainder of Jackson's political career. Baldwin withdrew from Congress in 1822 due to bad health and financial issues. Baldwin actively supported Jackson's 1828 presidential campaign in Pittsburgh but felt slighted when Jackson did not appoint him as a cabinet secretary. However, hurt feelings were repaired by 1830 when Jackson nominated Baldwin for associate justice.

Baldwin was generally at odds with the rest of the Court as an associate justice. Baldwin strongly disagreed with Marshall's agenda to extend the prominence and powers of the Court. Baldwin was known for his cutting views and aggressive dissents, which isolated him from his peers ideologically and socially. Baldwin, seeing that his perspectives were not gaining traction within the court, published a tract on his views on the necessity of a literal reading of the Constitution and the importance of the rights of business to a healthy nation in *A General View of the Origin and Nature of the Constitution and Government of the United States* (1837). The Marshall Court had developed a reputation for issuing only a majority opinion. However, Baldwin insisted on publishing dissents. Baldwin would create the mainstay of the Court through this insistence to produce both a majority and minority opinion on legal decisions as an accepted practice. Baldwin's fourteen-year tenure on the court produced two key dissents—*Worcester v. Georgia* (1832) and *Groves v. Slaughter* (1841)—before his death on April 21, 1844.

## Explanation and Analysis of the Document

### *The Majority Opinion*

Chief Justice Marshall opens his opinion by declaring that the matter before the court is of the utmost importance to define the middle ground between the extremes of states' rights and nationalists at a point where the nation is feeling considerable pressure. Marshall also notes that the issue causes reflection between the prevailing schools of thought regarding the reading of the Constitution—that neither constructionist nor liberal interpretations could accurately answer the matter in any definitive manner. Marshall rhetorically surmises the issue as the necessity for the Court to adjudicate the constitutional limits of "[t]he legislative power of a state" against "the personal liberty of a citizen." Marshall argues these are two matters and that each much be taken separately before the Court can decide on the more significant matter under consideration.

### Is the matter one under the jurisdiction of the Court?

Marshall outlines that the procedure and application of law in charging, trial, sentencing, and appeal processing by the state courts in relation to Worcester et al. was proper, but he holds short of blaming the lower court's decision for now. Having established that the case has been conducted under the Judicial Act and its amendments, Marshall has been brought firmly into the Court's jurisdiction by the state authorities and by the actions of the state authorities and the citizenship of Worcester and his fellow missionaries. Therefore, any such law designed by a state is unconstitutional and void. Marshall asserts that because of the path Georgia has taken, under Section 25 of the Judicial Act, "[i]t is too clear for controversy, that the act of congress by which this court is constituted, has given it the power, and of course imposed on it the duty of exercising jurisdiction in this case."

### Is the exercise of power by the legislature within its constitutional authority?

Marshall argues that it is not proper and is "repugnant to the said treaties" for the state of Georgia to rule the legitimacy of a treaty between the U.S. government and any foreign state. Therefore, any such law designed by a state is unconstitutional and void. Furthermore, Marshall argues that such laws overstep the authority of the state by assuming the constitutional power granted exclusively to Congress to treat both foreign nations and Indian tribes in Section 8 of Article I. Marshall also points out that any such law violates the Indian Trade and Intercourse Act of 1790 and its multiple amendments through 1812.

Marshall then supports this finding in a second way by citing Georgia's argument "that the residence, charged in the indictment, was under the authority of the president of the United States" and granted the missionaries' presence to "the permission and approval of the Cherokee nation." This, according to Marshall, argues that "the Cherokees, acknowledge their right as a sovereign nation to govern themselves and all persons who have settled within their territory, free from any

right of legislative interference by the several states composing the United States of America." Marshall asserts that this must be taken with latitude because cultural and linguistic differences exist between the two. Marshall, however, admonishes Georgia that its effort to interpret the form of government assumed by the Cherokee as "a surrender of self-government, would be, we think, a perversion of their necessary meaning, and a departure from the construction which has been uniformly put on [all Native American nations]."

Marshall connects the issue to common law as a direct line of inherited rights in the interaction between citizens and Native Americans as demonstrated by all European persons in the Americas since 1492 for a right to intercourse and defense but not conquest. "Certain it is, that our history furnishes no example, from the first settlement of our country, of any attempt on the part of the crown to interfere with the internal affairs of the Indians, farther than to keep out the agents of foreign powers, who, as traders or otherwise, might seduce them into foreign alliances. The king purchased their lands when they were willing to sell, at a price they were willing to take; but never coerced a surrender of them." Marshall asserts that the series of treaties between the U.S. government and the Native American tribes have placed the tribes "under the protection of the United States of America, and of no other sovereign whosoever."

Under such protection, Marshall argues, Congress has provided protections to the Native American territories within its borders, including the proper restraint of American citizens from encroaching upon Native American lands. Marshall points to the 1819 Indian Civilization Act, aimed at "providing against the further decline and final extinction of the Indian tribes adjoining to the frontier settlements of the United States, and for introducing among them the habits and arts of civilization." This act creates a demand for "capable persons, of good moral character, to instruct [Native Americans] in the mode of agriculture suited to their situation; and for teaching their children in reading, writing and arithmetic; and for performing such other duties as may be enjoined." This would be what the American Board missionaries had stated as their sole cause for establishing residency with consent from the Cherokee Nation.

"This act avowedly contemplates the preservation of the Indian nations as an object sought by the United States.

It proposes to effect this object by civilizing and converting them from hunters into agriculturists. Though the Cherokees had already made considerable progress in this improvement, it cannot be doubted that the general words of the act comprehend them. Their advance in the 'habits and arts of civilization,' rather encouraged perseverance in the laudable exertions still farther to meliorate their condition. This act furnishes strong additional evidence of a settled purpose to fix the Indians in their country by giving them security at home."

According to Marshall, the question presented to the Court is: Has Georgia interpreted its policing power correctly in a rightful, if disdainful, exercise of power, "or is it usurpation?" Marshall answers, after a sizable monologue, that "The Cherokee nation, then, is a distinct community . . . in which the laws of Georgia can have no force, and which the citizens of Georgia have no right to enter, but with the assent of the Cherokees themselves, or in conformity with treaties, and with the acts of congress."

### Can this court revise and reverse it?

Marshall concludes that the actions of the state of Georgia interfered with the proper exercise of federal authority and were thus unconstitutional. With that, Marshall answers the overarching question of jurisdiction succinctly: "It is the opinion of this court that the judgment of the superior court for the county of Gwinnett, in the state of Georgia, condemning Samuel A. Worcester to hard labour, in the penitentiary of the state of Georgia, for four years, was pronounced by that court under colour of a law which is void, as being repugnant to the constitution, treaties, and laws of the United States, and ought, therefore, to be reversed and annulled."

### The Dissenting Opinion

Associate Justice Baldwin did not write a formal opinion but stated very succinctly that in his opinion, the court had already ruled in *Cherokee Nation v. Georgia* that "an Indian tribe or nation within the United States is not a foreign state in the sense of the constitution, and cannot maintain an action in the courts of the United States." Additionally, Baldwin argued that due to Georgia's failure to appear or lodge a defense, the writ of error issued by the Supreme Court to the state of Georgia had not been properly returned. Because of this, in Baldwin's opinion, the Supreme Court did not have jurisdiction to render a legal decision.

Some historians have offered that Baldwin's failure to provide a formal opinion either to the court reporter or to any other entity was a recognition by Baldwin, and to the Democratic-Republicans generally, of how volatile any debate on states' rights was in the nation at that time. As support to this interpretation of Baldwin's actions, historians note that Baldwin similarly failed to offer a formal opinion as the lone dissenter in the decision rendered in *United States v. Amistad* (1841). Here with the decision that violence to force the manumission of enslaved people could be considered legal if undertaken by the enslaved themselves, Baldwin also sought to walk the razor's edge politically while finding methods to render his judicial duties appropriately.

## Impact

Although the Supreme Court's decision had struck down Georgia's 1830 laws, neither the state nor the federal government enforced the decision. President Andrew Jackson, a Southerner with firm beliefs in states' rights doctrine, sought to hold the nation together even after the Compromise of 1820 had allowed some political pressure for nullification to dissipate. Thus, Jackson had no desire to enforce the Court's decision—especially in light of Baldwin's dissenting opinion. Because of this lack of enforcement, the decision was largely lame in its actual effects. Worcester and Butler remained in prison until 1833 when a negotiated release was reached with Governor Wilson Lumpkin, who had won a second election to the office after Gilmer. The Cherokee were forcibly removed from their lands in Georgia due to a legally and morally dubious treaty between the U.S. government and a group of Cherokees purportedly acting on behalf of the tribe. Despite the efforts of Chief John Ross to declare the treaty void, President Jackson ordered the U.S. Army to supervise and escort the Cherokee from the Southeast to territories west of the Mississippi River in present-day Oklahoma. The forced relocation is more commonly known today as the Trail of Tears. It is considered by historians to be one of the more shameful events in American–Native American relations. Today the hardline ruling issued in *Worcester v. Georgia* has softened through successive decisions. Modern jurisprudence holds that states have limited rights to regulate Native American territories and members within their political boundaries.

## Questions for Further Study

1. How does the relationship between the Native American tribes and the U.S. government differ between Marshall and Baldwin's interpretations?

2. The Supreme Court is often asked to make decisions about the constitutionality of a case separate from the moral or ethical grounds of a case. Was the majority decision aimed primarily at the legal or moral grounds of the case? Why do you think so?

3. Baldwin had previously supported Jackson's violent tactics in the Seminole War when others challenged these as morally questionable. Was his dissent here a continuation of support for Jackson's polices toward Native Americans? Why do you think so?

4. After three attempts, what was the deciding factor in making in *Worcester v. Georgia*, and not *Tassel v. Georgia* or *Cherokee Nation v. Georgia*, a "proper" case for the Marshall court to hear and decide upon the conflict between the Cherokee Nation and the State of Georgia?

5. How could the outcome of *Worcester v. Georgia* have affected you if you were a tribal leader of another Native American tribe coming into increasing encroachment by American settlers?

## Further Reading

### Books

Andrew, John. *From Revivals to Removal: Jeremiah Evarts, the Cherokee Nation, and the Search for the Soul of America*. Athens: University of Georgia Press, 1992.

Garrison, Tim. *The Legal Ideology of Removal: The Southern Judiciary and the Sovereignty of Native American Nations*. Athens: University of Georgia Press, 2009.

Magliocca, Gerard. *Andrew Jackson and the Constitution: The Rise and Fall of Generational Regimes*. Lawrence: University Press of Kansas, 2011.

Robertson, Lindsay. *Conquest by Law: How the Discovery of America Dispossessed Indigenous Peoples of Their Lands*. New York: Oxford University Press, 2005.

Sedgwick, John. *Blood Moon: An American Epic of War and Splendor in the Cherokee Nation*. New York: Simon & Schuster, 2018.

Williams, David. *The Georgia Gold Rush: Twenty-Niners, Cherokees, and Gold Fever*. Columbia: University of South Carolina Press, 1995.

### Websites

"Account of S[amuel] A. Worcester's second Arrest, 1831 July 18." State Library Cherokee Collection, Tennessee State Library and Archives, Nashville, presented in the Digital Library of Georgia. Accessed February 17, 2023, http://dlg.usg.edu/record/dlg_zlna_ch050.

## Further Reading

### Websites

McBride, Alex. "Cherokee Indian Cases (1830s)." The Supreme Court: Supreme Court History: The First Hundred Years. December 2006. Accessed February 17, 2023, http://www.thirteen.org/wnet/supremecourt/antebellum/landmark_cherokee.html.

"Nullification Crisis." American Battlefield Trust. Accessed February 17, 2023, http://www.battlefields.org/learn/articles/nullification-crisis.

"Preludes to the Trail of Tears." National Park Service website. Accessed February 17, 2023, http://www.nps.gov/articles/000/preludes-trail-of-tears.htm.

Vile, John R. "Native Americans." The First Amendment Encyclopedia. Accessed February 17, 2023, http://mtsu.edu/first-amendment/article/1369/native-americans.

—Commentary by Bryant Macfarlane

# WORCESTER V. GEORGIA

## Document Text

### *Mr Chief Justice MARSHALL delivered the opinion of the Court*

This cause, in every point of view in which it can be placed, is of the deepest interest.

The defendant is a State, a member of the Union, which has exercised the powers of government over a people who deny its jurisdiction, and are under the protection of the United States.

The plaintiff is a citizen of the State of Vermont, condemned to hard labour for four years in the penitentiary of Georgia under colour of an act which he alleges to be repugnant to the Constitution, laws, and treaties of the United States.

The legislative power of a State, the controlling power of the Constitution and laws of the United States, the rights, if they have any, the political existence of a once numerous and powerful people, the personal liberty of a citizen, are all involved in the subject now to be considered.

It behooves this court, in every case, more especially in this, to examine into its jurisdiction with scrutinizing eyes before it proceeds to the exercise of a power which is controverted.

The first step in the performance of this duty is the inquiry whether the record is properly before the Court.

It is certified by the clerk of the court which pronounced the judgment of condemnation under which the plaintiff in error is imprisoned, and is also authenticated by the seal of the court. It is returned with, and annexed to, a writ of error issued in regular form, the citation being signed by one of the Associate Justices of the Supreme Court, and served on the Governor and Attorney General of the State more than thirty days before the commencement of the term to which the writ of error was returnable.

The Judicial Act (sec. 22, 25, 2 Laws U. S. 64, 65), so far as it prescribes the mode of proceeding, appears to have been literally pursued.

In February, 1797, a rule (6 Wheat.Rules) was made on this subject in the following words:

"It is ordered by the Court that the clerk of the Court to which any writ of error shall be directed may make return of the same by transmitting a true copy of the record, and of all proceedings in the same, under his hand and the seal of the Court."

This has been done. But the signature of the judge has not been added to that of the clerk. The law does not require it. The rule does not require it.

In the case of *Martin v. Hunter's Lessee*, 1 Wheat. 304, 14 U. S. 361, an exception was taken to the return of the refusal of the State court to enter a prior judgment of reversal by this Court because it was not made by the judge of the State court to which the writ was directed, but the exception was overruled, and the return was held sufficient. In *Buel v. Van Ness*, 8 Wheat. 312, also a writ of error to a State court, the record was authenticated in the same manner. No exception was taken to it. These were civil cases. But it has been truly said at the bar that, in regard to this process, the law makes no distinction between a criminal and civil case. The same return is required in both. If the sanction of the Court could be necessary for the establishment of this position, it has been silently given.

*M'Culloch v. Maryland*, 4 Wheat. 316, was a *qui tam* action brought to recover a penalty, and the record was authenticated by the seal of the Court and the signature of the clerk, without that of a judge. *Brown et al. v. The State of Maryland* was an indictment for a fine and forfeiture. The record in this case, too, was authenticated by the seal of the Court and the certificate of the clerk. The practice is both ways.

The record, then, according to the Judiciary Act and the rule and the practice of the Court, is regularly before us. The more important inquiry is does it exhibit a case cognizable by this tribunal?

The indictment charges the plaintiff in error and others, being white persons, with the offence of "residing within the limits of the Cherokee Nation without a license," and "without having taken the oath to support and defend the Constitution and laws of the State of Georgia."

The defendant in the State court appeared in proper person, and filed the following plea:

"And the said Samuel A. Worcester, in his own proper person, comes and says that this Court ought not to take further cognizance of the action and prosecution aforesaid because he says that, on the 15th day of July in the year 1831, he was, and still is, a resident in the Cherokee Nation, and that the said supposed crime or crimes, and each of them, were committed, if committed at all, at the town of New Echota, in the said Cherokee Nation, out of the jurisdiction of this Court, and not in the County Gwinnett, or elsewhere, within the jurisdiction of this Court, and this defendant saith that he is a citizen of the State of Vermont, one of the United States of America, and that he entered the aforesaid Cherokee Nation in the capacity of a duly authorised missionary of the American Board of Commissioners for Foreign Missions, under the authority of the President of the United States, and has not since been required by him to leave it; that he was, at the time of his arrest, engaged in preaching the gospel to the Cherokee Indians, and in translating the sacred scriptures into their language, with the permission and approval of the said Cherokee Nation, and in accordance with the humane policy of the Government of the United States for the civilization and improvement of the Indians; and that his residence there for this purpose is the residence charged in the aforesaid indictment; and this defendant further saith that this prosecution the State of Georgia ought not to have or maintain because he saith that several treaties have, from time to time, been entered into between the United States and the Cherokee Nation of Indians, to-wit, at Hopewell on the 28th day of November, 1785; at Holston on the 2d day of July, 1791; at Philadelphia on the 26th day of June, 1794; at Tellico on the 2d day of October, 1798; at Tellico on the 24th day of October, 1804; at Tellico on the 25th day of October, 1805; at Tellico on the 27th day of October, 1805; at Washington City on the 7th day of January, 1805; at Washington City on the 22d day of March, 1816; at the Chickasaw Council House on the 14th day of September, 1816; at the Cherokee Agency on the 8th day of July, 1817; and at Washington City on the 27th day of February, 1819: all which treaties have been duly ratified by the Senate of the United States of America, and by which treaties the United States of America acknowledge the said Cherokee Nation to be a sovereign nation, authorised to govern themselves and all persons who have settled within their territory free from any right of legislative interference by the several states composing the United States of America, in reference to acts done within their own territory, and by which treaties the whole of the territory now occupied by the Cherokee Nation on the east of the Mississippi has been solemnly guarantied to them, all of which treaties are existing treaties at this day, and in full force. By these treaties, and particularly by the Treaties of Hopewell and Holston, the aforesaid territory is acknowledged to lie without the jurisdiction of the several states composing the Union of the United States, and it is thereby specially stipulated that the citizens of the United States shall not enter the aforesaid territory, even on a visit, without a passport from the Governor of a State, or from someone duly authorised thereto by the President of the United States, all of which will more fully and at large appear by reference to the aforesaid treaties. And this defendant saith that the several acts charged in the bill of indictment were done or omitted to be done, if at all, within the said territory so recognized as belonging to the said nation and so, as aforesaid, held by them under the guarantee of the United States; that, for those acts, the defendant is not amenable to the laws of Georgia, nor to the jurisdiction of the Courts of the said state, and that the laws of the State of Georgia, which profess to add the said territory to the several adjacent counties of the said State and to extend the laws of Georgia over the said territory and persons inhabiting the same, and, in particular, the act on which this indictment against this defendant is grounded, to-wit,"

"An act entitled an act to prevent the exercise of assumed and arbitrary power by all persons under pretext of authority from the Cherokee Indians, and their laws, and to prevent white persons from residing within that part of the chartered limits of Georgia occupied by the Cherokee Indians, and to provide a guard for the protection of the gold mines, and to enforce the laws of the State within the aforesaid territory,"

"are repugnant to the aforesaid treaties, which, according to the Constitution of the United States, compose a part of the supreme law of the land; and that these laws of Georgia are, therefore, unconstitutional, void, and of no effect; that the said laws of Georgia are also unconstitutional and void because they impair the obligation of the various contracts formed by and between the aforesaid Cherokee Nation and the said United States of America, as above recited; also that the said laws of Georgia are unconstitutional and void because they interfere with, and attempt to regulate and control the intercourse with the said Cherokee Nation, which, by the said Constitution, belongs exclusively to the Congress of the United States; and because the said laws are repugnant to the statute of the United States, passed on the ___ day of March 1802, entitled 'An act to regulate trade and intercourse with the Indian tribes, and to preserve peace on the frontiers;' and that, therefore, this Court has no jurisdiction to cause this defendant to make further or other answer to the said bill of indictment, or further to try and punish this defendant for the said supposed offence or offences alleged in the bill of indictment, or any of them; and therefore this defendant prays judgment whether he shall be held bound to answer further to said indictment."

This plea was overruled by the Court. And the prisoner, being arraigned, plead not guilty. The jury found a verdict against him, and the Court sentenced him to hard labour in the penitentiary for the term of four years.

By overruling this plea, the Court decided that the matter it contained was not a bar to the action. The plea, therefore, must be examined for the purpose of determining whether it makes a case which brings the party within the provisions of the twenty-fifth section of the "Act to establish the judicial Courts of the United States."

The plea avers that the residence, charged in the indictment, was under the authority of the President of the United States, and with the permission and approval of the Cherokee Nation. That the treaties, subsisting between the United States, and the Cherokees, acknowledge their right as a sovereign nation to govern themselves and all persons who have settled within their territory, free from any right of legislative interference by the several states composing the United States of America. That the act under which the prosecution was instituted is repugnant to the said treaties, and is, therefore, unconstitutional and void. That the said act is also unconstitutional because it interferes with and attempts to regulate and control the intercourse with the Cherokee Nation, which belongs exclusively to Congress, and because also it is repugnant to the statute of the United States, entitled "An act to regulate trade and intercourse with the Indian tribes and to preserve peace on the frontiers."

Let the averments of this plea be compared with the twenty-fifth section of the Judicial Act.

That section enumerates the cases in which the final judgment or decree of a State court may be revised in the Supreme Court of the United States. These are

"where is drawn in question the validity of a treaty, or statute of, or an authority exercised under, the United States, and the decision is against their validity; or where is drawn in question the validity of a statute of, or an authority exercised under any State, on the ground of their being repugnant to the Constitution, treaties or laws of the United States, and the decision is in favour of such their validity; or where is drawn in question the construction of any clause of the Constitution, or of a treaty, or statute of, or commission held under the United States, and the decision is against the title, right, privilege or exemption, specially set up or claimed by either party under such clause of the said Constitution, treaty, statute or commission."

The indictment and plea in this case draw in question, we think, the validity of the treaties made by the United States with the Cherokee Indians; if not so, their construction is certainly drawn in question; and the decision has been, if not against their validity, "against the right, privilege or exemption, specially set up and claimed under them." They also draw into question the validity of a statute of the State of Georgia, "on the ground of its being repugnant to the Constitution, treaties and laws of the United States, and the decision is in favour of its validity."

It is, then, we think, too clear for controversy that the act of Congress by which this Court is constituted has given it the power, and of course imposed on it the duty, of exercising jurisdiction in this case. This duty, however unpleasant, cannot be avoided. Those who fill the judicial department have no discretion in selecting the subjects to be brought before them. We must examine the defence set up in this plea. We must inquire and decide whether the act of the Legislature of Georgia under which the plaintiff in error has been prosecuted and condemned be consistent with, or repugnant to, the Constitution, laws and treaties of the United States.

It has been said at the bar that the acts of the Legislature of Georgia seize on the whole Cherokee country, parcel it out among the neighbouring counties of the State, extend her code over the whole country, abolish its institutions and its laws, and annihilate its political existence.

If this be the general effect of the system, let us inquire into the effect of the particular statute and section on which the indictment is founded.

It enacts that

"all white persons, residing within the limits of the Cherokee Nation on the 1st day of March next, or at any time thereafter, without a license or permit from his Excellency the Governor, or from such agent as his Excellency the Governor shall authorise to grant such permit or license, and who shall not have taken the oath hereinafter required, shall be guilty of a high misdemeanour, and, upon conviction thereof, shall be punished by confinement to the penitentiary, at hard labour, for a term not less than four years."

The eleventh section authorises the Governor, should he deem it necessary for the protection of the mines or the enforcement of the laws in force within the Cherokee Nation, "to raise and organize a guard," &c.

The thirteenth section enacts,

"that the said guard or any member of them, shall be, and they are hereby, authorised and empowered to arrest any person legally charged with or detected in a violation of the laws of this State, and to convey, as soon as practicable, the person so arrested before a justice of the peace, judge of the superior, or justice of inferior Court of this State to be dealt with according to law."

The extraterritorial power of every legislature being limited in its action to its own citizens or subjects, the very passage of this act is an assertion of jurisdiction over the Cherokee Nation, and of the rights and powers consequent on jurisdiction.

The first step, then, in the inquiry which the Constitution and laws impose on this Court is an examination of the rightfulness of this claim.

America, separated from Europe by a wide ocean, was inhabited by a distinct people, divided into separate nations, independent of each other and of the rest of the world, having institutions of their own, and governing themselves by their own laws. It is difficult to comprehend the proposition that the inhabitants of either quarter of the globe could have rightful original claims of dominion over the inhabitants of the other, or over the lands they occupied, or that the discovery of either by the other should give the discoverer rights in the country discovered which annulled the preexisting rights of its ancient possessors.

After lying concealed for a series of ages, the enterprise of Europe, guided by nautical science, conducted some of her adventurous sons into this western world. They found it in possession of a people who had made small progress in agriculture or manufactures, and whose general employment was war, hunting, and fishing.

Did these adventurers, by sailing along the coast, and occasionally landing on it, acquire for the several governments to whom they belonged, or by whom they were commissioned, a rightful property in the soil, from the Atlantic to the Pacific, or rightful dominion over the numerous people who occupied it? Or has nature, or the great Creator of all things, conferred these rights over hunters and fishermen, on agriculturists and manufacturers?

But power, war, conquest, give rights, which, after possession, are conceded by the world, and which can never be controverted by those on whom they descend. We proceed, then, to the actual state of things, having glanced at their origin, because holding it in our recollection might shed some light on existing pretensions.

The great maritime powers of Europe discovered and visited different parts of this continent at nearly the same time. The object was too immense for any one of them to grasp the whole, and the claimants were too powerful to submit to the exclusive or unreasonable pretensions of any single potentate. To avoid bloody conflicts which might terminate disastrously to all, it was necessary for the nations of Europe to establish some principle which all would acknowledge, and which should decide their respective rights as between themselves. This principle, suggested by the actual state of things, was

"that discovery gave title to the government by whose subjects or by whose authority it was made against all other European governments, which title might be consummated by possession."

8 Wheat. 21 U. S. 573.

This principle, acknowledged by all Europeans because it was the interest of all to acknowledge it, gave to the nation making the discovery, as its inevitable consequence, the sole right of acquiring the soil and of making settlements on it. It was an exclusive principle which shut out the right of competition among those who had agreed to it, not one which could annul the previous rights of those who had not agreed to it. It regulated the right given by discovery among the European discoverers, but could not affect the rights of those already in possession, either as aboriginal occupants or as occupants by virtue of a discovery made before the memory of man. It gave the exclusive right to purchase, but did not found that right on a denial of the right of the possessor to sell.

The relation between the Europeans and the natives was determined in each case by the particular government which asserted and could maintain this preemptive privilege in the particular place. The United States succeeded to all the claims of Great Britain, both territorial and political, but no attempt, so far as is known, has been made to enlarge them. So far as they existed merely in theory, or were in their nature only exclusive of the claims of other European nations, they still retain their original character, and remain dormant. So far as they have been practically exerted, they exist in fact, are understood by both parties, are asserted by the one, and admitted by the other.

Soon after Great Britain determined on planting colonies in America, the King granted charters to companies of his subjects who associated for the purpose of carrying the views of the Crown into effect, and of enriching themselves. The first of these charters was made before possession was taken of any part of the country. They purport, generally, to convey the soil from the Atlantic to the South Sea. This soil was occupied by numerous and warlike nations, equally willing and able to defend their possessions. The extravagant and absurd idea that the feeble settlements made on the sea coast, or the companies under whom they were made, acquired legitimate power by them to govern the people, or occupy the lands from sea to sea did not enter the mind of any man. They were well understood to convey the title which, according to the common law of European sovereigns respecting America, they might rightfully convey, and no more. This was the exclusive right of purchasing such lands as the natives were willing to sell. The Crown could not be understood to grant what the Crown did not affect to claim; nor was it so understood.

The power of making war is conferred by these charters on the colonies, but defensive war alone seems to have been contemplated. In the first charter to the first and second colonies, they are empowered, "for their several defences, to encounter, expulse, repel, and resist, all persons who shall, without license," attempt to inhabit

"within the said precincts and limits of the said several colonies, or that shall enterprise or attempt at any time hereafter the least detriment or annoyance of the said several colonies or plantations."

The charter to Connecticut concludes a general power to make defensive war with these terms: "and upon just causes to invade and destroy the natives or other enemies of the said colony."

The same power, in the same words, is conferred on the government of Rhode Island.

---

This power to repel invasion, and, upon just cause, to invade and destroy the natives, authorizes offensive as well as defensive war, but only "on just cause." The very terms imply the existence of a country to be invaded, and of an enemy who has given just cause of war.

The charter to William Penn contains the following recital:

"and because, in so remote a country, near so many barbarous nations, the incursions as well of the savages themselves as of other enemies, pirates, and robbers may probably be feared; therefore we have given,"

&c. The instrument then confers the power of war.

These barbarous nations whose incursions were feared, and to repel whose incursions the power to make war was given, were surely not considered as the subjects of Penn, or occupying his lands during his pleasure.

The same clause is introduced into the charter to Lord Baltimore.

The charter to Georgia professes to be granted for the charitable purpose of enabling poor subjects to gain a comfortable subsistence by cultivating lands in the American provinces "at present waste and desolate." It recites:

"and whereas our provinces in North America have been frequently ravaged by Indian enemies, more especially that of South Carolina, which, in the late war by the neighbouring savages, was laid waste by fire and sword, and great numbers of the English inhabitants miserably massacred, and our loving subjects, who now inhabit there, by reason of the smallness of their numbers, will, in case of any new war, be exposed to the like calamities, inasmuch as their whole southern frontier continueth unsettled, and lieth open to the said savages."

These motives for planting the new colony are incompatible with the lofty ideas of granting the soil and all its inhabitants from sea to sea. They demonstrate the truth that these grants asserted a title against Europeans only, and were considered as blank paper so far as the rights of the natives were concerned. The power of war is given only for defence, not for conquest.

The charters contain passages showing one of their objects to be the civilization of the Indians, and their conversion to Christianity—objects to be accomplished by conciliatory conduct and good example, not by extermination.

The actual state of things and the practice of European nations on so much of the American continent as lies between the Mississippi and the Atlantic, explain their claims and the charters they granted. Their pretensions unavoidably interfered with each other; though the discovery of one was admitted by all to exclude the claim of any other, the extent of that discovery was the subject of unceasing contest. Bloody conflicts arose between them which gave importance and security to the neighbouring nations. Fierce and warlike in their character, they might be formidable enemies or effective friends. Instead of rousing their resentments by asserting claims to their lands or to dominion over their persons, their alliance was sought by flattering professions, and purchased by rich presents. The English, the French, and the Spaniards were equally competitors for their friendship and their aid. Not well acquainted with the exact meaning of words, nor supposing it to be material whether they were called the subjects or the children of their father in Europe; lavish in professions of duty and affection, in return for the rich presents they received; so long as their actual independence was untouched and their right to self-government acknowledged, they were willing to profess dependence on the power which furnished supplies of which they were in absolute need, and restrained dangerous intruders from entering their country. and this was probably the sense in which the term was understood by them.

Certain it is that our history furnishes no example, from the first settlement of our country, of any attempt on the part of the Crown to interfere with the internal affairs of the Indians farther than to keep out the agents of foreign powers, who, as traders or otherwise, might seduce them into foreign alliances. The King purchased their when they were willing to sell, at a price they were willing to take, but never coerced a surrender of them. He also purchased their alliance and dependence by subsidies, but never intruded into the interior of their affairs or interfered with their self-government so far as respected themselves only.

The general views of Great Britain with regard to the Indians were detailed by Mr Stuart, Superintendent of Indian affairs, in a speech delivered at Mobile, in presence of several persons of distinction, soon after the peace of 1763. Towards the conclusion, he says,

"Lastly, I inform you that it is the king's order to all his Governors and subjects to treat Indians with justice and humanity, and to forbear all encroachments on the territories allotted to them; accordingly, all individuals are prohibited from purchasing any of your lands; but, as you know that, as your white brethren cannot feed you when you visit them unless you give them ground to plant, it is expected that you will cede lands to the King for that purpose. But, whenever you shall be pleased to surrender any of your territories to his majesty, it must be done, for the future, at a public meeting of your nation, when the governors of the provinces or the superintendent shall be present, and obtain the consent of all your people. The boundaries of your hunting grounds will be accurately fixed, and no settlement permitted to be made upon them. As you may be assured that all treaties with your people will be faithfully kept, so it is expected that you, also, will be careful strictly to observe them."

The proclamation issued by the King of Great Britain in 1763, soon after the ratification of the articles of peace, forbids the Governors of any of the colonies to grant warrants of survey, or pass patents upon any lands whatever which, not having been ceded to, or purchased by, us (the King), as aforesaid, are reserved to the said Indians, or any of them.

The proclamation proceeds:

"And we do further declare it to be our royal will and pleasure, for the present, as aforesaid, to reserve, under our sovereignty, protection, and dominion, for the use of the said Indians, all the lands and territories lying to the westward of the sources of the rivers which fall into the sea, from the west and northwest as aforesaid: and we do hereby strictly forbid, on pain of our displeasure, all our loving subjects from making any purchases or settlements whatever, or taking possession of any of the lands above reserved, without our special leave and license for that purpose first obtained."

"And we do further strictly enjoin and require all persons whatever who have, either wilfully or inadvertently, seated themselves upon any lands within the countries above described, or upon any other lands which,

not having been ceded to, or purchased by us, are still reserved to the said Indians, as aforesaid, forthwith to remove themselves from such settlements."

A proclamation, issued by Governor Gage in 1772 contains the following passage:

"Whereas many persons, contrary to the positive orders of the King upon this subject, have undertaken to make settlements beyond the boundaries fixed by the treaties made with the Indian nations, which boundaries ought to serve as a barrier between the whites and the said nations, particularly on the Ouabache."

The proclamation orders such persons to quit those countries without delay.

Such was the policy of Great Britain towards the Indian nations inhabiting the territory from which she excluded all other Europeans; such her claims, and such her practical exposition of the charters she had granted. She considered them as nations capable of maintaining the relations of peace and war; of governing themselves, under her protection; and she made treaties with them the obligation of which she acknowledged.

This was the settled state of things when the war of our revolution commenced. The influence of our enemy was established; her resources enabled her to keep up that influence; and the colonists had much cause for the apprehension that the Indian nations would, as the allies of Great Britain, add their arms to hers. This, as was to be expected, became an object of great solicitude to Congress. Far from advancing a claim to their lands, or asserting any right of dominion over them, Congress resolved "that the securing and preserving the friendship of the Indian nations appears to be a subject of the utmost moment to these colonies."

The early journals of Congress exhibit the most anxious desire to conciliate the Indian nations. Three Indian departments were established; and commissioners appointed in each

"to treat with the Indians in their respective departments in the name and on the behalf of the United Colonies in order to preserve peace and friendship with the said Indians and to prevent their taking any part in the present commotions."

The most strenuous exertions were made to procure those supplies on which Indian friendships were supposed to depend, and every thing which might excite hostility was avoided.

The first treaty was made with the Delawares, in September, 1778.

The language of equality in which it is drawn evinces the temper with which the negotiation was undertaken and the opinion which then prevailed in the United States.

"1. That all offences or acts of hostilities by one or either of the contracting parties against the other be mutually forgiven, and buried in the depth of oblivion, never more to be had in remembrance."

"2. That a perpetual peace and friendship shall, from henceforth, take place and subsist between the contracting parties aforesaid, through all succeeding generations, and if either of the parties are engaged in a just and necessary war with any other nation or nations. that then each shall assist the other, in due proportion to their abilities, till their enemies are brought to reasonable terms of accommodation,"

&c.

3. The third article stipulates, among other things, a free passage for the American troops through the Delaware nation, and engages that they shall be furnished with provisions and other necessaries at their value.

"4. For the better security of the peace and friendship now entered into by the contracting parties against all infractions of the same by the citizens of either party to the prejudice of the other, neither party shall proceed to the infliction of punishments on the citizens of the other otherwise than by securing the offender or offenders, by imprisonment, or any other competent means, till a fair and impartial trial can be had by judges or juries of both parties, as near as can be to the laws, customs and usages of the contracting parties, and natural justice,"

&c.

5. The fifth article regulates the trade between the contracting parties in a manner entirely equal.

6. The sixth article is entitled to peculiar attention, as it contains a disclaimer of designs which were, at that time, ascribed to the United States by their enemies, and from the imputation of which Congress was then peculiarly anxious to free the government. It is in these words:

"Whereas the enemies of the United States have endeavoured by every artifice in their power to possess the Indians in general with an opinion that it is the design of the states aforesaid to extirpate the Indians and take possession of their country, to obviate such false suggestion, the United States do engage to guaranty to the aforesaid Nation of Delawares, and their heirs, all their territorial rights, in the fullest and most ample manner, as it hath been bounded by former treaties, as long as the said Delaware Nation shall abide by, and hold fast the chain of friendship now entered into."

The parties further agree that other tribes, friendly to the interest of the United States, may be invited to form a State, whereof the Delaware nation shall be the heads, and have a representation in Congress.

This treaty, in its language, and in its provisions, is formed, as near as may be, on the model of treaties between the Crowned heads of Europe.

The sixth article shows how Congress then treated the injurious calumny of cherishing designs unfriendly to the political and civil rights of the Indians.

During the War of the Revolution, the Cherokees took part with the British. After its termination, the United States, though desirous of peace, did not feel its necessity so strongly as while the war continued. Their political situation being changed, they might very well think it advisable to assume a higher tone, and to impress on the Cherokees the same respect for Congress which was before felt for the King of Great Britain. This may account for the language of the treaty of Hopewell. There is the more reason for supposing that the Cherokee chiefs were not very critical judges of the language, from the fact that every one makes his mark; no chief was capable of signing his name. It is probable the treaty was interpreted to them.

The treaty is introduced with the declaration that

"The commissioners plenipotentiary of the United States give peace to all the Cherokees, and receive them into the favour and protection of the United States of America, on the following conditions."

When the United States gave peace, did they not also receive it? Were not both parties desirous of it? If we consult the history of the day, does it not inform us that the United States were at least as anxious to obtain it as the Cherokees? We may ask, further: did the Cherokees come to the seat of the American government to solicit peace, or did the American commissioners go to them to obtain it? The treaty was made at Hopewell, not at New York. The word "give," then, has no real importance attached to it.

The first and second articles stipulate for the mutual restoration of prisoners, and are of course equal.

The third article acknowledges the Cherokees to be under the protection of the United States of America, and of no other power.

This stipulation is found in Indian treaties, generally. It was introduced into their treaties with Great Britain, and may probably be found in those with other European powers. Its origin may be traced to the nature of their connexion with those powers, and its true meaning is discerned in their relative situation.

The general law of European sovereigns respecting their claims in America limited the intercourse of Indians, in a great degree, to the particular potentate whose ultimate right of domain was acknowledged by the others. This was the general state of things in time of peace. It was sometimes changed in war. The consequence was that their supplies were derived chiefly from that nation, and their trade confined to it. Goods, indispensable to their comfort, in the shape of presents were received from the same hand. What was of still more importance, the strong hand of government was interposed to restrain the disorderly and licentious from intrusions into their country, from encroachments on their lands, and from those acts of violence which were often attended by reciprocal murder. The Indians perceived in this protection only what was beneficial to themselves—an engagement to punish aggressions on them. It involved, practically, no claim to their lands, no dominion over their persons. It merely bound the nation to the British Crown as a dependent ally claiming the protection of a powerful friend and neighbour and receiving the advantages of that protection without involving a surrender of their national character.

This is the true meaning of the stipulation, and is undoubtedly the sense in which it was made. Neither the British government nor the Cherokees ever understood it otherwise.

The same stipulation entered into with the United States is undoubtedly to be construed in the same manner. They receive the Cherokee Nation into their favor and protection. The Cherokees acknowledge themselves to be under the protection of the United States, and of no other power. Protection does not imply the destruction of the protected. The manner in which this stipulation was understood by the American government is explained by the language and acts of our first President.

The fourth article draws the boundary between the Indians and the citizens of the United States. But, in describing this boundary, the term "allotted" and the term "hunting ground" are used.

Is it reasonable to suppose that the Indians, who could not write and most probably could not read, who certainly were not critical judges of our language, should distinguish the word "allotted" from the words "marked out." The actual subject of contract was the dividing line between the two nations, and their attention may very well be supposed to have been confined to that subject. When, in fact, they were ceding lands to the United States, and describing the extent of their cession, it may very well be supposed that they might not understand the term employed as indicating that, instead of granting, they were receiving lands. If the term would admit of no other signification, which is not conceded, its being misunderstood is so apparent, results so necessarily from the whole transaction, that it must, we think, be taken in the sense in which it was most obviously used.

So with respect to the words "hunting grounds." Hunting was at that time the principal occupation of the Indians, and their land was more used for that purpose than for any other. It could not, however, be supposed that any intention existed of restricting the full use of the lands they reserved.

To the United States, it could be a matter of no concern whether their whole territory was devoted to hunting grounds or whether an occasional village and an occasional corn field, interrupted, and gave some variety to the scene.

These terms had been used in their treaties with Great Britain, and had never been misunderstood. They had never been supposed to imply a right in the British government to take their lands or to interfere with their internal government.

The fifth article withdraws the protection of the United States from any citizen who has settled, or shall settle, on the lands allotted to the Indians for their hunting grounds, and stipulates that, if he shall not remove within six months, the Indians may punish him.

The sixth and seventh articles stipulate for the punishment of the citizens of either country who may commit offences on or against the citizens of the other. The only inference to be drawn from them is that the United States considered the Cherokees as a nation.

The ninth article is in these words:

"For the benefit and comfort of the Indians, and for the prevention of injuries or oppressions on the part of the citizens or Indians, the United States, in Congress assembled, shall have the sole and exclusive right of regulating the trade with the Indians, and managing all their affairs, as they think proper."

To construe the expression "managing all their affairs" into a surrender of self-government would be, we think, a perversion of their necessary meaning, and a departure from the construction which has been uniformly put on them. The great subject of the article is the Indian trade. The influence it gave made it desirable that Congress should possess it. The commissioners brought forward the claim with the profession that their motive was "the benefit and comfort of the Indians, and the prevention of injuries or oppressions." This may be true as respects the regulation of their trade and as respects the regulation of all affairs connected with their trade, but cannot be true as respects the management of all their affairs. The most important of these are the cession of their lands and security against intruders on them. Is it credible that they should have considered themselves as surrendering to the United States the right to dictate their future cessions and the terms on which they should be made? or to compel their submission to the violence of disorderly and licentious intruders? It is equally inconceivable that they could have supposed themselves, by a phrase thus slipped into an article on another and most interesting subject, to have divested themselves of the right of self-government on subjects not connected with trade. Such a measure could not be "for their benefit and comfort," or for "the prevention of injuries and oppression." Such a construction would be inconsistent with the spirit of this and of all subsequent treaties, especially of those articles which recognise the right of the Cherokees to declare hostilities and to make war. It would convert a treaty of peace covertly into an act, annihilating the political existence of one of the parties. Had such a result been intended, it would have been openly avowed.

This treaty contains a few terms capable of being used in a sense which could not have been intended at the time, and which is inconsistent with the practical construction which has always been put on them; but its essential articles treat the Cherokees as a nation capable of maintaining the relations of peace and war, and ascertain the boundaries between them and the United States.

The treaty of Hopewell seems not to have established a solid peace. To accommodate the differences still existing between the State of Georgia and the Cherokee Nation, the Treaty of Holston was negotiated in July, 1791. The existing Constitution of the United States had been then adopted, and the Government, having more intrinsic capacity to enforce its just claims, was perhaps less mindful of high sounding expressions denoting superiority. We hear no more of giving peace to the Cherokees. The mutual desire of establishing permanent peace and friendship, and of removing all causes of war is honestly avowed, and, in pursuance of this desire, the first article declares that there shall be perpetual peace and friendship between all the citizens of the United States of America and all the individuals composing the Cherokee Nation.

The second article repeats the important acknowledgement that the Cherokee Nation is under the protection of the United States of America, and of no other sovereign whosoever.

The meaning of this has been already explained. The Indian nations were, from their situation, necessarily dependent on some foreign potentate for the supply of their essential wants and for their protection from lawless and injurious intrusions into their country. That power was naturally termed their protector. They had been arranged under the protection of Great Britain, but the extinguishment of the British power in their neighbourhood, and the establishment of that of the United States in its place, led naturally to the declaration on the part of the Cherokees that they were under the protection of the United States, and of no other power. They assumed the relation with the United States which had before subsisted with Great Britain.

This relation was that of a nation claiming and receiving the protection of one more powerful, not that of individuals abandoning their national character and submitting as subjects to the laws of a master.

The third article contains a perfectly equal stipulation for the surrender of prisoners.

The fourth article declares that "the boundary between the United States and the Cherokee Nation shall be as follows: beginning," &c. We hear no more of "allotments" or of "hunting grounds." A boundary is described, between nation and nation, by mutual consent. The national character of each, the ability of each to establish this boundary, is acknowledged by the other. To preclude forever all disputes, it is agreed that it shall be plainly marked by commissioners to be appointed by each party; and, in order to extinguish forever all claim of the Cherokees to the ceded lands, an additional consideration is to be paid by the United States. For this additional consideration, the Cherokees release all right to the ceded land forever.

By the fifth article, the Cherokees allow the United States a road through their country, and the navigation of the Tennessee river. The acceptance of these cessions is an acknowledgement of the right of the Cherokees to make or withhold them.

By the sixth article, it is agreed on the part of the Cherokees that the United States shall have the sole and exclusive right of regulating their trade. No claim is made to the management of all their affairs. This stipulation has already been explained. The observation may be repeated that the stipulation is itself an admission of their right to make or refuse it.

By the seventh article, the United States solemnly guaranty to the Cherokee Nation all their lands not hereby ceded.

The eighth article relinquishes to the Cherokees any citizens of the United States who may settle on their lands, and the ninth forbids any citizen of the United States to hunt on their lands or to enter their country without a passport.

The remaining articles are equal, and contain stipulations which could be made only with a nation admitted to be capable of governing itself.

This treaty, thus explicitly recognizing the national character of the Cherokees and their right of self-government, thus guarantying their lands, assuming the duty of protection, and of course pledging the faith of the United States for that protection, has been frequently renewed, and is now in full force.

To the general pledge of protection have been added several specific pledges deemed valuable by the Indians. Some of these restrain the citizens of the United States from encroachments on the Cherokee country, and provide for the punishment of intruders.

From the commencement of our government, Congress has passed acts to regulate trade and intercourse with the Indians; which treat them as nations, respect their rights, and manifest a firm purpose to afford that protection which treaties stipulate. All these acts, and especially that of 1802, which is still in force, manifestly consider the several Indian nations as distinct political communities, having territorial boundaries within which their authority is exclusive and having a right to all the lands within those boundaries which is not only acknowledged, but guarantied, by the United States.

In 1819, Congress passed an act for promoting those humane designs of civilizing the neighbouring Indians which had long been cherished by the Executive. It enacts,

"that, for the purpose of providing against the further decline and final extinction of the Indian tribes adjoining to the frontier settlements of the United States, and for introducing among them the habits and arts of civilization, the President of the United States shall be, and he is hereby, authorized, in every case where he shall judge improvement in the habits and condition of such Indians practicable, and that the means of instruction can be introduced with their own consent, to employ capable persons of good moral character to instruct them in the mode of agriculture suited to their situation, and for teaching their children in reading, writing and arithmetic, and for performing such other duties as may be enjoined, according to such instructions and rules as the President may give and prescribe for the regulation of their conduct in the discharge of their duties."

This act avowedly contemplates the preservation of the Indian nations as an object sought by the United States, and proposes to effect this object by civilizing and converting them from hunters into agriculturists. Though the Cherokees had already made considerable progress in this improvement, it cannot be doubted that the general words of the act comprehend them. Their advance in the "habits and arts of civilization," rather encouraged perseverance in the laudable exertions still farther to meliorate their condition. This act furnishes strong additional evidence of a settled purpose to fix the Indians in their country by giving them security at home.

The treaties and laws of the United States contemplate the Indian territory as completely separated from that of the States, and provide that all intercourse with them shall be carried on exclusively by the government of the Union. Is this the rightful exercise of power, or is it usurpation?

While these states were colonies, this power, in its utmost extent, was admitted to reside in the Crown. When our revolutionary struggle commenced, Congress was composed of an assemblage of deputies acting under specific powers granted by the legislatures, or conventions of the several colonies. It was a great popular movement, not perfectly organized; nor were the respective powers of those who were entrusted with the management of affairs accurately defined. The necessities of our situation produced a general conviction that those measures which concerned all must be transacted by a body in which the representatives of all were assembled, and which could command the confidence of all. Congress, therefore, was considered as invested with all the powers of war and peace, and Congress dissolved our connexion with the mother country, and declared these United Colonies to be independent states. Without any written definition of powers, they employed diplomatic agents to represent the United States at the several Courts of Europe; offered to negotiate treaties with them, and did actually negotiate treaties with France. From the same necessity, and on the same principles, Congress assumed the management of Indian affairs, first in the name of these United Colonies and, afterwards in the name of the United States. Early attempts were made at negotiation, and to regulate trade with them. These not proving successful, war was carried on under the direction and with the forces of the United States, and the efforts to make peace, by treaty, were earnest and incessant. The Confederation found Congress in the exercise of the same powers of peace and war, in our relations with Indian nations, as with those of Europe.

Such was the state of things when the Confederation was adopted. That instrument surrendered the powers of peace and war to Congress, and prohibited them to the States respectively, unless a State be actually invaded

"or shall have received certain advice of a resolution being formed by some nation of Indians to invade such State, and the danger is so imminent as not to admit of delay till the United States in Congress assembled can be consulted."

This instrument also gave the United States in Congress assembled the sole and exclusive right of

"regulating the trade and managing all the affairs with the Indians, not members of any of the States, provided that the legislative power of any State within its own limits be not infringed or violated."

The ambiguous phrases which follow the grant of power to the United States were so construed by the States of North Carolina and Georgia as to annul the power itself. The discontents and confusion resulting from these conflicting claims produced representations to Congress, which were referred to a committee, who made their report in 1787. The report does not assent to the construction of the two States, but recommends an accommodation, by liberal cessions of territory, or by an admission on their part of the powers claimed by Congress. The correct exposition of this article is rendered unnecessary by the adoption of our existing Constitution. That instrument confers on Congress the powers of war and peace; of making treaties, and of regulating commerce with foreign nations, and among the several States and with the Indian tribes. These powers comprehend all that is required for the regulation of our intercourse with the Indians. They are not limited by any restrictions on their free actions. The shackles imposed on this power in the Confederation are discarded.

The Indian nations had always been considered as distinct, independent political communities, retaining their original natural rights as the undisputed possessors of the soil from time immemorial, with the single exception of that imposed by irresistible power, which excluded them from intercourse with any other European potentate than the first discoverer of the coast of the particular region claimed, and this was a restriction which those European potentates imposed on themselves, as well as on the Indians. The very term "nation," so generally applied to them, means "a people distinct from others." The Constitution, by declaring treaties already made, as well as those to be made, to be the supreme law of the land, has adopted and sanctioned the previous treaties with the Indian nations, and consequently admits their rank among those powers who are capable of making treaties. The words "treaty" and "nation" are words of our own language, selected in our diplomatic and legislative proceedings by ourselves, having each a definite and well understood meaning. We have applied them to Indians, as we have applied them to the other nations of the earth. They are applied to all in the same sense.

Georgia, herself, has furnished conclusive evidence that her former opinions on this subject concurred with those entertained by her sister States, and by the Government of the United States. Various acts of her legislature have been cited in the argument, including the contract of cession made in the year 1802, all tending to prove her acquiescence in the universal conviction that the Indian nations possessed a full right to the lands they occupied until that right should be extinguished by the United States, with their consent; that their territory was separated from that of any State within whose chartered limits they might reside by a boundary line, established by treaties; that, within their boundary, they possessed rights with which no State could interfere; and that the whole power of regulating the intercourse with them was vested in the United States. A review of these acts on the part of Georgia would occupy too much time, and is the less necessary because they have been accurately detailed in the argument at the bar. Her new series of laws, manifesting her abandonment of these opinions, appears to have commenced in December, 1828.

In opposition to this original right, possessed by the undisputed occupants of every country; to this recognition of that right, which is evidenced by our history, in every change through which we have passed; is placed the charters granted by the monarch of a distant and distinct region, parceling out a territory in possession of others whom he could not remove and did not attempt to remove, and the cession made of his claims by the treaty of peace.

The actual state of things at the time, and all history since, explain these charters; and the King of Great Britain, at the treaty of peace, could cede only what belonged to his Crown. These newly asserted titles can derive no aid from the articles so often repeated in Indian treaties, extending to them, first, the protection of Great Britain, and afterwards that of the United States. These articles are associated with others recognizing their title to self-government. The very fact of repeated treaties with them recognizes it, and the settled doctrine of the law of nations is that a weaker power does not surrender its independence—its right to self-government—by associating with a stronger and taking its protection. A weak State, in order to provide for its safety, may place itself under the protection of one more powerful without stripping itself of the right of government and ceasing to be a State. Examples of this kind are not wanting in Europe. "Tributary and feudatory states," says Vattel,

"do not thereby cease to be sovereign and independent states, so long as self-government and sovereign and independent authority are left in the administration of the state."

At the present day, more than one state may be considered as holding its right of self-government under the guarantee and protection of one or more allies.

The Cherokee Nation, then, is a distinct community occupying its own territory, with boundaries accurately described, in which the laws of Georgia can have no force, and which the citizens of Georgia have no right to enter but with the assent of the Cherokees themselves, or in conformity with treaties and with the acts of Congress. The whole intercourse between the United States and this Nation, is, by our Constitution and laws, vested in the Government of the United States.

The act of the State of Georgia, under which the plaintiff in error was prosecuted, is consequently void, and the judgment a nullity. Can this Court revise, and reverse it?

If the objection to the system of legislation lately adopted by the Legislature of Georgia in relation to the

Cherokee Nation was confined to its extraterritorial operation, the objection, though complete so far as respected mere right, would give this Court no power over the subject. But it goes much further. If the review which has been taken be correct, and we think it is, the acts of Georgia are repugnant to the Constitution, laws, and treaties of the United States.

They interfere forcibly with the relations established between the United States and the Cherokee Nation, the regulation of which, according to the settled principles of our Constitution, are committed exclusively to the government of the Union.

They are in direct hostility with treaties, repeated in a succession of years, which mark out the boundary that separates the Cherokee country from Georgia, guaranty to them all the land within their boundary, solemnly pledge the faith of the United States to restrain their citizens from trespassing on it, and recognize the pre-existing power of the nation to govern itself.

They are in equal hostility with the acts of Congress for regulating this intercourse and giving effect to the treaties.

The forcible seizure and abduction of the plaintiff in error, who was residing in the nation with its permission and by authority of the President of the United States, is also a violation of the acts which authorise the chief magistrate to exercise this authority.

Will these powerful considerations avail the plaintiff in error? We think they will. He was seized and forcibly carried away while under guardianship of treaties guarantying the country in which he resided and taking it under the protection of the United States. He was seized while performing, under the sanction of the chief magistrate of the Union, those duties which the humane policy adopted by Congress had recommended. He was apprehended, tried, and condemned under colour of a law which has been shown to the repugnant to the Constitution, laws, and treaties of the United States. Had a judgment, liable to the same objections, been rendered for property, none would question the jurisdiction of this Court. It cannot be less clear when the judgment affects personal liberty, and inflicts disgraceful punishment, if punishment could disgrace when inflicted on innocence. The plaintiff in error is not less interested in the operation of this unconstitutional law than if it affected his property. He is not less entitled to the protection of the Constitution, laws, and treaties of his country.

This point has been elaborately argued and, after deliberate consideration, decided, in the case of *Cohens v. The Commonwealth of Virginia*, 6 Wheat. 264.

It is the opinion of this Court that the judgment of the Superior Court for the County of Gwinnett, in the State of Georgia, condemning Samuel A. Worcester to hard labour in the penitentiary of the State of Georgia for four years was pronounced by that Court under colour of a law which is void, as being repugnant to the Constitution, treaties, and laws of the United States, and ought, therefore, to be reversed and annulled.

---

### Glossary

**domestic community:** also called domestic dependent nation; a nation or government within and subservient to the United States

**jurisdiction:** authority; the territory within which one may exercise one's authority

**sovereign nation:** an independent or foreign nation; important in the concept of tribal sovereignty, which holds that Native American nations are distinct governments separate from the U.S. federal and state governments

# CHARLES RIVER BRIDGE V. WARREN BRIDGE

| DATE | CITATION |
|---|---|
| 1837 | 36 U.S. 420 |

| AUTHOR | SIGNIFICANCE |
|---|---|
| Roger B. Taney | Held that the Massachusetts legislature's decision to grant a charter to the proprietors of Warren Bridge, after having granted a similar charter to the Charles River Bridge Company, did not violate the contract clause of the Constitution |

| VOTE | |
|---|---|
| 5-2 | |

## Overview

 The three leading cases decided during Chief Justice Roger Taney's first term had all been argued while John Marshall was still serving as chief justice, and all would have been decided differently if Marshall had lived. (Marshall died in 1835; Taney was named chief justice in 1836.) Taney made certain all three were reargued and decided during his first month on the high bench—and he ensured that all three decisions bore his stamp. *Charles River Bridge v. Warren Bridge* was the most significant of these decisions and represented a clear departure from the Marshall tradition. The case was a contract dispute. Massachusetts had entered into a contract with the Charles River Bridge Company to build a bridge over the Charles River connecting Boston and Charlestown. Later, the Massachusetts legislature granted a charter to the Warren Bridge company to build a second bridge over the Charles River connecting the same two cities. Charles River Bridge filed suit, arguing that Massachusetts had violated its contract and thus had violated the contract clause of the Constitution, which states in Article I, Section 10, Clause 1: "No State shall enter into any Treaty, Alliance, or Confederation; grant Letters of Marque and Reprisal; coin Money; emit Bills of Credit; make any Thing but gold and silver Coin a Tender in Payment of Debts; pass any Bill of Attainder, ex post facto Law, or Law impairing the Obligation of Contracts, or grant any Title of Nobility." The key phrase for purposes of the case is "Law impairing the Obligation of Contracts." Essentially, Charles River argued that Massachusetts had passed a law that impaired its obligation under an existing contract.

## Context

In the wake of the American Revolution, investors petitioned the Massachusetts legislature for a charter to build a bridge over the Charles River. The bridge would link the growing cities of Boston and Charlestown, which had for decades relied on a ferry service provided by Harvard College and chartered by the Massachusetts Colony. In 1785 the commonwealth issued the charter, which authorized the Charles Bridge Company to charge tolls for forty years, after which the company was to return the bridge to the commonwealth. Construction began immediately and was complet-

***Warren Bridge depicted in 1843***
(Boston Public Library)

ed in 1786, and residents in the area began to realize benefits in the form of increased trade and decreased travel time. So too did the proprietors: the value of the company's stock rose sixfold by 1814, and by 1823 the value of the company was an estimated $280,000. From 1786 to 1827 the company collected more than $800,000 in tolls.

Witnessing the success of the Charles River Bridge, other communities petitioned the commonwealth for bridge charters. After one was granted in 1792, Charles River demanded to be compensated for lost revenue; Massachusetts in response extended the company's charter to seventy years. As other communities petitioned for bridge charters, the commonwealth repeatedly had to refute the claim of Charles River that its charter gave it a monopoly that was protected by the contract clause of the Constitution.

In 1823, merchants in Charlestown launched an effort to build a competing bridge over the Charles River, arguing that the existing bridge was dangerous and overcrowded and that the tolls were "burdensome, vexatious, and odious." Again, Charles River Bridge fought back, demanding compensation for lost revenue, but the political climate was such that legislators support-

ed the new bridge and approved the Warren Bridge charter in 1828. On the Boston side, the bridge was 915 feet from the existing bridge; on the Charlestown side, the distance was 260 feet. The Warren Bridge was granted the same toll schedule as the Charles River Bridge. The new bridge was completed in six months, and as predicted, the revenues of the Charles River Bridge Company began to decline.

Lawyers for the Charles River Bridge Company took the case to court. Initially, they were unable to get an injunction to halt the construction of the new bridge. They took the case to the state supreme court, arguing that the company's tolls were its only tangible property, that the old bridge was the successor to the exclusive Harvard ferry franchise, and that the new bridge charter was a violation of both the contract clause of the Constitution and the state constitutional prohibition against taking private property without compensation. The state supreme court dismissed the case, which then arrived at the door of the U.S. Supreme Court. The case was argued before the Marshall Court in 1831, but for various reasons it languished for six years. It was reargued in 1837 under the new chief justice, Roger B. Taney.

## About the Author

Roger Brooke Taney's legacy on the Supreme Court has been dominated by a bit of judicial overreaching that changed the course of history: his opinion in *Dred Scott v. Sandford*, also known as the Dred Scott Case. Taney served as the United States' fifth chief justice for nearly three decades, for much of that period expanding upon precedents set by his illustrious predecessor, John Marshall. He made important inroads in such areas as federal laws concerning corporations and the application of the Constitution's commerce clause, skillfully balancing the old demands of federalism with the new emphasis on states' rights that characterized the age of Andrew Jackson. Although he wrote more, and not insignificant, opinions after *Dred Scott*, Taney could not outlive the opprobrium that flowed from the decision that declared both that African Americans were not citizens and that the Missouri Compromise—a congressional effort to preserve the balance between slaveholding and non-slaveholding states—was invalid. As the noted Supreme Court historian R. Kent Newmyer has remarked, after *Dred Scott*, "there was nothing left but the grim logic of marching men."

Taney was born into a Catholic family that first settled in the Maryland Tidewater region in the middle of the seventeenth century. Taney's mother had an aristocratic background, but his father was descended from an indentured servant who worked his way up in the world. By the time of Taney's birth in 1777, his father was a wealthy tobacco planter who lavished an excellent education on his second son, who would be obliged to earn his own living. When he was only fifteen, Taney entered Dickinson College in Pennsylvania, from which he graduated as valedictorian in 1795. After three years of reading law in the offices of Judge Jeremiah Chase in Annapolis, Maryland, Taney was admitted to the state bar. That same year he embarked on a political career, serving first as a Federalist member of the Maryland House of Delegates. His career there proved short-lived when the 1800 election brought the Jeffersonian Republicans to power. Taney moved to Frederick, Maryland, where he maintained a successful legal practice. After several defeats he also reentered politics in 1816 as a state senator.

When the Federalist Party disintegrated, Taney joined the Democratic movement led by Andrew Jackson. Taney proved himself a party faithful by serving as state chairman of the committee to elect Jackson as president. In 1831, while Taney was serving as Maryland's attorney general, Jackson named him to the same position in his cabinet. Taney was also to serve concurrently as Jackson's acting secretary of war. A Jackson stalwart, Taney also played an important role in the president's war on the Bank of the United States in 1832: when Jackson decided to kill the bank by withdrawing federal deposits, it was Taney who fulfilled this mission after two successive secretaries of the treasury refused to comply with the order. A grateful Jackson sought to reward Taney, but the Senate, alienated by the president's unilateral maneuvers, declined to confirm Taney as secretary of the treasury and indefinitely postponed a decision on Taney's nomination to the Supreme Court as an associate justice. Jackson tried again a few months later, nominating Taney as the replacement for Chief Justice John Marshall, who had died on July 6, 1835. The Senate again delayed voting on Taney's nomination, but after a closed executive session, Taney was confirmed.

Following in the wake of the man known as the "Great Chief Justice," Taney had large shoes to fill. He had a reputation as a political hack who was expected to do Jackson's bidding on the Court, just as he had in the cabinet. As if to underscore his political orientation, when making his debut on the Court, Taney broke with tradition by appearing in long trousers—emblematic of radical democracy—rather than the knee breeches sported by his predecessors. But instead of undoing the constitutional nationalism that was the legacy of the Marshall Court, the Taney Court developed what had gone before by expanding it into a more equitable sovereignty shared with the states. The first three cases that came before the Taney Court had been argued during Marshall's tenure, and all three presented questions concerning the balance of powers between federal and state governance. Taney himself wrote the opinion of the Court for the most significant of these cases, *Charles River Bridge v. Warren Bridge*, which departed from Federalist doctrine by allowing that rights vested in states can sometimes override prohibitions memorialized in the Constitution's contracts clause. The Taney Court's gradualism and ability, as demonstrated in the License Cases, to craft compromises between state and federal authority earned the public's respect. Roger Brooke Taney was on course to become one of history's most respected jurists until the Court decided—perhaps unnecessarily—to take on the issue of slavery.

*Dred Scott* proved to be Taney's undoing—as it nearly did for the nation. Taney lived for another seven years, during which he wrote a number of laudable opinions, such as his 1861 opinion in *Ex parte Merryman*, a circuit court case condemning President Abraham Lincoln's suspension of the writ of habeas corpus. Lincoln simply ignored the decision; he could do so because *Dred Scott* had thoroughly undermined Taney's authority. Broken, embittered, and impoverished, Taney died while still in office on October 12, 1864—the same day his home state abolished slavery.

## Explanation and Analysis of the Document

In 1785 the Massachusetts legislature granted a charter to the Charles River Bridge Company to build a bridge connecting Boston with nearby Cambridge. The company was given the right to collect tolls for forty years (later extended to seventy years when another company proposed to build a competing bridge), after which time bridge ownership would revert to the state. The endeavor proved hugely successful, and the profits of the company's shareholders rose with the population of Boston and its environs. In 1828 the state granted a charter to the Warren Bridge Company to build another bridge nearby the Charles River Bridge, but this contract permitted the Warren Bridge Company to collect only enough tolls to pay for the bridge's construction, or only for a maximum of six years, after which the public would be permitted to use the new bridge free of charge. As might be expected, Charles River Bridge shareholders cried foul and filed suit, declaring that Massachusetts had violated the terms of its original contract, which they said implicitly conferred a monopoly on their company.

The Supreme Court of Massachusetts found against the Charles River Bridge Company, declining to grant an injunction preventing construction of the Warren Bridge. The Charles River Bridge Company then appealed its case to the U.S. Supreme Court, citing the Massachusetts constitutional guarantee of "life, liberty and property" as well as Article I, Section 10, of the Constitution, which reads in pertinent part: "No State shall . . . pass any Bill of Attainder, ex post facto Law,

or Law impairing the Obligation of Contracts." Construction of the Warren Bridge, the appellant claimed, would jeopardize both their property rights and public confidence in government undertakings. Some members of the Marshall Court, which originally heard arguments in the case, agreed with the appellant company, but owing largely to illness and vacancies on the Court, a decision in the case was postponed. When the case was reargued nearly six years later, some of those Marshall Court justices remained, but the new Taney Court was dominated by Jacksonian Democrats, who favored the kind of economic progress represented by the case of the Warren Bridge Company.

Chief Justice Taney wrote an opinion for the four-member majority. The opinion, which Charles River Bridge Company counsel Daniel Webster called both "smooth and plausible" and "cunning and jesuitical," manages to uphold the sanctity of contract while also advancing the interests of the state legislature, itself representing the sovereign power of the people. While asserting that the "rights of private property must be sacredly guarded," Taney also states that "the object and end of all government is to promote the happiness and prosperity of the community." Massachusetts had chartered the first bridge to promote the public good, but a second bridge was needed now for exactly the same reason. Both economic progress and equal opportunity require a ruling favoring the Warren Bridge Company, unless—and here is the heart of the matter—the contract included language expressly granting monopoly rights to the Charles River Bridge Company. It did not.

Conservative observers feared that American corporate law had been forever damaged, but in fact Taney had accomplished something subtle: by warning against the dangers of vested economic interests and political power, he made way for technological innovation that would advance both corporate and public welfare. Contrary to what the Marshall Court holdover Justice Joseph Story argued in dissent (joined by Smith Thompson), the majority's opinion actually increased incentives for economic investment. And although Taney insists that the Court must not engage in nullification of legislation passed to advance the public good, by emphasizing its support for corporate development, his opinion actually increased the Court's influence.

## Impact

Although many observers at the time, particularly conservative Whigs, disapproved of the Court's decision, many others regarded it as a solid, practical response to emerging policy needs. Taney noted changes in technologies and public improvements, such as the development of railroads. His view was that the law should promote change, not impede it, and that if the owners and operators of the Charles River Bridge Company could stop such changes, the courts would be overrun with suits seeking similar protections.

Thus, for example, a turnpike company could petition the courts to preserve its monopoly at the expense of the railroads. Investment capital would be discouraged. The public would lose the benefits of advances in science and technology and of risk taking on the part of entrepreneurs. The case was important because it took into account the importance of travel and trade against the importance of companies making profits. Additionally, it asserted the right of government to control waterways and the profits that could be earned from travel over them. The case, too, was a very early step in efforts to curb monopolies.

---

### Questions for Further Study

1. What positive effects did the Taney Court's decision in this case have for the nation?

2. Was granting a charter at this time considered legally the same as entering into a contract?

3. What obligation did any state have to its citizens with regard to public transport, given the growth of the population and of the economy at the time?

4. Was the Court's decision in this case fair? Why or why not?

---

### Further Reading

#### Books

Kutler, Stanley I. *Privilege and Creative Destruction: The Charles River Bridge Case,* rev. ed. New York: Norton, 1971.

Newmyer, Kent. *The Supreme Court under Marshall and Taney,* 2nd ed. Hoboken, NJ: Wiley-Blackwell, 2005.

#### Articles

Baker, Donald I. "Competition and Regulation: Charles River Bridge Recrossed." *Cornell Law Review* 60 (January 1975): 159, 165–77.

Ely, James W. "Whatever Happened to the Contract Clause?" *Charleston Law Review* 4, no. 2 (Winter 2010): 371–94.

Newmyer, Kent. "Justice Joseph Story: The Charles River Bridge Case and the Crisis of Republicanism." *American Journal of Legal History* 17, no. 3 (July 1973): 232–45.

—Commentary by Lisa Paddock and Michael J. O'Neal

# CHARLES RIVER BRIDGE V. WARREN BRIDGE

## Document Text

### TANEY, Ch. J., delivered the opinion of the Court

The questions involved in this case are of the gravest character, and the court have given to them the most anxious and deliberate consideration. The value of the right claimed by the plaintiffs is large in amount; and many persons may, no doubt, be seriously affected in their pecuniary interests, by any decision which the court may pronounce; and the questions which have been raised as to the power of the several states, in relation to the corporations they have chartered, are pregnant with important consequences; not only to the individuals who are concerned in the corporate franchises, but to the communities in which they exist. The court are fully sensible, that it is their duty, in exercising the high powers conferred on them by the constitution of the United States, to deal with these great and extensive interests, with the utmost caution; guarding, so far as they have the power to do so, the rights of property, and at the same time, carefully abstaining from any encroachment on the rights reserved to the states.

We are not now left to determine, for the first time, the rules by which public grants are to be construed in this country . . . the principle recognised, that in grants by the public, nothing passes by implication. . . .

The case now before the court is, in principle, precisely the same. It is a charter from a state; the act of incorporation is silent in relation to the contested power. The argument in favor of the proprietors of the Charles River bridge, is the same, almost in words, with that used by the Providence Bank; that is, that the power claimed by the state, if it exists, may be so used as to destroy the value of the franchise they have granted to the corporation. The argument must receive the same answer; and the fact that the power has been already exercised, so as to destroy the value of the franchise, cannot in any degree affect the principle. The existence of the power does not, and cannot, depend upon the circumstance of its having been exercised or not. . . .

While the rights of private property are sacredly guarded, we must not forget, that the community also have rights, and that the happiness and well-being of every citizen depends on their faithful preservation.

Adopting the rule of construction above stated as the settled one, we proceed to apply it to the charter of 1785, to the proprietors of the Charles River bridge. . . . There is no exclusive privilege given to them over the waters of Charles river, above or below their bridge; no right to erect another bridge themselves, nor to prevent other persons from erecting one, no engagement from the state, that another shall not be erected; and no undertaking not to sanction competition, nor to make improvements that may diminish the amount of its income. Upon all these subjects, the charter is silent; and nothing is said in it about a line of travel, so much insisted on in the argument, in which they are to have exclusive privileges. No words are used, from which an intention to grant any of these rights can be inferred; if the plaintiff is entitled to them, it must be implied, simply, from the nature of the grant; and cannot be inferred, from the words by which the grant is made. . . .

It results from this statement, that the legislature, in the very law extending the charter, asserts its rights to authorize improvements over Charles river which would take off a portion of the travel from this bridge and diminish its profits; and the bridge company accept the renewal thus given, and thus carefully connected with this assertion of the right on the part of the state. Can they, when holding their corporate existence under this law, and deriving their franchises altogether from it, add to the privileges expressed in their charter, an implied agreement, which is in direct conflict with a portion of the law from which they derive their corporate existence? Can the legislature be presumed to have taken upon themselves an implied obligation, contrary to its own acts and declarations contained in the same law? It would be difficult to find a case justifying such an implication, even between individuals; still less will it be found, where sovereign rights are concerned, and where the interests of a whole community would be deeply affected by such an implication. It would, indeed, be a strong exertion of judicial power, acting upon its own views of what justice required, and the parties ought to have done, to raise, by a sort of judicial coercion, an implied contract, and infer it from the nature of the very instrument in which the legislature appear to have taken pains to use words which disavow and repudiate any intention, on the part of the state, to make such a contract. . . .

Amid the multitude of cases which have occurred, and have been daily occurring, for the last forty or fifty years, this is the first instance in which such an implied contract has been contended for, and this court called upon to infer it, from an ordinary act of incorporation, containing nothing more than the usual stipulations and provisions to be found in every such law. The absence of any such controversy, when there must have been so many occasions to give rise to it, proves, that neither states, nor individuals, nor corporations, ever imagined that such a contract could be implied from such charters. It shows, that the men who voted for these laws, never imagined that they were forming such a contract; and if we maintain that they have made it, we must create it by a legal fiction, in opposition to the truth of the fact, and the obvious intention of the party. We cannot deal thus

with the rights reserved to the states; and by legal intendments and mere technical reasoning, take away from them any portion of that power over their own internal police and improvement, which is so necessary to their well-being and prosperity.

And what would be the fruits of this doctrine of implied contracts, on the part of the states, and of property in a line of travel, by a corporation, if it would now be sanctioned by this court? To what results would it lead us? . . . The millions of property which have been invested in railroads and canals, upon lines of travel which had been before occupied by turnpike corporations, will be put in jeopardy. We shall be thrown back to the improvements of the last century, and obliged to stand still, until the claims of the old turnpike corporations shall be satisfied; and they shall consent to permit these states to avail themselves of the lights of modern science, and to partake of the benefit of those improvements which are now adding to the wealth and prosperity, and the convenience and comfort, of every other part of the civilized world. Nor is this all. This court will find itself compelled to fix, by some arbitrary rule, the width of this new kind of property in a line of travel; for if such a right of property exists, we have no lights to guide us in marking out its extent, unless, indeed, we resort to the old feudal grants, and to the exclusive rights of ferries, by prescription, between towns; and are prepared to decide that when a turnpike road from one town to another, had been made, no railroad or canal, between these two points, could afterwards be established. This Court are not prepared to sanction principles which must lead to such results.

Many other questions, of the deepest importance, have been raised and elaborately discussed in the argument. It is not necessary, for the decision of this case, to express our opinion upon them; and the court deem it proper to avoid volunteering an opinion on any question, involving the construction of the constitution, where the case itself does not bring the question directly before them, and make it their duty to decide upon it. Some questions, also, of a purely technical character, have been made and argued, as to the form of proceeding and the right to relief. But enough appears on the record, to bring out the great question in contest; and it is the interest of all parties concerned, that the real controversy should be settled, without further delay: and as the opinion of the court is pronounced on the main question in dispute here, and disposes of the whole case, it is altogether unnecessary to enter upon the examination of the forms of proceeding, in which the parties have brought it before the court.

The judgment of the supreme judicial court of the commonwealth of Massachusetts, dismissing the plaintiffs' bill, must, therefore, be affirmed, with costs.

## Glossary

**franchises:** a legal term that generally refers to the rights of an organization to sell its products or services with permission from the local government

**implied contract:** a legal term referring to a contractual obligation arising out of the actions of the parties rather than from the wording of the written contract

**intendments:** ways in which the legal system interprets something, in particular the meaning of a law

**Providence Bank:** reference to an 1830 Supreme Court case, *Providence Bank v. Billings*, in which the Court ruled that the imposition of a state tax on a state-chartered bank was not inconsistent with the contracts clause of the Constitution and was therefore legal

# UNITED STATES V. AMISTAD

**DATE**
1841

**AUTHOR**
Joseph Story

**VOTE**
7-1

**CITATION**
40 U.S. 518

**SIGNIFICANCE**
Held that the illegally captured Africans aboard the schooner La Amistad, which was seized by a U.S. naval vessel, should be considered free since Spanish law forbid the slave trade. Therefore, since they were not slaves, they were free, kidnapped Africans and should be treated as foreign subjects in America's courts.

## Overview

Issued on March 9, 1841, the decision of the U.S. Supreme Court in the *United States v. Amistad* was the most significant one issued by the Court on the question of slavery before the *Dred Scott* decision of 1857. The case arose from the seizure of the schooner *La Amistad*, its passengers, and cargo in 1839 by a U.S. naval vessel. Among the passengers were fifty-three Africans, a slave named Antonio owned by the captain, and two Spaniards. The Spaniards claimed that the Africans were their slaves, but the Africans asserted they were free. For the next two years, American abolitionists provided legal counsel to the Africans, hoping to secure their freedom and to record a legal victory in the battle against slavery. Unlike the *Dred Scott* decision, in which Chief Justice Roger Taney would say that Blacks "had no rights which the white man was bound to respect," Justice Joseph Story's opinion in *Amistad*, based on "the eternal principles of justice and international law," held that "these negroes ought to be deemed free" because they

were entitled to equal justice in America's courts, just like any other foreign subject, no matter his or her color. The abolitionist movement claimed a victory and termed it a triumph of justice. The decision freed the Africans but not Antonio. In other words, the case was limited to its facts. The Africans were entitled to their freedom because they had been kidnapped and illegally sold into slavery, but those held legally to be slaves could not be freed. Henry Baldwin was the lone dissenter in the case.

## Context

In the early days of the Republic many Americans believed that slavery would eventually disappear, and there was some basis for such hope. As early as 1780, Pennsylvania began gradually emancipating all slaves born after that year, and Massachusetts banned slavery. Even Maryland and North Carolina banned the importation of slaves in the 1780s. But after the Rev-

***Sengbe Pieh, leader of the*** **Amistad** ***uprising***
(Wikimedia Commons)

olution, the slave-based economy of the South did not diminish. The invention of the cotton gin and other agricultural advances increased the demand for slave labor. While the northern states had mixed economies based on small farmers and merchants and a growing industrial base, the South's economy had become even more dependent on slave labor. Instead of becoming more united, the regions grew more polarized.

In 1820 the Missouri Compromise formalized the great divide between the regions on the issue of slavery. Under the terms of the Missouri Compromise, the North would consist of free states, but the South would consist of states where slavery remained legal. The growth of slavery also engendered a growth in antislavery sentiment outside the South. By the 1830s the American Anti-Slavery Society had attracted thousands of abolitionists. While abolitionists enjoyed little early political success, they resorted to aggressive propaganda campaigns and vigorous legal attacks to secure freedom for as many Blacks as possible.

In the South, there was less antislavery sentiment among whites. The Denmark Vesey Uprising in South Carolina in 1822 and Nat Turner's Rebellion in Virginia in 1831 demonstrated that there was strong desire for freedom among the South's slaves. But this Black resistance was met with white resistance. Southern planters drew inward and more strident in their support for slavery. Abolitionist literature was banned in some southern communities, and some states made it illegal to teach slaves to read and write. Throughout the 1830s numerous southern legislatures pleaded with northern states to control the abolitionists.

Slavery was also a troubling issue diplomatically. Even though the U.S. Congress banned the importation of slaves as of January 1, 1808, the slave population in the South grew from about 1 million in 1808 to over 2.4 million in 1840. The increase came primarily through natural population growth, but the illegal Caribbean slave trade provided inexpensive African slaves. Treaties between Spain and other countries prohibited the slave trade, but Cuba, a Spanish colony, became a major source of illegal slaves. With Cuba so close and white Americans so divided, America's slave trade ban was difficult to enforce and often simply ignored.

In this context it is not surprising that the plight of the Africans from *La Amistad* became both a national and an international issue. In the spring of 1839, more than five hundred Africans were kidnapped on the west coast of Africa and loaded onto the Portuguese slaver *Tecora* for the voyage to Cuba. During the 4,500-mile journey fewer than two-thirds survived. From the survivors, forty-nine adult men and four children were purchased by José Ruiz and Pedro Montez. Montez procured passports that permitted him to transport his "slaves" from Havana to Puerto Principe, Cuba, on *La Amistad*. If the "slaves" had been born in Cuba, these passports would have been legal. However, these Blacks were native-born Africans and were free under Spanish law. After the Africans were herded onto *La Amistad*, the schooner waited until nightfall to set sail, to avoid British patrols. Once the ship was under way, the Africans, under the leadership of a young man named Joseph Cinqué, overpowered the crew and killed the captain, two crewmen, and the cook. They spared the captain's slave, Antonio, as well as Montez and Ruiz because the two Spaniards promised to sail the Africans back to Africa. But the two men had other plans. At daylight they sailed east, but after dark they reversed course so that the vessel zigzagged west and north for two months. On August 25, 1839, the ship neared the coast of Long Island. When the ship anchored there, Cinqué and three others went ashore to obtain water. There they met two New Yorkers who tried to trick the Africans into bringing the schooner ashore so that the boat and its "cargo" could be claimed as salvage. But a U.S. naval officer spotted the schooner and intervened. The crew of the cutter USS *Washington* boarded *La Amistad* and discovered that it was a slave ship. Lieutenant Thomas Gedney ordered the seizure of *La Amistad*, its passengers, and its cargo and transported the ship to Connecticut. So began the complex legal case that ensued.

U.S. district court judge Andrew T. Judson conducted an inquiry. Montez and Ruiz asserted their claim using the Cuban passports and by informing the court that the Africans were slaves who had mutinied and murdered the captain and crew. Judson ordered that the Africans be held over for grand jury proceedings in September and said that the property claims could be decided then. Formal legal proceedings soon intensified. Numerous claims to salvage rights on the vessel and its cargo were filed on behalf of the crew of the USS *Washington*. A petition for a writ of habeas corpus was begun on behalf of the Africans. Federal criminal charges were filed against the Africans, and four civil actions in the courts of New York were filed by the Africans against the two Spaniards. Fortunately for the Africans, the seizure drew the interest of American abolitionists, who provided legal counsel and translators. Consequently, the subsequent legal proceedings pitted the Africans against an array of whites. Under admiralty law, the naval officers and the two New Yorkers theoretically had a claim for rescuing the distressed ship and claiming the ship as well as its cargo as salvage. However, if the Africans were not slaves, the claims would be greatly diminished in value. So even at the earliest stages of the case, the fight was over whether the Africans were free or slaves. If they were slaves, they could be seized and sold. If not, the Africans were free.

U.S. Supreme Court justice Smith Thompson, sitting as a circuit court judge, ruled that the alleged offenses had occurred on the high seas beyond the jurisdiction of American courts. However, Thompson refused to release the Africans and referred the matter to the U.S. district court to decide whether the Africans were slaves under Spanish law. Then Judson heard the salvage cases, which were drawn out, contentious, and

***Drawing of Kimbo, an African slave aboard* La Amistad**
(William H. Townsend)

dramatic. The parties to the cases included the U.S. government headed by President Martin Van Buren, the queen of Spain, the vice-consul of Spain, four Spanish civilians, more than forty Africans, two naval officers, and two white civilians from New York. Each had varying interests. Van Buren was up for reelection in 1840 and needed proslavery, southern votes. Under a treaty with Spain, the administration asserted that the U.S. government was obligated to seize the Africans and return them to Spain. The queen of Spain claimed that the ship and the Africans were property under Spanish law. The two Spaniards claimed the Africans as their property. Three other Spanish residents of Cuba also filed claims to certain goods. The vice-consul of Spain claimed Antonio as a slave on behalf of the deceased captain's heirs. The naval officers and the two New Yorkers claimed *La Amistad*, its cargo, and the Africans as salvage.

While the courts had to decide who had rights to the vessel and its nonhuman cargo, the real battle was between the Africans, represented by lawyers recruited by abolitionists, and the Spanish Crown, as represented by the U.S. government. Based on that evidence, the lawyers for the Africans argued that the passports presented by Montez and Ruiz were fraudulent. Sensing that public sentiment seemed to favor the Africans, the Van Buren administration tried to end the case. In an attempt to have the Blacks turned over to the administration as quickly as possible, U.S. District Attorney William S. Holabird contended that the Africans were "free men" whom the government must send back to Africa. That concession did not end the matter, because Ruiz and Montez still contended that the Africans were their property. Also, the Africans and their lawyers knew that allowing the Van Buren administration to take custody of them might result in their persecution by the Spanish for murder and piracy. Based on the evidence and the government's concession, the lower courts determined that the Africans had been born free in Sierra Leone and therefore had been illegally kidnapped into slavery.

By the time the case came to the U.S. Supreme Court, most of the admiralty claims had been resolved. The only parties left were Spain, represented by the government of the United States; Gedney, represented by private counsel; and the Africans, represented by Roger Baldwin and John Quincy Adams. By this time the administration had reversed course and argued that the Africans were slaves and thus that the administration was obligated to return them to Spain. Baldwin argued that international law guaranteed equal rights to all free men. He pointed out that the Africans had never resided in Cuba and never were subject to Spanish law. Baldwin continued to request that the case against the Africans be dismissed and that they be freed from jail. He urged the Supreme Court to reverse the lower court ruling that the Africans should be turned over to the president for return to Africa.

## About the Author

When the *Amistad* case was argued beginning in February 1841, the U.S. Supreme Court was composed of Chief Justice Roger Taney of Maryland, Smith Thompson of New York, John McLean of Ohio, Henry Baldwin of Pennsylvania, James Wayne of Georgia, Philip Barbour of Virginia, John Catron of Tennessee, John McKinley of Alabama, and Joseph Story of Massachusetts. Taney, Barbour, Catron, McKinley, and Wayne had all owned slaves. Moreover, McLean, Wayne, Baldwin, Taney, and McKinley had been appointed to the Court by Democratic presidents Andrew Jackson and Martin Van Buren. Generally Democrats supported the institution of slavery, and Van Buren's administration was adamantly opposed to freeing the *Amistad* Blacks.

But there were two members of the Court who were not only less friendly to slavery but were not friendly to Van Buren. Justice Smith Thompson was the circuit justice for Connecticut and as such had heard the petition and the appeals that had confirmed that the Blacks were free. The other justice was Joseph Story, author of the opinion in the case. When the case was argued in February and March 1841, Justice McKinley was ill, and during the course of the multiday arguments Justice Barbour died. So when the decision was announced, six justices joined in the opinion of Justice Story, and only one justice, Henry Baldwin, dissented.

Joseph Story, born on September 18, 1779, in Marblehead, Massachusetts, was appointed by President James Madison in 1811 at age thirty-two, the youngest person to ever serve on the Court. Despite his inexperience, he became one of the most distinguished justices in the history of the Court. By the time of the *Amistad* decision, he was the senior member. He was also a professor at Harvard Law School and the author of numerous legal treatises. Story had been an ally of Chief Justice John Marshall, and the two laid the cornerstones of the federal government and the judiciary. At the time of the *Amistad* case, Story's views on slavery were well known. He had spoken out publicly in a Salem, Massachusetts, town meeting against slavery and the Missouri Compromise. His judicial record clearly exhibited his distaste for the illegal slave trade. However, there were limits to Story's judicial philosophy. In 1842 he authored the lead opinion in *Prigg v. Pennsylvania*, which held that the Fugitive Slave Act of 1793 preempted all state law to the contrary. Story did attempt to limit his ruling by stating that states were not required to enforce the federal statute, only that states could not enact statutes that tried to subvert the federal act. However, Story's opinion earned him no credit with abolitionists. Despite his personal opinion of slavery, Story's opinions demonstrated his strict adherence to the law and facts. Story died on September 10, 1845.

## Explanation and Analysis of the Document

Story's opinion begins by summarizing the facts of the case in paragraph 1. Then, in paragraphs 2 through 7, Story summarizes the convoluted legal proceedings that resulted in the case's being heard before the U.S.

Supreme Court. To review briefly: At issue in the case was who was entitled to the ship and its cargo and what was to be the fate of the Africans on the ship. Were the Africans, in fact, slaves to be returned to the owner who claimed them, or were they free men who had been kidnapped from Africa illegally and hence to be freed to return to Africa?

The key paragraph in Story's summary of the legal proceedings to date is paragraph 6, which notes that on January 23, 1840, a district court had ruled on the various matters before it. In addition to the salvage claims, the court "decreed that they [that is, the "negroes"] should be delivered to the President of the United States, to be transported to Africa, pursuant to the act of 3d March, 1819." The act in question was the Act of March 3, 1819, Relative to the Slave Trade, which was crucial to the case and which read in part:

> Be it enacted by the Senate and House of Representatives of the United States of America, in Congress assembled, That the President of the United States be, and he is hereby, authorized, whenever he shall deem it expedient, to cause any of the armed vessels of the United States, to be employed to cruise on any of the coasts of the United States, or territories thereof, or of the coast of Africa, or elsewhere, where he may judge attempts may be made to carry on the slave trade by citizens or residents of the United States, in contravention of the acts of Congress prohibiting the same.

Paragraph 7 then notes that the district court ruling was appealed and that the appellate court simply affirmed the rulings of the district court. Accordingly, the case was appealed to the U.S. Supreme Court.

Story's analysis of the case and his ruling begin with paragraph 8, where he lays out what he perceives to be the two central issues in the case: whether, under the terms of the 1795 treaty with Spain (often called Pinckney's Treaty or, more formally, the Treaty of San Lorenzo or the Treaty of Madrid), sufficient proof was given as the to the ownership of the ship, its cargo, and the Africans; and whether the U.S. government has a right to intervene in the case. It should be noted that at this point in the proceedings, the United States, as one of the parties to the case, was simply attempting to defend the rights of Spain under the treaty; the U.S.

government was not, for example, asserting any ownership rights over the ship, cargo, and Africans, nor was it interested in prosecuting the Africans for their mutiny aboard the ship. A second party to the case, Lieutenant Thomas Gedney, was still trying to assert his right to the ship and cargo as salvage; in connection with this claim, the term "libel" is used, but in this context, the word refers simply to an admiralty lawsuit, or a lawsuit brought under the laws of the sea. Finally, the third party to the case consists of the Africans led by Cinqué, who were asserting that they were not slaves and should be granted their freedom.

From the standpoint of African American history and the history of the abolition of the slave trade, the core of Story's opinion begins with paragraph 12. In this paragraph, Story examines the U.S. treaty with Spain and searches for the clause in the treaty that would apply in this case. The treaty was designed to establish rights when, for example, a ship flying under one country's flag was pursued by pirates and had to put into a port of the other country. An alternative case would be a ship of one country that had to be rescued by a ship from the other because it was, for example, sinking. The purpose of the treaty was simply to agree that one country's property should be returned by the other. The facts in the *Amistad* case, though, did not conform precisely to any of the clauses in the treaty with Spain. Accordingly, it was up to the Supreme Court to determine what the property rights were. With regard to the ship and its cargo, the issue was relatively simple. The more complicated issue involved the Africans and whether they were "merchandise" under the terms of the treaty.

In paragraph 13, Story takes up this issue. He uses some Latin legal language, including the phrase *onus probandi*, which means "burden of proof." Additionally, he uses the phrase *casus foederis*, which literally means "case of the alliance" and refers to a situation in which the terms of an alliance between nations come into play. He concludes in this paragraph that "these negroes never were the lawful slaves of Ruiz or Montez, or of any other Spanish subjects." He goes on to say that "they are natives of Africa, and were kidnapped there, and were unlawfully transported to Cuba, in violation of the laws and treaties of Spain, and the most solemn edicts and declarations of that government." But then the question arises as to whether the Africans, because of their mutiny, were "pirates or robbers." In paragraph 14, Story concludes: "If, then, these negroes are not slaves, but are kidnapped Africans, who, by the laws of Spain itself, are entitled to their freedom, and were kidnapped and illegally" then "they cannot be deemed pirates or robbers in the sense of the law of nations, or the treaty with Spain, or the laws of Spain itself."

Paragraph 15 takes up the issue of the evidence that the Africans were the property of the Spaniards who claimed them. Story acknowledges that, in general, the U.S. government is obligated to accept any proof of ownership asserted by the citizens of another country and is not obligated to "look behind" any documents the presumed owner provides. Story concedes that the Spaniards' documents would normally be taken as "prima facie" evidence that they, in fact, owned the Africans. But Story goes on to reject the notion that the documents have to be accepted at face value. Such documents can be "impugned for fraud," and if they are found to be fraudulent, they do not have to be accepted as proof. Put simply, Story asserts that the ownership documents of the Spaniards are fraudulent, and therefore the U.S. government is under no obligation to accept them. In paragraph 16, then, Story concludes that if the Africans are not slaves but "free negroes," then the U.S. treaty with Spain is inoperative and "the United States are bound to respect their rights as much as those of Spanish subjects." He states that "the treaty with Spain never could have intended to take away the equal rights of all foreigners" and, on the basis of "the eternal principles of justice and international law," he concludes that "these negroes ought to be deemed free; and that the Spanish treaty interposes no obstacle to the just assertion of their rights."

Paragraph 17 takes up the question of what is to be done with the Africans. The problem Story faced was this: If Africans were brought into the country illegally in contravention of laws prohibiting the slave trade, then the United States, in the person of the president, was obligated to return them to Africa. The problem here was the circumstances under which the Africans had set foot on U.S. soil. They were not brought by slave traders. They, in essence, brought themselves by seizing the ship, and when they arrived in the United

States, they had no intention of becoming slaves. Accordingly, Story rules that the United States is under no obligation to return them to Africa.

Paragraph 19 briefly affirms the right of Lieutenant Gedney to salvage. That is, the Court ruled that because of his actions, he was entitled to claim the ship and its cargo under the maritime version of "finders keepers." Of course, Gedney did not want the actual physical property; what he wanted was the value of the property in money. Story affirms his right to salvage.

## Impact

Some historians believe that the *Amistad* case may have helped defeat Martin Van Buren in his quest to be reelected president in 1840. When the case came to his attention, he backed the initial U.S. position as formed by Secretary of State John Forsyth, which favored the claims of Spain and urged that the Africans be returned to Cuba as pirates, murderers, and escaped slaves. Both Van Buren, a Democrat, and his opponent, William Henry Harrison, courted the southern vote, and neither wanted to be perceived as soft on the issue of slavery. Although the *Amistad* case did not figure directly in the election campaign, it formed part of the backdrop of American regional politics in the pre–Civil War decades.

The outcome of the case galvanized the abolition movement, but it angered much of the South. As a legal precedent, the case has been cited only once in a subsequent U.S. Supreme Court decision. The reality was that the case had limited direct impact. It had freed the Africans, but not the slave Antonio. The evidence presented at the initial admiralty trial proved that the Africans were free and not slaves. Moreover, the U.S. attorney had admitted that they were not slaves but free. This admission foreclosed any further argument by the Van Buren administration on behalf of the Spanish. Consequently the case has to be seen as one decided strictly upon its facts. However, Story did use the international law on the slave trade to make clear that a free Black man had rights in American courts—an important holding in the ultimate collapse of the slave system.

## Questions for Further Study

1. In what sense was the *Amistad* case a victory for abolitionists?

2. The *Amistad* case was a highly complex one. Summarize the facts of the case and the legal issues it presented.

3. What were the international implications of the *Amistad* case? What role did issues involving the transportation of slaves and maritime law play in the outcome of the case?

4. What role did domestic politics play in attitudes toward the case and the U.S. government's position on it?

5. Why were Joseph Cinqué and the other Africans aboard the vessel not put on trial for murder and mutiny?

## Further Reading

### Books

Finkelman, Paul, ed. *Slavery, Race, and the American Legal System 1700–1872.* New York: Garland, 1988.

Jones, Howard. *Mutiny on the Amistad: The Saga of a Slave Revolt and Its Impact on American Abolition, Law, and Diplomacy.* New York: Oxford University Press, 1987.

Osagie, Iyunolu Folayan. *The Amistad Revolt: Memory, Slavery, and the Politics of Identity in the United States and Sierra Leone.* Athens: University of Georgia Press, 2000.

Rediker, Marcus. *The Amistad Rebellion: An Atlantic Odyssey of Slavery and Freedom.* New York: Viking, 2012.

### Articles

Jackson, Donald Dale. "Mutiny on the Amistad." *Smithsonian* 28 (December 1997): 114–124.

Jones, Howard. "Cinqué of the Amistad a Slave Trader? Perpetuating a Myth." *Journal of American History* 87, no. 3 (2000): 923–939.

### Websites

"The Amistad Case, 1839." Office of the Historian. Accessed March 2, 2023, https://history.state.gov/milestones/1830-1860/amistad.

—Commentary by W. Lewis Burke

# UNITED STATES V. AMISTAD

## Document Text

### Mr. Justice Story delivered the opinion of the Court

This is the case of an appeal from the decree of the Circuit Court of the District of Connecticut, sitting in admiralty. The leading facts, as they appear upon the transcript of the proceedings, are as follows: On the 27th of June, 1839, the schooner L'Amistad, being the property of Spanish subjects, cleared out from the port of Havana, in the island of Cuba, for Puerto Principe, in the same island. On board of the schooner were the captain, Ransom Ferrer, and Jose Ruiz, and Pedro Montez, all Spanish subjects. The former had with him a negro boy, named Antonio, claimed to be his slave. Jose Ruiz had with him forty-nine negroes, claimed by him as his slaves, and stated to be his property, in a certain pass or document, signed by the Governor General of Cuba. Pedro Montez had with him four other negroes, also claimed by him as his slaves, and stated to be his property, in a similar pass or document, also signed by the Governor General of Cuba. On the voyage, and before the arrival of the vessel at her port of destination, the negroes rose, killed the captain, and took possession of her. On the 26th of August, the vessel was discovered by Lieutenant Gedney, of the United States brig Washington, at anchor on the high seas, at the distance of half a mile from the shore of Long Island. A part of the negroes were then on shore at Culloden Point, Long Island; who were seized by Lieutenant Gedney, and brought on board. The vessel, with the negroes and other persons on board, was brought by Lieutenant Gedney into the district of Connecticut, and there libelled for salvage in the District Court of the United States. A libel for salvage was also filed by Henry Green and Pelatiah Fordham, of Sag Harbour, Long Island. On the 18th of September, Ruiz and Montez filed claims and libels, in which they asserted their ownership of the negroes as their slaves, and of certain parts of the cargo, and prayed that the same might be "delivered to them, or to the representatives of her Catholic majesty, as might be most proper." On the 19th of September, the Attorney of the United States, for the district of Connecticut, filed an information or libel, setting forth, that the Spanish minister had officially presented to the proper department of the government of the United States, a claim for the restoration of the vessel, cargo, and slaves, as the property of Spanish subjects, which had arrived within the jurisdictional limits of the United States, and were taken possession of by the said public armed brig of the United States; under such circumstances as made it the duty of the United States to cause the same to be restored to the true proprietors, pursuant to the treaty between the United States and Spain: and praying the Court, on its being made legally to appear that the claim of the Spanish minister was well founded, to make such order for the disposal of the vessel, cargo, and slaves, as would best enable the United States to comply with their treaty stipulations. But if it should appear, that the negroes were persons transported from Africa, in violation of the laws of the United States, and brought within the United States contrary to the same laws; he then prayed the Court to make such order for their removal to the coast of Africa, pursuant to the laws of the United States, as it should deem fit.

On the 19th of November, the Attorney of the United States filed a second information or libel, similar to the first, with the exception of the second prayer above set forth in his former one. On the same day, Antonio G. Vega, the vice-consul of Spain, for the state of Connecticut, filed his libel, alleging that Antonio was a slave, the property of the representatives of Ramon Ferrer, and praying the Court to cause him to be delivered to the said vice-consul, that he might be returned by him to his lawful owner in the island of Cuba.

On the 7th of January, 1840, the negroes, Cinque and others, with the exception of Antonio, by their counsel, filed an answer, denying that they were slaves, or the property of Ruiz and Montez, or that the Court could, under the Constitution or laws of the United States, or under any treaty, exercise any jurisdiction over their persons, by reason of the premises; and praying that they might be dismissed. They specially set forth and insist in this answer, that they were native born Africans; born free, and still of right ought to be free and not slaves; that they were, on or about the 15th of April, 1839, unlawfully kidnapped, and forcibly and wrongfully carried on board a certain vessel on the coast of Africa, which was unlawfully engaged in the slave trade, and were unlawfully transported in the same vessel to the island of Cuba, for the purpose of being there unlawfully sold as slaves; that Ruiz and Montez, well knowing the premises, made a pretended purchase of them: that afterwards, on or about the 28th of June, 1839, Ruiz and Montez, confederating with Ferrer, (captain of the Amistad,) caused them, without law or right, to be placed on board of the Amistad, to be transported to some place unknown to them, and there to be enslaved for life; that, on the voyage, they rose on the master, and took possession of the vessel, intending to return therewith to their native country, or to seek an asylum in some free state; and the vessel arrived, about the 26th of August, 1839, off Montauk Point, near Long Island; a part of them were sent onshore, and were seized by Lieutenant Gedney, and carried on board; and all of them were afterwards brought by him into the district of Connecticut.

On the 7th of January, 1840, Jose Antonio Tellincas, and Messrs. Aspe and Laca, all Spanish subjects, residing in Cuba, filed their claims, as owners to certain portions of the goods found on board of the schooner L'Amistad.

On the same day, all the libellants and claimants, by their counsel, except Jose Ruiz and Pedro Montez, (whose libels and claims, as stated of record, respectively, were pursued by the Spanish minister, the same being merged in his claims,) appeared, and the negroes also appeared by their counsel; and the case was heard on the libels, claims, answers, and testimony of witnesses.

On the 23d day of January, 1840, the District Court made a decree. By that decree, the Court rejected the claim of Green and Fordham for salvage, but allowed salvage to Lieutenant Gedney and others, on the vessel and cargo, of one-third of the value thereof, but not on the negroes, Cinque and others; it allowed the claim of Tellincas, and Aspe and Laca with the exception of the above-mentioned salvage; it dismissed the libels and claims of Ruiz and Montez, with costs, as being included under the claim of the Spanish minister; it allowed the claim of the Spanish vice-consul for Antonio, on behalf of Ferrer's representatives; it rejected the claims of Ruiz and Montez for the delivery of the negroes, but admitted them for the cargo, with the exception of the above-mentioned salvage; it rejected the claim made by the Attorney of the United States on behalf of the Spanish minister, for the restoration of the negroes under the treaty; but it decreed that they should be delivered to the President of the United States, to be transported to Africa, pursuant to the act of 3d March, 1819.

From this decree the District Attorney, on behalf of the United States, appealed to the Circuit Court, except so far as related to the restoration of the slave Antonio. The claimants, Tellincas, and Aspe and Laca, also appealed from that part of the decree which awarded salvage on the property respectively claimed by them. No appeal was interposed by Ruiz or Montez, or on behalf of the representatives of the owners of the Amistad. The Circuit Court, by a mere pro forma decree, affirmed the decree of the District Court, reserving the question of salvage upon the claims of Tellincas, and Aspe and Laca. And from that decree the present appeal has been brought to this Court.

The cause has been very elaborately argued, as well upon the merits, as upon a motion on behalf of the appellees to dismiss the appeal. On the part of the United States, it has been contended, 1. That due and sufficient proof concerning the property has been made to authorize the restitution of the vessel, cargo, and negroes to the Spanish subjects on whose behalf they are claimed pursuant to the treaty with Spain, of the 27th of October, 1795. 2. That the United States had a right to intervene in the manner in which they have done, to obtain a decree for the restitution of the property, upon the application of the Spanish minister. These propositions have been strenuously denied on the other side. Other collateral and incidental points have been stated, upon which it is not necessary at this moment to dwell.

Before entering upon the discussion of the main points involved in this interesting and important controversy, it may be necessary to say a few words as to the actual posture of the case as it now stands before us. In the first place, then, the only parties now before the Court on one side, are the United States, intervening for the sole purpose of procuring restitution of the property as Spanish property, pursuant to the treaty, upon the grounds stated by the other parties claiming the property in their respective libels. The United States do not assert any property in themselves, or any violation of their own rights, or sovereignty, or laws, by the acts complained of. They do not insist that these negroes have been imported into the United States, in contravention of our own slave trade acts. They do not seek to have these negroes delivered up for the purpose of being transported to Cuba as pirates or robbers, or as fugitive criminals found within our territories, who have been guilty of offences against the laws of Spain. They do not assert that the seizure, and bringing the vessel, and cargo, and negroes into port, by Lieutenant Gedney, for the purpose of adjudication, is a tortious act. They simply confine themselves to the right of the Spanish claimants to the restitution of their property, upon the facts asserted in their respective allegations.

In the next place, the parties before the Court on the other side as appellees, are Lieutenant Gedney, on his libel for salvage, and the negroes, (Cinque, and others,) asserting themselves, in their answer, not to be slaves, but free native Africans, kidnapped in their own country, and illegally transported by force from that country; and now entitled to maintain their freedom.

No question has been here made, as to the proprietary interests in the vessel, and cargo. It is admitted that they belong to Spanish subjects, and that they ought to be restored. The only point on this head is, whether the restitution ought to be upon the payment of salvage or not? The main controversy is, whether these negroes are the property of Ruiz and Montez, and ought to be delivered up; and to this, accordingly, we shall first direct our attention.

It has been argued on behalf of the United States, that the Court are bound to deliver them up, according to the treaty of 1795, with Spain, which has in this particular been continued in full force, by the treaty of 1819, ratified in 1821. The sixth article of that treaty, seems to have had, principally, in view cases where the property of the subjects of either state had been taken possession of within the territorial jurisdiction of the other, during war. The eighth article provides for cases where the shipping of the inhabitants of either state are forced, through stress of weather, pursuit of pirates, or enemies, or any other urgent necessity, to seek shelter in the ports of the other. There may well be some doubt entertained, whether the present case, in its actual circumstances, falls within the purview of this article. But it does not seem necessary, for reasons hereafter stated, absolutely to decide it. The ninth article provides, "that all ships and merchandise, of what nature soever, which shall be rescued out of the hands of any pirates or robbers, on the high seas, shall be brought into some port of either state, and shall be delivered to the custody of the officers of that port, in order to be taken care of and restored entire to the true proprietor, as soon as due and sufficient proof shall be made concerning the, property thereof." This is the article on which the main reliance is placed on behalf of the United States, for the restitution of these negroes. To bring the case within the article, it is essential to establish, First, That these negroes, under all the circumstances, fall within the description of merchandise, in the sense of the treaty. Secondly, That there has been a rescue of them on the high seas, out of the hands of the pirates and robbers; which, in the present case, can only be, by showing that they themselves are pirates and robbers; and, Thirdly, That Ruiz and Montez, the asserted proprietors, are the true proprietors, and have established their title by competent proof.

If these negroes were, at the time, lawfully held as slaves under the laws of Spain, and recognised by those laws as property capable of being lawfully bought and sold; we see no reason why they may not justly be deemed within the intent of the treaty, to be included under the denomination of merchandise, and, as such, ought to be restored to the claimants: for, upon that point, the laws of Spain would seem to furnish the proper rule of interpretation. But, admitting this, it is clear, in our opinion, that neither of the other essential facts and requisites has been established in proof; and the onus probandi of both lies upon the claimants to give rise to the casus foederis. It is plain beyond controversy, if we examine the evidence, that these negroes never were the lawful slaves of Ruiz or Montez, or of any other Spanish subjects. They are natives of Africa, and were kidnapped there, and were unlawfully transported to Cuba, in violation of the laws and treaties of Spain, and the most solemn edicts and declarations of that government. By those laws, and treaties, and edicts, the African slave trade is utterly abolished; the dealing in that trade is deemed a heinous crime; and the negroes thereby introduced into the dominions of Spain, are declared to be free. Ruiz and Montez are proved to have made the pretended purchase of these negroes, with a full knowledge of all the circumstances. And so cogent and irresistible is the evidence in this respect, that the District Attorney has admitted in open Court, upon the record, that these negroes were native Africans, and recently imported into Cuba, as alleged in their answers to the libels in the case. The supposed proprietary interest of Ruiz and Montez, is completely displaced, if we are at liberty to look at the evidence or the admissions of the District Attorney.

If, then, these negroes are not slaves, but are kidnapped Africans, who, by the laws of Spain itself, are entitled to their freedom, and were kidnapped and illegally carried to Cuba, and illegally detained and restrained on board of the Amistad; there is no pretence to say, that they are pirates or robbers. We may lament the dreadful acts, by which they asserted their liberty, and took possession of the Amistad, and endeavoured to regain their native country; but they cannot be deemed pirates or robbers in the sense of the law of nations, or the treaty with Spain, or the laws of Spain itself; at least so far as those laws have been brought to our knowledge. Nor do the libels of Ruiz or Montez assert them to be such.

This posture of the facts would seem, of itself, to put an end to the whole inquiry upon the merits. But it is argued, on behalf of the United States, that the ship, and cargo, and negroes were duly documented as belonging to Spanish subjects, and this Court have no right to look behind these documents; that full faith and credit is to be given to them; and that they are to be held conclusive evidence in this cause, even although it should be established by the most satisfactory proofs, that

they have been obtained by the grossest frauds and impositions upon the constituted authorities of Spain. To this argument we can, in no wise, assent. There is nothing in the treaty which justifies or sustains the argument. We do not here meddle with the point, whether there has been any connivance in this illegal traffic, on the part of any of the colonial authorities or subordinate officers of Cuba; because, in our view, such an examination is unnecessary, and ought not to be pursued, unless it were indispensable to public justice, although it has been strongly pressed at the bar. What we proceed upon is this, that although public documents of the government, accompanying property found on board of the private ships of a foreign nation, certainly are to be deemed prima facie evidence of the facts which they purport to state, yet they are always open to be impugned for fraud; and whether that fraud be in the original obtaining of these documents, or in the subsequent fraudulent and illegal use of them, when once it is satisfactorily established, it overthrows all their sanctity, and destroys them as proof. Fraud will vitiate any, even the most solemn transactions; and an asserted title to property, founded upon it, is utterly void. The very language of the ninth article of the treaty of 1795 requires the proprietor to make due and sufficient proof of his property. And how can that proof be deemed either due or sufficient, which is but a connected and stained tissue of fraud? This is not a mere rule of municipal jurisprudence. Nothing is more clear in the law of nations, as an established rule to regulate their rights, and duties, and Intercourse, than the doctrine, that the ship's papers are but prima facie evidence, and that, if they are shown to be fraudulent, they are not to be held proof of any valid title. This rule is familiarly applied, and, indeed, is of every-days occurrence in cases of prize, in the contests between belligerents and neutrals, as is apparent from numerous cases to be found in the Reports of this Court; and it is just as applicable to the transactions of civil intercourse between nations in times of peace. If a private ship, clothed with Spanish papers, should enter the ports of the United States, claiming the privileges, and immunities, and rights belonging to bona fide subjects of Spain, under our treaties or laws, and she should, in reality, belong to the subjects of another nation, which was not entitled to any such privileges, immunities, or rights, and the proprietors were seeking, by fraud, to cover their own illegal acts, under the flag of Spain; there can be no doubt, that it would be the duty of our

Courts to strip off the disguise, and to look at the case according to its naked realities. In the solemn treaties between nations, it can never be presumed that either state intends to provide the means of perpetrating or protecting frauds; but all the provisions are to be construed as intended to be applied to bona fide transactions. The seventeenth article of the treaty with Spain, which provides for certain passports and certificates, as evidence of property on board of the ships of both states, is, in its terms, applicable only to cases where either of the parties is engaged in a war. This article required a certain form of passport to be agreed upon by the parties, and annexed to the treaty. It never was annexed; and, therefore, in the case of the Amiable Isabella, 6 Wheaton, 1, it was held inoperative.

It is also a most important consideration in the present case, which ought not to be lost sight of, that, supposing these African negroes not to be slaves, but kidnapped, and free negroes, the treaty with Spain cannot be obligatory upon them; and the United States are bound to respect their rights as much as those of Spanish subjects. The conflict of rights between the parties under such circumstances, becomes positive and inevitable, and must be decided upon the eternal principles of justice and international law. If the contest were about any goods on board of this ship, to which American citizens asserted a title, which was denied by the Spanish claimants, there could be no doubt of the right of such American citizens to litigate their claims before any competent American tribunal, notwithstanding the treaty with Spain. A fortiori, the doctrine must apply where human life and human liberty are in issue; and constitute the very essence of the controversy. The treaty with Spain never could have intended to take away the equal rights of all foreigners, who should contest their claims before any of our Courts, to equal justice; or to deprive such foreigners of the protection given them by other treaties, or by the general law of nations. Upon the merits of the case, then, there does not seem to us to be any ground for doubt, that these negroes ought to be deemed free; and that the Spanish treaty interposes no obstacle to the just assertion of their rights.

There is another consideration growing out of this part of the case, which necessarily rises in judgment. It is observable, that the United States, in their original claim, filed it in the alternative, to have the negroes, if slaves and Spanish property, restored to the proprietors; or, if not slaves, but negroes who had been transported from Africa, in violation of the laws of the United States, and brought into the United States contrary to the same laws, then the Court to pass an order to enable the United States to remove such persons to the coast of Africa, to be delivered there to such agent as may be authorized to receive and provide for them. At a subsequent period, this last alternative claim was not insisted on, and another claim was interposed, omitting it; from which the conclusion naturally arises that it was abandoned. The decree of the District Court, however, contained an order for the delivery of the negroes to the United States; to be transported to the coast of Africa, under the act of the 3d of March, 1819, ch. 224. The United States do not now insist upon any affirmance of this part of the decree; and, in our judgment, upon the admitted facts, there is no ground to assert that the case comes within the purview of the act of 1819, or of any other of our prohibitory slave trade acts. These negroes were never taken from Africa, or brought to the United States in contravention of those acts. When the Amistad arrived she was in possession of the negroes, asserting their freedom; and in no sense could they possibly intend to import themselves here, as slaves, or for sale as slaves. In this view of the matter, that part of the decree of the District Court is unmaintainable, and must be reversed.

The view which has been thus taken of this case, upon the merits, under the first point, renders it wholly unnecessary for us to give any opinion upon the other point, as to the right of the United States to intervene in this case in the manner already stated. We dismiss this, therefore, as well as several minor points made at the argument.

As to the claim of Lieutenant Gedney for the salvage service, it is understood that the United States do not now desire to interpose any obstacle to the allowance of it, if it is deemed reasonable by the Court. It was a highly meritorious and useful service to the proprietors of the ship and cargo; and such as, by the general principles of maritime law, is always deemed a just foundation for salvage. The rate allowed by the Court, does not seem to us to have been beyond the exercise of a sound discretion, under the very peculiar and embarrassing circumstances of the case.

Upon the whole, our opinion is, that the decree of the Circuit Court, affirming that of the District Court, ought to be affirmed, except so far as it directs the negroes to be delivered to the President, to be transported to Africa, in pursuance of the act of the 3d of March, 1819; and, as to this, it ought to be reversed: and that the said negroes be declared to be free, and be dismissed from the custody of the Court, and go without delay.

### Mr. Justice Baldwin dissented

This cause came on to be heard on the transcript of the record from the Circuit Court of the United States, for the District of Connecticut, and was argued by counsel. On consideration whereof, it is the opinion of this Court, that there is error in that part of the decree of the Circuit Court, affirming the decree of the District Court, which ordered the said negroes to be delivered to the President of the United States, to be transported to Africa, in pursuance of the act of Congress, of the 3d of March, 1819; and that, as to that part, it ought to be reversed: and, in all other respects, that the said decree of the Circuit Court ought to be affirmed. It is therefore ordered adjudged, and decreed by this Court, that the decree of the said Circuit Court be, and the same is hereby, affirmed, except as to the part aforesaid, and as to that part, that it be reversed; and that the cause be remanded to the Circuit Court, with directions to enter, in lieu of that part, a decree, that the said negroes be, and are hereby, declared to be free, and that they be dismissed from the custody of the Court, and be discharged from the suit, and go thereof quit without delay.

## Glossary

**a fortiori:** a Latin phrase meaning roughly "with stronger or greater reason"

**act of the 3d of March, 1819:** Act of March 3, 1819, Relative to the Slave Trade, giving the president the power to block illegal transportation of slaves

**casus foederis:** Latin for "case of the alliance," referring to a situation in which the terms of an alliance between nations come into play

**clothed:** in law, refers to a pretense or fraud

**information:** in law, a lawsuit

**libel:** in maritime law, a lawsuit

**onus probandi:** Latin for "burden of proof"

**prima facie:** Latin for "at first sight," referring to a legal matter not needing proof unless contrary evidence is shown

**sitting in admiralty:** functioning as an admiralty court, or one that hears cases involving maritime law

**tortious act:** an act that subjects the doer to liability, or fault, in tort law

**treaty between the United States and Spain:** Pinckney's Treaty or, more formally, the Treaty of San Lorenzo or the Treaty of Madrid, signed in 1795

# PRIGG V. PENNSYLVANIA

| | |
|---|---|
| **DATE**<br>1842 | **CITATION**<br>41 U.S. 539 |
| **AUTHOR**<br>Joseph Story | **SIGNIFICANCE**<br>Held that the Fugitive Slave Act of 1793 precluded a Pennsylvania law preventing state officials from cooperating in returning fugitive slaves |
| **VOTE**<br>8-1 | |

## Overview

*Prigg v. Pennsylvania* was the first decision of the U.S. Supreme Court to interpret the fugitive slave clause of the U.S. Constitution and also the first decision to consider the constitutionality of the Fugitive Slave Act of 1793. In his "opinion of the Court," Justice Joseph Story of Massachusetts reached six major conclusions: that the federal Fugitive Slave Act of 1793 was constitutional in all its provisions; that no state could pass any law that added requirements to the federal law or impeded the return of fugitive slaves, such as requiring that a state judge hear the case; that masters or their agents had a constitutional right of self-help (the technical term was "recaption") to seize any fugitive slave anywhere and to bring that slave back to the South and that this could be done without complying with the provisions of the Fugitive Slave Act or even bringing the alleged fugitive before a judge; that if a captured fugitive slave was brought before a judge, he or she was entitled to only a summary proceeding to determine whether he or she was the person described in the papers provided by the master; that a judge was not to decide whether the person before him was a slave or free but only whether he or she was the person described in the papers; and that state officials should enforce but could not be required to enforce the Fugitive Slave Act.

With the exception of *Dred Scott v. Sandford* (1857), this was the Supreme Court's most important decision concerning slavery and race before the Civil War. Justice Story wrote an overwhelmingly proslavery opinion for the court, with the dissent of only one justice, John McLean of Ohio. However, most of the majority justices could not agree with each other on all the details. Thus, there were five separate opinions agreeing with the outcome but not necessarily agreeing with all of Justice Story's points. Chief Justice Roger B. Taney agreed with the result but so emphatically disagreed with some of Story's points that his opinion is sometimes mistakenly called a dissent. Only two justices in the majority failed to write an opinion.

## Context

*Prigg v. Pennsylvania* came to the U.S. Supreme Court as an appeal from a decision in Pennsylvania, where Edward Prigg, a citizen of Maryland, had been convicted of kidnapping a Black woman named Margaret Morgan and her children. Prigg claimed that Morgan and her children were slaves in Maryland, owned by Margaret Ashmore, who was the mother-in-law of one of the other original defendants, Nathan Bemis. In 1837, Prigg, Bemis, and two other men traveled to Pennsylvania and seized Morgan and her children. They brought the group before Pennsylvania Justice of the Peace Thomas Henderson and asked for a certificate that would allow them to take the fugitive slaves back to Maryland. This was the proper procedure under an 1826 Pennsylvania personal liberty law designed to prevent the kidnapping of free Blacks. Henderson refused to issue the certificate because he did not believe that Morgan was a slave. At this point Prigg and Bemis released Morgan and her children and then offered to take them home. Instead, Prigg and his companions took them all to Maryland, where they were eventually sold as slaves. A Pennsylvania grand jury indicted all four Maryland men for kidnapping. After two years of negotiations, Maryland agreed to return just one of them, Prigg, for trial. He was quickly convicted, and the Pennsylvania Supreme Court upheld this result. Prigg then appealed to the U.S. Supreme Court.

The facts of the case were complicated. Margaret Morgan was, in fact, the child of a slave woman, and under Maryland law that made her a slave as well. But shortly after the War of 1812, when she was just a child, her owner, John Ashmore, told Margaret's parents that they were free. From that point on, Margaret always considered herself a free person. In the 1820s she married Jerry Morgan, who was born free in Pennsylvania. In the 1830 census Margaret, her children, and her husband were listed as "free persons of color" living in Harford County, Maryland. In 1832 the Morgans all moved to York, Pennsylvania, where they lived until 1837, when Prigg and Bemis claimed them as slaves. In Pennsylvania, Margaret gave birth to at least one child and perhaps two. Under Pennsylvania law they were free, *even* if Margaret was a fugitive slave.

The circumstances of this case illustrate the complexity of returning fugitive slaves. Most people imagine fugitive slaves to have been literally on the run, captured by hard-charging slave hunters in hot pursuit of African Americans seeking their freedom. Certainly there were cases like that. But often those claimed as fugitive slaves had lived in the North for months or years and had established themselves within a community. Even if Margaret Morgan was technically a fugitive slave, by 1837 she was also the wife of a free Black citizen of Pennsylvania and the mother of one or two Pennsylvania-born free African American children. Returning her to bondage would affect more than just her life—it would directly affect her family and, indirectly, a whole community.

***Justice John McLean was the sole dissenter.***
(Matthew Brady)

The return of fugitive slaves presented enormous legal, political, moral, and emotional controversies for the United States. By 1812 the nation had become truly divided into two sections. All of the northern states had either ended slavery or were doing so through gradual abolition acts. The small antislavery movements in the South that sprang up during the Revolution had all but disappeared. The nation had become, as Abraham Lincoln characterized it in his "House Divided" speech (1858), "half slave and half free."

While slavery was dying out in the North, the free Black population was growing. Many white northerners were uncomfortable with the presence of free Blacks, and discrimination was significant. Still, almost all northerners disliked slavery, and most were appalled at the idea of holding people in bondage. Furthermore, the overwhelming majority of northerners were opposed to seeing their free Black neighbors kidnapped and sold as slaves. Many northerners felt the same way about fugitive slaves who were brave, lucky, and enterprising enough to escape from bondage and become free.

The federal Fugitive Slave Act of 1793 provided that masters or their agents could bring an alleged slave before any state or federal judge and obtain a certificate of removal on the basis of an affidavit from the state where the person was allegedly a slave. There was no hearing into the status of the alleged slave, no jury trial, and no real opportunity for the person claimed to prove that he or she was actually free or that the wrong person had been seized. The law contemplated a summary process. In addition, the federal law provided no punishment for people who seized Blacks and did not bring them before a judge or magistrate.

Starting in the 1790s there were persistent complaints from northern Blacks and their white allies that southerners were roaming the streets of cities like Philadelphia and New York or scouring rural areas near Virginia and Maryland, kidnapping free Blacks and hurrying them off to the South. There were also complaints that southerners were falsely claiming free people as fugitive slaves. Some of these people were free-born citizens of the northern states. Others were fugitive slaves who had recently escaped to the North. Some were like Margaret Morgan and her children, whose status was uncertain and murky. In response to kidnappings, starting in the 1820s the legislatures in a number of free states, including New Jersey, Pennsylvania, and New York, passed personal liberty laws to protect free Blacks. These laws made it a crime to remove a Black from the state without a judicial hearing by a state official. Thus Prigg was prosecuted under the Pennsylvania law after he removed Morgan and her children from the state without obtaining the proper papers from a state magistrate.

By the time Prigg's case reached the U.S. Supreme Court, state judges in New York and New Jersey had held that the Fugitive Slave Act of 1793 was unconstitutional. The New York courts believed that Congress had no power to pass the law and that the return of fugitive slaves was a matter left entirely to the states. In the case at hand, *Jack v. Martin* (1835), the New York court returned the slave Jack to his owner but did so under state law. In other words, New York accepted its constitutional obligation to return runaway slaves, but the state did not accept the idea that this should be done under federal law. In New Jersey the highly respected Chief Justice Joseph Hornblower questioned the constitutionality of the Fugitive Slave Act of 1793 in an unpublished opinion, complaining that it provided for a "summary and

dangerous proceeding" and afforded "but little protection of security to the free colored man, who may be falsely claimed as a fugitive from labor." Hornblower believed that even if the Congress had the power to pass the law, it was unconstitutional because it denied alleged fugitives due process and a jury trial.

Southerners complained that these laws made it impossible for them to recover their runaway slaves. They also argued that since Congress had passed a law on this subject, it was unfair to make them also comply with the rules set out by the different states. This argument was complicated by the fact that Prigg and Bemis had only partially followed the procedures set out under the 1793 law. They did bring Morgan before a judge, as the federal law required, but when he gave them a ruling they did not like, they took the law into their own hands and simply forced Morgan and her children to go to Maryland without any legal documents or the authorization of any court.

By 1841 slavery had become one of the most important and divisive issues in American politics. A small but growing abolitionist movement in the North was noisily calling for an end to slavery everywhere in the nation. The House of Representatives refused to even read antislavery petitions sent by abolitionists. More ominously for the South, northern politicians, such as New York's Governor William H. Seward, Congressmen Joshua Giddings of Ohio, and Congressman (and former president) John Quincy Adams of Massachusetts, were increasingly openly hostile to slavery. Southerners believed that they could never recover fugitive slaves, even though in the late 1830s there were famous cases in Maine and New York where masters did recover runaway slaves. It was in this context that Prigg's case went to the Supreme Court.

## About the Author

There are three authors of the opinions reprinted here: Joseph Story, Roger B. Taney, and John McLean. Joseph Story was born in 1779 and raised in a solidly middle-class family in Marblehead, Massachusetts (outside Boston). A hard-working and brilliant student, he graduated second in his class from Harvard University in 1798, at the age of nineteen. He then became a lawyer, held local offices, and served in Congress in 1808–1809. On November 15, 1811, President James Madison nominated him to the Supreme Court. He remained on the Court until his death on September 10, 1845.

Story was learned, scholarly, and a firm believer in a strong Supreme Court. He was Chief Justice John Marshall's closest ally on the Court. A northerner, Story personally opposed slavery and, in his early years, issued a number of opinions and charges to grand juries that supported a strict suppression of the illegal African slave trade. In 1820 he made a speech opposing the spread of slavery into the western territories. In addition to his Supreme Court duties, Story was a professor at Harvard Law School and the author of more than a dozen books and treatises on law. His most important was *Commentaries on the Constitution of the United States* (1833), a three-volume treatise that argued for a highly nationalist interpretation of the Constitution and rejected notions of states' rights. His decision in *Prigg* was consistent with these values because it nationalized the return of fugitive slaves and rejected the idea that the states could regulate this issue. It was totally at odds, however, with his opposition to slavery and deeply inconsistent with the values of most New Englanders, the section of the nation he represented on the Court.

Chief Justice Roger B. Taney was born in 1777 into a wealthy slaveholding planter family in Maryland. He graduated from Dickinson College in 1795 at age eighteen, practiced law, and served in the state legislature. He was initially a Federalist, but in the 1820s he became an avid supporter of Andrew Jackson. He served as Jackson's attorney general and secretary of the Treasury before becoming chief justice of the United States in 1836. As a young man, Taney had freed most of his own slaves and once defended a minister accused of giving antislavery sermons. However, while serving as Jackson's attorney general, he argued that free Blacks were not entitled to passports because they could never be considered citizens of the United States. By the early 1840s he was committed to supporting slavery, even if he did not own slaves. In 1857 he would write the opinion of the Court in *Dred Scott v. Sandford*, holding that free Blacks had no rights under the Constitution and could never be considered citizens of the nation. Taney was far more sympathetic to states' rights than Story and less supportive of a strong national government. His opinion in *Prigg* was inconsistent with these legal principles, since he rejected the idea that states should be able to protect their free Black citizens in fugitive slave

cases. However, his opinion in *Prigg* was consistent with his strong support for slavery. He died in 1864.

John McLean was born in 1785 in New Jersey but grew up on a small farm on the Ohio frontier. He had no formal education until age sixteen and never attended college. He edited a newspaper, practiced law, and then held a series of political offices, serving in Congress, on the Ohio Supreme Court, as commissioner of the General Land Office, and then as postmaster general under three successive presidents: James Monroe, John Quincy Adams, and Andrew Jackson. Even his opponents believed that McLean was the most competent and honest postmaster of his age. Shortly after he took office, President Jackson appointed McLean to the Supreme Court, where he served for thirty-two years, making him the twelfth-longest-serving justice in the first two and a quarter centuries of the Court's history. He died in 1861.

McLean was always antislavery and, as Ohio justice, wrote a strong opinion holding that any slave voluntarily brought into the state was free. Later in life he became related through marriage to Salmon P. Chase, the most important antislavery lawyer in the nation, who was nicknamed "the Attorney General for Fugitive Slaves." At the time McLean was on the Court, justices were required to "ride circuit," where they presided over federal court trials in the states of the circuit to which they were assigned. McLean, riding circuit in Ohio, Indiana, Illinois, and Michigan, heard more fugitive slave cases than any other justice. He took seriously his obligation to enforce the fugitive slave clause of the Constitution and the 1793 Fugitive Slave Act. However, he also believed in protecting the rights of free Blacks and preventing the enslavement of anyone unless there was an absolutely clear legal right to send that person into bondage. His opinion in *Prigg* is consistent with these views and with his vast experience with fugitive slave cases, which far exceeded the combined experience of Taney and Story.

## Explanation and Analysis of the Document

As noted, seven of the nine justices wrote opinions in this case. Eight of the nine justices believed that Prigg's conviction should be overturned. The main point of disagreement was between Story and Taney, on whether state officials could be required to participate in the return of fugitive slaves. McLean's dissent argued that the Pennsylvania law was constitutional and thus it was permissible to prosecute Prigg for kidnapping.

In his opinion Story reached six major conclusions: that the federal Fugitive Slave Act of 1793 was constitutional; that no state could pass any law that added requirements to the federal law or impeded the return of fugitive slaves; that people claiming fugitive slaves (masters or their agents) had a constitutionally protected common law right of recaption, or "self-help," which allowed a claimant to seize any fugitive slave anywhere and bring that slave back to the South without complying with the provisions of the Fugitive Slave Act; that a captured fugitive slave was entitled to only a summary proceeding to determine whether he or she was indeed the person described in the papers provided by the claimant; that a judge was not to decide whether the person before him was a slave or free but only whether he or she was the person described in the papers; and that state officials should, but could not be required to, enforce the Fugitive Slave Act.

When combined, these conclusions created an overwhelming proslavery result. Story's notion of self-help was the most important for slave owners and the most dangerous for free Blacks. Story claimed that the fugitive slave clause created "a positive, unqualified right on the part of the owner of the slave which no state law or regulation can in any way qualify, regulate, control, or restrain." In Story's view, under the Constitution,

> the owner of a slave is clothed with entire authority, in every State in the Union, to seize and recapture his slave whenever he can do it without any breach of the peace or any illegal violence. In this sense and to this extent, this clause of the Constitution may properly be said to execute itself, and to require no aid from legislation, state or national.

Under this extraordinary conclusion any southerner could seize any Black and remove that person to the South without any state interference, as long as no "breach of the peace" occurred.

One might presume that a "breach of the peace" would always occur when a Black, especially a free one, was seized by a slave catcher or kidnapper, but this was

hardly the case. In his dissent, Justice McLean pointed out the logical problems of limiting Story's right of self-help to instances in which there was no breach of the peace:

> But it is said, the master may seize his slave wherever he finds him, if by doing so he does not violate the public peace; that the relation of master and slave is not affected by the laws of the State to which the slave may have fled, and where he is found. If the master has a right to seize and remove the slave without claim, he can commit no breach of the peace by using all the force necessary to accomplish his object.

In other words, the logic of Story's opinion was that no amount of violence against an alleged slave would be illegal. Slavery was based on force, and thus it would never be a breach of the peace for a master to take his slave by brutal force.

Violent seizures at night or in isolated areas could be accomplished without anyone's observing a breach of the peace. This happened with Margaret Morgan and her children. One moment they were in a wagon on their way home after Justice Henderson had released them. The next moment, in the middle of the night on a rural road with no one to help them, they were overpowered by four men and taken to Maryland. Once a Black was shackled, intimidated, and perhaps beaten into submission, travel from the North to the South could be accomplished without any obvious breach of the peace. If state officials could not stop whites from transporting a Black in chains, then kidnapping of any Black could always be accomplished. Under such a rule anyone, especially children, might be kidnapped and enslaved. Kidnappings of this sort had led to the enactment of Pennsylvania's 1826 personal liberty law.

In his majority opinion, Justice Story ignored the fact that one or more of Morgan's children was born free in Pennsylvania. Instead, he held that the fugitive slave clause gave masters an absolute right to claim their runaway slaves without any interference from state laws or state officials. Thus, Pennsylvania's 1826 personal liberty law was unconstitutional. Story held that only Congress could regulate the return of fugitive slaves, as it had in the 1793 law. That law required a master to bring a slave before any magistrate or judge, federal or state, to obtain a certificate of removal to take the slave with him. Even though Story found this law to be constitutional—and all state laws supplementing it to be unconstitutional—he also held that a master did not have to follow the procedure set out in the 1793 law. Instead, Story asserted that under the Constitution itself masters had a right of "self-help." Thus, if a master found it convenient to return a fugitive slave without going before a judge, he could do so, as long as it was accomplished without a "breach of the peace." For free Blacks and their white allies this seemed like an invitation for kidnapping.

Story left the states powerless to prevent this type of kidnapping. His opinion effectively made the law of the South the law of the nation. In the South, race was a presumption of slave status; by giving masters and slave hunters a common law right of "recaption," Story nationalized this presumption. As a result, slave catchers could operate in the North without having to prove the seized person's slave status. The consequences for the nearly one hundred and seventy-five thousand free Blacks in the North could have been dire. In his dissenting opinion, Justice McLean protested the result, but his complaints fell on deaf ears.

Story also ruled that northern states should help enforce the federal law, but they could not be forced to do so. This was a logical outcome of his reading of the Constitution. It was also consistent with nineteenth-century notions of states' rights: that the national government could not compel the states to act in a certain way. Story emphatically declared that the northern states *should* enforce the law, but from his perspective whatever they did would be a useful outcome. If the northern states enforced the law, it would prove to the South that it had nothing to fear from a stronger union and a more powerful national government. If, on the other hand, the northern states did not enforce the law, the national government would have to create an enforcement system, and this would have the dual value of strengthening the national government—a lifetime goal of Story's—and emphatically tying the South to support a nationalization of law.

In his concurring opinion, Chief Justice Taney misstated Story's position. He claimed that Story would not allow the states to capture fugitive slaves. As the very end of Story's opinion shows, this is not true. Story wanted the states to help with the return of fugitive slaves. He just

did not believe they could be forced to do so.

## Impact

The impact of *Prigg* was mixed. Southerners were generally pleased with the outcome but complained that Justice Story's opinion undermined enforcement of the 1793 Fugitive Slave Act, because Story said that northern judges could not be required to enforce the law. Most northerners, especially abolitionists, other opponents of slavery, and free Blacks, were appalled by the decision. Northern opponents of slavery attacked the opinion for protecting slavery and failing to protect the liberties of free Blacks. In Story's home state of Massachusetts many of his colleagues were horrified by the opinion. John Quincy Adams spent a whole day reading all the opinions, saddened by the case and the fact the opinion had been written by someone from his own state. Abolitionists, predictably, denounced Story and the decision.

After Justice Story died, his son, who was himself antislavery, claimed that his father believed that the opinion was a "triumph of freedom" because it allowed northern states to refuse to participate in the return of fugitive slaves. However, there is no evidence to support this claim. In fact, it would have been utterly inconsistent for Story to have purposely undermined his opinion in that way. Moreover, there is other evidence to suggest that Story fully backed his opinion. Shortly after the case was decided, he wrote to Senator John M. Berrien of Georgia urging that he introduce legislation that would allow the federal courts to appoint commissioners to enforce any federal law that a state judge could enforce. Thus, if the state judges refused to hear cases under the 1793 law, the federal court commissioners could do so. Story naively believed such a law could be passed without even mentioning fugitive slaves.

Many northern judges and legislatures acted on Story's single line suggesting that the states *should* enforce the federal law but could not be required to do so. Starting in 1843, a number of free states prohibited law enforcement and judicial officers from hearing fugitive slave cases and closed their jails to slave catchers. This led to increasing demands from the South for a new fugitive slave law, which was finally passed in 1850. That law adopted Story's suggestion to authorize the appointment of federal commissioners in every state to enforce the law.

Justice McLean, who dissented from Story's opinion, may also have been harmed by the case. In 1844 he was proposed as a presidential candidate by the Whig Party. However, southern Whigs blocked any consideration of him because, they argued, he was hostile to slavery. McLean very much wanted to be president, and his fidelity to liberty may have cost him dearly.

In the end, this case was a disaster for African Americans. It left all free Blacks in the North vulnerable to kidnapping, with no chance that their state or local governments could interfere to protect them. It dramatically threatened the growing population of fugitive slaves in the North, who could now be seized without any warrant or legal procedure. It further allowed for cases of mistaken identity, because even if Blacks were brought before a court, alleged fugitives could not get a trial to prove their freedom. The case underscored that the proslavery clauses of the Constitution of 1787 were in full flower in the 1840s.

The greatest cost of the decision was born by the free Blacks of the North. They were now subject to capture and enslavement without any hope that local governments could protect them. Like Margaret Morgan and her children, they could be swept up by slave catchers, dragged to the South, and sold into lifetime bondage. When the dust from the case finally settled, Edward Prigg remained a free man, while Margaret Morgan and her children, including those born in the free state of Pennsylvania, remained slaves, sold into the Deep South, where they would toil away in anonymity, far from their family and friends.

---

## Questions for Further Study

1. Compare the portion of this opinion written by Justice Joseph Story with his opinion just a year earlier in *United States v. Amistad.* What inferences can you draw about Story's attitude toward slavery from the two cases?

2. Similarly, read the portion of this opinion written by Justice Roger Taney with his opinion in the landmark *Dred Scott v. Sandford.* What consistencies do you see in the two opinions? Are there any significant differences?

3. Read this document in connection with the Fugitive Slave Act of 1793 and the Fugitive Slave Act of 1850. What impact might Story's decision have had, directly or indirectly, on the later law?

4. It is often quipped that if one party to a legal dispute is entirely happy with the outcome, the court has probably not done its job properly. To what extent were both sides—North and South, supporters and opponents of slavery—unhappy with the decision in this case?

5. In what way way, if any, did the Court's decision in *Prigg v. Pennsylvania* contribute to the divisions that led to the U.S. Civil War?

## Further Reading

### Books

Finkelman, Paul. *An Imperfect Union: Slavery, Federalism, and Comity.* Chapel Hill: University of North Carolina Press, 1981.

Finkelman, Paul. *Supreme Injustice: Slavery in the Nation's Highest Court.* Cambridge, MA: Harvard University Press, 2018.

Finkelman, Paul. "Story Telling on the Supreme Court: Prigg v. Pennsylvania and Justice Joseph Story's Judicial Nationalism." In *Supreme Court Review,* 1994, ed. Dennis J. Hutchinson et al. Chicago: University of Chicago Press, 1995.

Hyman, Harold M., and William M. Wiecek. *Equal Justice under Law: Constitutional Development, 1835–1875.* New York: Harper and Row, 1982.

Morris, Thomas D. *Free Men All: The Personal Liberty Laws of the North, 1780–1861.* Baltimore: Johns Hopkins University Press, 1974.

Newmyer, R. Kent. *Supreme Court Justice Joseph Story: Statesman of the Old Republic.* Chapel Hill: University of North Carolina Press, 1985.

### Articles

Finkelman, Paul. "Sorting Out Prigg v. Pennsylvania." *Rutgers Law Journal* 24 (Spring 1993): 605–665.

Goldstein, Leslie Friedman. "A 'Triumph of Freedom' After All? Prigg v. Pennsylvania Re-examined." *Labor and History Review* 29, no. 3 (August 2011): 763–796.

### Websites

"Fugitive Slave Act of 1793." UShistory.org website. Accessed February 23, 2023, https://www.ushistory.org/presidentshouse/history/slaveact1793.php.

"Fugitive Slaves." Slavery in the North website. Accessed February 23, 2023, http://slavenorth.com/fugitive.htm.

—Commentary by Paul Finkelman

# PRIGG V. PENNSYLVANIA

## Document Text

### Joseph Story: Majority Opinion

This is a writ of error to the Supreme Court of Pennsylvania, brought under the 25th section of the Judiciary Act of 1789, ch. 20, for the purpose of revising the judgment of that court, in a case involving the construction of the Constitution and laws of the United States. The facts are briefly these:

The plaintiff in error was indicted in the Court of Oyer and Terminer for York County, for having, with force and violence, taken and carried away from that county, to the State of Maryland, a certain negro woman, named Margaret Morgan, with a design and intention of selling and disposing of, and keeping her, as a slave or servant for life, contrary to a statute of Pennsylvania, passed on the 26th of March, 1826. That statute, in the first section, in substance provides that, if any person or persons shall, from and after the passing of the act, by force and violence, take and carry away, or cause to be taken and carried away, and shall, by fraud or false pretence, seduce, or cause to be seduced, or shall attempt to take, carry away or seduce, any negro or mulatto from any part of that Commonwealth, with a design and intention of selling and disposing of, or causing to be sold, or of keeping and detaining, or of causing to be kept and detained, such negro or mulatto, as a slave or servant for life, or for any term whatsoever, every such person or persons, his or their aiders or abettors, shall, on conviction thereof, be deemed guilty of felony, and shall forfeit and pay a sum not less than five hundred, nor more than one thousand dollars, and moreover shall be sentenced to undergo

servitude for any term or terms of years, not less than seven years nor exceeding twenty-one years, and shall be confined and kept to hard labor, &c....

The plaintiff in error pleaded not guilty to the indictment, and, at the trial, the jury found a special verdict which in substance states that the negro woman, Margaret Morgan, was a slave for life, and held to labor and service under and according to the laws of Maryland, to a certain Margaret Ashmore, a citizen of Maryland; that the slave escaped and fled from Maryland into Pennsylvania in 1832; that the plaintiff in error, being legally constituted the agent and attorney of the said Margaret Ashmore, in 1837 caused the said negro woman to be taken and apprehended as a fugitive from labor by a state constable under a warrant from a Pennsylvania magistrate; that the said negro woman was thereupon brought before the said magistrate, who refused to take further cognizance of the case; and thereupon the plaintiff in error did remove, take and carry away the said negro woman and her children out of Pennsylvania into Maryland, and did deliver the said negro woman and her children into the custody and possession of the said Margaret Ashmore. The special verdict further finds that one of the children was born in Pennsylvania more than a year after the said negro woman had fled and escaped from Maryland....

Before proceeding to discuss the very important and interesting questions involved in this record, it is fit to say that the cause has been conduced in the court below, and has been brought here by the cooperation and sanction, both of the State of Maryland and the

State of Pennsylvania in the most friendly and courteous spirit, with a view to have those questions finally disposed of by the adjudication of this Court so that the agitations on this subject in both States, which have had a tendency to interrupt the harmony between them, may subside, and the conflict of opinion be put at rest. It should also be added that the statute of Pennsylvania of 1826 was (as has been suggested at the bar) passed with a view of meeting the supposed wishes of Maryland on the subject of fugitive slaves, and that, although it has failed to produce the good effects intended in its practical construction, the result was unforeseen and undesigned.

1. The question arising in the case as to the constitutionality of the statute of Pennsylvania, has been most elaborately argued at the bar. . . . Few questions which have ever come before this Court involve more delicate and important considerations, and few upon which the public at large may be presumed to feel a more profound and pervading interest. We have accordingly given them our most deliberate examination, and it has become my duty to state the result to which we have arrived, and the reasoning by which it is supported. . . .

There are two clauses in the Constitution upon the subject of fugitives, which stands in juxtaposition with each other and have been thought mutually to illustrate each other. They are both contained in the second section of the fourth Article, and are in the following words:

> A person charged in any State with treason, felony, or other crime who shall flee from justice and be found in another State shall, on demand of the executive authority of the State from which he fled, be delivered up, to be removed to the State having jurisdiction of the crime.

> No person held to service or labor in one State, under the laws thereof, escaping into another, shall, in consequence of any law or regulation therein, be discharged from such service or labor, but shall be delivered up on claim of the party to whom such service or labor may be due.

The last clause is that the true interpretation whereof is directly in judgment before us. Historically, it is well known that the object of this clause was to secure to the citizens of the slave-holding States the complete right and title of ownership in their slaves, as property, in every State in the Union into which they might escape from the State where they were held in servitude. The full recognition of this right and title was indispensable to the security of this species of property in all the slave-holding States, and indeed was so vital to the preservation of their domestic interests and institutions that it cannot be doubted that it constituted a fundamental article without the adoption of which the Union could not have been formed. Its true design was to guard against the doctrines and principles prevalent in the non-slaveholding States, by preventing them from intermeddling with, or obstructing, or abolishing the rights of the owners of slaves.

By the general law of nations, no nation is bound to recognize the state of slavery as to foreign slaves found within its territorial dominions, when it is in opposition to its own policy and institutions, in favor of the subjects of other nations where slavery is recognized. If it does it, it is as a matter of comity, and not as a matter of international right. The state of slavery is deemed to be a mere municipal regulation, founded upon and limited to the range of the territorial laws. This was fully recognized in *Somerset's Case* [Great Britain, 1771], . . . which decided before the American revolution. It is manifest from this consideration that, if the Constitution had not contained this clause, every non-slaveholding State in the Union would have been at liberty to have declared free all runaway slaves coming within its limits, and to have given them entire immunity and protection against the claims of their masters—a course which would have created the most bitter animosities and engendered perpetual strife between the different States. The clause was therefore of the last importance to the safety and security of the southern States, and could not have been surrendered by them, without endangering their whole property in slaves. The clause was accordingly adopted into the Constitution by the unanimous consent of the framers of it—a proof at once of its intrinsic and practical necessity.

How then are we to interpret the language of the clause? The true answer is in such a manner as, consistently with the words, shall fully and completely effectuate the whole objects of it. If, by one mode of interpretation, the right must become shadowy and unsubstantial, and without any remedial power adequate to the end, and, by another mode, it will attain its just end and secure its manifest purpose, it would seem, upon principles of reasoning, absolutely irresistible, that the latter ought to prevail. No court of justice can be authorized so to construe any clause of the Constitution as to defeat its obvious ends when another construction, equally accordant with the words and sense thereof, will enforce and protect them.

The clause manifestly contemplates the existence of a positive, unqualified right on the part of the owner of the slave which no state law or regulation can in any way qualify, regulate, control, or restrain. The slave is not to be discharged from service or labor in consequence of any state law or regulation. Now certainly, without indulging in any nicety of criticism upon words, it may fairly and reasonably be said that any state law or state regulation which interrupts, limits, delays, or postpones the right of the owner to the immediate possession of the slave and the immediate command of his service and labor operates pro tanto a discharge of the slave therefrom. The question can never be how much the slave is discharged from, but whether he is discharged from any, by the natural or necessary operation of state laws or state regulations. The question is not one of quantity or degree, but of withholding or controlling the incidents of a positive and absolute right.

We have said that the clause contains a positive and unqualified recognition of the right of the owner in the slave, unaffected by any state law or legislation whatsoever, because there is no qualification or restriction of it to be found therein, and we have no right to insert any which is not expressed and cannot be fairly implied. Especially are we estopped from so doing when the clause puts the right to the service or labor upon the same ground, and to the same extent, in every other State as in the State from which the slave escaped and in which he was held to the service or labor. If this be so, then all the incidents to that right attach also. The owner must, therefore, have the right to seize and repossess the slave, which the local laws of his own State confer upon him, as property, and we all know that this right of seizure and recaption is universally acknowledged in all the slaveholding States. Indeed, this is no more than a mere affirmance of the principles of the common law applicable to this very subject. [Blackstone's Commentaries] . . . lays it down as unquestionable doctrine.

"Recaption or reprisal [says he] is another species of remedy by the mere act of the party injured. This happens when anyone hath deprived another of his property in goods or chattels personal, or wrongfully detains one's wife, child or servant, in which case the owner of the goods, and the husband, parent or master, may lawfully claim and retake them wherever he happens to find them, so it be not in a riotous manner or attended with a breach of the peace."

Upon this ground, we have not the slightest hesitation in holding that, under and in virtue of the Constitution, the owner of a slave is clothed with entire authority, in every State in the Union, to seize and recapture his slave whenever he can do it without any breach of the peace or any illegal violence. In this sense and to this extent, this clause of the Constitution may properly be said to execute itself, and to require no aid from legislation, state or national.

But the clause of the Constitution does not stop here, nor, indeed, consistently with its professed objects, could it do so. Many cases must arise in which, if the remedy of the owner were confined to the mere right of seizure and recaption, he would be utterly without any adequate redress. He may not be able to lay his hands upon the slave. He may not be able to enforce his rights against persons who either secrete or conceal or withhold the slave. He may be restricted by local legislation as to the mode of proofs of his ownership, as to the courts in which he shall sue, and as to the actions which he may bring or the process he may use to compel the delivery of the slave. Nay, the local legislation may be utterly inadequate to furnish the appropriate redress, by authorizing no process in rem, or no specific mode of repossessing the slave, leaving the owner, at best, not that right which the Constitution designed to secure, a specific delivery and repossession of the slave, but a mere remedy in damages, and that, perhaps, against persons utterly insolvent or worthless. The state legislation may be entirely silent on the whole subject, and its ordinary remedial process framed with different views and objects, and this may be innocently, as well as designedly, done, since every State is perfectly competent, and has the exclusive right, to prescribe the remedies in its own judicial tribunals, to limit the time as well as the mode of redress, and to deny jurisdiction over cases which its own policy and its own institutions either prohibit or discountenance.

If, therefore, the clause of the Constitution had stopped at the mere recognition of the right, without providing or contemplating any means by which it might be established and enforced, in cases where it did not execute itself, it is plain that it would have been, in a great variety of cases, a delusive and empty annunciation. If it did not contemplate any action, either through state or national legislation, as auxiliaries to its more perfect enforcement in the form of remedy, or of protection, then, as there would be no duty on either to aid the right, it would be left to the mere comity of the States to act as they should please, and would depend for its security upon the changing course of public opinion, the mutations of public policy, and the general adaptations of remedies for purposes strictly according to the lex fori.

And this leads us to the consideration of the other part of the clause, which implies at once a guarantee and duty. It says, "but he [the slave] shall be delivered up on claim of the party to whom such service or labor may be due." Now we think it exceedingly difficult, if not impracticable, to read this language and not to feel that it contemplated some further remedial redress than that which might be administered at the hands of the owner himself. A claim is to be made! What is a claim? It is, in a just juridical sense, a demand of some matter, as of right, made by one person upon another, to do or to forbear to do some act or thing as a matter of duty. A more limited but, at the same time, an equally expressive, definition was given by Lord Dyer, as cited in *Stowel v. Zouch*, ... and it is equally applicable to the present case: that "a claim is a challenge by a man of the propriety or ownership of a thing which he has not in possession, but which is wrongfully detained from him."

The slave is to be delivered up on the claim. By whom to be delivered up? In what mode to be delivered up? How, if a refusal takes place, is the right of delivery to be enforced? Upon what proofs? What shall be the evidence of a rightful recaption or delivery? When and under what circumstances shall the possession of the owner, after it is obtained, be conclusive of his right, so as to preclude any further inquiry or examination into it by local tribunals or otherwise, while the slave, in possession of the owner, is in transitu to the State from which he fled?

These and many other questions will readily occur upon the slightest attention to the clause; and it is obvious that they can receive but one satisfactory answer. They require the aid of legislation to protect the right, to enforce the delivery, and to secure the subsequent possession of the slave. If, indeed, the Constitution guaranties the right, and if it requires the delivery upon the claim of the owner (as cannot well be doubted), the natural inference certainly is that the National Government is clothed with the appropriate authority and functions to enforce it. The fundamental principle, applicable to all cases of this sort, would seem to be that, where the end is required, the means are given; and where the duty is enjoined, the ability to perform it is contemplated to exist on the part of the functionaries to whom it is entrusted. The clause is found in the National Constitution, and not in that of any State. It does not point out any state functionaries, or any state action, to carry its provisions into effect. The States cannot, therefore, be compelled to enforce them, and it might well be deemed an unconstitutional exercise of the power of interpretation to insist that the States are bound to provide means to carry into effect the duties of the National Government, nowhere delegated or entrusted to them by the Constitution. On the contrary, the natural, if not the necessary, conclusion is, that the National Government, in the absence of all positive provisions to the contrary, is bound, through its own proper departments, legislative, judicial or executive, as the case may require, to carry into effect all the rights and duties imposed upon it by the Constitution. The remark of Mr. Madison, in the Federalist (No. 43), would seem in such cases to apply with peculiar force. "A right [says he] implies a remedy, and where else would the remedy be deposited than where it is deposited by the Constitution?"—meaning, as the context shows, in the Government of the United States.

It is plain, then, that where a claim is made by the owner, out of possession, for the delivery of a slave, it must be made, if at all, against some other person; and, inasmuch as the right is a right of property, capable of being recognized and asserted by proceedings before a court of justice, between parties adverse to each other, it constitutes, in the strictest sense, a controversy between the parties, and a case "arising under the Constitution" of the United States within the express delegation of judicial power given by that instrument. Congress, then, may call that power into activity for the very purpose of giving effect to that right; and, if so, then it may prescribe the mode and extent in which it shall be applied, and how and under what circumstances the proceedings shall afford a complete protection and guarantee to the right.

Congress has taken this very view of the power and duty of the National Government.... The result of their deliberations was the passage of the act of the 12th of February 1793, ch. 51, which, after having, in the first and second sections, provided by the case of fugitives from justice, by a demand to be made of the delivery, through the executive authority of the State where they are found, proceeds, in the third section, to provide that, when a person held to labor or service in any of the United States, shall escape into any other of the States or territories, the person to whom such labor or service may be due, his agent or attorney, is hereby empowered to seize or arrest such fugitive from labor, and take him or her before any judge of the circuit or district courts of the United States, residing or being within the State, or before any magistrate of a county, city or town corporate, wherein such seizure or arrest shall be made; and, upon proof to the satisfaction of such judge or magistrate, either by oral evidence or affidavit, &c., that the person so seized or arrested, doth, under the laws of the State or territory from which he or she fled, owe service or labor to the person claiming him or her, it shall be the duty of such judge or magistrate to give a certificate thereof to such claimant, his agent or attorney which shall be sufficient warrant for removing the said fugitive from labor to the State or territory from which he or she fled. The fourth section provides a penalty against any person who shall knowingly and willingly obstruct or hinder such claimant, his agent, or attorney in so seizing or arresting such fugitive from labor, or rescue such fugitive from the claimant, or his agent or attorney when so arrested, or who shall harbor or conceal such fugitive after notice that he is such; and it also saves to the person claiming such labor or service his right of action for or on account of such injuries.

In a general sense, this act may be truly said to cover the whole ground of the Constitution, both as to fugitives from justice and fugitive slaves—that is, it covers both the subjects in its enactments, not because it exhausts the remedies which may be applied by Congress to enforce the rights if the provisions of the act shall in practice be found not to attain the object of the Constitution; but because it points out fully all the modes of attaining those objects which Congress, in their discretion, have as yet deemed expedient or proper to meet the exigencies of the Constitution. If this be so, then it would seem, upon just principles of construction, that the legislation of Congress, if constitutional, must supersede all state legislation upon the same subject and, by necessary implication, prohibit it. For, if Congress have a constitutional power to regulate a particular subject, and they do actually regulate it in a given manner, and in a certain form, it cannot be that the state legislatures have a right to interfere and, as it were, by way of complement to the legislation of Congress, to prescribe additional regulations and what they may deem auxiliary provisions for the same purpose. In such a case, the legislation of Congress, in what it does prescribe, manifestly indicates that it does not intend that there shall be any further legislation to act upon the subject matter. Its silence as to what it does not do is as expressive of what its intention is as the direct provisions made by it.... [Thus,] it is not competent for state legislation to add to the provisions of Congress upon that subject, for that the will of Congress upon the whole subject is as clearly established by what it has not declared as by what it has expressed.

But it has been argued that the act of Congress is unconstitutional because it does not fall within the scope of any of the enumerated powers of legislation confided to that body, and therefore it is void. Stripped of its artificial and technical structure, the argument comes to this—that although rights are exclusively secured by, or duties are exclusively imposed upon, the National Government, yet, unless the power to enforce these rights or to execute these duties can be found among the express powers of legislation enumerated in the Constitution, they remain without any means of giving them effect by any act of Congress, and they must operate solely proprio vigore, however defective may be their operation—nay! even although, in a practical sense, they may become a nullity from the want of a proper remedy to enforce them or to provide against their violation. If this be the true interpretation of the Constitution, it must in a great measure fail to attain many of its avowed and positive objects as a security of rights and a recognition of duties. Such a limited construction of the Constitution has never yet been adopted as correct either in theory or practice. No one has ever supposed that Congress could constitutionally, by its legislation, exercise powers or enact laws beyond the powers delegated to it by the Constitution. But it has on various occasions exercised powers which were necessary and proper as means to carry into effect rights expressly given and duties expressly enjoined thereby. The end being required, it has been deemed a just and necessary implication that the means to accomplish it are given also, or, in other words, that the power flows as a necessary means to accomplish the end....

In respect to fugitives from justice, the Constitution, although it expressly provides that the demand shall be made by the executive authority of the State from which the fugitive has fled, is silent as to the party upon whom the demand is to be made and as to the mode in which it shall be made. This very silence occasioned embarrassments in enforcing the right and duty at an early period after the adoption of the Constitution; and produced a hesitation on the part of the executive authority of Virginia to deliver up a fugitive from justice upon the demand of the executive of Pennsylvania in the year 1791; and, as we historically know from the message of President Washington and the public documents of that period, it was the immediate cause of the passing of the Act of 1793, which designated the person (the state executive) upon whom the demand should be made, and the mode and proofs upon and in which it should be made. From that time down to the present hour, not a doubt has been breathed upon the constitutionality of this part of the act, and every executive in the Union has constantly acted upon and admitted its validity....

The same uniformity of acquiescence in the validity of the Act of 1793 upon the other part of the subject matter that of fugitive slaves has prevailed throughout the whole Union until a comparatively recent period. Nay, being from its nature and character more readily susceptible of being brought into controversy in courts of justice than the former, and of enlisting in opposition to it the feelings, and it may be, the prejudices, of some portions of the non-slaveholding States, it has naturally been brought under adjudication in several States in the Union, and particularly in Massachusetts, New York, and Pennsylvania, and, on all these occasions, its validity has been affirmed.... Under such circumstances, if the question were one of doubtful construction, such long acquiescence in it, such contemporaneous expositions of it, and such extensive and uniform recognition of its validity would, in our judgment, entitle the question to be considered at rest unless, indeed, the interpretation of the Constitution is

to be delivered over to interminable doubt throughout the whole progress of legislation and of national operations. Congress, the executive, and the judiciary have, upon various occasions, acted upon this as a sound and reasonable doctrine. ... The remaining question is whether the power of legislation upon this subject is exclusive in the National Government or concurrent in the States until it is exercised by Congress. In our opinion, it is exclusive....

In the first place, it is material to state (what has been already incidentally hinted at) that the right to seize and retake fugitive slaves and the duty to deliver them up, in whatever State of the Union they may be found, and, of course, the corresponding power in Congress to use the appropriate means to enforce the right and duty, derive their whole validity and obligation exclusively from the Constitution of the United States, and are there, for the first time, recognized and established in that peculiar character.

Before the adoption of the Constitution, no State had any power whatsoever over the subject except within its own territorial limits, and could not bind the sovereignty or the legislation of other States. ... It is, therefore, in a just sense, a new and positive right ... [and the] natural inference deductible from this consideration certainly is, in the absence of any positive delegation of power to the state legislatures that it belongs to the Legislative Department of the National Government, to which it owes its origin and establishment. It would be a strange anomaly and forced construction to suppose that the National Government meant to rely for the due fulfillment of its own proper duties, and the rights it intended to secure, upon state legislation, and not upon that of the Union. A fortiori, it would be more objectionable to suppose that a power which was to be the same throughout the Union should be confided to state sovereignty, which could not rightfully act beyond its own territorial limits....

[If] the States have a right, in the absence of legislation by Congress, to act upon the subject, each State is at liberty to prescribe just such regulations as suit its own policy, local convenience, and local feelings. The legislation of one State may not only be different from, but utterly repugnant to and incompatible with, that of another. The time and mode and limitation of the remedy, the proofs of the title, and all other incidents applicable thereto may be prescribed in one State which are rejected or disclaimed in another. One State may require the owner to sue in one mode, another in a different mode. One State may make a statute of limitations as to the remedy, in its own tribunals, short and summary; another may prolong the period and yet restrict the proofs. Nay, some States may utterly refuse to act upon the subject of all, and others may refuse to open its courts to any remedies *in rem* because they would interfere with their own domestic policy, institutions, or habits. The right, therefore, would never, in a practical sense, be the same in all the States. It would have no unity of purpose or uniformity of operation. The duty might be enforced in some States, retarded or limited in others, and denied as compulsory in many, if not in all. Consequences like these must have been foreseen as very likely to occur in the non-slaveholding States where legislation, if not silent on the subject and purely voluntary, could scarcely be presumed to be favorable to the exercise of the rights of the owner.

It is scarcely conceivable that the slaveholding States would have been satisfied with leaving to the legislation of the non-slaveholding States a power of regulation, in the absence of that of Congress, which would or might practically amount to a power to destroy the rights of the owner. If the argument, therefore, of a concurrent power in the States to act upon the subject matter, in the absence of legislation by Congress, be well founded, then, if Congress had never acted at all, or if the act of Congress should be repealed without providing a substitute, there would be a resulting authority in each of the States to regulate the whole subject at its pleasure, and to dole out its own remedial justice or withhold it at its pleasure and according to its own views of policy and expediency. Surely such a state of things never could have been intended under such a solemn guarantee of right and duty. On the other hand, construe the right of legislation as exclusive in Congress, and every evil and every danger vanishes. The right and the duty are then coextensive and uniform in remedy and operation throughout the whole Union. The owner has the same security, and the same remedial justice, and the same exemption from state regulation and control through however many States he may pass with his fugitive slave in his possession *in transitu* to his own domicile. But, upon the other supposition, the moment he passes the state line, he becomes amenable to the laws of another sovereignty whose regulations may greatly embarrass or delay the exercise of his rights, and even be repug-

nant to those of the State where he first arrested the fugitive. Consequences like these show that the nature and objects of the provisions imperiously require that, to make it effectual, it should be construed to be exclusive of state authority....

And we know no case in which the confusion and public inconvenience and mischiefs thereof could be more completely exemplified than the present.

These are some of the reasons, but by no means all, upon which we hold the power of legislation on this subject to be exclusive in Congress. To guard, however, against any possible misconstruction of our views, it is proper to state that we are by no means to be understood in any manner whatsoever to doubt or to interfere with the police power belonging to the States in virtue of their general sovereignty. That police power extends over all subjects within territorial limits of the States, and has never been conceded to the United States. It is wholly distinguishable from the right and duty secured by the provision now under consideration, which is exclusively derived from and secured by the Constitution of the United States and owes its whole efficacy thereto. We entertain no doubt whatsoever that the States, in virtue of their general police power, possesses full jurisdiction to arrest and restrain runaway slaves, and remove them from their borders, and otherwise to secure themselves against their depredations and evil example, as they certainly may do in cases of idlers, vagabonds and paupers. The rights of the owners of fugitive slaves are in no just sense interfered with or regulated by such a course, and, in many cases, the operations of this police power, although designed generally for other purposes—for protection, safety and peace of the State—may essentially promote and aid the interests of the owners. But such regulations can never be permitted to interfere with or to obstruct the just rights of the owner to reclaim his slave, derived from the Constitution of the United States, or with the remedies prescribed by Congress to aid and enforce the same.

Upon these grounds, we are of opinion that the act of Pennsylvania upon which this indictment is founded is unconstitutional and void. It purports to punish as a public offense against that State the very act of seizing and removing a slave by his master which the Constitution of the United States was designed to justify and uphold. The special verdict finds this fact, and the state courts have rendered judgment against the plaintiff in error upon that verdict. That judgment must, therefore, be reversed, and the cause remanded to the Supreme Court of Pennsylvania with directions to carry into effect the judgment of this Court rendered upon the special verdict, in favor of the plaintiff in error.

## Roger Taney: Concurrence

I concur in the opinion pronounced by the Court that the law of Pennsylvania, under which the plaintiff in error was indicted, is unconstitutional and void, and that the judgment against him must be reversed. But, as the questions before us arise upon the construction of the Constitution of the United States, and as I do not assent to all the principles contained in the opinion just delivered, it is proper to state the points on which I differ. . . .

The act of February 12th, 1793, is a constitutional exercise of this power, and every state law which requires the master, against his consent, to go before any state tribunal or officer before he can take possession of his property, or which authorizes a state officer to interfere with him when he is peaceably removing it from the State, is unconstitutional and void.

But, as I understand the opinion of the Court, it goes further, and decides that the power to provide a remedy for this right is vested exclusively in Congress, and that all laws upon the subject passed by a State since the adoption of the Constitution of the United States are null and void, even although they were intended in good faith to protect the owner in the exercise of his rights of property, and do not conflict in any degree with the act of Congress.

I do not consider this question as necessarily involved in the case before us, for the law of Pennsylvania under which the plaintiff in error was prosecuted is clearly in conflict with the Constitution of the United States, as well as with the law of 1793. But, as the question is discussed in the opinion of the Court, and as I do not assent either to the doctrine or the reasoning by which it is maintained, I proceed to state very briefly my objections.

The opinion of the Court maintains that the power over this subject is so exclusively vested in Congress that no State, since the adoption of the Constitution, can pass any law in relation to it. In other words, according to the opinion just delivered, the state authorities are prohibited from interfering for the purpose of protecting the right of the master and aiding him in the recovery of his property. I think the States are not prohibited, and that, on the contrary, it is enjoined upon them as a duty to protect and support the owner when he is endeavoring to obtain possession of his property found within their respective territories.

The language used in the Constitution does not, in my judgment, justify this construction given to it by the court. It contains no words prohibiting the several States from passing laws to enforce this right. They are, in express terms, forbidden to make any regulation that shall impair it, but there the prohibition stops. . . .

And why may not a State protect a right of property acknowledged by its own paramount law? Besides, the laws of the different States in all other cases constantly protect the citizens of other States in their rights of property when it is found within their respective territories, and no one doubts their power to do so. And, in the absence of any express prohibition, I perceive no reason for establishing by implication a different rule in this instance where, by the national compact, this right of property is recognized as an existing right in every State of the Union.

I do not speak of slaves whom their masters voluntarily take into a non-slaveholding State. That case is not before us. I speak of the case provided for in the Constitution—that is to say, the case of a fugitive who has escaped from the service of his owner and who has taken refuge and is found in another State. . . .

I cannot understand the rule of construction by which a positive and express stipulation for the security of certain individual rights of property in the several States is held to imply a prohibition to the States to pass any laws to guard and protect them. . . .

Indeed, if the state authorities are absolved from all obligation to protect this right, and may stand by and see it violated without an effort to defend it, the act of Congress of 1793 scarcely deserves the name of a remedy. The state officers mentioned in the law are not bound to execute the duties imposed upon them by Congress unless they choose to do so or are required to do so by a law of the State, and the state legislature has the power, if it thinks proper, to prohibit them. The Act of 1793, therefore, must depend altogether for its execution upon the officers of the United States named in it. And the master must take the fugitive, after he has seized him, before a judge of the district or circuit court, residing in the State, and exhibit his proofs, and procure from the judge his certificate of ownership, in order to obtain the protection in removing his property which this act of Congress profess to give.

Now, in many of the States, there is but one district judge, and there are only nine States which have judges of the Supreme Court residing within them. The fugitive will frequently be found by his owner in a place very distant from the residence of either of these judges, and would certainly be removed beyond his reach before a warrant could be procured from the judge to arrest him, even if the act of Congress authorized such a warrant. But it does not authorize the judge to issue a warrant to arrest the fugitive, but evidently relied on the state authorities to protect the owner in making the seizure. And it is only when the fugitive is arrested and brought before the judge that he is directed to take the proof and give the certificate of ownership. It is only necessary to state the provisions of this law in order to show how ineffectual and delusive is the remedy provided by Congress if state authority is forbidden to come to its aid....

Fugitives from the more southern States, when endeavoring to escape into Canada, very frequently pass through [other slave states]. . . .. But if the States are forbidden to legislate on this subject, and the power is exclusively in Congress, then these state laws are unconstitutional and void, and the fugitive can only be arrested according to the provisions of the act of Congress. By that law, the power to seize is given to no one but the owner, his agent, or attorney. And if the officers of the State are not justified in acting under the state laws, and cannot arrest the fugitive and detain him in prison without having first received an authority from the owner, the territory of the State must soon become an open pathway for the fugitives escaping from other states. For they are often in the act of passing through it by the time that the owner first discovers that they have absconded, and, in almost every instance, they would be beyond its borders (if they were allowed to pass through without interruption) before the master would be able to learn the road they had taken....

It is true that Maryland, as well as every other slaveholding State, has a deep interest in the faithful execution of the clause in question. But the obligation of the compact is not confined to them; it is equally binding upon the faith of every State in the Union, and has heretofore, in my judgment, been justly regarded as obligatory upon all.

I dissent, therefore, upon these grounds, from that part of the opinion of the Court which denies the obligation and the right of the state authorities to protect the master when he is endeavoring to seize a fugitive from his service in pursuance of the right given to him by the Constitution of the United States, provided the state law is not in conflict with the remedy provided by Congress.

## John McLean: Concurrence

As this case involves questions deeply interesting, if not vital, to the permanency of the Union of these States, and as I differ on one point from the opinion of the court, I deem it proper to state my own views on the subject....

The plaintiff, being a citizen of Maryland, with others, took Margaret Morgan, a colored woman and a slave, by force and violence, without the certificate required by the act of Congress, from the State of Pennsylvania, and brought her to the State of Maryland. By an amicable arrangement between the two States, judgment was entered against the defendant in the court where the indictment was found, and, on the cause's being removed to the Supreme Court of the State, that judgment, pro forma, was affirmed. And the case is now here for our examination and decision.

The last clause of the second section of the Fourth Article of the Constitution of the United States declares that

"No person held to service or labor in one State, under the laws thereof, escaping into another, shall, in consequence of any law or regulation therein, be discharged from such service or labor, but shall be delivered up, on claim of the party to whom such service or labor may be due."

This clause of the Constitution is now for the first time brought before this Court for consideration....

Does the provision in regard to the reclamation of fugitive slaves vest the power exclusively in the Federal Government?

This must be determined from the language of the Constitution and the nature of the power.

The language of the provision is general; it covers the whole ground, not in detail, but in principle. The States are inhibited from passing "any law or regulation which shall discharge a fugitive slave from the service of his master," and a positive duty is enjoined on them to deliver him up, "on claim of the party to whom his service may be due."

The nature of the power shows that it must be exclusive.

It was designed to protect the rights of the master, and against whom? Not against the State, nor the people of the State in which he resides, but against the people and the legislative action of other States where the fugitive from labor might be found. Under the Confederation, the master had no legal means of enforcing his rights in a State opposed to slavery. A disregard of rights thus asserted was deeply felt in the South; it produced great excitement, and would have led to results destructive of the Union. To avoid this, the constitutional guarantee was essential.

The necessity for this provision was found in the views and feelings of the people of the States opposed to slavery, and who, under such an influence, could not be expected favorably to regard the rights of the master. Now, by whom is this paramount law to be executed? . . .

I come now to a most delicate and important inquiry in this case, and that is whether the claimant of a fugitive from labor may seize and remove him by force out of the State in which he may be found, in defiance of its laws. I refer not to laws which are in conflict with the Constitution, or the Act of 1793. Such state laws, I have already said, are void. But I have reference to those laws which regulate the police of the State, maintain the peace of its citizens, and preserve its territory and jurisdiction from acts of violence. . . .

Both the Constitution and the Act of 1793 require the fugitive from labor to be delivered up on claim being made by the party or his agent to whom the service is due. Not that a suit should be regularly instituted; the proceeding authorized by the law is summary and informal. The fugitive is seized by the claimant, and taken before a judge or magistrate within the State, and on proof, parol or written that he owes labor to the claimant, it is made the duty of the judge or magistrate to give the certificate which authorizes the removal of the fugitive to the State from whence he absconded.

The counsel inquire of whom the claim shall be made. And they represent that the fugitive, being at large in the State, is in the custody of no one, nor under the protection of the State, so that the claim cannot be made, and consequently that the claimant may seize the fugitive and remove him out of the State.

A perusal of the act of Congress obviates this difficulty and the consequence which is represented as growing out of it.

The act is framed to meet the supposed case. The fugitive is presumed to be at large, for the claimant is authorized to seize him; after seizure, he is in custody; before it, he was not; and the claimant is required to take him before a judicial officer of the State; and it is before such officer his claim is to be made.

To suppose that the claim is not to be made, and indeed, cannot be, unless the fugitive be in the custody or possession of some public officer or individual is to disregard the letter and spirit of the Act of 1793. There is no act in the statute book more precise in its language and, as it would seem, less liable to misconstruction. In my judgment, there is not the least foundation in the act for the right asserted in the argument, to take the fugitive by force and remove him out of the State.

Such a proceeding can receive no sanction under the act, for it is in express violation of it. The claimant, having seized the fugitive, is required by the act to take him before a federal judge within the State, or a state magistrate within the county, city or town corporate, within which the seizure was made. Nor can there be any pretence that, after the seizure under the statute, the claimant may disregard the other express provision of it by taking the fugitive, without claim, out of the State. But it is said, the master may seize his slave wherever he finds him, if by doing so he does not violate the public peace; that the relation of master and slave is not affected by the laws of the State to which the slave may have fled and where he is found.

If the master has a right to seize and remove the slave without claim, he can commit no breach of the peace by using all the force necessary to accomplish his object.

It is admitted that the rights of the master, so far as regards the services of the slave, are not impaired by this change, but the mode of asserting them, in my opinion, is essentially modified. In the State where the service is due, the master needs no other law than the law of force to control the action of the slave. But can this law be applied by the master in a State which makes the act unlawful?

Can the master seize his slave and remove him out of the State, in disregard of its laws, as he might take his horse which is running at large? This ground is taken in the argument. Is there no difference in principle in these cases?

The slave, as a sensible and human being, is subject to the local authority into whatsoever jurisdiction he may go; he is answerable under the laws for his acts, and he may claim their protection; the State may protect him against all the world except the claim of his master. Should anyone commit lawless violence on the slave, the offender may unquestionably be punished; and should the slave commit murder, he may be detained and punished for it by the State in disregard of the claim of the master. Being within the jurisdiction of a State, a slave bears a very different relation to it from that of mere property.

In a State where slavery is allowed, every colored person is presumed to be a slave, and, on the same principle, in a non-slaveholding State, every person is presumed to be free, without regard to color. On this principle, the States, both slaveholding and non-slaveholding, legislate. The latter may prohibit, as Pennsylvania has done, under a certain penalty, the forcible removal of a colored person out of the State. Is such law in conflict with the Act of 1793?

The Act of 1793 authorizes a forcible seizure of the slave by the master not to take him out of the State, but to take him before some judicial officer within it. The law of Pennsylvania punishes a forcible removal of a colored person out of the State. Now here is no conflict between the law of the State and the law of Congress; the execution of neither law can, by any just interpretation, in my opinion, interfere with the execution of the other; the laws in this respect stand in harmony with each other.

It is very clear that no power to seize and forcibly remove the slave, without claim, is given by the act of Congress. Can it be exercised under the Constitution? Congress have legislated on the constitutional power, and have directed the mode in which it shall be executed. The act, it is admitted, covers the whole ground, and that it is constitutional there seems to be no reason to doubt. Now, under such circumstances, can the provisions of the act be disregarded, and an assumed power set up under the Constitution? This is believed to be wholly inadmissible by any known rule of construction.

The terms of the Constitution are general, and, like many other powers in that instrument, require legislation. In the language of this Court in *Martin v. Hunter's Lessee, . . .*

"the powers of the Constitution are expressed in general terms, leaving to the legislature, from time to time, to adopt its own means to effectuate legitimate objects, and to mould and model the exercise of its powers as its own wisdom and the public interests should require."

This Congress have done by the Act of 1793. It gives a summary and effectual mode of redress to the master, and is he not bound to pursue it? It is the legislative construction of the Constitution, and is it not a most authoritative construction? I was not prepared to hear the counsel contend that, notwithstanding this exposition of the Constitution, and ample remedy provided in the act, the master might disregard the act and set up his right under the Constitution. And, having taken this step, it was easy to take another and say that this right may be asserted by a forcible seizure and removal of the fugitive.

This would be a most singular constitutional provision. It would extend the remedy by recaption into another sovereignty, which is sanctioned neither by the common law nor the law of nations. If the master may lawfully seize and remove the fugitive out of the State where he may be found, without an exhibition of his claim, he may lawfully resist any force, physical or legal, which the State, or the citizens of the State, may interpose.

To hold that he must exhibit his claim in case of resistance is to abandon the ground assumed. He is engaged, it is said, in the lawful prosecution of a constitutional right; all resistance, then, by whomsoever made or in whatsoever form, must be illegal. Under such circumstances, the master needs no proof of his claim, though he might stand in need of additional physical power; having appealed to his power, he has only to collect a sufficient force to put down all resistance and attain his object; having done this, he not only stands acquitted and justified, but he has recourse for any injury he may have received in overcoming the resistance.

If this be a constitutional remedy, it may not always be a peaceful one. But if it be a rightful remedy that it may be carried to this extent no one can deny. And if it may be exercised without claim of right, why may it not be resorted to after the unfavorable decision of the judge or magistrate? This would limit the necessity of the exhibition of proof by the master to the single case where the slave was in the actual custody of some public officer. How can this be the true construction of the Constitution? That such a procedure is not sanctioned by the Act of 1793 has been shown. That act was passed expressly to guard against acts of force and violence.

I cannot perceive how anyone can doubt that the remedy given in the Constitution, if, indeed, it give any remedy, without legislation, was designed to be a peaceful one; a remedy sanctioned by judicial authority; a remedy guarded by the forms of law. But the inquiry is reiterated, is not the master entitled to his property? I answer that he is. His right is guarantied by the Constitution, and the most summary means for its enforcement is found in the act of Congress, and neither the State nor its citizens can obstruct the prosecution of this right.

The slave is found in a State where every man, Black or white, is presumed to be free, and this State, to preserve the peace of its citizens, and its soil and jurisdiction from acts of violence, has prohibited the forcible abduction of persons of color. Does this law conflict with the Constitution? It clearly does not, in its terms.

The conflict is supposed to arise out of the prohibition against the forcible removal of persons of color generally, which may include fugitive slaves. Prima facie it does not include slaves, as every man within the State is presumed to be free, and there is no provision in the act which embraces slaves. Its language clearly shows that it was designed to protect free persons of color within the State. But it is admitted there is no exception as to the forcible removal of slaves, and here the important and most delicate question arises between the power of the State and the assumed but not sanctioned power of the Federal Government.

No conflict can arise between the act of Congress and this State law; the conflict can only arise between the forcible acts of the master and the law of the State. The master exhibits no proof of right to the services of the slave, but seizes him and is about to remove him by force. I speak only of the force exerted on the slave. The law of the State presumes him to be free and prohibits his removal. Now, which shall give way, the master or the State? The law of the State does in no case discharge, in the language of the Constitution, the slave from the service of his master.

It is a most important police regulation. And if the master violate it, is he not amenable? The offense consists in the abduction of a person of color, and this is attempted to be justified upon the simple ground that the slave is property. That a slave is property must be admitted. The state law is not violated by the seizure of the slave by the master, for this is authorized by the act of Congress, but by removing him out of the State by force and without proof of right, which the act does not authorize. Now, is not this an act which a State may prohibit? The presumption, in a non-slaveholding State, is against the right of the master, and in favor of the freedom of the person he claims. This presumption may be rebutted, but until it is rebutted by the proof required in the Act of 1793, and also, in my judgment, by the Constitution, must not the law of the State be respected and obeyed?

The seizure which the master has a right to make under the act of Congress, is for the purpose of taking the slave before an officer. His possession the subject for which it was made.

The certificate of right to the service the subject for which it was made. The certificate of right to the service of the slave is undoubtedly for the protection of the master, but it authorizes the removal of the slave out of the State where he was found to the State from whence he fled, and, under the Constitution, this authority is valid in all the States.

The important point is shall the presumption of right set up by the master, unsustained by any proof or the presumption which arises from the laws and institutions of the State, prevail; this is the true issue. The sovereignty of the State is on one side, and the asserted interest of the master on the other; that interest is protected by the paramount law, and a special, a summary, and an effectual, mode of redress is given. But this mode is not pursued, and the remedy is taken into his own hands by the master.

The presumption of the State that the colored person is free may be erroneous in fact, and, if so, there can be no difficulty in proving it. But may not the assertion of the master be erroneous also, and, if so, how is his act of force to be remedied? The colored person is taken and forcibly conveyed beyond the jurisdiction of the State. This force, not being authorized by the act of Congress nor by the Constitution, may be prohibited by the State. As the act covers the whole power in the Constitution and carries out, by special enactments, its provisions, we are, in my judgment, bound by the act. We can no more, under such circumstances, administer a remedy under the Constitution in disregard of the act than we can exercise a commercial or other power in disregard of an act of Congress on the same subject.

This view respects the rights of the master and the rights of the State; it neither jeopards nor retards the reclamation of the slave; it removes all state action prejudicial to the rights of the master; and recognizes in the State a power to guard and protect its own jurisdiction and the peace of its citizen.

It appears in the case under consideration that the state magistrate before whom the fugitive was brought refused to act. In my judgment, he was bound to perform the duty required of him by a law paramount to any act, on the same subject, in his own State. But this refusal does not justify the subsequent action of the claimant; he should have taken the fugitive before a judge of the United States, two of whom resided within the State.

It may be doubted, whether the first section of the act of Pennsylvania under which the defendant was indicted, by a fair construction, applies to the case under consideration. The decision of the Supreme Court of that State was *pro forma*, and, of course, without examination. Indeed, I suppose, the case has been made up merely to bring the question before this Court. My opinion, therefore, does not rest so much upon the particular law of Pennsylvania as upon the inherent and sovereign power of a State to protect its jurisdiction and the peace of its citizens in any and every mode which its discretion shall dictate, which shall not conflict with a defined power of the Federal Government.

This cause came on to be heard on the transcript of the record from the Supreme Court of Pennsylvania, and was argued by counsel, on consideration whereof it is the opinion of this Court that the act of the Commonwealth of Pennsylvania upon which the indictment in this case is founded is repugnant to the Constitution and laws of the United States, and therefore, void, and that the judgment of the Supreme Court of Pennsylvania upon the special verdict found in the case ought to have been that the said Edward Prigg was not guilty. It is, therefore, ordered and adjudged by this Court that the judgment of the said Supreme Court of Pennsylvania be, and the same is hereby, reversed.

And this Court proceeding to render such judgment in the premises as the said Supreme Court of Pennsylvania ought to have rendered, do hereby order and adjudge that judgment upon the special verdict aforesaid be here entered that the said Edward Prigg is not guilty in manner and form as is charged against him in the said indictment, and that he go thereof quit, without day; and that this cause be remanded to the Supreme Court of Pennsylvania with directions accordingly, so that such other proceeding may be had therein as to law and justice shall appertain.

## Glossary

**a fortiori:** Latin for "with even stronger reason"

**act of the 12th of February 1793:** the Fugitive Slave Act of 1793

**Blackstone:** Sir William Blackstone, a preeminent jurist in eighteenth-century England and the author of *Commentaries on the Laws of England*

## Glossary

**comity:** legal reciprocity, or the principle that a jurisdiction will recognize the validity and effect of another jurisdiction's executive, legislative, and judicial acts

**Confederation:** the United States under the Articles of Confederation

**Court of Oyer and Terminer:** in the United States, the name given to courts of criminal jurisdiction in some states

**estopped:** legally prevented

**in rem:** Latin for "in a thing" and referring to a legal action in connection with a specific piece of property

**in transitu:** Latin for "in transit"

**jeopards:** jeopardizes

**lex fori:** Latin for "law of the forum," referring to the law of the jurisdiction where a case is pending

**Lord Dyer:** Sir James Dyer, a preeminent jurist in sixteenth-century England

**Madison:** James Madison, one of the authors of the Federalist Papers and the fourth U.S. president

**prima facie:** Latin for "at first sight," describing a fact that is presumed to be true unless disproved by contrary evidence

**pro forma:** Latin for "as a matter of form"

**pro tanto:** Latin for "only to that extent"; partially

**proprio vigore:** Latin for "by its own force or vigor"

**recaption:** self-help in seizing a fugitive slave

**take further cognizance:** hear, consider

**writ of error:** a judicial writ from an appellate court ordering the court of record to produce the records of trial; an appeal

# DRED SCOTT V. SANDFORD

| DATE | CITATION |
|---|---|
| 1857 | 60 U.S. 393 |
| **AUTHOR** | **SIGNIFICANCE** |
| Roger B. Taney | Infamous decision that held that blacks could never be citizens of the United States and have rights under the Constitution |
| **VOTE** | |
| 7-2 | |

## Overview

In March 1857 Chief Justice Roger B. Taney announced the opinion of the U.S. Supreme Court in *Dred Scott v. John F. A. Sandford*, which was the Court's most important decision ever issued on slavery. The decision had a dramatic effect on American politics as well as law. The case involved a Missouri slave named Dred Scott who claimed to be free because his master had taken him to what was then the Wisconsin Territory and is today the state of Minnesota. In the Missouri Compromise (also known as the Compromise of 1820), Congress has declared that there would be no slavery north of the state of Missouri. Thus, Scott claimed to be free because he had lived in a federal territory where slavery was not allowed. In an opinion that was more than fifty pages long, Chief Justice Taney held that Scott was still a slave, that the Missouri Compromise was unconstitutional, and that Congress had no power to ban slavery from a federal territory. In a part of the decision that shocked many northerners, Chief Justice Taney also held that blacks could never be citizens of the United States and that they had no rights under the Constitution. With notorious bluntness, Taney declared that blacks were "so far inferior, that they had no rights which the white man was bound to respect." The decision was criticized by many northerners and led many to support the new Republican Party. While it is an exaggeration to say the case caused the Civil War, Chief Justice Taney's decision certainly inflamed sectional tensions. It also helped lead to the nomination and election of Abraham Lincoln in 1860, which in turn led to secession and the war.

## Context

In the Northwest Ordinance of 1787 the Congress, under the Articles of Confederation, banned slavery from all of the territories north and west of the Ohio River. This area, known as the Northwest Territory, would ultimately become the states of Ohio, Indiana, Illinois, Michigan, and Wisconsin. At the time, the western boundary of the United States was the Mississippi River. The territory west of the Mississippi belonged to Spain.

In 1802 Spain ceded its territories north of Mexico to France, and in 1803 the United States acquired all this land through the Louisiana Purchase. Most of the Louisiana Purchase territory was directly west of the Ohio River and north of the point where the Ohio flowed into the Mississippi. In 1812 Louisiana entered the Union as a slave state without any controversy. In 1818 when Missouri sought admission to the Union as a slave state, however, a number of members of Congress from the North objected on the ground that Missouri should be governed by the Northwest Ordinance. This led to a protracted two-year debate over the status of slavery in Missouri. In the end Congress accepted a compromise developed by Representative Henry Clay of Kentucky. Known as the Missouri Compromise, the law allowed Missouri to enter the Union as a slave state and admitted Maine as a free state. The law also prohibited slavery north and west of Missouri.

At the time of these debates Dred Scott was a slave in Virginia. In 1830 his master, Peter Blow, moved to St. Louis, taking Dred Scott with him. In 1832 Peter Blow died, and shortly after that Dred Scott was sold to Captain John Emerson, a U.S. Army surgeon. In 1833 Emerson was sent to Fort Armstrong, which was located on the site of the modern-day city of Rock Island, Illinois. Scott might have claimed his freedom while at Fort Armstrong, because Illinois was a free state. Under the accepted rule of law at the time, slaves could usually become free if their masters voluntarily brought them to a free state. Indeed, as early as 1824 the Missouri Supreme Court had freed a slave named Winny because her master had taken her to Illinois. In 1836 the Missouri Supreme Court freed another slave woman, Rachel, because her master, who was in the army, had taken her to forts in present-day Michigan and Minnesota. However, Scott, who was illiterate, probably did not know he could be freed, and he made no effort to gain his freedom at this time.

In 1836 the army sent Emerson to Fort Snelling in what is today the city of St. Paul, Minnesota. At the time, this area was called the Wisconsin Territory, and slavery was illegal there under the Missouri Compromise. Once again, Scott might have claimed his freedom because of his residence in a free jurisdiction, but he did not. From 1836 to 1840 Scott lived at Fort Snelling, at Fort Jessup in Louisiana, and then again at Fort Snelling. During this time he married a slave named Harriet, who was then owned by Lawrence Taliaferro, the Indian agent at Fort Snelling. Taliaferro either sold or gave Harriet to Emerson so the newly married couple could be together. In 1838 Emerson married Irene Sanford.

**Dred Scott**
(Louis Schultze)

In 1840 Captain Emerson left the Scotts and their two daughters in St. Louis while he went to Florida during the Second Seminole War. In 1842 Emerson left the army and moved to Iowa, a free territory, but he left his slaves and his wife in St. Louis. In 1843 Dr. Emerson died, and ownership of the Scotts passed to Irene Sanford Emerson.

At this point Dred Scott attempted to purchase his freedom with the help of the sons of his former master, Peter Blow. However, Irene Emerson refused to allow Scott to buy his freedom. Thus, in 1846 a lawyer—the first of five who volunteered to help Scott—filed a suit in St. Louis Circuit Court, claiming that he had become free while living in both Illinois and the Wisconsin Territory (Minnesota) and that once free he could not be reenslaved when he returned to Missouri. By this time there had been numerous cases on the issue in the Missouri courts, and usually slaves who had lived in free states or territories were declared free. For technical reasons, however, Dred Scott did not get his hearing until 1850, about four years after he first sued for freedom. At that point a jury of twelve white men, sitting in the slave state of Missouri, declared Scott and his family to be free.

This should have ended the case, but Irene Emerson appealed to the Missouri Supreme Court in an effort to retain her property. The Scotts were a valuable asset. In addition, while the case had been pending, the Court had hired out the Scotts and kept their wages in an account. Thus, Irene Emerson was trying to keep four slaves plus the wages of Dred and Harriet for the previous four years.

Under the existing precedents Irene Emeson should not have held out much hope that she would win her case. However, a recent amendment to the Missouri Constitution provided for the election of the state supreme court, and in 1851 a new court took office. Two of the new justices were adamantly proslavery. It therefore seemed like the right time for Mrs. Emerson to challenge the decisions that had led to Scott's freedom.

In 1852 the Missouri Supreme Court, by a two-to-one vote, reversed the decision freeing Dred Scott. Reflecting his proslavery sentiments and his hostility to the growing antislavery movement in the North, Justice William Scott (who was not related to Dred Scott) declared that the state would no longer follow its own precedents on slavery. This decision revolutionized Missouri law, but it was consistent with decisions in some Deep South states, which had also abandoned the idea that slaves could become free if they were brought to free states.

Dred Scott's quest for freedom should have ended here, because there was no higher court where he could appeal the decision. Under American law at the time, Scott had no grounds for appealing to the U.S. Supreme Court because no constitutional issue had been raised in the case. The federal courts did not have jurisdiction over the status of slaves within the states.

By this time, however, Mrs. Emerson had moved east and married another physician, Dr. Calvin Chaffee of Springfield, Massachusetts. She could not take her slaves with her because slavery was illegal in Massachusetts. Moreover, her new husband was a firm opponent of slavery, and any discussion of her property interest in the Scotts might have undermined her new marriage. Thus, she either gave or sold the Scotts to her brother, John F. A. Sanford, who lived in New York City but had business interests in both St. Louis and New York. (He spelled his last name Sanford, but the clerk of the U.S. Supreme Court would add an extra "d" to his name, and thus the case would be known as *Dred Scott v. Sandford*.)

Sanford's residence in New York opened up the possibility that Dred Scott could now reopen his case in a federal court. Under the Constitution citizens of one state are allowed to sue citizens of another state. This is known as diversity jurisdiction, because there is a diversity (or difference) in the state citizenship of the people involved in the lawsuit. The framers of the Constitution believed that it was necessary for federal courts to be able to hear suits between citizens of different states because otherwise the people would fear that the courts of one state would favor the state's own citizens. The federal courts presumably would be neutral.

Thus, in 1853 Scott's newest lawyer filed a suit in federal court against John Sanford. Scott alleged that he was a "citizen" of Missouri and sued Sanford for assault and battery, asking for $10,000 in damages. Sanford responded with something called a plea in abatement. In this response Sanford argued that the court should abate (stop) the case immediately because, as Sanford argued, Dred Scott "was not a citizen of the State of Missouri, as alleged in his declaration, being a negro of African descent, whose ancestors were of pure African blood, and who were brought into this country and sold as slaves." In essence, Sanford argued that no Black person could be a citizen of Missouri, so even if Dred Scott was free, the federal court did not have jurisdiction to hear the case.

In 1854 U.S. District Judge Robert Wells rejected this argument. He held that *if* Dred Scott was free, then he should be considered a citizen for the purpose of diversity jurisdiction. This was the first and only victory Dred Scott had in the federal courts. After hearing all the evidence, Wells decided that Scott's status had to be determined by applying the law of Missouri. Since the Missouri Supreme Court had already held that Scott was not free, Judge Wells ruled against Scott. This set the stage for the case to go to the U.S. Supreme Court. In the December 1855 term the Supreme Court heard arguments in the case, but in the spring of 1856, with a presidential election looming, the Court declined to decide the case and instead asked for new arguments in the next term, beginning in December 1856, which was after the election.

While Dred Scott's case was making its way through the courts, slavery had emerged as the central issue of American politics. In 1820 the Missouri Compromise had settled the issue of slavery in the territories. Starting in 1836, however, the Republic of Texas requested to become part of the United States. Presidents Andrew Jackson and Martin Van Buren resisted accepting Texas because they knew that bringing Texas into the Union would reopen the issue of slavery in the West and probably would lead to a war with Mexico. In late 1844 President John Tyler, who was coming to the end of his term, managed to get Congress to accept Texas, which entered the Union in 1845. This immediately let to a confrontation with Mexico, which had never recognized Texas independence. In April 1846 American and Mexican troops clashed, and by May the two nations were at war. The war ended in September 1847, when General Zachary Taylor entered Mexico City. In the Treaty of Guadalupe Hidalgo, signed on February 2, 1848, Mexico recognized the Texas annexation and ceded all of its northern lands, which included all or part of the present-day states of California, Arizona, New Mexico, Nevada, Utah, and Colorado.

The acquisition of this territory, known as the Mexican Cession, led to a crisis in the Union as the nation debated the status of slavery in the new territories. Congress finally broke the deadlock with a series of statutes collectively known as the Compromise of 1850. These laws allowed slavery in the new territories but admitted California as a free state. This compromise did not satisfy the South, which wanted to repeal the restrictions on slavery in the Missouri Compromise. This was accomplished in 1854 with the passage of the Kansas-Nebraska Act. This law allowed the creation of territorial governments in the territories west and northwest of Missouri—including the present-day states of Kansas, Nebraska, South Dakota, and North Dakota—without regard to slavery. The law allowed the settlers of these territories to decide for themselves whether or not to allow slavery.

The Kansas-Nebraska Act had two immediate results. First was a revolution in politics and the emergence of a new political organization that became the Republican Party. By 1856 it was the dominant party in the North. Its main goal was to prevent the spread of slavery into the territories. Meanwhile, in Kansas a small civil war broke out between supporters and opponents of slavery. Known as Bleeding Kansas, the conflict claimed more than fifty lives in 1855 and 1856.

In 1856 the new Republican Party nominated John C. Frémont for the presidency. Frémont, nicknamed "the Pathfinder," was a national hero for his explorations in the West and his role in securing California during the Mexican-American War. Running on a slogan of "Free Soil, Free Labor, Free Speech, Free Men," Frémont and the new party carried eleven northern states. This was not enough to win but was nevertheless a very impressive showing for a brand-new party. The winning candidate, James Buchanan, was a Pennsylvanian but strongly sympathetic to the South and slavery. He supported opening all of the territories to slavery. In his inaugural address Buchanan declared that the issue of slavery in the territories was a question for the judicial branch and urged Americans to accept the outcome of the Court's pending ruling in the Dred Scott case. Buchanan could so confidently take this position because two justices on the court, Robert C. Grier and John Catron, had told him how the case would be decided. Two days later Chief Justice Taney announced the decision. Rather than settling the issue of slavery in the territories, the decision only made it more troublesome and controversial.

## About the Author

Roger Brooke Taney (pronounced Tawnee) had a long and distinguished career in American politics and law. He was born in 1777 into a wealthy slaveholding family on the eastern shore of Maryland. He served in the Maryland legislature as a Federalist, but in the 1820s he became a supporter of Andrew Jackson. He was attorney general in Jackson's administration and drafted what became Jackson's famous veto in 1831 of the bill to recharter the Second Bank of the United States. As a young lawyer he freed his own slaves because he had no use for them, but he never opposed slavery or favored abolition. As attorney general he prepared a detailed opinion for President Jackson asserting that free blacks were not entitled to passports and could never be considered citizens of the United States. Taney served briefly as secretary of the treasury, overseeing the removal of deposits from the Bank of the United States.

In 1837 Taney became chief justice of the United States, a position he held until 1864, longer than any other chief justice except John Marshall. As chief justice he was a staunch supporter of slavery and the interests of the southern states. By 1857, when he delivered his opinion in Dred Scott's case, Taney was deeply hostile to abolitionism and vigorously proslavery. In 1860 and 1861 he tacitly supported secession and opposed all of President Lincoln's efforts to maintain the Union, suppress the insurrection, and end slavery. When Taney died in 1864, the U.S. Senate refused to authorize a statue for him, as it had for other deceased justices. In arguing against the proposal for a statue, Senator Charles Sumner of Massachusetts declared that Taney had "administered justice at last wickedly, and degraded the judiciary of the country, and degraded the age." He predicted that "the name is to be hooted down the pages of history" (rpt. in Finkelman, 1997, p. 222).

## Explanation and Analysis of the Document

All nine justices wrote an opinion in this case. The opinions range in length from Justice Robert C. Grier's half-page concurrence to Justice Benjamin R. Curtis's seventy-page dissent. Chief Justice Taney's "Opinion of the Court" is fifty-four pages long. The nine opinions, along with a handful of pages summarizing the lawyers' arguments, consume 260 pages of *United States Supreme Court Reports*. In his opinion Chief Justice Taney declares that the Missouri Compromise is unconstitutional. This was only the second Supreme Court decision to strike down a federal law. The only other antebellum decision to strike down a federal act—*Marbury v. Madison* (1803)—held unconstitutional a minor portion of the Judiciary Act of 1789. Here the Court struck down a major statute.

In his opinion Chief Justice Taney discusses three issues: Black citizenship, the constitutionality of the Missouri Compromise, and the power of Congress to ban slavery from the territories. First he examines whether the question of citizenship is legitimately before the Court. The lower federal court had assumed that if Dred Scott was free, he was a citizen of the state where he lived, and he had a right to sue a citizen of another state in federal court. Taney rejects this conclusion. Since the 1830s he had believed that blacks could never be citizens of the United States. Now he had a chance to make his views the law.

Taney bases his argument entirely on race. In a very inaccurate history of the founding period, which ig-

nored the fact that free blacks had voted in a number of states at the time of the ratification of the Constitution, Taney asserts that at the founding of the nation blacks, whether enslaved or free, were without any political or legal rights. He declares that blacks

> are not included, and were not intended to be included, under the word "citizens" in the Constitution, and can therefore claim none of the rights and privileges which that instrument provides for and secures to citizens of the United States. On the contrary, they were at that time [1787] considered as a subordinate and inferior class of beings, who had been subjugated by the dominant race, and, whether emancipated or not, yet remained subject to their authority, and had no rights or privileges but such as those who held the power and the Government might choose to grant them.

In one of the most notoriously racist statements in American law, Taney declares that blacks are "so far inferior, that they had no rights which the white man was bound to respect." He therefore concludes that blacks could never be citizens of the United States, even if they were born in the country and considered to be citizens of the states in which they lived.

Taney then turns to the issue of slavery in the territories. Here he discusses the constitutionality of the Missouri Compromise and the status of slavery in the territories. His goal is to settle, in favor of the South, the status of slavery in the territories. To do this Taney had to overcome two strong arguments in favor of congressional power over slavery in the territories. First was the clause in the Constitution that explicitly gave Congress the power to regulate the territories. Second was the political tradition, dating from the Northwest Ordinance, that Congress had such a power. Taney accomplished this through an examination of two separate provisions of the Constitution: the territories clause and the Fifth Amendment.

The territories clause of the Constitution, Article IV, Section 3, Paragraph 2, provides that "Congress shall have Power to dispose of and make all needful Rules and Regulations respecting the Territory or other Property belonging to the United States." Congress had used this clause to govern the territories, prohibiting slavery in some territories and allowing it in others. As recently as 1854 Congress had passed the Kansas-Nebraska Act, allowing the settlers of a territory to allow or ban slavery as they wished. Almost all Americans assumed that Congress had the power to prohibit slavery in the territories. One American who did not was Chief Justice Taney.

In his opinion Taney interprets the territories clause to apply only to those territories the United States had owned in 1787. Taney writes that the clause is

> confined, and was intended to be confined, to the territory which at that time belonged to, or was claimed by, the United States, and was within their boundaries as settled by the treaty with Great Britain, and can have no influence upon a territory afterwards acquired from a foreign Government. It was a special provision for a known and particular territory, and to meet a present emergency, and nothing more.

Few scholars today find this argument even remotely plausible. This was also true in 1857. Justice John Catron, who agreed with Taney on almost every other point, dissented from the claim that Congress could not pass laws to regulate the territories. Nevertheless, Taney asserts that Congress had only the power to provide a minimal government in the territories, but nothing beyond that. Taney implies that allowing Congress to actually govern the territories would be equivalent to "establish[ing] or maintain[ing] colonies bordering on the United States or at a distance, to be ruled and governed at its own pleasure." Taney's argument here is absurd. By 1857 the United States had held some territory (what later became the eastern tip of Minnesota) for the entire period since the adoption of the Constitution without making it a state or treating it as a colony.

The weakness of his argument did not stop Taney, who was determined, as few justices have been, to reach a specific result. His goal was to prohibit the congressional regulation of slavery in the territories, and any argument, it seemed, would do the trick. However, if Congress could not govern the territories, then they would be governed by the settlers. What would happen if the settlers, such as those in Kansas, voted to prohibit slavery? Taney found an answer to this question in the Fifth Amendment to the U.S. Constitution,

which prohibits the government from taking private property without due process of law.

Thus, Taney argues that forbidding slavery in the territories violated the due process clause of the Fifth Amendment, which declares that under federal law no person could "be deprived of life, liberty, or property without due process of law." Taney asserts that "an act of Congress which deprives a citizen of the United States of his liberty or property, merely because he came himself or brought his property into a particular Territory of the United States, and who had committed no offence against the laws, could hardly be dignified with the name of due process of law."

This led Taney to assert that slavery was a special form of property with special constitutional protection. Thus he writes:

> the right of property in a slave is distinctly and expressly affirmed in the Constitution. The right to traffic in it, like an ordinary article of merchandise and property, was guarantied to the citizens of the United States, in every State that might desire it, for twenty years. And the Government in express terms is pledged to protect it in all future time, if the slave escapes from his owner. This is done in plain words—too plain to be misunderstood. And no word can be found in the Constitution which gives Congress a greater power over slave property, or which entitles property of that kind to less protection than property of any other description. The only power conferred is the power coupled with the duty of guarding and protecting the owner in his rights.

This was perhaps Chief Justice Taney's strongest argument. The Constitution of 1787 clearly protected slavery in a number of places. It was an important and unique kind of property, and thus it needed to be protected. Moreover, Taney's argument that all citizens should be able to bring their property with them into every federal territory was not wholly wrong. Indeed, the heart of Taney's argument was that slavery was an important part of American society; therefore slave owners had to have equal access to federal lands.

Chief Justice Taney thus declares that any prohibition on slavery in the territories violated the Fifth Amendment. Even the people of a territory could not ban slavery through the territorial legislature. Taney writes, "And if Congress itself cannot do this—if it is beyond the powers conferred on the Federal Government—it will be admitted, we presume, that it could not authorize a Territorial Government to exercise them. It could confer no power on any local Government, established by its authority, to violate the provisions of the Constitution." Like the Missouri Compromise, under Taney's interpretation of the Constitution, popular sovereignty also was unconstitutional.

Six other justices agreed with all or some of Taney's decision. Four were from the South, and two, Samuel Nelson of New York and Robert C. Grier of Pennsylvania, were northern Democrats with southern sympathies. Two justices, John McLean of Ohio and Benjamin R. Curtis of Massachusetts, issued stinging dissents. Both pointed out, at great length, that Taney's history was wrong and that blacks voted in a number of states at the time of the country's founding. Both justices pointed out that since African Americans voted for the ratification of the Constitution in 1787, it was hard to argue that they could not be considered citizens of the nation they helped to create. The dissenters also stressed that since 1787 no one had doubted that Congress could regulate the territories and ban slavery in them. On both grounds they may have had the better historical arguments but not the votes on the Court.

## Impact

Few cases have had such a huge impact on American politics. Most southerners cheered the decision. So did President Buchanan, who hoped the decision would bring peace to Kansas and destroy the Republican Party, since its main platform was prohibiting slavery in the territories. It also undercut Buchanan's rival in the Democratic Party, Senator Stephen A. Douglas. He had been the leading proponent of popular sovereignty in the territories, which would have allowed the settlers in the territories to decide for themselves whether they wanted slavery. This had been the basis of the Kansas-Nebraska Act, which Douglas sponsored. Under *Dred Scott*, however, popular sovereignty was unconstitutional because the territorial governments were prohibited from banning slavery. Douglas would give tacit support for the decision, but it undermined his political strength in the North.

Republicans around the nation attacked the decision. Horace Greeley, the Republican editor of the *New York Tribune*, responded to the decision with outrage, calling Taney's opinion "wicked," "atrocious," and "abominable" and a "collation of false statements and shallow sophistries." The paper's editor thought Taney's decision had no more validity than the opinions that might be expressed in any "Washington bar-room" (Fehrenbacher, 1978, p. 417). The *Chicago Tribune* declared that Taney's statements on Black citizenship were "inhuman dicta" (Fehrenbacher, 1978, p. 417). The Black abolitionist Frederick Douglass called it a "devilish decision—this judicial incarnation of wolfishness!" (rpt. in Finkelman, 1997, p. 174). He also believed, however, that the decision would lead more people to oppose slavery. In 1858 Abraham Lincoln, in his "House Divided" Speech, attacked the decision and warned that if Republicans were not elected to office, the "next Dred Scott decision" would lead to the nationalization of slavery. Lincoln predicted, "We shall *lie down* pleasantly dreaming that the people of *Missouri* are on the verge of making their state *free*; and we shall *awake* to the *reality*, instead that the *Supreme* Court has made *Illinois* a *slave* state." Lincoln was convinced that the "logical conclusion" of Taney's opinion was that "what one master might lawfully do with Dred Scott, in the free state of Illinois, every master might lawfully do with any other *one*, or *one thousand* slaves in Illinois, or in any other free state" (Finkelman, 1997, pp. 185–195).

The decision helped make Abraham Lincoln a national figure and led to his nomination and election as president in 1861. The nation would overrule *Dred Scott* with the adoption of the Thirteenth Amendment to the Constitution in 1865, which ended all slavery in the United States, and the Fourteenth Amendment in 1868, which made all people born in the United States citizens of the United States.

## Questions for Further Study

1. While most Americans find Taney's decision morally wrong, do any of his arguments make sense?

2. Why do you think Dred Scott did not try to gain his freedom when he lived in Illinois or at Fort Snelling?

3. What are the legacies of the decision today? Are there ways in which the ideas of Chief Justice Taney might still be alive in our culture?

## Further Reading

### *Books*

Ehrlich, Walter. *They Have No Rights: Dred Scott's Struggle for Freedom.* Westport, CT: Greenwood Press, 1979.

Fehrenbacher, Don E. *The Dred Scott Case: Its Significance in American Law and Politics.* New York: Oxford University Press, 1978.

Fehrenbacher, Don E. *The Slaveholding Republic: An Account of the United States Government's Relations to Slavery.* New York: Oxford University Press, 2001.

Finkelman, Paul. *An Imperfect Union: Slavery, Federalism, and Comity.* Chapel Hill: University of North Carolina Press, 1981.

Finkelman, Paul. *Slavery in the Courtroom: An Annotated Bibliography of American Cases.* Washington, DC: Government Printing Office, 1985.

Finkelman, Paul. *Dred Scott v. Sandford: A Brief History with Documents,* 2nd ed. Boston: Bedford/St. Martin's, 2016.

Herda, D. J. *Slavery and Citizenship: The Dred Scott Case.* Berkeley Heights, NJ: Enslow, 2017.

Jones, Martha S. *Birthright Citizens: A History of Race and Rights in Antebellum America.* New York: Cambridge University Press, 2018.

Konig, David Thomas, Paul Finkelman, and Christopher Alan Bracey, eds. T*he Dred Scott Case: Historical and Contemporary Perspectives on Race and Law.* Athens: Ohio University Press, 2010.

### *Articles*

Paquette, Robert L. "The Mind of Roger Taney: New Light on the Dred Scott Decision." *Academic Questions* 29 (2016): 34–48.

VanderVelde, Lea. "The Dred Scott Case in Context." *Journal of Supreme Court History* 40, no. 3 (2015): 263–281.

—Commentary by Paul Finkelman

# DRED SCOTT V. SANDFORD

## Document Text

### *Mr. Chief Justice Taney delivered the opinion of the Court*

This case has been twice argued. After the argument at the last term, differences of opinion were found to exist among the members of the court; and as the questions in controversy are of the highest importance, and the court was at that time much pressed by the ordinary business of the term, it was deemed advisable to continue the case, and direct a re-argument on some of the points, in order that we might have an opportunity of giving to the whole subject a more deliberate consideration. It has accordingly been again argued by counsel, and considered by the court; and I now proceed to deliver its opinion. There are two leading questions presented by the record: 1. Had the Circuit Court of the United States jurisdiction to hear and determine the case between these parties? And 2. If it had jurisdiction, is the judgment it has given erroneous or not? The plaintiff in error, who was also the plaintiff in the court below, was, with his wife and children, held as slaves by the defendant, in the State of Missouri; and he brought this action in the Circuit Court of the United States for that district, to assert the title of himself and his family to freedom. The declaration is in the form usually adopted in that State to try questions of this description, and contains the averment necessary to give the court jurisdiction; that he and the defendant are citizens of different States; that is, that he is a citizen of Missouri, and the defendant a citizen of New York. The defendant pleaded in abatement to the jurisdiction of the court, that the plaintiff was not a citizen of the State of Missouri, as alleged in his declaration, being a negro of

African descent, whose ancestors were of pure African blood, and who were brought into this country and sold as slaves. To this plea the plaintiff demurred, and the defendant joined in demurrer. The court overruled the plea, and gave judgment that the defendant should answer over. And he thereupon put in sundry pleas in bar, upon which issues were joined; and at the trial the verdict and judgment were in his favor. Whereupon the plaintiff brought this writ of error. Before we speak of the pleas in bar, it will be proper to dispose of the questions which have arisen on the plea in abatement. That plea denies the right of the plaintiff to sue in a court of the United States, for the reasons therein stated. If the question raised by it is legally before us, and the court should be of opinion that the facts stated in it disqualify the plaintiff from becoming a citizen, in the sense in which that word is used in the Constitution of the United States, then the judgment of the Circuit Court is erroneous, and must be reversed. It is suggested, however, that this plea is not before us; and that as the judgment in the court below on this plea was in favor of the plaintiff, he does not seek to reverse it, or bring it before the court for revision by his writ of error; and also that the defendant waived this defence by pleading over, and thereby admitted the jurisdiction of the court. But, in making this objection, we think the peculiar and limited jurisdiction of courts of the United States has not been adverted to. This peculiar and limited jurisdiction has made it necessary, in these courts, to adopt different rules and principles of pleading, so far as jurisdiction is concerned, from those which regulate courts of common law in England, and in the different States of the Union which have adopted the common-law rules.

In these last-mentioned courts, where their character and rank are analogous to that of a Circuit Court of the United States; in other words, where they are what the law terms courts of general jurisdiction; they are presumed to have jurisdiction, unless the contrary appears. No averment in the pleadings of the plaintiff is necessary, in order to give jurisdiction. If the defendant objects to it, he must plead it specially, and unless the fact on which he relies is found to be true by a jury, or admitted to be true by the plaintiff, the jurisdiction cannot be disputed in an appellate court.

Now, it is not necessary to inquire whether in courts of that description a party who pleads over in bar, when a plea to the jurisdiction has been ruled against him, does or does not waive his plea; nor whether upon a judgment in his favor on the pleas in bar, and a writ of error brought by the plaintiff, the question upon the plea in abatement would be open for revision in the appellate court. Cases that may have been decided in such courts, or rules that may have been laid down by common-law pleaders, can have no influence in the decision in this court. Because, under the Constitution and laws of the United States, the rules which govern the pleadings in its courts, in questions of jurisdiction, stand on different principles and are regulated by different laws.

This difference arises, as we have said, from the peculiar character of the Government of the United States. For although it is sovereign and supreme in its appropriate sphere of action, yet it does not possess all the powers which usually belong to the sovereignty of a nation. Certain specified powers, enumerated in the Constitution, have been conferred upon it; and neither the legislative, executive, nor judicial departments of the Government can lawfully exercise any authority beyond the limits marked out by the Constitution. And in regulating the judicial department, the cases in which the courts of the United States shall have jurisdiction are particularly and specifically enumerated and defined; and they are not authorized to take cognizance of any case which does not come within the description therein specified. Hence, when a plaintiff sues in a court of the United States, it is necessary that he should show, in his pleading, that the suit he brings is within the jurisdiction of the court, and that he is entitled to sue there. And if he omits to do this, and should, by any oversight of the Circuit Court, obtain a judgment in his favor, the judgment would be reversed in the appellate court for want of jurisdiction in the court below. The jurisdiction would not be presumed, as in the case of a common-law English or State court, unless the contrary appeared. But the record, when it comes before the appellate court, must show, affirmatively, that the inferior court had authority, under the Constitution, to hear and determine the case. And if the plaintiff claims a right to sue in a Circuit Court of the United States, under that provision of the Constitution which gives jurisdiction in controversies between citizens of different States, he must distinctly aver in his pleading that they are citizens of different States; and he cannot maintain his suit without showing that fact in the pleadings.

This point was decided in the case of *Bingham v. Cabot*, (in 3 Dall., 382,) and ever since adhered to by the court. And in *Jackson v. Ashton*, (8 Pet., 148,) it was held that the objection to which it was open could not be waived by the opposite party, because consent of parties could not give jurisdiction.

It is needless to accumulate cases on this subject. Those already referred to, and the cases of *Capron v. Van Noorden*, (in 2 Cr., 126,) and *Montalet v. Murray*, (4 Cr., 46,) are sufficient to show the rule of which we have spoken. The case of *Capron v. Van Noorden* strikingly illustrates the difference between a common-law court and a court of the United States.

If, however, the fact of citizenship is averred in the declaration, and the defendant does not deny it, and put it in issue by plea in abatement, he cannot offer evidence at the trial to disprove it, and consequently cannot avail himself of the objection in the appellate court, unless the defect should be apparent in some other part of the record. For if there is no plea in abatement, and the want of jurisdiction does not appear in any other part of the transcript brought up by the writ of error, the undisputed averment of citizenship in the declaration must be taken in this court to be true. In this case, the citizenship is averred, but it is denied by the defendant in the manner required by the rules of pleading, and the fact upon which the denial is based is admitted by the demurrer. And, if the plea and demurrer, and judgment of the court below upon it, are before us upon this record, the question to be decided is, whether the facts stated in the plea are sufficient to show that the plaintiff is not entitled to sue as a citizen in a court of the United States. We think they are before us. The plea in abatement and the judgment of the court upon it, are a part of the judicial proceedings in the Circuit Court, and are there recorded as such; and a writ of error always brings up to the superior court the whole record of the proceedings in the court below. And in the case of the *United States v. Smith*, (11 Wheat., 172,) this court said, that the case being brought up by writ of error, the whole record was under the consideration of this court. And this being the case in the present instance, the plea in abatement is necessarily under consideration; and it becomes, therefore, our duty to decide whether the facts stated in the plea are or are not sufficient to show that the plaintiff is not entitled to sue as a citizen in a court of the United States.

This is certainly a very serious question, and one that now for the first time has been brought for decision before this court. But it is brought here by those who have a right to bring it, and it is our duty to meet it and decide it.

The question is simply this: Can a negro, whose ancestors were imported into this country, and sold as slaves, become a member of the political community formed and brought into existence by the Constitution of the United States, and as such become entitled to all the rights, and privileges, and immunities, guarantied by that instrument to the citizen? One of which rights is the privilege of suing in a court of the United States in the cases specified in the Constitution.

It will be observed, that the plea applies to that class of persons only whose ancestors were negroes of the African race, and imported into this country, and sold and held as slaves. The only matter in issue before the court, therefore, is, whether the descendants of such slaves, when they shall be emancipated, or who are born of parents who had become free before their birth, are citizens of a State, in the sense in which the word citizen is used in the Constitution of the United States. And this being the only matter in dispute on the pleadings, the court must be understood as speaking in this opinion of that class only, that is, of those persons who are the descendants of Africans who were imported into this country, and sold as slaves.

The situation of this population was altogether unlike that of the Indian race. The latter, it is true, formed no part of the colonial communities, and never amalgamated with them in social connections or in government. But although they were uncivilized, they were yet a free and independent people, associated together in nations or tribes, and governed by their own laws. Many of these political communities were situated in territories to which the white race claimed the ultimate right of dominion. But that claim was acknowledged to be subject to the right of the Indians to occupy it as long as they thought proper, and neither the English nor colonial Governments claimed or exercised any dominion over the tribe or nation by whom it was occupied, nor claimed the right to the possession of the territory, until the tribe or nation consented to cede it. These Indian Governments were regarded and treated as foreign Governments, as much so as if an ocean had separated the red man from the white; and their freedom has constantly been acknowledged, from the time of the first emigration to the English colonies to the present day, by the different Governments which succeeded each other. Treaties have been negotiated with them, and their alliance sought for in war; and the people who compose these Indian political communities have always been treated as foreigners not living under our Government. It is true that the course of events has brought the Indian tribes within the limits of the United States under subjection to the white race; and it has been found necessary, for their sake as well as our own, to regard them as in a state of pupilage, and to legislate to a certain extent over them and the territory they occupy. But they may, without doubt, like the subjects of any other foreign Government, be naturalized by the authority of Congress, and become citizens of a State, and of the United States; and if an individual should leave his nation or tribe, and take up his abode among the white population, he would be entitled to all the rights and privileges which would belong to an emigrant from any other foreign people.

We proceed to examine the case as presented by the pleadings.

The words "people of the United States" and "citizens" are synonymous terms, and mean the same thing. They both describe the political body who, according to our republican institutions, form the sovereignty, and who hold the power and conduct the Government through their representatives. They are what we familiarly call the "sovereign people," and every citizen is one of this people, and a constituent member of this sovereignty.

The question before us is, whether the class of persons described in the plea in abatement compose a portion of this people, and are constituent members of this sovereignty? We think they are not, and that they are not included, and were not intended to be included, under the word "citizens" in the Constitution, and can therefore claim none of the rights and privileges which that instrument provides for and secures to citizens of the United States. On the contrary, they were at that time considered as a subordinate and inferior class of beings, who had been subjugated by the dominant race, and, whether emancipated or not, yet remained subject to their authority, and had no rights or privileges but such as those who held the power and the Government might choose to grant them.

It is not the province of the court to decide upon the justice or injustice, the policy or impolicy, of these laws. The decision of that question belonged to the political or law-making power; to those who formed the sovereignty and framed the Constitution. The duty of the court is, to interpret the instrument they have framed, with the best lights we can obtain on the subject, and to administer it as we find it, according to its true intent and meaning when it was adopted.

In discussing this question, we must not confound the rights of citizenship which a State may confer within its own limits, and the rights of citizenship as a member of the Union. It does not by any means follow, because he has all the rights and privileges of a citizen of a State, that he must be a citizen of the United States. He may have all of the rights and privileges of the citizen of a State, and yet not be entitled to the rights and privileges of a citizen in any other State. For, previous to the adoption of the Constitution of the United States, every State had the undoubted right to confer on whomsoever it pleased the character of citizen, and to endow him with all its rights. But this character of course was confined to the boundaries of the State, and gave him no rights or privileges in other States beyond those secured to him by the laws of nations and the comity of States. Nor have the several States surrendered the power of conferring these rights and privileges by adopting the Constitution of the United States. Each State may still confer them upon an alien, or any one it thinks proper, or upon any class or description of persons; yet he would not be a citizen in the sense in which that word is used in the Constitution of the United States, nor entitled to sue as such in one of its courts, nor to the privileges and immunities of a citizen in the other States. The rights which he would acquire would be restricted to the State which gave them. The Constitution has conferred on Congress the right to establish an uniform rule of naturalization, and this right is evidently exclusive, and has always been held by this court to be so. Consequently, no State, since the adoption of the Constitution, can by naturalizing an alien invest him with the rights and privileges secured to a citizen of a State under the Federal Government, although, so far as the State alone was concerned, he would undoubtedly be entitled to the rights of a citizen, and clothed with all the rights and immunities which the Constitution and laws of the State attached to that character.

It is very clear, therefore, that no State can, by any act or law of its own, passed since the adoption of the Constitution, introduce a new member into the political community created by the Constitution of the United States. It cannot make him a member of this community by making him a member of its own. And for the same reason it cannot introduce any person, or description of persons, who were not intended to be embraced in this new political family, which the Constitution brought into existence, but were intended to be excluded from it.

The question then arises, whether the provisions of the Constitution, in relation to the personal rights and privileges to which the citizen of a State should be entitled, embraced the negro African race, at that time in this country, or who might afterwards be imported, who had then or should afterwards be made free in any State; and to put it in the power of a single State to make him a citizen of the United States, and endue him with the full rights of citizenship in every other State without their consent? Does the Constitution of the United States act upon him whenever he shall be made free under the laws of a State, and raised there to the rank of a citizen, and immediately clothe him with all the privileges of a citizen in every other State, and in its own courts?

The court think the affirmative of these propositions cannot be maintained. And if it cannot, the plaintiff in error could not be a citizen of the State of Missouri, within the meaning of the Constitution of the United States, and, consequently, was not entitled to sue in its courts.

It is true, every person, and every class and description of persons, who were at the time of the adoption of the Constitution recognised as citizens in the several States, became also citizens of this new political body; but none other; it was formed by them, and for them and their posterity, but for no one else. And the personal rights and privileges guarantied to citizens of this new sovereignty were intended to embrace those only who were then members of the several State communities, or who should afterwards by birthright or otherwise become members, according to the provisions of the Constitution and the principles on which it was founded. It was the union of those who were at that time members of distinct and separate political communities into one political family, whose power, for certain specified purposes, was to extend over the whole territory of the United States. And it gave to each citizen rights and privileges outside of his State which he did not before possess, and placed him in every other State upon a perfect equality with its own citizens as to rights of person and rights of property; it made him a citizen of the United States.

It becomes necessary, therefore, to determine who were citizens of the several States when the Constitution was adopted. And in order to do this, we must recur to the Governments and institutions of the thirteen colonies, when they separated from Great Britain and formed new sovereignties, and took their places in the family of independent nations. We must inquire who, at that time, were recognised as the people or citizens of a State, whose rights and liberties had been outraged by the English Government; and who declared their independence, and assumed the powers of Government to defend their rights by force of arms.

In the opinion of the court, the legislation and histories of the times, and the language used in the Declaration of Independence, show, that neither the class of persons who had been imported as slaves, nor their descendants, whether they had become free or not, were then acknowledged as a part of the people, nor intended to be included in the general words used in that memorable instrument.

It is difficult at this day to realize the state of public opinion in relation to that unfortunate race, which prevailed in the civilized and enlightened portions of the world at the time of the Declaration of Independence, and when the Constitution of the United States was framed and adopted. But the public history of every European nation displays it in a manner too plain to be mistaken.

They had for more than a century before been regarded as beings of an inferior order, and altogether unfit to associate with the white race, either in social or political relations; and so far inferior, that they had no rights which the white man was bound to respect; and that the negro might justly and lawfully be reduced to slavery for his benefit. He was bought and sold, and treated as an ordinary article of merchandise and traffic, whenever a profit could be made by it. This opinion was at that time fixed and universal in the civilized portion of the white race. It was regarded as an axiom in morals as well as in politics, which no one thought of disputing, or supposed to be open to dispute; and men in every grade and position in society daily and habitually acted upon it in their private pursuits, as well as in matters of public concern, without doubting for a moment the correctness of this opinion.

And in no nation was this opinion more firmly fixed or more uniformly acted upon than by the English Government and English people. They not only seized them on the coast of Africa, and sold them or held them in slavery for their own use; but they took them as ordinary articles of merchandise to every country where they could make a profit on them, and were far more extensively engaged in this commerce than any other nation in the world.

The opinion thus entertained and acted upon in England was naturally impressed upon the colonies they founded on this side of the Atlantic. And, accordingly, a negro of the African race was regarded by them as an article of property, and held, and bought and sold as such, in every one of the thirteen colonies which united in the Declaration of Independence, and afterwards formed the Constitution of the United States. The slaves were more or less numerous in the different colonies, as slave labor was found more or less profitable. But no one seems to have doubted the correctness of the prevailing opinion of the time.

The legislation of the different colonies furnishes positive and indisputable proof of this fact.

It would be tedious, in this opinion, to enumerate the various laws they passed upon this subject. It will be sufficient, as a sample of the legislation which then generally prevailed throughout the British colonies, to give the laws of two of them; one being still a large slaveholding State, and the other the first State in which slavery ceased to exist.

The province of Maryland, in 1717, (ch. 13, s. 5,) passed a law declaring "that if any free negro or mulatto intermarry with any white woman, or if any white man shall intermarry with any negro or mulatto woman, such negro or mulatto shall become a slave during life, excepting mulattoes born of white women, who, for such intermarriage, shall only become servants for seven years, to be disposed of as the justices of the county court, where such marriage so happens, shall think fit; to be applied by them towards the support of a public school within the said county. And any white man or white woman who shall intermarry as aforesaid, with any negro or mulatto, such white man or white woman shall become servants during the term of seven years, and shall be disposed of by the justices as aforesaid, and be applied to the uses aforesaid."

The other colonial law to which we refer was passed by Massachusetts in 1705, (chap. 6.) It is entitled "An act for the better preventing of a spurious and mixed issue," &c.; and it provides, that "if any negro or mulatto shall presume to smite or strike any person of the English or other Christian nation, such negro or mulatto shall be severely whipped, at the discretion of the justices before whom the offender shall be convicted."

And "that none of her Majesty's English or Scottish subjects, nor of any other Christian nation, within this province, shall contract matrimony with any negro or mulatto; nor shall any person, duly authorized to solemnize marriage, presume to join any such in marriage, on pain of forfeiting the sum of fifty pounds; one moiety thereof to her Majesty, for and towards the support of the Government within this province, and the other moiety to him or them that shall inform and sue for the same, in any of her Majesty's courts of record within the province, by bill, plaint, or information."

We give both of these laws in the words used by the respective legislative bodies, because the language in which they are framed, as well as the provisions contained in them, show, too plainly to be misunderstood, the degraded condition of this unhappy race. They were still in force when the Revolution began,

and are a faithful index to the state of feeling towards the class of persons of whom they speak, and of the position they occupied throughout the thirteen colonies, in the eyes and thoughts of the men who framed the Declaration of Independence and established the State Constitutions and Governments. They show that a perpetual and impassable barrier was intended to be erected between the white race and the one which they had reduced to slavery, and governed as subjects with absolute and despotic power, and which they then looked upon as so far below them in the scale of created beings, that intermarriages between white persons and negroes or mulattoes were regarded as unnatural and immoral, and punished as crimes, not only in the parties, but in the person who joined them in marriage. And no distinction in this respect was made between the free negro or mulatto and the slave, but this stigma, of the deepest degradation, was fixed upon the whole race.

We refer to these historical facts for the purpose of showing the fixed opinions concerning that race, upon which the statesmen of that day spoke and acted. It is necessary to do this, in order to determine whether the general terms used in the Constitution of the United States, as to the rights of man and the rights of the people, was intended to include them, or to give to them or their posterity the benefit of any of its provisions.

The language of the Declaration of Independence is equally conclusive:

It begins by declaring that, "when in the course of human events it becomes necessary for one people to dissolve the political bands which have connected them with another, and to assume among the powers of the earth the separate and equal station to which the laws of nature and nature's God entitle them, a decent respect for the opinions of mankind requires that they should declare the causes which impel them to the separation."

It then proceeds to say: "We hold these truths to be self-evident: that all men are created equal; that they are endowed by their Creator with certain unalienable rights; that among them is life, liberty, and the pursuit of happiness; that to secure these rights, Governments are instituted, deriving their just powers from the consent of the governed."

The general words above quoted would seem to embrace the whole human family, and if they were used in a similar instrument at this day would be so understood. But it is too clear for dispute, that the enslaved African race were not intended to be included, and formed no part of the people who framed and adopted this declaration; for if the language, as understood in that day, would embrace them, the conduct of the distinguished men who framed the Declaration of Independence would have been utterly and flagrantly inconsistent with the principles they asserted; and instead of the sympathy of mankind, to which they so confidently appealed, they would have deserved and received universal rebuke and reprobation.

Yet the men who framed this declaration were great men—high in literary acquirements—high in their sense of honor, and incapable of asserting principles inconsistent with those on which they were acting. They perfectly understood the meaning of the language they used, and how it would be understood by others; and they knew that it would not in any part of the civilized world be supposed to embrace the negro race, which, by common consent, had been excluded from civilized Governments and the family of nations, and doomed to slavery. They spoke and acted according to the then established doctrines and principles, and in the ordinary language of the day, and no one misunderstood them. The unhappy black race were separated from the white by indelible marks, and laws long before established, and were never thought of or spoken of except as property, and when the claims of the owner or the profit of the trader were supposed to need protection.

This state of public opinion had undergone no change when the Constitution was adopted, as is equally evident from its provisions and language.

The brief preamble sets forth by whom it was formed, for what purposes, and for whose benefit and protection. It declares that it is formed by the people of the United States; that is to say, by those who were members of the different political communities in the several States; and its great object is declared to be to secure the blessings of liberty to themselves and their posterity. It speaks in general terms of the people of the United States, and of citizens of the several States, when it is providing for the exercise of the powers granted or the privileges secured to the citizen. It does not define what description of persons are intended to be included under these terms, or who shall be regarded as a citizen and one of the people. It uses them as terms so well understood, that no further description or definition was necessary.

But there are two clauses in the Constitution which point directly and specifically to the negro race as a separate class of persons, and show clearly that they were not regarded as a portion of the people or citizens of the Government then formed.

One of these clauses reserves to each of the thirteen States the right to import slaves until the year 1808, if it thinks proper. And the importation which it thus sanctions was unquestionably of persons of the race of which we are speaking, as the traffic in slaves in the United States had always been confined to them. And by the other provision the States pledge themselves to each other to maintain the right of property of the master, by delivering up to him any slave who may have escaped from his service, and be found within their respective territories. By the first above-mentioned clause, therefore, the right to purchase and hold this property is directly sanctioned and authorized for twenty years by the people who framed the Constitution. And by the second, they pledge themselves to maintain and uphold the right of the master in the manner specified, as long as the Government they then formed should endure. And these two provisions show, conclusively, that neither the description of persons therein referred to, nor their descendants, were embraced in any of the other provisions of the Constitution; for certainly these two clauses were not intended to confer on them or their posterity the blessings of liberty, or any of the personal rights so carefully provided for the citizen.

No one of that race had ever migrated to the United States voluntarily; all of them had been brought here as articles of merchandise. The number that had been emancipated at that time were but few in comparison with those held in slavery; and they were identified in the public mind with the race to which they belonged, and regarded as a part of the slave population rather than the free. It is obvious that they were not even in the minds of the framers of the Constitution when they were conferring special rights and privileges upon the citizens of a State in every other part of the Union.

Indeed, when we look to the condition of this race in the several States at the time, it is impossible to believe that these rights and privileges were intended to be extended to them.

It is very true, that in that portion of the Union where the labor of the negro race was found to be unsuited to the climate and unprofitable to the master, but few slaves were held at the time of the Declaration of Independence; and when the Constitution was adopted, it had entirely worn out in one of them, and measures had been taken for its gradual abolition in several others. But this change had not been produced by any change of opinion in relation to this race; but because it was discovered, from experience, that slave labor was unsuited to the climate and productions of these States: for some of the States, where it had ceased or nearly ceased to exist, were actively engaged in the slave trade, procuring cargoes on the coast of Africa, and transporting them for sale to those parts of the Union where their labor was found to be profitable, and suited to the climate and productions. And this traffic was openly carried on, and fortunes accumulated by it, without reproach from the people of the States where they resided. And it can hardly be supposed that, in the States where it was then countenanced in its worst form—that is, in the seizure and transportation—the people could have regarded those who were emancipated as entitled to equal rights with themselves.

And we may here again refer, in support of this proposition, to the plain and unequivocal language of the laws of the several States, some passed after the Declaration of Independence and before the Constitution was adopted, and some since the Government went into operation.

We need not refer, on this point, particularly to the laws of the present slaveholding States. Their statute books are full of provisions in relation to this class, in the same spirit with the Maryland law which we have before quoted. They have continued to treat them as an inferior class, and to subject them to strict police regulations, drawing a broad line of distinction between the citizen and the slave races, and legislating in relation to them upon the same principle which prevailed at the time of the Declaration of Independence. As relates to these States, it is too plain for argument, that they have never been regarded as a part of the people or citizens of the State, nor supposed to possess any political rights which the dominant race might not withhold or grant at their pleasure. And as long ago as 1822, the Court of Appeals of Kentucky decided that free negroes and mulattoes were not citizens within the meaning of the Constitution of the United States; and the correctness of this decision is recognized, and the same doctrine affirmed, in 1 Meigs's Tenn. Reports, 331.

And if we turn to the legislation of the States where slavery had worn out, or measures taken for its speedy abolition, we shall find the same opinions and principles equally fixed and equally acted upon.

Thus, Massachusetts, in 1786, passed a law similar to the colonial one of which we have spoken. The law of 1786, like the law of 1705, forbids the marriage of any white person with any negro, Indian, or mulatto, and inflicts a penalty of fifty pounds upon any one who shall join them in marriage; and declares all such marriage absolutely null and void, and degrades thus the unhappy issue of the marriage by fixing upon it the stain of bastardy. And this mark of degradation was renewed, and again impressed upon the race, in the careful and deliberate preparation of their revised code published in 1836. This code forbids any person from joining in marriage any white person with any Indian, negro, or mulatto, and subjects the party who shall offend in this respect, to imprisonment, not exceeding six months, in the common jail, or to hard labor, and to a fine of not less than fifty nor more than two hundred dollars; and, like the law of 1786, it declares the marriage to be absolutely null and void. It will be seen that the punishment is increased by the code upon the person who shall marry them, by adding imprisonment to a pecuniary penalty.

So, too, in Connecticut. We refer more particularly to the legislation of this State, because it was not only among the first to put an end to slavery within its own territory, but was the first to fix a mark of reprobation upon the African slave trade. The law last mentioned was passed in October, 1788, about nine months after the State had ratified and adopted the present Constitution of the United States; and by that law it prohibited its own citizens, under severe penalties, from engaging in the trade, and declared all policies of insurance on the vessel or cargo made in the State to be null and void. But, up to the time of the adoption of the Constitution, there is nothing in the legislation of the State indicating any change of opinion as to the relative rights and position of the white and black races in this country, or indicating that it meant to place the latter, when free, upon a level with its citizens. And certainly nothing which would have led the slaveholding States to suppose, that Connecticut designed to claim for them, under the new Constitution, the equal rights and privileges and rank of citizens in every other State.

The first step taken by Connecticut upon this subject was as early as 1774, wen it passed an act forbidding the further importation of slaves into the State. But the section containing the prohibition is introduced by the following preamble:

"And whereas the increase of slaves in this State is injurious to the poor, and inconvenient."

This recital would appear to have been carefully introduced, in order to prevent any misunderstanding of the motive which induced the Legislature to pass the law, and places it distinctly upon the interest and convenience of the white population—excluding the inference that it might have been intended in any degree for the benefit of the other.

And in the act of 1784, by which the issue of slaves, born after the time therein mentioned, were to be free at a certain age, the section is again introduced by a preamble assigning a similar motive for the act. It is in these words:

"Whereas sound policy requires that the abolition of slavery should be effected as soon as may be consistent with the rights of individuals, and the public safety and welfare"—showing that the right of property in the master was to be protected, and that the measure was one of policy, and to prevent the injury and inconvenience, to the whites, of a slave population in the State.

And still further pursuing its legislation, we find that in the same statute passed in 1774, which prohibited the further importation of slaves into the State, there is also a provision by which any negro, Indian, or mulatto servant, who was found wandering out of the town or place to which he belonged, without a written pass such as is therein described, was made liable to be seized by any one, and taken before the next authority to be examined and delivered up to his master—who was required to pay the charge which had accrued thereby. And a subsequent section of the same

law provides, that if any free negro shall travel without such pass, and shall be stopped, seized, or taken up, he shall pay all charges arising thereby. And this law was in full operation when the Constitution of the United States was adopted, and was not repealed till 1797. So that up to that time free negroes and mulattoes were associated with servants and slaves in the police regulations established by the laws of the State.

And again, in 1833, Connecticut passed another law, which made it penal to set up or establish any school in that State for the instruction of persons of the African race not inhabitants of the State, or to instruct or teach in any such school or institution, or board or harbor for that purpose, any such person, without the previous consent in writing of the civil authority of the town in which such school or institution might be.

And it appears by the case of *Crandall v. The State*, reported in 10 Conn. Rep., 340, that upon an information filed against Prudence Crandall for a violation of this law, one of the points raised in the defence was, that the law was a violation of the Constitution of the United States; and that the persons instructed, although of the African race, were citizens of other States, and therefore entitled to the rights and privileges of citizens in the State of Connecticut. But Chief Justice Dagget, before whom the case was tried, held, that persons of that description were not citizens of a State, within the meaning of the word citizen in the Constitution of the United States, and were not therefore entitled to the privileges and immunities of citizens in other States.

The case was carried up to the Supreme Court of Errors of the State, and the question fully argued there. But the case went off upon another point, and no opinion was expressed on this question.

We have made this particular examination into the legislative and judicial action of Connecticut, because, from the early hostility it displayed to the slave trade on the coast of Africa, we may expect to find the laws of that State as lenient and favorable to the subject race as those of any other State in the Union; and if we find that at the time the Constitution was adopted, they were not even there raised to the rank of citizens, but were still held and treated as property, and the laws relating to them passed with reference altogether to the interest and convenience of the white race, we shall hardly find them elevated to a higher rank anywhere else.

A brief notice of the laws of two other States, and we shall pass on to other considerations.

By the laws of New Hampshire, collected and finally passed in 1815, no one was permitted to be enrolled in the militia of the State, but free white citizens; and the same provision is found in a subsequent collection of the laws, made in 1855. Nothing could more strongly mark the entire repudiation of the African race. The alien is excluded, because, being born in a foreign country, he cannot be a member of the community until he is naturalized. But why are the African race, born in the State, not permitted to share in one of the highest duties of the citizen? The answer is obvious; he is not, by the institutions and laws of the State, numbered among its people. He forms no part of the sovereignty of the State, and is not therefore called on to uphold and defend it. Again, in 1822, Rhode Island, in its revised code, passed a law forbidding persons who were authorized to join persons in marriage, from joining in marriage any white person with any negro, Indian, or mulatto, under the penalty of two hundred dollars, and declaring all such marriages absolutely null and void; and the same law was again re-enacted in its revised code of 1844. So that, down to the last-mentioned period, the strongest mark of inferiority and degradation was fastened upon the African race in that State.

It would be impossible to enumerate and compress in the space usually allotted to an opinion of a court, the various laws, marking the condition of this race, which were passed from time to time after the Revolution, and before and since the adoption of the Constitution of the United States. In addition to those already referred to, it is sufficient to say, that Chancellor Kent, whose accuracy and research no one will question, states in the sixth edition of his *Commentaries*, (published in 1848, 2 vol., 258, note b,) that in no part of the country except Maine, did the African race, in point of fact, participate equally with the whites in the exercise of civil and political rights.

The legislation of the States therefore shows, in a manner not to be mistaken, the inferior and subject condition of that race at the time the Constitution was adopted, and long afterwards, throughout the thirteen States by which that instrument was framed; and it is hardly consistent with the respect due to these States, to suppose that they regarded at that time, as fellow-citizens and members of the sovereignty, a class of beings whom they had thus stigmatized; whom, as we are bound, out of respect to the State sovereignties, to assume they had deemed it just and necessary thus to stigmatize, and upon whom they had impressed such deep and enduring marks of inferiority and degradation; or, that when they met in convention to form the Constitution, they looked upon them as a portion of their constituents, or designed to include them in the provisions so carefully inserted for the security and protection of the liberties and rights of their citizens. It cannot be supposed that they intended to secure to them rights, and privileges, and rank, in the new political body throughout the Union, which every one of them denied within the limits of its own dominion. More especially, it cannot be believed that the large slaveholding States regarded them as included in the word citizens, or would have consented to a Constitution which might compel them to receive them in that character from another State. For if they were so received, and entitled to the privileges and immunities of citizens, it would exempt them from the operation of the special laws and from the police regulations which they considered to be necessary for their own safety. It would give to persons of the negro race, who were recognised as citizens in any one State of the Union, the right to enter every other State whenever they pleased, singly or in companies, without pass or passport, and without obstruction, to sojourn there as long as they pleased, to go where they pleased at every hour of the day or night without molestation, unless they committed some violation of law for which a white man would be punished; and it would give them the full liberty of speech in public and in private upon all subjects upon which its own citizens might speak; to hold public meetings upon political affairs, and to keep and carry arms wherever they went. And all of this would be done in the face of the subject race of the same color, both free and slaves, and inevitably producing discontent and insubordination among them, and endangering the peace and safety of the State.

It is impossible, it would seem, to believe that the great men of the slaveholding States, who took so large a share in framing the Constitution of the United States, and exercised so much influence in procuring its adoption, could have been so forgetful or regardless of their own safety and the safety of those who trusted and confided in them.

Besides, this want of foresight and care would have been utterly inconsistent with the caution displayed in providing for the admission of new members into this political family. For, when they gave to the citizens of each State the privileges and immunities of citizens in the several States, they at the same time took from the several States the power of naturalization, and confined that power exclusively to the Federal Government. No State was willing to permit another State to determine who should or should not be admitted as one of its citizens, and entitled to demand equal rights and privileges with their own people, within their own territories. The right of naturalization was therefore, with one accord, surrendered by the States, and confided to the Federal Government. And this power granted to Congress to establish an uniform rule of naturalization is, by the well-understood meaning of the word, confined to persons born in a foreign country, under a foreign Government. It is not a power to raise to the rank of a citizen any one born in the United States, who, from birth or parentage, by the laws of the country, belongs to an inferior and subordinate class. And when we find the States guarding themselves from the indiscreet or improper admission by other States of emigrants from other countries, by giving the power exclusively to Congress, we cannot fail to see that they could never have left with the States a much more important power—that is, the power of transforming into citizens a numerous class of persons, who in that character would be much more dangerous to the peace and safety of a large portion of the Union, than the few foreigners one of the States might improperly naturalize. The Constitution upon its adoption obviously took from the States all power by any subsequent legislation to introduce as a citizen into the political family of the United States any one, no matter where he was born, or what might be his character or condition; and it gave to Congress the power to confer this character upon those only who were born outside of the dominions of the United States. And no law of a State, therefore, passed since the Constitution was adopted, can give any right of citizenship outside of its own territory.

A clause similar to the one in the Constitution, in relation to the rights and immunities of citizens of one State in the other States, was contained in the Articles of Confederation. But there is a difference of language, which is worthy of note. The provision in the Articles of Confederation was, "that the free inhabitants of each of the States, paupers, vagabonds, and fugitives from justice, excepted, should be entitled to all the privileges and immunities of free citizens in the several States."

It will be observed, that under this Confederation, each State had the right to decide for itself, and in its own tribunals, whom it would acknowledge as a free inhabitant of another State. The term free inhabitant, in the generality of its terms, would certainly include one of the African race who had been manumitted. But no example, we think, can be found of his admission to all the privileges of citizenship in any State of the Union after these Articles were formed, and while they continued in force. And, notwithstanding the generality of the words "free inhabitants," it is very clear that, according to their accepted meaning in that day, they did not include the African race, whether free or not: for the fifth section of the ninth article provides that Congress should have the power "to agree upon the number of land forces to be raised, and to make requisitions from each State for its quota in proportion to the number of white inhabitants in such State, which requisition should be binding."

Words could hardly have been used which more strongly mark the line of distinction between the citizen and the subject; the free and the subjugated races. The latter were not even counted when the inhabitants of a State were to be embodied in proportion to its numbers for the general defence. And it cannot for a moment be supposed, that a class of persons thus separated and rejected from those who formed the sovereignty of the States, were yet intended to be included under the words "free inhabitants," in the preceding article, to whom privileges and immunities were so carefully secured in every State.

But although this clause of the Articles of Confederation is the same in principle with that inserted in the Constitution, yet the comprehensive word inhabitant, which might be construed to include an emancipated slave, is omitted; and the privilege is confined to citizens of the State. And this alteration in words would hardly have been made, unless a different meaning was intended to be conveyed, or a possible doubt removed. The just and fair inference is, that as this privilege was about to be placed under the protection of the General Government, and the words expounded by its tribunals, and all power in relation to it taken from the State and its courts, it was deemed prudent to describe with precision and caution the persons to whom this high privilege was given—and the word citizen was on that account substituted for the words free inhabitant. The word citizen excluded, and no doubt intended to exclude, foreigners who had not become citizens of some one of the States when the Constitution was adopted; and also every description of persons who were not fully recognised as citizens in the several States. This, upon any fair construction of the instruments to which we have referred, was evidently the object and purpose of this change of words.

To all this mass of proof we have still to add, that Congress has repeatedly legislated upon the same construction of the Constitution that we have given. Three laws, two of which were passed almost immediately after the Government went into operation, will be abundantly sufficient to show this. The two first are particularly worthy of notice, because many of the men who assisted in framing the Constitution, and took an active part in procuring its adoption, were then in the halls of legislation, and certainly understood what they meant when they used the words "people of the United States" and "citizen" in that well-considered instrument.

The first of these acts is the naturalization law, which was passed at the second session of the first Congress, March 26, 1790, and confines the right of becoming citizens "to aliens being free white persons."

Now, the Constitution does not limit the power of Congress in this respect to white persons. And they may, if they think proper, authorize the naturalization of any one, of any color, who was born under allegiance to another Government. But the language of the law above quoted, shows that citizenship at that time was perfectly understood to be confined to the white race; and that they alone constituted the sovereignty in the Government.

Congress might, as we before said, have authorized the naturalization of Indians, because they were aliens and foreigners. But, in their then untutored and savage state, no one would have thought of admitting them as citizens in a civilized community. And, moreover, the atrocities they had but recently committed, when they were the allies of Great Britain in the Revolutionary war, were yet fresh in the recollection of the people of the United States, and they were even then guarding themselves against the threatened renewal of Indian hostilities. No one supposed then that any Indian would ask for, or was capable of enjoying, the privileges of an American citizen, and the word white was not used with any particular reference to them.

Neither was it used with any reference to the African race imported into or born in this country; because Congress had no power to naturalize them, and therefore there was no necessity for using particular words to exclude them.

It would seem to have been used merely because it followed out the line of division which the Constitution has drawn between the citizen race, who formed and held the Government, and the African race, which they held in subjection and slavery, and governed at their own pleasure.

Another of the early laws of which we have spoken, is the first militia law, which was passed in 1792, at the first session of the second Congress. The language of this law is equally plain and significant with the one just mentioned. It directs that every "free able-bodied white male citizen" shall be enrolled in the militia. The word white is evidently used to exclude the African race, and the word "citizen" to exclude unnaturalized foreigners; the latter forming no part of the sovereignty, owing it no allegiance, and therefore under no obligation to defend it. The African race, however, born in the country, did owe allegiance to the Government, whether they were slave or free; but it is repudiated, and rejected from the duties and obligations of citizenship in marked language.

The third act to which we have alluded is even still more decisive; it was passed as late as 1813, (2 Stat., 809,) and it provides: "That from and after the termination of the war in which the United States are now engaged with Great Britain, it shall not be lawful to employ, on board of any public or private vessels of the United States, any person or persons except citizens of the United States, or persons of color, natives of the United States." Here the line of distinction is drawn in express words. Persons of color, in the judgment of Congress, were not included in the word citizens, and they are described as another and different class of persons, and authorized to be employed, if born in the United States.

And even as late as 1820, (chap. 104, sec. 8,) in the charter to the city of Washington, the corporation is authorized "to restrain and prohibit the nightly and other disorderly meetings of slaves, free negroes, and mulattoes," thus associating them together in its legislation; and after prescribing the punishment that may be inflicted on the slaves, proceeds in the following words: "And to punish such free negroes and mulattoes by penalties not exceeding twenty dollars for any one offence; and in case of the inability of any such free negro or mulatto to pay any such penalty and cost thereon, to cause him or her to be confined to labor for any time not exceeding six calendar months." And in a subsequent part of the same section, the act authorizes the corporation "to prescribe the terms and conditions upon which free negroes and mulattoes may reside in the city."

This law, like the laws of the States, shows that this class of persons were governed by special legislation directed expressly to them, and always connected with provisions for the government of slaves, and not with those for the government of free white citizens. And after such an uniform course of legislation as we have stated, by the colonies, by the States, and by Congress, running through a period of more than a century, it would seem that to call persons thus marked and stigmatized, "citizens" of the United States, "fellow-citizens," a constituent part of the sovereignty, would be an abuse of terms, and not calculated to exalt the character of an American citizen in the eyes of other nations.

The conduct of the Executive Department of the Government has been in perfect harmony upon this subject with this course of legislation. The question was brought officially before the late William Wirt, when he was the Attorney General of the United States, in 1821, and he decided that the words "citizens of the United States" were used in the acts of Congress in the same sense as in the Constitution; and that free persons of color were not citizens, within the meaning of the Constitution and laws; and this opinion has been confirmed by that of the late Attorney General, Caleb Cushing, in a recent case, and acted upon by the Secretary of State, who refused to grant passports to them as "citizens of the United States."

But it is said that a person may be a citizen, and entitled to that character, although he does not possess all the rights which may belong to other citizens; as, for example, the right to vote, or to hold particular offices; and that yet, when he goes into another State, he is entitled to be recognised there as a citizen, although the State may measure his rights by the rights which it allows to persons of a like character or class resident in the State, and refuse to him the full rights of citizenship.

This argument overlooks the language of the provision in the Constitution of which we are speaking.

Undoubtedly, a person may be a citizen, that is, a member of the community who form the sovereignty, although he exercises no share of the political power, and is incapacitated from holding particular offices. Women and minors, who form a part of the political family, cannot vote; and when a property qualification is required to vote or hold a particular office, those who have not the necessary qualification cannot vote or hold the office, yet they are citizens.

So, too, a person may be entitled to vote by the law of the State, who is not a citizen even of the State itself. And in some of the States of the Union foreigners not naturalized are allowed to vote. And the State may give the right to free negroes and mulattoes, but that does not make them citizens of the State, and still less of the United States. And the provision in the Constitution giving privileges and immunities in other States, does not apply to them.

Neither does it apply to a person who, being the citizen of a State, migrates to another State. For then he becomes subject to the laws of the State in which he lives, and he is no longer a citizen of the State from which he removed. And the State in which he resides may then, unquestionably, determine his status or condition, and place him among the class of persons who are not recognised as citizens, but belong to an inferior and subject race; and may deny him the privileges and immunities enjoyed by its citizens.

But so far as mere rights of person are concerned, the provision in question is confined to citizens of a State who are temporarily in another State without taking up their residence there. It gives them no political rights in the State, as to voting or holding office, or in any other respect. For a citizen of one State has no right to participate in the government of another. But if he ranks as a citizen in the State to which he belongs, within the meaning of the Constitution of the United States, then, whenever he goes into another State, the Constitution clothes him, as to the rights of person, will all the privileges and immunities which belong to citizens of the State. And if persons of the African race are citizens of a State, and of the United States, they would be entitled to all of these privileges and immunities in every State, and the State could not restrict them; for they would hold these privileges and immunities under the paramount authority of the Federal Government, and its courts would be bound to maintain and enforce them, the Constitution and laws of the State to the contrary notwithstanding. And if the States could limit or restrict them, or place the party in an inferior grade, this clause of the Constitution would be unmeaning, and could have no operation; and would give no rights to the citizen when in another State. He would have none but what the State itself chose to allow him. This is evidently not the construction or meaning of the clause in question. It guaranties rights to the citizen, and the State cannot withhold them. And these rights are of a character and would lead to consequences which make it absolutely certain that the African race were not included under the name of citizens of a State, and were not in the contemplation of the framers of the Constitution when these privileges and immunities were provided for the protection of the citizen in other States.

The case of *Legrand v. Darnall* (2 Peters, 664) has been referred to for the purpose of showing that this court has decided that the descendant of a slave may sue as a citizen in a court of the United States; but the case itself shows that the question did not arise and could not have arisen in the case.

It appears from the report, that Darnall was born in Maryland, and was the son of a white man by one of his slaves, and his father executed certain instruments to manumit him, and devised to him some landed property in the State. This property Darnall afterwards sold to Legrand, the appellant, who gave his notes for the purchase-money. But becoming afterwards apprehensive that the appellee had not been emancipated according to the laws of Maryland, he refused to pay the notes until he could be better satisfied as to Darnall's right to convey. Darnall, in the mean time, had taken up his residence in Pennsylvania, and brought suit on the notes, and recovered judgment in the Circuit Court for the district of Maryland.

The whole proceeding, as appears by the report, was an amicable one; Legrand being perfectly willing to pay the money, if he could obtain a title, and Darnall not wishing him to pay unless he could make him a good one. In point of fact, the whole proceeding was under the direction of the counsel who argued the case for the appellee, who was the mutual friend of the parties, and confided in by both of them, and whose only object was to have the rights of both parties established by judicial decision in the most speedy and least expensive manner.

Legrand, therefore, raised no objection to the jurisdiction of the court in the suit at law, because he was himself anxious to obtain the judgment of the court upon his title. Consequently, there was nothing in the record before the court to show that Darnall was of African descent, and the usual judgment and award of execution was entered. And Legrand thereupon filed his bill on the equity side of the Circuit Court, stating that Darnall was born a slave, and had not been legally emancipated, and could not therefore take the land devised to him, nor make Legrand a good title; and praying an injunction to restrain Darnall from proceeding to execution on the judgment, which was granted. Darnall answered, averring in his answer that he was a free man, and capable of conveying a good title. Testimony was taken on this point, and at the hearing the Circuit Court was of opinion that Darnall was a free man and his title good, and dissolved the injunction and dismissed the bill; and that decree was affirmed here, upon the appeal of Legrand.

Now, it is difficult to imagine how any question about the citizenship of Darnall, or his right to sue in that character, can be supposed to have arisen or been decided in that case. The fact that he was of African descent was first brought before the court upon the bill in equity. The suit at law had then passed into judgment and award of execution, and the Circuit Court, as a court of law, had no longer any authority over it. It was a valid and legal judgment, which the court that rendered it had not the power to reverse or set aside. And unless it had jurisdiction as a court of equity to restrain him from using its process as a court of law, Darnall, if he thought proper, would have been at liberty to proceed on his judgment, and compel the payment of the money, although the allegations in the bill were true, and he was incapable of making a title. No other court could have enjoined him, for certainly no State equity court could interfere in that way with the judgment of a Circuit Court of the United States.

But the Circuit Court as a court of equity certainly had equity jurisdiction over its own judgment as a court of law, without regard to the character of the parties; and had not only the right, but it was its duty—no matter who were the parties in the judgment—to prevent them from proceeding to enforce it by execution, if the court was satisfied that the money was not justly and equitably due. The ability of Darnall to convey did not depend upon his citizenship, but upon his title to freedom. And if he was free, he could hold and convey property, by the laws of Maryland, although he was not a citizen. But if he was by law still a slave, he could not. It was therefore the duty of the court, sitting as a court of equity in the latter case, to prevent him from using its process, as a court of common law, to compel the payment of the purchase-money, when it was evident that the purchaser must lose the land. But if he was free, and could make a title, it was equally the duty of the court not to suffer Legrand to keep the land, and refuse the payment of the money, upon the ground that Darnall was incapable of suing or being sued as a citizen in a court of the United States. The character or citizenship of the parties had no connection with the question of jurisdiction, and the matter in dispute had no relation to the citizenship of Darnall. Nor is such a question alluded to in the opinion of the court.

Besides, we are by no means prepared to say that there are not many cases, civil as well as criminal, in which a Circuit Court of the United States may exercise jurisdiction, although one of the African race is a party; that broad question is not before the court. The question with which we are now dealing is, whether a person of the African race can be a citizen of the United States, and become thereby entitled to a special privilege, by virtue of his title to that character, and which, under the Constitution, no one but a citizen can claim. It is manifest that the case of Legrand and Darnall has no bearing on that question, and can have no application to the case now before the court.

This case, however, strikingly illustrates the consequences that would follow the construction of the Constitution which would give the power contended

for to a State. It would in effect give it also to an individual. For if the father of young Darnall had manumitted him in his lifetime, and sent him to reside in a State which recognised him as a citizen, he might have visited and sojourned in Maryland when he pleased, and as long as he pleased, as a citizen of the United States; and the State officers and tribunals would be compelled, by the paramount authority of the Constitution, to receive him and treat him as one of its citizens, exempt from the laws and police of the State in relation to a person of that description, and allow him to enjoy all the rights and privileges of citizenship, without respect to the laws of Maryland, although such laws were deemed by it absolutely essential to its own safety.

The only two provisions which point to them and include them, treat them as property, and make it the duty of the Government to protect it; no other power, in relation to this race, is to be found in the Constitution; and as it is a Government of special, delegated, powers, no authority beyond these two provisions can be constitutionally exercised. The Government of the United States had no right to interfere for any other purpose but that of protecting the rights of the owner, leaving it altogether with the several States to deal with this race, whether emancipated or not, as each State may think justice, humanity, and the interests and safety of society, require. The States evidently intended to reserve this power exclusively to themselves.

No one, we presume, supposes that any change in public opinion or feeling, in relation to this unfortunate race, in the civilized nations of Europe or in this country, should induce the court to give to the words of the Constitution a more liberal construction in their favor than they were intended to bear when the instrument was framed and adopted. Such an argument would be altogether inadmissible in any tribunal called on to interpret it. If any of its provisions are deemed unjust, there is a mode prescribed in the instrument itself by which it may be amended; but while it remains unaltered, it must be construed now as it was understood at the time of its adoption. It is not only the same in words, but the same in meaning, and delegates the same powers to the Government, and reserves and secures the same rights and privileges to the citizen; and as long as it continues to exist in its present form, it speaks not only in the same words, but with the same meaning and intent with which it spoke when it came from the hands of its framers, and was voted on and adopted by the people of the United States. Any other rule of construction would abrogate the judicial character of this court, and make it the mere reflex of the popular opinion or passion of the day. This court was not created by the Constitution for such purposes. Higher and graver trusts have been confided to it, and it must not falter in the path of duty.

What the construction was at that time, we think can hardly admit of doubt. We have the language of the Declaration of Independence and of the Articles of Confederation, in addition to the plain words of the Constitution itself; we have the legislation of the different States, before, about the time, and since, the Constitution was adopted; we have the legislation of Congress, from the time of its adoption to a recent period; and we have the constant and uniform action of the Executive Department, all concurring together, and leading to the same result. And if anything in relation to the construction of the Constitution can be regarded as settled, it is that which we now give to the word "citizen" and the word "people."

And upon a full and careful consideration of the subject, the court is of opinion, that, upon the facts stated in the plea in abatement, Dred Scott was not a citizen of Missouri within the meaning of the Constitution of the United States, and not entitled as such to sue in its courts; and, consequently, that the Circuit Court had no jurisdiction of the case, and that the judgment on the plea in abatement is erroneous.

We are aware that doubts are entertained by some of the members of the court, whether the plea in abatement is legally before the court upon this writ of error; but if that plea is regarded as waived, or out of the case upon any other ground, yet the question as to the jurisdiction of the Circuit Court is presented on the face of the bill of exception itself, taken by the plaintiff at the trial; for he admits that he and his wife were born slaves, but endeavors to make out his title to freedom and citizenship by showing that they were taken by their owner to certain places, hereinafter mentioned, where slavery could not by law exist, and that they thereby became free, and upon their return to Missouri became citizens of that State.

Now, if the removal of which he speaks did not give them their freedom, then by his own admission he is still a slave; and whatever opinions may be entertained in favor of the citizenship of a free person of the African race, no one supposes that a slave is a citizen of the State or of the United States. If, therefore, the acts done by his owner did not make them free persons, he is still a slave, and certainly incapable of suing in the character of a citizen.

The principle of law is too well settled to be disputed, that a court can give no judgment for either party, where it has no jurisdiction; and if, upon the showing of Scott himself, it appeared that he was still a slave, the case ought to have been dismissed, and the judgment against him and in favor of the defendant for costs, is, like that on the plea in abatement, erroneous, and the suit ought to have been dismissed by the Circuit Court for want of jurisdiction in that court.

But, before we proceed to examine this part of the case, it may be proper to notice an objection taken to the judicial authority of this court to decide it; and it has been said, that as this court has decided against the jurisdiction of the Circuit Court on the plea in abatement, it has no right to examine any question presented by the exception; and that anything it may say upon that part of the case will be extra-judicial, and mere obiter dicta.

This is a manifest mistake; there can be no doubt as to the jurisdiction of this court to revise the judgment of a Circuit Court, and to reverse it for any error apparent on the record, whether it be the error of giving judgment in a case over which it had no jurisdiction, or any other material error; and this, too, whether there is a plea in abatement or not.

The objection appears to have arisen from confounding writs of error to a State court, with writs of error to a Circuit Court of the United States. Undoubtedly, upon a writ of error to a State court, unless the record shows a case that gives jurisdiction, the case must be dismissed for want of jurisdiction in this court. And if it is dismissed on that ground, we have no right to examine and decide upon any question presented by the bill of exceptions, or any other part of the record. But writs of error to a State court, and to a Circuit Court of the United States, are regulated by different laws, and stand upon entirely different principles. And in a writ of error to a Circuit Court of the United States, the whole record is before this court for examination and decision; and if the sum in controversy is large enough to give jurisdiction, it is not only the right, but it is the judicial duty of the court, to examine the whole case as presented by the record; and if it appears upon its face that any material error or errors have been committed by the court below, it is the duty of this court to reverse the judgment, and remand the case. And certainly an error in passing a judgment upon the merits in favor of either party, in a case which it was not authorized to try, and over which it had no jurisdiction, is as grave an error as a court can commit.

The plea in abatement is not a plea to the jurisdiction of this court, but to the jurisdiction of the Circuit Court. And it appears by the record before us, that the Circuit Court committed an error, in deciding that it had jurisdiction, upon the facts in the case, admitted by the pleadings. It is the duty of the appellate tribunal to correct this error; but that could not be done by dismissing the case for want of jurisdiction here—for that would leave the erroneous judgment in full force, and the injured party without remedy. And the appellate court therefore exercises the power for which alone appellate courts are constituted, by reversing the judgment of the court below for this error. It exercises its proper and appropriate jurisdiction over the judgment and proceedings of the Circuit Court, as they appear upon the record brought up by the writ of error.

The correction of one error in the court below does not deprive the appellate court of the power of examining further into the record, and correcting any other material errors which may have been committed by the inferior court. There is certainly no rule of law—nor any practice—nor any decision of a court—which even questions this power in the appellate tribunal. On the contrary, it is the daily practice of this court, and of all appellate courts where they reverse the judgment of an inferior court for error, to correct by its opinions whatever errors may appear on the record material to the case; and they have always held it to be their duty to do so where the silence of the court might lead to misconstruction or future controversy, and the point has been relied on by either side, and argued before the court.

In the case before us, we have already decided that the Circuit Court erred in deciding that it had jurisdiction upon the facts admitted by the pleadings. And it appears that, in the further progress of the case, it acted upon the erroneous principle it had decided on

the pleadings, and gave judgment for the defendant, where, upon the facts admitted in the exception, it had no jurisdiction.

We are at a loss to understand upon what principle of law, applicable to appellate jurisdiction, it can be supposed that this court has not judicial authority to correct the last-mentioned error, because they had before corrected the former; or by what process of reasoning it can be made out, that the error of an inferior court in actually pronouncing judgment for one of the parties, in a case in which it had no jurisdiction, cannot be looked into or corrected by this court, because we have decided a similar question presented in the pleadings. The last point is distinctly presented by the facts contained in the plaintiff's own bill of exceptions, which he himself brings here by this writ of error. It was the point which chiefly occupied the attention of the counsel on both sides in the argument—and the judgment which this court must render upon both errors is precisely the same. It must, in each of them, exercise jurisdiction over the judgment, and reverse it for the errors committed by the court below; and issue a mandate to the Circuit Court to conform its judgment to the opinion pronounced by this court, by dismissing the case for want of jurisdiction in the Circuit Court. This is the constant and invariable practice of this court, where it reverses a judgment for want of jurisdiction in the Circuit Court.

It can scarcely be necessary to pursue such a question further. The want of jurisdiction in the court below may appear on the record without any plea in abatement. This is familiarly the case where a court of chancery has exercised jurisdiction in a case where the plaintiff had a plain and adequate remedy at law, and it so appears by the transcript when brought here by appeal. So also where it appears that a court of admiralty has exercised jurisdiction in a case belonging exclusively to a court of common law. In these cases there is no plea in abatement. And for the same reason, and upon the same principles, where the defect of jurisdiction is patent on the record, this court is bound to reverse the judgment, although the defendant has not pleaded in abatement to the jurisdiction of the inferior court.

The cases of *Jackson v. Ashton* and of *Capron v. Van Noorden*, to which we have referred in a previous part of this opinion, are directly in point. In the last-mentioned case, Capron brought an action against Van Noorden in a Circuit Court of the United States, without showing, by the usual averments of citizenship, that the court had jurisdiction. There was no plea in abatement put in, and the parties went to trial upon the merits. The court gave judgment in favor of the defendant with costs. The plaintiff thereupon brought his writ of error, and this court reversed the judgment given in favor of the defendant, and remanded the case with directions to dismiss it, because it did not appear by the transcript that the Circuit Court had jurisdiction.

The case before us still more strongly imposes upon this court the duty of examining whether the court below has not committed an error, in taking jurisdiction and giving a judgment for costs in favor of the defendant; for in *Capron v. Van Noorden* the judgment was reversed, because it did not appear that the parties were citizens of different States. They might or might not be. But in this case it does appear that the plaintiff was born a slave; and if the facts upon which he relies have not made him free, then it appears affirmatively on the record that he is not a citizen, and consequently his suit against Sandford was not a suit between citizens of different States, and the court had no authority to pass any judgment between the parties. The suit ought, in this view of it, to have been dismissed by the Circuit Court, and its judgment in favor of Sandford is erroneous, and must be reversed.

It is true that the result either way, by dismissal or by a judgment for the defendant, makes very little, if any, difference in a pecuniary or personal point of view to either party. But the fact that the result would be very nearly the same to the parties in either form of judgment, would not justify this court in sanctioning an error in the judgment which is patent on the record, and which, if sanctioned, might be drawn into precedent, and lead to serious mischief and injustice in some future suit.

We proceed, therefore, to inquire whether the facts relied on by the plaintiff entitled him to his freedom. The case, as he himself states it, on the record brought here by his writ of error, is this:

The plaintiff was a negro slave, belonging to Dr. Emerson, who was a surgeon in the army of the United States. In the year 1834, he took the plaintiff from the State of Missouri to the military post at Rock Island, in the State of Illinois, and held him there as a slave until

the month of April or May, 1836. At the time last mentioned, said Dr. Emerson removed the plaintiff from said military post at Rock Island to the military post at Fort Snelling, situate on the west bank of the Mississippi river, in the Territory known as Upper Louisiana, acquired by the United States of France, and situate north of the latitude of thirty-six degrees thirty minutes north, and north of the State of Missouri. Said Dr. Emerson held the plaintiff in slavery at said Fort Snelling, from said last-mentioned date until the year 1838.

In the year 1835, Harriet, who is named in the second count of the plaintiff's declaration, was the negro slave of Major Taliaferro, who belonged to the army of the United States. In that year, 1835, said Major Taliaferro took said Harriet to said Fort Snelling, a military post, situated as hereinbefore stated, and kept her there as a slave until the year 1836, and then sold and delivered her as a slave, at said Fort Snelling, unto the said Dr. Emerson hereinbefore named. Said Dr. Emerson held said Harriet in slavery at said Fort Snelling until the year 1838.

In the year 1836, the plaintiff and Harriet intermarried, at Fort Snelling, with the consent of Dr. Emerson, who then claimed to be their master and owner. Eliza and Lizzie, named in the third count of the plaintiff's declaration, are the fruit of that marriage. Eliza is about fourteen years old, and was born on board the steamboat Gipsey, north of the north line of the State of Missouri, and upon the river Mississippi. Lizzie is about seven years old, and was born in the State of Missouri, at the military post called Jefferson Barracks.

In the year 1838, said Dr. Emerson removed the plaintiff and said Harriet, and their said daughter Eliza, from said Fort Snelling to the State of Missouri, where they have ever since resided.

Before the commencement of this suit, said Dr. Emerson sold and conveyed the plaintiff, and Harriet, Eliza, and Lizzie, to the defendant, as slaves, and the defendant has ever since claimed to hold them, and each of them, as slaves.

In considering this part of the controversy, two questions arise: 1. Was he, together with his family, free in Missouri by reason of the stay in the territory of the United States hereinbefore mentioned? And 2. If they were not, is Scott himself free by reason of his removal to Rock Island, in the State of Illinois, as stated in the above admissions?

We proceed to examine the first question.

The act of Congress, upon which the plaintiff relies, declares that slavery and involuntary servitude, except as a punishment for crime, shall be forever prohibited in all that part of the territory ceded by France, under the name of Louisiana, which lies north of thirty-six degrees thirty minutes north latitude, and not included within the limits of Missouri. And the difficulty which meets us at the threshold of this part of the inquiry is, whether Congress was authorized to pass this law under any of the powers granted to it by the Constitution; for if the authority is not given by that instrument, it is the duty of this court to declare it void and inoperative, and incapable of conferring freedom upon any one who is held as a slave under the have of any one of the States.

The counsel for the plaintiff has laid much stress upon that article in the Constitution which confers on Congress the power "to dispose of and make all needful rules and regulations respecting the territory or other property belonging to the United States;" but, in the judgment of the court, that provision has no bearing on the present controversy, and the power there given, whatever it may be, is confined, and was intended to be confined, to the territory which at that time belonged to, or was claimed by, the United States, and was within their boundaries as settled by the treaty with Great Britain, and can have no influence upon a territory afterwards acquired from a foreign Government. It was a special provision for a known and particular territory, and to meet a present emergency, and nothing more.

A brief summary of the history of the times, as well as the careful and measured terms in which the article is framed, will show the correctness of this proposition.

It will be remembered that, from the commencement of the Revolutionary war, serious difficulties existed between the States, in relation to the disposition of large and unsettled territories which were included in the chartered limits of some of the States. And some of the other States, and more especially Maryland, which had no unsettled lands, insisted that as the unoccupied lands, if wrested from Great Britain, would owe

their preservation to the common purse and the common sword, the money arising from them ought to be applied in just proportion among the several States to pay the expenses of the war, and ought not to be appropriated to the use of the State in whose chartered limits they might happen to lie, to the exclusion of the other States, by whose combined efforts and common expense the territory was defended and preserved against the claim of the British Government.

These difficulties caused much uneasiness during the war, while the issue was in some degree doubtful, and the future boundaries of the United States yet to be defined by treaty, if we achieved our independence.

The majority of the Congress of the Confederation obviously concurred in opinion with the State of Maryland, and desired to obtain from the States which claimed it a cession of this territory, in order that Congress might raise money on this security to carry on the war. This appears by the resolution passed on the 6th of September, 1780, strongly urging the States to cede these lands to the United States, both for the sake of peace and union among themselves, and to maintain the public credit; and this was followed by the resolution of October 10th, 1780, by which Congress pledged itself, that if the lands were ceded, as recommended by the resolution above mentioned, they should be disposed of for the common benefit of the United States, and be settled and formed into distinct republican States, which should become members of the Federal Union, and have the same rights of sovereignty, and freedom, and independence, as other States.

But these difficulties became much more serious after peace took place, and the boundaries of the United States were established. Every State, at that time, felt severely the pressure of its war debt; but in Virginia, and some other States, there were large territories of unsettled lands, the sale of which would enable them to discharge their obligations without much inconvenience; while other States, which had no such resource, saw before them many years of heavy and burdensome taxation; and the latter insisted, for the reasons before stated, that these unsettled lands should be treated as the common property of the States, and the proceeds applied to their common benefit.

The letters from the statesmen of that day will show how much this controversy occupied their thoughts, and the dangers that were apprehended from it. It was the disturbing element of the time, and fears were entertained that it might dissolve the Confederation by which the States were then united.

These fears and dangers were, however, at once removed, when the State of Virginia, in 1784, voluntarily ceded to the United States the immense tract of country lying northwest of the river Ohio, and which was within the acknowledged limits of the State. The only object of the State, in making this cession, was to put an end to the threatening and exciting controversy, and to enable the Congress of that time to dispose of the lands, and appropriate the proceeds as a common fund for the common benefit of the States. It was not ceded, because it was inconvenient to the State to hold and govern it, nor from any expectation that it could be better or more conveniently governed by the United States.

The example of Virginia was soon afterwards followed by other States, and, at the time of the adoption of the Constitution, all of the States, similarly situated, had ceded their unappropriated lands, except North Carolina and Georgia. The main object for which these cessions were desired and made, was on account of their money value, and to put an end to a dangerous controversy, as to who was justly entitled to the proceeds when the lands should be sold. It is necessary to bring this part of the history of these cessions thus distinctly into view, because it will enable us the better to comprehend the phraseology of the article in the Constitution, so often referred to in the argument.

Undoubtedly the powers of sovereignty and the eminent domain were ceded with the land. This was essential, in order to make it effectual, and to accomplish its objects. But it must be remembered that, at that time, there was no Government of the United States in existence with enumerated and limited powers; what was then called the United States, were thirteen separate, sovereign, independent States, which had entered into a league or confederation for their mutual protection and advantage, and the Congress of the United States was composed of the representatives of these separate sovereignties, meeting together, as equals, to discuss and decide on certain measures which the States, by the Articles of Confederation, had agreed to submit to their decision. But this Confederation had none of the attributes of sovereignty in legislative, executive, or judicial power. It was little more than a congress of am-

bassadors, authorized to represent separate nations, in matters in which they had a common concern.

It was this Congress that accepted the cession from Virginia. They had no power to accept it under the Articles of Confederation. But they had an undoubted right, as independent sovereignties, to accept any cession of territory for their common benefit, which all of them assented to; and it is equally clear, that as their common property, and having no superior to control them, they had the right to exercise absolute dominion over it, subject only to the restrictions which Virginia had imposed in her act of cession. There was, as we have said, no Government of the United States then in existence with special enumerated and limited powers. The territory belonged to sovereignties, who, subject to the limitations above mentioned, had a right to establish any form of government they pleased, by compact or treaty among themselves, and to regulate rights of person and rights of property in the territory, as they might deem proper. It was by a Congress, representing the authority of these several and separate sovereignties, and acting under their authority and command, (but not from any authority derived from the Articles of Confederation,) that the instrument usually called the ordinance of 1787 was adopted; regulating in much detail the principles and the laws by which this territory should be governed; and among other provisions, slavery is prohibited in it. We do not question the power of the States, by agreement among themselves, to pass this ordinance, nor its obligatory force in the territory, while the confederation or league of the States in their separate sovereign character continued to exist.

This was the state of things when the Constitution of the United States was formed. The territory ceded by Virginia belonged to the several confederated States as common property, and they had united in establishing in it a system of government and jurisprudence, in order to prepare it for admission as States, according to the terms of the cession. They were about to dissolve this federative Union, and to surrender a portion of their independent sovereignty to a new Government, which, for certain purposes, would make the people of the several States one people, and which was to be supreme and controlling within its sphere of action throughout the United States; but this Government was to be carefully limited in its powers, and to exercise no authority beyond those expressly granted by the

Constitution, or necessarily to be implied from the language of the instrument, and the objects it was intended to accomplish; and as this league of States would, upon the adoption of the new Government, cease to have any power over the territory, and the ordinance they had agreed upon be incapable of execution, and a mere nullity, it was obvious that some provision was necessary to give the new Government sufficient power to enable it to carry into effect the objects for which it was ceded, and the compacts and agreements which the States had made with each other in the exercise of their powers of sovereignty. It was necessary that the lands should be sold to pay the war debt; that a Government and system of jurisprudence should be maintained in it, to protect the citizens of the United States who should migrate to the territory, in their rights of person and of property. It was also necessary that the new Government, about to be adopted, should be authorized to maintain the claim of the United States to the unappropriated lands in North Carolina and Georgia, which had not then been ceded, but the cession of which was confidently anticipated upon some terms that would be arranged between the General Government and these two States. And, moreover, there were many articles of value besides this property in land, such as arms, military stores, munitions, and ships of war, which were the common property of the States, when acting in their independent characters as confederates, which neither the new Government nor any one else would have a right to take possession of, or control, without authority from them; and it was to place these things under the guardianship and protection of the new Government, and to clothe it with the necessary powers, that the clause was inserted in the Constitution which give Congress the power "to dispose of and make all needful rules and regulations respecting the territory or other property belonging to the United States." It was intended for a specific purpose, to provide for the things we have mentioned. It was to transfer to the new Government the property then held in common by the States, and to give to that Government power to apply it to the objects for which it had been destined by mutual agreement among the States before their league was dissolved. It applied only to the property which the States held in common at that time, and has no reference whatever to any territory or other property which the new sovereignty might afterwards itself acquire.

The language used in the clause, the arrangement and combination of the powers, and the somewhat unusual phraseology it uses, when it speaks of the political power to be exercised in the government of the territory, all indicate the design and meaning of the clause to be such as we have mentioned. It does not speak of any territory, nor of Territories, but uses language which, according to its legitimate meaning, points to a particular thing. The power is given in relation only to the territory of the United States—that is, to a territory then in existence, and then known or claimed as the territory of the United States. It begins its enumeration of powers by that of disposing, in other words, making sale of the lands, or raising money from them, which, as we have already said, was the main object of the cession, and which is accordingly the first thing provided for in the article. It then gives the power which was necessarily associated with the disposition and sale of the lands—that is, the power of making needful rules and regulations respecting the territory. And whatever construction may now be given to these words, every one, we think, must admit that they are not the words usually employed by statesmen in giving supreme power of legislation. They are certainly very unlike the words used in the power granted to legislate over territory which the new Government might afterwards itself obtain by cession from a State, either for its seat of Government, or for forts, magazines, arsenals, dock yards, and other needful buildings.

And the same power of making needful rules respecting the territory is, in precisely the same language, applied to the other property belonging to the United States—associating the power over the territory in this respect with the power over movable or personal property—that is, the ships, arms, and munitions of war, which then belonged in common to the State sovereignties. And it will hardly be said, that this power, in relation to the last-mentioned objects, was deemed necessary to be thus specially given to the new Government, in order to authorize it to make needful rules and regulations respecting the ships it might itself build, or arms and munitions of war it might itself manufacture or provide for the public service.

No one, it is believed, would think a moment of deriving the power of Congress to make needful rules and regulations in relation to property of this kind from this clause of the Constitution. Nor can it, upon any fair construction, be applied to any property but that which the new Government was about the receive from the confederated States. And if this be true as to this property, it must be equally true and limited as to the territory, which is so carefully and precisely coupled with it—and like it referred to as property in the power granted. The concluding words of the clause appear to render this construction irresistible; for, after the provisions we have mentioned, it proceeds to say, "that nothing in the Constitution shall be so construed as to prejudice any claims of the United States, or of any particular State."

Now, as we have before said, all of the States, except North Carolina and Georgia, had made the cession before the Constitution was adopted, according to the resolution of Congress of October 10, 1780. The claims of other States, that the unappropriated lands in these two States should be applied to the common benefit, in like manner, was still insisted on, but refused by the States. And this member of the clause in question evidently applies to them, and can apply to nothing else. It was to exclude the conclusion that either party, by adopting the Constitution, would surrender what they deemed their rights. And when the latter provision relates so obviously to the unappropriated lands not yet ceded by the States, and the first clause makes provision for those then actually ceded, it is impossible, by any just rule of construction, to make the first provision general, and extend to all territories, which the Federal Government might in any way afterwards acquire, when the latter is plainly and unequivocally confined to a particular territory; which was a part of the same controversy, and involved in the same dispute, and depended upon the same principles. The union of the two provisions in the same clause shows that they were kindred subjects; and that the whole clause is local, and relates only to lands, within the limits of the United States, which had been or then were claimed by a State; and that no other territory was in the mind of the framers of the Constitution, or intended to be embraced in it. Upon any other construction it would be impossible to account for the insertion of the last provision in the place where it is found, or to comprehend why, or for what object, it was associated with the previous provision.

This view of the subject is confirmed by the manner in which the present Government of the United States dealt with the subject as soon as it came into existence. It must be borne in mind that the same States that formed the Confederation also formed and adopted the new Government, to which so large a portion of their former sovereign powers were surrendered. It must also be borne in mind that all of these same States which had then ratified the new Constitution were represented in the Congress which passed the first law for the government of this territory; and many of the members of that legislative body had been deputies from the States under the Confederation—had united in adopting the ordinance of 1787, and assisted in forming the new Government under which they were then acting, and whose powers they were then exercising. And it is obvious from the law they passed to carry into effect the principles and provisions of the ordinance, that they regarded it as the act of the States done in the exercise of their legitimate powers at the time. The new Government took the territory as it found it, and in the condition in which it was transferred, and did not attempt to undo anything that had been done. And, among the earliest laws passed under the new Government, is one reviving the ordinance of 1787, which had become inoperative and a nullity upon the adoption of the Constitution. This law introduces no new form or principles for its government, but recites, in the preamble, that it is passed in order that this ordinance may continue to have full effect, and proceeds to make only those rules and regulations which were needful to adapt it to the new Government, into whose hands the power had fallen. It appears, therefore, that this Congress regarded the purposes to which the land in this Territory was to be applied, and the form of government and principles of jurisprudence which were to prevail there, while it remained in the Territorial state, as already determined on by the States when they had full power and right to make the decision; and that the new Government, having received it in this condition, ought to carry substantially into effect the plans and principles which had been previously adopted by the States, and which no doubt the States anticipated when they surrendered their power to the new Government. And if we regard this clause of the Constitution as pointing to this Territory, with a Territorial Government already established in it, which had been ceded to the States for the purposes hereinbefore mentioned—every word in it is perfectly appropriate and easily understood, and the provisions it contains are in perfect harmony with the objects for which it was ceded, and with the condition of its government as a Territory at the time.

We can, then, easily account for the manner in which the first Congress legislated on the subject—and can also understand why this power over the territory was associated in the same clause with the other property of the United States, and subjected to the like power of making needful rules and regulations. But if the clause is construed in the expanded sense contended for, so as to embrace any territory acquired from a foreign nation by the present Government, and to give it in such territory a despotic and unlimited power over persons and property, such as the confederated States might exercise in their common property, it would be difficult to account for the phraseology used, when compared with other grants of power—and also for its association with the other provisions in the same clause.

The Constitution has always been remarkable for the felicity of its arrangement of different subjects, and the perspicuity and appropriateness of the language it uses. But if this clause is construed to extend to territory acquired by the present Government from a foreign nation, outside of the limits of any charter from the British Government to a colony, it would be difficult to say, why it was deemed necessary to give the Government the power to sell any vacant lands belonging to the sovereignty which might be found within it; and if this was necessary, why the grant of this power should precede the power to legislate over it and establish a Government there; and still more difficult to say, why it was deemed necessary so specially and particularly to grant the power to make needful rules and regulations in relation to any personal or movable property it might acquire there. For the words, other property necessarily, by every known rule of interpretation, must mean property of a different description from territory or land. And the difficulty would perhaps be insurmountable in endeavoring to account for the last member of the sentence, which provides that "nothing in this Constitution shall be so construed as to prejudice any claims of the United States or any particular State," or to say how any particular State could have claims in or to a territory ceded by a foreign Government, or to account for associating this provision with the preceding provisions of the clause, with which it would appear to have no connection.

The words "needful rules and regulations" would seem, also, to have been cautiously used for some definite object. They are not the words usually employed by statesmen, when they mean to give the powers of sovereignty, or to establish a Government, or to authorize its establishment. Thus, in the law to renew and keep alive the ordinance of 1787, and to re-establish the Government, the title of the law is: "An act to provide for the government of the territory northwest of the river Ohio." And in the Constitution, when granting the power to legislate over the territory that may be selected for the seat of Government independently of a State, it does not say Congress shall have power "to make all needful rules and regulations respecting the territory;" but it declares that "Congress shall have power to exercise exclusive legislation in all cases whatsoever over such District (not exceeding ten miles square) as may, by cession of particular States and the acceptance of Congress, become the seat of the Government of the United States."

The words "rules and regulations" are usually employed in the Constitution in speaking of some particular specified power which it means to confer on the Government, and not, as we have seen, when granting general powers of legislation. As, for example, in the particular power to Congress "to make rules for the government and regulation of the land and naval forces, or the particular and specific power to regulate commerce;" "to establish an uniform rule of naturalization;" "to coin money and regulate the value thereof." And to construe the words of which we are speaking as a general and unlimited grant of sovereignty over territories which the Government might afterwards acquire, is to use them in a sense and for a purpose for which they were not used in any other part of the instrument. But if confined to a particular Territory, in which a Government and laws had already been established, but which would require some alterations to adapt it to the new Government, the words are peculiarly applicable and appropriate for that purpose. The necessity of this special provision in relation to property and the rights or property held in common by the confederated States, is illustrated by the first clause of the sixth article. This clause provides that "all debts, contracts, and engagements entered into before the adoption of this Constitution, shall be as valid against the United States under this Government as under the Confederation." This provision, like the one under consideration, was indispensable if the new Constitution was adopted. The new Government was not a mere change in a dynasty, or in a form of government, leaving the nation or sovereignty the same, and clothed with all the rights, and bound by all the obligations of the preceding one. But, when the present United States came into existence under the new Government, it was a new political body, a new nation, then for the first time taking its place in the family of nations. It took nothing by succession from the Confederation. It had no right, as its successor, to any property or rights of property which it had acquired, and was not liable for any of its obligations. It was evidently viewed in this light by the framers of the Constitution. And as the several States would cease to exist in their former confederated character upon the adoption of the Constitution, and could not, in that character, again assemble together, special provisions were indispensable to transfer to the new Government the property and rights which at that time they held in common; and at the same time to authorize it to lay taxes and appropriate money to pay the common debt which they had contracted; and this power could only be given to it by special provisions in the Constitution. The clause in relation to the territory and other property of the United States provided for the first, and the clause last quoted provided for the other. They have no connection with the general powers and rights of sovereignty delegated to the new Government, and can neither enlarge nor diminish them. They were inserted to meet a present emergency, and not to regulate its powers as a Government.

Indeed, a similar provision was deemed necessary, in relation to treaties made by the Confederation; and when in the clause next succeeding the one of which we have last spoken, it is declared that treaties shall be the supreme law of the land, care is taken to include, by express words, the treaties made by the confederated States. The language is: "and all treaties made, or which shall be made, under the authority of the United States, shall be the supreme law of the land."

Whether, therefore, we take the particular clause in question, by itself, or in connection with the other provisions of the Constitution, we think it clear, that it applies only to the particular territory of which we have spoken, and cannot, by any just rule of interpretation, be extended to territory which the new Government might afterwards obtain from a foreign nation. Consequently, the power which Congress may have lawfully exercised in this Territory, while it remained under a Territorial Government, and which may have been sanctioned by judicial decision, can furnish no justification and no argument to support a similar exercise of power over territory afterwards acquired by the Federal Government. We put aside, therefore, any argument, drawn from precedents, showing the extent of the power which the General Government exercised over slavery in this Territory, as altogether inapplicable to the case before us.

But the case of the *American and Ocean Insurance Companies v. Canter* ( 1 Pet., 511) has been quoted as establishing a different construction of this clause of the Constitution. There is, however, not the slightest conflict between the opinion now given and the one referred to; and it is only by taking a single sentence out of the latter and separating it from the context, that even an appearance of conflict can be shown. We need not comment on such a mode of expounding an opinion of the court. Indeed it most commonly misrepresents instead of expounding it. And this is fully exemplified in the case referred to, where, if one sentence is taken by itself, the opinion would appear to be in direct conflict with that now given; but the words which immediately follow that sentence show that the court did not mean to decide the point, but merely affirmed the power of Congress to establish a Government in the Territory, leaving it an open question, whether that power was derived from this clause in the Constitution, or was to be necessarily inferred from a power to acquire territory by cession from a foreign Government. The opinion on this part of the case is short, and we give the whole of it to show how well the selection of a single sentence is calculated to mislead.

The passage referred to is in page 542, in which the court, in speaking of the power of Congress to establish a Territorial Government in Florida until it should become a State, uses the following language:

> "In the mean time Florida continues to be a Territory of the United States, governed by that clause of the Constitution which empowers Congress to make all needful rules and regulations respecting the territory or other property of the United States. Perhaps the power of governing a Territory belonging to the United States, which has not, by becoming a State, acquired the means of self-government, may result, necessarily, from the facts that it is not within the jurisdiction of any

particular State, and is within the power and jurisdiction of the United States. The right to govern may be the inevitable consequence of the right to acquire territory. Whichever may be the source from which the power is derived, the possession of it is unquestionable."

It is thus clear, from the whole opinion on this point, that the court did not mean to decide whether the power was derived from the clause in the Constitution, or was the necessary consequence of the right to acquire. They do decide that the power in Congress is unquestionable, and in this we entirely concur, and nothing will be found in this opinion to the contrary. The power stands firmly on the latter alternative put by the court—that is, as "the inevitable consequence of the right to acquire territory."

And what still more clearly demonstrates that the court did not mean to decide the question, but leave it open for future consideration, is the fact that the case was decided in the Circuit Court by Mr. Justice Johnson, and his decision was affirmed by the Supreme Court. His opinion at the circuit is given in full in a note to the case, and in that opinion he states, in explicit terms, that the clause of the Constitution applies only to the territory then within the limits of the United States, and not to Florida, which had been acquired by cession from Spain. This part of his opinion will be found in the note in page 517 of the report. But he does not dissent from the opinion of the Supreme Court; thereby showing that, in his judgment, as well as that of the court, the case before them did not call for a decision on that particular point, and the court abstained from deciding it. And in a part of its opinion subsequent to the passage we have quoted, where the court speak of the legislative power of Congress in Florida, they still speak with the same reserve. And in page 546, speaking of the power of Congress to authorize the Territorial Legislature to establish courts there, the court say: "They are legislative courts, created in virtue of the general right of sovereignty which exists in the Government, or in virtue of that clause which enables Congress to make all needful rules and regulations respecting the territory belonging to the United States."

It has been said that the construction given to this clause is new, and now for the first time brought forward. The case of which we are speaking, and which has been so much discussed, shows that the fact is otherwise. It shows that precisely the same question came before Mr. Justice Johnson, at his circuit, thirty years ago—was fully considered by him, and the same construction given to the clause in the Constitution which is now given by this court. And that upon an appeal from his decision the same question was brought before this court, but was not decided because a decision upon it was not required by the case before the court.

There is another sentence in the opinion which has been commented on, which even in a still more striking manner shows how one may mislead or be misled by taking out a single sentence from the opinion of a court, and leaving out of view what precedes and follows. It is in page 546, near the close of the opinion, in which the court say: "In legislating for them," ( the territories of the United States,) "Congress exercises the combined powers of the General and of a State Government." And it is said, that as a State may unquestionably prohibit slavery within its territory, this sentence decides in effect that Congress may do the same in a Territory of the United States, exercising there the powers of a State, as well as the power of the General Government.

The examination of this passage in the case referred to, would be more appropriate when we come to consider in another part of this opinion what power Congress can constitutionally exercise in a Territory, over the rights of person or rights of property of a citizen. But, as it is in the same case with the passage we have before commented on, we dispose of it now, as it will save the court from the necessity of referring again to the case. And it will be seen upon reading the page in which this sentence is found, that it has no reference whatever to the power of Congress over rights of person or rights of property—but relates altogether to the power of establishing judicial tribunals to administer the laws constitutionally passed, and defining the jurisdiction they may exercise.

The law of Congress establishing a Territorial Government in Florida, provided that the Legislature of the Territory should have legislative powers over "all rightful objects of legislation; but no law should be valid which was inconsistent with the laws and Constitution of the United States."

Under the power thus conferred, the Legislature of Florida passed an act, erecting a tribunal at Key West to decide cases of salvage. And in the case of which we are speaking, the question arose whether the Territorial Legislature could be authorized by Congress to establish such a tribunal, with such powers; and one of the parties, among other objections, insisted that Congress could not under the Constitution authorize the Legislature of the Territory to establish such a tribunal with such powers, but that it must be established by Congress itself; and that a sale of cargo made under its order, to pay salvors, was void, as made without legal authority, and passed no property to the purshaser. It is in disposing of this objection that the sentence relied on occurs, and the court begin that part of the opinion by stating with great precision the point which they are about to decide.

They say: "It has been contended that by the Constitution of the United States, the judicial power of the United States extends to all cases of admiralty and maritime jurisdiction; and that the whole of the judicial power must be vested 'in one Supreme Court, and in such inferior courts as Congress shall from time to time ordain and establish.' Hence it has been argued that Congress cannot vest admiralty jurisdiction in courts created by the Territorial Legislature."

And after thus clearly stating the point before them, and which they were about to decide, they proceed to show that these Territorial tribunals were not constitutional courts, but merely legislative, and that Congress might, therefore, delegate the power to the Territorial Government to establish the court in question; and they conclude that part of the opinion in the following words: "Although admiralty jurisdiction can be exercised in the States in those courts only which are established in pursuance of the third article of the Constitution, the same limitation does not extend to the Territories. In legislating for them, Congress exercises the combined powers of the General and State Governments."

Thus it will be seen by these quotations from the opinion, that the court, after stating the question it was about to decide in a manner too plain to be misunderstood, proceeded to decide it, and announced, as the opinion of the tribunal, that in organizing the judicial department of the Government in a Territory of the United States, Congress does not act under, and is not restricted by,

the third article in the Constitution, and is not bound, in a Territory, to ordain and establish courts in which the judges hold their offices during good behaviour, but may exercise the discretionary power which a State exercises in establishing its judicial department, and regulating the jurisdiction of its courts, and may authorize the Territorial Government to establish, or may itself establish, courts in which the judges hold their offices for a term of years only; and may vest in them judicial power upon subjects confided to the judiciary of the United States. And in doing this, Congress undoubtedly exercises the combined power of the General and a State Government. It exercises the discretionary power of a State Government in authorizing the establishment of a court in which the judges hold their appointments for a term of years only, and not during good behaviour; and it exercises the power of the General Government in investing that court with admiralty jurisdiction, over which the General Government had exclusive jurisdiction in the Territory.

No one, we presume, will question the correctness of that opinion; nor is there anything in conflict with it in the opinion now given. The point decided in the case cited has no relation to the question now before the court. That depended on the construction of the third article of the Constitution, in relation to the judiciary of the United States, and the power which Congress might exercise in a Territory in organizing the judicial department of the Government. The case before us depends upon other and different provisions of the Constitution, altogether separate and apart from the one above mentioned. The question as to what courts Congress may ordain or establish in a Territory to administer laws which the Constitution authorizes it to pass, and what laws it is or is not authorized by the Constitution to pass, are widely different—are regulated by different and separate articles of the Constitution, and stand upon different principles. And we are satisfied that no one who reads attentively the page in Peters's Reports to which we have referred, can suppose that the attention of the court was drawn for a moment to the question now before this court, or that it meant in that case to say that Congress had a right to prohibit a citizen of the United States from taking any property which he lawfully held into a Territory of the United States.

This brings us to examine by what provision of the Constitution the present Federal Government, under its delegated and restricted powers, is authorized to acquire territory outside of the original limits of the United States, and what powers it may exercise therein over the person or property of a citizen of the United States, while it remains a Territory, and until it shall be admitted as one of the States of the Union.

There is certainly no power given by the Constitution to the Federal Government to establish or maintain colonies bordering on the United States or at a distance, to be ruled and governed at its own pleasure; nor to enlarge its territorial limits in any way, except by the admission of new States. That power is plainly given; and if a new State is admitted, it needs no further legislation by Congress, because the Constitution itself defines the relative rights and powers, and duties of the State, and the citizens of the State, and the Federal Government. But no power is given to acquire a Territory to be held and governed permanently in that character.

And indeed the power exercised by Congress to acquire territory and establish a Government there, according to its own unlimited discretion, was viewed with great jealousy by the leading statesmen of the day. And in the Federalist, (No. 38,) written by Mr. Madison, he speaks of the acquisition of the Northwestern Territory by the confederated States, by the cession from Virginia, and the establishment of a Government there, as an exercise of power not warranted by the Articles of Confederation, and dangerous to the liberties of the people. And he urges the adoption of the Constitution as a security and safeguard against such an exercise of power.

We do not mean, however, to question the power of Congress in this respect. The power to expand the territory of the United States by the admission of new States is plainly given; and in the construction of this power by all the departments of the Government, it has been held to authorize the acquisition of territory, not fit for admission at the time, but to be admitted as soon as its population and situation would entitle it to admission. It is acquired to become a State, and not to be held as a colony and governed by Congress with absolute authority; and as the propriety of admitting a new State is committed to the sound discretion of Congress, the power to acquire territory for that purpose, to be held by the United States until it is in a suitable condition to become a State upon an equal footing with the other States, must rest upon the same

discretion. It is a question for the political department of the Government, and not the judicial; and whatever the political departent of the Government shall recognise as within the limits of the United States, the judicial department is also bound to recognise, and to administer in it the laws of the United States, so far as they apply, and to maintain in the Territory the authority and rights of the Government, and also the personal rights and rights of property of individual citizens, as secured by the Constitution. All we mean to say on this point is, that, as there is no express regulation in the Constitution defining the power which the General Government may exercise over the person or property of a citizen in a Territory thus acquired, the court must necessarily look to the provisions and principles of the Constitution, and its distribution of powers, for the rules and principles by which its decision must be governed.

Taking this rule to guide us, it may be safely assumed that citizens of the United States who migrate to a Territory belonging to the people of the United States, cannot be ruled as mere colonists, dependent upon the will of the General Government, and to be governed by any laws it may think proper to impose. The principle upon which our Governments rest, and upon which alone they continue to exist, is the union of States, sovereign and independent within their own limits in their internal and domestic concerns, and bound together as one people by a General Government, possessing certain enumerated and restricted powers, delegated to it by the people of the several States, and exercising supreme authority within the scope of the powers granted to it, throughout the dominion of the United States. A power, therefore, in the General Government to obtain and hold colonies and dependent territories, over which they might legislate without restriction, would be inconsistent with its own existence in its present form. Whatever it acquires, it acquires for the benefit of the people of the several States who created it. It is their trustee acting for them, and charged with the duty of promoting the interests of the whole people of the Union in the exercise of the powers specifically granted.

At the time when the Territory in question was obtained by cession from France, it contained no population fit to be associated together and admitted as a State; and it therefore was absolutely necessary to hold possession of it, as a Territory belonging to the

United States, until it was settled and inhabited by a civilized community capable of self-government, and in a condition to be admitted on equal terms with the other States as a member of the Union. But, as we have before said, it was acquired by the General Government, as the representative and trustee of the people of the United States, and it must therefore be held in that character for their common and equal benefit; for it was the people of the several States, acting through their agent and representative, the Federal Government, who in fact acquired the Territory in question, and the Government holds it for their common use until it shall be associated with the other States as a member of the Union.

But until that time arrives, it is undoubtedly necessary that some Government should be established, in order to organize society, and to protect the inhabitants in their persons and property; and as the people of the United States could act in this matter only through the Government which represented them, and the through which they spoke and acted when the Territory was obtained, it was not only within the scope of its powers, but it was its duty to pass such laws and establish such a Government as would enable those by whose authority they acted to reap the advantages anticipated from its acquisition, and to gather there a population which would enable it to assume the position to which it was destined among the States of the Union. The power to acquire necessarily carries with it the power to preserve and apply to the purposes for which it was acquired. The form of government to be established necessarily rested in the discretion of Congress. It was their duty to establish the one that would be best suited for the protection and security of the citizens of the United States, and other inhabitants who might be authorized to take up their abode there, and that must always depend upon the existing condition of the Territory, as to the number and character of its inhabitants, and their situation in the Territory. In some cases a Government, consisting of persons appointed by the Federal Government, would best subserve the interests of the Territory, when the inhabitants were few and scattered, and new to one another. In other instances, it would be more advisable to commit the powers of self-government to the people who had settled in the Territory, as being the most competent to determine what was best for their own interests. But some form of civil authority would

be absolutely necessary to organize and preserve civilized society, and prepare it to become a State; and what is the best form must always depend on the condition of the Territory at the time, and the choice of the mode must depend upon the exercise of a discretionary power by Congress, acting within the scope of its constitutional authority, and not infringing upon the rights of person or rights of property of the citizen who might go there to reside, or for any other lawful purpose. It was acquired by the exercise of this discretion, and it must be held and governed in like manner, until it is fitted to be a State.

But the power of Congress over the person or property of a citizen can never be a mere discretionary power under our Constitution and form of Government. The powers of the Government and the rights and privileges of the citizen are regulated and plainly defined by the Constitution itself. And when the Territory becomes a part of the United States, the Federal Government enters into possession in the character impressed upon it by those who created it. It enters upon it with its powers over the citizen strictly defined, and limited by the Constitution, from which it derives its own existence, and by virtue of which alone it continues to exist and act as a Government and sovereignty. It has no power of any kind beyond it; and it cannot, when it enters a Territory of the United States, put off its character, and assume discretionary or despotic powers which the Constitution has denied to it. It cannot create for itself a new character separated from the citizens of the United States, and the duties it owes them under the provisions of the Constitution. The Territory being a part of the United States, the Government and the citizen both enter it under the authority of the Constitution, with their respective rights defined and marked out; and the Federal Government can exercise no power over his person or property, beyond what that instrument confers, nor lawfully deny any right which it has reserved.

A reference to a few of the provisions of the Constitution will illustrate this proposition.

For example, no one, we presume, will contend that Congress can make any law in a Territory respecting the establishment of religion, or the free exercise thereof, or abridging the freedom of speech or of the press, or the right of the people of the Territory peaceably to assemble, and to petition the Government for the redress of grievances.

Nor can Congress deny to the people the right to keep and bear arms, nor the right to trial by jury, nor compel any one to be a witness against himself in a criminal proceeding.

These powers, and others, in relation to rights of person, which it is not necessary here to enumerate, are, in express and positive terms, denied to the General Government; and the rights of private property have been guarded with equal care. Thus the rights of property are united with the rights of person, and placed on the same ground by the fifth amendment to the Constitution, which provides that no person shall be deprived of life, liberty, and property, without due process of law. And an act of Congress which deprives a citizen of the United States of his liberty or property, merely because he came himself or brought his property into a particular Territory of the United States, and who had committed no offence against the laws, could hardly be dignified with the name of due process of law.

So, too, it will hardly be contended that Congress could by law quarter a soldier in a house in a Territory without the consent of the owner, in time of peace; nor in time of war, but in a manner prescribed by law. Nor could they by law forfeit the property of a citizen in a Territory who was convicted of treason, for a longer period than the life of the person convicted; nor take private property for public use without just compensation.

The powers over person and property of which we speak are not only not granted to Congress, but are in express terms denied, and they are forbidden to exercise them. And this prohibition is not confined to the States, but the words are general, and extend to the whole territory over which the Constitution gives it power to legislate, including those portions of it remaining under Territorial Government, as well as that covered by States. It is a total absence of power everywhere within the dominion of the United States, and places the citizens of a Territory, so far as these rights are concerned, on the same footing with citizens of the States, and guards them as firmly and plainly against any inroads which the General Government might attempt, under the plea of implied or incidental powers.

And if Congress itself cannot do this—if it is beyond the powers conferred on the Federal Government—it will be admitted, we presume, that it could not authorize a Territorial Government to exercise them. It could confer no power on any local Government, established by its authority, to violate the provisions of the Constitution.

It seems, however, to be supposed, that there is a difference between property in a slave and other property, and that different rules may be applied to it in expounding the Constitution of the United States. And the laws and usages of nations, and the writings of eminent jurists upon the relation of master and slave and their mutual rights and duties, and the powers which Governments may exercise over it, have been dwelt upon in the argument.

But in considering the question before us, it must be borne in mind that there is no law of nations standing between the people of the United States and their Government, and interfering with their relation to each other. The powers of the Government, and the rights of the citizen under it, are positive and practical regulations plainly written down. The people of the United States have delegated to it certain enumerated powers, and forbidden it to exercise others. It has no power over the person or property of a citizen but what the citizens of the United States have granted. And no laws or usages of other nations, or reasoning of statesmen or jurists upon the relations of master and slave, can enlarge the powers of the Government, or take from the citizens the rights they have reserved. And if the Constitution recognises the right of property of the master in a slave, and makes no distinction between that description of property and other property owned by a citizen, no tribunal, acting under the authority of the United States, whether it be legislative, executive, or judicial, has a right to draw such a distinction, or deny to it the benefit of the provisions and guarantees which have been provided for the protection of private property against the encroachments of the Government.

Now, as we have already said in an earlier part of this opinion, upon a different point, the right of property in a slave is distinctly and expressly affirmed in the Constitution. The right to traffic in it, like an ordinary article of merchandise and property, was guarantied to the citizens of the United States, in every State that might desire it, for twenty years. And the Government in express terms is pledged to protect it in all future time, if the slave escapes from his owner. This is done in plain words—too plain to be misunderstood. And no word can be found in the Constitution which gives Congress a greater power over slave property, or which entitles property of that kind to less protection that property of any other description. The only power conferred is the power coupled with the duty of guarding and protecting the owner in his rights.

Upon these considerations, it is the opinion of the court that the act of Congress which prohibited a citizen from holding and owning property of this kind in the territory of the United States north of the line therein mentioned, is not warranted by the Constitution, and is therefore void; and that neither Dred Scott himself, nor any of his family, were made free by being carried into this territory; even if they had been carried there by the owner, with the intention of becoming a permanent resident.

We have so far examined the case, as it stands under the Constitution of the United States, and the powers thereby delegated to the Federal Government.

But there is another point in the case which depends on State power and State law. And it is contended, on the part of the plaintiff, that he is made free by being taken to Rock Island, in the State of Illinois, independently of his residence in the territory of the United States; and being so made free, he was not again reduced to a state of slavery by being brought back to Missouri.

Our notice of this part of the case will be very brief; for the principle on which it depends was decided in this court, upon much consideration, in the case of *Strader et al. v. Graham*, reported in 10th Howard, 82. In that case, the slaves had been taken from Kentucky to Ohio, with the consent of the owner, and afterwards brought back to Kentucky. And this court held that their status or condition, as free or slave, depended upon the laws of Kentucky, when they were brought back into that State, and not of Ohio; and that this court had no jurisdiction to revise the judgment of a State court upon its own laws. This was the point directly before the court, and the decision that this court had not jurisdiction turned upon it, as will be seen by the report of the case.

So in this case. As Scott was a slave when taken into the State of Illinois by his owner, and was there held

as such, and brought back in that character, his status, as free or slave, depended on the laws of Missouri, and not of Illinois.

It has, however, been urged in the argument, that by the laws of Missouri he was free on his return, and that this case, therefore, cannot be governed by the case of *Strader et al. v. Graham*, where it appeared, by the laws of Kentucky, that the plaintiffs continued to be slaves on their return from Ohio. But whatever doubts or opinions may, at one time, have been entertained upon this subject, we are satisfied, upon a careful examination of all the cases decided in the State courts of Missouri referred to, that it is now firmly settled by the decisions of the highest court in the State, that Scott and his family upon their return were not free, but were, by the laws of Missouri, the property of the defendant; and that the Circuit Court of the United States had no jurisdiction, when, by the laws of the State, the plaintiff was a slave, and not a citizen.

Moreover, the plaintiff, it appears, brought a similar action against the defendant in the State court of Missouri, claiming the freedom of himself and his family upon the same grounds and the same evidence upon which he relies in the case before the court. The case was carried before the Supreme Court of the State; was fully argued there; and that court decided that neither the plaintiff nor his family were entitled to freedom, and were still the slaves of the defendant; and reversed the judgment of the inferior State court, which had given a different decision. If the plaintiff supposed that this judgment of the Supreme Court of the State was erroneous, and that this court had jurisdiction to revise and reverse it, the only mode by which he could legally bring it before this court was by writ of error directed to the Supreme Court of the State, requiring it to transmit the record to this court. If this had been done, it is too plain for argument that the writ must have been dismissed for want of jurisdiction in this court. The case of *Strader and others v. Graham* is directly in point; and, indeed, independent of any decision, the language of the 25th section of the act of 1789 is too clear and precise to admit of controversy.

But the plaintiff did not pursue the mode prescribed by law for bringing the judgment of a State court before this court for revision, but suffered the case to be remanded to the inferior State court, where it is still continued, and is, by agreement of parties, to await the judgment of this court on the point. All of this appears on the record before us, and by the printed report of the case.

And while the case is yet open and pending in the inferior State court, the plaintiff goes into the Circuit Court of the United States, upon the same case and the same evidence, and against the same party, and proceeds to judgment, and then brings here the same case from the Circuit Court, which the law would not have permitted him to bring directly from the State court. And if this court takes jurisdiction in this form, the result, so far as the rights of the respective parties are concerned, is in every respect substantially the same as if it had in open violation of law entertained jurisdiction over the judgment of the State court upon a writ of error, and revised and reversed its judgment upon the ground that its opinion upon the question of law was erroneous. It would ill become this court to sanction such an attempt to evade the law, or to exercise an appellate power in this circuitous way, which it is forbidden to exercise in the direct and regular and invariable forms of judicial proceedings.

Upon the whole, therefore, it is the judgment of this court, that it appears by the record before us that the plaintiff in error is not a citizen of Missouri, in the sense in which that word is used in the Constitution; and that the Circuit Court of the United States, for that reason, had no jurisdiction in the case, and could give no judgment in it. Its judgment for the defendant must, consequently, be reversed, and a mandate issued, directing the suit to be dismissed for want of jurisdiction.

---

### Glossary

**jurisdiction:** the power or right of a court to hear a case

**mulatto:** a person of mixed European and African ancestry; technically, a mulatto was considered half European and half African, but the term was more loosely used to describe all people with some African and some European ancestry

---

# ABLEMAN V. BOOTH

<table>
<tr><td>

**DATE**
1859

**AUTHOR**
Roger Brooke Taney

**VOTE**
9-0

</td><td>

**CITATION**
62 U.S. 506

**SIGNIFICANCE**
Upheld the constitutionality of the Fugitive Slave Law of 1850 and held that state courts could not issue a writ of habeas corpus to remove a prisoner from federal custody

</td></tr>
</table>

## Overview

In *Ableman v. Booth*, the Supreme Court upheld the constitutionality of the federal Fugitive Slave Law of 1850. The law authorized the federal government—at taxpayer expense—to seize alleged fugitive slaves, incarcerate them, and transport them back to the states they had come from. Hearings under the law were summary and often conducted without any attorney representing the alleged fugitives, who were not allowed to testify on their own behalf. The law provided for the appointment of federal commissioners in every county in the nation to preside over these summary hearings and then return fugitives to the South (or set the alleged fugitive free if the commissioners ruled against the slaveowner). Commissioners received a fee of $5.00 if they ruled in favor of the alleged slave, and $10.00 if the ruled in favor of the slaveowner.

The law was enormously unpopular in the North and led to protests and spontaneous or planned actions that liberated, or attempted to liberate, Black people seized as fugitives. In 1854 a group of three U.S. deputy marshals and a Missouri slaveowner, Bennami S. Garland, went to Racine, Wisconsin, where Garland seized Joshua Glover as Garland's fugitive slave and brought him, "all bruised and bloodied," to a jail in Milwaukee. He was held in secret, having been taken to the jail at night, but by morning news of the arrest spread. The next day Sherman Miller Booth (1812–1904), a graduate of Yale University, a longtime abolitionist, and a newspaper editor, distributed a handbill that declared, in part: "Citizens of Milwaukee! Shall we have Star Chamber proceedings here? and shall a Man be dragged back to Slavery from our Free Soil, *without an open trial of his right to Liberty?*" Booth then rode through the streets of the city, in Paul Revere fashion, yelling, "To the rescue! Slave catchers are in our midst," urging everyone he saw to gather at the courthouse at two o'clock that afternoon. The secret nature of the arrest led many in the city to fear Glover would be sent back to slavery without even a judicial hearing. A large crowd gathered and heard impassioned speeches from Booth and others. A lawyer who was trying to help Glover told the crowd that the U.S. marshal had declared he would refuse to comply with a writ of habeas corpus from a state judge to bring Glover into court for a fair hearing. Shortly after this, the crowd charged the jail, removed Glover, and eventually sent him to

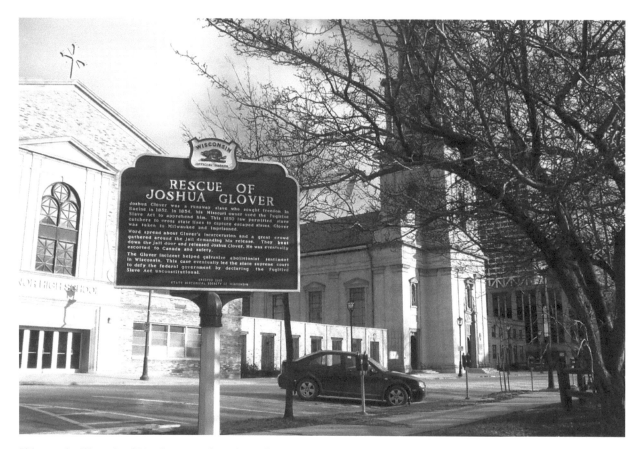

**Wisconsin Historical Marker in Milwaukee identifying where fugitive slave Joshua Glover was rescued by a mob incited by Sherman Booth**
(Wikimedia Commons)

Canada. The U.S. marshal, Stephen V. Ableman, then arrested Sherman Booth and others who had helped organized the rescue, subjecting them to possible fines of $1,000 (about $40,000 in 2023) and six months in prison. As the most prominent leader of the rescue, Booth would become the main target of Ableman and the federal government.

Shortly after the arrest, Justice Abram D. Smith of the Wisconsin Supreme Court issued a writ of habeas corpus, directing Marshal Ableman to release Booth. The U.S. attorney opposed this writ, arguing that a state court could not release someone held in federal custody. Justice Smith asserted that "every citizen has a right to call upon the state authority for protection," and a state "judicial officer" had a duty to "to see that no citizen is imprisoned within the limits of the state . . . except by proper legal and constitutional authority." In many ways this case was a mirror image of the arguments of Virginia in *Martin v. Hunter's Lessee* and *Cohens v. Virginia,* as a jurist in a northern state argued a states' rights position to challenge the constitution-

ality of a federal law that protected slavery. Smith declared the 1850 act to be unconstitutional. While this was a challenge to the federal government, it was not a rejection of the authority of the federal courts, since in 1854 no federal court had actually considered the constitutionality of the new law. Thus, the state court was free to interpret the law as it wished.

Meanwhile, a federal grand jury indicted Booth and others for rescuing Glover. In January 1855 Booth was convicted. U.S. District Judge Andrew G. Miller sentenced Booth to a month in the county jail and a $1,000 fine. The rescue and all these proceedings made national news and gained the attention of the administration of President Franklin Pierce. His attorney general, Caleb Cushing, was already planning to go to the U.S. Supreme Court to overturn the acts of the Wisconsin Supreme Court and did not act after Booth's conviction. However, after another Wisconsin decision led to Booth being let out of jail on a state writ of habeas corpus, the U.S. government decided to appeal to the U.S. Supreme Court.

In response, the Wisconsin Supreme Court refused to send the record of the case to Washington. The case festered until 1858, when the opinions in the Booth cases were published in the official reports of the Wisconsin Supreme Court. The United States Supreme Court used the printed opinions as the "record" of the case. In 1859 the Supreme Court unanimously overturned the Wisconsin decision, and Booth was rearrested and incarcerated in the federal customs house in Milwaukee. He remained in jail after his one-month sentence because he refused to pay his fine. Finally, President James Buchanan remitted his fine (but did not pardon him), and Booth was released from jail the day before Abraham Lincoln was inaugurated on March 4, 1861. Buchanan realized that keeping Booth in jail simply made him martyr and increased antislavery agitation. Booth continued to support Black rights, and in 1865 he successfully litigated to enfranchise Blacks on the same basis as whites in Wisconsin, winning *Gillespie v. Palmer* in the Wisconsin Supreme Court. He went on to a long career in journalism with the Newspaper Union and the *Chicago Tribune*.

Chief Justice Taney's opinion in *Ableman v. Booth* was one of the strongest ever written in asserting the supremacy of the federal government and the federal courts. Usually seen as a supporter for states' rights, he rejected the idea in this opinion.

## Context

Article IV, Section 2, Clause 3 of the U.S. Constitution provides that "No Person held to Service or Labour in one State, under the Laws thereof, escaping into another, shall, in Consequence of any Law or Regulation therein, be discharged from such Service or Labour, but shall be delivered up on Claim of the Party to whom such Service or Labour may be due." The language of the clause suggests that such delivery would be implemented by state-to-state negotiations, similarly to the way fugitives from justice would be extradited when one state requested them from another. The placement of the clause in Article IV, Section 2, supports this understanding, since that section of the Constitution dealt entirely with state-to-state relations and, unlike all other sections in Article IV, delegated no power to Congress.

Despite these linguistic and structural implications, in 1793 Congress passed a Fugitive Slave Law that set out the procedure for removing an alleged fugitive slave. With very few federal judges—most states had only one—the law relied on state jurists for its enforcement. The law provided that state judges would issue a "certificate of removal" for someone claiming a fugitive slave "upon proof to the satisfaction of such Judge or magistrate, either by oral testimony or affidavit taken before and certified by a magistrate of any such State or Territory," that the person was indeed a fugitive slave. The law did not set out any procedure or process, and the law seemed to assume these would be summary hearings without a jury and possibly without a lawyer representing the alleged slave. Anyone interfering with the return of a fugitive could be fined $500 and also be subject to a civil lawsuit for the value of the enslaved person.

Starting in the 1820s the northern states passed "personal liberty laws" to provide due process protections for alleged fugitive and to prevent the kidnapping of their free Black neighbors. In *Prigg v. Pennsylvania*, Justice Joseph Story struck down all these state laws, holding that slaveowners were free to seize and transport their fugitives without any judicial hearing. At this point many northern states declared they would not allow their courts, jails, or police officials to help recover fugitive slaves.

In 1850 Congress passed a new Fugitive Slave Law, which created the first national law enforcement bureaucracy in U.S. history. It called for the appointment of federal commissioners in every county to enforce the law and allowed them to call on the U.S. marshal, the U.S. Army, the U.S. Navy, and state militias to capture and transport fugitives. Under the law, alleged fugitives were prohibited from testifying in their own behalf and denied a jury trial. The law specifically prohibited the use of a writ of habeas corpus to challenge the incarceration of an alleged fugitive. This was in direct violation of the language of the U.S. Constitution, Article I, Section 9, Clause 2, which specifically declares: "The Privilege of the Writ of Habeas Corpus shall not be suspended, unless when in Cases of Rebellion or Invasion the public Safety may require it." The law did, however, prohibit the application for a writ of habeas corpus for people like Booth, who were arrested for violating the law. Finally, as noted above, commissioners received ten dollars if they returned a person to slavery, but only five dollars if they denied the claim of the person trying to take a Black person to the South as a slave. To many, this seemed like a blatant attempt to corrupt the hearings by bribing the commissioners.

From its passage in September 1850 until the Civil War, the law led to rescues and riots in a number of places in the North, including Boston, Massachusetts; Christiana, Pennsylvania; Syracuse, New York; and Oberlin-Wellington, Ohio. The Milwaukee rescue of Joshua Glover was one of the most important of these and gained national attention.

The Wisconsin court's willingness to challenge the constitutionality of the 1850 law was not a direct attack on the Supreme Court or even the Constitution, because no court had ever adjudicated the new statute, and many provisions, such as the denial of a jury trial, the right of an alleged slave to testify, and the suspension of the writ of habeas corpus, seemed to violate the Constitution. Furthermore, at this time there was no set rule whether state courts could grant a writ of habeas corpus to a person in federal custody.

## About the Author

The author of this opinion, Chief Justice Roger Brooke Taney, came from a wealthy slaveholding family in Maryland. He graduated from college in 1796, at age nineteen, at a time when most Americans did not even attend high school. He studied law under Jeremiah Townley Chase, a leading Maryland politician, and married Anne Phoebe Charlton Key, the sister of Francis Scott Key, who would later write "The Star Spangled Banner." The Keys were also a wealthy family, and more politically important than the Taneys. Initially a Federalist, Taney rose quickly in Maryland's political and legal community, serving as a state senator and attorney general of the state. Before 1820 he freed some, but not all, of the slaves he inherited, because as a lawyer he did not need so many. Nonetheless, there would always be slaves in his household.

Taney was an early supporter of Andrew Jackson and in 1831 became Jackson's acting secretary of war. In July 1831 he became attorney general of the United States. In 1832, as attorney general, he wrote an opinion to President Jackson asserting that no Black person could ever be a citizen. He told the president that Blacks had no political or legal rights except those they

might "enjoy" at the "sufferance" and "mercy" of whites and that Blacks, "even when free," were a "degraded class" whose "privileges" were "accorded to them as a matter of kindness and benevolence rather than right." In 1857, in *Dred Scott v. Sandford*, Taney would use almost identical language to turn his hostility to free African Americans into precedent in constitutional law. As attorney general, he drafted Andrew Jackson's famous veto of the bill to recharter the Bank of the United States, and as acting secretary of the treasury he hurriedly removed federal deposits from the bank, which eventually helped put the nation into a major depression following the Panic of 1837.

In 1836 Taney became chief justice of the U.S. Supreme Court. He would serve until 1864. On the Court, Taney generally supported states' rights in economic matters and limitations on the federal government. He favored local control of the economy rather than the expansive notion of a national economy reflected in the opinions of John Marshall. He was aggressively proslavery and deeply opposed to abolitionism. His brother-in-law, Francis Scott Key, as the U.S. attorney for the District of Columbia, prosecuted whites who possessed antislavery literature. Such case never came before the Supreme Court, but privately Taney supported them. Taney is most remembered for his deeply racist opinion in *Dred Scott*, which he wrote just two years before the *Booth* case. Despite the fact the free Blacks voted on the same basis as whites in eight states when the Constitution was ratified, Taney asserted in *Dred Scott* that they were never part of the American political community and, moreover, could *never be* part of that community. He asserted that Blacks "no rights which the white man was bound to respect." He was so committed to making Blacks, even free Blacks, second-class citizens that he harassed and berated Justice Benjamin Robbins Curtis, one of the two dissenters in *Dred Scott*, to the point that Curtis resigned from the Court a few months after the decision.

Taney's views on states' rights were inconsistent in cases involving slavery. For example, in *Prigg v. Pennsylvania* (1842) he asserted in a concurring opinion that the federal government should have the power to force the northern states to spend their resources to help capture fugitive slaves. Similarly, in *Ableman v. Booth* he completely rejected Wisconsin's claim that it could protect its own citizens from an arbitrary federal law. However, in his last slavery case before the Civil

War, *Kentucky v. Dennison* (1861), he protected states' rights in order prevent the Lincoln administration from ordering state governors to help defend the United States from an expect war with the Confederate States. During the Civil War, he did everything in his power to obstruct the Lincoln administration's efforts to preserve the Union. He secretly wrote an opinion declaring the Emancipation Proclamation unconstitutional, but no case ever reached his court, and the draft remained unused in his private papers.

## Explanation and Analysis of the Document

Shortly after Glover's rescue, the federal commissioner in Wisconsin, Winfield Smith, charged Sherman Booth with violating the 1850 law. Initially one of Booth's supporters guaranteed Booth's appearance in court for a trial, and he was let out on bail. However, on May 26 Booth surrendered to the U.S. marshal, and he was put back in jail. The next day Booth applied for a write of habeas corpus from Justice Abram Smith, directed at the Marshal Ableman. Booth asserted that the 1850 law was unconstitutional, and thus his arrest was illegal. Shortly after this, Justice Smith ruled in Booth's favor, and the Wisconsin Supreme Court ordered the U.S. marshal to release him. This set up a conflict between the state and the federal government and allowed Booth to challenge the constitutionality of the 1850 law. In June, Marshal Ableman appealed to the full Wisconsin court to overrule Justice Smith. In July the full Wisconsin court sided with Booth, who remained free. Ableman then turned to the U.S. Supreme Court to overturn the Wisconsin court. The Supreme Court then ordered Wisconsin to send the record of the case to Washington for review and ordered Booth to respond to Ableman's arguments.

In the meantime, Booth had been indicted under the 1850 law and was once more arrested. He once again asked for writ of habeas corpus, but the Wisconsin court declined to issue the writ. The Wisconsin court believed the actions of Commissioner Smith (no relation to Wisconsin Supreme Court justice Smith) had been unconstitutional, but in this second requestion for a writ of habeas corpus, titled *Ex parte Sherman M. Booth*, the Wisconsin court respected the power of the federal government to indict Booth and try him. In January 1855

the federal government put Booth on trial, and despite eloquent arguments of his lawyer on the immorality of the 1850 law, the jury convicted Booth. The U.S. district judge, Andrew G. Millers, sentence Booth to thirty days in the county jail and a $1,000 fine.

In late January 1855, Booth and his codefendant John Ryecraft, who had also been convicted, asked the Wisconsin Supreme Court for another writ of habeas corpus. In February the state Supreme Court heard the case. The U.S. government did not send a lawyer, apparently refusing to acknowledge that the Wisconsin Supreme Court could overrule the federal court. Justice Smith asserted at this time that "[t]he power to guard and protect the liberty of the individual citizen is inherent in every government; one which it cannot relinquish, which was reserved to the states [and] without which they could not exist, because it is obvious that they could claim no allegiance or support from their citizens whom they had not the power to protect." A unanimous Wisconsin court concluded that the federal government had no jurisdiction over Booth because it had not properly charged him with a federal crime, because the indictment failed to assert that Glover was a slave, and because the federal government never provided any evidence that he was one. Once again, the Wisconsin Supreme Court set Booth free.

The federal government then appealed to the U.S. Supreme Court, and the Supreme Court sent what is called a writ of error to the Wisconsin court, requiring that it send the record of the case to Washington. The Wisconsin court ordered its clerks not to rely to the Supreme Court. This was a clear violation of the Judiciary Act of 1793, which required states to comply with a writ of error from the Supreme Court. Wisconsin, in effect, was nullifying a federal law.

In May 1856 Chief Justice Taney postponed any consideration of the case to give the Wisconsin court time to send the record. This was an election year, and Taney and the slaveholding majority on the Court may have been reluctant to have a major confrontation over the fugitive slave law leading up to the election. For the same reason, that spring the Court declined to decide the case of *Dred Scott v. Sandford* but held it over for reargument, which would occur after the 1856 election.

The Court finally heard arguments in the case in January 1859, nearly two years after the court issued its controversial decision in *Dred Scott* in March 1857. The Wisconsin Supreme Court still had not sent the record of the Booth case to the Supreme Court. But by this time the Wisconsin Supreme Court had published its opinions in the Booth case, and the Taney Court accepted this printed report as the "record" of the case.

Chief Justice Taney, speaking for a unanimous Court, set out this history in great detail at the first eight pages of his opinion. He then arrived at the key legal question: Could a state court remove a prisoner from federal custody on a writ of habeas corpus? Taney summarized this issue: "the State court have . . . determined that their decision is final and conclusive upon all the courts of the United States, and ordered their clerk to disregard and refuse obedience to the writ of error issued by this court, pursuant to the [Judiciary] act of Congress of 1789, to bring here for examination and revision the judgment of the State court."

Taney could not have been shocked by such arguments, since southern states courts had been making similar arguments since the early part of the century. Furthermore, slave-state politicians had been arguing for such state powers almost since the beginning of the country. But Taney ignored all this history and asserted, disingenuously, "These propositions are new in the jurisprudence of the United States, as well as of the States; and the supremacy of the State courts over the courts of the United States, in cases arising under the Constitution and laws of the United States, is now for the first time asserted and acted upon in the Supreme Court of a State." They were hardly new. Thomas Jefferson and James Madison had made similar arguments in the Virginia and Kentucky Resolutions of 1798 and 1799. (Indeed, a protest meeting denounced the arrest of both Glover and Booth by directly quoting the Virginia and Kentucky resolutions.) Lawyers for Virginia had made similar arguments in *Martin v. Hunter's Lessee* and *Cohens v. Virginia*.

Taney answered these arguments with an assertation of the supremacy of the federal courts as powerful as anything John Marshall had articulated. He asserted that what Wisconsin was trying to do would destroy all federal law and that "no offence against the laws of the United States can be punished by their own courts, without the permission and according to the judgment of the courts of the State in which the party happens to be imprisoned." Upholding the Wisconsin court

would, in effect, destroy the nation: "It would seem to be hardly necessary to do more than state the result to which these decisions of the State courts must inevitably lead. It is, of itself, a sufficient and conclusive answer; for no one will suppose that a Government which has now lasted nearly seventy years, enforcing its laws by its own tribunals, and preserving the union of the States, could have lasted a single year, or fulfilled the high trusts committed to it, if offences against its laws could not have been punished without the consent of the State in which the culprit was found."

Taney described the national government as being "supreme, and strong enough to execute its own laws by its own tribunals, without interruption from a State or from State authorities. And it was evident that anything short of this would be inadequate to the main objects for which the Government was established; and that local interests, local passions or prejudices, incited and fostered by individuals for sinister purposes, would lead to acts of aggression and injustice by one State upon the rights of another, which would ultimately terminate in violence and force, unless there was a common arbiter between them, armed with power enough to protect and guard the rights of all, by appropriate laws, to be carried into execution peacefully by its judicial tribunals." As Chief Justice Marshall had in *Cohens v. Virginia*, Taney quoted the Supremacy Clause of the Constitution: "this Constitution, and the laws of the United States which shall be passed in pursuance thereof, and all treaties made, or which shall be made, under the authority of the United States, shall be the supreme law of the land, and the judges in every State shall be bound thereby, anything in the Constitution or laws of any State to the contrary notwithstanding."

After describing the supremacy of the Supreme Court for a few pages, he added that Fugitive Slave Law of 1850 was fully constitutional in all its provisions and that the Wisconsin Supreme Court was reversed.

In some ways Taney's opinion stood in stark contrast to his opinion in *Dred Scott v. Sandford* (1857), where he had struck down the Compromise of 1820, also called the Missouri Compromise, which had been the basis of all federal regulation of the federal territories, in order to accommodate the claim of Missouri that it could ignore the 1820 law. In other words, Taney was happy to protect slavery by striking down a major federal law and support the states' rights claims of

Missouri, and he was also happy to reject the states' rights claims of Wisconsin to support slavery and the Fugitive Slave Law of 1850.

Despite the context this case and its proslavey implications, few constitutional scholars would disagree with the result or Taney's argument. If the states could easily overrule or ignore federal laws, the United States could not exist as country. However, as noted, two years later, in *Kentucky v. Dennison*, Taney would reject the text of the Constitution to support states' rights because that would protect slavery.

## Impact

The immediate impact of this case was the confirmation, by the U.S. Supreme Court, that the fugitive slave law of 1850 was constitutional, although that was not the main issue in the case. There are strong reasons to think the law was not in fact constitutional, but given the makeup of the court—five slaveowners, three proslavery northern Democrats, and one antislavery justice from Ohio—it was unlikely the Court would even consider overturning the law.

The more significant impact was Chief Justice Taney's powerful assertion of the supremacy of the Supreme Court and the absolute obligation for the state courts to cooperate with a case brought to the Supreme Court. This was the first case in which the Supreme Court held that state courts could not issue a writ of habeas corpus to release prisoners from federal custody. This makes it an important and enduring case to this day.

Southerners and northern Democrats, who generally supported the South and opposed any antislavery activity, were delighted by Taney's opinion. They argued that the case supported "law and order" and required that the free states support the fugitive slave law, although in reality the case stood for the proposition that the northern states could not interfere with its enforcement. A Democratic paper asserted that the actions of the Wisconsin court had been "totally illegal and virtually revolutionary." The paper was happy that this "revolutionary" act had been stopped by the Supreme Court.

Republican papers denounced the opinion. The *New York Evening Post* declared Taney's opinion was "fatal to the reserved rights of the States" and "nothing more dangerous to the securities of the individual, can well be conceived, than the authority claimed for [the federal courts] in the recent decision of Judge Taney." Wisconsin's legislature passed a resolution condemning the decision as "an act of undelegated power, and therefore without authority, void, and of no force." Wisconsin declared that the states "being sovereign and independent have the unquestionable right to judge [the Constitution's] infraction; and that a positive defiance of those sovereignties, of all unauthorized acts done or attempted to be done under color of that instrument, is the rightful remedy."

Positions on states' rights and federal power had been reversed. Since the late 1790s, southern states and Democrats had support states' rights with language almost identical to what the Wisconsin legislature said, often talking about the "sovereign and independent" nature of the states. Now northerners and opponents of slavery were making such arguments, while reliably states'-rights politicians and editorialists in the South were condemning such claims.

Meanwhile, Booth remained in jail until August 1860, when a mob overwhelmed his jailors and freed him. He did not leave the state or try to hide from the federal marshal but traveled openly, giving speeches and openly carrying a pistol, which he called his "little *habeas corpus*," while large crowds shielded him from capture. Federal authorities recaptured him in October, and he remained incarcerated until President Buchanan remitted his fine in March 1861 and he was released.

Taney wrote a dramatically proslavery decision supporting federal supremacy and attacking states' rights. This was useful to the South and slavery in 1859, but by the time Lincoln entered the White House, seven Deep South states had seceded (four more would soon follow), and national power was in the hands of a man who hated slavery—he famously wrote "If slavery is not wrong, than nothing is wrong"—and was fully prepared to use federal power to preserve the Union and insure the supremacy of the Constitution against the Confederate states and against slavery.

The U.S. Supreme Court has cited *Booth* in only 32 cases, but four of them were important for civil liberties and civil rights. In 1872, in *Tarble's Case*, the Supreme

Court relied heavily on *Ableman v. Booth* to overturn a habeas corpus decision from Wisconsin. The case involved Edward Tarble, who lied about his age and gave a false name to enlist in the U.S. Army when he was under the age of eighteen. His father asked for a writ of habeas corpus from the Wisconsin courts to have the Army release him and return Edward to his father, who was still his legal guardian. The Wisconsin Supreme Court sided with Tarble, and in an 8–1 decision the U.S. Supreme Court reversed Wisconsin's decision, citing and quoting from the *Booth* case. This decision was not tainted by the Fugitive Slave Law but simply affirmed that the states could not use habeas corpus to remove someone from federal custody.

In *Ex parte Siebold* (1880), the court upheld federal conviction of a corrupt election official in Maryland. He had been charged under the Reconstruction-era enforcement laws designed to protect white voters. The Court cited *Booth* in support of its refusal to issue a writ of habeas corpus for the convicted election official.

In the Civil Rights Cases (1883), the Court struck down the federal Civil Rights Act of 1875, which prohibited racial discrimination on railroads, in hotels, and in other places of public accommodation. In an important dissent, Justice John Marshall Harlan argued that Congress had the power to pass such a law. He pointed out that before the Civil War, Congress protected the rights of slaveowners to chase down fugitive slaves in the North. He quoted *Booth*, noting that the Court had upheld the 1850 fugitive slave law because the law was, "in all of its provisions, fully authorized by the Constitution of the United States." He argued that under the Fourteenth Amendment, the Court should apply this standard to protect the civil rights of free Blacks.

An equally ironic, but more successful, use of the case occurred a century after the *Booth* decision, in *Cooper v. Aaron* (1958), which came out of the attempt to integrate the public schools in Little Rock, Arkansas. Governor Orville Faubus of Arkansas prevented the integration of Central High School in Little Rock, asserting that the Supreme Court's decision in *Brown v. Board of Education* (1954) did not apply to his state because Arkansas had not been a party to the case. Quoting *Marbury v. Madison* (1803), a unanimous Supreme Court explained to the governor that the Constitution was "the fundamental and paramount law of the nation" and that "it is emphatically the province and duty of the judicial department to say what the law is." A few sentences later, the Court reminded Governor Faubus and the Little Rock school board that under the supremacy clause of the Constitution, all state officials were "solemnly committed by oath taken pursuant to Article VI, Clause 3, "to support this Constitution." The Court then noted: "Chief Justice Taney's opinion in *Booth*, speaking for a unanimous Court in 1859, said that this requirement" in the supremacy clause to support the Constitution "reflected the framers' 'anxiety to preserve it [the Constitution] in full force, in all its powers, and to guard against resistance to or evasion of its authority, on the part of a State.'"

Thus, a decision aimed at protecting slavery and incarcerating someone who freed a slave ironically provided part of the basis, a century later, to support school integration and the power of the federal government and the Supreme Court to help end legalized segregation in the former slave states.

## Questions for Further Study

1. The U.S. Constitution declared that fugitive slaves should be "delivered upon the Claim" of a slave owner. This was supported by the Fugitive Slave Law of 1850. How does this case raise the fundamental question of when it is permissible to break the law to protect human rights and human dignity?

2. In 1854 when this case began, there were very few federal judges in the United States. Under Taney's opinion, if you were in federal custody, then to receive a writ of habeas corpus, you had to apply to a federal judge. With so few federal judges, it might be very difficult for a prison to apply to a federal court for relief. Should the Court have considered this in flatly denying the right of a state to issue a writ of habeas corpus for someone in federal custody? Please explain.

3. This case is ultimately about protecting slavery, but it is remembered as being about the supremacy of the Constitution, the Court, and the laws of Congress. Which do you think it should it be remembered for?

4. This case is seen as a high point of northern states' arguments against slavery and of proslavery nationalism. During the Civil War, Jefferson Davis, the Confederate president, and other southerners claimed they were seceding to protect states' rights. However, in Booth they had cheered the Supreme Court's vigorous opposition to states' rights and support for a strong national government. How does this affect the notion that the Civil War was about states' rights?

## Further Reading

### *Books*

Baker, R. Howard. *Rescue of Joshua Glover: A Fugitive Slave, The Constitution, and the Coming of the Civil War.* Athens, OH: Ohio University Press, 2006.

Campbell, Stanley W. *The Slave Catchers: Enforcement of the Fugitive Slave Law of 1850.* Chapel Hill: University of North Carolina Press, 1970.

Current, Richard. *History of Wisconsin,* Volume 2: *The Civil War Era, 1848–1873. Madison: Wisconsin State Historical Society, 1976.*

Finkelman, Paul. *An Imperfect Union: Slavery, Federalism and Comity.* Chapel Hill: University of North Carolina Press, 1981.

Finkelman, Paul. *Slavery in the Courtroom.* Washington, DC: Library of Congress, 1985.

Finkelman, Paul. *Supreme Injustice: Slavery in the Nation's Highest Court.* Cambridge: Harvard University Press, 2018.

Lubet, Steven. *Fugitive Justice: Runaways, Rescuers, and Slavery on Trial.* Cambridge: Harvard University Press, 2010.

Morris, Thomas D. *Free Men All: The Personal Liberty Laws of the North, 1780 to 1861.* Baltimore: Johns Hopkins University Press, 1974.

## Further Reading

### Articles

Maltz, Earl. "Slavery, Federalism, and the Constitution: Ableman v. Booth and the Struggle over Fugitive Slaves." *Cleveland State Law Review* 56 (2008) 83.

Parrish, Jenni. "The Booth Cases: Final Step to the Civil War." *Willamette Law Review* 29 (1993): 237.

Ranney, Joseph A. "'Suffering the Agonies of Their Righteousness': The Rise and Fall of the States Rights Movement in Wisconsin, 1854–1861." *Wisconsin Magazine of History* 75, no. 2 (1992): 83.

—Commentary by Paul Finkelman

# ABLEMAN V. BOOTH

## Document Text

### *Mr. Chief Justice TANEY delivered the opinion of the Court*

The plaintiff in error in the first of these cases is the marshal of the United States for the district of Wisconsin, and the two cases have arisen out of the same transaction, and depend, to some extent, upon the same principles. On that account, they have been argued and considered together; and the following are the facts as they appear in the transcripts before us:

Sherman M. Booth was charged before Winfield Smith, a commissioner duly appointed by the District Court of the United States for the district of Wisconsin, with having, on the 11th day of March, 1854, aided and abetted, at Milwaukee, in the said district, the escape of a fugitive slave from the deputy marshal, who had him in custody under a warrant issued by the district judge of the United States for that district, under the act of Congress of September 18, 1850.

Upon the examination before the commissioner, he was satisfied that an offence had been committed as charged, and that there was probable cause to believe that Booth had been guilty of it, and thereupon held him to bail to appear and answer before the District Court of the United States for the district of Wisconsin on the first Monday in July then next ensuing. But on the 26th of May, his bail or surety in the recognisance delivered him to the marshal, in the presence of the commissioner, and requested the commissioner to recommit Booth to the custody of the marshal, and he having failed to recognise again for his appearance before the District Court, the commissioner committed him to the custody of the marshal, to be delivered to the keeper of the jail until he should be discharged by due course of law.

Booth made application on the next day, the 27th of May, to A. D. Smith, one of the justices of the Supreme Court of the State of Wisconsin, for a writ of habeas corpus, stating that he was restrained of his liberty by Stephen V. R. Ableman, marshal of the United States for that district, under the warrant of commitment hereinbefore mentioned, and alleging that his imprisonment was illegal because the act of Congress of September 18, 1850, was unconstitutional and void, and also that the warrant was defective, and did not describe the offence created by that act, even if the act were valid.

Upon this application, the justice, on the same day, issued the writ of habeas corpus, directed to the marshal, requiring him forthwith to have the body of Booth before him (the said justice) together with the time and cause of his imprisonment. The marshal thereupon, on the day above mentioned, produced Booth and made his return, stating that he was received into his custody as marshal on the day before, and held in custody by virtue of the warrant of the commissioner above mentioned, a copy of which he annexed to and returned with the writ.

To this return Booth demurred, as not sufficient in law to justify his detention. And upon the hearing the justice decided that his detention was illegal, and ordered the marshal to discharge him and set him at liberty, which was accordingly done.

Afterwards, on the 9th of June in the same year, the marshal applied to the Supreme Court of the State for a certiorari, setting forth in his application the proceedings hereinbefore mentioned, and charging that the release of Booth by the justice was erroneous and unlawful, and praying that his proceedings might be brought before the Supreme Court of the State for revision.

The certiorari was allowed on the same day, and the writ was accordingly issued on the 12th of the same month, and returnable on the third Tuesday of the month, and on the 20th, the return was made by the justice, stating the proceedings as hereinbefore mentioned.

The case was argued before the Supreme Court of the State, and, on the 19th of July, it pronounced its judgment, affirming the decision of the associate justice discharging Booth from imprisonment, with costs against Ableman, the marshal.

Afterwards, on the 26th of October, the marshal sued out a writ of error, returnable to this court on the first Monday of December, 1854, in order to bring the judgment here for revision, and the defendant in error was regularly cited to appear on that day, and the record and proceedings were certified to this court by the clerk of the State court in the usual form, in obedience to the writ of error. And on the 4th of December, Booth, the defendant in error, filed a memorandum in writing in this court, stating that he had been cited to appear here in this case, and that he submitted it to the judgment of this court on the reasoning in the argument and opinions in the printed pamphlets therewith sent.

After the judgment was entered in the Supreme Court of Wisconsin, and before the writ of error was sued out, the State court entered on its record that, in the final judgment it had rendered, the validity of the act of Congress of September 18, 1850, and of February 12, 1793, and the authority of the marshal to hold the defendant in his custody under the process mentioned in his return to the writ of habeas corpus were respectively drawn in question, and the decision of the court in the final judgment was against their validity, respectively.

This certificate was not necessary to give this court jurisdiction, because the proceedings, upon their face, show that these questions arose, and how they were decided, but it shows that, at that time, the Supreme Court of Wisconsin did not question their obligation

to obey the writ of error, nor the authority of this court to reexamine their judgment in the cases specified. And the certificate is given for the purpose of placing distinctly on the record the points that were raised and decided in that court, in order that this court might have no difficulty in exercising its appellate power and pronouncing its judgment upon all of them.

We come now to the second case. At the January term of the District Court of the United States for the district of Wisconsin, after Booth had been set at liberty and after the transcript of the proceedings in the case above mentioned had been returned to and filed in this court, the grand jury found a bill of indictment against Booth for the offence with which he was charged before the commissioner and from which the State court had discharged him. The indictment was found on the 4th of January, 1855. On the 9th, a motion was made by counsel on behalf of the accused to quash the indictment, which was overruled by the court, and he thereupon pleaded not guilty, upon which issue was joined. On the 10th, a jury was called and appeared in court, when he challenged the array, but the challenge was overruled and the jury empaneled. The trial, it appears, continued from day to day, until the 13th, when the jury found him guilty in the manner and form in which he stood indicted in the fourth and fifth counts. On the 16th, he moved for a new trial and in arrest of judgment, which motions were argued on the 20th, and on the 23d the court overruled the motions and sentenced the prisoner to be imprisoned for one month, and to pay a fine of $1,000 and the costs of prosecution, and that he remain in custody until the sentence was complied with.

We have stated more particularly these proceedings from a sense of justice to the District Court, as they show that every opportunity of making his defence was afforded him, and that his case was fully heard and considered.

On the 26th of January, three days after the sentence was passed, the prisoner by his counsel filed his petition in the Supreme Court of the State, and with his petition filed a copy of the proceedings in the District Court, and also affidavits from the foreman and one other member of the jury who tried him, stating that their verdict was guilty on the fourth and fifth counts, and not guilty on the other three, and stated in his petition that his imprisonment was illegal because the fugitive slave law was unconstitutional, that the District Court had no jurisdiction to try or punish him for the matter charged against him, and that the proceedings and sentence of that court were absolute nullities in law. Various other objections to the proceedings are alleged which are unimportant in the questions now before the court, and need not, therefore, be particularly stated. On the next day, the 27th, the court directed two writs of habeas corpus to be issued, one to the marshal and one to the sheriff of Milwaukee, to whose actual keeping the prisoner was committed by the marshal, by order of the District Court. The habeas corpus directed each of them to produce the body of the prisoner and make known the cause of his imprisonment immediately after the receipt of the writ.

On the 30th of January the marshal made his return, not acknowledging the jurisdiction but stating the sentence of the District Court as his authority; that the prisoner was delivered to, and was then in the actual keeping of the sheriff of Milwaukee county by order of the court, and he therefore had no control of the body of the prisoner; and if the sheriff had not received him, he should have so reported to the District Court, and should have conveyed him to some other place or prison, as the court should command.

On the same day, the sheriff produced the body of Booth before the State court, and returned that he had been committed to his custody by the marshal by virtue of a transcript, a true copy of which was annexed to his return, and which was the only process or authority by which he detained him.

This transcript was a full copy of the proceedings and sentence in the District Court of the United States, as hereinbefore stated. To this return the accused, by his counsel, filed a general demurrer.

The court ordered the hearing to be postponed until the 2d of February, and notice to be given to the district attorney of the United States. It was accordingly heard on that day, and on the next (February 3d), the court decided that the imprisonment was illegal, and ordered and adjudged that Booth be, and he was by that judgment, forever discharged from that imprisonment and restraint, and he was accordingly set at liberty.

On the 21st of April next following, the Attorney General of the United States presented a petition to the

Chief Justice of the Supreme Court, stating briefly the facts in the case and at the same time presenting an exemplification of the proceedings hereinbefore stated, duly certified by the clerk of the State court and averring in his petition that the State court had no jurisdiction in the case, and praying that a writ of error might issue to bring its judgment before this court to correct the error. The writ of error was allowed and issued, and, according to the rules and practice of the court, was returnable on the first Monday of December, 1855, and a citation for the defendant in error to appear on that day was issued by the Chief Justice at the same time.

No return having been made to this writ, the Attorney General, on the 1st of February, 1856, filed affidavits showing that the writ of error had been duly served on the clerk of the Supreme Court of Wisconsin, at his office, on the 30th of May, 1855, and the citation served on the defendant in error on the 28th of June, in the same year. And also the affidavit of the district attorney of the United States for the district of Wisconsin, setting forth that when he served the writ of error upon the clerk, as above mentioned, he was informed by the clerk, and has also been informed by one of the justices of the Supreme Court, which released Booth,

*"that the court had directed the clerk to make no return to the writ of error, and to enter no order upon the journals or records of the court concerning the same."*

And, upon these proofs, the Attorney General moved the court for an order upon the clerk to make return to the writ of error, on or before the first day of the next ensuing term of this court. The rule was accordingly laid, and, on the 22d of July, 1856, the Attorney General filed with the clerk of this court the affidavit of the marshal of the district of Wisconsin that he had served the rule on the clerk on the 7th of the month above mentioned, and no return having been made, the Attorney General, on the 27th of February, 1857, moved for leave to file the certified copy of the record of the Supreme Court of Wisconsin, which he had produced with his application for the writ of error, and to docket the case in this court in conformity with a motion to that effect made at the last term. And the court thereupon, on the 6th of March, 1857, ordered the copy of the record filed by the Attorney General to be received and entered on the docket of this court, to have the same effect and legal operation as if returned by the clerk with the writ of error, and that the case stand for argument at the next ensuing term, without further notice to either party.

The case was accordingly docketed, but was not reached for argument in the regular order and practice of the court until the present term.

This detailed statement of the proceedings in the different courts has appeared to be necessary in order to form a just estimate of the action of the different tribunals in which it has been heard, and to account for the delay in the final decision of a case, which, from its character, would seem to have demanded prompt action. The first case, indeed, was reached for trial two terms ago. But as the two cases are different portions of the same prosecution for the same offence, they unavoidably, to some extent, involve the same principles of law, and it would hardly have been proper to hear and decide the first before the other was ready for hearing and decision. They have accordingly been argued together, by the Attorney General of the United States, at the present term. No counsel has in either case appeared for the defendant in error. But we have the pamphlet arguments filed and referred to by Booth in the first case, as hereinbefore mentioned, also the opinions and arguments of the Supreme Court of Wisconsin, and of the judges who compose it, in full, and are enabled, therefore, to see the grounds on which they rely to support their decisions.

It will be seen from the foregoing statement of facts that a judge of the Supreme Court of the State of Wisconsin in the first of these cases, claimed and exercised the right to supervise and annul the proceedings of a commissioner of the United States, and to discharge a prisoner who had been committed by the commissioner for an offence against the laws of this Government, and that this exercise of power by the judge was afterwards sanctioned and affirmed by the Supreme Court of the State.

In the second case, the State court has gone a step further, and claimed and exercised jurisdiction over the proceedings and judgment of a District Court of the United States, and, upon a summary and collateral proceeding by habeas corpus, has set aside and annulled its judgment and discharged a prisoner who had been tried and found guilty of an offence against the laws of the United States and sentenced to imprisonment by the District Court.

And it further appears that the State court have not only claimed and exercised this jurisdiction, but have also determined that their decision is final and conclusive upon all the courts of the United States, and ordered their clerk to disregard and refuse obedience to the writ of error issued by this court, pursuant to the act of Congress of 1789, to bring here for examination and revision the judgment of the State court.

These propositions are new in the jurisprudence of the United States, as well as of the States; and the supremacy of the State courts over the courts of the United States, in cases arising under the Constitution and laws of the United States, is now for the first time asserted and acted upon in the Supreme Court of a State.

The supremacy is not, indeed, set forth distinctly and broadly, in so many words, in the printed opinions of the judges. It is intermixed with elaborate discussions of different provisions in the fugitive slave law, and of the privileges and power of the writ of habeas corpus. But the paramount power of the State court lies at the foundation of these decisions, for their commentaries upon the provisions of that law, and upon the privileges and power of the writ of habeas corpus, were out of place, and their judicial action upon them without authority of law, unless they had the power to revise and control the proceedings in the criminal case of which they were speaking, and their judgments releasing the prisoner and disregarding the writ of error from this court can rest upon no other foundation.

If the judicial power exercised in this instance has been reserved to the States, no offence against the laws of the United States can be punished by their own courts without the permission and according to the judgment of the courts of the State in which the party happens to be imprisoned, for if the Supreme Court of Wisconsin possessed the power it has exercised in relation to offences against the act of Congress in question, it necessarily follows that they must have the same judicial authority in relation to any other law of the United States, and, consequently, their supervising and controlling power would embrace the whole criminal code of the United States, and extend to offences against our revenue laws, or any other law intended to guard the different departments of the General Government from fraud or violence. And it would embrace all crimes, from the highest to the lowest; including felonies, which are punished with death, as well as misdemeanors, which are punished by imprisonment. And, moreover, if the power is possessed by the Supreme Court of the State of Wisconsin, it must belong equally to every other State in the Union when the prisoner is within its territorial limits, and it is very certain that the State courts would not always agree in opinion, and it would often happen that an act which was admitted to be an offence, and justly punished, in one State would be regarded as innocent, and indeed as praiseworthy, in another.

It would seem to be hardly necessary to do more than state the result to which these decisions of the State courts must inevitably lead. It is, of itself, a sufficient and conclusive answer, for no one will suppose that a Government which has now lasted nearly seventy years, enforcing its laws by its own tribunals and preserving the union of the States, could have lasted a single year, or fulfilled the high trusts committed to it, if offences against its laws could not have been punished without the consent of the State in which the culprit was found.

The judges of the Supreme Court of Wisconsin do not distinctly state from what source they suppose they have derived this judicial power. There can be no such thing as judicial authority unless it is conferred by a Government or sovereignty, and if the judges and courts of Wisconsin possess the jurisdiction they claim, they must derive it either from the United States or the State. It certainly has not been conferred on them by the United States, and it is equally clear it was not in the power of the State to confer it, even if it had attempted to do so, for no State can authorize one of its judges or courts to exercise judicial power, by habeas corpus or otherwise, within the jurisdiction of another and independent Government. And although the State of Wisconsin is sovereign within its territorial limits to a certain extent, yet that sovereignty is limited and restricted by the Constitution of the United States. And the powers of the General Government, and of the State, although both exist and are exercised within the same territorial limits, are yet separate and distinct sovereignties, acting separately and independently of each other within their respective spheres. And the sphere of action appropriated to the United States is as far beyond the reach of the judicial process issued by a State judge or a State court, as if the line of division was traced by landmarks and monuments visible to the eye. And the State of Wisconsin had no more

power to authorize these proceedings of its judges and courts than it would have had if the prisoner had been confined in Michigan, or in any other State of the Union, for an offence against the laws of the State in which he was imprisoned.

It is, however, due to the State to say that we do not find this claim of paramount jurisdiction in the State courts over the courts of the United States asserted or countenanced by the Constitution or laws of the State. We find it only in the decisions of the judges of the Supreme Court. Indeed, at the very time these decisions were made, there was a statute of the State which declares that a person brought up on a habeas corpus shall be remanded if it appears that he is confined:

"1st. By virtue of process, by any court or judge of the United States, in a case where such court or judge has exclusive jurisdiction; or,"

"2d. By virtue of the final judgment or decree of any competent court of civil or criminal jurisdiction."

Even, therefore, if these cases depended upon the laws of Wisconsin, it would be difficult to find in these provisions such a grant of judicial power as the Supreme Court claims to have derived from the State.

But, as we have already said, questions of this kind must always depend upon the Constitution and laws of the United States, and not of a State. The Constitution was not formed merely to guard the States against danger from foreign nations, but mainly to secure union and harmony at home, for if this object could be attained, there would be but little danger from abroad, and, to accomplish this purpose, it was felt by the statesmen who framed the Constitution and by the people who adopted it that it was necessary that many of the rights of sovereignty which the States then possessed should be ceded to the General Government, and that, in the sphere of action assigned to it, it should be supreme, and strong enough to execute its own laws by its own tribunals, without interruption from a State or from State authorities. And it was evident that anything short of this would be inadequate to the main objects for which the Government was established, and that local interests, local passions or prejudices, incited and fostered by individuals for sinister purposes, would lead to acts of aggression and injustice by one State upon the rights of another, which would ultimately terminate in violence and force unless there was a common arbiter between them, armed with power enough to protect and guard the rights of all by appropriate laws to be carried into execution peacefully by its judicial tribunals.

The language of the Constitution by which this power is granted is too plain to admit of doubt or to need comment. It declares that

"this Constitution, and the laws of the United States which shall be passed in pursuance thereof, and all treaties made, or which shall be made, under the authority of the United States, shall be the supreme law of the land, and the judges in every State shall be bound thereby, anything in the Constitution or laws of any State to the contrary notwithstanding."

But the supremacy thus conferred on this Government could not peacefully be maintained unless it was clothed with judicial power equally paramount in authority to carry it into execution, for if left to the courts of justice of the several States, conflicting decisions would unavoidably take place, and the local tribunals could hardly be expected to be always free from the local influences of which we have spoken. And the Constitution and laws and treaties of the United States, and the powers granted to the Federal Government, would soon receive different interpretations in different States, and the Government of the United States would soon become one thing in one State and another thing in another. It was essential, therefore, to its very existence as a Government that it should have the power of establishing courts of justice, altogether independent of State power, to carry into effect its own laws, and that a tribunal should be established in which all cases which might arise under the Constitution and laws and treaties of the United States, whether in a State court or a court of the United States, should be finally and conclusively decided. Without such a tribunal, it is obvious that there would be no uniformity of judicial decision, and that the supremacy, (which is but another name for independence) so carefully provided in the clause of the Constitution above referred to could not possibly be maintained peacefully unless it was associated with this paramount judicial authority.

Accordingly, it was conferred on the General Government in clear, precise, and comprehensive terms. It is declared that its judicial power shall (among other

subjects enumerated) extend to all cases in law and equity arising under the Constitution and laws of the United States, and that, in such cases, as well as the others there enumerated, this court shall have appellate jurisdiction both as to law and fact, with such exceptions and under such regulations as Congress shall make. The appellate power, it will be observed, is conferred on this court in all cases or suits in which such a question shall arise. It is not confined to suits in the inferior courts of the United States, but extends to all cases where such a question arises, whether it be in a judicial tribunal of a State or of the United States. And it is manifest that this ultimate appellate power in a tribunal created by the Constitution itself was deemed essential to secure the independence and supremacy of the General Government in the sphere of action assigned to it, to make the Constitution and laws of the United States uniform, and the same in every State, and to guard against evils which would inevitably arise from conflicting opinions between the courts of a State and of the United States, if there was no common arbiter authorized to decide between them.

The importance which the framers of the Constitution attached to such a tribunal, for the purpose of preserving internal tranquillity, is strikingly manifested by the clause which gives this court jurisdiction over the sovereign States which compose this Union when a controversy arises between them. Instead of reserving the right to seek redress for injustice from another State by their sovereign powers, they have bound themselves to submit to the decision of this court, and to abide by its judgment. And it is not out of place to say here that experience has demonstrated that this power was not unwisely surrendered by the States, for, in the time that has already elapsed since this Government came into existence, several irritating and angry controversies have taken place between adjoining States in relation to their respective boundaries, and which have sometimes threatened to end in force and violence but for the power vested in this court to hear them and decide between them.

The same purposes are clearly indicated by the different language employed when conferring supremacy upon the laws of the United States, and jurisdiction upon its courts. In the first case, it provides that

"this Constitution, and the laws of the United States *which shall be made in pursuance thereof,* shall be the supreme law of the land, and obligatory upon the judges in every State."

The words in italics show the precision and foresight which marks every clause in the instrument. The sovereignty to be created was to be limited in its powers of legislation, and if it passed a law not authorized by its enumerated powers, it was not to be regarded as the supreme law of the land, nor were the State judges bound to carry it into execution. And as the courts of a State, and the courts of the United States, might, and indeed certainly would, often differ as to the extent of the powers conferred by the General Government, it was manifest that serious controversies would arise between the authorities of the United States and of the States, which must be settled by force of arms unless some tribunal was created to decide between them finally and with out appeal.

The Constitution has accordingly provided, as far as human foresight could provide, against this danger. And, in conferring judicial power upon the Federal Government, it declares that the jurisdiction of its courts shall extend to all cases arising under "this Constitution" and the laws of the United States -- leaving out the words of restriction contained in the grant of legislative power which we have above noticed. The judicial power covers every legislative act of Congress, whether it be made within the limits of its delegated powers or be an assumption of power beyond the grants in the Constitution.

This judicial power was justly regarded as indispensable not merely to maintain the supremacy of the laws of the United States, but also to guard the States from any encroachment upon their reserved rights by the General Government. And as the Constitution is the fundamental and supreme law, if it appears that an act of Congress is not pursuant to and within the limits of the power assigned to the Federal Government, it is the duty of the courts of the United States to declare it unconstitutional and void. The grant of judicial power is not confined to the administration of laws passed in pursuance to the provisions of the Constitution, nor confined to the interpretation of such laws, but, by the very terms of the grant, the Constitution is under their view when any act of Congress is brought before them, and it is their duty to declare the law void, and refuse to execute it, if it is not pursuant to the legislative powers conferred upon Congress. And as the final

appellate power in all such questions is given to this court, controversies as to the respective powers of the United States and the States, instead of being determined by military and physical force, are heard, investigated, and finally settled with the calmness and deliberation of judicial inquiry. And no one can fail to see that, if such an arbiter had not been provided in our complicated system of government, internal tranquillity could not have been preserved, and if such controversies were left to arbitrament of physical force, our Government, State and National, would soon cease to be Governments of laws, and revolutions by force of arms would take the place of courts of justice and judicial decisions.

In organizing such a tribunal, it is evident that every precaution was taken which human wisdom could devise to fit it for the high duty with which it was intrusted. It was not left to Congress to create it by law, for the States could hardly be expected to confide in the impartiality of a tribunal created exclusively by the General Government without any participation on their part. And as the performance of its duty would sometimes come in conflict with individual ambition or interests and powerful political combinations, an act of Congress establishing such a tribunal might be repealed in order to establish another more subservient to the predominant political influences or excited passions of the day. This tribunal, therefore, was erected, and the powers of which we have spoken conferred upon it, not by the Federal Government, but by the people of the States, who formed and adopted that Government and conferred upon it all the powers, legislative, executive, and judicial, which it now possesses. And in order to secure its independence and enable it faithfully and firmly to perform its duty, it engrafted it upon the Constitution itself, and declared that this court should have appellate power in all cases arising under the Constitution and laws of the United States. So long, therefore, as this Constitution shall endure, this tribunal must exist with it, deciding in the peaceful forms of judicial proceeding the angry and irritating controversies between sovereignties which, in other countries, have been determined by the arbitrament of force.

These principles of constitutional law are confirmed and illustrated by the clause which confers legislative power upon Congress. That power is specifically given in article 1, section 8, paragraph 18, in the following words:

"To make all laws which shall be necessary and proper to carry into execution the foregoing powers, and all other powers vested by this Constitution in the Government of the United States, or in any department or officer thereof."

Under this clause of the Constitution, it became the duty of Congress to pass such laws as were necessary and proper to carry into execution the powers vested in the judicial department. And in the performance of this duty, the First Congress, at its first session, passed the act of 1789, ch. 20, entitled *An act to establish the judicial courts of the United States.* It will be remembered that many of the members of the Convention were also members of this Congress, and it cannot be supposed that they did not understand the meaning and intention of the great instrument which they had so anxiously and deliberately considered, clause by clause, and assisted to frame. And the law they passed to carry into execution the powers vested in the judicial department of the Government proves past doubt that their interpretation of the appellate powers conferred on this court was the same with that which we have now given, for, by the 25th section of the act of 1789, Congress authorized writs of error to be issued from this court to a State court whenever a right had been claimed under the Constitution or laws of the United States and the decision of the State court was against it. And to make this appellate power effectual and altogether independent of the action of State tribunals, this act further provides that, upon writs of error to a State court, instead of remanding the cause for a final decision in the State court, this court may, at their discretion, if the cause shall have been once remanded before, proceed to a final decision of the same and award execution.

These provisions in the act of 1789 tell us, in language not to be mistaken, the great importance which the patriots and statement of the First Congress attached to this appellate power, and the foresight and care with which they guarded its free and independent exercise against interference or obstruction by States or State tribunals.

In the case before the Supreme Court of Wisconsin, a right was claimed under the Constitution and laws of the United States, and the decision was against the right claimed, and it refuses obedience to the writ of error, and regards its own judgment as final. It has not only reversed and annulled the judgment of the District Court of the United States, but it has reversed and annulled the provisions of the Constitution itself, and the act of Congress of 1789, and made the superior and appellate tribunal the inferior and subordinate one.

We do not question the authority of State court or judge who is authorized by the laws of the State to issue the writ of habeas corpus to issue it in any case where the party is imprisoned within its territorial limits, provided it does not appear, when the application is made, that the person imprisoned is in custody under the authority of the United States. The court or judge has a right to inquire, in this mode of proceeding, for what cause and by what authority the prisoner is confined within the territorial limits of the State sovereignty. And it is the duty of the marshal or other person having the custody of the prisoner to make known to the judge or court, by a proper return, the authority by which he holds him in custody. This right to inquire by process of habeas corpus, and the duty of the officer to make a return, grows necessarily out of the complex character of our Government and the existence of two distinct and separate sovereignties within the same territorial space, each of them restricted in its powers and each within its sphere of action, prescribed by the Constitution of the United States, independent of the other. But, after the return is made and the State judge or court judicially apprized that the party is in custody under the authority of the United States, they can proceed no further. They then know that the prisoner is within the dominion and jurisdiction of another Government, and that neither the writ of habeas corpus nor any other process issued under State authority can pass over the line of division between the two sovereignties. He is then within the dominion and exclusive jurisdiction of the United States. If he has committed an offence against their laws, their tribunals alone can punish him. If he is wrongfully imprisoned, their judicial tribunals can release him and afford him redress. And although, as we have said, it is the duty of the marshal or other person holding him to make known, by a proper return, the authority under which he detains him, it is at the same time imperatively his duty to obey the process of the United States, to hold the prisoner in custody under it, and to refuse obedience to the mandate or process of any other Government. And consequently it is his duty not to take the prisoner, nor suffer him to be taken, before a State judge or court upon a habeas corpus issued under State authority. No State judge or court, after they are judicially informed that the party is imprisoned under the authority of the United States, has any right to interfere with him or to require him to be brought before them. And if the authority of a State, in the form of judicial process or otherwise, should attempt to control the marshal or other authorized officer or agent of the United States in any respect, in the custody of his prisoner, it would be his duty to resist it, and to call to his aid any force that might be necessary to maintain the authority of law against illegal interference. No judicial process, whatever form it may assume, can have any lawful authority outside of the limits of the jurisdiction of the court or judge by whom it is issued, and an attempt to enforce it beyond these boundaries is nothing less than lawless violence.

Nor is there anything in this supremacy of the General Government, or the jurisdiction of its judicial tribunals to awaken the jealousy or offend the natural and just pride of State sovereignty. Neither this Government nor the powers of which we are speaking were forced upon the States. The Constitution of the United States, with all the powers conferred by it on the General Government and surrendered by the States, was the voluntary act of the people of the several States, deliberately done for their own protection and safety against injustice from one another. And their anxiety to preserve it in full force, in all its powers, and to guard against resistance to or evasion of its authority on the part of a State is proved by the clause which requires that the members of the State Legislatures and all executive and judicial officers of the several States (as well as those of the General Government) shall be bound, by oath or affirmation, to support this Constitution. This is the last and closing clause of the Constitution, and inserted when the whole frame of Government, with the powers hereinbefore specified, had been adopted by the Convention, and it was in that form, and with these powers, that the Constitution was submitted to the people of the several States for their consideration and decision.

Now, it certainly can be no humiliation to the citizen of a republic to yield a ready obedience to the laws as administered by the constituted authorities. On the contrary, it is among his first and highest duties as a citizen, because free government cannot exist without it. Nor can it be inconsistent with the dignity of a sov-

ereign State to observe faithfully, and in the spirit of sincerity and truth, the compact into which it voluntarily entered when it became a State of this Union. On the contrary, the highest honor of sovereignty is untarnished faith. And certainly no faith could be more deliberately and solemnly pledged than that which every State has plighted to the other States to support the Constitution as it is, in all its provisions, until they shall be altered in the manner which the Constitution itself prescribes. In the emphatic language of the pledge required, it is *to support this Constitution.* And no power is more clearly conferred by the Constitution and laws of the United States than the power of this court to decide, ultimately and finally, all cases arising under such Constitution and laws, and for that purpose to bring here for revision, by writ of error, the judgment of a State court, where such questions have arisen, and the right claimed under them denied by the highest judicial tribunal in the State.

We are sensible that we have extended the examination of these decisions beyond the limits required by any intrinsic difficulty in the questions. But the decisions in question were made by the supreme judicial tribunal of the State, and when a court so elevated in its position has pronounced a judgment which, if it could be maintained, would subvert the very foundations of this Government, it seemed to be the duty of this court, when exercising its appellate power, to show plainly the grave errors into which the State court has fallen and the consequences to which they would inevitably lead.

But it can hardly be necessary to point out the errors which followed their mistaken view of the jurisdiction they might lawfully exercise, because, if there was any defect of power in the commissioner, or in his mode of proceeding, it was for the tribunals of the United States to revise and correct it, and not for a State court. And as regards the decision of the District Court, it had exclusive and final jurisdiction by the laws of the United States, and neither the regularity of its proceedings nor the validity of its sentence could be called in question in any other court, either of a State or the United States, by habeas corpus or any other process.

But although we think it unnecessary to discuss these questions, yet, as they have been decided by the State court, and are before us on the record, and we are not willing to be misunderstood, it is proper to say that, in the judgment of this court, the act of Congress commonly called the fugitive slave law is, in all of its provisions, fully authorized by the Constitution of the United States, that the commissioner had lawful authority to issue the warrant and commit the party, and that his proceedings were regular and conformable to law. We have already stated the opinion and judgment of the court as to the exclusive jurisdiction of the District Court and the appellate powers which this court is authorized and required to exercise. And if any argument was needed to show the wisdom and necessity of this appellate power, the cases before us sufficiently prove it, and at the same time emphatically call for its exercise.

The judgment of the Supreme Court of Wisconsin must therefore be reversed in each of the cases now before the court.

## Glossary

**certiorari:** a higher court's review of a lower court's decision

**demurrer:** an objection; a type of challenge in court that asserts that a case should be dismissed because of insufficient facts

**fugitive slave:** a person who had escaped or was attempting to escape bondage

**habeas corpus:** the presentation of a person in court; the requirement that a person under arrest be brought to a court or before a judge to determine whether the person should be detained or released

**summary:** speedy; immediate

**writ:** a legal order

# EX PARTE MILLIGAN

| DATE | CITATION |
|---|---|
| 1866 | 71 U.S. 2 |

| AUTHOR | SIGNIFICANCE |
|---|---|
| David Davis | Established that presidential authority had legal limits on suspending individual rights under the law, even during war |

| VOTE | |
|---|---|
| 9-0 | |

## Overview

Argued on March 5, 1866, and decided on April 3, 1866, the case of *Ex parte Milligan* is a landmark decision that reaffirmed the limits of presidential power in the administration of order in the wake of the American Civil War. Lambdin Milligan was arrested for anti-Union activities in Indiana on October 5, 1864. Milligan was a citizen of Indiana, which had remained part of the Union. In December of that same year, Milligan was sentenced to death by a military tribunal. In May 1865, President Andrew Johnson commuted Milligan's sentence to life imprisonment. Milligan did not argue his guilt or innocence but instead challenged that the military tribunal for Milligan was unconstitutional when civil courts were operating simultaneously in the same jurisdiction. The federal circuit courts could not decide if Milligan's trial was constitutional and referred the case to the U.S. Supreme Court for a ruling. The Supreme Court agreed that the military tribunal had overstepped its authority, and Milligan was released from prison.

## Context

After the beginning of the American Civil War on April 12, 1861, President Abraham Lincoln sought ways to hold the Union together despite the many challenges to its continued existence. Confederate sympathizers and an anti-war faction of Democrats in the North continued to threaten the effective order of the Union. The states and territories were divided under military districts, and the influence of military officers in daily life increased significantly. When several riots broke out in mid-April in Baltimore, Maryland, between militiamen traveling to Washington, D.C., and anti-war factions, civil authorities asked Lincoln to stop all military movements through Maryland. Arguing that such action would further imperil the nation's capital, Lincoln refused to stop troop movements through the state. Lincoln and others feared that anti-war and pro-Confederate agitation in Maryland would cause the state to secede through violence.

On April 19, Lincoln sought the legal advice of Attorney General Edward Bates to determine if the situation authorized increased legal powers to the president. Article I of the Constitution contains a clause that provides for the temporary suspension of legal rights "when in

***1867 photograph of the Chase Court***
(Alexander Gardner)

cases of rebellion or invasion" to protect the general safety of the people. Bates agreed that the situation did meet the test. Lincoln delegated the authority to suspend the legal right to habeas corpus—the right for a detained person to request a speedy trial to determine if their continued detention is warranted—to army officers along the Maryland routes of transport leading to Washington.

On April 29, the Maryland legislature voted to remain in the Union but directed that the federal government refrain from using the state for troop movement. Maryland militiamen under the command of Lieutenant John Merryman destroyed railroad bridges, which hampered the swift movement of troops through the state. Union volunteers arrested John Merryman in Baltimore under charges of treason and transported Merryman to Fort McHenry. Lawyers representing Merryman traveled to Washington to seek an order to present Merryman to a court. U.S. Supreme Court Chief Justice Roger Taney (who also served as the fed-

eral court judge for the District of Maryland) ordered the military commander of Fort McHenry to produce Merryman in court in Baltimore the next day. When the military refused to do so, Taney argued that constitutionally only the legislature—not the president—had the authority to suspend rights under Article I. Lincoln argued that because Congress was currently in recess, he had such authority. After reconvening in July 1861, arguing that no official had declared martial law, Congress refused to authorize the president such power. By February 1862, Lincoln ordered Merryman and other Maryland political prisoners to be released, offering amnesty if they took a loyalty oath to the Union.

With the hopes of a quick resolution of the war dashed after the First Battle of Bull Run in August 1862, calls for increased state militia contributions to the defense of the Union met with steep opposition. In September 1862, Lincoln issued Proclamation 94, which both suspended habeas corpus across the nation and subjected anyone interfering with raising troops or aiding the Confederacy to martial law. By March 1863, Congress recognized that the war required increased powers to be afforded to the president. Under the Habeas Corpus Suspension Act, Congress afforded the president of the United States the right to suspend habeas corpus. In September 1863, Lincoln suspended habeas corpus to any case involving prisoners of war, spies, aiders or abettors of the enemy, or military personnel. In February 1864, the U.S. Supreme Court unanimously upheld the constitutionality of the suspension of habeas corpus and the inability of citizens charged by a military tribunal to appeal to a higher court in *Ex parte Vallandigham*.

Lambdin Milligan, a lawyer and leader of an anti-war organization, was arrested along with several other prominent critics of Lincoln by a military posse in Indiana on October 5, 1864, for anti-Union activities. On October 21, the military commission convened in Indianapolis. Milligan and two others were sentenced to death, while a fourth was sentenced to hard labor for the remainder of the war. In early April 1865, Lincoln and the Military District Commander of Indiana modified the sentence of hard labor to restriction to a small geographic area and a loyalty oath. Milligan and the others began a concerted effort to secure pardons for their actions. In May 1865, the decision in *Ex parte Vallandigham* would be challenged when a petition was filed with the District Court of Indiana for a writ of habeas corpus. Just days before Milligan's scheduled execution on May 16, 1865, President Johnson commuted Milligan's sentence to life imprisonment. Between October and December 1865, President Johnson would restore civil law and reinstate habeas corpus to states and territories that had remained in the Union. Milligan did not argue his guilt or innocence but instead challenged that the military tribunal was unconstitutional when civil courts were operating simultaneously in the same jurisdiction. Milligan's legal representation was an influential group that included David Field, brother of Associate Justice Stephen Field, future president James Garfield, and Jerimiah Black, the former U.S. attorney general and secretary of state. Milligan argued that a federal grand jury had convened in Indianapolis during his trial, yet he had not been indicted. The U.S. Supreme Court agreed with Milligan, and he was released from prison.

## About the Author

David Davis was born March 9, 1815, to David Davis, a successful Maryland physician, and Ann Mercer Davis. He made his way west to Ohio and attended Kenyon College, graduating in 1832. Returning east to Massachusetts, Davis read law with a prominent probate judge and fell in love with his daughter Sarah. Inspired by the law, Davis enrolled in Yale Law School, graduating in 1835. Davis moved to Illinois, established a private law practice, and, by mid-1838, married Sarah. The couple would have two children and be married for over 40 years. Much of Davis's success within society would be attributable to the efforts of Sarah, who became a prominent Bloomington citizen in her own right.

He unsuccessfully ran as a Whig before being elected as a Republican to the Illinois state legislature in 1845. He served on the Illinois Constitutional Convention in 1847 and was influential in changing the appointment of judges to popular vote. In 1848, he was elected to the Eighth Circuit Court seat in Springfield, Illinois, serving three terms until his departure in December 1862. In this position, Davis heard cases argued by Abraham Lincoln and Stephen Douglas. Fiercely supportive of abolition and personally embarrassed by the failure of the Whig party to correct the issue, Davis was deeply impressed by Lincoln. The men grew close, and Davis became the campaign manager for Lincoln's 1860 Republican presidential nomination. Davis would serve as executor of Lincoln's will after his April 14, 1865, assassination.

Lincoln nominated Davis to the U.S. Supreme Court seat vacated by John Campbell on December 1, 1862. Davis was confirmed by Senate just seven days later. Davis served on the Supreme Court for 14 years but felt uninspired by the work and even flirted briefly with a presidential campaign. Aside from his landmark majority opinion in *Ex parte Milligan* (1866), he is best known for his minority opinion in *Hepburn v. Griswold* (1870), in which he argued paper currency was unconstitutional, and his impact on the Hayes-Tilden Presidential Election Committee. Anticipating Davis would vote along party lines, the Democratically controlled Illinois Senate attempted to influence the commission's outcome by appointing the Republican Davis to the Senate in 1877. As senator, Davis would be elected to serve as president pro tempore, in which position, after the 1881 assassination of James Garfield left the vice presidency vacant, he would become affectionately and unofficially known as "Mr. Vice President."

Davis did not seek reelection and, returning to Bloomington, Illinois, withdrew from public life in 1883. Davis and his family had constructed a large Victorian mansion—named Clover Lawn—and at the time of his death in 1886, he was one of the largest landholders in Illinois, with a personal fortune of nearly five million dollars.

## Explanation and Analysis of the Document

Justice Davis's opinion seeks to answer four fundamental questions presented by the case. First, is an issue of a writ of habeas corpus required? Second, did the military commission have jurisdiction over the offense when it convened and sentenced Milligan? Third, did the grounds under which Milligan was charged meet the test to be tried, or should he be freed from correctional custody? Finally, did the circuit court have jurisdiction to hear the case or its appeal?

Justice Davis begins by addressing the basis for habeas corpus. This, he argues, is based on the legislature's passage of the Judiciary Act of 1789, which conferred the constitutional power of the courts to inquire into the cause of an individual's detainment or arrest; secure the right of the individual against unreasonable search and seizure; ensure the evidence presented merits a warrant for probable cause before arrest; and if indicted, ensure a speedy trial by jury. Davis outlines the accepted legal precedent in which writ may be applied for by a prisoner or which a court may consider and determine, based upon the facts of the case if the individual should continue to be imprisoned or be freed. This also means that if the prisoner feels that an error of judgment has occurred, they may appeal to a higher court. Davis ends his opening by defining the constraints and restraints of habeas corpus as a matter of law, not discretion.

Having clearly outlined the precedents inherent in the right of habeas corpus afforded by the Constitution, Davis begins to present the context in which the Civil War had affected the legal limits of the federal authorities. Davis argues that Lincoln and Congress had passed the Habeas Corpus Act of 1863 with a clear intention under the suspension clause that the act would become invalid after restoring peace. The second and third sections of the act required that a person arrested after the passage of the act was entitled to his discharge if not indicted or presented by the grand jury convened at the first subsequent term of the Circuit or District Court of the United States for the District. Davis argues that military commissions had no jurisdiction under the congressionally approved act to try, convict, or sentence for any criminal offense a citizen who was neither a resident of a rebellious state nor a prisoner of war, nor a person in the military or naval service. Davis outlines that the Confederacy did not invade the state of Illinois, and the federal courts were open to exercising their judicial functions throughout the war.

Finally, Davis argues that at no point may a citizen not connected with military service or a resident in a state where the courts are open and in the proper exercise of their jurisdiction, even when the privilege of the writ of habeas corpus is suspended, be tried, convicted, or sentenced other than by the ordinary courts of law. Having clearly outlined the limits of federal authority granted under the Constitution, Davis begins to outline the facts of the case: Milligan's arrest on October 5, 1864, in his home state of Illinois by order of the military commandant of Illinois Brevet Major-General Hovey; the charges of conspiracy, treason, and conspiracy to commit armed rebellion against the United States; and the connections between Milligan and the secret societies known as the Order of American Knights or Sons of Liberty. Davis points out that Milligan, a lawyer, raised an objection to the authority of the military commission but was overruled by the justice. Milligan filed a petition in the Circuit Court of Indiana based upon the fact that he was not presented to a federal grand jury within twenty days as required, in violation of the Habeas Corpus Act.

Justice Davis's opinion effectively argues that martial law and civil law cannot have jurisdiction over the individual. Constitutionally, martial law can only be called into action when civil law cannot adequately secure public or private safety and rights. However, the presence of martial law can only exist under the articles of war as prescribed by Congress and supersedes local law only as a sanction suitable for a temporary period. Military governance thus can only exist when the civil government cannot or will not exercise its functions because of military operations in the geographical area. Congress, then, had the power to delegate authority for martial law, including tribunals. However, this delegation of authority only extended to crimes against the security and safety of Union forces. However, none of these provisions for altering individual rights were present in Illinois when Milligan was arrested, tried, and sentenced. Furthermore, the Habeas Corpus Act only allowed citizens to be detained, not tried or executed, under the jurisdiction of martial law. Individuals who resided in areas that had supported the usurpation of civil law as part of the Confederate cause had demonstrated their inability to punish guilty parties and liberate innocent parties with assurity and were therefore subject to martial law.

## Impact

*Ex parte Milligan* was hugely impactful in that it reinforced the rights of the individual while establishing limitations on federal power. However, the U.S. Supreme Court was also mindful of the times in which it was operating. The court sought to correct errors for citizens who had not forfeited their rights but enforced the legitimacy of military tribunals and governance in the occupied South. The decision created a clear delineation between military governance and martial law, which continues to shape how Americans view the military's role in establishing stable civil governments in nations after periods of war.

After Milligan and his fellows were released, Milligan filed a civil lawsuit against Hovey, the military commandant who had ordered his arrest. *Milligan v. Hovey* (1871) is notable for two reasons. First, Hovey hired future president Benjamin Harrison to defend him, which helped establish Harrison's reputation as a fierce defender of American values of civil rights and the just rule of law. Second, the case stands out as establishing the precedent of federal civil rights protection as a civil and legal matter. Despite Harrison's portrayal of Milligan as nothing short of a traitor to his nation and its values, the jury awarded Milligan five dollars in damages and court costs for his unlawful imprisonment.

*Ex parte Milligan* proved to be a foundational decision with a significant influence on *Ex parte Quirin* (1942) and *Hamdi v. Rumsfeld* (2004), which upheld the line established in *Milligan* between the jurisdiction for actions of lawful and unlawful citizens during times of war. Both *Quirin* and *Hamdi v. Rumsfeld* recognized the federal government's authority to detain enemy combatants, even if they are citizens, provided that the federal government recognized the right to due process and the individual right to challenge their status as an enemy before an impartial authority.

---

### Questions for Further Study

1. Did the Supreme Court demonstrate an inconsistency in its interpretation of constitutional authority to suspend habeas corpus decisions in *Ex parte Vallandigham* and *Ex parte Milligan*? Why or why not?

2. How did Davis's relationship with Lincoln factor into his opinion?

3. Having witnessed the extreme measures the federal government was willing to go to in times of war, was the decision in Milligan intentionally constructed to avoid the risk of future abuses of power? Defend your position.

4. Why is the right to apply to a court for due process so important?

5. Does the sentence of a military tribunal of non-military personnel in a time of war still hold after the war is concluded, or should a civil authority review these cases? Why?

## Further Reading

### Books

Gregory, Anthony. *The Power of Habeas Corpus in America: From the King's Prerogative to the War on Terror.* New York: Cambridge University Press, 2013.

Kelly, Darwin. *Milligan's Fight against Lincoln.* New York: Exposition Press, 1973.

Neely, Mark, Jr. *The Fate of Liberty: Abraham Lincoln and Civil Liberties.* New York: Oxford University Press, 1991.

Rehnquist, William. *All the Laws but One: Civil Liberties in Wartime.* New York: Vintage Books, 2007.

Winger, Stewart, and Jonathan White. *Ex Parte Milligan Reconsidered: Race and Civil Liberties from the Lincoln Administration to the War on Terror.* Lawrence: University Press of Kansas, 2020.

### Websites

"Ex parte Milligan." Civil War on the Western Border. Kansas City Public Library. Accessed February 15, 2023, http://civilwaronthewesternborder.org/timeline/ex-parte-milligan.

McBride, Alex. "Landmark Cases: Ex parte Milligan (1866)." The Supreme Court: Supreme Court History: The First Hundred Years. December 2006. Accessed February 15, 2023, http://www.thirteen.org/wnet/supreme-court/antebellum/landmark_exparte.html.

—Commentary by Bryant Macfarlane

# EX PARTE MILLIGAN

## Document Text

### *Mr. Justice DAVIS delivered the opinion of the Court*

On the 10th day of May, 1865, Lambdin P. Milligan presented a petition to the Circuit Court of the United States for the District of Indiana to be discharged from an alleged unlawful imprisonment. The case made by the petition is this: Milligan is a citizen of the United States; has lived for twenty years in Indiana, and, at the time of the grievances complained of, was not, and never had been, in the military or naval service of the United States. On the 5th day of October, 1864, while at home, he was arrested by order of General Alvin P. Hovey, commanding the military district of Indiana, and has ever since been kept in close confinement.

On the 21st day of October, 1864, he was brought before a military commission, convened at Indianapolis by order of General Hovey, tried on certain charges and specifications, found guilty, and sentenced to be hanged, and the sentence ordered to be executed on Friday, the 19th day of May, 1865.

On the 2d day of January, 1865, after the proceedings of the military commission were at an end, the Circuit Court of the United States for Indiana met at Indianapolis and empaneled a grand jury, who were charged to inquire whether the laws of the United States had been violated. and, if so, to make presentments. The court adjourned on the 27th day of January, having, prior thereto, discharged from further service the grand jury, who did not find any bill of indictment or make any presentment against Milligan for any offence whatever, and, in fact, since his imprisonment, no bill of indictment has been found or presentment made against him by any grand jury of the United States.

Milligan insists that said military commission had no jurisdiction to try him upon the charges preferred, or upon any charges whatever, because he was a citizen of the United States and the State of Indiana, and had not been, since the commencement of the late Rebellion, a resident of any of the States whose citizens were arrayed against the government, and that the right of trial by jury was guaranteed to him by the Constitution of the United States.

The prayer of the petition was that, under the act of Congress approved March 3d, 1863, entitled, "An act relating to habeas corpus and regulating judicial proceedings in certain cases," he may be brought before the court and either turned over to the proper civil tribunal to be proceeded against according to the law of the land or discharged from custody altogether.

With the petition were filed the order for the commission, the charges and specifications, the findings of the court, with the order of the War Department reciting that the sentence was approved by the President of the United States, and directing that it be carried into execution without delay. The petition was presented and filed in open court by the counsel for Milligan; at the same time, the District Attorney of the United States for Indiana appeared and, by the agreement of counsel, the application was submitted to the court. The opinions of the judges of the Circuit Court were opposed on three questions, which are certified to the Supreme Court:

1st. "On the facts stated in said petition and exhibits, ought a writ of habeas corpus to be issued?" 2d. "On the facts stated in said petition and exhibits, ought the said Lambdin P. Milligan to be discharged from custody as in said petition prayed?"

3d. "Whether, upon the facts stated in said petition and exhibits, the military commission mentioned therein had jurisdiction legally to try and sentence said Milligan in manner and form as in said petition and exhibits is stated?"

The importance of the main question presented by this record cannot be overstated, for it involves the very framework of the government and the fundamental principles of American liberty.

During the late wicked Rebellion, the temper of the times did not allow that calmness in deliberation and discussion so necessary to a correct conclusion of a purely judicial question. *Then,* considerations of safety were mingled with the exercise of power, and feelings and interests prevailed which are happily terminated. *Now* that the public safety is assured, this question, as well as all others, can be discussed and decided without passion or the admixture of any element not required to form a legal judgment. We approach the investigation of this case fully sensible of the magnitude of the inquiry and the necessity of full and cautious deliberation.

But we are met with a preliminary objection. It is insisted that the Circuit Court of Indiana had no authority to certify these questions, and that we are without jurisdiction to hear and determine them.

The sixth section of the "Act to amend the judicial system of the United States," approved April 29, 1802, declares

"that whenever any question shall occur before a Circuit Court upon which the opinions of the judges shall be opposed, the point upon which the disagreement shall happen shall, during the same term, upon the request of either party or their counsel, be stated under the direction of the judges and certified under the seal of the court to the Supreme Court at their next session to be held thereafter, and shall by the said court be finally decided, and the decision of the Supreme Court and their order in the premises shall be remitted to the Circuit Court and be there entered of record, and shall

have effect according to the nature of the said judgment and order: *Provided,* That nothing herein contained shall prevent the cause from proceeding, if, in the opinion of the court, further proceedings can be had without prejudice to the merits."

It is under this provision of law that a Circuit Court has authority to certify any question to the Supreme Court for adjudication. The inquiry, therefore, is, whether the case of Milligan is brought within its terms.

It was admitted at the bar that the Circuit Court had jurisdiction to entertain the application for the writ of habeas corpus and to hear and determine it, and it could not be denied, for the power is expressly given in the 14th section of the Judiciary Act of 1789, as well as in the later act of 1863. Chief Justice Marshall, in Bollman's case, construed this branch of the Judiciary Act to authorize the courts as well as the judges to issue the writ for the purpose of inquiring into the cause of the commitment, and this construction has never been departed from. But it is maintained with earnestness and ability that a certificate of division of opinion can occur only in a *cause,* and that the proceeding by a party moving for a writ of habeas corpus does not become a cause *until after the writ has been issued and a return made.*

Independently of the provisions of the act of Congress of March 3, 1863, relating to habeas corpus, on which the petitioner bases his claim for relief and which we will presently consider, can this position be sustained?

It is true that it is usual for a court, on application for a writ of habeas corpus, to issue the writ, and, on the return, to dispose of the case, but the court can elect to waive the issuing of the writ and consider whether, upon the facts presented in the petition, the prisoner, if brought before it, could be discharged. One of the very points on which the case of Tobias Watkins, reported in 3 Peters, turned was whether, if the writ was issued, the petitioner would be remanded upon the case which he had made.

The Chief Justice, in delivering the opinion of the court, said:

"The cause of imprisonment is shown as fully by the petitioner as it could appear on the return of the writ; consequently, the writ ought not to be awarded if the court is satisfied that the prisoner would be remanded to prison."

The judges of the Circuit Court of Indiana were therefore warranted by an express decision of this court in refusing the writ if satisfied that the prisoner. on his own showing. was rightfully detained.

But, it is contended, if they differed about the lawfulness of the imprisonment, and could render no judgment, the prisoner is remediless, and cannot have the disputed question certified under the act of 1802. His remedy is complete by writ of error or appeal, if the court renders a final judgment refusing to discharge him; but if he should be so unfortunate as to be placed in the predicament of having the court divided on the question whether he should live or die, he is hopeless, and without remedy. He wishes the vital question settled not by a single judge at his chambers, but by the highest tribunal known to the Constitution, and yet the privilege is denied him because the Circuit Court consists of two judges, instead of one.

Such a result was not in the contemplation of the legislature of 1802, and the language used by it cannot be construed to mean any such thing. The clause under consideration was introduced to further the ends of justice by obtaining a speedy settlement of important questions where the judges might be opposed in opinion.

The act of 1802 so changed the judicial system that the Circuit Court, instead of three, was composed of two judges, and, without this provision or a kindred one, if the judges differed, the difference would remain, the question be unsettled, and justice denied. The decisions of this court upon the provisions of this section have been numerous. In *United States v. Daniel,* the court, in holding that a division of the judges on a motion for a new trial could not be certified, say: "That the question must be one which arises in a cause depending before the court relative to a proceeding belonging to the cause." Testing Milligan's case by this rule of law, is it not apparent that it is rightfully here, and that we are compelled to answer the questions on which the judges below were opposed in opinion? If, in the sense of the law, the proceeding for the writ of habeas corpus was the "*cause*" of the party applying for it, then it is evident that the "cause" was pending before the court, and that the questions certified arose out of it, belonged to it, and were matters of right, and not of discretion.

But it is argued that the proceeding does not ripen into a cause until there are two parties to it.

This we deny. It was the *cause* of Milligan when the petition was presented to the Circuit Court. It would have been the *cause* of both parties if the court had issued the writ and brought those who held Milligan in custody before it. Webster defines the word "cause" thus: "A suit or action in court; any legal process which a party institutes to obtain his demand, or by which he seeks his right, or supposed right"—and he says,

"this is a legal, scriptural, and popular use of the word, coinciding nearly with case, from *cado,* and action, from *ago,* to urge and drive."

In any legal sense, action, suit, and cause, are convertible terms. Milligan supposed he had a right to test the validity of his trial and sentence, and the proceeding which he set in operation for that purpose was his "cause" or "suit." It was the only one by which he could recover his liberty. He was powerless to do more; he could neither instruct the judges nor control their action, and should not suffer, because, without fault of his, they were unable to render a judgment. But the true meaning to the term "suit" has been given by this court. One of the questions in *Weston v. City Council of Charleston,* was whether a writ of prohibition was a suit, and Chief Justice Marshall says:

"The term is certainly a comprehensive one, and is understood to apply to any proceeding in a court of justice by which an individual pursues that remedy which the law affords him."

Certainly Milligan pursued the only remedy which the law afforded him.

Again, in *Cohens v. Virginia,* he says: "In law language, a suit is the prosecution of some demand in a court of justice." Also,

"To commence a suit is to demand something by the institution of process in a court of justice, and to prosecute the suit is to continue that demand."

When Milligan demanded his release by the proceeding relating to habeas corpus, he commenced a suit, and he has since prosecuted it in all the ways known to the law. One of the questions in *Holmes v. Jennison, et al.,* was whether, under the 25th section of the Judiciary Act, a proceeding for a writ of habeas corpus was a "suit." Chief Justice Taney held that,

"if a party is unlawfully imprisoned, the writ of habeas corpus is his appropriate legal remedy. It is his suit in court to recover his liberty."

There was much diversity of opinion on another ground of jurisdiction, but that, in the sense of the 25th section of the Judiciary Act, the proceeding by habeas corpus was a suit was not controverted by any except Baldwin, Justice, and he thought that "suit" and "cause," as used in the section, mean the same thing.

The court do not say that a return must be made and the parties appear and begin to try the case before it is a suit. When the petition is filed and the writ prayed for, it is a *suit*—the suit of the party making the application. If it is a suit under the 25th section of the Judiciary Act when the proceedings are begun, it is, by all the analogies of the law, equally a suit under the 6th section of the act of 1802.

But it is argued that there must be two parties to the suit, because the point is to be stated upon the request of "either party or their counsel."

Such a literal and technical construction would defeat the very purpose the legislature had in view, which was to enable any party to bring the case here when the point in controversy was a matter of right, and not of discretion, and the words "either party," in order to prevent a failure of justice, must be construed as words of enlargement, and not of restriction. Although this case is here *ex parte*, it was not considered by the court below without notice having been given to the party supposed to have an interest in the detention of the prisoner. The statements of the record show that this is not only a fair, but conclusive, inference. When the counsel for Milligan presented to the court the petition for the writ of habeas corpus, Mr. Hanna, the District Attorney for Indiana, also appeared, and, by agreement, the application was submitted to the court, who took the case under advisement, and on the next day announced their inability to agree, and made the certificate. It is clear that Mr. Hanna did not represent the petitioner, and why is his appearance entered? It admits of no other solution than this—that he was informed of the application, and appeared on behalf of the government to contest it. The government was

the prosecutor of Milligan, who claimed that his imprisonment was illegal and sought, in the only way he could, to recover his liberty. The case was a grave one, and the court unquestionably directed that the law officer of the government should be informed of it. He very properly appeared, and, as the facts were uncontroverted and the difficulty was in the application of the law, there was no useful purpose to be obtained in issuing the writ. The cause was therefore submitted to the court for their consideration and determination.

But Milligan claimed his discharge from custody by virtue of the act of Congress "relating to habeas corpus, and regulating judicial proceedings in certain cases," approved March 3d, 1863. Did that act confer jurisdiction on the Circuit Court of Indiana to hear this case?

In interpreting a law, the motives which must have operated with the legislature in passing it are proper to be considered. This law was passed in a time of great national peril, when our heritage of free government was in danger.

An armed rebellion against the national authority, of greater proportions than history affords an example of, was raging, and the public safety required that the privilege of the writ of habeas corpus should be suspended. The President had practically suspended it, and detained suspected persons in custody without trial, but his authority to do this was questioned. It was claimed that Congress alone could exercise this power, and that the legislature, and not the President, should judge of the political considerations on which the right to suspend it rested. The privilege of this great writ had never before been withheld from the citizen, and, as the exigence of the times demanded immediate action, it was of the highest importance that the lawfulness of the suspension should be fully established. It was under these circumstances, which were such as to arrest the attention of the country, that this law was passed. The President was authorized by it to suspend the privilege of the writ of habeas corpus whenever, in his judgment, the public safety required, and he did, by proclamation, bearing date the 15th of September, 1863, reciting, among other things, the authority of this statute, suspend it. The suspension of the writ does not authorize the arrest of anyone, but simply denies to one arrested the privilege of this writ in order to obtain his liberty.

It is proper therefore to inquire under what circumstances the courts could rightfully refuse to grant this writ, and when the citizen was at liberty to invoke its aid.

The second and third sections of the law are explicit on these points. The language used is plain and direct, and the meaning of the Congress cannot be mistaken. The public safety demanded, if the President thought proper to arrest a suspected person, that he should not be required to give the cause of his detention on return to a writ of habeas corpus. But it was not contemplated that such person should be detained in custody beyond a certain fixed period unless certain judicial proceedings, known to the common law, were commenced against him. The Secretaries of State and War were directed to furnish to the judges of the courts of the United States a list of the names of all parties, not prisoners of war, resident in their respective jurisdictions, who then were or afterwards should be held in custody by the authority of the President, and who were citizens of states in which the administration of the laws in the Federal tribunals was unimpaired. After the list was furnished, if a grand jury of the district convened and adjourned, and did not indict or present one of the persons thus named, he was entitled to his discharge, and it was the duty of the judge of the court to order him brought before him to be discharged if he desired it. The refusal or omission to furnish the list could not operate to the injury of anyone who was not indicted or presented by the grand jury, for, if twenty days had elapsed from the time of his arrest and the termination of the session of the grand jury, he was equally entitled to his discharge as if the list were furnished, and any credible person, on petition verified by affidavit, could obtain the judge's order for that purpose.

Milligan, in his application to be released from imprisonment, averred the existence of every fact necessary under the terms of this law to give the Circuit Court of Indiana jurisdiction. If he was detained in custody by the order of the President otherwise than as a prisoner of war, if he was a citizen of Indiana and had never been in the military or naval service, and the grand jury of the district had met, after he had been arrested, for a period of twenty days, and adjourned without taking any proceedings against him, then the court had the right to entertain his petition and determine the lawfulness of his imprisonment. Because

the word "court" is not found in the body of the second section, it was argued at the bar that the application should have been made to a judge of the court, and not to the court itself; but this is not so, for power is expressly conferred in the last proviso of the section on the court equally with a judge of it to discharge from imprisonment. It was the manifest design of Congress to secure a certain remedy by which anyone deprived of liberty could obtain it if there was a judicial failure to find cause of offence against him. Courts are not, always in session, and can adjourn on the discharge of the grand jury, and before those who are in confinement could take proper steps to procure their liberation. To provide for this contingency, authority was given to the judges out of court to grant relief to any party who could show that, under the law, he should be no longer restrained of his liberty.

It was insisted that Milligan's case was defective because it did not state that the list was furnished to the judges, and therefore it was impossible to say under which section of the act it was presented.

It is not easy to see how this omission could affect the question of jurisdiction. Milligan could not know that the list was furnished, unless the judges volunteered to tell him, for the law did not require that any record should be made of it or anybody but the judges informed of it. Why aver the fact when the truth of the matter was apparent to the court without an averment? How can Milligan be harmed by the absence of the averment when he states that he was under arrest for more than sixty days before the court and grand jury, which should have considered his case, met at Indianapolis? It is apparent therefore that, under the Habeas Corpus Act of 1863, the Circuit Court of Indiana had complete jurisdiction to adjudicate upon this case, and, if the judges could not agree on questions vital to the progress of the cause, they had the authority (as we have shown in a previous part of this opinion), and it was their duty, to certify those questions of disagreement to this court for final decision. It was argued that a final decision on the questions presented ought not to be made, because the parties who were directly concerned in the arrest and detention of Milligan were not before the court, and their rights might be prejudiced by the answer which should be given to those questions. But this court cannot know what return will be made to the writ of habeas corpus when issued, and it is very clear that no one is concluded upon any question that may be raised to that return. In the sense of the law of 1802 which authorized a certificate of division, a final decision means final upon the points certified, final upon the court below, so that it is estopped from any adverse ruling in all the subsequent proceedings of the cause.

But it is said that this case is ended, as the presumption is that Milligan was hanged in pursuance of the order of the President.

Although we have no judicial information on the subject, yet the inference is that he is alive, for otherwise learned counsel would not appear for him and urge this court to decide his case. It can never be, in this country of written constitution and laws, with a judicial department to interpret them, that any chief magistrate would be so far forgetful of his duty as to order the execution of a man who denied the jurisdiction that tried and convicted him after his case was before Federal judges with power to decide it, who, being unable to agree on the grave questions involved, had, according to known law, sent it to the Supreme Court of the United States for decision. But even the suggestion is injurious to the Executive, and we dismiss it from further consideration. There is therefore nothing to hinder this court from an investigation of the merits of this controversy.

The controlling question in the case is this: upon the facts stated in Milligan's petition and the exhibits filed, had the military commission mentioned in it jurisdiction legally to try and sentence him? Milligan, not a resident of one of the rebellious states or a prisoner of war, but a citizen of Indiana for twenty years past and never in the military or naval service, is, while at his home, arrested by the military power of the United States, imprisoned, and, on certain criminal charges preferred against him, tried, convicted, and sentenced to be hanged by a military commission, organized under the direction of the military commander of the military district of Indiana. Had this tribunal the legal power and authority to try and punish this man?

No graver question was ever considered by this court, nor one which more nearly concerns the rights of the whole people, for it is the birthright of every American citizen when charged with crime to be tried and punished according to law. The power of punishment is alone through the means which the laws have provided for that purpose, and, if they are ineffectual, there is an immunity from punishment, no matter how great an offender the individual may be or how much his crimes may have shocked the sense of justice of the country or endangered its safety. By the protection of the law, human rights are secured; withdraw that protection and they are at the mercy of wicked rulers or the clamor of an excited people. If there was law to justify this military trial, it is not our province to interfere; if there was not, it is our duty to declare the nullity of the whole proceedings. The decision of this question does not depend on argument or judicial precedents, numerous and highly illustrative as they are. These precedents inform us of the extent of the struggle to preserve liberty and to relieve those in civil life from military trials. The founders of our government were familiar with the history of that struggle, and secured in a written constitution every right which the people had wrested from power during a contest of ages. By that Constitution and the laws authorized by it, this question must be determined. The provisions of that instrument on the administration of criminal justice are too plain and direct to leave room for misconstruction or doubt of their true meaning. Those applicable to this case are found in that clause of the original Constitution which says "That the trial of all crimes, except in case of impeachment, shall be by jury," and in the fourth, fifth, and sixth articles of the amendments. The fourth proclaims the right to be secure in person and effects against unreasonable search and seizure, and directs that a judicial warrant shall not issue "without proof of probable cause supported by oath or affirmation." The fifth declares

"that no person shall be held to answer for a capital or otherwise infamous crime unless on presentment by a grand jury, except in cases arising in the land or naval forces, or in the militia, when in actual service in time of war or public danger, nor be deprived of life, liberty, or property without due process of law."

And the sixth guarantees the right of trial by jury, in such manner and with such regulations that, with upright judges, impartial juries, and an able bar, the innocent will be saved and the guilty punished. It is in these words:

"In all criminal prosecutions the accused shall enjoy the right to a speedy and public trial by an impartial jury of the state and district wherein the crime shall have been committed, which district shall have been previously ascertained by law, and to be informed of the nature and cause of the accusation, to be confronted with the witnesses against him, to have compulsory process for obtaining witnesses in his favor, and to have the assistance of counsel for his defence."

These securities for personal liberty thus embodied were such as wisdom and experience had demonstrated to be necessary for the protection of those accused of crime. And so strong was the sense of the country of their importance, and so jealous were the people that these rights, highly prized, might be denied them by implication, that, when the original Constitution was proposed for adoption, it encountered severe opposition, and, but for the belief that it would be so amended as to embrace them, it would never have been ratified.

Time has proven the discernment of our ancestors, for even these provisions, expressed in such plain English words that it would seem the ingenuity of man could not evade them, are now, after the lapse of more than seventy years, sought to be avoided. Those great and good men foresaw that troublous times would arise when rulers and people would become restive under restraint, and seek by sharp and decisive measures to accomplish ends deemed just and proper, and that the principles of constitutional liberty would be in peril unless established by irrepealable law. The history of the world had taught them that what was done in the past might be attempted in the future. The Constitution of the United States is a law for rulers and people, equally in war and in peace, and covers with the shield of its protection all classes of men, at all times and under all circumstances. No doctrine involving more pernicious consequences was ever invented by the wit of man than that any of its provisions can be suspended during any of the great exigencies of government. Such a doctrine leads directly to anarchy or despotism, but the theory of necessity on which it is based is false, for the government, within the Constitution, has all the powers granted to it which are necessary to preserve its existence, as has been happily proved by the result of the great effort to throw off its just authority.

Have any of the rights guaranteed by the Constitution been violated in the case of Milligan?, and, if so, what are they?

Every trial involves the exercise of judicial power, and from what source did the military commission that tried him derive their authority? Certainly no part of judicial power of the country was conferred on them, because the Constitution expressly vests it "in one supreme court and such inferior courts as the Congress may from time to time ordain and establish," and it is not pretended that the commission was a court ordained and established by Congress. They cannot justify on the mandate of the President, because he is controlled by law, and has his appropriate sphere of duty, which is to execute, not to make, the laws, and there is "no unwritten criminal code to which resort can be had as a source of jurisdiction."

But it is said that the jurisdiction is complete under the "laws and usages of war."

It can serve no useful purpose to inquire what those laws and usages are, whence they originated, where found, and on whom they operate; they can never be applied to citizens in states which have upheld the authority of the government, and where the courts are open and their process unobstructed. This court has judicial knowledge that, in Indiana, the Federal authority was always unopposed, and its courts always open to hear criminal accusations and redress grievances, and no usage of war could sanction a military trial there for any offence whatever of a citizen in civil life in nowise connected with the military service. Congress could grant no such power, and, to the honor of our national legislature be it said, it has never been provoked by the state of the country even to attempt its exercise. One of the plainest constitutional provisions was therefore infringed when Milligan was tried by a court not ordained and established by Congress and not composed of judges appointed during good behavior.

Why was he not delivered to the Circuit Court of Indiana to be proceeded against according to law? No reason of necessity could be urged against it, because Congress had declared penalties against the offences charged, provided for their punishment, and directed that court to hear and determine them. And soon after this military tribunal was ended, the Circuit Court met, peacefully transacted its business, and adjourned. It needed no bayonets to protect it, and required no military aid to execute its judgments. It was held in a state, eminently distinguished for patriotism, by judges commissioned during the Rebellion, who were provided with juries, upright, intelligent, and selected by a marshal appointed by the President. The government had no right to conclude that Milligan, if guilty, would not receive in that court merited punishment, for its records disclose that it was constantly engaged in the trial of similar offences, and was never interrupted in its administration of criminal justice. If it was dangerous, in the distracted condition of affairs, to leave Milligan unrestrained of his liberty because he "conspired against the government, afforded aid and comfort to rebels, and incited the people to insurrection," the law said arrest him, confine him closely, render him powerless to do further mischief, and then present his case to the grand jury of the district, with proofs of his guilt, and, if indicted, try him according to the course of the common law. If this had been done, the Constitution would have been vindicated, the law of 1863 enforced, and the securities for personal liberty preserved and defended.

Another guarantee of freedom was broken when Milligan was denied a trial by jury. The great minds of the country have differed on the correct interpretation to be given to various provisions of the Federal Constitution, and judicial decision has been often invoked to settle their true meaning; but, until recently, no one ever doubted that the right of trial by jury was fortified in the organic law against the power of attack. It is *now* assailed, but if ideas can be expressed in words and language has any meaning, *this right*—one of the most valuable in a free country—is preserved to everyone accused of crime who is not attached to the army or navy or militia in actual service. The sixth amendment affirms that, "in all criminal prosecutions, the accused shall enjoy the right to a speedy and public trial by an impartial jury," language broad enough to embrace all persons and cases; but the fifth, recognizing the necessity of an indictment or presentment before anyone can be held to answer for high crimes, "*excepts* cases arising in the land or naval forces, or in the militia, when in actual service, in time of war or public danger," and the framers of the Constitution doubtless meant to limit the right of trial by jury in the sixth amendment to those persons who were subject to indictment or presentment in the fifth.

The discipline necessary to the efficiency of the army and navy required other and swifter modes of trial than are furnished by the common law courts, and, in pursuance of the power conferred by the Constitution, Congress has declared the kinds of trial, and the manner in which they shall be conducted, for offences committed while the party is in the military or naval service. Everyone connected with these branches of the public service is amenable to the jurisdiction which Congress has created for their government, and, while thus serving, surrenders his right to be tried by the civil courts. *All other persons,* citizens of states where the courts are open, if charged with crime, are guaranteed the inestimable privilege of trial by jury. This privilege is a vital principle, underlying the whole administration of criminal justice; it is not held by sufferance, and cannot be frittered away on any plea of state or political necessity. When peace prevails, and the authority of the government is undisputed, there is no difficulty of preserving the safeguards of liberty, for the ordinary modes of trial are never neglected, and no one wishes it otherwise; but if society is disturbed by civil commotion—if the passions of men are aroused and the restraints of law weakened, if not disregarded—these safeguards need, and should receive, the watchful care of those intrusted with the guardianship of the Constitution and laws. In no other way can we transmit to posterity unimpaired the blessings of liberty, consecrated by the sacrifices of the Revolution.

It is claimed that martial law covers with its broad mantle the proceedings of this military commission. The proposition is this: that, in a time of war, the commander of an armed force (if, in his opinion, the exigencies of the country demand it, and of which he is to judge) has the power, within the lines of his military district, to suspend all civil rights and their remedies and subject citizens, as well as soldiers to the rule of *his will,* and, in the exercise of his lawful authority, cannot be restrained except by his superior officer or the President of the United States.

If this position is sound to the extent claimed, then, when war exists, foreign or domestic, and the country is subdivided into military departments for mere convenience, the commander of one of them can, if he chooses, within his limits, on the plea of necessity, with the approval of the Executive, substitute military force for and to the exclusion of the laws, and punish all persons as he thinks right and proper, without fixed or certain rules.

The statement of this proposition shows its importance, for, if true, republican government is a failure, and there is an end of liberty regulated by law. Martial law established on such a basis destroys every guarantee of the Constitution, and effectually renders the "military independent of and superior to the civil power"—the attempt to do which by the King of Great Britain was deemed by our fathers such an offence that they assigned it to the world as one of the causes which impelled them to declare their independence. Civil liberty and this kind of martial law cannot endure together; the antagonism is irreconcilable, and, in the conflict, one or the other must perish.

This nation, as experience has proved, cannot always remain at peace, and has no right to expect that it will always have wise and humane rulers sincerely attached to the principles of the Constitution. Wicked men, ambitious of power, with hatred of liberty and contempt of law, may fill the place once occupied by Washington and Lincoln, and if this right is conceded, and the calamities of war again befall us, the dangers to human liberty are frightful to contemplate. If our fathers had failed to provide for just such a contingency, they would have been false to the trust reposed in them. They knew—the history of the world told them—the nation they were founding, be its existence short or long, would be involved in war; how often or how long continued human foresight could not tell, and that unlimited power, wherever lodged at such a time, was especially hazardous to freemen. For this and other equally weighty reasons, they secured the inheritance they had fought to maintain by incorporating in a written constitution the safeguards which time had proved were essential to its preservation. Not one of these safeguards can the President or Congress or the Judiciary disturb, except the one concerning the writ of habeas corpus.

It is essential to the safety of every government that, in a great crisis like the one we have just passed through, there should be a power somewhere of suspending the writ of habeas corpus. In every war, there are men of previously good character wicked enough to counsel their fellow-citizens to resist the measures deemed necessary by a good government to sustain its just authority and overthrow its enemies, and their influence may lead to dangerous combinations. In the emergency of the times, an immediate public investigation according to law may not be possible, and yet the period to the country may be too imminent to suffer such persons to go at large. Unquestionably, there is then an exigency which demands that the government, if

it should see fit in the exercise of a proper discretion to make arrests, should not be required to produce the persons arrested in answer to a writ of habeas corpus. The Constitution goes no further. It does not say, after a writ of habeas corpus is denied a citizen, that he shall be tried otherwise than by the course of the common law; if it had intended this result, it was easy, by the use of direct words, to have accomplished it. The illustrious men who framed that instrument were guarding the foundations of civil liberty against the abuses of unlimited power; they were full of wisdom, and the lessons of history informed them that a trial by an established court, assisted by an impartial jury, was the only sure way of protecting the citizen against oppression and wrong. Knowing this, they limited the suspension to one great right, and left the rest to remain forever inviolable. But it is insisted that the safety of the country in time of war demands that this broad claim for martial law shall be sustained. If this were true, it could be well said that a country, preserved at the sacrifice of all the cardinal principles of liberty, is not worth the cost of preservation. Happily, it is not so.

It will be borne in mind that this is not a question of the power to proclaim martial law when war exists in a community and the courts and civil authorities are overthrown. Nor is it a question what rule a military commander, at the head of his army, can impose on states in rebellion to cripple their resources and quell the insurrection. The jurisdiction claimed is much more extensive. The necessities of the service during the late Rebellion required that the loyal states should be placed within the limits of certain military districts and commanders appointed in them, and it is urged that this, in a military sense, constituted them the theater of military operations, and as, in this case, Indiana had been and was again threatened with invasion by the enemy, the occasion was furnished to establish martial law. The conclusion does not follow from the premises. If armies were collected in Indiana, they were to be employed in another locality, where the laws were obstructed and the national authority disputed. On her soil there was no hostile foot; if once invaded, that invasion was at an end, and, with it, all pretext for martial law. Martial law cannot arise from a *threatened* invasion. The necessity must be actual and present, the invasion real, such as effectually closes the courts and deposes the civil administration.

It is difficult to see how the *safety* for the country required martial law in Indiana. If any of her citizens were plotting treason, the power of arrest could secure them until the government was prepared for their trial, when the courts were open and ready to try them. It was as easy to protect witnesses before a civil as a military tribunal, and as there could be no wish to convict except on sufficient legal evidence, surely an ordained and establish court was better able to judge of this than a military tribunal composed of gentlemen not trained to the profession of the law.

It follows from what has been said on this subject that there are occasions when martial rule can be properly applied. If, in foreign invasion or civil war, the courts are actually closed, and it is impossible to administer criminal justice according to law, *then,* on the theatre of active military operations, where war really prevails, there is a necessity to furnish a substitute for the civil authority, thus overthrown, to preserve the safety of the army and society, and as no power is left but the military, it is allowed to govern by martial rule until the laws can have their free course. As necessity creates the rule, so it limits its duration, for, if this government is continued *after* the courts are reinstated, it is a gross usurpation of power. Martial rule can never exist where the courts are open and in the proper and unobstructed exercise of their jurisdiction. It is also confined to the locality of actual war. Because, during the late Rebellion, it could have been enforced in Virginia, where the national authority was overturned and the courts driven out, it does not follow that it should obtain in Indiana, where that authority was never disputed and justice was always administered. And so, in the case of a foreign invasion, martial rule may become a necessity in one state when, in another, it would be "mere lawless violence." We are not without precedents in English and American history illustrating our views of this question, but it is hardly necessary to make particular reference to them.

From the first year of the reign of Edward the Third, when the Parliament of England reversed the attainder of the Earl of Lancaster because he could have been tried by the courts of the realm, and declared

"that, in time of peace, no man ought to be adjudged to death for treason or any other offence without being arraigned and held to answer, and that regularly when the king's courts are open it is a time of peace in judgment of law,"

down to the present day, martial law, as claimed in this case, has been condemned by all respectable English jurists as contrary to the fundamental laws of the land and subversive of the liberty of the subject.

During the present century, an instructive debate on this question occurred in Parliament, occasioned by the trial and conviction by court-martial, at Demerara, of the Rev. John Smith, a missionary to the negroes, on the alleged ground of aiding and abetting a formidable rebellion in that colony. Those eminent statesmen Lord Brougham and Sir James Mackintosh participated in that debate, and denounced the trial as illegal because it did not appear that the courts of law in Demerara could not try offences, and that, "when the laws can act, every other mode of punishing supposed crimes is itself an enormous crime."

So sensitive were our Revolutionary fathers on this subject, although Boston was almost in a state of siege, when General Gage issued his proclamation of martial law, they spoke of it as an "attempt to supersede the course of the common law, and, instead thereof, to publish and order the use of martial law." The Virginia Assembly also denounced a similar measure on the part of Governor Dunmore

"as an assumed power which the king himself cannot exercise, because it annuls the law of the land and introduces the most execrable of all systems, martial law."

In some parts of the country, during the war of 1812, our officers made arbitrary arrests and, by military tribunals, tried citizens who were not in the military service. These arrests and trials, when brought to the notice of the courts, were uniformly condemned as illegal. The cases of *Smith v. Shaw* and *McConnell v. Hampden* (reported in 12 Johnson) are illustrations, which we cite not only for the principles they determine but on account of the distinguished jurists concerned in the decisions, one of whom for many years occupied a seat on this bench.

It is contended, that *Luther v. Borden,* decided by this court, is an authority for the claim of martial law advanced in this case. The decision is misapprehended. That case grew out of the attempt in Rhode Island to supersede the old colonial government by a revolutionary proceeding. Rhode Island, until that period, had no other form of local government than the charter granted by King Charles II in 1663, and, as that limited the right of suffrage, and did not provide for its own amendment, many citizens became dissatisfied because the legislature would not afford the relief in their power, and, without the authority of law, formed a new and independent constitution and proceeded to assert its authority by force of arms. The old government resisted this, and, as the rebellion was formidable, called out the militia to subdue it and passed an act declaring martial law. Borden, in the military service of the old government, broke open the house of Luther, who supported the new, in order to arrest him. Luther brought suit against Borden, and the question was whether, under the constitution and laws of the state, Borden was justified. This court held that a state "may use its military power to put down an armed insurrection too strong to be controlled by the civil authority," and, if the legislature of Rhode Island thought the period so great as to require the use of its military forces and the declaration of martial law, there was no ground on which this court could question its authority, and, as Borden acted under military orders of the charter government, which had been recognized by the political power of the country, and was upheld by the state judiciary, he was justified in breaking into and entering Luther's house. This is the extent of the decision. There was no question in issue about the power of declaring martial law under the Federal Constitution, and the court did not consider it necessary even to inquire "to what extent nor under what circumstances that power may by exercised by a state."

We do not deem it important to examine further the adjudged cases, and shall therefore conclude without any additional reference to authorities.

To the third question, then, on which the judges below were opposed in opinion, an answer in the negative must be returned.

It is proper to say, although Milligan's trial and conviction by a military commission was illegal, yet, if guilty of the crimes imputed to him, and his guilt had been ascertained by an established court and impartial jury, he deserved severe punishment. Open resistance to the measures deemed necessary to subdue a great rebellion, by those who enjoy the protection of government, and have not the excuse even of prejudice of section to plead in their favor, is wicked; but that resistance becomes an enormous crime when it assumes the form

of a secret political organization, armed to oppose the laws, and seeks by stealthy means to introduce the enemies of the country into peaceful communities, there to light the torch of civil war and thus overthrow the power of the United States. Conspiracies like these, at such a juncture, are extremely perilous, and those concerned in them are dangerous enemies to their country, and should receive the heaviest penalties of the law as an example to deter others from similar criminal conduct. It is said the severity of the laws caused them; but Congress was obliged to enact severe laws to meet the crisis, and as our highest civil duty is to serve our country when in danger, the late war has proved that rigorous laws, when necessary, will be cheerfully obeyed by a patriotic people, struggling to preserve the rich blessings of a free government.

The two remaining questions in this case must be answered in the affirmative. The suspension of the privilege of the writ of habeas corpus does not suspend the writ itself. The writ issues as a matter of course, and, on the return made to it, the court decides whether the party applying is denied the right of proceeding any further with it.

If the military trial of Milligan was contrary to law, then he was entitled, on the facts stated in his petition, to be discharged from custody by the terms of the act of Congress of March 3d, 1863. The provisions of this law having been considered in a previous part of this opinion, we will not restate the views there presented. Milligan avers he was a citizen of Indiana, not in the military or naval service, and was detained in close confinement, by order of the President, from the 5th day of October, 1864, until the 2d day of January, 1865, when the Circuit Court for the District of Indiana, with a grand jury, convened in session at Indianapolis, and afterwards, on the 27th day of the same month, adjourned without finding an indictment or presentment against him. If these averments were true (and their truth is conceded for the purposes of this case), the court was required to liberate him on taking certain oaths prescribed by the law, and entering into recognizance for his good behavior.

But it is insisted that Milligan was a prisoner of war, and therefore excluded from the privileges of the statute. It is not easy to see how he can be treated as a prisoner of war when he lived in Indiana for the past twenty years, was arrested there, and had not been, during the late troubles, a resident of any of the states in rebellion. If in Indiana he conspired with bad men to assist the enemy, he is punishable for it in the courts of Indiana; but, when tried for the offence, he cannot plead the rights of war, for he was not engaged in legal acts of hostility against the government, and only such persons, when captured, are prisoners of war. If he cannot enjoy the immunities attaching to the character of a prisoner of war, how can he be subject to their pains and penalties?

This case, as well as the kindred cases of Bowles and Horsey, were disposed of at the last term, and the proper orders were entered of record. There is therefore no additional entry required.

### The CHIEF JUSTICE delivered the following opinion

Four members of the court, concurring with their brethren in the order heretofore made in this cause, but unable to concur in some important particulars with the opinion which has just been read, think it their duty to make a separate statement of their views of the whole case.

We do not doubt that the Circuit Court for the District of Indiana had jurisdiction of the petition of Milligan for the writ of habeas corpus.

Whether this court has jurisdiction upon the certificate of division admits of more question. The construction of the act authorizing such certificates, which has hitherto prevailed here, denies jurisdiction in cases where the certificate brings up the whole cause before the court. But none of the adjudicated cases is exactly in point, and we are willing to resolve whatever doubt may exist in favor of the earliest possible answers to questions involving life and liberty. We agree, therefore, that this court may properly answer questions certified in such a case as that before us.

The crimes with which Milligan was charged were of the gravest character, and the petition and exhibits in the record, which must here be taken as true, admit his guilt. But whatever his desert of punishment may be, it is more important to the country and to every citizen that he should not be punished under an illegal sentence, sanctioned by this court of last resort, than that he should be punished at all. The laws which protect the liberties of the whole people must not be

violated or set aside in order to inflict, even upon the guilty, unauthorized though merited justice.

The trial and sentence of Milligan were by military commission convened in Indiana during the fall of 1864. The action of the commission had been under consideration by President Lincoln for some time when he himself became the victim of an abhorred conspiracy. It was approved by his successor in May, 1865, and the sentence was ordered to be carried into execution. The proceedings therefore had the fullest sanction of the executive department of the government.

This sanction requires the most respectful and the most careful consideration of this court. The sentence which it supports must not be set aside except upon the clearest conviction that it cannot be reconciled with the Constitution and the constitutional legislation of Congress.

We must inquire, then, what constitutional or statutory provisions have relation to this military proceeding.

The act of Congress of March 3d, 1863, comprises all the legislation which seems to require consideration in this connection. The constitutionality of this act has not been questioned and is not doubted.

The first section authorized the suspension, during the Rebellion, of the writ of habeas corpus throughout the United States by the President. The two next sections limited this authority in important respects.

The second section required that lists of all persons, being citizens of states in which the administration of the laws had continued unimpaired in the Federal courts, who were then held or might thereafter be held as prisoners of the United States, under the authority of the President, otherwise than as prisoners of war, should be furnished to the judges of the Circuit and District Courts. The lists transmitted to the judges were to contain the names of all persons, residing within their respective jurisdictions, charged with violation of national law. And it was required, in cases where the grand jury in attendance upon any of these courts should terminate its session without proceeding by indictment or otherwise against any prisoner named in the list, that the judge of the court should forthwith make an order that such prisoner, desiring a discharge, should be brought before him or the court to be discharged on entering into recognizance, if required, to keep the peace and for good behavior, or to appear, as the court might direct, to be further dealt with according to law. Every officer of the United States having custody of such prisoners was required to obey and execute the judge's order under penalty, for refusal or delay, of fine and imprisonment.

The third section provided, in case lists of persons other than prisoners of war then held in confinement, or thereafter arrested, should not be furnished within twenty days after the passage of the act, or, in cases of subsequent arrest, within twenty days after the time of arrest, that any citizen, after the termination of a session of the grand jury without indictment or presentment, might, by petition alleging the facts and verified by oath, obtain the judge's order of discharge in favor of any person so imprisoned on the terms and conditions prescribed in the second section.

It was made the duty of the District Attorney of the United States to attend examinations on petitions for discharge.

It was under this act that Milligan petitioned the Circuit Court for the District of Indiana for discharge from imprisonment.

The holding of the Circuit and District Courts of the United States in Indiana had been uninterrupted. The administration of the laws in the Federal courts had remained unimpaired. Milligan was imprisoned under the authority of the President, and was not a prisoner of war. No list of prisoners had been furnished to the judges, either of the District or Circuit Courts, as required by the law. A grand jury had attended the Circuit Courts of the Indiana district while Milligan was there imprisoned, and had closed its session without finding any indictment or presentment or otherwise proceeding against the prisoner.

His case was thus brought within the precise letter and intent of the act of Congress, unless it can be said that Milligan was not imprisoned by authority of the President, and nothing of this sort was claimed in argument on the part of the government.

It is clear upon this statement that the Circuit Court was bound to hear Milligan's petition for the writ of habeas corpus, called in the act an order to bring the prisoner before the judge or the court, and to issue the writ, or, in the language of the act, to make the order.

The first question, therefore—ought the writ to issue?—must be answered in the affirmative.

And it is equally clear that he was entitled to the discharge prayed for.

It must be borne in mind that the prayer of the petition was not for an absolute discharge, but to be delivered from military custody and imprisonment, and if found probably guilty of any offence, to be turned over to the proper tribunal for inquiry and punishment, or, if not found thus probably guilty, to be discharged altogether.

And the express terms of the act of Congress required this action of the court. The prisoner must be discharged on giving such recognizance as the court should require, not only for good behavior, but for appearance, as directed by the court, to answer and be further dealt with according to law.

The first section of the act authorized the suspension of the writ of habeas corpus generally throughout the United States. The second and third sections limited this suspension, in certain cases, within states where the administration of justice by the Federal courts remained unimpaired. In these cases, the writ was still to issue, and, under it, the prisoner was entitled to his discharge by a circuit or district judge or court unless held to bail for appearance to answer charges. No other judge or court could make an order of discharge under the writ. Except under the circumstances pointed out by the act, neither circuit nor district judge or court could make such an order. But under those circumstances, the writ must be issued, and the relief from imprisonment directed by the act must be afforded. The commands of the act were positive, and left no discretion to court or judge.

An affirmative answer must therefore be given to the second question, namely: ought Milligan to be discharged according to the prayer of the petition?

That the third question, namely: had the military commission in Indiana, under the facts stated, jurisdiction to try and sentence Milligan? must be answered negatively is an unavoidable inference from affirmative answers to the other two.

The military commission could not have jurisdiction to try and sentence Milligan if he could not be detained in prison under his original arrest or under sentence after the close of a session of the grand jury without indictment or other proceeding against him.

Indeed, the act seems to have been framed on purpose to secure the trial of all offences of citizens by civil tribunals in states where these tribunals were not interrupted in the regular exercise of their functions.

Under it, in such states, the privilege of the writ might be suspended. Any person regarded as dangerous to the public safety might be arrested and detained until after the session of a grand jury. Until after such session, no person arrested could have the benefit of the writ, and even then no such person could be discharged except on such terms, as to future appearance, as the court might impose. These provisions obviously contemplate no other trial or sentence than that of a civil court, and we could not assert the legality of a trial and sentence by a military commission, under the circumstances specified in the act and described in the petition, without disregarding the plain directions of Congress.

We agree therefore that the first two questions certified must receive affirmative answers, and the last a negative. We do not doubt that the positive provisions of the act of Congress require such answers. We do not think it necessary to look beyond these provisions. In them, we find sufficient and controlling reasons for our conclusions.

But the opinion which has just been read goes further, and, as we understand it, asserts not only that the military commission held in Indiana was not authorized by Congress, but that it was not in the power of Congress to authorize it, from which it may be thought to follow that Congress has no power to indemnify the officers who composed the commission against liability in civil courts for acting as members of it.

We cannot agree to this.

We agree in the proposition that no department of the government of the United States—neither President, nor Congress, nor the Courts—possesses any power not given by the Constitution.

We assent fully to all that is said in the opinion of the inestimable value of the trial by jury, and of the other constitutional safeguards of civil liberty. And we concur also in what is said of the writ of habeas corpus and of its suspension, with two reservations: (1) that, in our judgment, when the writ is suspended, the Executive is authorized to arrest, as well as to detain, and (2) that there are cases in which, the privilege of the writ being suspended, trial and punishment by military commission, in states where civil courts are open, may be authorized by Congress, as well as arrest and detention.

We think that Congress had power, though not exercised, to authorize the military commission which was held in Indiana.

We do not think it necessary to discuss at large the grounds of our conclusions. We will briefly indicate some of them.

The Constitution itself provides for military government, as well as for civil government. And we do not understand it to be claimed that the civil safeguards of the Constitution have application in cases within the proper sphere of the former.

What, then, is that proper sphere? Congress has power to raise and support armies, to provide and maintain a navy, to make rules for the government and regulation of the land and naval forces, and to provide for governing such part of the militia as may be in the service of the United States.

It is not denied that the power to make rules for the government of the army and navy is a power to provide for trial and punishment by military courts without a jury. It has been so understood and exercised from the adoption of the Constitution to the present time.

Nor, in our judgment, does the fifth, or any other amendment, abridge that power. "Cases arising in the land and naval forces, or in the militia in actual service in time of war or public danger," are expressly excepted from the fifth amendment, "that no person shall be held to answer for a capital or otherwise infamous crime, unless on a presentment or indictment of a grand jury," and it is admitted that the exception applies to the other amendments as well as to the fifth.

Now we understand this exception to have the same import and effect as if the powers of Congress in relation to the government of the army and navy and the militia had been recited in the amendment, and cases within those powers had been expressly excepted from its operation. The states, most jealous of encroachments upon the liberties of the citizen, when proposing additional safeguards in the form of amendments, excluded specifically from their effect cases arising in the government of the land and naval forces. Thus, Massachusetts proposed that

"no person shall be tried for any crime by which he would incur an infamous punishment or loss of life until he be first indicted by a grand jury except in such cases as may arise in the government and regulation of the land forces."

The exception in similar amendments proposed by New York, Maryland, and Virginia was in the same or equivalent terms. The amendments proposed by the states were considered by the first Congress, and such as were approved in substance were put in form and proposed by that body to the states. Among those thus proposed and subsequently ratified was that which now stands as the fifth amendment of the Constitution. We cannot doubt that this amendment was intended to have the same force and effect as the amendment proposed by the states. We cannot agree to a construction which will impose on the exception in the fifth amendment a sense other than that obviously indicated by action of the state conventions.

We think, therefore, that the power of Congress in the government of the land and naval forces and of the militia is not at all affected by the fifth or any other amendment. It is not necessary to attempt any precise definition of the boundaries of this power. But may it not be said that government includes protection and defence, as well as the regulation of internal administration? And is it impossible to imagine cases in which citizens conspiring or attempting the destruction or great injury of the national forces may be subjected by Congress to military trial and punishment in the just exercise of this undoubted constitutional power? Congress is but the agent of the nation, and does not the security of individuals against the abuse of this, as of every other, power depend on the intelligence and virtue of the people, on their zeal for public and private liberty, upon official responsibility secured by law, and upon the frequency of elections, rather than upon doubtful constructions of legislative powers?

But we do not put our opinion that Congress might authorize such a military commission as was held in

Indiana upon the power to provide for the government of the national forces.

Congress has the power not only to raise and support and govern armies, but to declare war. It has therefore the power to provide by law for carrying on war. This power necessarily extends to all legislation essential to the prosecution of war with vigor and success except such as interferes with the command of the forces and the conduct of campaigns. That power and duty belong to the President as commander-in-chief. Both these powers are derived from the Constitution, but neither is defined by that instrument. Their extent must be determined by their nature and by the principles of our institutions.

The power to make the necessary laws is in Congress, the power to execute in the President. Both powers imply many subordinate and auxiliary powers. Each includes all authorities essential to its due exercise. But neither can the President, in war more than in peace, intrude upon the proper authority of Congress, nor Congress upon the proper authority of the President. Both are servants of the people, whose will is expressed in the fundamental law. Congress cannot direct the conduct of campaigns, nor can the President, or any commander under him, without the sanction of Congress, institute tribunals for the trial and punishment of offences, either of soldiers or civilians, unless in cases of a controlling necessity, which justifies what it compels, or at least insures acts of indemnity from the justice of the legislature.

We by no means assert that Congress can establish and apply the laws of war where no war has been declared or exists.

Where peace exists, the laws of peace must prevail. What we do maintain is that, when the nation is involved in war, and some portions of the country are invaded, and all are exposed to invasion, it is within the power of Congress to determine in what states or district such great and imminent public danger exists as justifies the authorization of military tribunals for the trial of crimes and offences against the discipline or security of the army or against the public safety.

In Indiana, for example, at the time of the arrest of Milligan and his co-conspirators, it is established by the papers in the record, that the state was a military district, was the theatre of military operations, had been actually invaded, and was constantly threatened with invasion. It appears also that a powerful secret association, composed of citizens and others, existed within the state, under military organization, conspiring against the draft and plotting insurrection, the liberation of the prisoners of war at various depots, the seizure of the state and national arsenals, armed cooperation with the enemy, and war against the national government.

We cannot doubt that, in such a time of public danger, Congress had power under the Constitution to provide for the organization of a military commission and for trial by that commission of persons engaged in this conspiracy. The fact that the Federal courts were open was regarded by Congress as a sufficient reason for not exercising the power, but that fact could not deprive Congress of the right to exercise it. Those courts might be open and undisturbed in the execution of their functions, and yet wholly incompetent to avert threatened danger or to punish, with adequate promptitude and certainty, the guilty conspirators.

In Indiana, the judges and officers of the courts were loyal to the government. But it might have been otherwise. In times of rebellion and civil war, it may often happen, indeed, that judges and marshals will be in active sympathy with the rebels, and courts their most efficient allies.

We have confined ourselves to the question of power. It was for Congress to determine the question of expediency. And Congress did determine it. That body did not see fit to authorize trials by military commission in Indiana, but, by the strongest implication, prohibited them. With that prohibition we are satisfied, and should have remained silent if the answers to the questions certified had been put on that ground, without denial of the existence of a power which we believe to be constitutional and important to the public safety—a denial which, as we have already suggested, seems to draw in question the power of Congress to protect from prosecution the members of military commissions who acted in obedience to their superior officers and whose action, whether warranted by law or not, was approved by that upright and patriotic President under whose administration the Republic was rescued from threatened destruction.

We have thus far said little of martial law, nor do we propose to say much. What we have already said sufficiently indicates our opinion that there is no law for the government of the citizens, the armies or the navy of the United States, within American jurisdiction, which is not contained in or derived from the Constitution. And wherever our army or navy may go beyond our territorial limits, neither can go beyond the authority of the President or the legislation of Congress.

There are under the Constitution three kinds of military jurisdiction: one to be exercised both in peace and war, another to be exercised in time of foreign war without the boundaries of the United States, or in time of rebellion and civil war within states or districts occupied by rebels treated as belligerents, and a third to be exercised in time of invasion or insurrection within the limits of the United States or during rebellion within the limits of states maintaining adhesion to the National Government, when the public danger requires its exercise. The first of these may be called jurisdiction under MILITARY LAW, and is found in acts of Congress prescribing rules and articles of war or otherwise providing for the government of the national forces; the second may be distinguished as MILITARY GOVERNMENT, superseding, as far as may be deemed expedient, the local law and exercised by the military commander under the direction of the President, with the express or implied sanction of Congress, while the third may be denominated MARTIAL LAW PROPER, and is called into action by Congress, or temporarily, when the action of Congress cannot be invited, and, in the case of justifying or excusing peril, by the President in times of insurrection or invasion or of civil or foreign war, within districts or localities where ordinary law no longer adequately secures public safety and private rights.

We think that the power of Congress, in such times and in such localities, to authorize trials for crimes against the security and safety of the national forces may be derived from its constitutional authority to raise and support armies and to declare war, if not from its constitutional authority to provide for governing the national forces.

We have no apprehension that this power, under our American system of government, in which all official authority is derived from the people and exercised under direct responsibility to the people, is more likely to be abused than the power to regulate commerce or the power to borrow money. And we are unwilling to give our assent by silence to expressions of opinion which seem to us calculated, though not intended, to cripple the constitutional powers of the government, and to augment the public dangers in times of invasion and rebellion.

Mr. Justice WAYNE, Mr. Justice SWAYNE, and Mr. Justice MILLER concur with me in these views.

## Glossary

**ex parte:** on behalf of or for the benefit of one party

**habeas corpus:** the requirement that a person under arrest be brought to a court or before a judge to determine whether the person should be detained or released

**military commission:** a military court, particularly one organized in wartime, to try civilians

**writ:** a legal order

# SLAUGHTERHOUSE CASES

| DATE<br>1873 | CITATION<br>83 U.S. 36 |
| --- | --- |
| AUTHOR<br>Samuel Freeman Miller | SIGNIFICANCE<br>Held that the privileges or immunities clause of the Fourteenth Amendment did not extend protection for rights under state laws, effectively rendering the intended protections of the amendment ineffective and providing a foundation for the emergence of Jim Crow laws |
| VOTE<br>5-4 | |

## Overview

 The *Slaughterhouse Cases*, a consolidation of multiple lawsuits, argued that because of a Louisiana law forming a sanctioned corporate monopoly over the butchering trade, individual butchers would lose their right to practice their profession and earn a living as citizens. Argued February 3–5, 1873, and decided April 14, 1873, the decision rendered in the *Slaughterhouse Cases* is a unique example of a single U.S. Supreme Court decision that effectively reversed the political and popular will of the drafters of the amendment. The decision came just five years after ratification and less than a decade after the beginning of the American Civil War. Unlike the Constitution itself or many of its amendments, the intended meaning of the Thirteenth, Fourteenth, and Fifteenth Amendments were well known in 1873. Most, if not all, of the framers of these clauses and protections were alive and still very much part of the nation's political life. The *Slaughterhouse* decision argued that there was a fundamental difference between being a citizen of a state and a citizen of the nation—that everyone held dual citizenship as a citizen of each. Because of this duality, the Fourteenth Amendment's assurance of rights held only to the rights controlled by the federal government, such as those narrowly outlined in Article IV, Section 2 of the U.S. Constitution. Thus, the extension of rights under such amendments was fundamentally aimed at extending these protections to formerly enslaved people, not to alter states' rights.

## Context

In July 1868, Louisiana became the fourth former Confederate state readmitted to the Union, with a new state constitution that not only included a bill of rights but eliminated Black Codes (laws that restricted the rights of African Americans) and included protections from the Thirteenth, Fourteenth, and Fifteenth Amendments under the Reconstruction Acts of 1867–68. While the Louisiana Constitution of 1868 did not solve racial discrimination nor eliminate political corruption, the document did extend more protections and rights to its citizens than the previous five state constitutions. Despite such progress, the state remained under military occupation as part of the Fifth Military District until 1877.

THE DEATH CHAMBER.

***1860 wood engraving of a slaughterhouse scene***
(Library of Congress)

In 1869, New Orleans had nearly 200,000 people living in it and was one of the largest cities not only in Louisiana but in the American South. With such a large population came repeated periods of disease and other social ills. One of the most significant issues was the fouling of the New Orleans water supply by dumping animal waste and blood from slaughterhouses upstream and across the city. The resulting cholera and yellow fever outbreaks endangered the people living in the city and affected the city's lucrative shipping industry. The newly readmitted state sought to demonstrate its political effectiveness to the military governor of the Fifth Military District and the federal government by preserving and protecting the safety, health, and welfare of its citizens, as required by the Tenth Amendment, by granting a twenty-five-year monopoly to the Crescent City Livestock Landing and Slaughterhouse Company to run a slaughterhouse twenty-five miles downstream of New Orleans. Similar arrangements were already in operation in large cities like New York, San Francisco, Boston, Milwaukee, and Philadelphia.

Crescent City would not run the livestock yard and slaughter operation but rented space on its premises to butchers at a rate set by the Louisiana legislature. The charter required an inspector appointed by the governor to inspect all livestock before butchering to ensure the quality of product available to all citizens. All of these conditions, so the Louisiana Legislature argued, were set to assure the quality of facilities, quality of products, output volume, price of livestock, and general health and welfare through the centralization and improvement of slaughterhouse production. The charter to operate required all existing butchering spaces in the city to be closed and set harsh penalties against Crescent City should they refuse to rent space to any individual or entity.

Several members of the Butchers' Benevolent Association, a local trade union, argued that such an arrangement would cost them their right to practice their trade and earn a living. These members argued that such an arrangement created an unequal opportunity for city residents by artificially restricting who could practice a legal profession through the policing power of the state. When argued in front of the Louisiana Supreme Court on January 11, 1872, the case was denied, and the plaintiffs appealed to the U.S. Supreme Court. For the appeal, the plaintiffs from the Butchers' Benevolent Association hired the New Orleans–based former Supreme Court justice John Archibald Campbell as their lawyer.

John Archibald Campbell, a native Alabamian with no previous judicial experience, had been appointed to the U.S. Supreme Court by President Millard Fillmore in 1853 to moderate sectionalist agitation within the Southern presence in the national capital. Campbell was highly influential in *Marshall v. Baltimore & Ohio Railroad Company* (1853), *Piqua Branch of the State Bank of Ohio v. Knoop* (1854), *Dodge v. Woolsey* (1855), *Dred Scott v. Sandford* (1857), and *Christ's Church Hospital v. County of Philadelphia* (1860), in which he argued that corporations were not citizens and that federal jurisdiction was constantly a threat to the rights of states as intended by the framers of the U.S. Constitution. In addition to his views on the domination of the rights of individuals over corporations, Campbell argued that states had the right to change policies to keep pace with the evolving state of modern conditions to protect individual liberties from the invasive efforts of corporations.

Acting as a mediator between the nascent Confederacy and the federal government, Campbell was angered by what he saw as President Abraham Lincoln's overtly aggressive policy on the resupply of Fort Sumpter as the start of a needless war between the states. In reaction, Campbell resigned his seat on the U.S. Supreme Court in late April 1861 and, rebuffed from his native Alabama as a Unionist, settled in New Orleans. By October 1862, Campbell was appointed the assistant secretary of war by Confederate president Jefferson Davis and, despite his efforts to create a negotiated peace throughout the war, would serve in this role until the end of the American Civil War. After the *Ex parte Garland* (1867) decision that the U.S. Legislature Supplementary Act of January 24, 1865—which removed judiciary officials who had sided with the Confederacy through legislative power—was unconstitutional, Campbell soon became widely recognized as one of the most gifted constitutional lawyers in the nation.

Campbell's appeal on behalf of the Butchers' Benevolent Association to the U.S. Supreme Court was based on a violation of its rights under the Thirteenth and Fourteenth Amendments to the U.S. Constitution. Campbell argued that the monopoly created by the state charter created a sanction of involuntary servitude for the butchers operating in the city in violation of the Thirteenth Amendment. Furthermore, Campbell argued that such a charter abridged the privileges or immunities clause of the Fourteenth Amendment by depriving them of equal protection under the law and their liberty and property without due process.

## About the Author

### *The Majority Author*

Justice Samuel Freeman Miller, who authored the majority opinion, and Justice Stephen Johnson Field, who wrote the minority opinion, were nothing if not prolific in their overlapping tenure on the U.S. Supreme Court. Both Miller and Field would remain the most vocal and influential crafters of jurisprudence, only recently surpassed in the number of opinions by Justices John P. Stevens and Clarence Thomas.

Justice Samuel Freeman Miller, joined by Justices Nathan Clifford, William Strong, Ward Hunt, and David Davis, authored the majority opinion. Born April 5, 1816, in Richmond, Kentucky, to a farming family, Miller earned his medical degree from Transylvania University in Lexington, Kentucky, in 1838. Miller practiced medicine in Barbourville, Kentucky, while privately studying law, passing the bar in 1847. Miller was an active supporter of the abolition of slavery and moved to Iowa in 1850. In Iowa, Miller freed his slaves and became involved in the organization of the new Republican Party and the Unitarian Church. His political organizing for the 1860 presidential campaign of Abraham Lincoln resulted in his nomination to the U.S. Supreme Court on July 16, 1862. Miller's reputation and Lincoln's support resulted in a senatorial confirmation the same day with less than an hour of debate on the nomination. Miller would prove to be a judicial supporter of Abraham Lincoln's wartime policies, including the suspension of *habeas corpus* and the expansion of judicial powers to military commissions.

When Chief Justice Salmon P. Chase died in 1873, jurists from across the nation broadly advocated for the nomination of Samuel F. Miller to the position. However, President Ulysses S. Grant was determined to select fellow Ohio lawyer, politician, and diplomat Morrison R. Waite for the position. Despite not being appointed chief justice, Miller would continue to be a well-respected and intellectual force in the Waite court. When the contentious presidential election of 1876 proved to be unable to be resolved through the general election or electoral college processes, Congress created a fifteen-member federal electoral commission from an equal number of sitting senators, congressmen, and justices. Justices Miller and Field both served on the commission, which would ultimately elect Republican Rutherford B. Hayes as the nineteenth president of the United States. During the 1880s, the Republican Party considered Miller several times for its presidential candidate, but a formal nomination would never occur. Miller served as the president of the National Conference of the Unitarian Church in 1884 while still serving as a justice. Miller would die as a seated justice in 1890.

During his thirty-four-year tenure on the U.S. Supreme Court, Miller became an influential figure in the narrow post–Civil War interpretation of the Fourteenth Amendment. In addition to writing the majority opinion in the *Slaughterhouse Cases* (1873), he wrote the majority opinion in *Bradwell v. Illinois* (1873) and joined in the majority on *United States v. Cruikshank* (1876), the *Civil Rights Cases* (1883), and *In re Burrus* (1890). In each of these cases, Miller's narrow reading of the Fourteenth Amendment continually limited the federal government's effectiveness in protecting individual rights against discrimination or deprivation of liberties by state or private actors. Miller was also influential in protecting states' rights from federal oversight in interpreting state law, in *Murdock v. Memphis* (1874). However, during his tenure, Miller was not single-minded in his interpretation of federal protections of specific rights. In *Ex parte Yarbrough* (1884), *United States v. Kagama* (1886), *Wabash v. Illinois* (1886), and *In re Neagle* (1890), Miller would join the majority in asserting the dominance of federal over state prerogatives.

### The Dissenting Author

Justice Stephen Johnson Field was born in Haddam, Connecticut, in 1816. Field was born the sixth of nine children of David Field, a Congregationalist minister, and Submit Dickinson, a teacher. Field grew up in Stockbridge, Massachusetts, until the age of thirteen, when he joined his sister and brother-in-law as Congregationalist missionaries in Turkey. Despite his upbringing in the Congregationalist faith, Field gained a reputation as a vengeful man and easily made enemies throughout his life. Returning to Massachusetts after several years in Turkey, Field attended Williams College before apprenticing to Harmanus Bleecker in Albany, New York, then to his brother David in New York City, where he passed the bar. Field practiced law with his brother in New York City until the Gold Rush of 1848 beckoned Field to California. Just three days after Field's arrival in Marysville, California, Field was elected *alcalde*—a civil servant who was a combination of mayor and jurist in the Mexican law system. Field practiced law and implemented harsh penalties such as whipping and other brutal forms of public punishment for crimes to preserve order and peace in the rough gold rush town at the center of California's gold territory. In 1850, Field was elected to the California State Assembly but lost an 1851 election for California State Senate. In 1857, Field was elected to the California Supreme Court. In 1858, Field was challenged by fellow California Supreme Court justice William T. Barbour to a duel; though neither man actually fired a shot, Field soon was known to have altered his suit jackets to accommodate the accurate aiming and firing of pistols from inside the pockets. By 1859, Field became chief justice after David Terry, the former chief justice, had killed Senator David Broderick in a duel.

In the late 1850s, Field's brother Cyrus became a well-known inventor and multimillionaire, while his brother David became active in organizing the new Republican Party. By the early 1860s, the population of the American West had snowballed, and the judicial system became far too unwieldy to manage. Congress responded in 1863 with the Tenth Circuit Act that reorganized the judicial system, created a tenth federal circuit court, and increased the number of seated U.S. Supreme Court justices from nine to ten. With the expansion, Lincoln aimed to balance the Court politically and regionally by nominating Field as the tenth justice on March 6, 1863. Field was confirmed by Senate just four days later.

Field was a judicial forerunner in establishing the principle of substantive due process. Field would set the precedence for substantial due process in his opinions in the *Slaughterhouse Cases* (1873), *Munn v. Illinois* (1876), *Pennoyer v. Neff* (1878), *Strauder v. West Virginia* (1880), *In re Look Tin Sing* (1884), *Chew Heong v. United States* (1884), and *Mugler v. Kansas* (1887). Throughout these opinions, Field argued that the courts had the obligation under the Fifth and Fourteenth Amendments to protect individual rights—even if not explicitly outlined within the Constitution—in both the procedural and substance of the law. Field also was vocal in his interpretation of the Constitution's limits of authority in taxation (*Pollock v. Farmer's Loan and Trust Company* [1895]) and limitations on federal injunctions on business (*United States v. E.C. Knight Company* [1895]). However, Field was also a man of his time, and several of Field's opinions contained racist ideology, especially in reference to Chinese immigrants. Most notably, and in stark opposition to the principle of substantial due process, Field argued in favor of the majority in upholding racially motivated policies in *Chae Chan Ping v. United States* (1889) and *Plessy v. Ferguson* (1896).

As a respected jurist and prominent Californian, Field was selected as a founding trustee of Stanford University and saw the aims of establishing the first coeducational and nondenominational institution of higher learning in California realized in 1891. Field insisted on remaining on the bench to become the Court's longest-serving member. Despite his fellow justices' urgings to retire and his clear challenges with senility in his later years, Field would achieve his aim and retire on December 1, 1897, after over thirty-four years of service as a U.S. Supreme Court justice. Field's service record would be surpassed only by Justice William O. Douglas in the mid-twentieth century. Field died on April 9, 1899, in Washington, D.C.

## Explanation and Analysis of the Document

### *The Majority Opinion*

Justice Samuel F. Miller begins the opinion by noting that the case is a collection of claims filed by individual butchers rolled into a singular argument against the State of Louisiana as an error in granting an exclusive charter to Crescent City Livestock Landing and Slaughterhouse Company. Justice Miller notes that the initial argument was presented in January 1872 to the U.S. Supreme Court with one justice absent and that no consensus could be reached among the remaining justices. Thus, the argument was rescheduled for a full bench in February 1873. Miller notes that in the intervening time, several of the initial complainants had come to an agreement with the Crescent City Livestock Landing and Slaughterhouse Company outside the courtroom. However, Justice Miller notes that the settlement of some parties does not bind all parties to dismissal. With that, Justice Miller makes it clear that the argument being presented is that in granting a charter to Crescent City Livestock Landing and Slaughterhouse Company, the State of Louisiana violated the "most important provisions of the thirteenth and fourteenth articles of amendment of the Constitution of the United States."

Justice Miller then summarizes the March 8, 1869, legislation titled "An act to protect the health of the city of New Orleans, to locate the stock landings and slaughter houses, and to incorporate the Crescent City Live Stock Landing and Slaughter House Company." Section one forbids the slaughtering of animals for food in New Orleans and its surrounding parishes except by the corporation created by the act. Section two names the owners, gives the business title, and confers corporate powers under Louisiana law. The third section outlines the requirement of the company to erect stockyards, stock landings, and slaughterhouses to slaughter 500 animals daily. This section also places a June 1, 1869, deadline to complete such facilities by the company. Section four confers the monopoly for stock landings and slaughter to the company in the area. This section also sets fixed prices on steamboat landings and for each animal landed. Section five orders the closure of all other stock landings and slaughterhouses by June 1, 1869, and outlines the fines for violation. This section also sets forward fixed prices for butchers operating in their facility and requires the inspection of animals before slaughter. Miller then summarizes the plaintiff's objection as "conferring odious and exclusive privileges upon a small number of persons at the expense of the great body of the community of New Orleans," which deprives the butchers the right to exercise their trade and places the "daily subsistence of the population of the city" at grave risk.

Having outlined the facts of the case, Miller then begins his opinion. Miller begins with an acknowledgment that the act does create a period of exclusive privileges. However, Miller argues, this does not deprive the butchers of the right to practice their trade nor endanger the city's people. Next, Miller notes that the act effectively divides the exclusive privilege into two parts. The first is for the operation of stock landings and stockyards, and the second is for the slaughterhouse operation. For the first, Miller argues that such arrangements "for the safety and comfort of the people and the care of the animals, be limited to proper places." Furthermore, the proper operations of such facilities require exclusive use of land, and the owner should receive fair compensation for such use. Miller then turns to the core of the argument that the creation of the slaughterhouse privilege violates the civil and individual rights of citizens.

Miller argues that it is both the right and the duty of the legislative body to define proper areas to conduct lawful business—what is referred to as police power. He acknowledges that the "wisdom of the monopoly granted by the legislature may be open to question," but the creation of a monopoly does not deprive the butcher's ability to practice their trade—only where they may exert their labor. What Miller finds to be at the center of this constitutional question is how the federal government can adequately create and monitor boundaries for such policing power when these are primarily local issues. Miller argues that Congress does have the exclusive right to regulate commerce, but only between citizens of the United States and foreign nations—that the internal regulation of trade and associated policing power belong to the states, not to Congress. Should the state aim to accomplish a specific goal and see fit to appoint a corporation, it has the right to create it and endow it with the powers necessary to effect the desired and lawful purpose.

Miller argues that the "true meaning" of the framers of the Thirteenth, Fourteenth, and Fifteenth Amendments was aimed at bestowing the rights and privileges of national citizenship to formerly enslaved people, not to create additional guarantees of human rights to all citizens. Miller argues that nowhere within the Constitution is citizenship defined. Thus, the Fourteenth Amendment clearly outlines that "All persons born or naturalized in the United States, and subject to the jurisdiction thereof, are citizens of the United States and of the State wherein they reside." Citizenship to a state requires that the individual establish residency within the political borders of a state. National citizenship is conferred to every individual born or naturalized within the national border. Thus, according to Miller, the

individual carries two separate and distinct citizenships: one of the United States and one of a State.

The language of the Fourteenth Amendment's privileges or immunities clause that "No State shall make or enforce any law which shall abridge the privileges or immunities of citizens of the United States" is at the heart of Miller's opinion. With support from case law, Miller argues that the State of Louisiana did not create a violation of rights for its citizens that it would not have enforced on any citizen of the United States who established residency within the state. Furthermore, the act did not prohibit the free movement of citizens who did not want to abide by the constraints placed by the legislature on its citizens. This, Miller argues, means "An act to protect the health of the city of New Orleans, to locate the stock landings and slaughter houses, and to incorporate the Crescent City Live Stock Landing and Slaughter House Company" not only was constitutionally sound but also reaffirmed that "the existence of the State with powers for domestic and local government, including the regulation of civil rights—the rights of person and of property—was essential to the perfect working of our complex form of government."

## Dissenting Opinions

Justice Stephen Field (joined by Salmon Chase, Noah Swayne, and Joseph Bradley) argued in his dissent that although the plaintiff's argument was abstract, it did have "some support in the fundamental law of the country." Field begins his argument by first concurring with the majority decision that the State of Louisiana was not improperly exercising its duty to create constraints on its citizens through police power to ensure the "health, good order, morals, peace, and safety of society" in the creation of animal inspection and stock-landing requirements. However, according to Field, all other constraints created by the act did not promote these aims. Field contends that if a corporation can carry out such a volume of slaughtering while not endangering the public, it would similarly not endanger the public if other persons also practiced the legal slaughtering of animals under the same conditions as the corporation.

Furthermore, according to Field, the provisions of the Thirteenth, Fourteenth, and Fifteenth Amendments were not confined to formerly enslaved people alone but protected American citizens universally from parallel forms of servitude such as "serfage, vassalage, villeinage, peonage, and all other forms of compulsory service for the mere benefit or pleasure of others." Field argues that in the creation of a monopoly, the State of Louisiana did indeed make a "discrimination between classes of persons, which deprives the one class of their freedom or their property, or which makes a caste of them to subserve the power, pride, avarice, vanity, or vengeance of others." This violated the right to equal treatment under the law secured in the Fourteenth Amendment. As though directly speaking to Justice Miller, Field asserted: "The [Fourteenth] amendment does not attempt to confer any new privileges or immunities upon citizens or to enumerate or define those already existing. It assumes that there are such privileges and immunities which belong of right to citizens as such, and ordains that they shall not be abridged by State legislation." Field argues that all pursuits, professions, and vocations are open to all citizens of the United States and may only be limited universally. The State must regulate professions or pursuits for the public health, good order, and general economic prosperity of all its citizens. According to Field, the State of Louisiana directly violated the principles and values for which the nation stood.

Swayne and Bradley, in addition to joining Field's dissent, wrote separate dissents as well.

## Impact

The decision in the *Slaughterhouse Cases* served to counter the protections inherent in the Fourteenth Amendment effectively. Depicted by some as a vindication of states' rights against federal overreach, many others argued that such a narrow reading of the Fourteenth Amendment was unnecessary to protect the union from itself and that the states had been aware of the potential for censure of their policing powers by the federal authority when they adopted the Fourteenth Amendment. The *Slaughterhouse Cases* are unique in American law as they effectively declawed a constitutional amendment less than five years after its ratification. The decision provided a foundation for the emergence of Jim Crow laws in the post-Reconstruction South. The resulting nullification of the protections outlined in the privileges and immunities clause has not stopped plaintiffs from seeking protections under the Fourteenth Amendment. The effective loss of the privileges and immunities clause through the *Slaughterhouse Cases* decision created a precedent that generally remains the same today as it was in 1873. This has caused litigants to reframe their efforts to secure general rights from government infringement by framing their argument under the Fourteenth Amendment's due process clause, such as in the *Obergefell v. Hodges* (2015) decision that secured same-sex marriage rights for all Americans.

### Questions for Further Study

1. What impact did the American Civil War have on the interpretations offered by Justices Miller and Field?

2. Can a person have two separate citizenships, as Justice Miller argued? Why or why not?

3. Why would the framers of the Fourteenth Amendment have elected not to specifically outline the privileges and immunities that the amendment was trying to protect?

4. Was Justice Field's interpretation of the Thirteenth Amendment too radical, or was Justice Miller's interpretation too conservative? Why?

5. The *Slaughterhouse Cases* unquestionably impacted civil rights, especially for African Americans in the South. What other group(s) of Americans might have been negatively affected because of the decision? Why?

## Further Reading

### Books

Brandwein, Pamela. *Rethinking the Judicial Settlement of Reconstruction.* New York: Cambridge University Press, 2014.

Labbé, Ronald, and Jonathan Lurie. *The Slaughterhouse Cases: Regulation, Reconstruction, and the Fourteenth Amendment.* Lawrence: University Press of Kansas, 2003.

Ross, Michael. *Justice of Shattered Dreams: Samuel Freeman Miller and the Supreme Court during the Civil War Era.* Baton Rouge: Louisiana State University Press, 2003.

Wurman, Ilan. *The Second Founding: An Introduction to the Fourteenth Amendment.* New York: Cambridge University Press, 2020.

### Websites

Konkoly, Toni. "Slaughterhouse Cases (1873)." Supreme Court History: Law, Power, and Personality. December 2006. Accessed February 17, 2023. http://www.thirteen.org/wnet/supremecourt/personality/landmark_slaughterhouse.html.

"The Slaughterhouse Cases (1873)." Landmark Cases: Historic Supreme Court Decisions. Accessed February 17, 2023. http://landmarkcases.c-span.org/Case/3/The-Slaughterhouse-Cases.

—Commentary by Bryant Macfarlane

# SLAUGHTERHOUSE CASES

## Document Text

### Mr. Justice MILLER . . . delivered the opinion of the Court

These cases are brought here by writs of error to the Supreme Court of the State of Louisiana. They arise out of the efforts of the butchers of New Orleans to resist the Crescent City Livestock Landing and Slaughter-House Company in the exercise of certain powers conferred by the charter which created it, and which was granted by the legislature of that State.

The cases named on a preceding page, with others which have been brought here and dismissed by agreement, were all decided by the Supreme Court of Louisiana in favor of the Slaughter-House Company, as we shall hereafter call it for the sake of brevity, and these writs are brought to reverse those decisions.

The records were filed in this court in 1870, and were argued before it at length on a motion made by plaintiffs in error for an order in the nature of an injunction or supersedeas, pending the action of the court on the merits. The opinion on that motion is reported in 77 U. S. 10 Wallace 273.

On account of the importance of the questions involved in these cases, they were, by permission of the court, taken up out of their order on the docket and argued in January, 1872. At that hearing, one of the justices was absent, and it was found, on consultation, that there was a diversity of views among those who were present. Impressed with the gravity of the questions raised in the argument, the court, under these circumstances, ordered that the cases be placed on the calendar and reargued before a full bench. This argument was had early in February last.

Preliminary to the consideration of those questions is a motion by the defendant to dismiss the cases on the ground that the contest between the parties has been adjusted by an agreement made since the records came into this court, and that part of that agreement is that these writs should be dismissed. This motion was heard with the argument on the merits, and was much pressed by counsel. It is supported by affidavits and by copies of the written agreement relied on. It is sufficient to say of these that we do not find in them satisfactory evidence that the agreement is binding upon all the parties to the record who are named as plaintiffs in the several writs of error, and that there are parties now before the court, in each of the three cases, the names of which appear on a preceding page, who have not consented to their dismissal, and who are not bound by the action of those who have so consented. They have a right to be heard, and the motion to dismiss cannot prevail.

The records show that the plaintiffs in error relied upon, and asserted throughout the entire course of the litigation in the State courts, that the grant of privileges in the charter of defendant, which they were contesting, was a violation of the most important provisions of the thirteenth and fourteenth articles of amendment of the Constitution of the United States. The jurisdiction and the duty of this court to review the judgment of the State court on those questions is clear, and is imperative.

The statute thus assailed as unconstitutional was passed March 8th, 1869, and is entitled

> "An act to protect the health of the city of New Orleans, to locate the stock landings and slaughterhouses, and to incorporate the Crescent City Livestock Landing aud Slaughter-House Company."

The first section forbids the landing or slaughtering of animals whose flesh is intended for food within the city of New Orleans and other parishes and boundaries named and defined, or the keeping or establishing any slaughterhouses or abattoirs within those limits except by the corporation thereby created, which is also limited to certain places afterwards mentioned. Suitable penalties are enacted for violations of this prohibition.

The second section designates the corporators, gives the name to the corporation, and confers on it the usual corporate powers.

The third and fourth sections authorize the company to establish and erect within certain territorial limits, therein defined, one or more stockyards, stock landings, and slaughterhouses, and imposes upon it the duty of erecting, on or before the first day of June, 1869, one grand slaughterhouse of sufficient capacity for slaughtering five hundred animals per day.

It declares that the company, after it shall have prepared all the necessary buildings, yards, and other conveniences for that purpose, shall have the sole and exclusive privilege of conducting and carrying on the livestock landing and slaughterhouse business within the limits and privilege granted by the act, and that all such animals shall be landed at the stock landings and slaughtered at the slaughterhouses of the company, and nowhere else. Penalties are enacted for infractions of this provision, and prices fixed for the maximum charges of the company for each steamboat and for each animal landed.

Section five orders the closing up of all other stock landings and slaughterhouses after the first day of June, in the parishes of Orleans, Jefferson, and St. Bernard, and makes it the duty of the company to permit any person to slaughter animals in their slaughterhouses under a heavy penalty for each refusal. Another section fixes a limit to the charges to be made by the company for each animal so slaughtered in their building, and another provides for an inspection of all animals intended to be so slaughtered by an officer appointed by the governor of the State for that purpose.

These are the principal features of the statute, and are all that have any bearing upon the questions to be decided by us.

This statute is denounced not only as creating a monopoly and conferring odious and exclusive privileges upon a small number of persons at the expense of the great body of the community of New Orleans, but it is asserted that it deprives a large and meritorious class of citizens—the whole of the butchers of the city—of the right to exercise their trade, the business to which they have been trained and on which they depend for the support of themselves and their families, and that the unrestricted exercise of the business of butchering is necessary to the daily subsistence of the population of the city.

But a critical examination of the act hardly justifies these assertions.

It is true that it grants, for a period of twenty-five years, exclusive privileges. And whether those privileges are at the expense of the community in the sense of a curtailment of any of their fundamental rights, or even in the sense of doing them an injury, is a question open to considerations to be hereafter stated. But it is not true that it deprives the butchers of the right to exercise their trade, or imposes upon them any restriction incompatible with its successful pursuit, or furnishing the people of the city with the necessary daily supply of animal food.

The act divides itself into two main grants of privilege, the one in reference to stock landings and stockyards, and the other to slaughterhouses. That the landing of livestock in large droves, from steamboats on the bank of the river, and from railroad trains, should, for the safety and comfort of the people and the care of the animals, be limited to proper places, and those not numerous it needs no argument to prove. Nor can it be injurious to the general community that, while the duty of making ample preparation for this is imposed upon a few men, or a corporation, they should, to enable them to do it successfully, have the exclusive right of providing such landing places, and receiving a fair compensation for the service.

It is, however, the slaughterhouse privilege which is mainly relied on to justify the charges of gross injustice to the public and invasion of private right.

It is not, and cannot be successfully controverted that it is both the right and the duty of the legislative body—the supreme power of the State or municipality—to prescribe and determine the localities where the business of slaughtering for a great city may be conducted. To do this effectively, it is indispensable that all persons who slaughter animals for food shall do it in those places *and nowhere else.*

The statute under consideration defines these localities and forbids slaughtering in any other. It does not, as has been asserted, prevent the butcher from doing his own slaughtering. On the contrary, the Slaughter-House Company is required, under a heavy penalty, to permit any person who wishes to do so to slaughter in their houses, and they are bound to make ample provision for the convenience of all the slaughtering for the entire city. The butcher then is still permitted to slaughter, to prepare, and to sell his own meats; but he is required to slaughter at a specified place, and to pay a reasonable compensation for the use of the accommodations furnished him at that place.

The wisdom of the monopoly granted by the legislature may be open to question, but it is difficult to see a justification for the assertion that the butchers are deprived of the right to labor in their occupation, or the people of their daily service in preparing food, or how this statute, with the duties and guards imposed upon the company, can be said to destroy the business of the butcher, or seriously interfere with its pursuit.

The power here exercised by the legislature of Louisiana is, in its essential nature, one which has been, up to the present period in the constitutional history of this country, always conceded to belong to the States, however it may *now* be questioned in some of its details.

> "Unwholesome trades, slaughterhouses, operations offensive to the senses, the deposit of powder, the application of steam power to propel cars, the building with combustible materials, and the burial of the dead, may all,"

says Chancellor Kent,

> "be interdicted by law, in the midst of dense masses of population, on the general and rational principle that every person ought so to use his property as not to injure his neighbors, and that private interests must be made subservient to the general interests of the community."

This is called the police power, and it is declared by Chief Justice Shaw that it is much easier to perceive and realize the existence and sources of it than to mark its boundaries, or prescribe limits to its exercise.

This power is, and must be from its very nature, incapable of any very exact definition or limitation. Upon it depends the security of social order, the life and health of the citizen, the comfort of an existence in a thickly populated community, the enjoyment of private social life, and the beneficial use of property. "It extends," says another eminent judge, "to the protection of the lives, limbs, health, comfort, and quiet of all persons, and the protection of all property within the State, . . . and persons and property are subjected to all kinds of restraints and burdens in order to secure the general comfort, health, and prosperity of the State. Of the perfect right of the legislature to do this, no question ever was, or, upon acknowledged general principles, ever can be made, so far as natural persons are concerned."

The regulation of the place and manner of conducting the slaughtering of animals, and the business of butchering within a city, and the inspection of the animals to be killed for meat, and of the meat afterwards, are among the most necessary and frequent exercises of this power. It is not, therefore, needed that we should seek for a comprehensive definition, but rather look for the proper source of its exercise.

In *Gibbons v. Ogden,* Chief Justice Marshall, speaking of inspection laws passed by the States, says:

> "They form a portion of that immense mass of legislation which controls everything within the territory of a State not surrendered to the General Government—all which can be most advantageously administered by the States themselves. Inspection laws, quarantine laws, health laws of every description, as well as laws for regulating the internal commerce of a State, and those which respect turnpike roads, ferries, &c., are component parts. No direct general power over these objects is granted to Congress, and consequently they remain subject to State legislation."

The exclusive authority of State legislation over this subject is strikingly illustrated in the case of the *City of*

*New York v. Miln.* In that case, the defendant was prosecuted for failing to comply with a statute of New York which required of every master of a vessel arriving from a foreign port in that of New York City to report the names of all his passengers, with certain particulars of their age, occupation, last place of settlement, and place of their birth. It was argued that this act was an invasion of the exclusive right of Congress to regulate commerce. And it cannot be denied that such a statute operated at least indirectly upon the commercial intercourse between the citizens of the United States and of foreign countries. But notwithstanding this, it was held to be an exercise of the police power properly within the control of the State, and unaffected by the clause of the Constitution which conferred on Congress the right to regulate commerce.

To the same purpose are the recent cases of the *The License Tax,* and *United States v. De Witt.* In the latter case, an act of Congress which undertook as a part of the internal revenue laws to make it a misdemeanor to mix for sale naphtha and illuminating oils, or to sell oil of petroleum inflammable at less than a prescribed temperature, was held to be void because, as a police regulation, the power to make such a law belonged to the States, and did not belong to Congress.

It cannot be denied that the statute under consideration is aptly framed to remove from the more densely populated part of the city the noxious slaughterhouses, and large and offensive collections of animals necessarily incident to the slaughtering business of a large city, and to locate them where the convenience, health, and comfort of the people require they shall be located. And it must be conceded that the means adopted by the act for this purpose are appropriate, are stringent, and effectual. But it is said that, in creating a corporation for this purpose, and conferring upon it exclusive privileges—privileges which it is said constitute a monopoly—the legislature has exceeded its power. If this statute had imposed on the city of New Orleans precisely the same duties, accompanied by the same privileges, which it has on the corporation which it created, it is believed that no question would have been raised as to its constitutionality. In that case the effect on the butchers in pursuit of their occupation and on the public would have been the same as it is now. Why cannot the legislature confer the same powers on another corporation, created for a lawful and useful public object, that it can on the municipal

corporation already existing? That wherever a legislature has the right to accomplish a certain result, and that result is best attained by means of a corporation, it has the right to create such a corporation, and to endow it with the powers necessary to effect the desired and lawful purpose, seems hardly to admit of debate. The proposition is ably discussed and affirmed in the case of *McCulloch v. The State of Maryland* in relation to the power of Congress to organize the Bank of the United States to aid in the fiscal operations of the government.

It can readily be seen that the interested vigilance of the corporation created by the Louisiana legislature will be more efficient in enforcing the limitation prescribed for the stock landing and slaughtering business for the good of the city than the ordinary efforts of the officers of the law.

Unless, therefore, it can be maintained that the exclusive privilege granted by this charter to the corporation is beyond the power of the legislature of Louisiana, there can be no just exception to the validity of the statute. And, in this respect, we are not able to see that these privileges are especially odious or objectionable. The duty imposed as a consideration for the privilege is well defined, and its enforcement well guarded. The prices or charges to be made by the company are limited by the statute, and we are not advised that they are, on the whole, exorbitant or unjust.

The proposition is therefore reduced to these terms: can any exclusive privileges be granted to any of its citizens, or to a corporation, by the legislature of a State?

The eminent and learned counsel who has twice argued the negative of this question has displayed a research into the history of monopolies in England and the European continent only equalled by the eloquence with which they are denounced.

But it is to be observed that all such references are to monopolies established by the monarch in derogation of the rights of his subjects, or arise out of transactions in which the people were unrepresented, and their interests uncared for. The great *Case of Monopolies,* reported by Coke and so fully stated in the brief, was undoubtedly a contest of the commons against the monarch. The decision is based upon the ground that it was against common law, and the argument was aimed at the unlawful assumption of power by the crown, for whoever doubted the authority of Parliament to change or modify the common law? The discussion in the House of Commons cited from Macaulay clearly establishes that the contest was between the crown and the people represented in Parliament.

But we think it may be safely affirmed that the Parliament of Great Britain, representing the people in their legislative functions, and the legislative bodies of this country, have, from time immemorial to the present day, continued to grant to persons and corporations exclusive privileges—privileges denied to other citizens—privileges which come within any just definition of the word monopoly, as much as those now under consideration, and that the power to do this has never been questioned or denied. Nor can it be truthfully denied that some of the most useful and beneficial enterprises set on foot for the general good have been made successful by means of these exclusive rights, and could only have been conducted to success in that way.

It may, therefore, be considered as established that the authority of the legislature of Louisiana to pass the present statute is ample unless some restraint in the exercise of that power be found in the constitution of that State or in the amendments to the Constitution of the United States, adopted since the date of the decisions we have already cited.

If any such restraint is supposed to exist in the constitution of the State, the Supreme Court of Louisiana having necessarily passed on that question, it would not be open to review in this court.

The plaintiffs in error, accepting this issue, allege that the statute is a violation of the Constitution of the United States in these several particulars:

That it creates an involuntary servitude forbidden by the thirteenth article of amendment;

That it abridges the privileges and immunities of citizens of the United States;

That it denies to the plaintiffs the equal protection of the laws; and,

That it deprives them of their property without due process of law, contrary to the provisions of the first section of the fourteenth article of amendment.

This court is thus called upon for the first time to give construction to these articles.

We do not conceal from ourselves the great responsibility which this duty devolves upon us. No questions so far-reaching and pervading in their consequences, so profoundly interesting to the people of this country, and so important in their bearing upon the relations of the United States, of the several States to each other, and to the citizens of the States and of the United States, have been before this court during the official life of any of its present members. We have given every opportunity for a full hearing at the bar; we have discussed it freely and compared views among ourselves; we have taken ample time for careful deliberation, and we now propose to announce the judgments which we have formed in the construction of those articles, so far as we have found them necessary to the decision of the cases before us, and beyond that, we have neither the inclination nor the right to go.

Twelve articles of amendment were added to the Federal Constitution soon after the original organization of the government under it in 1789. Of these, all but the last were adopted so soon afterwards as to justify the statement that they were practically contemporaneous with the adoption of the original; and the twelfth, adopted in eighteen hundred and three, was so nearly so as to have become, like all the others, historical and of another age. But within the first eight years, three other articles of amendment of vast importance have been added by the voice of the people to that now venerable instrument.

The most cursory glance at these articles discloses a unity of purpose, when taken in connection with the history of the times, which cannot fail to have an important bearing on any question of doubt concerning their true meaning. Nor can such doubts, when any reasonably exist, be safely and rationally solved without a reference to that history, for in it is found the occasion and the necessity for recurring again to the great source of power in this country, the people of the States, for additional guarantees of human rights,

additional powers to the Federal government; additional restraints upon those of the States. Fortunately, that history is fresh within the memory of us all, and its leading features, as they bear upon the matter before us, free from doubt.

The institution of African slavery, as it existed in about half the States of the Union, and the contests pervading the public mind for many years between those who desired its curtailment and ultimate extinction and those who desired additional safeguards for its security and perpetuation, culminated in the effort, on the part of most of the States in which slavery existed, to separate from the Federal government and to resist its authority. This constituted the war of the rebellion, and whatever auxiliary causes may have contributed to bring about this war, undoubtedly the overshadowing and efficient cause was African slavery.

In that struggle, slavery, as a, legalized social relation, perished. It perished as a necessity of the bitterness and force of the conflict. When the armies of freedom found themselves upon the soil of slavery, they could do nothing less than free the poor victims whose enforced servitude was the foundation of the quarrel. And when hard-pressed in the contest, these men ( for they proved themselves men in that terrible crisis) offered their services and were accepted by thousands to aid in suppressing the unlawful rebellion, slavery was at an end wherever the Federal government succeeded in that purpose. The proclamation of President Lincoln expressed an accomplished fact as to a large portion of the insurrectionary districts when he declared slavery abolished in them all. But the war being over, those who had succeeded in reestablishing the authority of the Federal government were not content to permit this great act of emancipation to rest on the actual results of the contest or the proclamation of the Executive, both of which might have been questioned in after times, and they determined to place this main and most valuable result in the Constitution of the restored Union as one of its fundamental articles. Hence, the thirteenth article of amendment of that instrument.

Its two short sections seem hardly to admit of construction, so vigorous is their expression and so appropriate to the purpose we have indicated.

"1. Neither slavery nor involuntary servitude, except as a punishment for crime, whereof the party shall have been duly convicted, shall exist within the United States or any place subject to their jurisdiction."

"2. Congress shall have power to enforce this article by appropriate legislation."

To withdraw the mind from the contemplation of this grand yet simple declaration of the personal freedom of all the human race within the jurisdiction of this government—a declaration designed to establish the freedom of four millions of slaves—and with a microscopic search endeavor to find in it a reference to servitudes which may have been attached to property in certain localities requires an effort, to say the least of it.

That a personal servitude was meant is proved by the use of the word "involuntary," which can only apply to human beings. The exception of servitude as a punishment for crime gives an idea of the class of servitude that is meant. The word servitude is of larger meaning than slavery, as the latter is popularly understood in this country, and the obvious purpose was to forbid all shades and conditions of African slavery. It was very well understood that, in the form of apprenticeship for long terms, as it had been practiced in the West India Islands, on the abolition of slavery by the English government, or by reducing the slaves to the condition of serfs attached to the plantation, the purpose of the article might have been evaded if only the word slavery had been used. The case of the apprentice slave, held under a law of Maryland, liberated by Chief Justice Chase on a writ of habeas corpus under this article, illustrates this course of observation. And it is all that we deem necessary to say on the application of that article to the statute of Louisiana, now under consideration.

The process of restoring to their proper relations with the Federal government and with the other States those which had sided with the rebellion, undertaken under the proclamation of President Johnson in 1865 and before the assembling of Congress, developed the fact that, notwithstanding the formal recognition by those States of the abolition of slavery, the condition of the slave race would, without further protection of the Federal government, be almost as bad as it was before. Among the first acts of legislation adopted by several of the States in the legislative bodies which claimed to be in their normal relations with the Federal government were laws which imposed upon the colored race onerous disabilities and burdens and curtailed their rights in the pursuit of life, liberty, and property to such an extent that their freedom was of little value, while they had lost the protection which they had received from their former owners from motives both of interest and humanity.

They were in some States forbidden to appear in the towns in any other character than menial servants. They were required to reside on and cultivate the soil without the right to purchase or own it. They were excluded from many occupations of gain, and were not permitted to give testimony in the courts in any case where a white man was a party. It was said that their lives were at the mercy of bad men, either because the laws for their protection were insufficient or were not enforced.

These circumstances, whatever of falsehood or misconception may have been mingled with their presentation, forced upon the statesmen who had conducted the Federal government in safety through the crisis of the rebellion, and who supposed that, by the thirteenth article of amendment, they had secured the result of their labors, the conviction that something more was necessary in the way of constitutional protection to the unfortunate race who had suffered so much. They accordingly passed through Congress the proposition for the fourteenth amendment, and they declined to treat as restored to their full participation in the government of the Union the States which had been in insurrection until they ratified that article by a formal vote of their legislative bodies.

Before we proceed to examine more critically the provisions of this amendment, on which the plaintiffs in error rely, let us complete and dismiss the history of the recent amendments, as that history relates to the general purpose which pervades them all. A few years' experience satisfied the thoughtful men who had been the authors of the other two amendments that, notwithstanding the restraints of those articles on the States and the laws passed under the additional powers granted to Congress, these were inadequate for the protection of life, liberty, and property, without which freedom to the slave was no boon. They were in all those States denied the right of suffrage. The laws were administered by the white man alone. It was urged that a race of men distinctively marked, as was the negro, living in the midst of another and dominant race, could never be fully secured in their person and their property without the right of suffrage.

Hence, the fifteenth amendment, which declares that

> "the right of a citizen of the United States to vote shall not be denied or abridged by any State on account of race, color, or previous condition of servitude."

The negro having, by the fourteenth amendment, been declared to be a citizen of the United States, is thus made a voter in every State of the Union.

We repeat, then, in the light of this recapitulation of events, almost too recent to be called history, but which are familiar to us all, and on the most casual examination of the language of these amendments, no one can fail to be impressed with the one pervading purpose found in them all, lying at the foundation of each, and without which none of them would have been even suggested; we mean the freedom of the slave race, the security and firm establishment of that freedom, and the protection of the newly made freeman and citizen from the oppressions of those who had formerly exercised unlimited dominion over him. It is true that only the fifteenth amendment, in terms, mentions the negro by speaking of his color and his slavery. But it is just as true that each of the other articles was addressed to the grievances of that race, and designed to remedy them as the fifteenth.

We do not say that no one else but the negro can share in this protection. Both the language and spirit of these articles are to have their fair and just weight in any question of construction. Undoubtedly while negro slavery alone was in the mind of the Congress which proposed the thirteenth article, it forbids any other kind of slavery, now or hereafter. If Mexican peonage or the Chinese coolie labor system shall develop slavery of the Mexican of Chinese race within our territory, this amendment may safely be trusted to make it void. And so, if other rights are assailed by the States which properly and necessarily fall within the protection of these articles, that protection will apply, though the party interested may not be of African descent. But what we do say, and what we wish to be understood, is that, in any fair and just construction of any section or phrase of these amendments, it is necessary to look to the purpose which we have said was the pervading spirit of them all, the evil which they were designed to remedy, and the process of continued addition to the Constitution, until that purpose was supposed to be accomplished as far as constitutional law can accomplish it.

The first section of the fourteenth article to which our attention is more specially invited opens with a definition of citizenship—not only citizenship of the United States, but citizenship of the States. No such definition was previously found in the Constitution, nor had any attempt been made to define it by act of Congress. It had been the occasion of much discussion in the courts, by the executive departments, and in the public journals. It had been said by eminent judges that no man was a citizen of the United States except as he was a citizen of one of the States composing the Union. Those, therefore, who had been born and resided always in the District of Columbia or in the Territories, though within the United States, were not citizens. Whether this proposition was sound or not had never been judicially decided. But it had been held by this court, in the celebrated *Dred Scott* case, only a few years before the outbreak of the civil war, that a man of African descent, whether a slave or not, was not and could not be a citizen of a State or of the United States. This decision, while it met the condemnation of some of the ablest statesmen and constitutional lawyers of the country, had never been overruled, and if was to be accepted as a constitutional limitation of the right of citizenship, then all the negro race who had recently been made freemen were still not only not citizens, but were incapable of becoming so by anything short of an amendment to the Constitution.

To remove this difficulty primarily, and to establish clear and comprehensive definition of citizenship which should declare what should constitute citizenship of the United States and also citizenship of a State, the first clause of the first section was framed.

"All persons born or naturalized in the United States, and subject to the jurisdiction thereof, are citizens of the United States and of the State wherein they reside."

The first observation we have to make on this clause is that it puts at rest both the questions which we stated to have been the subject of differences of opinion. It declares that persons may be citizens of the United States without regard to their citizenship of a particular State, and it overturns the *Dred Scott* decision by making all persons born within the United States and subject to its jurisdiction citizens of the United States. That its main purpose was to establish the citizenship of the negro

can admit of no doubt. The phrase, "subject to its jurisdiction" was intended to exclude from its operation children of ministers, consuls, and citizens or subjects of foreign States born within the United States.

The next observation is more important in view of the arguments of counsel in the present case. It is that the distinction between citizenship of the United States and citizenship of a State is clearly recognized and established.

Not only may a man be a citizen of the United States without being a citizen of a State, but an important element is necessary to convert the former into the latter. He must reside within the State to make him a citizen of it, but it is only necessary that he should be born or naturalized in the United States to be a citizen of the Union.

It is quite clear, then, that there is a citizenship of the United States, and a citizenship of a State, which are distinct from each other, and which depend upon different characteristics or circumstances in the individual.

We think this distinction and its explicit recognition in this amendment of great weight in this argument, because the next paragraph of this same section, which is the one mainly relied on by the plaintiffs in error, speaks only of privileges and immunities of citizens of the United States, and does not speak of those of citizens of the several States. The argument, however, in favor of the plaintiffs rests wholly on the assumption that the citizenship is the same, and the privileges and immunities guaranteed by the clause are the same.

The language is, "No State shall make or enforce any law which shall abridge the privileges or immunities of citizens of *the United States*." It is a little remarkable, if this clause was intended as a protection to the citizen of a State against the legislative power of his own State, that the word citizen of the State should be left out when it is so carefully used, and used in contradistinction to citizens of the United States in the very sentence which precedes it. It is too clear for argument that the change in phraseology was adopted understandingly and, with a purpose.

Of the privileges and immunities of the citizen of the United States, and of the privileges and immunities of the citizen of the State, and what they respectively are, we will presently consider; but we wish to state here that it is only the former which are placed by this clause under the protection of the Federal Constitution, and that the latter, whatever they may be, are not intended to have any additional protection by this paragraph of the amendment.

If, then, there is a difference between the privileges and immunities belonging to a citizen of the United States as such and those belonging to the citizen of the State as such, the latter must rest for their security and protection where they have heretofore rested, for they are not embraced by this paragraph of the amendment.

The first occurrence of the words "privileges and immunities" in our constitutional history is to be found in the fourth of the articles of the old Confederation.

It declares

"that the better to secure and perpetuate mutual friendship and intercourse among the people of the different States in this Union, the free inhabitants of each of these States, paupers, vagabonds, and fugitives from justice excepted, shall be entitled to all the privileges and immunities of free citizens in the several States, and the people of each State shall have free ingress and regress to and from any other State, and shall enjoy therein all the privileges of trade and commerce, subject to the same duties, impositions, and restrictions as the inhabitants thereof respectively."

In the Constitution of the United States, which superseded the Articles of Confederation, the corresponding provision is found in section two of the fourth article, in the following words: "The citizens of each State shall be entitled to all the privileges and immunities of citizens of the several States."

There can be but little question that the purpose of both these provisions is the same, and that the privileges and immunities intended are the same in each. In the article of the Confederation, we have some of these specifically mentioned, and enough perhaps to give some general idea of the class of civil rights meant by the phrase.

Fortunately, we are not without judicial construction of this clause of the Constitution. The first and the leading case on the subject is that of *Corfield v. Cory-*

*ell,* decided by Mr. Justice Washington in the Circuit Court for the District of Pennsylvania in 1823.

"The inquiry," he says,

"is what are the privileges and immunities of citizens of the several States? We feel no hesitation in confining these expressions to those privileges and immunities which are fundamental; which belong of right to the citizens of all free governments, and which have at all times been enjoyed by citizens of the several States which compose this Union, from the time of their becoming free, independent, and sovereign. What these fundamental principles are it would be more tedious than difficult to enumerate. They may all, however, be comprehended under the following general heads: protection by the government, with the right to acquire and possess property of every kind and to pursue and obtain happiness and safety, subject, nevertheless, to such restraints as the government may prescribe for the general good of the whole."

This definition of the privileges and immunities of citizens of the States is adopted in the main by this court in the recent case of *Ward v. The State of Maryland,* while it declines to undertake an authoritative definition beyond what was necessary to that decision. The description, when taken to include others not named, but which are of the same general character, embraces nearly every civil right for the establishment and protection of which organized government is instituted. They are, in the language of Judge Washington, those rights which are fundamental. Throughout his opinion, they are spoken of as rights belonging to the individual as a citizen of a State. They are so spoken of in the constitutional provision which he was construing. And they have always been held to be the class of rights which the State governments were created to establish and secure.

In the case of *Paul v. Virginia,* the court, in expounding this clause of the Constitution, says that

"the privileges and immunities secured to citizens of each State in the several States by the provision in question are those privileges and immunities which are common to the citizens in the latter States under the constitution and laws by virtue of their being citizens."

The constitutional provision there alluded to did not create those rights, which it called privileges and immunities of citizens of the States. It threw around them in that clause no security for the citizen of the State in which they were claimed or exercised. Nor did it profess to control the power of the State governments over the rights of its own citizens.

Its sole purpose was to declare to the several States that, whatever those rights, as you grant or establish them to your own citizens, or as you limit or qualify or impose restrictions on their exercise, the same, neither more nor less, shall be the measure of the rights of citizens of other States within your jurisdiction.

It would be the vainest show of learning to attempt to prove by citations of authority that, up to the adoption of the recent amendments, no claim or pretence was set up that those rights depended on the Federal government for their existence or protection beyond the very few express limitations which the Federal Constitution imposed upon the States—such, for instance, as the prohibition against *ex post facto* laws, bills of attainder, and laws impairing the obligation of contracts. But, with the exception of these and a few other restrictions, the entire domain of the privileges and immunities of citizens of the States, as above defined, lay within the constitutional and legislative power of the States, and without that of the Federal government. Was it the purpose of the fourteenth amendment, by the simple declaration that no State should make or enforce any law which shall abridge the privileges and immunities of citizens of the United States, to transfer the security and protection of all the civil rights which we have mentioned, from the States to the Federal government? And where it is declared that Congress Shall have the power to enforce that article, was it intended to bring within the power of Congress the entire domain of civil rights heretofore belonging exclusively to the States?

All this and more must follow if the proposition of the plaintiffs in error be sound. For not only are these rights subject to the control of Congress whenever, in its discretion, any of them are supposed to be abridged by State legislation, but that body may also pass laws in advance, limiting and restricting the exercise of legislative power by the States, in their most ordinary and usual functions, as in its judgment it may think proper on all such subjects. And still further, such a construction followed by the reversal of the judgments of the Supreme Court of Louisiana in these cases, would constitute this court a perpetual censor upon all legislation of the States, on the civil rights of their own citizens, with authority to nullify such as it did not approve as consistent with those rights, as they existed at the time of the adoption of this amendment. The argument, we admit, is not always the most conclusive which is drawn from the consequences urged against the adoption of a particular construction of an instrument. But when, as in the case before us, these consequences are so serious, so far-reaching and pervading, so great a departure from the structure and spirit of our institutions; when the effect is to fetter and degrade the State governments by subjecting them to the control of Congress in the exercise of powers heretofore universally conceded to them of the most ordinary and fundamental character; when, in fact, it radically changes the whole theory of the relations of the State and Federal governments to each other and of both these governments to the people, the argument has a force that is irresistible in the absence of language which expresses such a purpose too clearly to admit of doubt.

We are convinced that no such results were intended by the Congress which proposed these amendments, nor by the legislatures of the States which ratified them.

Having shown that the privileges and immunities relied on in the argument are those which belong to citizens of the States as such, and that they are left to the State governments for security and protection, and not by this article placed under the special care of the Federal government, we may hold ourselves excused from defining the privileges and immunities of citizens of the United States which no State can abridge until some case involving those privileges may make it necessary to do so.

But lest it should be said that no such privileges and immunities are to he found if those we have been considering are excluded, we venture to suggest some which owe their existence to the Federal government, its national character, its Constitution, or its laws.

One of these is well described in the case of *Crandall v. Nevada.* It is said to be the right of the citizen of this great country, protected by implied guarantees of its Constitution,

> "to come to the seat of government to assert any claim he may have upon that government, to transact any business he may have with it, to seek its protection, to share its offices, to engage in administering its functions. He has the right of free access to its seaports, through which operations of foreign commerce are conducted, to the sub-treasuries, land offices, and courts of justice in the several States."

And quoting from the language of Chief Justice Taney in another case, it is said

> "that, *for all the great purposes for which the Federal government* was established, we are one people, with one common country, *we are all citizens of the United States;*"

and it is, as such citizens, that their rights are supported in this court in *Crandall v. Nevada.*

Another privilege of a citizen of the United States is to demand the care and protection of the Federal government over his life, liberty, and property when on the high seas or within the jurisdiction of a foreign government. Of this there can be no doubt, nor that the right depends upon his character as a citizen of the United States. The right to peaceably assemble and petition for redress of grievances, the privilege of the writ of habeas corpus, are rights of the citizen guaranteed by the Federal Constitution. The right to use the navigable waters of the United States, however they may penetrate the territory of the several States, all rights secured to our citizens by treaties with foreign nations, are dependent upon citizenship of the United States, and not citizenship of a State. One of these privileges is conferred by the very article under consideration. It is that a citizen of the United States can, of his own volition, become a citizen of any State of the Union by a *bona fide* residence therein, with the same rights as other citizens of that State. To these may be added the rights secured by the thirteenth and fifteenth articles of amendment, and by the other clause of the fourteenth, next to be considered.

But it is useless to pursue this branch of the inquiry, since we are of opinion that the rights claimed by these plaintiffs in error, if they have any existence, are not privileges and immunities of citizens of the United States within the meaning of the clause of the thirteenth amendment under consideration.

> "All persons born or naturalized in the United States, and subject to the jurisdiction thereof, are citizens of the United States and of the State wherein they reside. No State shall make or enforce any law which shall abridge the privileges or immunities of citizens of the United States; nor shall any State deprive any person of life, liberty, or property without due process of law, nor deny to any person within its jurisdiction the equal protection of its laws."

The argument has not been much pressed in these cases that the defendant's charter deprives the plaintiffs of their property without due process of law, or that it denies to them the equal protection of the law. The first of these paragraphs has been in the Constitution since the adoption of the fifth amendment, as a restraint upon the Federal power. It is also to be found in some form of expression in the constitutions of nearly all the States as a restraint upon the power of the States. This law, then, has practically been the same as it now is during the existence of the government, except so far as the present amendment may place the restraining power over the States in this matter in the hands of the Federal government.

We are not without judicial interpretation, therefore, both State and National, of the meaning of this clause. And it is sufficient to say that under no construction of that provision that we have ever seen, or any that we deem admissible, can the restraint imposed by the State of Louisiana upon the exercise of their trade by the butchers of New Orleans be held to be a deprivation of property within the meaning of that provision.

"Nor shall any State deny to any person within its jurisdiction the equal protection of the laws."

In the light of the history of these amendments, and the pervading purpose of them, which we have already discussed, it is not difficult to give a meaning to this clause. The existence of laws in the States where the newly emancipated negroes resided, which discriminated with gross injustice and hardship against them as a class, was the evil to be remedied by this clause, and by it such laws are forbidden.

If, however, the States did not conform their laws to its requirements, then by the fifth section of the article of amendment Congress was authorized to enforce it by suitable legislation. We doubt very much whether any action of a State not directed by way of discrimination against the negroes as a class, or on account of their race, will ever be held to come within the purview of this provision. It is so clearly a provision for that race and that emergency that a strong case would be necessary for its application to any other. But as it is a State that is to be dealt with, and not alone the validity of its laws, we may safely leave that matter until Congress shall have exercised its power, or some case of State oppression, by denial of equal justice in its courts, shall have claimed a decision at our hands. We find no such case in the one before us, and do not deem it necessary to go over the argument again, as it may have relation to this particular clause of the amendment.

In the early history of the organization of the government, its statesmen seem to have divided on the line which should separate the powers of the National government from those of the State governments, and though this line has never been very well defined in public opinion, such a division has continued from that day to this.

The adoption of the first eleven amendments to the Constitution so soon after the original instrument was accepted shows a prevailing sense of danger at that time from the Federal power. And it cannot be denied that such a jealousy continued to exist with many patriotic men until the breaking out of the late civil war. It was then discovered that the true danger to the perpetuity of the Union was in the capacity of the State organizations to combine and concentrate all the powers of the State, and of contiguous States, for a determined resistance to the General Government.

Unquestionably this has given great force to the argument, and added largely to the number of those who believe in the necessity of a strong National government.

But, however pervading this sentiment, and however it may have contributed to the adoption of the amendments we have been considering, we do not see in those amendments any purpose to destroy the main features

of the general system. Under the pressure of all the excited feeling growing out of the war, our statesmen have still believed that the existence of the State with powers for domestic and local government, including the regulation of civil rights the rights of person and of property was essential to the perfect working of our complex form of government, though they have thought proper to impose additional limitations on the States, and to confer additional power on that of the Nation.

But whatever fluctuations may be seen in the history of public opinion on this subject during the period of our national existence, we think it will be found that this court, so far as its functions required, has always held with a steady and an even hand the balance between State and Federal power, and we trust that such may continue to be the history of its relation to that subject so long as it shall have duties to perform which demand of it a construction of the Constitution or of any of its parts. The judgments of the Supreme Court of Louisiana in these cases are

AFFIRMED.

## Mr. Justice FIELD, dissenting

I am unable to agree with the majority of the court in these cases, and will proceed to state the reasons of my dissent from their judgment.

The cases grow out of the act of the legislature of the

State of Louisiana, entitled

> "An act to protect the health of the city of New Orleans, to locate the stock-landings and slaughterhouses, and to incorporate 'The Crescent City Live-Stock Landing and Slaughter-House Company,'"

which was approved on the eighth of March, 1869, and went into operation on the first of June following. The act creates the corporation mentioned in its title, which is composed of seventeen persons designated by name, and invests them and their successors with the powers usually conferred upon corporations in addition to their special and exclusive privileges. It first declares that it shall not be lawful, after the first day of June, 1869, to

> "land, keep, or slaughter any cattle, beeves, calves, sheep, swine, or other animals, or to

have, keep, or establish any stock-landing, yards, slaughterhouses, or abattoirs within the city of New Orleans or the parishes of Orleans, Jefferson, and St. Bernard,"

except as provided in the act, and imposes a penalty of two hundred and fifty dollars for each violation of its provisions. It then authorizes the corporation mentioned to establish and erect within the parish of St. Bernard and the corporate limits of New Orleans, below the United States barracks, on the east side of the Mississippi, or at any point below a designated railroad depot on the west side of the river,

> "wharves, stables, sheds, yards, and buildings, necessary to land, stable, shelter, protect, and preserve all kinds of horses, mules, cattle, and other animals,"

and provides that cattle and other animals, destined for sale or slaughter in the city of New Orleans or its environs shall be landed at the landings and yards of the company, and be there yarded, sheltered, and protected, if necessary, and that the company shall be entitled to certain prescribed fees for the use of its wharves, and for each animal landed, and be authorized to detain the animals until the fees are paid, and, if not paid within fifteen days, to take proceedings for their sale. Every person violating any of these provisions, or landing, yarding, or keeping animals elsewhere, is subjected to a fine of two hundred and fifty dollars.

The act then requires the corporation to erect a grand slaughterhouse of sufficient dimensions to accommodate all butchers, and in which five hundred animals may be slaughtered a day, with a sufficient number of sheds and stables for the stock received at the port of New Orleans, at the same time authorizing the company to erect other landing-places and other slaughterhouses at any points consistent with the provisions of the act.

The act then provides that, when the slaughterhouses and accessory buildings have been completed and thrown open for use, public notice thereof shall be given for thirty days, and within that time,

> "all other stock-landings and slaughterhouses within the parishes of Orleans, Jefferson, and St. Bernard shall be closed, and it shall no longer be lawful to slaughter cattle, hogs, calves,

sheep, or goats, the meat of which is determined [destined] for sale within the parishes aforesaid, under a penalty of one hundred dollars for each and every offence."

The act then provides that the company shall receive for every animal slaughtered in its buildings certain prescribed fees, besides the head, feet, gore, and entrails of all animals except of swine.

Other provisions of the act require the inspection of the animals before they are slaughtered, and allow the construction of railways to facilitate communication with the buildings of the company and the city of New Orleans.

But it is only the special and exclusive privileges conferred by the act that this court has to consider in the cases before it. These privileges are granted for the period of twenty-five years. Their exclusive character not only follows from the provisions I have cited, but it is declared in express terms in the act. In the third section, the language is that the corporation

> "shall have the sole and exclusive privilege of conducting and carrying on the livestock, landing, and slaughterhouse business within the limits and privileges granted by the provisions of the act."

And in the fourth section, the language is that, after the first of June, 1869, the company shall have "the exclusive privilege of having landed at their landing-places all animals intended for sale or slaughter in the parishes of Orleans and Jefferson," and "the exclusive privilege of having slaughtered" in its slaughterhouses all animals the meat of which is intended for sale in these parishes.

In order to understand the real character of these special privileges, it is necessary to know the extent of country and of population which they affect. The parish of Orleans contains an area of country of 150 square miles; the parish of Jefferson 384 square miles, and the parish of St. Bernard 620 square miles. The three parishes together contain an area of 1154 square miles, and they have a population of between two and three hundred thousand people.

The plaintiffs in error deny the validity of the act in question so far as it confers the special and exclusive privileges mentioned. The first case before us was brought by an association of butchers in the three parishes against the corporation to prevent the assertion and enforcement of these privileges. The second case was instituted by the attorney general of the State, in the name of the State, to protect the corporation in the enjoyment of these privileges and to prevent an association of stock dealers and butchers from acquiring a tract of land in the same district with the corporation upon which to erect suitable buildings for receiving, keeping, and slaughtering cattle and preparing animal food for market. The third case was commenced by the corporation itself to restrain the defendants from carrying on a business similar to its own in violation of its alleged exclusive privileges.

The substance of the averments of the plaintiffs in error is this: that, prior to the passage of the act in question, they were engaged in the lawful and necessary business of procuring and bringing to the parishes of Orleans, Jefferson, and St. Bernard animals suitable for human food, and in preparing such food for market; that, in the prosecution of this business, they had provided in these parishes suitable establishments for landing, sheltering, keeping, and slaughtering cattle and the sale of meat; that, with their association about four hundred persons were connected, and that, in the parishes named, about a thousand persons were thus engaged in procuring, preparing, and selling animal food. And they complain that the business of landing, yarding, and keeping, within the parishes named, cattle intended for sale or slaughter, which was lawful for them to pursue before the first day of June, 1869, is made by that act unlawful for anyone except the corporation named, and that the business of slaughtering cattle and preparing animal food for market, which it was lawful for them to pursue in these parishes before that day, is made by that act unlawful for them to pursue afterwards except in the buildings of the company, and upon payment of certain prescribed fees, and a surrender of a valuable portion of each animal slaughtered. And they contend that the lawful business of landing, yarding, sheltering, and keeping cattle intended for sale or slaughter, which they in common with every individual in the community of the three parishes had a right to follow, cannot be thus taken from them and given over for a period of twenty-five years to the sole and exclusive enjoyment of a corporation of seventeen persons or of anybody else. And they also contend that the lawful and necessary

business of slaughtering cattle and preparing animal food for market, which they and all other individuals had a right to follow, cannot be thus restricted within this territory of 1154 square miles to the buildings of this corporation, or be subjected to tribute for the emolument of that body.

No one will deny the abstract justice which lies in the position of the plaintiffs in error, and I shall endeavor to show that the position has some support in the fundamental law of the country.

It is contended in justification for the act in question that it was adopted in the interest of the city, to promote its cleanliness and protect its health, and was the legitimate exercise of what is termed the police power of the State. That power undoubtedly extends to all regulations affecting the health, good order, morals, peace, and safety of society, and is exercised on a great variety of subjects, and in almost numberless ways. All sorts of restrictions and burdens are imposed under it, and, when these are not in conflict with any constitutional prohibitions or fundamental principles, they cannot be successfully assailed in a judicial tribunal. With this power of the State and its legitimate exercise I shall not differ from the majority of the court. But under the pretence of prescribing a police regulation, the State cannot be permitted to encroach upon any of the just rights of the citizen, which the Constitution intended to secure against abridgment.

In the law in question there are only two provisions which can properly be called police regulations—the one which requires the landing and slaughtering of animals below the city of New Orleans, and the other which requires the inspection of the animals before they are slaughtered. When these requirements are complied with, the sanitary purposes of the act are accomplished. In all other particulars, the act is a mere grant to a corporation created by it of special and exclusive privileges by which the health of the city is in no way promoted. It is plain that if the corporation can, without endangering the health of the public, carry on the business of landing, keeping, and slaughtering cattle within a district below the city embracing an area of over a thousand square miles, it would not endanger the public health if other persons were also permitted to carry on the same business within the same district under similar conditions as to the inspection of the animals. The health of the city might require the removal from its limits and suburbs of all buildings for keeping and slaughtering cattle, but no such object could possibly justify legislation removing such buildings from a large part of the State for the benefit of a single corporation. The pretence of sanitary regulations for the grant of the exclusive privileges is a shallow one which merits only this passing notice.

It is also sought to justify the act in question on the same principle that exclusive grants for ferries, bridges, and turnpikes are sanctioned. But it can find no support there. Those grants are of franchises of a public character appertaining to the government. Their use usually requires the exercise of the sovereign right of eminent domain. It is for the government to determine when one of them shall be granted, and the conditions upon which it shall be enjoyed. It is the duty of the government to provide suitable roads, bridges, and ferries for the convenience of the public, and if it chooses to devolve this duty to any extent, or in any locality, upon particular individuals or corporations, it may of course stipulate for such exclusive privileges connected with the franchise as it may deem proper, without encroaching upon the freedom or the just rights of others. The grant, with exclusive privileges, of a right thus appertaining to the government, is a very different thing from a grant, with exclusive privileges, of a right to pursue one of the ordinary trades or callings of life, which is a right appertaining solely to the individual.

Nor is there any analogy between this act of Louisiana and the legislation which confers upon the inventor of a new and useful improvement an exclusive right to make and sell to others his invention. The government in this way only secures to the inventor the temporary enjoyment of that which, without him, would not have existed. It thus only recognizes in the inventor a temporary property in the product of his own brain.

The act of Louisiana presents the naked case, unaccompanied by any public considerations, where a right to pursue a lawful and necessary calling, previously enjoyed by every citizen, and in connection with which a thousand persons were daily employed, is taken away and vested exclusively for twenty-five years, for an extensive district and a large population, in a single corporation, or its exercise is for that period restricted to the establishments of the corporation, and there allowed only upon onerous conditions.

If exclusive privileges of this character can be granted to a corporation of seventeen persons, they may, in the discretion of the legislature, be equally granted to single individual. If they may be granted for twenty-five years, they may be equally granted for a century, and in perpetuity. If they may be granted for the landing and keeping of animals intended for sale or slaughter, they may be equally granted for the landing and storing of grain and other products of the earth, or for any article of commerce. If they may be granted for structures in which animal food is prepared for market, they may be equally granted for structures in which farinaceous or vegetable food is prepared. They may be granted for any of the pursuits of human industry, even in its most simple and common forms. Indeed, upon the theory on which the exclusive privileges granted by the act in question are sustained, there is no monopoly, in the most odious form, which may not be upheld.

The question presented is, therefore, one of the gravest importance not merely to the parties here, but to the whole country. It is nothing less than the question whether the recent amendments to the Federal Constitution protect the citizens of the United States against the deprivation of their common rights by State legislation. In my judgment, the fourteenth amendment does afford such protection, and was so intended by the Congress which framed and the States which adopted it.

The counsel for the plaintiffs in error have contended with great force that the act in question is also inhibited by the thirteenth amendment.

That amendment prohibits slavery and involuntary servitude, except as a punishment for crime, but I have not supposed it was susceptible of a construction which would cover the enactment in question. I have been so accustomed to regard it as intended to meet that form of slavery which had previously prevailed in this country, and to which the recent civil war owed its existence, that I was not prepared, nor am I yet, to give to it the extent and force ascribed by counsel. Still it is evidence that the language of the amendment is not used in a restrictive sense. It is not confined to African slavery alone. It is general and universal in its application. Slavery of white men as well as of black men is prohibited, and not merely slavery in the strict sense of the term, but involuntary servitude in every form.

The words "involuntary servitude" have not been the subject of any judicial or legislative exposition, that I am aware of, in this country, except that which is found in the Civil Rights Act, which will be hereafter noticed. It is, however, clear that they include something more than slavery in the strict sense of the term; they include also serfage, vassalage, villenage, peonage, and all other forms of compulsory service for the mere benefit or pleasure of others. Nor is this the full import of the terms. The abolition of slavery and involuntary servitude was intended to make everyone born in this country a freeman, and, as such, to give to him the right to pursue the ordinary avocations of life without other restraint than such as affects all others, and to enjoy equally with them the fruits of his labor. A prohibition to him to pursue certain callings, open to others of the same age, condition, and sex, or to reside in places where others are permitted to live, would so far deprive him of the rights of a freeman, and would place him, as respects others, in a condition of servitude. A person allowed to pursue only one trade or calling, and only in one locality of the country, would not be, in the strict sense of the term, in a condition of slavery, but probably none would deny that he would be in a condition of servitude. He certainly would not possess the liberties nor enjoy the privileges of a freeman. The compulsion which would force him to labor even for his own benefit only in one direction, or in one place, would be almost as oppressive and nearly as great an invasion of his liberty as the compulsion which would force him to labor for the benefit or pleasure of another, and would equally constitute an element of servitude. The counsel of the plaintiffs in error therefore contend that

> "wherever a law of a State, or a law of the United States, makes a discrimination between classes of persons which deprives the one class of their freedom or their property or which makes a caste of them to subserve the power, pride, avarice, vanity, or vengeance of others,"

there involuntary servitude exists within the meaning of the thirteenth amendment.

It is not necessary, in my judgment, for the disposition of the present case in favor of the plaintiffs in error, to accept as entirely correct this conclusion of counsel. It, however, finds support in the act of Congress known as the Civil Rights Act, which was framed and adopted upon a construction of the thirteenth amendment, giving to its language a similar breadth. That amendment was ratified on the eighteenth of December, 1865, and, in April of the following year, the Civil Rights Act was passed. Its first section declares that all persons born in the United States, and not subject to any foreign power, excluding Indians not taxed, are "citizens of the United States," and that

> "such citizens, of every race and color, without regard to any previous condition of slavery, or involuntary servitude, except as a punishment for crime whereof the party shall have been duly convicted, shall have the same right in every State and Territory in the United States to make and enforce contracts, to sue, be parties, and give evidence, to inherit, purchase, lease, sell, hold, and convey real and personal property, and to full and equal benefit of all laws and proceedings for the security of person and property, as enjoyed by white citizens."

This legislation was supported upon the theory that citizens of the United States, as such, were entitled to the rights and privileges enumerated, and that to deny to any such citizen equality in these rights and privileges with others was, to the extent of the denial, subjecting him to an involuntary servitude. Senator Trumbull, who drew the act and who was its earnest advocate in the Senate, stated, on opening the discussion upon it in that body, that the measure was intended to give effect to the declaration of the amendment, and to secure to all persons in the United States practical freedom. After referring to several statutes passed in some of the Southern States discriminating between the freedmen and white citizens, and after citing the definition of civil liberty given by Blackstone, the Senator said:

> "I take it that any statute which is not equal to all, and which deprives any citizen of civil rights which are secured to other citizens, is an unjust encroachment upon his liberty, and it is in fact a badge of servitude which by the Constitution is prohibited."

By the act of Louisiana, within the three parishes named, a territory exceeding one thousand one hundred square miles, and embracing over two hundred thousand people, every man who pursues the business of preparing animal food for market must take his animals to the buildings of the favored company, and must perform his work in them, and for the use of the buildings must pay a prescribed tribute to the company, and leave with it a valuable portion of each animal slaughtered. Every man in these parishes who has a horse or other animal for sale must carry him to the yards and stables of this company and for their use pay a like tribute. He is not allowed to do his work in his own buildings, or to take his animals to his own stables or keep them in his own yards, even though they should be erected in the same district as the buildings, stables, and yards of the company, and that district embraces over eleven hundred square miles. The prohibitions imposed by this act upon butchers and dealers in cattle in these parishes, and the special privileges conferred upon the favored corporation, are similar in principle and as odious in character as the restrictions imposed in the last century upon the peasantry in some parts of France, where, as says a French writer, the peasant was prohibited

> "to hunt on his own lands, to fish in his own waters, to grind at his own mill, to cook at his own oven, to dry his clothes on his own machines, to whet his instruments at his own grindstone, to make his own wine, his oil, and his cider at his own press, . . . or to sell his commodities at the public market."

The exclusive right to all these privileges was vested in the lords of the vicinage. "The history of the most execrable tyranny of ancient times," says the same writer, "offers nothing like this. This category of oppressions cannot be applied to a free man, or to the peasant, except in violation of his rights."

But if the exclusive privileges conferred upon the Louisiana corporation can be sustained, it is not perceived why exclusive privileges for the construction and keeping of ovens, machines, grindstones, wine-presses, and for all the numerous trades and pursuits for the prosecution of which buildings are required, may not be equally bestowed upon other corporations or private individuals, and for periods of indefinite duration.

It is not necessary, however, as I have said, to rest my objections to the act in question upon the terms and meaning of the thirteenth amendment. The provisions of the fourteenth amendment, which is properly a supplement to the thirteenth, cover, in my judgment, the case before us, and inhibit any legislation which confers special and exclusive privileges like these under consideration. The amendment was adopted to obviate objections which had been raised and pressed with great force to the validity of the Civil Rights Act, and to place the common rights of American citizens under the protection of the National government. It first declares that

> "all persons born or naturalized in the United States, and subject to the jurisdiction thereof, are citizens of the United States and of the State wherein they reside."

It then declares that

> "no State shall make or enforce any law which shall abridge the privileges or immunities of citizens of the United States, nor shall any State deprive any person of life, liberty, or property, without due process of law, nor deny to any person within its jurisdiction the equal protection of the laws."

The first clause of this amendment determines who are citizens of the United States, and how their citizenship is created. Before its enactment, there was much diversity of opinion among jurists and statesmen whether there was any such citizenship independent of that of the State, and, if any existed, as to the manner in which it originated. With a great number, the opinion prevailed that there was no such citizenship independent of the citizenship of the State. Such was the opinion of Mr. Calhoun and the class represented by him. In his celebrated speech in the Senate upon the Force Bill in 1833, referring to the reliance expressed by a senator upon the fact that we are citizens of the United States, he said:

"If by citizen of the United States he means a citizen at large, one whose citizenship extends to the entire geographical limits of the country without having a local citizenship in some State or Territory, a sort of citizen of the world, all I have to say is that such a citizen would be a perfect nondescript; that not a single individual of this description can be found in the entire mass of our population. Notwithstanding all the pomp and display of eloquence on the occasion, every citizen is a citizen of some State or Territory, and, as such, under an express provision of the Constitution, is entitled to all privileges and immunities of citizens in the several States; and it is in this and no other sense that we are citizens of the United States."

In the Dred Scott case, this subject of citizenship of the United States was fully and elaborately discussed. The exposition in the opinion of Mr. Justice Curtis has been generally accepted by the profession of the country as the one containing the soundest views of constitutional law. And he held that, under the Constitution, citizenship of the United States in reference to natives was dependent upon citizenship in the several States, under their constitutions and laws.

The Chief Justice, in that case, and a majority of the court with him, held that the words "people of the United States" and "citizens" were synonymous terms; that the people of the respective States were the parties to the Constitution; that these people consisted of the free inhabitants of those States; that they had provided in their Constitution for the adoption of a uniform rule of naturalization; that they and their descendants and persons naturalized were the only persons who could be citizens of the United States, and that it was not in the power of any State to invest any other person with citizenship so that he could enjoy the privileges of a citizen under the Constitution, and that therefore the descendants of persons brought to this country and sold as slaves were not, and could not be, citizens within the meaning of the Constitution.

The first clause of the fourteenth amendment changes this whole subject, and removes it from the region of discussion and doubt. It recognizes in express terms, if it does not create, citizens of the United States, and it makes their citizenship dependent upon the place of their birth, or the fact of their adoption, and not upon the constitution or laws of any State or the condition of their ancestry. A citizen of a State is now only a citizen of the United States residing in that State. The fundamental rights, privileges, and immunities which belong to him as a free man and a free citizen now belong to him as a citizen of the United States, and are not dependent upon his citizenship of any State. The exercise of these rights and privileges, and the degree of enjoyment received from such exercise, are always more or less affected by the condition and the local institutions of the State, or city, or town where he resides. They are thus affected in a State by the wisdom of its laws, the ability of its officers, the efficiency of its mag-

istrates, the education and morals of its people, and by many other considerations. This is a result which follows from the constitution of society, and can never be avoided, but in no other way can they be affected by the action of the State, or by the residence of the citizen therein. They do not derive their existence from its legislation, and cannot be destroyed by its power.

The amendment does not attempt to confer any new privileges or immunities upon citizens, or to enumerate or define those already existing. It assumes that there are such privileges and immunities which belong of right to citizens as such, and ordains that they shall not be abridged by State legislation. If this inhibition has no reference to privileges and immunities of this character, but only refers, as held by the majority of the court in their opinion, to such privileges and immunities as were before its adoption specially designated in the Constitution or necessarily implied as belonging to citizens of the United States, it was a vain and idle enactment, which accomplished nothing and most unnecessarily excited Congress and the people on its passage. With privileges and immunities thus designated or implied no State could ever have interfered by its laws, and no new constitutional provision was required to inhibit such interference. The supremacy of the Constitution and the laws of the United States always controlled any State legislation of that character. But if the amendment refers to the natural and inalienable rights which belong to all citizens, the inhibition has a profound significance and consequence.

What, then, are the privileges and immunities which are secured against abridgment by State legislation?

In the first section of the Civil Rights Act, Congress has given its interpretation to these terms, or at least has stated some of the rights which, in its judgment, these terms include; it has there declared that they include the right

> "to make and enforce contracts, to sue, be parties and give evidence, to inherit, purchase, lease, sell, hold, and convey real and personal property, and to full and equal benefit of all laws and proceedings for the security of person and property."

That act, it is true, was passed before the fourteenth amendment, but the amendment was adopted, as I have already said, to obviate objections to the act, or, speaking more accurately, I should say, to obviate objections to legislation of a similar character, extending the protection of the National government over the common rights of all citizens of the United States. Accordingly, after its ratification, Congress reenacted the act under the belief that whatever doubts may have previously existed of its validity, they were removed by the amendment.

The terms "privileges" and "immunities" are not new in the amendment; they were in the Constitution before the amendment was adopted. They are found in the second section of the fourth article, which declares that "the citizens of each State shall be entitled to all privileges and immunities of citizens in the several States," and they have been the subject of frequent consideration in judicial decisions. In *Corfield v. Coryell*, Mr. Justice Washington said he had

"no hesitation in confining these expressions to those privileges and immunities which were, in their nature, fundamental, which belong of right to citizens of all free governments, and which have at all times been enjoyed by the citizens of the several States which compose the Union, from the time of their becoming free, independent, and sovereign;"

and, in considering what those fundamental privileges were, he said that perhaps it would be more tedious than difficult to enumerate them, but that they might be

> "all comprehended under the following general heads: protection by the government; the enjoyment of life and liberty, with the right to acquire and possess property of every kind, and to pursue and obtain happiness and safety, subject, nevertheless, to such restraints as the government may justly prescribe for the general good of the whole."

This appears to me to be a sound construction of the clause in question. The privileges and immunities designated are those which of right belong to the citizens of all free governments. Clearly among these must be placed the right to pursue a lawful employment in a lawful manner, without other restraint than such as equally affects all persons. In the discussions in Congress upon the passage of the Civil Rights Act, repeated reference

was made to this language of Mr. Justice Washington. It was cited by Senator Trumbull with the observation that it enumerated the very rights belonging to a citizen of the United States set forth in the first section of the act, and with the statement that all persons born in the United States, being declared by the act citizens of the United States, would thenceforth be entitled to the rights of citizens, and that these were the great fundamental rights set forth in the act; and that they were set forth "as appertaining to every freeman."

The privileges and immunities designated in the second section of the fourth article of the Constitution are, then, according to the decision cited, those which of right belong to the citizens of all free governments, and they can be enjoyed under that clause by the citizens of each State in the several States upon the same terms and conditions as they are enjoyed by the citizens of the latter States. No discrimination can be made by one State against the citizens of other States in their enjoyment, nor can any greater imposition be levied than such as is laid upon its own citizens. It is a clause which insures equality in the enjoyment of these rights between citizens of the several States whilst in the same State.

Nor is there anything in the opinion in the case of *Paul v. Virginia*, which at all militates against these views, as is supposed by the majority of the court. The act of Virginia of 1866 which was under consideration in that case provided that no insurance company not incorporated under the laws of the State should carry on its business within the State without previously obtaining a license for that purpose, and that it should not receive such license until it had deposited with the treasurer of the State bonds of a specified character, to an amount varying from thirty to fifty thousand dollars. No such deposit was required of insurance companies incorporated by the State, for carrying on their business within the State; and in the case cited, the validity of the discriminating provisions of the statute of Virginia between her own corporations and the corporations of other States was assailed. It was contended that the statute in this particular was in conflict with that clause of the Constitution which declares that "the citizens of each State shall be entitled to all privileges and immunities of citizens in the several States." But the court answered, that corporations were not citizens within the meaning of this clause; that the term citizens as there used applied only to natural persons, members of the body politic owing allegiance to the State, not to artificial persons created by the legislature and possessing only the attributes which the legislature had prescribed; that, though it had been held that where contracts or rights of property were to be enforced by or against a corporation, the courts of the United States would, for the purpose of maintaining jurisdiction, consider the corporation as representing citizens of the State, under the laws of which it was created, and to this extent would treat a corporation was a citizen within the provision of the Constitution extending the judicial power of the United States to controversies between citizens of different States, it had never been held in any case which had come under its observation, either in the State or Federal courts, that a corporation was a citizen within the meaning of the clause in question, entitling the citizens of each State to the privileges and immunities of citizens in the several States. And the court observed that the privileges and immunities secured by that provision were those privileges and immunities which were common to the citizens in the latter States, under their constitution and laws, by virtue of their being citizens; that special privileges enjoyed by citizens in their own States were not secured in other States by the provision; that it was not intended by it to give to the laws of one State any operation in other States; that they could have no such operation except by the permission, expressed or implied, of those States; and that the special privileges which they conferred must, therefore, be enjoyed at home unless the assent of other States to their enjoyment therein were given. And so the court held that a corporation, being a grant of special privileges to the corporators, had no legal existence beyond the limits of the sovereignty where created, and that the recognition of its existence by other States, and the enforcement of its contracts made therein, depended purely upon the assent of those States, which could be granted upon such terms and conditions as those States might think proper to impose.

The whole purport of the decision was that citizens of one State do not carry with them into other States any special privileges or immunities, conferred by the laws of their own States, of a corporate or other character. That decision has no pertinency to the questions involved in this case. The common privileges and immunities which of right belong to all citizens, stand on a very different footing. These the citizens of each State

do carry with them into other States, and are secured by the clause in question in their enjoyment upon terms of equality with citizens of the latter States. This equality in one particular was enforced by this court in the recent case of *Ward v. The State of Maryland*, reported in the 12th of Wallace. A statute of that State required the payment of a larger sum from a nonresident trader for a license to enable him to sell his merchandise in the State than it did of a resident trader, and the court held that the statute, in thus discriminating against the nonresident trader, contravened the clause securing to the citizens of each State the privileges and immunities of citizens of the several States. The privilege of disposing of his property, which was an essential incident to his ownership possessed by the nonresident, was subjected by the statute of Maryland to a greater burden than was imposed upon a like privilege of her own citizens. The privileges of the nonresident were in this particular abridged by that legislation.

What the clause in question did for the protection of the citizens of one State against hostile and discriminating legislation of other States, the fourteenth amendment does for the protection of every citizen of the United States against hostile and discriminating legislation against him in favor of others, whether they reside in the same or in different States. If, under the fourth article of the Constitution, equality of privileges and immunities is secured between citizens of different States, under the fourteenth amendment, the same equality is secured between citizens of the United States.

It will not be pretended that, under the fourth article of the Constitution, any State could create a monopoly in any known trade or manufacture in favor of her own citizens, or any portion of them, which would exclude an equal participation in the trade or manufacture monopolized by citizens of other States. She could not confer, for example, upon any of her citizens the sole right to manufacture shoes, or boots, or silk, or the sole right to sell those articles in the State so as to exclude nonresident citizens from engaging in a similar manufacture or sale. The nonresident citizens could claim equality of privilege under the provisions of the fourth article with the citizens of the State exercising the monopoly as well as with others, and thus, as respects them, the monopoly would cease. If this were not so, it would be in the power of the State to exclude at any time the citizens of other States from participation in particular branches of commerce or trade, and extend the exclusion from time to time so as effectually to prevent any traffic with them.

Now what the clause in question does for the protection of citizens of one State against the creation of monopolies in favor of citizens of other States, the fourteenth amendment does for the protection of every citizen of the United States against the creation of any monopoly whatever. The privileges and immunities of citizens of the United States, of every one of them, is secured against abridgment in any form by any State. The fourteenth amendment places them under the guardianship of the National authority. All monopolies in any known trade or manufacture are an invasion of these privileges, for they encroach upon the liberty of citizens to acquire property and pursue happiness, and were held void at common law in the great *Case of Monopolies,* decided during the reign of Queen Elizabeth.

A monopoly is defined

> "to be an institution or allowance from the sovereign power of the State by grant, commission, or otherwise, to any person or corporation, for the sole buying, selling, making, working, or using of anything, whereby any person or persons, bodies politic or corporate, are sought to be restrained of any freedom or liberty they had before, or hindered in their lawful trade."

All such grants relating to any known trade or manufacture have been held by all the judges of England, whenever they have come up for consideration, to be void at common law as destroying the freedom of trade, discouraging labor and industry, restraining persons from getting an honest livelihood, and putting it into the power of the grantees to enhance the price of commodities. The definition embraces, it will be observed, not merely the sole privilege of buying and selling particular articles, or of engaging in their manufacture, but also the sole privilege of using anything by which others may be restrained of the freedom or liberty they previously had in any lawful trade, or hindered in such trade. It thus covers in every particular the possession and use of suitable yards, stables, and buildings for keeping and protecting cattle and other animals, and for their slaughter. Such establishments are essential to the free and successful prosecution by any butcher of the lawful trade of preparing animal food for market. The exclusive privilege of supplying such yards, buildings, and other conveniences for the prosecution of this business in a large district of country, granted by the act of Louisiana to seventeen persons, is as much a monopoly as though the act had granted to the company the exclusive privilege of buying and selling the animals themselves. It equally restrains the butchers in the freedom and liberty they previously had and hinders them in their lawful trade.

The reasons given for the judgment in the *Case of Monopolies* apply with equal force to the case at bar. In that case, a patent had been granted to the plaintiff giving him the sole right to import playing cards, and the entire traffic in them, and the sole right to make such cards within the realm. The defendant, in disregard of this patent, made and sold some gross of such cards and imported others, and was accordingly sued for infringing upon the exclusive privileges of the plaintiff. As to a portion of the cards made and sold within the realm, he pleaded that he was a haberdasher in London and a free citizen of that city, and, as such, had a right to make and sell them. The court held the plea good and the grant void, as against the common law and divers acts of Parliament. "All trades," said the court,

> "as well mechanical as others, which prevent idleness (the bane of the commonwealth) and exercise men and youth in labor for the maintenance of themselves and their families, and for the increase of their substance, to serve the queen when occasion shall require, are profitable for the commonwealth, and therefore the grant to the plaintiff to have the sole making of them is *against the common law and the benefit and liberty of the subject.*"

The case of Davenant and Hurdis was cited in support of this position. In that case, a company of merchant tailors in London, having power by charter to make ordinances for the better rule and government of the company so that they were consonant to law and reason, made an ordinance that any brother of the society who should have any cloth dressed by a clothworker not being a brother of the society should put one-half of his cloth to some brother of the same society who exercised the art of a clothworker, upon pain of forfeiting ten shillings,

"and it was adjudged that the ordinance, although

it had the countenance of a charter, was against the common law, *because it was against the liberty of the subject; for every subject, by the law, has freedom and liberty to put his cloth to be dressed by what clothworker he pleases, and cannot be restrained to certain persons, for that, in effect, would be a monopoly,* and, therefore, such ordinance, by color of a charter or any grant by charter to such effect, would be void. "

Although the court, in its opinion, refers to the increase in prices and deterioration in quality of commodities which necessarily result from the grant of monopolies, the main ground of the decision was their interference with the liberty of the subject to pursue for his maintenance and that of his family any lawful trade or employment. This liberty is assumed to be the natural right of every Englishman.

The struggle of the English people against monopolies forms one of the most interesting and instructive chapters in their history. It finally ended in the passage of the statute of 21st James I, by which it was declared

> "that all monopolies and all commissions, grants, licenses, charters, and letters-patent, to any person or persons, bodies politic or corporate whatsoever, of or for the sole buying, selling, making, working, or using of anything"

within the realm or the dominion of Wales were altogether contrary to the laws of the realm and utterly void, with the exception of patents for new inventions for a limited period, and for printing, then supposed to belong to the prerogative of the king, and for the preparation and manufacture of certain articles and ordnance intended for the prosecution of war.

The common law of England, as is thus seen, condemned all monopolies in any known trade or manufacture, and declared void all grants of special privileges whereby others could be deprived of any liberty which they previously had, or be hindered in their lawful trade. The statute of James I, to which I have referred, only embodied the law as it had been previously declared by the courts of England, although frequently disregarded by the sovereigns of that country.

The common law of England is the basis of the jurisprudence of the United States. It was brought to this country by the colonists, together with the English statutes, and was established here so far as it was applicable to their condition. That law and the benefit of such of the English statutes as existed at the time of their colonization, and which they had by experience found to be applicable to their circumstances, were claimed by the Congress of the United Colonies in 1774 as a part of their "indubitable rights and liberties."

Of the statutes the benefits of which was thus claimed, the statute of James I against monopolies was one of the most important. And when the Colonies separated from the mother country, no privilege was more fully recognized or more completely incorporated into the fundamental law of the country than that every free subject in the British empire was entitled to pursue his happiness by following any of the known established trades and occupations of the country, subject only to such restraints as equally affected all others. The immortal document which proclaimed the independence of the country declared as self-evident truths that the Creator had endowed all men

> "with certain inalienable rights, and that among these are life, liberty, and the pursuit of happiness; and that to secure these rights governments are instituted among men."

If it be said that the civil law, and not the common law, is the basis of the jurisprudence of Louisiana, I answer that the decree of Louis XVI, in 1776, abolished all monopolies of trades and all special privileges of corporations, guilds, and trading companies, and authorized every person to exercise, without restraint, his art, trade, or profession, and such has been the law of France and of her colonies ever since, and that law prevailed in Louisiana at the time of her cession to the United States. Since then, notwithstanding the existence in that State of the civil law as the basis of her jurisprudence, freedom of pursuit has been always recognized as the common right of her citizens. But were this otherwise, the fourteenth amendment secures the like protection to all citizens in that State against any abridgment of their common rights, as in other States. That amendment was intended to give practical effect to the declaration of 1776 of inalienable rights, rights which are the gift of the Creator, which the law does not confer, but only recognizes. If the trader in London could plead that he was a free citizen of that city against the enforcement to his injury of monopolies, surely, under the fourteenth amendment, every citizen of the United States should be able to plead his citizenship of the republic as a protection against any similar invasion of his privileges and immunities.

So fundamental has this privilege of every citizen to be free from disparaging and unequal enactments in the pursuit of the ordinary avocations of life been regarded that few instances have arisen where the principle has been so far violated as to call for the interposition of the courts. But whenever this has occurred, with the exception of the present cases from Louisiana, which are the most barefaced and flagrant of all, the enactment interfering with the privilege of the citizen has been pronounced illegal and void. When a case under the same law under which the present cases have arisen came before the Circuit Court of the United States in the District of Louisiana, there was no hesitation on the part of the court in declaring the law, in its exclusive features, to be an invasion of one of the fundamental privileges of the citizen. The presiding justice, in delivering the opinion of the court, observed that it might be difficult to enumerate or define what were the essential privileges of a citizen of the United States, which a State could not by its laws invade, but that, so far as the question under consideration was concerned, it might be safely said that

> "it is one of the privileges of every American citizen to adopt and follow such lawful industrial pursuit, not injurious to the community, as he may see fit, without unreasonable regulation or molestation and without being restricted by any of those unjust, oppressive, and odious monopolies or exclusive privileges which have been condemned by all free governments."

And again:

> "There is no more sacred right of citizenship than the right to pursue unmolested a lawful employment in a lawful manner. It is nothing more nor less than the sacred right of labor."

In the *City of Chicago v. Rumpff,* which was before the Supreme Court of Illinois, we have a case similar in all its features to the one at bar. That city being authorized by its charter to regulate and license the slaughtering of animals within its corporate limits, the common council passed what was termed an ordinance in reference thereto, whereby a particular building was designated for the slaughtering of all animals intended for sale or consumption in the city, the owners of which were granted the exclusive right for a specified period to have all such animals slaughtered at their establishment, they to be paid a specific sum for the privilege of slaughtering there by all persons exercising it. The validity of this action of the corporate authorities was assailed on the ground of the grant of exclusive privileges, and the court said:

> "The charter authorizes the city authorities to license or regulate such establishments. Where that body has made the necessary regulations, required for the health or comfort of the inhabitants, all persons inclined to pursue such an occupation should have an opportunity of conforming to such regulations, otherwise the ordinance would be unreasonable, and tend to oppression. Or, if they should regard it for the interest of the city that such establishments should be licensed, the ordinance should be so framed that all persons desiring it might obtain licenses by conforming to the prescribed terms and regulations for the government of such business. We regard it neither as a regulation nor a license of the business to confine it to one building or to give it to one individual. Such an action is oppressive, and creates a monopoly that never could have been contemplated by the General Assembly. It impairs the rights of all other persons, and cuts them off from a share in not only a legal, but a necessary, business. Whether we consider this as an ordinance or a contract, it is equally unauthorized as being opposed to the rules governing the adoption of municipal by-laws. The principle of equality of rights to the corporators is violated by this contract. If the common council may require all of the animals for the consumption of the city to be slaughtered in a single building, or on a particular lot, and the owner be paid a specific sum for the privilege, what would prevent the making a similar contract with some other person that all of the vegetables, or fruits, the flour, the groceries, the dry goods, or other commodities should be sold on his lot and he receive a compensation for the privilege? We can see no difference in principle."

It is true that the court in this opinion was speaking of

a municipal ordinance, and not of an act of the legislature of a State. But, as it is justly observed by counsel, a legislative body is no more entitled to destroy the equality of rights of citizens, nor to fetter the industry of a city, than a municipal government. These rights are protected from invasion by the fundamental law.

In the case of the *Norwich Gaslight Company v. The Norwich City Gas Company,* which was before the Supreme Court of Connecticut, it appeared that the common council of the city of Norwich had passed a resolution purporting to grant to one Treadway, his heirs and assigns, for the period of fifteen years, the right to lay gas pipes in the streets of that city, declaring that no other person or corporation should, by the consent of the common council, lay gas pipes in the streets during that time. The plaintiffs, having purchased of Treadway, undertook to assert an exclusive right to use the streets for their purposes, as against another company which was using the streets for the same purposes. And the court said:

> "As, then, no consideration whatever, either of a public or private character, was reserved for the grant; and as the business of manufacturing and selling gas is an ordinary business, like the manufacture of leather, or any other article of trade in respect to which the government has no exclusive prerogative, we think that, so far as the restriction of other persons than the plaintiffs from using the streets for the purpose of distributing gas by means of pipes can fairly be viewed as intended to operate as a restriction upon its free manufacture and sale, it comes directly within the definition and description of a monopoly, and, although we have no direct constitutional provision against a monopoly, yet the whole theory of a free government is opposed to such grants, and it does not require even the aid which may be derived from the Bill of Rights, the first section of which declares 'that no man or set of men are entitled to exclusive public emoluments or privileges from the community,' to render them void."

In the *Mayor of the City of Hudson v. Thorne,* an application was made to the chancellor of New York to dissolve an injunction restraining the defendants from erecting a building in the city of Hudson upon a vacant lot owned by them, intended to be used as a hay-press. The common council of the city had passed an ordinance directing that no person should erect, or construct, or cause to be erected or constructed, any wooden or frame barn, stable, or hay-press of certain dimensions within certain specified limits in the city without its permission. It appeared, however, that there were such buildings already in existence, not only in compact parts of the city but also within the prohibited limits, the occupation of which for the storing and pressing of hay the common council did not intend to restrain. And the chancellor said:

> "If the manufacture of pressed hay within the compact parts of the city is dangerous in causing or promoting fires, the common council have the power expressly given by their charter to prevent the carrying on of such manufacture; but as all by-laws must be reasonable, the common council cannot make a by-law which shall permit one person to carry on the dangerous business and prohibit another who has an equal right from pursuing the same business."

In all these cases, there is a recognition of the equality of right among citizens in the pursuit of the ordinary avocations of life, and a declaration that all grants of exclusive privileges, in contravention of this equality, are against common right, and void.

This equality of right, with exemption from all disparaging and partial enactments, in the lawful pursuits of life, throughout the whole country, is the distinguishing privilege of citizens of the United States. To them, everywhere, all pursuits, all professions, all avocations are open without other restrictions than such as are imposed equally upon all others of the same age, sex, and condition. The State may prescribe such regulations for every pursuit and calling of life as will promote the public health, secure the good order and advance the general prosperity of society, but, when once prescribed, the pursuit or calling must be free to be followed by every citizen who is within the conditions designated, and will conform to the regulations. This is the fundamental idea upon which our institutions rest, and, unless adhered to in the legislation of the country, our government will be a republic only in name. The fourteenth amendment, in my judgment, makes it essential to the validity of the legislation of every State that this equality of right should be respected. How widely this equality has been departed from, how entirely rejected and trampled upon by the act of Louisiana, I have already shown. And it is to me a matter of profound regret that its validity is recognized by a majority of this court, for by it the right of free labor, one of the most sacred and imprescriptible rights of man, is violated. As stated by the Supreme Court of Connecticut in the case cited, grants of exclusive privileges, such as is made by the act in question, are opposed to the whole theory of free government, and it requires no aid from any bill of rights to render them void. That only is a free government, in the American sense of the term, under which the inalienable right of every citizen to pursue his happiness is unrestrained, except by just, equal, and impartial laws.

I am authorized by the CHIEF JUSTICE, Mr. Justice SWAYNE, and Mr. Justice BRADLEY to state that they concur with me in this dissenting opinion.

### *Mr. Justice BRADLEY, also dissenting*

I concur in the opinion which has just been read by Mr. Justice Field, but desire to add a few observations for the purpose of more fully illustrating my views on the important question decided in these cases, and the special grounds on which they rest.

The fourteenth amendment to the Constitution of the United States, section 1, declares that no State shall make or enforce any law which shall abridge the privileges and immunities of citizens of the United States.

The legislature of Louisiana, under pretence of making a police regulation for the promotion of the public health, passed an act conferring upon a corporation, created by the act, the exclusive right, for twenty-five years, to have and maintain slaughterhouses, landings for cattle, and yards for confining cattle intended for slaughter, within the parishes of Orleans, Jefferson, and St. Bernard, a territory containing nearly twelve hundred square miles, including the city of New Orleans; and prohibiting all other persons from building, keeping, or having slaughterhouses, landings for cattle, and yards for confining cattle intended for slaughter within the said limits; and requiring that all cattle and other animals to be slaughtered for food in that district should be brought to the slaughterhouses and works of the favored company to be slaughtered, and a payment of a fee to the company for such act.

It is contended that this prohibition abridges the privileges and immunities of citizens of the United States, especially of the plaintiffs in error, who were particularly affected thereby, and whether it does so or not is the simple question in this case. And the solution of this question depends upon the solution of two other questions, to-wit:

First. Is it one of the rights and privileges of a citizen of the United States to pursue such civil employment as he may choose to adopt, subject to such reasonable regulations as may be prescribed by law?

Secondly. Is a monopoly, or exclusive right, given to one person to the exclusion of all others, to keep slaughterhouses, in a district of nearly twelve hundred square miles, for the supply of meat for a large city, a reasonable regulation of that employment which the legislature has a right to impose?

The first of these questions is one of vast importance, and lies at the very foundations of our government. The question is now settled by the fourteenth amendment itself, that citizenship of the United States is the primary citizenship in this country, and that State citizenship is secondary and derivative, depending upon citizenship of the United States and the citizen's place of residence. The States have not now, if they ever had, any power to restrict their citizenship to any classes or persons. A citizen of the United States has a perfect constitutional right to go to and reside in any State he chooses, and to claim citizenship therein, and an equality of rights with every other citizen, and the whole power of the nation is pledged to sustain him in that right. He is not bound to cringe to any superior, or to pray for any act of grace, as a means of enjoying all the rights and privileges enjoyed by other citizens. And when the spirit of lawlessness, mob violence, and sectional hate can be so completely repressed as to give full practical effect to this right, we shall be a happier nation, and a more prosperous one, than we now are. Citizenship of the United States ought to be, and, according to the Constitution, is, a sure and undoubted title to equal rights in any and every States in this Union, subject to such regulations as the legislature may rightfully prescribe. If a man be denied full equality before the law, he is denied one of the essential rights of citizenship as a citizen of the United States.

Every citizen, then, being primarily a citizen of the United States, and, secondarily, a citizen of the State where he resides, what, in general, are the privileges and immunities of a citizen of the United States? Is the right, liberty, or privilege of choosing any lawful employment one of them?

If a State legislature should pass a law prohibiting the inhabitants of a particular township, county, or city, from tanning leather or making shoes, would such a law violate any privileges or immunities of those inhabitants as citizens of the United States, or only their privileges and immunities as citizens of that particular State? Or if a State legislature should pass a law of caste, making all trades and professions, or certain enumerated trades and professions, hereditary, so that no one could follow any such trades or professions except that which was pursued by his father, would such a law violate the privileges and immunities of the people of that State as citizens of the United States, or only as citizens of the State? Would they have no redress but to appeal to the courts of that particular State?

This seems to me to be the essential question before us for consideration. And, in my judgment, the right of any citizen to follow whatever lawful employment he chooses to adopt (submitting himself to all lawful regulations) is one of his most valuable rights, and one which the legislature of a State cannot invade, whether restrained by its own constitution or not.

The right of a State to regulate the conduct of its citizens is undoubtedly a very broad and extensive one, and not to be lightly restricted. But there are certain fundamental rights which this right of regulation cannot infringe. It may prescribe the manner of their exercise, but it cannot subvert the rights themselves. I speak now of the rights of citizens of any free government. Granting for the present that the citizens of one government cannot claim the privileges of citizens in another government, that, prior to the union of our North American States, the citizens of one State could not claim the privileges of citizens in another State, or that, after the union was formed, the citizens of the United States, as such, could not claim the privileges of citizens in any particular State, yet the citizens of each of the States and the citizens of the United States would be entitled to certain privileges and immunities as citizens at the hands of their own government—privileges and immunities which their own governments respectively would be bound to respect and maintain. In this free country, the people of which inherited certain traditional rights

and privileges from their ancestors, citizenship means something. It has certain privileges and immunities attached to it which the government, whether restricted by express or implied limitations, cannot take away or impair. It may do so temporarily by force, but it cannot do so by right. And these privileges and immunities attach as well to citizenship of the United States as to citizenship of the States.

The people of this country brought with them to its shores the rights of Englishmen, the rights which had been wrested from English sovereigns at various periods of the nation's history. One of these fundamental rights was expressed in these words, found in Magna Charta:

> "No freeman shall be taken or imprisoned, or be disseized of his freehold or liberties or free customs, or be outlawed or exiled, or any otherwise destroyed; nor will we pass upon him or condemn him but by lawful judgment of his peers or by the law of the land."

English constitutional writers expound this article as rendering life, liberty, and property inviolable except by due process of law. This is the very right which the plaintiffs in error claim in this case. Another of these rights was that of habeas corpus, or the right of having any invasion of personal liberty judicially examined into, at once, by a competent judicial magistrate. Blackstone classifies these fundamental rights under three heads, as the absolute rights of individuals, to-wit: the right of personal security, the right of personal liberty, and the right of private property. And, of the last, he says:

> "The third absolute right, inherent in every Englishman, is that of property, which consists in the free use, enjoyment, and disposal of all his acquisitions, without any control or diminution save only by the laws of the land."

The privileges and immunities of Englishmen were established and secured by long usage and by various acts of Parliament. But it may be said that the Parliament of England has unlimited authority, and might repeal the laws which have from time to time been enacted. Theoretically, this is so, but practically it is not. England has no written constitution, it is true, but it has an unwritten one, resting in the acknowledged, and frequently declared, privileges of Parliament and the people, to violate which in any material respect would produce a revolution in an hour. A violation of one of the fundamental principles of that constitution in the Colonies, namely, the principle that recognizes the property of the people as their own, and which, therefore, regards all taxes for the support of government as gifts of the people through their representatives, and regards taxation without representation as subversive of free government, was the origin of our own revolution.

This, it is true, was the violation of a political right, but personal rights were deemed equally sacred, and were claimed by the very first Congress of the Colonies, assembled in 1774, as the undoubted inheritance of the people of this country; and the Declaration of Independence, which was the first political act of the American people in their independent sovereign capacity, lays the foundation of our National existence upon this broad proposition:

> "That all men are created equal; that they are endowed by their Creator with certain inalienable rights; that among these are life, liberty, and the pursuit of happiness."

Here again we have the great three-fold division of the rights of freemen, asserted as the rights of man. Rights to life, liberty, and the pursuit of happiness are equivalent to the rights of life, liberty, and property. These are the fundamental rights which can only be taken away by due process of law, and which can only be interfered with, or the enjoyment of which can only be modified, by lawful regulations necessary or proper for the mutual good of all; and these rights, I contend, belong to the citizens of every free government.

For the preservation, exercise, and enjoyment of these rights the individual citizen, as a necessity, must be left free to adopt such calling, profession, or trade as may seem to him most conducive to that end. Without this right, he cannot be a freeman. This right to choose one's calling is an essential part of that liberty which it is the object of government to protect, and a calling, when chosen, is a man's property and right. Liberty and property are not protected where these rights are arbitrarily assailed.

I think sufficient has been said to show that citizenship is not an empty name, but that, in this country, at least,

it has connected with it certain incidental rights, privileges, and immunities of the greatest importance. And to say that these rights and immunities attach only to State citizenship, and not to citizenship of the United States, appears to me to evince a very narrow and insufficient estimate of constitutional history and the rights of men, not to say the rights of the American people.

On this point, the often-quoted language of Mr. Justice Washington, in *Corfield v. Coryell,* is very instructive. Being called upon to expound that clause in the fourth article of the Constitution which declares that "the citizens of each State shall be entitled to all the privileges and immunities of citizens in the several States," he says:

> "The inquiry is what are the privileges and immunities of citizens in the several States? We feel no hesitation in confining these expressions to those privileges and immunities which are, in their nature, fundamental, which belong, of right, to the citizens of all free governments, and which have at all times been enjoyed by the citizens of the several States which compose this Union from the time of their becoming free, independent, and sovereign. What these fundamental privileges are it would perhaps be more tedious than difficult to enumerate. They may, however, be all comprehended under the following general heads: protection by the government; the enjoyment of life and liberty, with the right to acquire and possess property of every kind, and to pursue and obtain happiness and safety, subject, nevertheless, to such restraints as the government may justly prescribe for the general good of the whole; the right of a citizen of one State to pass through, or to reside in, any other State for purposes of trade, agriculture, professional pursuits, or otherwise; to claim the benefit of the writ of habeas corpus; to institute and maintain actions of any kind in the courts of the State; to take, hold, and dispose of property, either real or personal; and an exemption from higher taxes or impositions than are paid by the other citizens of the State, may be mentioned as some of the particular privileges and immunities of citizens which are clearly embraced by the general description of privileges deemed to be fundamental."

It is pertinent to observe that both the clause of the Constitution referred to and Justice Washington, in his comment on it, speak of the privileges and immunities of citizens in a State, not of citizens of a State. It is the privileges and immunities of citizens, that is, of citizens as such, that are to be accorded to citizens of other States when they are found in any State; or, as Justice Washington says,

> "privileges and immunities which are, in their nature, fundamental; which belong, of right, to the citizens of all free governments."

It is true the courts have usually regarded the clause referred to as securing only an equality of privileges with the citizens of the State in which the parties are found. Equality before the law is undoubtedly one of the privileges and immunities of every citizen. I am not aware that any case has arisen in which it became necessary to vindicate any other fundamental privilege of citizenship; although rights have been claimed which were not deemed fundamental, and have been rejected as not within the protection of this clause. Be this, however, as it may, the language of the clause is as I have stated it, and seems fairly susceptible of a broader interpretation than that which makes it a guarantee of mere equality of privileges with other citizens.

But we are not bound to resort to implication, or to the constitutional history of England, to find an authoritative declaration of some of the most important privileges and immunities of citizens of the United States. It is in the Constitution itself. The Constitution, it is true, as it stood prior to the recent amendments, specifies, in terms, only a few of the personal privileges and immunities of citizens, but they are very comprehensive in their character. The States were merely prohibited from passing bills of attainder, *ex post facto* laws, laws impairing the obligation of contracts, and perhaps one or two more. But others of the greatest consequence were enumerated, although they were only secured, in express terms, from invasion by the Federal government; such as the right of habeas corpus, the right of trial by jury, of free exercise of religious worship, the right of free speech and a free press, the right peaceably to assemble for the discussion of public measures, the right to be secure against unreasonable searches and seizures, and above all, and including almost all the rest, the right of *not being deprived of life, liberty, or property without due process of law.* These and still oth-

ers are specified in the original Constitution, or in the early amendments of it, as among the privileges and immunities of citizens of the United States, or, what is still stronger for the force of the argument, the rights of all persons, whether citizens or not.

But even if the Constitution were silent, the fundamental privileges and immunities of citizens, as such, would be no less real and no less inviolable than they now are. It was not necessary to say in words that the citizens of the United States should have and exercise all the privileges of citizens; the privilege of buying, selling, and enjoying property; the privilege of engaging in any lawful employment for a livelihood; the privilege of resorting to the laws for redress of injuries, and the like. Their very citizenship conferred these privileges, if they did not possess them before. And these privileges they would enjoy whether they were citizens of any State or not. Inhabitants of Federal territories and new citizens, made such by annexation of territory or naturalization, though without any status as citizens of a State, could, nevertheless, as citizens of the United States, lay claim to every one of the privileges and immunities which have been enumerated, and among these none is more essential and fundamental than the right to follow such profession or employment as each one may choose, subject only to uniform regulations equally applicable to all.

II. The next question to be determined in this case is: is a monopoly or exclusive right, given to one person, or corporation, to the exclusion of all others, to keep slaughterhouses in a district of nearly twelve hundred square miles, for the supply of meat for a great city, a reasonable regulation of that employment which the legislature has a right to impose?

The keeping of a slaughterhouse is part of, and incidental to, the trade of a butcher—one of the ordinary occupations of human life. To compel a butcher, or rather all the butchers of a large city and an extensive district, to slaughter their cattle in another person's slaughterhouse and pay him a toll therefor is such a restriction upon the trade as materially to interfere with its prosecution. It is onerous, unreasonable, arbitrary, and unjust. It has none of the qualities of a police regulation. If it were really a police regulation, it would undoubtedly be within the power of the legislature. That portion of the act which requires all slaughterhouses to be located below the city, and to be subject to inspection, &c.,

is clearly a police regulation. That portion which allows no one but the favored company to build, own, or have slaughterhouses is not a police regulation, and has not the faintest semblance of one. It is one of those arbitrary and unjust laws, made in the interest of a few scheming individuals, by which some of the Southern States have, within the past few years, been so deplorably oppressed and impoverished. It seems to me strange that it can be viewed in any other light.

The granting of monopolies, or exclusive privileges to individuals or corporations is an invasion of the right of others to choose a lawful calling, and an infringement of personal liberty. It was so felt by the English nation as far back as the reigns of Elizabeth and James. A fierce struggle for the suppression of such monopolies, and for abolishing the prerogative of creating them, was made, and was successful. The statute of 21st James abolishing monopolies was one of those constitutional landmarks of English liberty which the English nation so highly prizes and so jealously preserves. It was a part of that inheritance which our fathers brought with them. This statute abolished all monopolies except grants for a term of years to the inventors of new manufactures. This exception is the groundwork of patents for new inventions and copyrights of books. These have always been sustained as beneficial to the state. But all other monopolies were abolished as tending to the impoverishment of the people and to interference with their free pursuits. And ever since that struggle, no English-speaking people have ever endured such an odious badge of tyranny.

It has been suggested that this was a mere legislative act, and that the British Parliament, as well as our own legislatures, have frequently disregarded it by granting exclusive privileges for erecting ferries, railroads, markets, and other establishments of a public kind. It requires but a slight acquaintance with legal history to know that grants of this kind of franchises are totally different from the monopolies of commodities or of ordinary callings or pursuits. These public franchises can only be exercised under authority from the government, and the government may grant them on such conditions as it sees fit. But even these exclusive privileges are becoming more and more odious, and are getting to be more and more regarded as wrong in principle, and as inimical to the just rights and greatest good of the people. But to cite them as proof of the power of legislatures to create mere monopolies, such as no free and enlight-

ened community any longer endures, appears to me, to say the least, very strange and illogical.

Lastly: can the Federal courts administer relief to citizens of the United States whose privileges and immunities have been abridged by a State? Of this I entertain no doubt. Prior to the fourteenth amendment, this could not be done, except in a few instances, for the want of the requisite authority.

As the great mass of citizens of the United States were also citizens of individual States, many of their general privileges and immunities would be the same in the one capacity as in the other. Having this double citizenship, and the great body of municipal laws intended for the protection of person and property being the laws of the State, and no provision being made, and no machinery provided by the Constitution, except in a few specified cases, for any interference by the General Government between a State and its citizens, the protection of the citizen in the enjoyment of his fundamental privileges and immunities (except where a citizen of one State went into another State) was largely left to State laws and State courts, where they will still continue to be left unless actually invaded by the unconstitutional acts or delinquency of the State governments themselves.

Admitting, therefore, that formerly the States were not prohibited from infringing any of the fundamental privileges and immunities of citizens of the United States, except in a few specified cases, that cannot be said now, since the adoption of the fourteenth amendment. In my judgment, it was the intention of the people of this country in adopting that amendment to provide National security against violation by the States of the fundamental rights of the citizen.

The first section of this amendment, after declaring that all persons born or naturalized in the United States, and subject to its jurisdiction, are citizens of the United States and of the State wherein they reside, proceeds to declare further that

> "no State shall make or enforce any law which shall abridge the privileges or immunities of citizens of the United States; nor shall any State deprive any person of life, liberty, or property, without due process of law, nor deny to any person within its jurisdiction the equal protection of the laws;"

and that Congress shall have power to enforce by appropriate legislation the provisions of this article.

Now here is a clear prohibition on the States against making or enforcing any law which shall abridge the privileges or immunities of citizens of the United States.

If my views are correct with regard to what are the privileges and immunities of citizens, it follows conclusively that any law which establishes a sheer monopoly, depriving a large class of citizens of the privilege of pursuing a lawful employment, does abridge the privileges of those citizens.

The amendment also prohibits any State from depriving any person (citizen or otherwise) of life, liberty, or property, without due process of law.

In my view, a law which prohibits a large class of citizens from adopting a lawful employment, or from following a lawful employment previously adopted, does deprive them of liberty as well as property, without due process of law. Their right of choice is a portion of their liberty; their occupation is their property. Such a law also deprives those citizens of the equal protection of the laws, contrary to the last clause of the section.

The constitutional question is distinctly raised in these cases; the constitutional right is expressly claimed; it was violated by State law, which was sustained by the State court, and we are called upon in a legitimate and proper way to afford redress. Our jurisdiction and our duty are plain and imperative.

It is futile to argue that none but persons of the African race are intended to be benefited by this amendment. They may have been the primary cause of the amendment, but its language is general, embracing all citizens, and I think it was purposely so expressed.

The mischief to be remedied was not merely slavery and its incidents and consequences, but that spirit of insubordination and disloyalty to the National government which had troubled the country for so many years in some of the States, and that intolerance of free speech and free discussion which often rendered life and property insecure, and led to much unequal legislation. The amendment was an attempt to give voice to the strong National yearning for that time and that condition of things, in which American citizenship should be a sure guaranty of safety, and in which every citizen of the United States might stand erect on every portion of its soil, in the full enjoyment of every right and privilege belonging to a freeman, without fear of violence or molestation.

But great fears are expressed that this construction of the amendment will lead to enactments by Congress interfering with the internal affairs of the States, and establishing therein civil and criminal codes of law for the government of the citizens, and thus abolishing the State governments in everything but name; or else, that it will lead the Federal courts to draw to their cognizance the supervision of State tribunals on every subject of judicial inquiry, on the plea of ascertaining whether the privileges and immunities of citizens have not been abridged.

In my judgment, no such practical inconveniences would arise. Very little, if any, legislation on the part of Congress would be required to carry the amendment into effect. Like the prohibition against passing a law impairing the obligation of a contract, it would execute itself. The point would be regularly raised in a suit at law, and settled by final reference to the Federal court. As the privileges and immunities protected are only those fundamental ones which belong to every citizen, they would soon become so far defined as to cause but a slight accumulation of business in the Federal courts. Besides, the recognized existence of the law would prevent its frequent violation. But even if the business of the National courts should be increased, Congress could easily supply the remedy by increasing their number and efficiency. The great question is what is the true construction of the amendment? When once we find that, we shall find the means of giving it effect. The argument from inconvenience ought not to have a very controlling influence in questions of this sort. The National will and National interest are of far greater importance.

In my opinion the judgment of the Supreme Court of Louisiana ought to be reversed.

### Mr. Justice SWAYNE, dissenting

I concur in the dissent in these cases and in the views expressed by my brethren, Mr. Justice Field and Mr. Justice Bradley. I desire, however, to submit a few additional remarks.

The first eleven amendments to the Constitution were intended to be checks and limitations upon the government which that instrument called into existence.

They had their origin in a spirit of jealousy on the part of the States which existed when the Constitution was adopted. The first ten were proposed in 1789 by the first Congress at its first session after the organization of the government. The eleventh was proposed in 1794, and the twelfth in 1803. The one last mentioned regulates the mode of electing the President and Vice-President. It neither increased nor diminished the power of the General Government, and may be said in that respect to occupy neutral ground. No further amendments were made until 1865, a period of more than sixty years. The thirteenth amendment was proposed by Congress on the 1st of February, 1865, the fourteenth on the 16th of June, 1866, and the fifteenth on the 27th of February, 1869. These amendments are a new departure, and mark an important epoch in the constitutional history of the country. They trench directly upon the power of the States, and deeply affect those bodies. They are, in this respect, at the opposite pole from the first eleven.

Fairly construed, these amendments may be said to rise to the dignity of a new Magna Charta. The thirteenth blotted out slavery and forbade forever its restoration. It struck the fetters from four millions of human beings, and raised them at once to the sphere of freemen. This was an act of grace and justice performed by the Nation. Before the war, it could have been done only by the States where the institution existed, acting severally and separately from each other. The power then rested wholly with them. In that way, apparently, such a result could never have occurred. The power of Congress did not extend to the subject, except in the Territories.

The fourteenth amendment consists of five sections. The first is as follows:

> "All persons born or naturalized within the United States, and subject to the jurisdiction thereof, are citizens of the United States and of the State wherein they reside. No State shall make any law which shall abridge the privileges or immunities of citizens of the United States, nor shall any State deprive any person of life, liberty, or property, without due process of law, nor deny to any person within its jurisdiction the equal protection of the laws."

The fifth section declares that Congress shall have power to enforce the provisions of this amendment by appropriate legislation.

The fifteenth amendment declares that the right to vote shall not be denied or abridged by the United States, or by any State, on account of race, color, or previous condition of servitude. Until this amendment was adopted the subject to which it relates was wholly within the jurisdiction of the States. The General Government was excluded from participation.

The first section of the fourteenth amendment is alone involved in the consideration of these cases. No searching analysis is necessary to eliminate its meaning. Its language is intelligible and direct. Nothing can be more transparent. Every word employed has an established signification. There is no room for construction. There is nothing to construe. Elaboration may obscure, but cannot make clearer, the intent and purpose sought to be carried out.

(1) Citizens of the States and of the United States are defined.

(2) It is declared that no State shall, by law, abridge the privileges or immunities of citizens of the United States.

(3) That no State shall deprive any person, whether a citizen or not, of life, liberty, or property, without due process of law, nor deny to any person within its jurisdiction the equal protection of the laws.

A citizen of a State is *ipso facto* a citizen of the United States. No one can be the former without being also the latter; but the latter, by losing his residence in one State without acquiring it in another, although he continues to be the latter, ceases for the time to be the former. "The privileges and immunities" of a citizen of the United States include, among other things, the fundamental rights of life, liberty, and property, and also the rights which pertain to him by reason of his membership of the Nation. The citizen of a State has the same fundamental rights as a citizen of the United States, and also certain others, local in their character, arising from his relation to the State, and, in addition, those which belong to the citizen of the United States, he being in that relation also. There may thus be a double citizenship, each having some rights peculiar to itself. It is only over those which belong to the citizen of the United States that the category here in question throws the shield of its protection. All those which belong to the citizen of a State, except as a bills of attainder, *ex post facto* laws, and laws impairing the obligation of contracts, are left to the guardianship of the bills of rights, constitutions, and laws of the States respectively. Those rights may all be enjoyed in every State by the citizens of every other State by virtue of clause 2, section 4, article 1, of the Constitution of the United States as it was originally framed. This section does not in anywise affect them; such was not its purpose.

In the next category, obviously *ex industria,* to prevent, as far as may be, the possibility of misinterpretation, either as to persons or things, the phrases "citizens of the United States" and "privileges and immunities" are dropped, and more simple and comprehensive terms are substituted. The substitutes are "any person," and "life," "liberty," and "property," and "the equal protection of the laws." Life, liberty, and property are forbidden to be taken "without due process of law," and "equal protection of the laws" is guaranteed to all. Life is the gift of God, and the right to preserve it is the most sacred of the rights of man. Liberty is freedom from all restraints but such as are justly imposed by law. Beyond that line lies the domain of usurpation and tyranny. Property is everything which has an exchangeable value, and the right of property includes the power to dispose of it according to the will of the owner. Labor is property, and as such merits protection. The right to make it available is next in importance to the rights of life and liberty. It lies to a large extent at the foundation of most other forms of property, and of all solid individual and national prosperity. "Due process of law" is the application of the law as it exists in the fair and regular course of administrative procedure. "The equal protection of the laws" places all upon a footing of legal equality and gives the same protection to all for the preservation of life, liberty, and property, and the pursuit of happiness.

It is admitted that the plaintiffs in error are citizens of the United States, and persons within the jurisdiction of Louisiana. The cases before us, therefore, present but two questions.

(1) Does the act of the legislature creating the monopoly in question abridge the privileges and immunities of the plaintiffs in error as citizens of the United States?

(2) Does it deprive them of liberty or property without due process of law, or deny them the equal protection of the laws of the State, they being persons "within its jurisdiction?"

Both these inquiries I remit for their answer as to the facts to the opinions of my brethren, Mr. Justice Field and Mr. Justice Bradley. They are full and conclusive upon the subject. A more flagrant and indefensible invasion of the rights of many for the benefit of a few has not occurred in the legislative history of the country. The response to both inquiries should be in the affirmative. In my opinion, the cases, as presented in the record, are clearly within the letter and meaning of both the negative categories of the sixth section. The judgments before us should, therefore, be reversed.

These amendments are all consequences of the late civil war. The prejudices and apprehension as to the central government which prevailed when the Constitution was adopted were dispelled by the light of experience. The public mind became satisfied that there was less danger of tyranny in the head than of anarchy and tyranny in the members. The provisions of this section are all eminently conservative in their character. They are a bulwark of defence, and can never be made an engine of oppression. The language employed is unqualified in its scope. There is no exception in its terms, and there can be properly none in their application. By the language "citizens of the United States" was meant all such citizens; and by "any person" was meant all persons within the jurisdiction of the State. No distinction is intimated on account of race or color. This court has no authority to interpolate a limitation that is neither expressed nor implied. Our duty is to execute the law, not to make it. The protection provided was not intended to be confined to those of any particular race or class, but to embrace equally all races, classes, and conditions of men. It is objected that the power conferred is novel and large. The answer is that the novelty was known, and the measure deliberately adopted. The power is beneficent in its nature, and cannot be abused. It is such as should exist in every well-ordered system of polity. Where could it be more appropriately lodged than in the hands to which it is confided? It is necessary to enable the government of the nation to secure to everyone within its jurisdiction the rights and privileges enumerated, which, according to the plainest considerations of reason and justice and the fundamental principles of the social compact all are entitled to enjoy. Without such authority, any government claiming to be national is glaringly defective. The construction adopted by the majority of my brethren is, in my judgment, much too narrow. It defeats, by a limitation not anticipated, the intent of those by whom the instrument was framed and of those by whom it was adopted. To the extent of that limitation, it turns, as it were, what was meant for bread into a stone. By the Constitution as it stood before the war, ample protection was given against oppression by the Union, but little was given against wrong and oppression by the States. That want was intended to be supplied by this amendment. Against the former, this court has been called upon more than once to interpose. Authority of the same amplitude was intended to be conferred as to the latter. But this arm of our jurisdiction is, in these cases, stricken down by the judgment just given. Nowhere than in this court ought the will of the nation, as thus expressed, to be more liberally construed or more cordially executed. This determination of the majority seems to me to lie far in the other direction.

I earnestly hope that the consequences to follow may prove less serious and far-reaching than the minority fear they will be.

---

### Glossary

**abridge:** reduce

**police power:** the right and the duty of a government or legislative body to define proper areas to conduct lawful business

**privileges or immunities clause:** Section 1, sentence 2 of the Fourteenth Amendment, which states, in part: "No State shall make or enforce any law which shall abridge the privileges or immunities of citizens of the United States"

**writ:** a legal order

---

# UNITED STATES V. CRUIKSHANK

| DATE | CITATION |
|---|---|
| 1875 | 92 U.S. 542 |

| AUTHOR | SIGNIFICANCE |
|---|---|
| Morrison Waite | Held that, despite the Fourteenth Amendment's due process and equal protection clauses, the U.S. Bill of Rights did not limit the power of state governments or private individuals |

| VOTE | |
|---|---|
| 5-4 | |

## Overview

*United States v. Cruikshank et al.* involved an effort to bring to justice three men accused of participating in the slaughter of some one hundred Blacks in Colfax, Louisiana, on April 13, 1873, one of the most sensational incidents of Reconstruction political violence. During Reconstruction, the decade-long period after the Civil War, the federal government passed laws to protect Blacks from violence and intimidation as they sought to exercise the right to vote. Nonetheless, in *Cruikshank*, the Supreme Court affirmed a lower federal court's decision to invalidate the result of a previous verdict of guilty and ordered the release of the defendants.

While the Court's decision rested in large part upon its criticism of a poorly drafted indictment, the narrow grounds upon which it based its decision hampered federal efforts to protect Blacks from violence. Coupled with another Court decision, *United States v. Reese*, the *Cruikshank* decision marked a significant step in the federal government's retreat from Reconstruction. It would be nearly a century before new legislation reaffirmed the federal government's ability and will to protect African Americans in exercising their right

to vote. Nathan Clifford agreed with the majority on some measures but disagreed on others in his concurrence/dissent, and was joined by David Davis, Joseph P. Bradley, and Ward Hunt.

## Context

In the five years following the end of the Civil War, Congress adopted several measures that together removed race as a barrier to African Americans' right to vote. The change was piecemeal in approach but revolutionary in impact. In March and July 1867 and March 1868, the Reconstruction Acts provided for the enfranchisement of African Americans so as to allow them to participate in fresh elections to establish new state constitutions in ten former Confederate states. African Americans also won election as delegates to these conventions, and the ten state constitutions that eventually emerged from this process secured their right to vote. In July 1868 the Fourteenth Amendment guaranteed citizenship for former slaves and equal protection under the law for all, and, while recognizing that the right of suffrage remained one reserved to the states, it provided that a state's representation

***1876 photo of the Waite Court***
(Samuel Montague Fassett)

in the House of Representatives would be reduced in proportion to the state's restrictions upon suffrage. That year, over half a million African Americans voted in the presidential election, providing the Republican candidate Ulysses S. Grant with his popular majority—though he would have still claimed victory in the Electoral College had Blacks not voted in such numbers.

Although Republicans achieved much with the enfranchisement of most southern Blacks, Blacks still could not vote in many other states, including key northern states such as Ohio and Pennsylvania. Republican efforts to secure suffrage for Blacks in several northern states between 1865 and 1868 usually fell short of success. With Grant elected, Republicans turned to amending the Constitution once more, this time to remove barriers to voting for American citizens based on "race, color, or previous condition of servitude," as the Fifteenth Amendment would state. Such phrasing recognized that states remained the primary determiners of suffrage qualifications for their citizens but forbade those states from depriving Black citizens of

the right to vote based on their race. As constitutional amendments are ratified by state legislatures, not by popular vote, and the Republicans then controlled enough state legislatures for ratification, the Fifteenth Amendment became part of the Constitution in 1870.

Southern white supremacist terrorists first targeted Black voters during the 1868 presidential contest. By 1870 Congress decided to take action, and on May 31 it passed the Enforcement Act of 1870, designed to provide federal protection for Black voters and the means to prosecute white terrorists. In April 1871 another Enforcement Act, also known as the Ku Klux Klan Act, authorized President Grant to suspend the writ of habeas corpus in the effort to subdue such domestic terrorism: Grant used these powers to pursue the Klan in South Carolina in the fall of 1871. However, the Ku Klux Klan Act was of limited duration, and it expired in 1872. That year, a presidential election year, violence broke out in Louisiana during a closely contested local election whose results were disputed. Both Democrats and Republicans claimed victory; with Congress declining to count the state's electoral vote, it remained unclear for weeks which party would gain control of the state government, including the governorship. Eventually the Republicans prevailed—but not without outbreaks of violence, the most sensational of which happened in Colfax, in Grant Parish.

Established in 1869 and named after the nation's eighteenth president, Grant Parish is located along the Red River, north of New Orleans, in the heart of Louisiana; the county seat located at Colfax is named after Grant's first vice president, Schuyler Colfax. It soon witnessed its share of political friction and violence: Both parties claimed victory in the 1872 elections. Clashes between Blacks and whites subsequently increased, and in the early spring, Blacks seeking protection began flocking to the shelter of the Colfax courthouse. Efforts to prevent a confrontation proved futile, and some three hundred whites gathered outside the courthouse. On Easter Sunday, April 13, 1873, the whites first demanded that the Blacks surrender; when that proved unavailing, they allowed women and children to depart. Soon after, a firefight between the two sides commenced. Eventually the whites launched an assault on the courthouse, set it on fire, and tracked down those Blacks who had fled from the building, killing some and capturing others. That night, the whites slaughtered the remaining Black prisoners. Estimates of the dead for the entire day ranged from fifty to some four hundred Black men; a federal investigation settling upon 105 known dead Black men, with the fates of dozens more remaining unknown.

Federal officials indicted ninety-eight men under the terms of the Enforcement Act of 1870, among them, William J. Cruikshank, John P. Hadnot, and William D. Irwin, who, along with six other men, had been taken into custody by federal authorities. The nine men were tried in New Orleans before the U.S. circuit court judge William B. Woods. The prosecuting district attorney, James R. Beckwith, with a view to presenting a clean case, carefully narrowed the number of victims to two—Levi Nelson and Alexander Tillman, who had not been involved in resisting the whites by force. (Indeed, Nelson survived the massacre and testified for the government.) A first trial acquitted one defendant, while Woods declared a mistrial for the other eight defendants when the jury was unable to agree on a verdict. Those eight men underwent a second trial in May 1874, and on June 10 three men—Cruikshank, Hadnot,

and Irwin—were found guilty of violating section 6 of the Enforcement Act of 1870, which stipulated that if two or more people conspired to violate the provisions of the act or to "oppress" any citizen by trying to prevent him from exercising his rights under federal law or the Constitution, such an act would be punished as a felony, with possible fines and imprisonment.

During the second trial, Judge Woods was joined for short periods of time by the Supreme Court associate justice Joseph P. Bradley, who appeared in New Orleans as part of his duties as a federal circuit-court judge—an onerous additional duty performed by all justices of the Supreme Court at the time. Woods was inclined to uphold the convictions, but Bradley dissented and was determined to explain why. His detailed opinion carefully defined federal power to enforce the Thirteenth, Fourteenth, and Fifteenth Amendments. He argued that while violence inflicted for racial reasons was well within the jurisdiction of federal law, that motive had to be proved: It was insufficient to argue simply that conflict between people of different races must be due to the racial difference. Unless race as a motive could be established, cases of criminal violence should be handled in state court. Turning to the case at hand, Bradley argued that as the indictment did not expressly specify that Nelson and Tillman's rights as U.S. citizens had been violated owing to their race, there was no justification to treat them under federal law. It was an opinion narrow in its reasoning but broad in its implications. As the district attorney who prosecuted the case later complained, "If the demolished indictment is not good, I am incompetent to frame a good one"; Bradley had come close to implying just that. As Bradley and Woods divided on the propriety of the convictions, the punishment was placed in abeyance, or "arrested," while the Supreme Court heard the case.

Between the time of the massacre at Colfax in April 1873 and the Supreme Court's release of its decision nearly three years later, Republican Reconstruction policy suffered a series of serious setbacks that all but doomed the federal government's efforts to protect African Americans as free people, as citizens, and as voters and officeholders. In several southern states, including Alabama, Arkansas, Mississippi, and Texas, Republicans lost their hold on power as the result of political circumstances, terrorism, and internal friction. In Louisiana and Mississippi, violence played a key role in Democrats' resurgence; although Republicans barely held on to power in Louisiana, they lost it in Mississippi, where the Democrats embraced as a slogan a pledge that they would regain power peaceably if they could and forcibly if they must. An economic depression in 1873 had long-term effects and, combined with debates over monetary policy and tales of Republican corruption and malfeasance, resulted in the Democrats' reclaiming control of the House of Representatives in 1874, shutting down any further efforts to pass legislation to protect Black citizens from violence and intimidation.

Even President Grant, who had once expressed his willingness to protect Black rights, allowed frustration to get the better of him. In a special message to the Senate in January 1875, he made specific reference to the Colfax massacre, "a butchery of citizens . . . which in bloodthirstiness and barbarity is hardly surpassed by any acts of savage warfare." Nearly two years later, he declared that while critics of Reconstruction waxed eloquent about the missteps of southern Republican regimes, "every one of the Colfax miscreants goes unwhipped of justice, and no way can be found in this boasted land of civilization and Christianity to punish the perpetrators of this bloody and monstrous crime." Grant at length grew exasperated with the fractious behavior of southern Republicans and eroding support in the North for protecting the fruits of victory. When Mississippi's governor requested that federal troops be dispatched to his state in 1875, the president declined, explaining that "the whole public are tired out with these annual autumnal outbreaks in the South" and would no longer support such federal intervention policy. In fact, Grant himself had nominated Bradley to the Supreme Court in 1870, and it was his administration's Department of Justice, led by Attorney General George H. Williams, that did not seem equal to the task at hand, as much because of its lack of legal skill as a paucity of resources.

The chief justice when *Cruikshank* was argued from March 30 to April 1, 1875, was Morrison J. Waite, appointed by President Grant. Waite's eight associate justices, aside from Nathan Clifford, were all Republican appointees, though two, David Davis and Stephen J. Field (both Abraham Lincoln's nominees), could no longer be counted as Republicans themselves. Samuel F. Miller and Noah H. Swayne, both also Lincoln nominees, had each hoped to be tapped as the next chief justice; the remaining justices, Ward Hunt, Wil-

liam Strong, and Joseph P. Bradley, had been named by Grant. It was Bradley whose vote while on circuit-court duty in Louisiana brought *Cruikshank* to the Supreme Court, and he hoped his detailed 1874 opinion would guide the Court's decision and reasoning. Although ideally justices were to rise above their partisan roots, it was generally assumed that they would most often lean in the direction of their previous party affiliation and view cases in that light. When Congress passed legislation establishing an electoral commission to help resolve the disputed election of 1876, among the five commission members from the Court it was assumed that Clifford and Field would cast their votes for the Democratic case while Miller and Strong would side with the Republican claimant. When the supposedly independent Davis stepped aside to accept election as U.S. senator from Illinois, Democrats wondered whether his replacement, none other than Bradley, would also favor the Republicans. Some Democrats believed otherwise, in part because of Bradley's actions in the course of events that brought the *Cruikshank* case before the Court, for he had thereby defied Republican preferences.

In 1873 all of the associate justices who heard the arguments in the *Cruikshank* case had participated in deciding what became known as the Slaughter-House Cases, with Miller delivering the opinion for a slim five-to-four majority on April 14, 1873—the day after the massacre at Colfax. The cases involved a series of suits testing the constitutionality of a Louisiana law that attempted to regulate the state's slaughterhouse industry by establishing a private corporation that would exercise sole control over the industry by allocating space to area slaughterhouses. The suits cited the Fourteenth Amendment in support of their claim that the legislation was invalid. Miller's opinion, allowing the Louisiana law and the controlling corporation to stand, argued that the Fourteenth Amendment's privileges and immunities clause affects only those rights a person holds as part of U.S. citizenship, not as citizens of a state; furthermore, the primary objective of that clause was rather to protect the federal rights of former slaves. Thus, the Fourteenth Amendment did not protect the butchers' interests, namely, to freely pursue their chosen vocation, against the interests of the state. Miller's concept of dual citizenship would appear again in *Cruikshank*, this time as adverse to the former slaves. Clifford, Strong, Hunt, and Davis had agreed with Miller, while Field, Swayne, and Bradley dissented, along with Waite's predecessor, Salmon P. Chase.

While many members of the Court at first glance seemed sympathetic to the ends of Reconstruction policy, Bradley's circuit-court opinion on the Colfax massacre defendants, coming in the wake of Miller's reasoning in the Slaughter-House Cases, suggested that a majority of the justices were in favor of a strict and narrow explication of congressional legislation, which did not augur well for the prosecution. Moreover, the government's short brief for *Cruikshank* proved less than compelling in its argument, especially as it sidestepped Bradley's circuit-court opinion, failed to mention either African Americans or the Fifteenth Amendment, and mentioned the Enforcement Acts only in passing. It instead focused on just two counts of the indictment that concerned "conspiracy," arguing that an effort to conspire to deprive anyone of their constitutional rights was punishable under federal law. In contrast, the four briefs filed by the defense—including one by Justice Field's brother, David Dudley Field—argued at length that the pertinent sections of the Enforcement Act of 1870 were unconstitutional and that the Bill of Rights, far from conferring upon citizens specific rights, simply prohibited their infringement by the federal government and did not apply to state governments. The lawyer Field went so far as to attack the constitutionality of all postwar civil rights legislation, and he sought to bring his arguments before the public by publishing his brief.

All in all, by the time the Supreme Court heard the arguments in the *Cruikshank* case at the end of March 1875, the political foundations of Reconstruction, flawed as they were, were beginning to erode. By the time the Court released its opinion in March 1876, what had begun as a fighting withdrawal by Reconstruction's supporters was turning into a full-scale retreat to ensure the political survival of the Republican Party in the 1876 presidential contest.

## About the Author

Chief Justice Morrison R. Waite composed the Court's opinion in *United States v. Cruikshank*. At first he had hoped to entrust Associate Justice Nathan Clifford with drafting the Court's opinion, but Clifford's draft, presented to the justices in November 1875, fell short

of offering a comprehensive overview of the issues at stake and based the Court's ruling on narrow grounds.

The son of a judge, Waite, born on November 19, 1816, was a native of Connecticut and an 1837 graduate of Yale who moved to Ohio after graduation, eventually settling in Toledo. Originally a Whig in politics, he became a Republican, but his sole brush with political office came when he served a term in the Ohio Senate. In 1871 he served on the legal team that presented the United States' case at a Geneva tribunal convened to settle U.S. claims of damages caused by the CSS *Alabama*, built by Great Britain to serve the Confederacy. Three years later, in the wake of several frustrated attempts to nominate a new chief justice of the United States, President Grant settled upon Waite, who won confirmation despite critical commentary that he would not be up to the task. Along with *United States v. Reese*, *United States v. Cruikshank* provided Waite with his first substantial test as chief justice. After *Cruikshank*, Waite went on to serve twelve more years as chief justice. When he died on March 23, 1888, he left behind a solid but unspectacular record. If his performance surprised those critics who had criticized Grant for nominating a nonentity, it nevertheless fell short of the greatness achieved by other chief justices.

## Explanation and Analysis of the Document

Waite's opinion outlines a concept of dual citizenship first developed by the Supreme Court in 1873 in the Slaughter-House Cases. A citizen owed allegiance to both the federal and state governments and, in turn, could expect those governments to protect the specific rights attributable to each jurisdiction. Under this construction it was left to the states to prosecute cases of murder, manslaughter, and homicide as well as most infringements of civil rights.

Although Waite argues that the Fifteenth Amendment in itself does not guarantee the right to vote, he concedes that the amendment's second section constructed a new constitutional right that could be protected by the federal government, namely, that voters not suffer discrimination "on account of race, color, or previous condition of servitude." Yet such wording, he contends, means that the fact that Cruikshank and his collaborators were charged with murdering Black Republican voters was not sufficient to bring them under the scope of the Enforcement Act of 1870: Prosecutors had to charge—and prove—that the victims were murdered because of their race. The right not to be discriminated against as such was the only relevant right protected under federal law. But the prosecutors did not demonstrate violation of this right in this instance. The chief justice asserts that the indictments were so vague that they did not sufficiently meet the Fourth Amendment standard of informing the accused of the offense for which they were being tried. Had the indictment specified that race was the basis upon which the accused murdered the victims, then and only then would the actions of the accused have come under the Enforcement Acts.

Waite's opinion mentions the sixteen counts on which Cruikshank, Hadnot, and Irwin were convicted. The first eight counts charged that the defendants "banded together" to deprive Levi Nelson and Alexander Tillman of their rights, while the ninth through sixteenth counts charged, equivalently, that the defendants "conspired" to deprive Nelson and Tillman of their rights. The defendants were charged with seeking to deprive Nelson and Tillman of, in the first and ninth counts, the right to assemble peacefully; in the second and tenth counts, of the right to keep and bear arms; in the third and tenth counts, of the right to not be deprived of life and liberty without due process of law; in the fourth and twelfth counts, of equal rights and equal treatment under law; in the fifth and thirteenth counts, of their rights as citizens by reason of their race; in the sixth and fourteenth counts, of their right to vote; in the seventh and fifteenth counts, of the right to vote without suffering harm; and in the eighth and sixteenth counts, of the free exercise of their rights secured by federal law and the Constitution.

In his opinion, Waite carefully goes through the sixteen counts, which were framed with section 6 of the Enforcement Act of 1870 in mind. That section states that if two or more people "shall band or conspire together" to intimidate or harm "any citizen" to prevent that citizen from exercising his rights secured by the Constitution and federal law, those people could be found guilty of a felony and could be fined, imprisoned, or both. Citing the Slaughter-House Cases, Waite distinguishes between the rights of citizens protected by the federal government and those protected by state government. He reads the Bill of Rights as operating to restrain the federal government, not state governments, and thus quickly sets aside those charges dealing with the right to assemble peacefully and to bear arms. He rather summarily dismisses those counts that addressed the victims' right not to be deprived of life or liberty without due process, arguing that state governments were to protect those rights. Repeatedly he offers a narrow view of federal power based upon his interpretation of the Fourteenth Amendment; time and again, he argues that the victims needed to seek recourse at the state level.

Waite also criticizes the indictment as too vague in what it alleged. He rejects the fourth and twelfth counts, charging that they failed to claim race as the reason the defendants attempted to deprive Nelson and Tillman of their civil rights, even as he admits that the Fifteenth Amendment did establish a new right, that of exempting citizens from racial discrimination in their effort to exercise the right to vote. He employs the same justification as the reason the defendants attempted to deprive Nelson and Tillman of the right to vote, thus setting aside the sixth and fourteenth counts; He repeats that reasoning in dismissing the seventh and fifteenth counts, which charged the defendants with endangering Nelson and Tillman because they had voted.

This left two pairs of counts: the fifth and thirteenth, which concerned whether Tillman and Nelson had been deprived of their rights as citizens because of their race, and the eighth and sixteenth, which simply said that they had been deprived of their rights as U.S. citizens. Here Waite finds that section 6 of the Enforcement Act of 1870 went beyond the grant of authority extended to Congress in the Fifteenth Amendment by failing to specify race, rendering the section inappropriate; in turn, he finds the counts "too vague and general" and "so defective that no judgment of conviction should be pronounced upon them."

Waite's opinion develops the notion of federalism and dual sovereignty, reminding Americans that the Court would not nationalize all rights and grant them federal protection. Having failed to specify the federal right being violated as specified in the Enforcement Act of 1870, the indictment, in Waite's opinion, was insufficient and could not sustain a conviction. The Fourteenth Amendment offered minimal protection, as it called for federal intervention to remedy state inaction or violation of the Bill of Rights, but, again, the prosecution did not demonstrate the relevant unlawful activity, namely, any such inaction or violation on the part of the state. In sum, although Waite was willing to accept the responsibility of the federal government to protect a voter from finding his right to vote challenged or blocked owing to his race, the chief justice's decision placed a heavy burden of proof on prosecutors by requiring that they specify that motive and demonstrate it.

## Impact

The *Cruikshank* decision marked yet another milepost on the Republican retreat from Reconstruction. With the Democrats in control of the House of Representatives, there would be no chance for Republicans to pass new enforcement legislation. Meanwhile, by the time the decision appeared, the Grant administration was engulfed by charges of corruption involving cabinet members and the White House staff. Although the decision itself did not rule on the constitutionality of the Enforcement Act of 1870, the opinion ensured that its clauses would be construed strictly and narrowly. A second opinion released by the Court on the same day the *Cruikshank* decision was issued, *United States v. Reese*, bore more directly upon the Enforcement Act of 1870. In *Reese*, strictly interpreting the scope and meaning of that legislation, Waite found it insufficient to protect the right outlined in the Fifteenth Amendment, that is, the right to vote as not abridged due to race, color, or previous condition of servitude. The prosecution had charged that Kentucky election officials had violated the law in refusing to allow William Garner, an African American, to vote, but it could not be demonstrated that they did so because of Garner's race.

By March 1876, only three southern states remained under Republican rule: South Carolina, Louisiana, and Florida. Without the threat of federal prosecution, terrorist forces continued to target Black voters, tipping the scale toward Democratic candidates. Had southern Blacks been allowed to vote freely in the election of 1876, the Republican candidate Rutherford B. Hayes would have then secured the presidency. Instead, the Democratic candidate Samuel J. Tilden claimed a majority of the popular vote, falling just one electoral vote short of the presidency owing to disputed voting returns in the three Republican states still remaining in the South. Through the resulting Compromise of 1877, Hayes was awarded the disputed votes and the presidency in exchange for the promise that federal troops would be removed from the three southern Republican-led states. Grant and then Hayes duly removed the troops from Florida, South Carolina, and Louisiana, and by the summer of 1877 the southern states were all under Democratic rule. Not until the twentieth century would the federal government once more use force and the law to assure Blacks their right to vote.

## Questions for Further Study

1. In what way did the Court's decision in this case represent a retreat from Reconstruction and the protection of African Americans afforded by the Fourteenth and Fifteenth Amendments to the Constitution?

2. An ongoing source of dispute in the United States concerns the respective powers of the federal government and those of the states. How did *United States v. Cruikshank* reflect this struggle?

3. What events led to the Colfax massacre of 1873? Why did the Supreme Court become involved in what could have been regarded as a Louisiana matter?

4. What political consequences did the Court's decision in this case have? How might the history of Reconstruction and the post–Civil War South have been different if the Court had reached a different decision?

5. What could the U.S. government have done differently in enforcing the civil rights of African Americans in the post–Civil War South? If you had been president during the 1870s, what would you have done?

## Further Reading

### Books

Escott, Paul D. *Black Suffrage: Lincoln's Last Goal.* Charlottesville: University of Virginia Press, 2022.

Fairman, Charles. *Reconstruction and Reunion, 1864–88.* Cambridge, U.K.: Cambridge University Press, 2010.

Goldman, Robert M. *Reconstruction and Black Suffrage: Losing the Vote in Reese and Cruikshank.* Lawrence: University Press of Kansas, 2001.

Kaczorowski, Robert J. *The Politics of Judicial Interpretation: The Federal Courts, Department of Justice and Civil Rights, 1866–1876.* Dobbs Ferry, N.Y.: Oceana Publications, 1985.

Keith, LeeAnna. *The Colfax Massacre: The Untold Story of Black Power, White Terror, and the Death of Reconstruction.* New York: Oxford University Press, 2008.

Lane, Charles. *The Day Freedom Died: The Colfax Massacre, the Supreme Court, and the Betrayal of Reconstruction.* New York: Henry Holt, 2008.

Simpson, Brooks D. *The Reconstruction Presidents.* Lawrence: University Press of Kansas, 1998.

### Websites

"The Colfax Massacre." Black Past. Accessed March 2, 2023, https://www.blackpast.org/african-american-history/colfax-massacre-1873/.

"The 1873 Colfax Massacre Crippled the Reconstruction Era." Smithsonian Magazine. Accessed March 2, 2023, https://www.smithsonianmag.com/smart-news/1873-colfax-massacre-crippled-reconstruction-180958746/.

—Commentary by Brooks D. Simpson

# UNITED STATES V. CRUIKSHANK

## Document Text

### *Mr. Chief Justice Waite delivered the opinion of the Court*

This case comes here with a certificate by the judges of the Circuit Court for the District of Louisiana that they were divided in opinion upon a question which occurred at the hearing. It presents for our consideration an indictment containing sixteen counts, divided into two series of eight counts each, based upon sect. 6 of the Enforcement Act of May 31, 1870. That section is as follows:—

"That if two or more persons shall band or conspire together, or go in disguise upon the public highway, or upon the premises of another, with intent to violate any provision of this act, or to injure, oppress, threaten, or intimidate any citizen, with intent to prevent or hinder his free exercise and enjoyment of any right or privilege granted or secured to him by the Constitution or laws of the United States, or because of his having exercised the same, such persons shall be held guilty of felony, and, on conviction thereof, shall be fined or imprisoned, or both, at the discretion of the court—the fine not to exceed $5,000, and the imprisonment not to exceed ten years—and shall, moreover, be thereafter ineligible to, and disabled from holding, any office or place of honor, profit, or trust created by the Constitution or laws of the United States."

The question certified arose upon a motion in arrest of judgment after a verdict of guilty generally upon the whole sixteen counts, and is stated to be whether "the said sixteen counts of said indictment are severally good and sufficient in law, and contain charges of criminal matter indictable under the laws of the United States."

The general charge in the first eight counts is that of "banding," and in the second eight that of "conspiring" together to injure, oppress, threaten, and intimidate Levi Nelson and Alexander Tillman, citizens of the United States, of African descent and persons of color, with the intent thereby to hinder and prevent them in their free exercise and enjoyment of rights and privileges "granted and secured" to them "in common with all other good citizens of the United States by the Constitution and laws of the United States."

The offences provided for by the statute in question do not consist in the mere "banding" or "conspiring" of two or more persons together, but in their banding or conspiring with the intent, or for any of the purposes, specified. To bring this case under the operation of the statute, therefore, it must appear that the right, the enjoyment of which the conspirators intended to hinder or prevent, was one granted or secured by the Constitution or laws of the United States. If it does not so appear, the criminal matter charged has not been made indictable by any act of Congress.

We have in our political system a government of the United States and a government of each of the several States. Each one of these governments is distinct from the others, and each has citizens of its own who owe it allegiance and whose rights, within its jurisdiction, it must protect. The same person may be at the same time a citizen of the United States and a citizen of a State, but his rights of citizenship under one of these governments will be different from those he has under the other. *Slaughter-House Cases*, 16 Wall. 74.

Citizens are the members of the political community to which they belong. They are the people who compose the community, and who, in their associated capacity, have established or submitted themselves to the dominion of a government for the promotion of their general welfare and the protection of their individual as well as their collective rights. In the formation of a government, the people may confer upon it such powers as they choose. The government, when so formed, may, and when called upon should, exercise all the powers it has for the protection of the rights of its citizens and the people within its jurisdiction, but it can exercise no other. The duty of a government to afford protection is limited always by the power it possesses for that purpose.

Experience made the fact known to the people of the United States that they required a national government for national purposes. The separate governments of the separate States, bound together by the articles of confederation alone, were not sufficient for the promotion of the general welfare of the people in respect to foreign nations, or for their complete protection as citizens of the confederated States. For this reason, the people of the United States, "in order to form a more perfect union, establish justice, insure domestic tranquillity, provide for the common defence, promote the general welfare, and secure the blessings of liberty" to themselves and their posterity (Const. Preamble), ordained and established the government of the United States, and defined its powers by a Constitution, which they adopted as its fundamental law, and made its rule of action.

The government thus established and defined is to some extent a government of the States in their political capacity. It is also, for certain purposes, a government of the people. Its powers are limited in number, but not in degree. Within the scope of its powers, as enumerated and defined, it is supreme, and above the States; but beyond, it has no existence. It was erected for special purposes, and endowed with all the powers necessary for its own preservation and the accomplishment of the ends its people had in view. It can neither grant nor secure to its citizens any right or privilege not expressly or by implication placed under its jurisdiction.

The people of the United States resident within any State are subject to two governments—one State and the other National—but there need be no conflict between the two. The powers which one possesses the other does not. They are established for different purposes, and have separate jurisdictions. Together, they make one whole, and furnish the people of the United States with a complete government, ample for the protection of all their rights at home and abroad. True, it may sometimes happen that a person is amenable to both jurisdictions for one and the same act. Thus, if a marshal of the United States is unlawfully resisted while executing the process of the courts within a State, and the resistance is accompanied by an assault on the officer, the sovereignty of the United States is violated by the resistance, and that of the State by the breach of peace in the assault. So, too, if one passes counterfeited coin of the United States within a State, it may be an offence against the United States and the State: the United States because it discredits the coin, and the State because of the fraud upon him to whom it is passed. This does not, however, necessarily imply that the two governments possess powers in common, or bring them into conflict with each other. It is the natural consequence of a citizenship which owes allegiance to two sovereignties and claims protection from both. The citizen cannot complain, because he has voluntarily submitted himself to such a form of government. He owes allegiance to the two departments, so to speak, and, within their respective spheres, must pay the penalties which each exacts for disobedience to its laws. In return, he can demand protection from each within its own jurisdiction.

The Government of the United States is one of delegated powers alone. Its authority is defined and limited by the Constitution. All powers not granted to it by that instrument are reserved to the States or the people. No rights can be acquired under the Constitution or laws of the United States, except such as the Government of the United States has the authority to grant or secure. All that cannot be so granted or secured are left under the protection of the States. We now proceed to an examination of the indictment, to ascertain whether the several rights, which it is alleged the defendants intended to interfere with, are such as had been in law and in fact granted or secured by the Constitution or laws of the United States.

The first and ninth counts state the intent of the defendants to have been to hinder and prevent the citizens named in the free exercise and enjoyment of their "lawful right and privilege to peaceably assemble together with each other and with other citizens of the United States for a peaceful and lawful purpose."

The right of the people peaceably to assemble for lawful purposes existed long before the adoption of the Constitution of the United States. In fact, it is, and always has been, one of the attributes of citizenship under a free government. It "derives its source," to use the language of Chief Justice Marshall in 22 U. S. 211, "from those laws whose authority is acknowledged by civilized man throughout the world." It is found wherever civilization exists. It was not, therefore, a right granted to the people by the Constitution. The Government of the United States, when established, found it in existence, with the obligation on the part of the States to afford it protection. As no direct power over it was granted to Congress, it remains, according to the ruling in *Gibbons v. Ogden*, id., 22 U. S. 203, subject to State jurisdiction.

Only such existing rights were committed by the people to the protection of Congress as came within the general scope of the authority granted to the national government.

The first amendment to the Constitution prohibits Congress from abridging "the right of the people to assemble and to petition the government for a redress of grievances." This, like the other amendments proposed and adopted at the same time, was not intended to limit the powers of the State governments in respect to their own citizens, but to operate upon the National Government alone. *Barron v. The City of Baltimore*, 7 Pet. 250; *Lessee of Livingston v. Moore*, id., 551; *Fox v. Ohio*, 5 How. 434; *Smith v. Maryland*, 18 id. 76; *Withers v. Buckley*, 20 id. 90; *Pervear v. The Commonwealth*, 5 Wall. 479; *Twitchell v. The Commonwealth*, 7 id. 321; *Edwards v. Elliott*, 21 id. 557. It is now too late to question the correctness of this construction. As was said by the late Chief Justice, in *Twitchell v. The Commonwealth*, 7 Wall. 325, "the scope and application of these amendments are no longer subjects of discussion here." They left the authority of the States just where they found it, and added nothing to the already existing powers of the United States.

The particular amendment now under consideration assumes the existence of the right of the people to assemble for lawful purposes, and protects it against encroachment by Congress. The right was not created by the amendment; neither was its continuance guaranteed, except as against congressional interference. For their protection in its enjoyment, therefore, the people must look to the States. The power for that purpose was originally placed there, and it has never been surrendered to the United States.

The right of the people peaceably to assemble for the purpose of petitioning Congress for a redress of grievances, or for any thing else connected with the powers or the duties of the national government, is an attribute of national citizenship, and, as such, under the protection of, and guaranteed by, the United States. The very idea of a government republican in form implies a right on the part of its citizens to meet peaceably for consultation in respect to public affairs and to petition for a redress of grievances. If it had been alleged in these counts that the object of the defendants was to prevent a meeting for such a purpose, the case would have been within the statute, and within the scope of the sovereignty of the United States. Such, however, is not the case. The offence, as stated in the indictment, will be made out, if it be shown that the object of the conspiracy was to prevent a meeting for any lawful purpose whatever.

The second and tenth counts are equally defective. The right there specified is that of "bearing arms for a lawful purpose." This is not a right granted by the Constitution. Neither is it in any manner dependent upon that instrument for its existence. The second amendment declares that it shall not be infringed, but this, as has been seen, means no more than that it shall not be infringed by Congress. This is one of the amendments that has no other effect than to restrict the powers of the national government, leaving the people to look for their protection against any violation by their fellow citizens of the rights it recognizes, to what is called, in *The City of New York v. Miln*, 11 Pet. 139, the "powers which relate to merely municipal legislation, or what was, perhaps, more properly called internal police," "not surrendered or restrained" by the Constitution of the United States.

The third and eleventh counts are even more objectionable. They charge the intent to have been to deprive the citizens named, they being in Louisiana, "of their respective several lives and liberty of person without due process of law." This is nothing else than alleging a conspiracy to falsely imprison or murder citizens of the United States, being within the territorial jurisdiction of the State of Louisiana. The rights of life and personal liberty are natural rights of man. "To secure these rights," says the Declaration of Independence, "governments are instituted among men, deriving their just powers from the consent of the governed." The very highest duty of the States, when they entered into the Union under the Constitution, was to protect all persons within their boundaries in the enjoyment of these "unalienable rights with which they were endowed by their Creator." Sovereignty, for this purpose, rests alone with the States. It is no more the duty or within the power of the United States to punish for a conspiracy to falsely imprison or murder within a State, than it would be to punish for false imprisonment or murder itself.

The Fourteenth Amendment prohibits a State from depriving any person of life, liberty, or property without due process of law, but this adds nothing to the rights of one citizen as against another. It simply furnishes an additional guaranty against any encroachment by the States upon the fundamental rights which belong to every citizen as a member of society. As was said by Mr. Justice Johnson, in *Bank of Columbia v. Okely*, 4 Wheat. 244, it secures "the individual from the arbitrary exercise of the powers of government, unrestrained by the established principles of private rights and distributive justice."

These counts in the indictment do not call for the exercise of any of the powers conferred by this provision in the amendment.

The fourth and twelfth counts charge the intent to have been to prevent and hinder the citizens named, who were of African descent and persons of color, in "the free exercise and enjoyment of their several right and privilege to the full and equal benefit of all laws and proceedings, then and there, before that time, enacted or ordained by the said State of Louisiana and by the United States, and then and there, at that time, being in force in the said State and District of Louisiana aforesaid, for the security of their respective persons and property, then and there, at that time enjoyed at and within said State and District of Louisiana by white persons, being citizens of said State of Louisiana and the United States, for the protection of the persons and property of said white citizens."

There is no allegation that this was done because of the race or color of the persons conspired against. When stripped of its verbiage, the case as presented amounts to nothing more than that the defendants conspired to prevent certain citizens of the United States, being within the State of Louisiana, from enjoying the equal protection of the laws of the State and of the United States.

The Fourteenth Amendment prohibits a State from denying to any person within its jurisdiction the equal protection of the laws; but this provision does not, any more than the one which precedes it, and which we have just considered, add anything to the rights which one citizen has under the Constitution against another. The equality of the rights of citizens is a principle of republicanism. Every republican government is in duty bound to protect all its citizens in the enjoyment of this principle, if within its power. That duty was originally assumed by the States, and it still remains there. The only obligation resting upon the United States is to see that the States do not deny the right. This the amendment guarantees, but no more. The power of the national government is limited to the enforcement of this guaranty.

No question arises under the Civil Rights Act of April 9, 1866 (14 Stat. 27), which is intended for the protection of citizens of the United States in the enjoyment of certain rights, without discrimination on account of race, color, or previous condition of servitude, because, as has already been stated, it is nowhere alleged in these counts that the wrong contemplated against the rights of these citizens was on account of their race or color.

Another objection is made to these counts that they are too vague and uncertain. This will be considered hereafter, in connection with the same objection to other counts.

The sixth and fourteenth counts state the intent of the defendants to have been to hinder and prevent the citizens named, being of African descent, and colored, "in the free exercise and enjoyment of their several and respective right and privilege to vote at any election to be thereafter by law had and held by the people in and of the said State of Louisiana, or by the people of and in the parish of Grant aforesaid."

In 88 U. S. 214, we hold that the Fifteenth Amendment has invested the citizens of the United States with a new constitutional right, which is, exemption from discrimination in the exercise of the elective franchise on account of race, color, or previous condition of servitude. From this, it appears that the right of suffrage is not a necessary attribute of national citizenship, but that exemption from discrimination in the exercise of that right on account of race, &c., is. The right to vote in the States comes from the States, but the right of exemption from the prohibited discrimination comes from the United States. The first has not been granted or secured by the Constitution of the United States, but the last has been.

Inasmuch, therefore, as it does not appear in these counts that the intent of the defendants was to prevent these parties from exercising their right to vote on account of their race, &c., it does not appear that it was their intent to interfere with any right granted or secured by the Constitution or laws of the United States. We may suspect that race was the cause of the hostility, but it is not so averred. This is material to a description of the substance of the offence, and cannot be supplied by implication. Everything essential must be charged positively, and not inferentially. The defect here is not in form, but in substance.

The seventh and fifteenth counts are no better than the sixth and fourteenth. The intent here charged is to put the parties named in great fear of bodily harm, and to injure and oppress them, because, being and having been in all things qualified, they had voted "at an election before that time had and held according to law by the people of the said State of Louisiana, in said State, to-wit, on the fourth day of November, A.D. 1872, and at divers other elections by the people of the State, also before that time had and held according to law."

There is nothing to show that the elections voted at were any other than State elections, or that the conspiracy was formed on account of the race of the parties against whom the conspirators were to act. The charge as made is really of nothing more than a conspiracy to commit a breach of the peace within a State. Certainly it will not be claimed that the United States have the power or are required to do mere police duty in the States. If a State cannot protect itself against domestic violence, the United States may, upon the call of the executive, when the legislature cannot be convened, lend their assistance for that purpose. This is a guaranty of the Constitution (art. 4, sect. 4), but it applies to no case like this.

We are therefore of the opinion that the first, second, third, fourth, sixth, seventh, ninth, tenth, eleventh, twelfth, fourteenth, and fifteenth counts do not contain charges of a criminal nature made indictable under the laws of the United States, and that consequently they are not good and sufficient in law. They do not show that it was the intent of the defendants, by their conspiracy, to hinder or prevent the enjoyment of any right granted or secured by the Constitution.

We come now to consider the fifth and thirteenth and the eighth and sixteenth counts, which may be brought together for that purpose. The intent charged in the fifth and thirteenth is "to hinder and prevent the parties in their respective free exercise and enjoyment of the rights, privileges, immunities, and protection granted and secured to them respectively as citizens of the United States, and as citizens of said State of Louisiana . . . for the reason that they, . . . being then and there citizens of said State and of the United States, were persons of African descent and race, and persons of color, and not white citizens thereof;" and in the eighth and sixteenth, to hinder and prevent them "in their several and respective free exercise and enjoyment of every, each, all, and singular the several rights and privileges granted and secured to them by the Constitution and laws of the United States."

The same general statement of the rights to be interfered with is found in the fifth and thirteenth counts.

According to the view we take of these counts, the question is not whether it is enough, in general, to describe a statutory offence in the language of the statute, but whether the offence has here been described at all. The statute provides for the punishment of those who conspire "to injure, oppress, threaten, or intimidate any citizen, with intent to prevent or hinder his free exercise and enjoyment of any right or privilege granted or secured to him by the Constitution or laws of the United States."

These counts in the indictment charge, in substance that the intent in this case was to hinder and prevent these citizens in the free exercise and enjoyment of "every, each, all, and singular" the rights granted them by the Constitution, &c. There is no specification of any particular right. The language is broad enough to cover all.

---

In criminal cases, prosecuted under the laws of the United States, the accused has the constitutional right "to be informed of the nature and cause of the accusation." Amend. VI. In *United States v. Mills*, 7 Pet. 142, this was construed to mean that the indictment must set forth the offence "with clearness and all necessary certainty, to apprise the accused of the crime with which he stands charged;" and in *United States v. Cook*, 17 Wall. 174 that "every ingredient of which the offence is composed must be accurately and clearly alleged." It is an elementary principle of criminal pleading that, where the definition of an offence, whether it be at common law or by statute, "includes generic terms, it is not sufficient that the indictment shall charge the offence in the same generic terms as in the definition, but it must state the species—it must descend to particulars."

The object of the indictment is, first, to furnish the accused with such a description of the charge against him as will enable him to make his defence, and avail himself of his conviction or acquittal for protection against a further prosecution for the same cause; and, second, to inform the court of the facts alleged, so that it may decide whether they are sufficient in law to support a conviction, if one should be had. For this, facts are to be stated, not conclusions of law alone. A crime is made up of acts and intent; and these must be set forth in the indictment, with reasonable particularity of time, place, and circumstances.

It is a crime to steal goods and chattels, but an indictment would be bad that did not specify with some degree of certainty the articles stolen. This because the accused must be advised of the essential particulars of the charge against him, and the court must be able to decide whether the property taken was such as was the subject of larceny. So, too, it is in some States a crime for two or more persons to conspire to cheat and defraud another out of his property, but it has been held that an indictment for such an offence must contain allegations setting forth the means proposed to be used to accomplish the purpose. This because, to make such a purpose criminal, the conspiracy must be to cheat and defraud in a mode made criminal by statute; and, as all cheating and defrauding has not been made criminal, it is necessary for the indictment to state the means proposed, in order that the court may see that they are in fact illegal. *State v. Parker*, 43 N. H. 83; *State v. Keach*, 40 Vt. 118; *Alderman v. The People*, 4 Mich. 414; *State v. Roberts*, 34 Me. 32. In Maine, it is an offence for two or more to conspire with the intent unlawfully and wickedly to commit any crime punishable by imprisonment in the State prison (*State v. Roberts*), but we think it will hardly be claimed that an indictment would be good under this statute which charges the object of the conspiracy to have been "unlawfully and wickedly to commit each, every, all, and singular the crimes punishable by imprisonment in the State prison." All crimes are not so punishable. Whether a particular crime be such a one or not is a question of law. The accused has, therefore, the right to have a specification of the charge against him in this respect in order that he may decide whether he should present his defence by motion to quash, demurrer, or plea, and the court that it may determine whether the facts will sustain the indictment. So here, the crime is made to consist in the unlawful combination with an intent to prevent the enjoyment of any right granted or secured by the Constitution, &c. All rights are not so granted or secured. Whether one is so or not is a question of law, to be decided by the court, not the prosecutor. Therefore, the indictment should state the particulars, to inform the court as well as the accused. It must be made to appear—that is to say, appears from the indictment, without going further—that the acts charged will, if proved, support a conviction for the offence alleged.

But it is needless to pursue the argument further. The conclusion is irresistible that these counts are too vague and general. They lack the certainty and precision required by the established rules of criminal pleading. It follows that they are not good and sufficient in law. They are so defective that no judgment of conviction should be pronounced upon them.

*The order of the Circuit Court arresting the judgment upon the verdict is, therefore, affirmed; and the cause remanded, with instructions to discharge the defendants.*

## Glossary

**articles of confederation:** the initial constitution of the United States, replaced by the present Constitution because they gave too much power to the states and not enough to the federal government

**Chief Justice Marshall:** John Marshall, the early-nineteenth-century chief justice whose decisions defined many of the powers of the federal government

**demurrer:** a court pleading filed by a defendant stating that the facts of the case do not support the plaintiff's accusations

**Enforcement Act of May 31, 1870:** one of three federal laws passed to protect the civil rights of African Americans, especially the right to vote

**Justice Johnson:** Associate Justice William Johnson

**quash:** the action of voiding a legal proceeding or court decision

# REYNOLDS V. UNITED STATES

| DATE | CITATION |
|------|----------|
| 1879 | 98 U.S. 145 |

| AUTHOR | SIGNIFICANCE |
|--------|--------------|
| Morrison R. Waite | Held that a religious belief or religiously imposed duty is not a valid defense to a crime, in this case, polygamy |

| VOTE | |
|------|--|
| 9-0 | |

## Overview

Argued on November 14–15, 1878, *Reynolds v. United States* was a key case in the history of litigation bearing on the First Amendment, specifically the free exercise of religious beliefs. The case involved polygamy as practiced by the Church of Jesus Christ of Latter-day Saints (LDS), commonly referred to as the Mormon Church. In 1862, the federal Morrill Anti-Bigamy Act was passed, outlawing the practice of polygamy in the United States, including U.S. territories. One George Reynolds was charged in Utah Territory with violating the act by taking a wife while still married to another woman. He argued in court that his religious duty as a Mormon required him to marry multiple women and that therefore the law was a violation of his civil rights under the First Amendment to the Constitution. The case presented the question of whether a religious duty was a defense against a criminal charge.

## Context

In 1852, the Mormon Church, relying on passages from the Old Testament and from Mormon scripture, officially endorsed plural marriage. The Republican

Party, however, announced in its platform in 1856 that it was opposed to what it called the "twin relics of barbarism," slavery and polygamy. As opposition to plural marriage grew, Congress passed the Morrill Anti-Bigamy Act in 1862. The act criminalized polygamy in the United States and in U.S. territories, including Utah Territory, where polygamy was a common practice. Mormons, however, saw the law as unconstitutional, specifically as an infringement on their right to the "free exercise" of religion guaranteed by the First Amendment to the Constitution. Federal officials in Utah Territory believed that it would be difficult to get convictions under the law because of the influence of Mormons in the territory's judicial system.

Prosecutors and church officials in Utah joined forces to create a case that would test the constitutionality of the law. The case began when Utah resident George Reynolds, a member of the Mormon Church, was charged with violating the anti-bigamy law. A federal court found him guilty, fined him $500, and sentenced him to two years of hard labor. In court, Reynolds argued that he was simply following one of the central tenets of his religion and that he had in effect been instructed by the church's leadership to

**Photograph of a Mormon man and his three wives**
Wikimedia Commons)

take multiple wives. He appealed his conviction to the U.S. Supreme Court.

Interestingly, the Court until this time had never interpreted the meaning of the free-exercise clause in the First Amendment. The Court, in affirming Reynolds's conviction in *Reynolds v. United States* (1879), concluded that the Constitution protected beliefs but not actions that were prohibited by law. What followed was a decade of case law on polygamy that became known as "the Raid." In *Miles v. United States* (1880), the Court suggested that anti-bigamy laws should be amended to make prosecutions easier. Congress followed this recommendation by passing the Edmunds Act, also called the Edmunds Anti-Polygamy Act of 1882, named after Vermont senator George F. Edmunds. The new law forbade "bigamous" or "unlawful cohabitation," in this way removing the need to prove that an actual unlawful second marriage had taken place. The act reinforced the 1862 Morrill Act by making the offence of unlawful cohabitation easier to prove. It also made it illegal for polygamists or those who cohabited to vote, hold public office, or serve on juries in federal territories.

In his annual message to Congress in 1885, President Grover Cleveland chimed in by commenting on the is-sue of polygamy in Utah. He stated that "the strength, the perpetuity, and the destiny of the nation rest upon our homes, established by the law of God, guarded by parental care, regulated by parental authority, and sanctified by parental love." He added: "These are not the homes of polygamy. . . . There is no feature of this practice or the system which sanctions it which is not opposed to all that is of value in our institutions."

The 1882 law led to three cases that reached the Court in 1885. *Murphy v. Ramsey* upheld the disenfranchisement of polygamists (that is, denying them the right to vote). In *Clawson v. United States*, the Court affirmed the exclusion of Mormons from juries. *Cannon v. United States* sharpened the definition of "unlawful cohabitation." With regard to *Cannon*, the problem the Court faced was that a charge of bigamy required proof of separate marriages, but many polygamous Mormon marriages took place in secret, making it nearly impossible to gather evidence. This problem was circumvented by criminalizing "cohabitation with more than one woman." While Mormons argued that prosecution for cohabitation required proof of sexual relations, the Court rejected this view, stating that cohabitation involved "holding out to the world two women as . . . wives."

Matters did not end there. New legislation was passed in 1887 when Congress passed the Edmunds-Tucker Act, sponsored by Senator Edmunds and Congressman John Randolph Tucker of Virginia. The act had a number of provisions. It disincorporated the LDS and confiscated its funds; it required prospective voters, jurors, and public officials to take an anti-polygamy oath; it vacated territorial laws that allowed illegitimate children to inherit; it required civil marriage licenses; it set aside the common law spousal privilege for polygamists, in this way requiring wives to testify against their husbands; it disenfranchised women, who in 1870 had been granted the right to vote in Utah; and it replace local judges with federally appointed judges.

In *Late Corporation of the Church of Jesus Christ of Latter-day Saints v. United States* (1890), the Court, in unmistakable terms, rejected the argument that the 1885 act infringed on religious liberties, comparing polygamy to human sacrifice, religious assassinations, and "other open offenses against the enlightened sentiment of mankind." In *Davis v. Beason* (1890) the Court upheld an Idaho law that disenfranchised all Mormons, whether they were polygamists or not. In the wake of these defeats in the legislature and the courts, which threatened the very existence of the church, Mormon president Wilford Woodruff issued the "Manifesto" in which he called on Mormons to obey the laws banning polygamy. In the early twentieth century, the church began to excommunicate polygamists, although the practice continued, and indeed continues in the twenty-first century.

## About the Author

Morrison Remick Waite was born on November 27, 1816, in Lyme, Connecticut. Waite attended nearby Bacon Academy before enrolling, as many of his forebears had, at Yale University, where he graduated in 1837. He then struck out for the western frontier and landed in Maumee City, Ohio, to study law with Samuel Young and eventually become Young's partner. In 1840 he married Amelia Warner, and the two had five children. In 1848 Waite moved his family to nearby Toledo, Ohio, where he established a successful corporate and business law practice with his younger brother.

Waite's appointment as chief justice of the U.S. Supreme Court was surprising in light of his relative lack of prominence in public affairs. He sat briefly on the Toledo City Council and served a single term (1849–50) in the Ohio state legislature. Twice, in 1846 and 1862, he ran unsuccessfully for Congress. He was active in Republican Party politics, and during the Civil War he made speeches and wrote petitions in support of the Union. His only notable public service was in 1871, when President Ulysses S. Grant appointed him to a three-member delegation to the Geneva Arbitration in Europe. The goal of this body was to settle compensation claims between Great Britain and the United States arising out of the Civil War.

Waite was serving as president of the Ohio Constitutional Convention in 1873 when word reached him that Grant had appointed him chief justice of the Supreme Court to fill the vacancy left by Salmon Chase. Grant, whose administration was marred by charges of corruption, turned to Waite, a fresh face in Washington, D.C., who did not carry the political baggage of many of Grant's cronies. He was confirmed unanimously in the Senate in January 1874.

Waite went on to a successful fourteen-year tenure as chief justice. He was an efficient manager and an extraordinarily hard worker. Under his leadership the Court decided nearly 3,500 cases, and Waite himself wrote 872 opinions. He was able to impose a measure of unanimity on the Court, and among his opinions, only 2 percent were dissents from the majority. Given this large number of cases, the Waite court ruled on nearly every issue imaginable, but two issues stand out for their significance in constitutional history. One concerned the Court's role in economic and business regulation. After the Civil War the Court grappled repeatedly with the question of who, if anyone, had the power to regulate large corporations and business trusts. Waite believed that the public interest demanded that businesses and corporations be regulated and insisted that government had the power to regulate. Writing for the Court in *Munn v. Illinois* (1876), he argued that the state had the power to regulate private property and commerce when that commerce was "affected with a public interest." *Munn* altered the course of business regulation in the United States.

A second major issue the Waite court had to grapple with was Reconstruction—the period immediately after the Civil War from 1865 to 1877 referring to the reconstruction of society in the former Confederate states—and the application of the Reconstruction amendments as they affected freedmen in the South. The amendments failed to stamp out harassment of African Americans who attempted to vote or take part in politics, so Congress passed the Enforcement Acts of 1870–71, making specified acts against potential voters crimes. Against the backdrop, Waite ruled in two important cases. One was *United States v. Cruikshank* (1876), which overturned the conviction in Louisiana of three men accused of using violence and fraud to deny African Americans the right to vote. The other case was *United States v. Reese* (1876), which declared portions of the Enforcement Acts unconstitutional because they did not require proof that the reason for denying voting rights was race.

While these decisions were setbacks for civil rights, Waite was not hostile to African Americans. He believed that racial divisions in the post–Civil War South would recede as Blacks gained further education, and to this end he was an active supporter of philanthropic organizations that funded colleges for Blacks in the South and lobbied Congress to provide additional funds. Further, in other cases involving civil rights he showed a more progressive attitude. In *Strauder v. West Virginia* (1879), for example, he struck down all-white juries, and in the same year in *Neal v. Delaware* he ruled that state judges could not exclude African Americans from juries.

Waite continued to carry a crushing workload to the end of his life. Exhausted and ill, he insisted on appearing in court on March 20, 1888, to read an opinion he had drafted. He was unable to do so and died on March 23, 1888.

## Explanation and Analysis of the Document

Supreme Court cases, like those heard at any court of appeal, are based on the assertion by one of the parties that the lower court had erred in some way, often in the interpretation or application of the law. In his decision in *Reynolds v. United States*, Chief Justice Waite begins by outlining the "assignments of error," which in essence are the questions or issues the Court was called on to adjudicate. Justice Waite takes up each of the questions in turn.

1. Was the indictment bad because found by a grand jury of less than sixteen persons?

Justice Waite dismisses this issue by noting that the act of Congress "in relation to courts and judicial officers in the Territory of Utah" (1874) regulates the qualifications of jurors but not the number of jurors in a grand jury. However, the revised statues of the territory specified that a grand jury in a circuit or district court must have a minimum of sixteen jurors; the grand jury in the case before the Court had only fifteen. Justice Waite notes a minimum number of jurors was not "designed to regulate the impaneling of grand juries in all court where offenders against the laws of the United States could be tried." Accordingly, he does not find this to be a relevant objection.

2. Were the challenges of certain petit jurors by the accused improperly overruled?

One of the claims of appellant Reynolds was that challenges of some of the jurors were improperly overruled. These challenges were based on the belief that the potential juror was biased against the defendant or had reached a conclusion in the case without having heard the evidence. Accordingly, the defendant's right to a trial by an impartial jury was violated. Justice Waite cites cases bearing on the issue of the impartiality of jurors, noting that in all these cases, the courts conceded that "if hypothetical only, the partiality is not so manifest as to necessarily set the juror aside." A potential juror may have an impression about the case, but his mind may remain open to a "fair consideration of the testimony." He notes that because of the prevalence of newspapers and "universal education," any case of public interest will be brought to the attention of a potential juror. Those who are best fitted to be jurors will almost certainly have heard or read of the case and will likely have formed an impression. The issue a court faces is "whether the nature and strength of the opinion formed are such as in law necessarily to raise the presumption of partiality." He concludes that "unless [Reynolds] shows the actual existence of such an opinion in the mind of the juror as will raise the presumption of partiality, the juror need not necessarily be set aside, and it will not be error in the court to refuse to do so." This issue, then, does not provide grounds for setting aside the verdict of the lower court.

3. Were the challenges of certain other jurors by the government improperly sustained?

The third issue Justice Waite addresses is whether government challenges of certain other jurors were improperly sustained. This issue was easily addressed, for Waite points out that "it is apparent that all the jurors to whom the challenges related were or had been living in polygamy. It needs no argument to show that such a jury could not have gone into the box entirely free from bias and prejudice." These jurors were "incompetent and properly excluded" so "it matters not here upon what form of challenge they were set aside."

4. Was the testimony of Amelia Jane Schofield, given at a former trial for the same offence, but under another indictment, improperly admitted in evidence?

The fourth issue raises a thorny legal issue. Waite begins by summarizing the constitutional issue, stating that "the Constitution does not guarantee an accused person against the legitimate consequences of his own wrongful acts." Rather, it grants him the right to confront the witnesses against him. If the accused keeps the witnesses away or conceals them, he has no grounds for complaint. After examining the case law and legal history of this issue, Justice Waite turns to the facts:

> that the absent witness [Schofield] was the alleged second wife of the accused; that she had testified on a former trial for the same offence under another indictment; that she had no home, except with the accused; that, at some time before the trial, a subpoena had been issued for her, but, by mistake, she was named as Mary Jane Schobold; that an officer who knew the witness personally went to the house of the accused to serve the subpoena, and on his arrival inquired for her, either by the name of Mary Jane Schofield or Mrs. Reynolds; that he was told by the accused she was not at home; that he then said, "Will you tell me where she is?" that the reply was "No; that will be for you to find out"; that the officer then remarked she was making him considerable trouble, and that she would get into trouble herself; and the accused replied, "Oh, no; she won't, till the subpoena is served upon her."

The name was corrected and a new subpoena issued, but again, the witness was kept away. When the case was called the next day, the court ruled that the evidence she had sworn to at a former trial was admissible. Waite concludes that her former testimony is admissible because at the former trial, Reynolds was present and had full opportunity to cross examine the witness.

5. Should the accused have been acquitted if he married the second time because he believed it to be his religious duty?

The fifth issue is the core constitutional issue, that which bears on the First Amendment right to the "free exercise" of religious beliefs. Waite begins by examining the scriptural justification for polygamy as understood by the Mormon Church. The legal question, then, is

> whether religious belief can be accepted as a justification of an overt act made criminal by the law of the land. The inquiry is not as to the power of Congress to prescribe criminal laws for the Territories, but as to the guilt of one who knowingly violates a law which has been properly enacted if he entertains a religious belief that the law is wrong.

Waite provides a detailed examination of the First Amendment as it pertains to the U.S. territories. He notes that the Constitution does not define "religion," prompting him to examine the history of religious belief in the fledgling United States as well as the history of the relationship between religious belief and the law. He calls attention to the "Memorial and Remonstrance" of James Madison and the Virginia law guaranteeing religious freedom written by Thomas Jefferson. He also quotes Jefferson's famous letter to the Danbury Baptist Association (1802):

> Believing with you that religion is a matter which lies solely between man and his God; that he owes account to none other for his faith or his worship; that the legislative powers of the government reach actions only, and not opinions—I contemplate with sovereign reverence that act of the whole American people which declared that their legislature should 'make no law respecting an establishment of religion or prohibiting the free exercise thereof,' thus building a wall of separation between church and State.

The conclusion to be drawn is that Congress has no legislative authority over mere *opinion*. It does, however, have the power to regulate *actions* that violate social duties or subvert good order.

Waite proceeds to examine polygamy, calling it "odious" in the nations of Europe and stating that "from the earliest history of England, polygamy has been treated as an offence against society" punishable by death in England and Wales. Waite then arrives at the core of the religious liberty issue, stating that

> it is impossible to believe that the constitutional guaranty of religious freedom was intended to prohibit legislation in respect to this most important feature of social life. Marriage, while from its very nature a sacred obligation, is nevertheless, in most civilized nations, a civil contract, and usually regulated by law. Upon it society may be said to be built, and out of its fruits spring social relations and social obligations and duties with which government is necessarily required to deal.

He goes on to note that polygamy creates a patriarchal society that "fetters" the people in a form of "despotism." He adds: "Laws are made for the government of actions, and while they cannot interfere with mere religious belief and opinions, they may with practices." He concludes that "when the offence consists of a positive act which is knowingly done, it would be dangerous to hold that the offender might escape punishment because he religiously believed the law which he had broken ought never to have been made."

6. Did the court err in that part of the charge which directed the attention of the jury to the consequences of polygamy?

The sixth question Justice Waite examines is whether the lower court erred in directing the jury's attention to the consequences of polygamy. The lower court issued this instruction to the jury:

> I think it not improper . . . that you should consider what are to be the consequences to the innocent victims of this delusion. As this contest goes on, they multiply, and there are pure-minded women and there are innocent children—innocent in a sense even beyond the degree of the innocence of childhood itself. These are to be the sufferers; and as jurors fail to do their duty, and as these cases come up in the Territory of Utah, just so do these victims multiply and spread themselves over the land.

Waite rejected this claim, noting that Congress passed the statute prohibiting polygamy precisely because of the "evil consequences" polygamy had. The lower court said nothing that was intended to inflame the passions or prejudices of the jury. It merely called the attention of the jury to the "peculiar character" of the crime with which Reynolds was charged.

Waite concluded that "no error was committed by the court below" and affirmed the lower court's judgment.

The opinion includes a brief objection raised by Justice Samuel J. Field, who believed that the introduction of the testimony of Amelia Jane Schofield was admitted without sufficient foundation.

Also appended to the case is a note that a petition for rehearing the case was filed based on the lower court's sentence of hard labor. Waite agrees that "the act of Congress under which the indictment was found provides for punishment by imprisonment only." Accordingly, he sets aside the lower court's sentence as it pertained to hard labor.

---

## Questions for Further Study

1. On what fundamental basis was the U.S. government opposed to polygamy?

2. What was the principal argument that Mormons made in defense of polygamy?

3. To what extent does Justice Waite appeal to legal and legislative tradition in arriving at his opinion in the case?

4. Was the verdict in this case a violation of the religious rights of the Mormon Church?

---

## Further Reading

### Books

Alley, Robert S. *The Constitution and Religion: Leading Supreme Court Cases on Church and State.* Amherst, NY: Prometheus Books, 1999: 414–19.

Embry, Jessie L. "Polygamy." In *Utah History Encyclopedia,* edited by Allan Kent Powell. Salt Lake City: University of Utah Press, 1994.

Firmage, Edwin Brown, and Richard Collin Mangrum. *Zion in the Courts: A Legal History of the Church of Jesus Christ of Latter-day Saints, 1830–1900.* Urbana: University of Illinois Press, 1988.

Gordon, Sarah Barringer. *The Mormon Question: Polygamy and Constitutional Conflict in Nineteenth Century America.* Chapel Hill: University of North Carolina Press, 2002.

Riggs, Robert E. "Reynolds v. United States." In *The Encyclopedia of Mormonism,* edited by Daniel H. Ludlow. New York: Macmillan, 1992.

### Articles

Clayton, James L. "The Supreme Court, Polygamy and the Enforcement of Morals in Nineteenth Century America: An Analysis of Reynolds v. United States." *Journal of Mormon Thought* 12, no. 4 (Winter 1979): 46–61.

Drakeman, Donald L. "Reynolds v. United States: The Historical Construction of Constitutional Reality." *Constitutional Commentary* 21 (2004): 697–726. https://scholarship.law.umn.edu/cgi/viewcontent.cgi?article=1286&context=concomm.

Guynn, Randall D., and Gene C. Schaerr. "The Mormon Polygamy Cases." *Sunstone Magazine,* September 1987: 8–17.

Harmer-Dionne, Elizabeth. "Once a Peculiar People: Cognitive Dissonance and the Suppression of Mormon Polygamy as a Case Study Negating the Belief–Action Distinction." *Stanford Law Review* 50 (April 1998): 1295–1347.

McConnell, Michael W. "The Origins and Historical Understanding of Free Exercise of Religion." *Harvard Law Review* 103 (1990): 1409–1517.

### Websites

"What Does 'Free Exercise' of Religion Mean under the First Amendment?" Freedom Forum Institute. Accessed February 24, 2023, https://www.freedomforuminstitute.org/about/faq/what-does-free-exercise-of-religion-mean-under-the-first-amendment/.

—Commentary by Michael J. O'Neal

# REYNOLDS V. UNITED STATES

## Document Text

### *MR. CHIEF JUSTICE WAITE delivered the opinion of the Court*

The assignments of error, when grouped, present the following questions:

1. Was the indictment bad because found by a grand jury of less than sixteen persons?

2. Were the challenges of certain petit jurors by the accused improperly overruled?

3. Were the challenges of certain other jurors by the government improperly sustained?

4. Was the testimony of Amelia Jane Schofield, given at a former trial for the same offence, but under another indictment, improperly admitted in evidence?

5. Should the accused have been acquitted if he married the second time, because he believed it to be his religious duty?

6. Did the court err in that part of the charge which directed the attention of the jury to the consequences of polygamy?

These questions will be considered in their order.

1. As to the grand jury.

The indictment was found in the District Court of the third judicial district of the Territory. The act of Congress "in relation to courts and judicial officers in the Territory of Utah," approved June 23, 1874 (18 Stat. 253), while regulating the qualifications of jurors in the Territory and prescribing the mode of prepar-

ing the lists from which grand and petit jurors are to be drawn, as well as the manner of drawing, makes no provision in respect to the number of persons of which a grand jury shall consist. Sect. 808, Revised Statutes, requires that a grand jury impaneled before any district or circuit court of the United States shall consist of not less than sixteen nor more than twenty-three persons, while a statute of the Territory limits the number in the district courts of the Territory to fifteen. Comp.Laws Utah, 1876, 357. The grand jury which found this indictment consisted of only fifteen persons, and the question to be determined is whether the section of the Revised Statutes referred to or the statute of the Territory governs the case.

By sect. 1910 of the Revised Statutes, the district courts of the Territory have the same jurisdiction in all cases arising under the Constitution and laws of the United States as is vested in the circuit and district courts of the United States; but this does not make them circuit and district courts of the United States. We have often so decided. *American Insurance Co. v. Canter,* 1 Pet. 511; *Benner et al. v. Porter,* 9 How. 235; *Clinton v. Englebrecht,* 13 Wall. 434. They are courts of the Territories, invested for some purposes with the powers of the courts of the United States. Writs of error and appeals lie from them to the Supreme Court of the Territory, and from that court as a territorial court to this in some cases.

Sect. 808 was not designed to regulate the impaneling of grand juries in all courts where offenders against the laws of the United States could be tried, but only in the circuit and district courts. This leaves the territorial courts free to act in obedience to the requirements of the territorial laws in force for the time being. *Clinton v. Englebrecht, supra; 85 U. S. Toombs,* 18 Wall. 648. As Congress may at any time assume control of the matter, there is but little danger to be anticipated from improvident territorial legislation in this particular. We are therefore of the opinion that the court below no more erred in sustaining this indictment than it did at a former term, at the instance of this same plaintiff in error, in adjudging another bad which was found against him for the same offence by a grand jury composed of twenty-three persons. 1 Utah 226.

2. As to the challenges by the accused.

By the Constitution of the United States (Amend. VI.), the accused was entitled to a trial by an impartial jury. A juror to be impartial must, to use the language of Lord Coke, "be indifferent as he stands unsworn." Co. Litt. 155*b.* Lord Coke also says that a principal cause of challenge is

> "so called because, if it be found true, it standeth sufficient of itself, without leaving anything to the conscience or discretion of the triers"

(*id.,* 156*b*); or, as stated in Bacon's Abridgment, "it is grounded on such a manifest presumption of partiality that, if found to be true, it unquestionably sets aside the . . . juror." Bac.Abr., tit. Juries, E.1.

> "If the truth of the matter alleged is admitted, the law pronounces the judgment; but if denied, it must be made out by proof to the satisfaction of the court or the triers."

*Id.,* E.12. To make out the existence of the fact, the juror who is challenged may be examined on his *voire dire,* and asked any questions that do not tend to his infamy or disgrace.

All of the challenges by the accused were for principal cause. It is good ground for such a challenge that a juror has formed an opinion as to the issue to be tried. The courts are not agreed as to the knowledge upon which the opinion must rest in order to render the juror incompetent, or whether the opinion must be accompanied by malice or ill will; but all unite in holding that it must be founded on some evidence, and be more than a mere impression. Some say it must be positive (Gabbet, Criminal Law, 391); others, that it must be decided and substantial (Armistead's Case, 11 Leigh

(Va.) 659; *Wormley's Case,* 10 Gratt. (Va.) 658; *Neely v. The People,* 13 Ill. 685); others, fixed (*State v. Benton,* 2 Dev. & B. (N.C.) L. 196); and still others deliberate and settled (*Staup v. Commonwealth,* 74 Pa.St. 458; *Curley v. Commonwealth,* 84 *id.* 151). All concede, however, that, if hypothetical only, the partiality is not so manifest as to necessarily set the juror aside. Mr. Chief Justice Marshall, in Burr's Trial (1 Burr's Trial 416), states the rule to be that

> "light impressions, which may fairly be presumed to yield to the testimony that may be offered, which may leave the mind open to a fair consideration of the testimony, constitute no sufficient objection to a juror, but that those strong and deep impressions which close the mind against the testimony that may be offered in opposition to them, which will combat that testimony and resist its force, do constitute a sufficient objection to him."

The theory of the law is that a juror who has formed an opinion cannot be impartial. Every opinion which he may entertain need not necessarily have that effect. In these days of newspaper enterprise and universal education, every case of public interest is almost, as a matter of necessity, brought to the attention of all the intelligent people in the vicinity, and scarcely anyone can be found among those best fitted for jurors who has not read or heard of it, and who has not some impression or some opinion in respect to its merits. It is clear, therefore, that upon the trial of the issue of fact raised by a challenge for such cause, the court will practically be called upon to determine whether the nature and strength of the opinion formed are such as in law necessarily to raise the presumption of partiality. The question thus presented is one of mixed law and fact, and to be tried, as far as the facts are concerned, like any other issue of that character, upon the evidence. The finding of the trial court upon that issue ought not to be set aside by a reviewing court, unless the error is manifest. No less stringent rules should be applied by the reviewing court in such a case than those which govern in the consideration of motions for new trial because the verdict is against the evidence. It must be made clearly to appear that upon the evidence the court ought to have found the juror had formed such an opinion that he could not, in law, be deemed impartial. The case must be one in which it is manifest the law left nothing to the "conscience or discretion" of the court.

The challenge in this case most relied upon in the argument here is that of Charles Read. He was sworn on his *voire dire,* and his evidence,{1} taken as a whole, shows that he "believed" he had formed an opinion which he had never expressed, but which he did not think would influence his verdict on hearing the testimony. We cannot think this is such a manifestation of partiality as to leave nothing to the "conscience or discretion" of the triers. The reading of the evidence leaves the impression that the juror had some hypothetical opinion about the case, but it falls far short of raising a manifest presumption of partiality. In considering such questions in a reviewing court, we ought not to be unmindful of the fact we have so often observed in our experience, that jurors not unfrequently seek to excuse themselves on the ground of having formed an opinion, when, on examination, it turns out that no real disqualification exists. In such cases, the manner of the juror while testifying is oftentimes more indicative of the real character of his opinion than his words. That is seen below, but cannot always be spread upon the record. Care should, therefore, be taken in the reviewing court not to reverse the ruling below upon such a question of fact, except in a clear case. The affirmative of the issue is upon the challenger. Unless he shows the actual existence of such an opinion in the mind of the juror as will raise the presumption of partiality, the juror need not necessarily be set aside, and it will not be error in the court to refuse to do so. Such a case, in our opinion, was not made out upon the challenge of Read. The fact that he had not expressed his opinion is important only as tending to show that he had not formed one which disqualified him. If a positive and decided opinion had been formed, he would have been incompetent even though it had not been expressed. Under these circumstances, it is unnecessary to consider the case of Ransohoff, for it was confessedly not as strong as that of Read.

3. As to the challenges by the government.

The questions raised upon these assignments of error are not whether the district attorney should have been permitted to interrogate the jurors while under examination upon their *voire dire* as to the fact of their living in polygamy. No objection was made below to the questions, but only to the ruling of the court upon the challenges after the testimony taken in answer to the questions was in. From the testimony, it is apparent that all the jurors to whom the challenges related were or had been living in polygamy. It needs no argument to show that such a jury could not have gone into the box entirely free from bias and prejudice, and that, if the challenge was not good for principal cause, it was for favor. A judgment will not be reversed simply because a challenge good for favor was sustained in form for cause. As the jurors were incompetent and properly excluded, it matters not here upon what form of challenge they were set aside. In one case, the challenge was for favor. In the courts of the United States, all challenges are tried by the court without the aid of triers (Rev.Stat. sect. 819), and we are not advised that the practice in the territorial courts of Utah is different.

4. As to the admission of evidence to prove what was sworn to by Amelia Jane Schofield on a former trial of the accused for the same offence but under a different indictment.

The Constitution gives the accused the right to a trial at which he should be confronted with the witnesses against him; but if a witness is absent by his own wrongful procurement, he cannot complain if competent evidence is admitted to supply the place of that which he has kept away. The Constitution does not guarantee an accused person against the legitimate consequences of his own wrongful acts. It grants him the privilege of being confronted with the witnesses against him; but if he voluntarily keeps the witnesses away, he cannot insist on his privilege. If, therefore, when absent by his procurement, their evidence is supplied in some lawful way, he is in no condition to assert that his constitutional rights have been violated.

In *Lord Morley's Case* (6 State Trials, 770), as long ago as the year 1666, it was resolved in the House of Lords

> "that, in case oath should be made that any witness, who had been examined by the coroner and was then absent, was detained by the means or procurement of the prisoner, and the opinion of the judges asked whether such examination might be read, we should answer, that, if their lordships were satisfied by the evidence they had heard that the witness was detained by means or procurement of the prisoner, then the examination might be read; but whether he was detained by means or procurement of the prisoner was matter

of fact, of which we were not the judges, but their lordships."

This resolution was followed in *Harrison's Case* (12 *id.* 851), and seems to have been recognized as the law in England ever since. In *Regina v. Scaife* (17 Ad. & El.N.S. 242), all the judges agreed that, if the prisoner had resorted to a contrivance to keep a witness out of the way, the deposition of the witness, taken before a magistrate and in the presence of the prisoner, might be read. Other cases to the same effect are to be found, and in this country the ruling has been in the same way. *Drayton v. Wells,* 1 Nott & M. (S.C.) 409; *Williams v. The State,* 19 Ga. 403. So that now, in the leading textbooks, it is laid down that, if a witness is kept away by the adverse party, his testimony, taken on a former trial between the same parties upon the same issues, may be given in evidence. 1 Greenl. Evid., sect. 163; 1 Taylor, Evid., sect. 446. Mr. Wharton (1 Whart.Evid., sect. 178) seemingly limits the rule somewhat, and confines it to cases where the witness has been corruptly kept away by the party against whom he is to be called, but in reality his statement is the same as that of the others; for in all it is implied that the witness must have been wrongfully kept away. The rule has its foundation in the maxim that no one shall be permitted to take advantage of his own wrong, and, consequently, if there has not been, in legal contemplation, a wrong committed, the way has not been opened for the introduction of the testimony. We are content with this long-established usage, which, so far as we have been able to discover, has rarely been departed from. It is the outgrowth of a maxim based on the principles of common honesty, and, if properly administered, can harm no one.

Such being the rule, the question becomes practically one of fact, to be settled as a preliminary to the admission of secondary evidence. In this respect, it is like the preliminary question of the proof of loss of a written instrument, before secondary evidence of the contents of the instrument can be admitted. In *Lord Morley's Case* (*supra*), it would seem to have been considered a question for the trial court alone, and not subject to review on error or appeal; but without deeming it necessary in this case to go so far as that, we have no hesitation in saying that the finding of the court below is, at least, to have the effect of a verdict of a jury upon a question of fact, and should not be disturbed unless the error is manifest.

The testimony shows that the absent witness was the alleged second wife of the accused; that she had testified on a former trial for the same offence under another indictment; that she had no home, except with the accused; that, at some time before the trial, a subpoena had been issued for her, but, by mistake, she was named as Mary Jane Schobold; that an officer who knew the witness personally went to the house of the accused to serve the subpoena, and on his arrival inquired for her, either by the name of Mary Jane Schofield or Mrs. Reynolds; that he was told by the accused she was not at home; that he then said, "Will you tell me where she is?" that the reply was "No; that will be for you to find out;" that the officer then remarked she was making him considerable trouble, and that she would get into trouble herself; and the accused replied, "Oh, no; she won't, till the subpoena is served upon her," and then, after some further conversation, that "She does not appear in this case."

It being discovered after the trial commenced that a wrong name had been inserted in the subpoena, a new subpoena was issued with the right name, at nine o'clock in the evening. With this, the officer went again to the house, and there found a person known as the first wife of the accused. He was told by her that the witness was not there, and had not been for three weeks. He went again the next morning, and, not finding her or being able to ascertain where she was by inquiring in the neighborhood, made return of that fact to the court. At ten o'clock that morning, the case was again called, and, the foregoing facts being made to appear, the court ruled that evidence of what the witness had sworn to at the former trial was admissible.

In this we see no error. The accused was himself personally present in court when the showing was made, and had full opportunity to account for the absence of the witness, if he would, or to deny under oath that he had kept her away. Clearly, enough had been proven to cast the burden upon him of showing that he had not been instrumental in concealing or keeping the witness away. Having the means of making the necessary explanation, and having every inducement to do so if he would, the presumption is that he considered it better to rely upon the weakness of the case made against him than to attempt to develop the strength of his own. Upon the testimony as it stood, it is clear to our minds that the judgment should not be reversed because secondary evidence was admitted.

This brings us to the consideration of what the former testimony was, and the evidence by which it was proven to the jury.

It was testimony given on a former trial of the same person for the same offence, but under another indictment. It was substantially testimony given at another time in the same cause. The accused was present at the time the testimony was given, and had full opportunity of cross-examination. This brings the case clearly within the well established rules. The cases are fully cited in 1 Whart.Evid., sect. 177.

The objection to the reading by Mr. Patterson of what was sworn to on the former trial does not seem to have been because the paper from which he read was not a true record of the evidence as given, but because the foundation for admitting the secondary evidence had not been laid. This objection, as has already been seen, was not well taken.

5. As to the defence of religious belief or duty.

On the trial, the plaintiff in error, the accused, proved that, at the time of his alleged second marriage, he was, and for many years before had been, a member of the Church of Jesus Christ of Latter-Day Saints, commonly called the Mormon Church, and a believer in its doctrines; that it was an accepted doctrine of that church

> "that it was the duty of male members of said church, circumstances permitting, to practise polygamy; . . . that this duty was enjoined by different books which the members of said church believed to be of divine origin, and, among others, the Holy Bible, and also that the members of the church believed that the practice of polygamy was directly enjoined upon the male members thereof by the Almighty God, in a revelation to Joseph Smith, the founder and prophet of said church; that the failing or refusing to practise polygamy by such male members of said church, when circumstances would admit, would be punished, and that the penalty for such failure and refusal would be damnation in the life to come."

He also proved

> "that he had received permission from the recognized authorities in said church to enter into

polygamous marriage; . . . that Daniel H. Wells, one having authority in said church to perform the marriage ceremony, married the said defendant on or about the time the crime is alleged to have been committed, to some woman by the name of Schofield, and that such marriage ceremony was performed under and pursuant to the doctrines of said church."

Upon this proof, he asked the court to instruct the jury that, if they found from the evidence that he

> "was married as charged—if he was married—in pursuance of and in conformity with what he believed at the time to be a religious duty, that the verdict must be 'not guilty.'"

This request was refused, and the court did charge

> "that there must have been a criminal intent, but that if the defendant, under the influence of a religious belief that it was right—under an inspiration, if you please, that it was right—deliberately married a second time, having a first wife living, the want of consciousness of evil intent—the want of understanding on his part that he was committing a crime—did not excuse him, but the law inexorably in such case implies the criminal intent."

Upon this charge and refusal to charge, the question is raised whether religious belief can be accepted as a justification of an overt act made criminal by the law of the land. The inquiry is not as to the power of Congress to prescribe criminal laws for the Territories, but as to the guilt of one who knowingly violates a law which has been properly enacted if he entertains a religious belief that the law is wrong.

Congress cannot pass a law for the government of the Territories which shall prohibit the free exercise of religion. The first amendment to the Constitution expressly forbids such legislation. Religious freedom is guaranteed everywhere throughout the United States, so far as congressional interference is concerned. The question to be determined is, whether the law now under consideration comes within this prohibition.

The word "religion" is not defined in the Constitution. We must go elsewhere, therefore, to ascertain its meaning, and nowhere more appropriately, we think, than to the history of the times in the midst of which the provision was adopted. The precise point of the inquiry is what is the religious freedom which has been guaranteed.

Before the adoption of the Constitution, attempts were made in some of the colonies and States to legislate not only in respect to the establishment of religion, but in respect to its doctrines and precepts as well. The people were taxed, against their will, for the support of religion, and sometimes for the support of particular sects to whose tenets they could not and did not subscribe. Punishments were prescribed for a failure to attend upon public worship, and sometimes for entertaining heretical opinions. The controversy upon this general subject was animated in many of the States, but seemed at last to culminate in Virginia. In 1784, the House of Delegates of that State, having under consideration "a bill establishing provision for teachers of the Christian religion," postponed it until the next session, and directed that the bill should be published and distributed, and that the people be requested "to signify their opinion respecting the adoption of such a bill at the next session of assembly."

This brought out a determined opposition. Amongst others, Mr. Madison prepared a "Memorial and Remonstrance," which was widely circulated and signed, and in which he demonstrated "that religion, or the duty we owe the Creator," was not within the cognizance of civil government. Semple's Virginia Baptists, Appendix. At the next session, the proposed bill was not only defeated, but another, "for establishing religious freedom," drafted by Mr. Jefferson, was passed. 1 Jeff. Works, 45; 2 Howison, Hist. of Va. 298. In the preamble of this act (12 Hening's Stat. 84) religious freedom is defined, and, after a recital

> "that to suffer the civil magistrate to intrude his powers into the field of opinion, and to restrain the profession or propagation of principles on supposition of their ill tendency is a dangerous fallacy which at once destroys all religious liberty,"

it is declared

> "that it is time enough for the rightful purposes of civil government for its officers to interfere when principles break out into overt acts against peace and good order."

In these two sentences is found the true distinction between what properly belongs to the church and what to the State.

In a little more than a year after the passage of this statute, the convention met which prepared the Constitution of the United States. Of this convention, Mr. Jefferson was not a member, he being then absent as minister to France. As soon as he saw the draft of the Constitution proposed for adoption, he, in a letter to a friend, expressed his disappointment at the absence of an express declaration insuring the freedom of religion (2 Jeff.Works 355), but was willing to accept it as it was, trusting that the good sense and honest intentions of the people would bring about the necessary alterations.

1 Jeff. Works 79. Five of the States, while adopting the Constitution, proposed amendments. Three—New Hampshire, New York, and Virginia—included in one form or another a declaration of religious freedom in the changes they desired to have made, as did also North Carolina, where the convention at first declined to ratify the Constitution until the proposed amendments were acted upon. Accordingly, at the first session of the first Congress, the amendment now under consideration was proposed with others by Mr. Madison. It met the views of the advocates of religious freedom, and was adopted. Mr. Jefferson afterwards, in reply to an address to him by a committee of the Danbury Baptist Association (8 *id.* 113), took occasion to say:

> "Believing with you that religion is a matter which lies solely between man and his God; that he owes account to none other for his faith or his worship; that the legislative powers of the government reach actions only, and not opinions—I contemplate with sovereign reverence that act of the whole American people which declared that their legislature should 'make no law respecting an establishment of religion or prohibiting the free exercise thereof,' thus building a wall of separation between church and State. Adhering to this expression of the supreme will of the nation in behalf of the rights of conscience, I shall see with sincere satisfaction the progress of those sentiments which tend to restore man to all his natural rights, convinced he has no natural right in opposition to his social duties."

Coming as this does from an acknowledged leader of the advocates of the measure, it may be accepted almost as an authoritative declaration of the scope and effect of the amendment thus secured. Congress was deprived of all legislative power over mere opinion, but was left free to reach actions which were in violation of social duties or subversive of good order.

Polygamy has always been odious among the northern and western nations of Europe, and, until the establishment of the Mormon Church, was almost exclusively a feature of the life of Asiatic and of African people. At common law, the second marriage was always void (2 Kent, Com. 79), and from the earliest history of England, polygamy has been treated as an offence against society. After the establishment of the ecclesiastical courts, and until the time of James I, it was punished through the instrumentality of those tribunals not merely because ecclesiastical rights had been violated, but because upon the separation of the ecclesiastical courts from the civil the ecclesiastical were supposed to be the most appropriate for the trial of matrimonial causes and offences against the rights of marriage, just as they were for testamentary causes and the settlement of the estates of deceased persons.

By the statute of 1 James I (c. 11), the offence, if committed in England or Wales, was made punishable in the civil courts, and the penalty was death. As this statute was limited in its operation to England and Wales, it was at a very early period reenacted, generally with some modifications, in all the colonies. In connection with the case we are now considering, it is a significant fact that, on the 8th of December, 1788, after the passage of the act establishing religious freedom, and after the convention of Virginia had recommended as an amendment to the Constitution of the United States the declaration in a bill of rights that "all men have an equal, natural, and unalienable right to the free exercise of religion, according to the dictates of conscience," the legislature of that State substantially enacted the statute of James I., death penalty included, because, as recited in the preamble, "it hath been doubted whether bigamy or poligamy be punishable by the laws of this Commonwealth." 12 Hening's Stat. 691. From that day to this, we think it may safely be said there never has been a time in any State of the Union when polygamy has not been an offence against society, cognizable by the civil courts and punishable with more or less severity. In the face of all this

evidence, it is impossible to believe that the constitutional guaranty of religious freedom was intended to prohibit legislation in respect to this most important feature of social life. Marriage, while from its very nature a sacred obligation, is nevertheless, in most civilized nations, a civil contract, and usually regulated by law. Upon it society may be said to be built, and out of its fruits spring social relations and social obligations and duties with which government is necessarily required to deal. In fact, according as monogamous or polygamous marriages are allowed, do we find the principles on which the government of the people, to a greater or less extent, rests. Professor, Lieber says, polygamy leads to the patriarchal principle, and which, when applied to large communities, fetters the people in stationary despotism, while that principle cannot long exist in connection with monogamy. Chancellor Kent observes that this remark is equally striking and profound. 2 Kent, Com. 81, note (e). An exceptional colony of polygamists under an exceptional leadership may sometimes exist for a time without appearing to disturb the social condition of the people who surround it; but there cannot be a doubt that, unless restricted by some form of constitution, it is within the legitimate scope of the power of every civil government to determine whether polygamy or monogamy shall be the law of social life under its dominion.

In our opinion, the statute immediately under consideration is within the legislative power of Congress. It is constitutional and valid as prescribing a rule of action for all those residing in the Territories, and in places over which the United States have exclusive control. This being so, the only question which remains is whether those who make polygamy a part of their religion are excepted from the operation of the statute. If they are, then those who do not make polygamy a part of their religious belief may be found guilty and punished, while those who do, must be acquitted and go free. This would be introducing a new element into criminal law. Laws are made for the government of actions, and while they cannot interfere with mere religious belief and opinions, they may with practices. Suppose one believed that human sacrifices were a necessary part of religious worship; would it be seriously contended that the civil government under which he lived could not interfere to prevent a sacrifice? Or if a wife religiously believed it was her duty to burn herself upon the funeral pile of her dead husband;

would it be beyond the power of the civil government to prevent her carrying her belief into practice?

So here, as a law of the organization of society under the exclusive dominion of the United States, it is provided that plural marriages shall not be allowed. Can a man excuse his practices to the contrary because of his religious belief?

To permit this would be to make the professed doctrines of religious belief superior to the law of the land, and, in effect, to permit every citizen to become a law unto himself. Government could exist only in name under such circumstances.

A criminal intent is generally an element of crime, but every man is presumed to intend the necessary and legitimate consequences of what he knowingly does. Here, the accused knew he had been once married, and that his first wife was living. He also knew that his second marriage was forbidden by law. When, therefore, he married the second time, he is presumed to have intended to break the law. And the breaking of the law is the crime. Every act necessary to constitute the crime was knowingly done, and the crime was therefore knowingly committed. Ignorance of a fact may sometimes be taken as evidence of a want of criminal intent, but not ignorance of the law. The only defence of the accused in this case is his belief that the law ought not to have been enacted. It matters not that his belief was a part of his professed religion; it was still belief, and belief only.

In *Regina v. Wagstaff* (10 Cox Crim.Cases, 531), the parents of a sick child, who omitted to call in medical attendance because of their religious belief that what they did for its cure would be effective, were held not to be guilty of manslaughter, while it was said the contrary would have been the result if the child had actually been starved to death by the parents under the notion that it was their religious duty to abstain from giving it food. But when the offence consists of a positive act which is knowingly done, it would be dangerous to hold that the offender might escape punishment because he religiously believed the law

which he had broken ought never to have been made. No case, we believe, can be found that has gone so far.

6. As to that part of the charge which directed the attention of the jury to the consequences of polygamy.

The passage complained of is as follows:

> "I think it not improper, in the discharge of your duties in this case, that you should consider what are to be the consequences to the innocent victims of this delusion. As this contest goes on, they multiply, and there are pure-minded women and there are innocent children—innocent in a sense even beyond the degree of the innocence of childhood itself. These are to be the sufferers; and as jurors fail to do their duty, and as these cases come up in the Territory of Utah, just so do these victims multiply and spread themselves over the land."

While every appeal by the court to the passions or the prejudices of a jury should be promptly rebuked, and while it is the imperative duty of a reviewing court to take care that wrong is not done in this way, we see no just cause for complaint in this case. Congress, in 1862 (12 Stat. 501), saw fit to make bigamy a crime in the Territories. This was done because of the evil consequences that were supposed to flow from plural marriages. All the court did was to call the attention of the jury to the peculiar character of the crime for which the accused was on trial, and to remind them of the duty they had to perform. There was no appeal to the passions, no instigation of prejudice. Upon the showing made by the accused himself, he was guilty of a violation of the law under which he had been indicted, and the effort of the court seems to have been not to withdraw the minds of the jury from the issue to be tried, but to bring them to it; not to make them partial, but to keep them impartial.

Upon a careful consideration of the whole case, we are satisfied that no error was committed by the court below.

*Judgment affirmed.*

## Glossary

**challenge:** in a jury trial, the elimination of a potential juror because of possible bias

**petit jurors:** citizens in a jury that hears evidence in a trial and determines guilt or innocence or fault

**polygamy:** the practice of having two or more spouses, usually wives, at the same time

**subpoena:** an order to attend court

# CIVIL RIGHTS CASES

| DATE | CITATION |
|------|----------|
| 1883 | 109 U.S. 3 |

| AUTHOR | SIGNIFICANCE |
|--------|--------------|
| Joseph P. Bradley | Held that the Thirteenth and Fourteenth Amendments did not allow Congress to outlaw discrimination based on race by private parties |

| VOTE | |
|------|--|
| 9-0 | |

## Overview

In the *Civil Rights Cases* decision of 1883, the U.S. Supreme Court limited the powers of Congress with its finding that the equal protection clause of the Fourteenth Amendment did not pertain to actions involving private parties. This case decided five similar discrimination cases that had been grouped together as the *Civil Rights Cases* when they were heard by the Supreme Court. These cases involved African Americans who had been denied access to whites-only facilities in railroads, hotels, and theaters. All five cases were related to the Civil Rights Act of 1875, which the majority of justices declared unconstitutional in the *Civil Rights Cases* decision, which was delivered by Joseph P. Bradley. Nearly ninety years later, Congress would revive that legislation with the enactment of the Civil Rights Act of 1964. One of the most frequently examined decisions of the nineteenth century, the *Civil Rights Cases* decision dealt a dramatic blow to African Americans because it significantly narrowed the legal reach of the pivotal Fourteenth Amendment, which had provided for equal protection under the Constitution for African Americans.

John Marshall Harlan served thirty-three years, ten months, and four days on the U.S. Supreme Court, one of the longest tenures of all who have sat on the high bench. During that period, he wrote his share of opinions for the Court majority, yet he is best remembered for his dissents—for their passion, for their prescience, and for the sheer fact that the most significant among them, those concerning civil rights, were written by a southerner and former slaveholder. Harlan's passion for the Constitution led him to fight for the Union during the Civil War; it may also have accounted for his expansive reading of the Civil War Amendments, particularly the Fourteenth Amendment.

Harlan had the foresight to maintain in his dissenting opinion in the *Civil Rights Cases* that the "colored race" was entitled to the same right in public accommodations as any other member of the public, but in 1883 what most impressed his audience was the former slaveholder's willingness to stand alone as the voice of conscience, delivering his opinion with fervor and directness.

## Context

The American Civil War freed nearly four million slaves. While historians continue to debate the causes of the war, as President Abraham Lincoln made clear in his Second Inaugural Address, "These slaves constituted a peculiar and powerful interest. All knew that this interest was somehow the cause of the war." Eleven southern states seceded from the Union to form the Confederate States of America, nominally to protect "states' rights" but more specifically to preserve the institution of slavery. Even after four years of bloodshed, Confederate defeat, and the ratification of the Thirteenth Amendment abolishing slavery, southern states stubbornly resisted northern attempts to grant Blacks civil, political, and social rights. Throughout the period known as Reconstruction (until the mid-1870s Republicans in Congress passed a great deal of legislation, and two more amendments to the Constitution (the Fourteenth and Fifteenth Amendments), all with an eye toward expanding American citizenship to include former slaves. Of these many initiatives, none has had more positive or lasting effect than the Fourteenth Amendment, the five sections of which are notable for providing the "due process" and "equal protection" clauses that serve as the basis for over two-thirds of all cases that go before the Supreme Court today.

Under the leadership of such Radical Republicans from the Midwest and New England as John Bingham, Charles Sumner, and Thaddeus Stevens, Congress had passed the Civil Rights Act of 1866, which reversed the Supreme Court's decision in 1857 in *Dred Scott v. Sandford*, in which the Court had ruled that African Americans could not be considered citizens of the United States. The Civil Rights Act of 1866 deemed "all persons born in the United States" to be American citizens. Congress then established constitutional protection of that act with the Fourteenth Amendment, the ratification of which Congress demanded of former Confederate states before they could be readmitted to the Union. The equal protection clause of the Fourteenth Amendment's vital first section—"no state shall . . . deny to any person within its jurisdiction equal protection of the laws"—enforced the Declaration of Independence's principle that "all men are created equal." The Fourteenth Amendment extended legal protection to African Americans and ensured both equality

***John Marshall Harlan was the sole dissenter in the case.***
(Library of Congress)

and protection of all U.S. citizens, although the meaning of the terms *equality* and *protection* would soon prove to be the focus of considerable debate.

The Civil Rights Act of 1875 was controversial from the moment Senator Charles Sumner of Massachusetts first proposed it in 1870. The original bill had attempted to eliminate all forms of segregation, which Sumner viewed as inherently discriminatory. Sumner's proposed legislation also sought to redefine what most Americans took to be "social rights" as civil rights. The concept that Congress could regulate the actions of individuals or privately held companies proved to be especially contentious; Democrats and Republicans alike insisted that such provisions were unconstitutional and would never be upheld by the Supreme Court. Many legislators objected to the bill's initial provisions for desegregation in schools, churches, and cemeteries, all of which were omitted from the final version passed by the lame-duck second session of the Forty-third Congress.

The Civil Rights Act of 1875 met with mixed treatment from federal circuit courts prior to being ruled unconstitutional by the Supreme Court in 1883. During the late 1870s and early 1880s, as many as one hundred cases related to the act's provisions were tried and appealed before federal judges in Pennsylvania, Texas, Maryland, and Kentucky—all of which ruled the act constitutional. Divided federal courts in New York, Tennessee, Missouri, Kansas, and other states referred issues arising from the act to the Supreme Court. Although the Supreme Court had already considered the meaning of *equal protection* in three jury cases of 1880, it was not until the *Civil Rights Cases* ruling that the Court put forth the critically important doctrine of "state action," which limited federal guarantees of equal protection in favor of the laws and customs of individual states.

## About the Author

All of the Supreme Court justices who heard the *Civil Rights Cases* had been appointed and confirmed under Republican presidential administrations. Two of Lincoln's appointees, Samuel Freeman Miller and Stephen Johnson Field, remained on the Court in 1883. Miller was the only Democrat on the nation's highest bench. Justice John Marshall Harlan had been a Democrat before the Civil War but had become a Republican during Reconstruction. The other judges included Chief Justice Morrison Remick Waite and, in order of seniority, William Burnham Woods, Stanley Matthews, Horace Gray, and Samuel Blatchford. Joseph P. Bradley wrote the majority opinion in the *Civil Rights Cases* decision, while Justice Harlan offered the lone dissent.

Joseph P. Bradley was born on March 14, 1813, in Berne, New York. He studied at Rutgers University before taking up the practice of law through various apprenticeships in Newark, New Jersey, where he passed the bar in 1839. Bradley married Mary Hornblower, the daughter of the chief justice of the New Jersey Supreme Court, and soon became a prominent patent and commercial lawyer. In 1862 he waged an unsuccessful campaign for Congress as a conservative Republican who refused to support either emancipation or civil rights for Blacks, despite his aversion to slavery. While there was reason to suspect Bradley's views before his appointment to the Supreme Court under President Ulysses S. Grant in 1870, few could have anticipated the many anti–civil rights decisions in which Bradley's reasoning would prevail. By joining the majority, Bradley attacked the Enforcement Act of 1870 (which

protected Black voters) in *United States v. Reese* (1875) and *United States v. Cruikshank* (1876). In *United States v. Harris* (1883), Bradley again joined the Court's majority limiting the scope of the Ku Klux Klan Act of 1871, an attempt by Congress to outlaw conspiracies against African Americans. In his majority opinion for the *Civil Rights Cases*, Bradley pronounced the Civil Rights Act of 1875 unconstitutional. Bradley died on January 22, 1892.

Named for the "Great Chief Justice" of the United States and ardent Federalist John Marshall, John Marshall Harlan was born into a prominent Kentucky family with Whig Party affiliations. Harlan was the first U.S. Supreme Court justice to earn a law degree, which he received from Transylvania University in 1853, after graduating from Centre College in 1850. Harlan joined his father's Frankfort, Kentucky, law practice and his father's political party. The elder Harlan was a slaveholder and crony of the Whig leader Henry Clay, who supported gradual emancipation. John Marshall Harlan inherited James Harlan's paternalistic attitude toward slavery as well as some of his father's slaves. He would have inherited his father's position among the Whigs had the party not come apart in the 1850s over the issue of whether slavery should be allowed to expand into the American territories. Instead, father and son joined the nativist Know-Nothings, a short-lived political party in the 1850s that was fueled by fear that the nation was being overrun by Irish Catholic immigrants.

In 1858, Harlan, running as a Know-Nothing, was elected county judge. Over the next few years he voiced a number of racist and states' rights opinions that would later come back to haunt him. With the advent of the Civil War in 1861, however, Harlan discovered his true political orientation. A staunch supporter of the Union, he raised a company of infantry volunteers and joined the Union army. He did so out of unswerving loyalty to the Constitution, not any abolitionist sentiments. He threatened to resign his colonel's commission if President Abraham Lincoln signed the Emancipation Proclamation, but he did not do so until James Harlan's death in 1863 obliged him to take over his father's unfinished business. The same year, running as a Constitutional Unionist, Harlan won election as Kentucky's attorney general. After the war ended, the party, made up largely of conservative former Whigs who wanted to avoid disunion over slavery, lost its reason for being. In 1868, like many former Whigs,

Harlan joined the Republicans, where he quickly embraced his new party's antislavery platform.

Despite failing to win the governorship of Kentucky in 1871 and 1875, Harlan remained active in Republican political circles. In 1876, heading up the Kentucky delegation, he attended the Republican National Convention, where his support for Rutherford B. Hayes helped the latter secure the party's nomination. The close 1876 presidential contest between Hayes and Samuel J. Tilden dragged on for months, but shortly after it was settled in Hayes's favor, the new president appointed Harlan to head a commission charged with ending Republican rule in Louisiana, thus enforcing the political compromise that had resulted in Hayes's election. Consistent with his policy of ending Reconstruction and promoting North-South reconciliation, in 1877 Hayes nominated Harlan, a Unionist son of border-state Kentucky, to serve on the Supreme Court. Important documents from Harlan's tenure on the Supreme Court include his dissents in a number of landmark cases.

## Explanation and Analysis of the Document

### Joseph P. Bradley: Majority Opinion

The five cases consolidated in the *Civil Rights Cases* were *United States v. Stanley, United States v. Ryan, United States v. Nichols, United States v. Singleton,* and *Robinson & Wife v. Memphis and Charleston Railroad Company.* The *Stanley* and *Nichols* cases concerned indictments for denying access to inns or hotels; the *Ryan* and *Singleton* cases addressed access to theaters, one in San Francisco and the other in New York City. The *Robinson* case had originally been brought in Tennessee and involved the refusal of the Memphis and Charleston Railroad Company to allow Mrs. Robinson to travel in a ladies' train car. U.S. Solicitor General Samuel F. Phillips submitted all but the *Robinson* case as a group on November 7, 1882; briefs regarding the Robinson case were submitted on March 29, 1883.

The five related lawsuits in the *Civil Rights Cases* all had to do with Section 1 of the Civil Rights Act of 1875, which stated:

> All persons within the jurisdiction of the

United States shall be entitled to the full and equal enjoyment of the accommodations, advantages, facilities, and privileges of inns, public conveyances on land or water, theaters, or other places of public amusement; subject only to the conditions and limitations established by law, and applicable alike to citizens of every race and color, regardless of any previous condition of servitude.

Section 2 of the act stipulated:

> Any person who shall violate [Section 1] . . . shall . . . forfeit and pay the sum of five hundred dollars to the person aggrieved thereby . . . and shall also, for every such offense, be deemed guilty of a misdemeanor, and upon conviction thereof, shall be fined not less than five hundred nor more than one thousand dollars, or shall be imprisoned not less than thirty days nor more than one year.

Writing for the majority of justices, Justice Bradley no longer argued for a broad view of the Fourteenth Amendment, which he had proposed in previous cases. With the *Civil Rights Cases* majority opinion, Bradley echoed the narrow position of the *Slaughterhouse Cases* (1873) majority opinion, which held that state authority was primary and national authority was secondary or "corrective." He rejected the radical pro-nationalist, expansive-rights view and contended instead that the Civil Rights Act of 1875 was an impermissible attempt by Congress to regulate the private conduct of individuals with respect to racial discrimination. The act, Bradley wrote, "does not profess to be corrective of any constitutional wrong committed by the States." Regarding Section 4 of the act, he held that even private interference with such rights as voting, jury service, or appearing as witnesses in state court were not within Congress's control. Anyone faced with such interference had to look to state courts for relief.

The Court had two important missions in issuing this ruling: to contain the power of Congress in enacting legislation and to safeguard states' rights. The first became a prerequisite for the second. With respect to the first, Bradley stipulated that "legislation which Congress is authorized to adopt . . . is not general . . . but corrective legislation." To emphasize this point, Bradley repeated the word corrective ten more times.

As for the second objective, Bradley almost buried the following point in the opinion's text: "Legislation cannot properly cover the whole domain of rights appertaining to life, liberty, and property, defining them and providing for their vindication.... It would be to make Congress take the place of the State legislatures and to supersede them." Federal limitation of state authority through acts of Congress was what the Court most wanted to prevent. While the Court's majority did not challenge the Fourteenth Amendment's applicability to state laws and actions, it also did not tolerate congressional oversight of what it considered private actions regulated under state laws.

Bradley argued that while private actors broke laws, their actions could not destroy civil rights; only states could do that. In other words, "civil rights ... cannot be impaired by the wrongful acts of individuals, unsupported by state authority in the shape of laws, customs, or judicial or executive proceedings. The wrongful act of an individual ... is simply a private wrong, or a crime of that individual." According to this reasoning, demonstrations of white supremacy and incidents of segregation and violence against Blacks were wrongful private acts and did not generate anything akin to a state action, that is, the denial of civil rights, which could be remedied only by a corrective governmental action.

In the event confusion might persist on the distinction between wrongful private acts and deprivation of civil rights, Bradley provided several specific examples:

> An individual cannot deprive a man of his right to vote, to hold property, to buy and sell, to sue in the courts, or to be a witness or a juror; he may, by force or fraud, interfere with the enjoyment of the right in a particular case; he may commit an assault against the person, or commit murder, or use ruffian violence at the polls, or slander the good name of a fellow citizen; but, unless protected in these wrongful acts by some shield of State law or State authority, he cannot destroy or injure the right; he will only render himself amenable to satisfaction or punishment ... [according to] the laws of the State where the wrongful acts are committed.

In sum, an individual's civil rights could not be de-

stroyed by the acts of others. Any damage done had to be handled as a crime by the state where the offense had occurred.

Bradley also rejected the argument that the Thirteenth Amendment allowed Congress to pass the Civil Rights Act, since denial of access to public accommodations did not constitute slavery. According to the Court, such a broad construction of the Thirteenth Amendment would run "the slavery argument into the ground to make it apply to every act of discrimination." Bradley then went on to assert:

> When a man has emerged from slavery, and by the aid of beneficent legislation has shaken off the inseparable concomitants of that state, there must be some stage in the progress of his elevation when he takes the rank of a mere citizen, and ceases to be the special favorite of the laws, and when his rights as a citizen, or a man, are to be protected in the ordinary modes by which other men's rights are protected.

Gone from the Civil Rights Cases majority opinion was the generous spirit of Bradley's circuit-court opinion in an antecedent to the *Slaughterhouse Cases*. In 1870, three years before the Supreme Court struck down the privileges and immunities clause of the Fourteenth Amendment in the *Slaughterhouse Cases* ruling, Bradley had issued judicial relief for a "flagrant case of violation of the fundamental rights of labor" in *Livestock Dealers' & Butchers Association v. Crescent City Live-Stock Landing & Slaughterhouse Co., et al.,* often called the *Crescent City Case*. Here he had reasoned that where the Constitution "has provided a remedy, we ought not to shrink from granting the appropriate relief." Gone, too, was Bradley's earlier view that Congress had been authorized to enforce the Fourteenth Amendment with "appropriate legislation." Gone was the perception that "those who framed the article were not themselves aware" of its breadth. Gone was the belief that the Fourteenth Amendment went beyond the "privileges and immunities" of the original Constitution and embraced potentially far more. Gone was the principle that "the privileges and immunities of all citizens shall be absolutely unabridged, unimpaired." Gone as well was the conviction of Bradley's opinion in *United States v. Cruikshank,* which stated "that Congress has the power to secure [the rights of Blacks] not only as against the unfriendly operation of state laws, but against outrage . . . on the part of individuals, irrespective of state laws."

## John Marshall Harlan: Dissent

Justice John Marshall Harlan was the sole justice who dissented from the majority opinion. Although Justice Bradley had forsaken the pro–civil rights stance of his *Crescent City Case* opinion and *Slaughterhouse Cases* dissent, Justice Harlan used Bradley's reasoning in those cases as a starting point for his dissent in the *Civil Rights Cases*. While by the 1880s many Republicans had abandoned Radical Reconstruction and the extension of civil rights, Harlan had grown more committed to alleviating the plight of African Americans. Few, if any, nineteenth-century Supreme Court opinions have proved to be more prescient or memorable than Harlan's dissent in the *Civil Rights Cases*.

With a cherished pen and inkwell, the same pen that Chief Justice Roger Taney had used to write the majority opinion in *Dred Scott v. Sandford*, Harlan composed his dissent in the *Civil Rights Cases*. He forcefully rejected the majority opinion as "entirely too narrow and artificial," protesting that the Thirteenth Amendment gave Congress sufficient power to legislate beyond matters of bondage to address all "badges of slavery." At thirty-six pages and considerably longer than the majority opinion, Harlan's dissent characterized the *Civil Rights Cases* decision as at best tepid jurisprudential progress.

Harlan took aim at the Court majority's tandem mission with two goals of his own: a detailed critique of the view of congressional authority as "corrective" and recognition of "the enlarged powers conferred by the recent amendments upon the general government." He began his dissent with the observation that the Court had, in effect, sacrificed the recent Reconstruction Amendments (the Thirteenth, Fourteenth, and Fifteenth Amendments) to the Constitution and concluded, among other important points, that "the rights which Congress, by the act of 1875, endeavored to secure and protect are legal, not social rights."

Harlan stressed a number of Court decisions that conflicted with the majority opinion, particularly with respect to the Court's authority to overturn congressional legislation. In *Fletcher v. Peck*, the Court had maintained that to determine whether Congress had transgressed its constitutional power was "a question of much delicacy, which ought seldom, if ever, to be decided in the affirmative." In the *Sinking Fund Cases*—where railroad companies challenged a lower court injunction against them for trying to pay a stock dividend in alleged violation of recent legislation—the Court had held that declaring an act of Congress void "should never be made except in a clear case" and "every possible presumption is in favor of the validity of a statute." The Court's decision in *Prigg v. Commonwealth of Pennsylvania* held that "when the end is required the means are given" to Congress, though in that case "the end" had meant support for slavery and slaveholders. In *Ableman v. Booth*, the Court had sustained the constitutionality of the Fugitive Slave Act of 1850 "upon the implied power of Congress to enforce" the property claims of slaveholders. Harlan's point was that when slaveholders controlled the federal government, the Court had sustained the authority of Congress to legislate in favor of slavery; however, when it came to enforcement of the Constitution and civil rights in the years after Reconstruction, the Court was doing just the opposite—ruling to impede the legislative authority of Congress.

Perhaps the Court was at least a little embarrassed to be blocking civil rights legislation, especially once Harlan pointed out the litany of recent rulings that appeared to contradict the majority opinion. According to the Court in *Strauder v. West Virginia* and *Ex parte Virginia*, the purpose of the Reconstruction Amendments "was to raise the colored race from that condition of inferiority . . . into perfect equality of civil rights." In both *United States v. Cruikshank* and *United States v. Reese*, the Court had held that the Fifteenth Amendment "invested the citizens of the United States with a new constitutional right, which is exemption from discrimination" and that "the right to vote comes from the States; but the right of exemption from the prohibited discrimination comes from the United States."

According to Harlan, "exemption from discrimination . . . is a new constitutional right" conferred by the nation; Congress shall provide for the "form and manner" of protecting this right. Overwhelmed by the Court's contradictions and conservatism, Harlan posed this question: "Are the powers of the national legislature to be restrained in proportion as the rights and privileges, derived from the nation, are valuable?" One can sense Harlan's extreme frustration with the Court in his concluding comment:

The one underlying purpose of congressional legislation has been to enable the Black race to take the rank of mere citizens. The difficulty has been to compel a recognition of the legal right of the Black race to take the rank of citizens, and to secure the enjoyment of privileges belonging, under the law, to them as a component part of the people for whose welfare and happiness government is ordained.

If the Court had wanted to protect civil rights, legal precedent already existed. In his presentation to the justices, Solicitor General Phillips brought up *Munn v. Illinois* (1876), in which the Court had held that government regulation of privately owned grain elevators was "necessary for the public good" and had also affirmed broad police powers for government: "Under the powers inherent in every sovereignty, a government may regulate the conduct of its citizens toward each other." In his *Civil Rights Cases* dissent, Justice Harlan likewise observed that in *Munn v. Illinois* the Court had ruled that private property is no longer only a private concern when it becomes "affected with a public interest." Accordingly, the Court might well have viewed inns and railroads as public enterprises and thus under the purview of Congress.

Moreover, the Court could have looked to the commerce clause of the Constitution (Article I, Section 8). Justice Harlan noted just that regarding the Robinson case: "Might not the act of 1875 be maintained in that case, as applicable at least to commerce between the States, notwithstanding [that] it does not . . . profess to have been passed . . . to regulate commerce?" When Salmon Chase was chief justice from 1864 to 1873, the Court did not alter the interpretation of the commerce clause. In the *Civil Rights Cases* majority opinion, Justice Bradley acknowledged that "Congress is clothed with direct and plenary powers of legislation" under the commerce clause. However, he did not appear to accept that the three Reconstruction Amendments bolstered Congress's legislative plenary powers. Thus, Bradley dismissed whether inns and public conveyances were encompassed under Congress's legislative authority under the commerce clause as "a question which is not now before us." Nevertheless, the Court could have found the Civil Rights Act of 1875 constitutional under the commerce clause, especially in light of its *Munn v. Illinois* ruling.

That Bradley interpreted the Fourteenth Amendment as merely "corrective" elicited Harlan's harshest criticism.

Harlan observed that the entire amendment hardly assumed what Bradley claimed was an exclusively negative or "corrective" form simply because of the clause in Section 1 beginning with "no state shall." The historian Carter Woodson offered this candid assessment: "The court was too evasive or too stupid to observe that the first clause of this amendment was an affirmative. . . . Such sophistry deserves the condemnation of all fair-minded people." The Court also might have interpreted the Civil Rights Act and the Reconstruction Amendments in light of factors such as history and legislative intent. Or as Harlan put it, borrowing from an old adage: "It is not the words of the law but the internal sense of it that makes the law; the letter of the law is the body; the sense and reason of the law is the soul."

## Impact

The *Civil Rights Cases* decision closed the first chapter of the civil rights struggle in the United States. The majority ruling negated Section 5 of the Fourteenth Amendment, which had mandated Congress to enforce the amendment with "appropriate legislation." Yet again, the Court abrogated Congress's ability to protect and enforce civil liberties, as it had already previously ruled in the *Reese, Cruikshank,* and *Harris* cases. This ruling was as much a setback for Congress as it was for African Americans. With this fierce gesture, the Court applied the brakes on the development of national government and the extension of civil rights.

News of the Court's decision elicited a mixture of smugness and indifference to the principle of equal protection. The *Atlanta Constitution* reported:

> We do not hope to compass with words the deep and perfect satisfaction with which the decision of the United States Supreme Court on the Civil-Rights Bill will be received throughout the South. . . . It was against the mischievous intrusion of the negro into places set apart for white people that we protested.

Frederick Douglass saw the mischief elsewhere: "The decision is to the direction and interest of the Old Calhoun doctrine of State rights as against Federal authority. . . . The decision has resulted largely from confusing social with civil rights." The *Chicago Tribune* agreed with Douglass: "The Constitution in its present shape does not warrant Congressional regulation of social affairs . . . which individuals regulate to suit themselves." The *Washington Post* published statements attributed to Lee Nance, "an intelligent and well-informed colored resident of this city," who was quoted as having said, "'I would say that I am bothered more about where and how I can get enough money with which to pay for a good, square meal, than I am about where I will eat it.'" The *Post* then editorialized that "there are other issues of more concern to the colored people . . . than the social and sentimental questions passed upon by the court." While acknowledging the existence of prejudice against African Americans, *Harper's Weekly* maintained: "Colored citizens . . . need not regret the fate of the Civil Rights Bill. The wrongs under which they suffer are not to be remedied by law."

From the perspective of more than one well-respected editor, the Civil Rights Act of 1875 never had a chance. *The Nation* under the editor E. L. Godkin had championed civil rights for African Americans, but by 1883 Godkin, like much of the rest of America, had grown weary of the fight. On October 18, 1883, the magazine published this assessment:

> The Act was forced through Congress. . . . It was as clear then as it is now to almost every candid-minded man, that the Fourteenth Amendment, on which the promoters of the Act professed to base it, was really directed against State legislation, and not against the acts of individuals. . . . The Civil Rights Act was really

rather an admonition, or statement of moral obligation, than a legal command. Probably nine-tenths of those who voted for it knew very well that whenever it came before the Supreme Court it would be torn to pieces.

The *Cleveland Gazette* perhaps offered the most succinct, if solemn, pronouncement: The Civil Rights Bill "lingered unconsciously nearly nine years and died on the 15th of October, 1883."

The Court's narrow reading of the Fourteenth Amendment in the *Civil Rights Cases* decision destroyed movements toward integration and helped usher in racial segregation that would continue through the post–World War II years in much of the United States. That Justice Bradley and his colleagues did not view segregation as a "badge of slavery" brings up the question that if segregation is not such a badge, what is? The Court's ruling erased civil rights enforcement from the Republican agenda and mandated federal withdrawal from civil rights enforcement, a policy that would not begin to be reversed until well after World War II. Interestingly, when framing the Civil Rights Act of 1964, Congress relied on its powers under the commerce clause of the Constitution—one of the same arguments brought up by Justice Harlan in his famous dissent in the Civil Rights Cases. In passing the Civil Rights Act of 1964, Congress circumvented not only the legal precedent of the Civil Rights Cases decision but also the Supreme Court's limitation on congressional power to enforce "equal protection" under the law.

---

## Questions for Further Study

1. In what ways did the Court's decision in the *Civil Rights Cases* undermine the protections the Fourteenth Amendment to the U.S. Constitution afforded African Americans?

2. Using this document alongside the Thirteenth Amendment, the Fourteenth Amendment, the Fifteenth Amendment, the Ku Klux Klan Act, and *United States v. Cruikshank*, prepare a time line of fifteen key events from 1865 to 1883 that affected African Americans. Be prepared to defend your choices.

3. What was the basis of the Court's reasoning in ruling as it did in the *Civil Rights Cases*?

4. What factors in the social, economic, or political environment might have led the Supreme Court to rule as it did in the *Civil Rights Cases*?

## Further Reading

### Books

Beatty, Jack. *Age of Betrayal: The Triumph of Money in America, 1865–1900.* New York: Alfred A. Knopf, 2007.

Blackmon, Douglas A. *Slavery by Another Name: The Re-Enslavement of Black Americans from the Civil War to World War II,* New York: Anchor Books, 2009.

Elliott, Mark. *Color-Blind Justice: Albion Tourgée and the Quest for Racial Equality from the Civil War to Plessy v. Ferguson.* New York: Oxford University Press, 2006.

Garraty, John A., ed. *Quarrels That Have Shaped the Constitution.* New York: Harper & Row, 1964.

Miller, Loren. *The Petitioners: The Story of the Supreme Court of the United States and the Negro.* New York: Pantheon Books, 1966.

Urofsky, Melvin I., and Paul Finkelman. *A March of Liberty: A Constitutional History of the United States.* Vol. 1: *From the Founding to 1890.* 2nd ed. New York: Oxford University Press, 2002.

### Articles

Frantz, Laurent B. "Congressional Power to Enforce the Fourteenth Amendment against Private Acts." *Yale Law Journal* 73, no. 8 (July 1964): 1353–1384.

Hartz, Louis. "John M. Harlan in Kentucky, 1855–1877: The Story of His Pre-Court Career." *Filson Club History Quarterly* 14 (January 1940): 17–40.

Lado, Marianne L. Engelman. "A Question of Justice: African-American Legal Perspectives on the 1883 Civil Rights Cases." *Chicago-Kent Law Review* 70 (1995): 1123–1195.

McPherson, James M. "Abolitionists and the Civil Rights Act of 1875." *Journal of American History* 52, no. 3 (December 1965): 493–510.

Robinson, S. "African American Citizenship, the 1883 Civil Rights Cases and the Creation of the Jim Crow South." *History* 102, (March 2017): 225–241.

Scott, John Anthony. "Justice Bradley's Evolving Concept of the Fourteenth Amendment from the Slaughterhouse Cases to the Civil Rights Cases." *Rutgers Law Review* 25 (Summer 1971): 552–569.

Woodson, Carter. "Fifty Years of Negro Citizenship as Qualified by the United States Supreme Court." *Journal of Negro History* 6, no. 1 (January 1921): 1–53.

### Websites

"Civil Rights Cases, 1883." C-Span website. Accessed March 1, 2023, https://landmarkcases.c-span.org/Case/17/Civil-Rights-Cases.

—Commentary by R. Owen Williams and Lisa Paddock

# CIVIL RIGHTS CASES

## Document Text

### MR. JUSTICE BRADLEY delivered the opinion of the Court

After stating the facts in the above language, he continued:

It is obvious that the primary and important question in all the cases is the constitutionality of the law, for if the law is unconstitutional, none of the prosecutions can stand.

The sections of the law referred to provide as follows:

"SEC. 1. That all persons within the jurisdiction of the United States shall be entitled to the full and equal enjoyment of the accommodations, advantages, facilities, and privileges of inns, public conveyances on land or water, theatres, and other places of public amusement, subject only to the conditions and limitations established by law and applicable alike to citizens of every race and color, regardless of any previous condition of servitude."

"SEC. 2. That any person who shall violate the foregoing section by denying to any citizen, except for reasons by law applicable to citizens of every race and color, and regardless of any previous condition of servitude, the full enjoyment of any of the accommodations, advantages, facilities, or privileges in said section enumerated, or by aiding or inciting such denial, shall for every such offence, forfeit and pay the sum of five hundred dollars to the person aggrieved thereby, to be recovered in an action of debt, with full costs, and shall also, for every such offence, be deemed guilty of

a misdemeanor, and, upon conviction thereof, shall be fined not less than five hundred nor more than one thousand dollars, or shall be imprisoned not less than thirty days nor more than one year, *Provided,* That all persons may elect to sue for the penalty aforesaid, or to proceed under their rights at common law and by State statutes, and having so elected to proceed in the one mode or the other, their right to proceed in the other jurisdiction shall be barred. But this provision shall not apply to criminal proceedings, either under this act or the criminal law of any State; *and provided further,* that a judgment for the penalty in favor of the party aggrieved, or a judgment upon an indictment, shall be a bar to either prosecution respectively."

Are these sections constitutional? The first section, which is the principal one, cannot be fairly understood without attending to the last clause, which qualifies the preceding part.

The essence of the law is not to declare broadly that all persons shall be entitled to the full and equal enjoyment of the accommodations, advantages, facilities, and privileges of inns, public conveyances, and theatres, but that such enjoyment shall not be subject to any conditions applicable only to citizens of a particular race or color, or who had been in a previous condition of servitude. In other words, it is the purpose of the law to declare that, in the enjoyment of the accommodations and privileges of inns, public conveyances, theatres, and other places of public amusement, no distinction shall be made between citizens of different race or color or between those who have, and those who have not, been slaves. Its effect is to declare that, in all inns, public conveyances, and places of amusement, colored citizens, whether formerly slaves or not, and citizens of other races, shall have the same accommodations and privileges in all inns, public conveyances, and places of amusement as are enjoyed by white citizens, and vice versa. The second section makes it a penal offence in any person to deny to any citizen of any race or color, regardless of previous servitude, any of the accommodations or privileges mentioned in the first section.

Has Congress constitutional power to make such a law? Of course, no one will contend that the power to pass it was contained in the Constitution before the adoption of the last three amendments. The power is sought, first, in the Fourteenth Amendment, and the views and arguments of distinguished Senators, advanced whilst the law was under consideration, claiming authority to pass it by virtue of that amendment, are the principal arguments adduced in favor of the power. We have carefully considered those arguments, as was due to the eminent ability of those who put them forward, and have felt, in all its force, the weight of authority which always invests a law that Congress deems itself competent to pass. But the responsibility of an independent judgment is now thrown upon this court, and we are bound to exercise it according to the best lights we have.

The first section of the Fourteenth Amendment (which is the one relied on), after declaring who shall be citizens of the United States, and of the several States, is prohibitory in its character, and prohibitory upon the States. It declares that:

"No State shall make or enforce any law which shall abridge the privileges or immunities of citizens of the United States; nor shall any State deprive any person of life, liberty, or property without due process of law; nor deny to any person within its jurisdiction the equal protection of the laws."

It is State action of a particular character that is prohibited. Individual invasion of individual rights is not the subject matter of the amendment. It has a deeper and broader scope. It nullifies and makes void all State legislation, and State action of every kind, which impairs the privileges and immunities of citizens of the United States or which injures them in life, liberty or property

without due process of law, or which denies to any of them the equal protection of the laws. It not only does this, but, in order that the national will, thus declared, may not be a mere *brutum fulmen*, the last section of the amendment invests Congress with power to enforce it by appropriate legislation. To enforce what? To enforce the prohibition. To adopt appropriate legislation for correcting the effects of such prohibited State laws and State acts, and thus to render them effectually null, void, and innocuous. This is the legislative power conferred upon Congress, and this is the whole of it. It does not invest Congress with power to legislate upon subjects which are within the domain of State legislation, but to provide modes of relief against State legislation, or State action, of the kind referred to. It does not authorize Congress to create a code of municipal law for the regulation of private rights, but to provide modes of redress against the operation of State laws and the action of State officers executive or judicial when these are subversive of the fundamental rights specified in the amendment. Positive rights and privileges are undoubtedly secured by the Fourteenth Amendment, but they are secured by way of prohibition against State laws and State proceedings affecting those rights and privileges, and by power given to Congress to legislate for the purpose of carrying such prohibition into effect, and such legislation must necessarily be predicated upon such supposed State laws or State proceedings, and be directed to the correction of their operation and effect. A quite full discussion of this aspect of the amendment may be found in *United Sates v. Cruikshank*, 92 U. S. 542; *Virginia v. Rives*, 100 U. S. 313, and *Ex parte Virginia*, 100 U. S. 339.

An apt illustration of this distinction may be found in some of the provisions of the original Constitution. Take the subject of contracts, for example. The Constitution prohibited the States from passing any law impairing the obligation of contracts. This did not give to Congress power to provide laws for the general enforcement of contracts, nor power to invest the courts of the United States with jurisdiction over contracts, so as to enable parties to sue upon them in those courts. It did, however, give the power to provide remedies by which the impairment of contracts by State legislation might be counteracted and corrected, and this power was exercised. The remedy which Congress actually provided was that contained in the 25th section of the Judiciary Act of 1789, 1 Stat. 8, giving to the Supreme Court of the United States jurisdiction by writ of error to review the final decisions of State courts whenever they should sustain the validity of a State statute or authority alleged to be repugnant to the Constitution or laws of the United States. By this means, if a State law was passed impairing the obligation of a contract and the State tribunals sustained the validity of the law, the mischief could be corrected in this court. The legislation of Congress, and the proceedings provided for under it, were corrective in their character. No attempt was made to draw into the United States courts the litigation of contracts generally, and no such attempt would have been sustained. We do not say that the remedy provided was the only one that might have been provided in that case. Probably Congress had power to pass a law giving to the courts of the United States direct jurisdiction over contracts alleged to be impaired by a State law, and under the broad provisions of the act of March 3d 1875, ch. 137, 18 Stat. 470, giving to the circuit courts jurisdiction of all cases arising under the Constitution and laws of the United States, it is possible that such jurisdiction now exists. But under that, or any other law, it must appear as well by allegation, as proof at the trial, that the Constitution had been violated by the action of the State legislature. Some obnoxious State law passed, or that might be passed, is necessary to be assumed in order to lay the foundation of any federal remedy in the case, and for the very sufficient reason that the constitutional prohibition is against *State laws* impairing the obligation of contracts.

And so, in the present case, until some State law has been passed, or some State action through its officers or agents has been taken, adverse to the rights of citizens sought to be protected by the Fourteenth Amendment, no legislation of the United States under said amendment, nor any proceeding under such legislation, can be called into activity, for the prohibitions of the amendment are against State laws and acts done under State authority. Of course, legislation may, and should, be provided in advance to meet the exigency when it arises, but it should be adapted to the mischief and wrong which the amendment was intended to provide against, and that is State laws, or State action of some kind, adverse to the rights of the citizen secured by the amendment. Such legislation cannot properly cover the whole domain of rights appertaining to life, liberty and property, defining them and pro-

viding for their vindication. That would be to establish a code of municipal law regulative of all private rights between man and man in society. It would be to make Congress take the place of the State legislatures and to supersede them. It is absurd to affirm that, because the rights of life, liberty, and property (which include all civil rights that men have) are, by the amendment, sought to be protected against invasion on the part of the State without due process of law, Congress may therefore provide due process of law for their vindication in every case, and that, because the denial by a State to any persons of the equal protection of the laws is prohibited by the amendment, therefore Congress may establish laws for their equal protection. In fine, the legislation which Congress is authorized to adopt in this behalf is not general legislation upon the rights of the citizen, but corrective legislation, that is, such as may be necessary and proper for counteracting such laws as the States may adopt or enforce, and which, by the amendment, they are prohibited from making or enforcing, or such acts and proceedings as the States may commit or take, and which, by the amendment, they are prohibited from committing or taking. It is not necessary for us to state, if we could, what legislation would be proper for Congress to adopt. It is sufficient for us to examine whether the law in question is of that character.

An inspection of the law shows that it makes no reference whatever to any supposed or apprehended violation of the Fourteenth Amendment on the part of the States. It is not predicated on any such view. It proceeds *ex directo* to declare that certain acts committed by individuals shall be deemed offences, and shall be prosecuted and punished by proceedings in the courts of the United States. It does not profess to be corrective of any constitutional wrong committed by the States; it does not make its operation to depend upon any such wrong committed. It applies equally to cases arising in States which have the justest laws respecting the personal rights of citizens, and whose authorities are ever ready to enforce such laws, as to those which arise in States that may have violated the prohibition of the amendment. In other words, it steps into the domain of local jurisprudence, and lays down rules for the conduct of individuals in society towards each other, and imposes sanctions for the enforcement of those rules, without referring in any manner to any supposed action of the State or its authorities.

If this legislation is appropriate for enforcing the prohibitions of the amendment, it is difficult to see where it is to stop. Why may not Congress, with equal show of authority, enact a code of laws for the enforcement and vindication of all rights of life, liberty, and property? If it is supposable that the States may deprive persons of life, liberty, and property without due process of law (and the amendment itself does suppose this), why should not Congress proceed at once to prescribe due process of law for the protection of every one of these fundamental rights, in every possible case, as well as to prescribe equal privileges in inns, public conveyances, and theatres? The truth is that the implication of a power to legislate in this manner is based upon the assumption that, if the States are forbidden to legislate or act in a particular way on a particular subject, and power is conferred upon Congress to enforce the prohibition, this gives Congress power to legislate generally upon that subject, and not merely power to provide modes of redress against such State legislation or action. The assumption is certainly unsound. It is repugnant to the Tenth Amendment of the Constitution, which declares that powers not delegated to the United States by the Constitution, nor prohibited by it to the States, are reserved to the States respectively or to the people.

We have not overlooked the fact that the fourth section of the act now under consideration has been held by this court to be constitutional. That section declares

"that no citizen, possessing all other qualifications which are or may be prescribed by law, shall be disqualified for service as grand or petit juror in any court of the United States, or of any State, on account of race, color, or previous condition of servitude, and any officer or other person charged with any duty in the selection or summoning of jurors who shall exclude or fail to summon any citizen for the cause aforesaid, shall, on conviction thereof, be deemed guilty of a misdemeanor, and be fined not more than five thousand dollars."

In *Ex parte Virginia,* 100 U. S. 339, it was held that an indictment against a State officer under this section for excluding persons of color from the jury list is sustainable. But a moment's attention to its terms will show that the section is entirely corrective in its character. Disqualifications for service on juries are only created by the law, and the first part of the section is aimed at certain disqualifying laws, namely, those which make mere race or color a disqualification, and the second clause is directed against those who, assuming to use the authority of the State government, carry into effect such a rule of disqualification. In the Virginia case, the State, through its officer, enforced a rule of disqualification which the law was intended to abrogate and counteract. Whether the statute book of the State actually laid down any such rule of disqualification or not, the State, through its officer, enforced such a rule, and it is against such State action, through its officers and agents, that the last clause of the section is directed.

This aspect of the law was deemed sufficient to divest it of any unconstitutional character, and makes it differ widely from the first and second sections of the same act which we are now considering.

These sections, in the objectionable features before referred to, are different also from the law ordinarily called the "Civil Rights Bill," originally passed April 9th, 1866, 14 Stat. 27, ch. 31, and reenacted with some modifications in sections 16, 17, 18, of the Enforcement Act, passed ay 31st, 1870, 16 Stat. 140, ch. 114. That law, as reenacted, after declaring that all persons within the jurisdiction of the United States shall have the same right in every State and Territory to make and enforce contracts, to sue, be parties, give evidence, and to the full and equal benefit of all laws and proceedings for the security of persons and property as is enjoyed by white citizens, and shall be subject to like punishment, pains, penalties, taxes, licenses and exactions of every kind, and none other, any law, statute, ordinance, regulation or custom to the contrary notwithstanding, proceeds to enact that any person who, under color of any law, statute, ordinance, regulation or custom, shall subject, or cause to be subjected, any inhabitant of any State or Territory to the deprivation of any rights secured or protected by the preceding section (above quoted), or to different punishment, pains, or penalties, on account of such person's being an alien, or by reason of his color or race, than is prescribed for the punishment of citizens, shall be deemed guilty of a misdemeanor, and subject to fine and imprisonment as specified in the act. This law is clearly corrective in its character, intended to counteract and furnish redress against State laws and proceedings, and customs having the force of law, which sanction the wrongful acts specified. In the Revised Statutes, it is true, a very important clause, to-wit, the words "any law, statute, ordinance, regulation or custom to the contrary notwithstanding," which gave the declaratory section its point and effect, are omitted; but the penal part, by which the declaration is enforced, and which is really the effective part of the law, retains the reference to State laws by making the penalty apply only to those who should subject parties to a deprivation of their rights under color of any statute, ordinance, custom, etc., of any State or Territory, thus preserving the corrective character of the legislation. Rev. St. §§ 177, 1978, 1979, 5510. The Civil Rights Bill here referred to is analogous in its character to what a law would have been under the original Constitution, declaring that the validity of contracts should not be impaired, and that, if any person bound by a contract should refuse to comply with it, under color or pretence that it had been rendered void or invalid by a State law, he should be liable to an action upon it in the courts of the United States, with the addition of a penalty for setting up such an unjust and unconstitutional defence.

In this connection, it is proper to state that civil rights, such as are guaranteed by the Constitution against State aggression, cannot be impaired by the wrongful acts of individuals, unsupported by State authority in the shape of laws, customs, or judicial or executive proceedings. The wrongful act of an individual, unsupported by any such authority, is simply a private wrong, or a crime of that individual; an invasion of the rights of the injured party, it is true, whether they affect his person, his property, or his reputation; but if not sanctioned in some way by the State, or not done under State authority, his rights remain in full force, and may presumably be vindicated by resort to the laws of the State for redress. An individual cannot deprive a man of his right to vote, to hold property, to buy and sell, to sue in the courts, or to be a witness or a juror; he may, by force or fraud, interfere with the enjoyment of the right in a particular case; he may commit an assault against the person, or commit murder, or use ruffian violence at the polls, or slander the good name of a fellow citizen; but, unless protected in these wrongful acts by some shield of State law or State authority, he cannot destroy or injure the right; he will only render himself amenable to satisfaction or punishment, and amenable therefor to the laws of the State where the wrongful acts are committed. Hence, in all those cases where the Constitution seeks to protect the rights of the citizen against discriminative and unjust laws of the State by prohibiting such laws, it is not individual

offences, but abrogation and denial of rights, which it denounces and for which it clothes the Congress with power to provide a remedy. This abrogation and denial of rights for which the States alone were or could be responsible was the great seminal and fundamental wrong which was intended to be remedied. And the remedy to be provided must necessarily be predicated upon that wrong. It must assume that, in the cases provided for, the evil or wrong actually committed rests upon some State law or State authority for its excuse and perpetration.

Of course, these remarks do not apply to those cases in which Congress is clothed with direct and plenary powers of legislation over the whole subject, accompanied with an express or implied denial of such power to the States, as in the regulation of commerce with foreign nations, among the several States, and with the Indian tribes, the coining of money, the establishment of post offices and post roads, the declaring of war, etc. In these cases, Congress has power to pass laws for regulating the subjects specified in every detail, and the conduct and transactions of individuals in respect thereof. But where a subject is not submitted to the general legislative power of Congress, but is only submitted thereto for the purpose of rendering effective some prohibition against particular State legislation or State action in reference to that subject, the power given is limited by its object, and any legislation by Congress in the matter must necessarily be corrective in its character, adapted to counteract and redress the operation of such prohibited State laws or proceedings of State officers.

If the principles of interpretation which we have laid down are correct, as we deem them to be (and they are in accord with the principles laid down in the cases before referred to, as well as in the recent case of *United States v. Harris*, 106 U. S. 629), it is clear that the law in question cannot be sustained by any grant of legislative power made to Congress by the Fourteenth Amendment. That amendment prohibits the States from denying to any person the equal protection of the laws, and declares that Congress shall have power to enforce, by appropriate legislation, the provisions of the amendment. The law in question, without any reference to adverse State legislation on the subject, declares that all persons shall be entitled to equal accommodations and privileges of inns, public conveyances, and places of public amusement, and imposes a penalty upon any individual who shall deny to any citizen such equal accommodations and privileges. This is not corrective legislation; it is primary and direct; it takes immediate and absolute possession of the subject of the right of admission to inns, public conveyances, and places of amusement. It supersedes and displaces State legislation on the same subject, or only allows it permissive force. It ignores such legislation, and assumes that the matter is one that belongs to the domain of national regulation. Whether it would not have been a more effective protection of the rights of citizens to have clothed Congress with plenary power over the whole subject is not now the question. What we have to decide is whether such plenary power has been conferred upon Congress by the Fourteenth Amendment, and, in our judgment, it has not.

We have discussed the question presented by the law on the assumption that a right to enjoy equal accommodation and privileges in all inns, public conveyances, and places of public amusement is one of the essential rights of the citizen which no State can abridge or interfere with. Whether it is such a right or not is a different question which, in the view we have taken of the validity of the law on the ground already stated, it is not necessary to examine.

We have also discussed the validity of the law in reference to cases arising in the States only, and not in reference to cases arising in the Territories or the District of Columbia, which are subject to the plenary legislation of Congress in every branch of municipal regulation. Whether the law would be a valid one as applied to the Territories and the District is not a question for consideration in the cases before us, they all being cases arising within the limits of States. And whether Congress, in the exercise of its power to regulate commerce amongst the several States, might or might not pass a law regulating rights in public conveyances passing from one State to another is also a question which is not now before us, as the sections in question are not conceived in any such view. But the power of Congress to adopt direct and primary, as distinguished from corrective, legislation on the subject in hand is sought, in the second place, from the Thirteenth Amendment, which abolishes slavery. This amendment declares

"that neither slavery, nor involuntary servitude, except as a punishment for crime, whereof the party shall have been duly convicted, shall exist within the United States, or any place subject to their jurisdiction,"

and it gives Congress power to enforce the amendment by appropriate legislation.

This amendment, as well as the Fourteenth, is undoubtedly self-executing, without any ancillary legislation, so far as its terms are applicable to any existing state of circumstances. By its own unaided force and effect, it abolished slavery and established universal freedom. Still, legislation may be necessary and proper to meet all the various cases and circumstances to be affected by it, and to prescribe proper modes of redress for its violation in letter or spirit. And such legislation may be primary and direct in its character, for the amendment is not a mere prohibition of State laws establishing or upholding slavery, but an absolute declaration that slavery or involuntary servitude shall not exist in any part of the United States.

It is true that slavery cannot exist without law, any more than property in lands and goods can exist without law, and, therefore, the Thirteenth Amendment may be regarded as nullifying all State laws which establish or uphold slavery. But it has a reflex character also, establishing and decreeing universal civil and political freedom throughout the United States, and it is assumed that the power vested in Congress to enforce the article by appropriate legislation clothes Congress with power to pass all laws necessary and proper for abolishing all badges and incidents of slavery in the United States, and, upon this assumption ,it is claimed that this is sufficient authority for declaring by law that all persons shall have equal accommodations and privileges in all inns, public conveyances, and places of amusement, the argument being that the denial of such equal accommodations and privileges is, in itself, a subjection to a species of servitude within the meaning of the amendment. Conceding the major proposition to be true, that Congress has a right to enact all necessary and proper laws for the obliteration and prevention of slavery with all its badges and incidents, is the minor proposition also true, that the denial to any person of admission to the accommodations and privileges of an inn, a public conveyance, or a theatre does subject that person to any form of servitude, or tend to fasten upon him any badge of slavery? If it does not, then power to pass the law is not found in the Thirteenth Amendment.

In a very able and learned presentation of the cognate question as to the extent of the rights, privileges and immunities of citizens which cannot rightfully be abridged by state laws under the Fourteenth Amendment, made in a former case, a long list of burdens and disabilities of a servile character, incident to feudal vassalage in France, and which were abolished by the decrees of the National Assembly, was presented for the purpose of showing that all inequalities and observances exacted by one man from another were servitudes or badges of slavery which a great nation, in its effort to establish universal liberty, made haste to wipe out and destroy. But these were servitudes imposed by the old law, or by long custom, which had the force of law, and exacted by one man from another without the latter's consent. Should any such servitudes be imposed by a state law, there can be no doubt that the law would be repugnant to the Fourteenth, no less than to the Thirteenth, Amendment, nor any greater doubt that Congress has adequate power to forbid any such servitude from being exacted.

But is there any similarity between such servitudes and a denial by the owner of an inn, a public conveyance, or a theatre of its accommodations and privileges to an individual, even though the denial be founded on the race or color of that individual? Where does any slavery or servitude, or badge of either, arise from such an act of denial? Whether it might not be a denial of a right which, if sanctioned by the state law, would be obnoxious to the prohibitions of the Fourteenth Amendment is another question. But what has it to do with the question of slavery?

It may be that, by the Black Code (as it was called), in the times when slavery prevailed, the proprietors of inns and public conveyances were forbidden to receive persons of the African race because it might assist slaves to escape from the control of their masters. This was merely a means of preventing such escapes, and was no part of the servitude itself. A law of that kind could not have any such object now, however justly it might be deemed an invasion of the party's legal right as a citizen, and amenable to the prohibitions of the Fourteenth Amendment.

The long existence of African slavery in this country gave us very distinct notions of what it was and what were its necessary incidents. Compulsory service of the slave for the benefit of the master, restraint of his movements except by the master's will, disability to hold property, to make contracts, to have a standing in court, to be a witness against a white person, and such like burdens and incapacities were the inseparable incidents of the institution. Severer punishments for crimes were imposed on the slave than on free persons guilty of the same offences. Congress, as we have seen, by the Civil Rights Bill of 1866, passed in view of the Thirteenth Amendment before the Fourteenth was adopted, undertook to wipe out these burdens and disabilities, the necessary incidents of slavery constituting its substance and visible form, and to secure to all citizens of every race and color, and without regard to previous servitude, those fundamental rights which are the essence of civil freedom, namely, the same right to make and enforce contracts, to sue, be parties, give evidence, and to inherit, purchase, lease, sell and convey property as is enjoyed by white citizens. Whether this legislation was fully authorized by the Thirteenth Amendment alone, without the support which it afterward received from the Fourteenth Amendment, after the adoption of which it was reenacted with some additions, it is not necessary to inquire. It is referred to for the purpose of showing that, at that time (in 1866), Congress did not assume, under the authority given by the Thirteenth Amendment, to adjust what may be called the social rights of men and races in the community, but only to declare and vindicate those fundamental rights which appertain to the essence of citizenship, and the enjoyment or deprivation of which constitutes the essential distinction between freedom and slavery.

We must not forget that the province and scope of the Thirteenth and Fourteenth amendments are different: the former simply abolished slavery; the latter prohibited the States from abridging the privileges or immunities of citizens of the United States, from depriving them of life, liberty, or property without due process of law, and from denying to any the equal protection of the laws. The amendments are different, and the powers of Congress under them are different. What Congress has power to do under one it may not have power to do under the other. Under the Thirteenth Amendment, it has only to do with slavery and its incidents. Under the Fourteenth Amendment, it has power to counteract and render nugatory all State laws and proceedings which have the effect to abridge any of the privileges or immunities of citizens of the

United States, or to deprive them of life, liberty or property without due process of law, or to deny to any of them the equal protection of the laws. Under the Thirteenth Amendment, the legislation, so far as necessary or proper to eradicate all forms and incidents of slavery and involuntary servitude, may be direct and primary, operating upon the acts of individuals, whether sanctioned by State legislation or not; under the Fourteenth, as we have already shown, it must necessarily be, and can only be, corrective in its character, addressed to counteract and afford relief against State regulations or proceedings.

The only question under the present head, therefore, is whether the refusal to any persons of the accommodations of an inn or a public conveyance or a place of public amusement by an individual, and without any sanction or support from any State law or regulation, does inflict upon such persons any manner of servitude or form of slavery as those terms are understood in this country? Many wrongs may be obnoxious to the prohibitions of the Fourteenth Amendment which are not, in any just sense, incidents or elements of slavery. Such, for example, would be the taking of private property without due process of law, or allowing persons who have committed certain crimes (horse stealing, for example) to be seized and hung by the *posse comitatus* without regular trial, or denying to any person, or class of persons, the right to pursue any peaceful avocations allowed to others. What is called class legislation would belong to this category, and would be obnoxious to the prohibitions of the Fourteenth Amendment, but would not necessarily be so to the Thirteenth, when not involving the idea of any subjection of one man to another. The Thirteenth Amendment has respect not to distinctions of race or class or color, but to slavery. The Fourteenth Amendment extends its protection to races and classes, and prohibits any State legislation which has the effect of denying to any race or class, or to any individual, the equal protection of the laws.

Now, conceding for the sake of the argument that the admission to an inn, a public conveyance, or a place of public amusement on equal terms with all other citizens is the right of every man and all classes of men, is it any more than one of those rights which the states, by the Fourteenth Amendment, are forbidden to deny to any person? And is the Constitution violated until the denial of the right has some State sanction or authority?

Can the act of a mere individual, the owner of the inn, the public conveyance or place of amusement, refusing the accommodation, be justly regarded as imposing any badge of slavery or servitude upon the applicant, or only as inflicting an ordinary civil injury, properly cognizable by the laws of the State and presumably subject to redress by those laws until the contrary appears?

After giving to these questions all the consideration which their importance demands, we are forced to the conclusion that such an act of refusal has nothing to do with slavery or involuntary servitude, and that, if it is violative of any right of the party, his redress is to be sought under the laws of the State, or, if those laws are adverse to his rights and do not protect him, his remedy will be found in the corrective legislation which Congress has adopted, or may adopt, for counteracting the effect of State laws or State action prohibited by the Fourteenth Amendment. It would be running the slavery argument into the ground to make it apply to every act of discrimination which a person may see fit to make as to the guests he will entertain, or as to the people he will take into his coach or cab or car, or admit to his concert or theatre, or deal with in other matters of intercourse or business. Innkeepers and public carriers, by the laws of all the States, so far as we are aware, are bound, to the extent of their facilities, to furnish proper accommodation to all unobjectionable persons who in good faith apply for them. If the laws themselves make any unjust discrimination amenable to the prohibitions of the Fourteenth Amendment, Congress has full power to afford a remedy under that amendment and in accordance with it.

When a man has emerged from slavery, and, by the aid of beneficent legislation, has shaken off the inseparable concomitants of that state, there must be some stage in the progress of his elevation when he takes the rank of a mere citizen and ceases to be the special favorite of the laws, and when his rights as a citizen or a man are to be protected in the ordinary modes by which other men's rights are protected. There were thousands of free colored people in this country before the abolition of slavery, enjoying all the essential rights of life, liberty and property the same as white citizens, yet no one at that time thought that it was any invasion of his personal status as a freeman because he was not admitted to all the privileges enjoyed by white citizens, or because he was subjected to discriminations in the enjoyment of accommodations in inns, public conveyances and places of amusement. Mere discriminations on account of race or color were not regarded as badges of slavery. If, since that time, the enjoyment of equal rights in all these respects has become established by constitutional enactment, it is not by force of the Thirteenth Amendment (which merely abolishes slavery), but by force of the Thirteenth and Fifteenth Amendments.

On the whole, we are of opinion that no countenance of authority for the passage of the law in question can be found in either the Thirteenth or Fourteenth Amendment of the Constitution, and no other ground of authority for its passage being suggested, it must necessarily be declared void, at least so far as its operation in the several States is concerned.

This conclusion disposes of the cases now under consideration. In the cases of the *United States v. Michael Ryan,* and of *Richard A. Robinson and Wife v. The Memphis & Charleston*

Page 109 U. S. 26

*Railroad Company,* the judgments must be affirmed. In the other cases, the answer to be given will be that the first and second sections of the act of Congress of March 1st, 1875, entitled "An Act to protect all citizens in their civil and legal rights," are unconstitutional and void, and that judgment should be rendered upon the several indictments in those cases accordingly.

*And it is so ordered.*

## MR. JUSTICE HARLAN dissenting

The opinion in these cases proceeds, it seems to me, upon grounds entirely too narrow and artificial. I cannot resist the conclusion that the substance and spirit of the recent amendments of the Constitution have been sacrificed by a subtle and ingenious verbal criticism.

"It is not the words of the law, but the internal sense of it that makes the law; the letter of the law is the body; the sense and reason of the law is the soul."

Constitutional provisions, adopted in the interest of liberty and for the purpose of securing, through national legislation, if need be, rights inhering in a state of freedom and belonging to American citizenship have been so construed as to defeat the ends the people desired to accomplish, which they attempted to accomplish, and which they supposed they had accomplished by

changes in their fundamental law. By this I do not mean that the determination of these cases should have been materially controlled by considerations of mere expediency or policy. I mean only, in this form, to express an earnest conviction that the court has departed from the familiar rule requiring, in the interpretation of constitutional provisions, that full effect be given to the intent with which they were adopted.

The purpose of the first section of the act of Congress of March 1, 1875, was to prevent race discrimination in respect of the accommodations and facilities of inns, public conveyances, and places of public amusement. It does not assume to define the general conditions and limitations under which inns, public conveyances, and places of public amusement may be conducted, but only declares that such conditions and limitations, whatever they may be, shall not be applied so as to work a discrimination solely because of race, color, or previous condition of servitude. The second section provides a penalty against anyone denying, or aiding or inciting the denial, of any citizen, of that equality of right given by the first section except for reasons by law applicable to citizens of every race or color and regardless of any previous condition of servitude.

There seems to be no substantial difference between my brethren and myself as to the purpose of Congress, for they say that the essence of the law is not to declare broadly that all persons shall be entitled to the full and equal enjoyment of the accommodations, advantages, facilities, and privileges of inns, public conveyances, and theatres, but that such enjoyment shall not be subject to conditions applicable only to citizens of a particular race or color, or who had been in a previous condition of servitude. The effect of the statute, the court says, is that colored citizens, whether formerly slaves or not, and citizens of other races shall have the same accommodations and privileges in all inns, public conveyances, and places of amusement as are enjoyed by white persons, and vice versa.

The court adjudges, I think erroneously, that Congress is without power, under either the Thirteenth or Fourteenth Amendment, to establish such regulations, and that the first and second sections of the statute are, in all their parts, unconstitutional and void.

Whether the legislative department of the government has transcended the limits of its constitutional powers, "is at all times," said this court in *Fletcher v. Peck*, 6 Cr. 128,

> "a question of much delicacy which ought seldom, if ever, to be decided in the affirmative in a doubtful case.... The opposition between the Constitution and the law should be such that the judge feels a clear and strong conviction of their incompatibility with each other."

More recently, in *Sinking Fund Cases*, 99 U. S. 718, we said:

> "It is our duty, when required in the regular course of judicial proceedings, to declare an act of Congress void if not within the legislative power of the United States, but this declaration should never be made except in a clear case. Every possible presumption is in favor of the validity of a statute, and this continues until the contrary is shown beyond a rational doubt. One branch of the government cannot encroach on the domain of another without danger. The safety of our institutions depends in no small degree on a strict observance of this salutary rule."

Before considering the language and scope of these amendments, it will be proper to recall the relations subsisting, prior to their adoption, between the national government and the institution of slavery, as indicated by the provisions of the Constitution, the legislation of Congress, and the decisions of this court. In this mode, we may obtain keys with which to open the mind of the people and discover the thought intended to be expressed.

In section 2 of article IV of the Constitution, it was provided that

> "no person held to service or labor in one State, under the laws thereof, escaping into another, shall, in consequence of any law or regulation therein, be discharged from such service or labor, but shall be delivered up on claim of the party to whom such service or labor may be due."

Under the authority of this clause, Congress passed the Fugitive Slave Law of 1793, establishing a mode for the recovery of fugitive slaves and prescribing a penalty against any person who should knowingly and will-ingly obstruct or hinder the master, his agent, or attorney in seizing, arresting, and recovering the fugitive, or who should rescue the fugitive from him, or who should harbor or conceal the slave after notice that he was a fugitive.

In *Prigg v. Commonwealth of Pennsylvania*, 16 Pet. 539, this court had occasion to define the powers and duties of Congress in reference to fugitives from labor. Speaking by MR. JUSTICE STORY, it laid down these propositions:

That a clause of the Constitution conferring a right should not be so construed as to make it shadowy or unsubstantial, or leave the citizen without a remedial power adequate for its protection when another construction equally accordant with the words and the sense in which they were used would enforce and protect the right granted;

That Congress is not restricted to legislation for the execution of its expressly granted powers, but, for the protection of rights guaranteed by the Constitution, may employ such means, not prohibited, as are necessary and proper, or such as are appropriate, to attain the ends proposed;

That the Constitution recognized the master's right of property in his fugitive slave, and, as incidental thereto, the right of seizing and recovering him, regardless of any State law or regulation or local custom whatsoever; and,

That the right of the master to have his slave, thus escaping, delivered up on claim, being guaranteed by the Constitution, the fair implication was that the national government was clothed with appropriate authority and functions to enforce it.

The court said

> "The fundamental principle, applicable to all cases of this sort, would seem to be that, when the end is required the means are given, and when the duty is enjoined, the ability to perform it is contemplated to exist on the part of the functionary to whom it is entrusted."

Again,

> "It would be a strange anomaly and forced construction to suppose that the national govern-

ment meant to rely for the due fulfillment of its own proper duties, and the rights which it intended to secure, upon State legislation, and not upon that of the Union. *A fortiori,* it would be more objectionable to suppose that a power which was to be the same throughout the Union should be confided to State sovereignty, which could not rightfully act beyond its own territorial limits "

The act of 1793 was, upon these grounds, adjudged to be a constitutional exercise of the powers of Congress.

It is to be observed from the report of Priggs' case that Pennsylvania, by her attorney general, pressed the argument that the obligation to surrender fugitive slaves was on the States and for the States, subject to the restriction that they should not pass laws or establish regulations liberating such fugitives; that the Constitution did not take from the States the right to determine the status of all persons within their respective jurisdictions; that it was for the State in which the alleged fugitive was found to determine, through her courts or in such modes as she prescribed, whether the person arrested was, in fact, a freeman or a fugitive slave; that the sole power of the general government in the premises was, by judicial instrumentality, to restrain and correct, not to forbid and prevent in the absence of hostile State action, and that, for the general government to assume primary authority to legislate on the subject of fugitive slaves, to the exclusion of the States, would be a dangerous encroachment on State sovereignty. But to such suggestions, this court turned a deaf ear, and adjudged that primary legislation by Congress to enforce the master's right was authorized by the Constitution.

We next come to the Fugitive Slave Act of 1850, the constitutionality of which rested, as did that of 1793, solely upon the implied power of Congress to enforce the master's rights. The provisions of that act were far in advance of previous legislation. They placed at the disposal of the master seeking to recover his fugitive slave substantially the whole power of the nation. It invested commissioners, appointed under the act, with power to summon the *posse comitatus* for the enforcement of its provisions, and commanded all good citizens to assist in its prompt and efficient execution whenever their services were required as part of the *posse comitatus.* Without going into the details of that act, it is

sufficient to say that Congress omitted from it nothing which the utmost ingenuity could suggest as essential to the successful enforcement of the master's claim to recover his fugitive slave. And this court, in *Ableman v. Booth,* 21 How. 506, adjudged it to be "in all of its provisions, fully authorized by the Constitution of the United States."

The only other case, prior to the adoption of the recent amendments, to which reference will be made, is that of *Dred Scott v. Sanford,* 19 How. 399. That case was instituted in a circuit court of the United States by Dred Scott, claiming to be a citizen of Missouri, the defendant being a citizen of another State. Its object was to assert the title of himself and family to freedom. The defendant pleaded in abatement that Scott—being of African descent, whose ancestors, of pure African blood, were brought into this country and sold as slaves—was not a citizen. The only matter in issue, said the court, was whether the descendants of slaves thus imported and sold, when they should be emancipated, or who were born of parents who had become free before their birth, are citizens of a State in the sense in which the word "citizen" is used in the Constitution of the United States.

In determining that question, the court instituted an inquiry as to who were citizens of the several States at the adoption of the Constitution and who at that time were recognized as the people whose rights and liberties had been violated by the British government. The result was a declaration by this court, speaking by Chief Justice Taney, that the legislation and histories of the times, and the language used in the Declaration of Independence, showed

> "that neither the class of persons who had been imported as slaves nor their descendants, whether they had become free or not, were then acknowledged as a part of the people, nor intended to be included in the general words used in that instrument;"

that

> "they had for more than a century before been regarded as beings of an inferior race, and altogether unfit to associate with the white race either in social or political relations, and so far inferior that they had no rights which the white man was bound to respect, and that the

negro might justly and lawfully be reduced to slavery for his benefit;"

that he was "bought and sold, and treated as an ordinary article of merchandise and traffic, whenever a profit could be made by it;" and, that

> "this opinion was at that time fixed and universal in the civilized portion of the white race. It was regarded as an axiom in morals, as well as in politics, which no one thought of disputing, or supposed to be open to dispute, and men in every grade and position in society daily and habitually acted upon it in their private pursuits, as well as in matters of public concern, without for a moment doubting the correctness of this opinion."

The judgment of the court was that the words "people of the United States" and "citizens" meant the same thing, both describing

> "the political body who, according to our republican institutions, form the sovereignty and hold the power and conduct the government through their representatives;"

that

"they are what we familiarly call the 'sovereign people,' and every citizen is one of this people and a constituent member of this sovereignty;"

but that the class of persons described in the plea in abatement did not compose a portion of this people, were not "included, and were not intended to be included, under the word *citizens' in the Constitution;" that, therefore, they could "claim none of the rights and privileges which that instrument provides for and secures to citizens of the United States;" that,*

> "on the contrary, they were at that time considered as a subordinate and inferior class of beings who had been subjugated by the dominant race and, whether emancipated or not, yet remained subject to their authority, and had no rights or privileges but such as those who held the power and the government might choose to grant them."

Such were the relations which formerly existed between the government, whether national or state, and the descendants, whether free or in bondage, of those of African blood who had been imported into this country and sold as slaves.

The first section of the Thirteenth Amendment provides that

> "neither slavery nor involuntary servitude, except as a punishment for crime, whereof the party shall have been duly convicted, shall exist within the United States, or any place subject to their jurisdiction."

Its second section declares that "Congress shall have power to enforce this article by appropriate legislation." This amendment was followed by the Civil Rights Act of April 9, 1866, which, among other things, provided that

> "all persons born in the United States, and not subject to any foreign power, excluding Indians not taxed, are hereby declared to be citizens of the United States."

14 Stat. 27. The power of Congress, in this mode, to elevate the enfranchised race to national citizenship was maintained by the supporters of the act of 1866 to be as full and complete as its power, by general statute, to make the children, being of full age, of persons naturalized in this country, citizens of the United States without going through the process of naturalization. The act of 1866 in this respect was also likened to that of 1843, in which Congress declared

> "that the Stockbridge tribe of Indians, and each and every one of them, shall be deemed to be and are hereby declared to be, citizens of the United States to all intents and purposes, and shall be entitled to all the rights, privileges, and immunities of such citizens, and shall in all respects be subject to the laws of the United States."

If the act of 1866 was valid in conferring national citizenship upon all embraced by its terms, then the colored race, enfranchised by the Thirteenth Amendment, became citizens of the United States prior to the adoption of the Fourteenth Amendment. But, in the view which I take of the present case, it is not necessary to examine this question.

The terms of the Thirteenth Amendment are absolute and universal. They embrace every race which then was, or might thereafter be, within the United States. No race, as such, can be excluded from the benefits or rights thereby conferred. Yet it is historically true that that amendment was suggested by the condition, in this country, of that race which had been declared by this court to have had—according to the opinion entertained by the most civilized portion of the white race at the time of the adoption of the Constitution—"no rights which the white man was bound to respect," none of the privileges or immunities secured by that instrument to citizens of the United States. It had reference, in peculiar sense, to a people which (although the larger part of them were in slavery) had been invited by an act of Congress to aid in saving from overthrow a government which, theretofore, by all of its departments, had treated them as an inferior race, with no legal rights or privileges except such as the white race might choose to grant them.

These are the circumstances under which the Thirteenth Amendment was proposed for adoption. They are now recalled only that we may better understand what was in the minds of the people when that amendment was considered, and what were the mischiefs to be remedied and the grievances to be redressed by its adoption.

We have seen that the power of Congress, by legislation, to enforce the master's right to have his slave delivered up on claim was *implied* from the recognition of that right in the national Constitution. But the power conferred by the Thirteenth Amendment does not rest upon implication or inference. Those who framed it were not ignorant of the discussion, covering many years of our country's history, as to the constitutional power of Congress to enact the Fugitive Slave Laws of 1793 and 1850. When, therefore, it was determined, by a change in the fundamental law, to uproot the institution of slavery wherever it existed in the land and to establish universal freedom, there was a fixed purpose to place the authority of Congress in the premises beyond the possibility of a doubt. Therefore, *ex industria,* power to enforce the Thirteenth Amendment by appropriate legislation was expressly granted. Legislation for that purpose, my brethren concede, may be direct and primary. But to what specific ends may it be directed? This court has uniformly held that the national government has the power, whether expressly given or not, to secure and protect rights conferred or guaranteed by the Constitution. *United States v. Reese,* 92 U. S. 214; *Strauder v. West Virginia,* 100 U. S. 303. That doctrine ought not now to be abandoned when the inquiry is not as to an implied power to protect the master's rights, but what may Congress, under powers expressly granted, do for the protection of freedom and the rights necessarily inhering in a state of freedom.

The Thirteenth Amendment, it is conceded, did something more than to prohibit slavery as an *institution* resting upon distinctions of race and upheld by positive law. My brethren admit that it established and decreed universal *civil freedom* throughout the United States. But did the freedom thus established involve nothing more than exemption from actual slavery? Was nothing more intended than to forbid one man from owning another as property? Was it the purpose of the nation simply to destroy the institution, and then remit the race, theretofore held in bondage, to the several States for such protection, in their civil rights, necessarily growing out of freedom, as those States, in their discretion, might choose to provide? Were the States against whose protest the institution was destroyed to be left free, so far as national interference was concerned, to make or allow discriminations against that race, as such, in the enjoyment of those fundamental rights which, by universal concession, inhere in a state of freedom?

Had the Thirteenth Amendment stopped with the sweeping declaration in its first section against the existence of slavery and involuntary servitude except for crime, Congress would have had the power, by implication, according to the doctrines of *Prigg v. Commonwealth of Pennsylvania,* repeated in *Strauder v. West Virginia,* to protect the freedom established, and consequently, to secure the enjoyment of such civil rights as were fundamental in freedom. That it can exert its authority to that extent is made clear, and was intended to be made clear, by the express grant of power contained in the second section of the Amendment.

That there are burdens and disabilities which constitute badges of slavery and servitude, and that the power to enforce by appropriate legislation the Thirteenth Amendment may be exerted by legislation of a direct and primary character for the eradication not simply of the institution, but of its badges and incidents, are propositions which ought to be deemed indisputable.

They lie at the foundation of the Civil Rights Act of 1866. Whether that act was authorized by the Thirteenth Amendment alone, without the support which it subsequently received from the Fourteenth Amendment, after the adoption of which it was reenacted with some additions, my brethren do not consider it necessary to inquire. But I submit, with all respect to them, that its constitutionality is conclusively shown by their opinion. They admit, as I have said, that the Thirteenth Amendment established freedom; that there are burdens and disabilities, the necessary incidents of slavery, which constitute its substance and visible form; that Congress, by the act of 1866, passed in view of the Thirteenth Amendment, before the Fourteenth was adopted, undertook to remove certain burdens and disabilities, the necessary incidents of slavery, and to secure to all citizens of every race and color, and without regard to previous servitude, those fundamental rights which are the essence of civil freedom, namely, the same right to make and enforce contracts, to sue, be parties, give evidence, and to inherit, purchase, lease, sell, and convey property as is enjoyed by white citizens; that, under the Thirteenth Amendment, Congress has to do with slavery and its incidents, and that legislation, so far as necessary or proper to eradicate all forms and incidents of slaver and involuntary servitude, may be direct and primary, operating upon the acts of individuals, whether sanctioned by State legislation or not. These propositions being conceded, it is impossible, as it seems to me, to question the constitutional validity of the Civil Rights Act of 1866. I do not contend that the Thirteenth Amendment invests Congress with authority, by legislation, to define and regulate the entire body of the civil rights which citizens enjoy, or may enjoy, in the several States. But I hold that, since slavery, as the court has repeatedly declared, *Slaughterhouse Cases,* 16 Wall. 36; *Strauder West Virginia,* 100 U. S. 303, was the moving or principal cause of the adoption of that amendment, and since that institution rested wholly upon the inferiority, as a race, of those held in bondage, their freedom necessarily involved immunity from, and protection against, all discrimination against them, because of their race, in respect of such civil rights as belong to freemen of other races. Congress, therefore, under its express power to enforce that amendment by appropriate legislation, may enact laws to protect that people against the deprivation, *because of their race,* of any civil rights granted to other freemen in the same State, and such

legislation may be of a direct and primary character, operating upon States, their officers and agents, and also upon at least such individuals and corporations as exercise public functions and wield power and authority under the State.

To test the correctness of this position, let us suppose that, prior to the adoption of the Fourteenth Amendment, a State had passed a statute denying to freemen of African descent, resident within its limits, the same right which was accorded to white persons of making and enforcing contracts and of inheriting, purchasing, leasing, selling and conveying property; or a statute subjecting colored people to severer punishment for particular offences than was prescribed for white persons, or excluding that race from the benefit of the laws exempting homesteads from execution. Recall the legislation of 1865-1866 in some of the States, of which this court in the *Slaughterhouse Cases* said that it imposed upon the colored race onerous disabilities and burdens; curtailed their rights in the pursuit of life, liberty and property to such an extent that their freedom was of little value; forbade them to appear in the towns in any other character than menial servants; required them to reside on and cultivate the soil, without the right to purchase or own it; excluded them from many occupations of gain, and denied them the privilege of giving testimony in the courts where a white man was a party. 16 Wall. 83 U. S. 57. Can there be any doubt that all such enactments might have been reached by direct legislation upon the part of Congress under its express power to enforce the Thirteenth Amendment? Would any court have hesitated to declare that such legislation imposed badges of servitude in conflict with the civil freedom ordained by that amendment? That it would have been also in conflict with the Fourteenth Amendment because inconsistent with the fundamental rights of American citizenship does not prove that it would have been consistent with the Thirteenth Amendment.

What has been said is sufficient to show that the power of Congress under the Thirteenth Amendment is not necessarily restricted to legislation against slavery as an institution upheld by positive law, but may be exerted to the extent, at least, of protecting the liberated race against discrimination in respect of legal rights belonging to freemen where such discrimination is based upon race.

It remains now to inquire what are the legal rights of colored persons in respect of the accommodations, privileges and facilities of public conveyances, inns, and places of public amusement?

*First,* as to public conveyances on land and water. In *New Jersey Steam Navigation Co. v. Merchants' Bank,* 6 How. 344, this court, speaking by Mr. Justice Nelson, said that a common carrier is

> "in the exercise of a sort of public office, and has public duties to perform, from which he should not be permitted to exonerate himself without the assent of the parties concerned."

To the same effect is *Munn v. Illinois,* 94 U. S. 113. In *Olcott v. Supervisor,* 16 Wall. 678, it was ruled that railroads are public highways, established by authority of the State for the public use; that they are nonetheless public highways because controlled and owned by private corporations; that it is a part of the function of government to make and maintain highways for the convenience of the public; that no matter who is the agent, or what is the agency, the function performed is *that of the State;* that, although the owners may be private companies, they may be compelled to permit the public to use these works in the manner in which they can be used; that, upon these grounds alone have the courts sustained the investiture of railroad corporations with the State's right of eminent domain, or the right of municipal corporations, under legislative authority, to assess, levy and collect taxes to aid in the construction of railroads. So in *Township of Queensbury v. Culver,* 19 Wall. 83, it was said that a municipal subscription of railroad stock was in aid of the construction and maintenance of a public highway, and for the promotion of a public use. Again, in *Township of Pine Grove v. Talcott,* 19 Wall. 666: "Though the corporation [railroad] was private, its work was public, as much so as if it were to be constructed by the State." To the like effect are numerous adjudications in this and the State courts with which the profession is familiar. The Supreme Judicial Court of Massachusetts, in *Inhabitants of Worcester v. The Western R.R. Corporation,* 4 Met. 564, said in reference to a railroad:

> "The establishment of that great thoroughfare is regarded as a public work, established by public authority, intended for the public use and benefit, the use of which is secured to the whole community, and constitutes, therefore, like a canal, turnpike, or highway, a public easement. . . . It is true that the real and personal property, necessary to the establishment and management of the railroad is vested in the corporation, but it is in trust for the public."

In *Erie, Etc., R.R. Co. v. Casey,* 26 Penn. St. 287, the court, referring to an act repealing the charter of a railroad, and under which the State took possession of the road, said:

> "It is a public highway, solemnly devoted to public use. When the lands were taken, it was for such use, or they could not have been taken at all. . . . Railroads established upon land taken by the right of eminent domain by authority of the commonwealth, created by her laws as thoroughfares for commerce, are her highways. No corporation has property in them, though it may have franchises annexed to and exercisable within them."

In many courts it has been held that, because of the public interest in such a corporation, the land of a railroad company cannot be levied on and sold under execution by a creditor. The sum of the adjudged cases is that a railroad corporation is a governmental agency, created primarily for public purposes and subject to be controlled for the public benefit. Upon this ground, the State, when unfettered by contract, may regulate, in its discretion, the rates of fares of passengers and freight. And upon this ground, too, the State may regulate the entire management of railroads in all matters affecting the convenience and safety of the public, as, for example, by regulating speed, compelling stops of prescribed length at stations, and prohibiting discriminations and favoritism. If the corporation neglect or refuse to discharge its duties to the public, it may be coerced to do so by appropriate proceedings in the name or in behalf of the State.

Such being the relations these corporations hold to the public, it would seem that the right of a colored person to use an improved public highway upon the terms accorded to freemen of other races is as fundamental, in the state of freedom established in this country, as are any of the rights which my brethren concede to be so far fundamental as to be deemed the essence of civil freedom. "Personal liberty consists," says Blackstone, "in the power of locomotion, of changing situation, or removing one's person to whatever places one's own inclination may direct, without restraint unless by due course of law."

But of what value is this right of locomotion if it may be clogged by such burdens as Congress intended by the act of 1875 to remove? They are burdens which lay at the very foundation of the institution of slavery as it once existed. They are not to be sustained except upon the assumption that there is, in this land of universal liberty, a class which may still be discriminated against, even in respect of rights of a character so necessary and supreme that, deprived of their enjoyment in common with others, a freeman is not only branded as one inferior and infected, but, in the competitions of life, is robbed of some of the most essential means of existence, and all this solely because they belong to a particular race which the nation has liberated. The Thirteenth Amendment alone obliterated the race line so far as all rights fundamental in a state of freedom are concerned.

*Second,* as to inns. The same general observations which have been made as to railroads are applicable to inns. The word "inn" has a technical legal signification. It means, in the act of 1875, just what it meant at common law. A mere private boarding house is not an inn, nor is its keeper subject to the responsibilities, or entitled to the privileges, of a common innkeeper.

> "To constitute one an innkeeper within the legal force of that term, he must keep a house of entertainment or lodging for all travelers or wayfarers who might choose to accept the same, being of good character or conduct."

Redfield on Carriers, etc., § 7. Says Judge Story:

> "An innkeeper may be defined to be the keeper of a common inn for the lodging and entertainment of travelers and passengers, their horses and attendants. An innkeeper is bound to take in all travelers and wayfaring persons, and to entertain them, if he can accommodate them, for a reasonable compensation, and he must guard their goods with proper diligence. . . . If an innkeeper improperly refuses to receive or provide for a guest, he is liable to be indicted therefor. . . . They (carriers of passengers) are

no more at liberty to refuse a passenger, if they have sufficient room and accommodations, than an innkeeper is to refuse suitable room and accommodations to a guest."

"Story on Bailments §§ 475-476."

In *Rex v. Ivens,* 7 Carrington & Payne 213, 32 E.C.L. 49, the court, speaking by Mr. Justice Coleridge, said:

> "An indictment lies against an innkeeper who refuses to receive a guest, he having at the time room in his house and either the price of the guest's entertainment being tendered to him or such circumstances occurring as will dispense with that tender. This law is founded in good sense. The innkeeper is not to select his guest. He has no right to say to one, you shall come to my inn, and to another, you shall not, as everyone coming and conducting himself in a proper manner has a right to be received, and, for this purpose innkeepers are a sort of public servants, they having, in return a kind of privilege of entertaining travelers and supplying them with what they want."

These authorities are sufficient to show that a keeper of an inn is in the exercise of a *quasi*-public employment. The law gives him special privileges. and he is charged with certain duties and responsibilities to the public. The public nature of his employment forbids him from discriminating against any person asking admission as a guest on account of the race or color of that person.

*Third.* As to places of public amusement. It may be argued that the managers of such places have no duties to perform with which the public are, in any legal sense, concerned, or with which the public have any right to interfere, and that the exclusion of a black man from a place of public amusement on account of his race, or the denial to him on that ground of equal accommodations at such places, violates no legal right for the vindication of which he may invoke the aid of the courts. My answer is that places of public amusement, within the meaning of the act of 1875, are such as are established and maintained under direct license of the law. The authority to establish and maintain them comes from the public. The colored race is a part of that public. The local government granting the license represents them as well as all other races within its jurisdiction. A license from the public to establish a place of public amusement imports in law equality of right at such places among all the members of that public. This must be so unless it be—which I deny—that the common municipal government of all the people may, in the exertion of its powers, conferred for the benefit of all, discriminate or authorize discrimination against a particular race solely because of its former condition of servitude.

I also submit, whether it can be said—in view of the doctrines of this court as announced in *Munn v. State of Illinois,* 94 U. S. 113, and reaffirmed in *Peik v. Chicago & N.W. Railway Co.,* 94 U. S. 164, 169 [argument of counsel—omitted], that the management of places of public amusement is a purely private matter, with which government has no rightful concern? In the *Munn* case, the question was whether the State of Illinois could fix, by law, the maximum of charges for the storage of grain in certain warehouses in that State—the *private property of individual citizens.* After quoting a remark attributed to Lord Chief Justice Hale, to the effect that, when private property is "affected with a public interest, it ceases to be *juris privati* only," the court says:

> "Property does become clothed with a public interest when used in a manner to make it of public consequence and affect the community at large. When, therefore, one devotes his property to a use in which the public has an interest, he, in effect, grants to the public an interest in that use, and must submit to be controlled by the public for the common good to the extent of the interest he has thus created. He may withdraw his grant by discontinuing the use, but, so long as he maintains the use, he must submit to the control."

The doctrines of *Munn v. Illinois* have never been modified by this court, and I am justified upon the authority of that case in saying that places of public amusement, conducted under the authority of the law, are clothed with a public interest because used in a manner to make them of public consequence and to affect the community at large. The law may therefore regulate, to some extent, the mode in which they shall be conducted, and, consequently, the public have rights in respect of such places which may be vindicated by the law. It is consequently not a matter purely of private concern.

Congress has not, in these matters, entered the domain of State control and supervision. It does not, as I have said, assume to prescribe the general conditions and limitations under which inns, public conveyances, and places of public amusement shall be conducted or managed. It simply declares, in effect, that, since the nation has established universal freedom in this country for all time, there shall be no discrimination, based merely upon race or color, in respect of the accommodations and advantages of public conveyances, inns, and places of public amusement.

I am of the opinion that such discrimination practised by corporations and individuals in the exercise of their public or *quasi*-public functions is a badge of servitude the imposition of which Congress may prevent under its power, by appropriate legislation, to enforce the Thirteenth Amendment; and consequently, without reference to its enlarged power under the Fourteenth Amendment, the act of March 1, 1875, is not, in my judgment, repugnant to the Constitution.

It remains now to consider these cases with reference to the power Congress has possessed since the adoption of the Fourteenth Amendment. Much that has been said as to the power of Congress under the Thirteenth Amendment is applicable to this branch of the discussion, and will not be repeated.

Before the adoption of the recent amendments, it had become, as we have seen, the established doctrine of this court that negroes, whose ancestors had been imported and sold as slaves, could not become citizens of a State, or even of the United States, with the rights and privileges guaranteed to citizens by the national Constitution; further, that one might have all the rights and privileges of a citizen of a State without being a citizen in the sense in which that word was used in the national Constitution, and without being entitled to the privileges and immunities of citizens of the several States. Still further, between the adoption of the Thirteenth Amendment and the proposal by Congress of the Fourteenth Amendment, on June 16, 1866, the statute books of several of the States, as we have seen, had become loaded down with enactments which, under the guise of Apprentice, Vagrant, and contract regulations, sought to keep the colored race in a condition, practically, of servitude. It was openly announced that whatever might be the rights which persons of that race had as freemen, under the guarantees of the national Constitution, they could not become citizens of a State, with the privileges belonging to citizens, except by the consent of such State; consequently, that their civil rights as citizens of the State depended entirely upon State legislation. To meet this new peril to the black race, that the purposes of the nation might not be doubted or defeated, and by way of further enlargement of the power of Congress, the Fourteenth Amendment was proposed for adoption.

Remembering that this court, in the *Slaughterhouse Cases,* declared that the one pervading purpose found in all the recent amendments, lying at the foundation of each and without which none of them would have been suggested, was

> "the freedom of the slave race, the security and firm establishment of that freedom, and the protection of the newly made freeman and citizen from the oppression of those who had formerly exercised unlimited dominion over him"

-- that each amendment was addressed primarily to the grievances of that race—let us proceed to consider the language of the Fourteenth Amendment.

Its first and fifth sections are in these words:

> "SEC. 1. All persons born or naturalized in the United States, and subject to the jurisdiction thereof, are citizens of the United States and of the State wherein they reside. No State shall make or enforce any law which shall abridge the privileges or immunities of citizens of the United States; nor shall any State deprive any person of life, liberty, or property, without due process of law; nor deny to any person within its jurisdiction the equal protection of the laws."

"* * * *"

"SEC. 5. That Congress shall have power to enforce, by appropriate legislation, the provisions of this article."

It was adjudged in *Strauder v. West Virginia,* 100 U. S. 303, and *Ex parte Virginia,* 100 U. S. 339, and my brethren concede, that positive rights and privileges were intended to be secured, and are, in fact, secured, by the Fourteenth Amendment.

But when, under what circumstances, and to what extent may Congress, by means of legislation, exert its power to enforce the provisions of this amendment? The theory of the opinion of the majority of the court— the foundation upon which their reasoning seems to rest—is that the general government cannot, in advance of hostile State laws or hostile State proceedings, actively interfere for the protection of my of the rights, privileges, and immunities secured by the Fourteenth Amendment. It is said that such rights, privileges, and immunities are secured by way of *prohibition* against State laws and State proceedings affecting such rights and privileges, and by power given to Congress to legislate for the purpose of carrying *such prohibition* into effect; also, that congressional legislation must necessarily be predicated upon such supposed State laws or State proceedings, and be directed to the correction of their operation and effect.

In illustration of its position, the court refers to the clause of the Constitution forbidding the passage by a State of any law impairing the obligation of contracts. That clause does not, I submit, furnish a proper illustration of the scope and effect of the fifth section of the Fourteenth Amendment. No express power is given Congress to enforce, by primary direct legislation, the prohibition upon State laws impairing the obligation of contracts. Authority is, indeed, conferred to enact all necessary and proper laws for carrying into execution the enumerated powers of Congress and all other powers vested by the Constitution in the government of the United States or in any department or officer thereof. And, as heretofore shown, there is also, by necessary implication, power in Congress, by legislation, to protect a right derived from the national Constitution. But a prohibition upon a State is not a power in *Congress* or *in the national government.* It is simply a *denial of power* to the State. And the only mode in which the inhibition upon State laws impairing the obligation of contracts can be enforced is indirectly, through the courts in suits where the parties raise some question as to the constitutional validity of such laws. The judicial power of the United States extends to such suits for the reason that they are suits arising under the Constitution. The Fourteenth Amendment presents the first instance in our history of the investiture of Congress with affirmative power, by *legislation,* to *enforce* an express prohibition upon the States. It is not said that the *judicial* power of the nation may be exerted for the enforcement of that amendment. No enlargement of the judicial power was required, for it is clear that, had the fifth section of the Fourteenth Amendment been entirely omitted, the judiciary could have stricken down all State laws and nullified all State proceedings in hostility to rights and privileges secured or recognized by that amendment. The power given is, in terms, by congressional legislation, to enforce the provisions of the amendment.

The assumption that this amendment consists wholly of prohibitions upon State laws and State proceedings in hostility to its provisions is unauthorized by its language. The first clause of the first section --

"All persons born or naturalized in the United States, and subject to the jurisdiction thereof, are citizens of the United States, and of the State wherein they reside"

-- is of a distinctly affirmative character. In its application to the colored race, previously liberated, it created and granted as well citizenship of the United States as citizenship of the State in which they respectively resided. It introduced all of that race whose ancestors had been imported and sold as slaves at once into the political community known as the "People of the United States." They became instantly citizens of the United States and of their respective States. Further, they were brought by this supreme act of the nation within the direct operation of that provision of the Constitution which declares that "the citizens of each State shall be entitled to all privileges and immunities of citizens in the several States." Art. 4, § 2.

The citizenship thus acquired by that race in virtue of an affirmative grant from the nation may be protected not alone by the judicial branch of the government, but by congressional legislation of a primary direct character, this because the power of Congress is not restricted to the enforcement of prohibitions upon State laws or State action. It is, in terms distinct and positive, to enforce "the *provisions of this article*" of amendment; not simply those of a prohibitive character, but the provisions—*all* of the provisions—affirmative and prohibitive, of the amendment. It is, therefore, a grave misconception to suppose that the fifth section of the amendment has reference exclusively to

express prohibitions upon State laws or State action. If any right was created by that amendment, the grant of power through appropriate legislation to enforce its provisions authorizes Congress, by means of legislation operating throughout the entire Union, to guard, secure, and protect that right.

It is therefore an essential inquiry what, if any, right, privilege or immunity was given, by the nation to colored persons when they were made citizens of the State in which they reside? Did the constitutional grant of State citizenship to that race, of its own force, invest them with any rights, privileges and immunities whatever? That they became entitled, upon the adoption of the Fourteenth Amendment, "to all privileges and immunities of citizens in the several States," within the meaning of section 2 of article 4 of the Constitution, no one, I suppose, will for a moment question. What are the privileges and immunities to which, by that clause of the Constitution, they became entitled? To this it may be answered generally, upon the authority of the adjudged cases, that they are those which are fundamental in citizenship in a free republican government, such as are "common to the citizens in the latter States under their constitutions and laws by virtue of their being citizens." Of that provision it has been said, with the approval of this court, that no other one in the Constitution has tended so strongly to constitute the citizens of the United States one people. *Ward v. Maryland,* 12 Wall. 418; *Corfield v. Coryell,* 4 Wash.C.C. 371; *Paul v. Virginia,* 8 Wall. 168; *Slaughter-house Cases,* 16 *id.* 36.

Although this court has wisely forborne any attempt by a comprehensive definition to indicate all of the privileges and immunities to which the citizen of a State is entitled of right when within the jurisdiction of other States, I hazard nothing, in view of former adjudications, in saying that no State can sustain her denial to colored citizens of other States, while within her limits, of privileges or immunities fundamental in republican citizenship upon the ground that she accords such privileges and immunities only to her white citizens, and withholds them from her colored citizens. The colored citizens of other States, within the jurisdiction of that State, could claim, in virtue of section 2 of article 4 of the Constitution, every privilege and immunity which that State secures to her white citizens. Otherwise it would be in the power of any State, by discriminating class legislation against its own citizens of a particular race or color, to withhold from citizens of other States belonging to that proscribed race, when within her limits, privileges and immunities of the character regarded by all courts as fundamental in citizenship, and that too when the constitutional guaranty is that the citizens of each State shall be entitled to "all privileges and immunities of citizens of the several States." No State may, by discrimination against a portion of its own citizens of a particular race, in respect of privileges and immunities fundamental in citizenship, impair the constitutional right of citizens of other States, of whatever race, to enjoy in that State all such privileges and immunities as are there accorded to her most favored citizens. A colored citizen of Ohio or Indiana, while in the jurisdiction of Tennessee, is entitled to enjoy any privilege or immunity, fundamental in citizenship, which is given to citizens of the white race in the latter State. It is not to be supposed that anyone will controvert this proposition.

But what was secured to colored citizens of the United States—as between them and their respective States—by the national grant to them of State citizenship? With what rights, privileges, or immunities did this grant invest them? There is one, if there be no other—exemption from race discrimination in respect of any civil right belonging to citizens of the white race in the same State. That, surely, is their constitutional privilege when within the jurisdiction of other States. And such must be their constitutional right in their own State, unless the recent amendments be splendid baubles thrown out to delude those who deserved fair and generous treatment at the hands of the nation. Citizenship in this country necessarily imports at least equality of civil rights among citizens of every race in the same State. It is fundamental in American citizenship that, in respect of such rights, there shall be no discrimination by the State, or its officers, or by individuals or corporations exercising public functions or authority, against any citizen because of his race or previous condition of servitude. In *United States v. Cruikshank,* 92 U. S. 542, it was said at page 92 U. S. 555, that the rights of life and personal liberty are natural rights of man, and that "the equality of the rights of citizens is a principle of republicanism." And in *Ex parte Virginia,* 100 U. S. 334, the emphatic language of this court is that

> "one great purpose of these amendments was to raise the colored race from that condition of inferiority and servitude in which most of

them had previously stood into perfect equality of civil rights with all other persons within the jurisdiction of the States."

So, in *Strauder v. West Virginia,* 100 U.S. at 100 U. S. 306, the court, alluding to the Fourteenth Amendment, said:

> "This is one of a series of constitutional provisions having a common purpose, namely, securing to a race recently emancipated, a race that, through many generations, had been held in slavery, all the civil rights that the superior race enjoy."

Again, in *Neal v. Delaware,* 103 U. S. 386, it was ruled that this amendment was designed primarily

> "to secure to the colored race, thereby invested with the rights, privileges, and responsibilities of citizenship, the enjoyment of all the civil rights that, under the law, are enjoyed by white persons."

The language of this court with reference to the Fifteenth Amendment adds to the force of this view. In *United States v. Cruikshank,* it was said:

> "In *United States v. Reese,* 92 U. S. 214, we held that the Fifteenth Amendment has invested the citizens of the United States with a new constitutional right, which is exemption from discrimination in tho exercise of the elective franchise, on account of race, color, or previous condition of servitude. From this it appears that the right of suffrage is not a necessary attribute of national citizenship, but that exemption from discrimination in the exercise of that right on account of race, &c., is. The right to vote in the States comes from the States, but the right of exemption from the prohibited discrimination comes from the United States. The first has not been granted or secured by the Constitution of the United States, but the last has been."

Here, in language at once clear and forcible, is stated the principle for which I contend. It can scarcely be claimed that exemption from race discrimination, in respect of civil rights, against those to whom State citizenship was granted by the nation, is any less, for the colored race, a new constitutional right, derived from and secured by the national Constitution, than is exemption from such discrimination in the exercise of the elective franchise. It cannot be that the latter is an attribute of national citizenship, while the other is not essential in national citizenship or fundamental in State citizenship.

If, then, exemption from discrimination in respect of civil rights is a new constitutional right, secured by the grant of State citizenship to colored citizens of the United States—and I do not see how this can now be questioned—why may not the nation, by means of its own legislation of a primary direct character, guard, protect, and enforce that right? It is a right and privilege which the nation conferred. It did not come from the States in which those colored citizens reside. It has been the established doctrine of this court during all its history, accepted as essential to the national supremacy, that Congress, in the absence of a positive delegation of power to the State legislatures, may, by its own legislation, enforce and protect any right derived from or created by the national Constitution. It was so declared in *Prigg v. Commonwealth of Pennsylvania.* It was reiterated in *United States v. Reese,* 92 U. S. 214, where the court said that

> "rights and immunities created by and dependent upon the Constitution of the United States can be protected by Congress. The form and manner of the protection may be such as Congress, in the legitimate exercise of its discretion, shall provide. These may be varied to meet the necessities of the particular right to be protected."

It was distinctly reaffirmed in *Strauder v. West Virginia,* 100 U.S. at 100 U. S. 310, where we said that

> "a right or immunity created by the Constitution or only guaranteed by it, even without any express delegation of power, may be protected by Congress."

How then can it be claimed, in view of the declarations of this court in former cases, that exemption of colored citizens, within their States, from race discrimination in respect of the civil rights of citizens is not an immunity created or derived from the national Constitution?

This court has always given a broad and liberal construction to the Constitution, so as to enable Con-

gress, by legislation, to enforce rights secured by that instrument. The legislation which Congress may enact in execution of its power to enforce the provisions of this amendment is such as may be appropriate to protect the right granted. The word appropriate was undoubtedly used with reference to its meaning, as established by repeated decisions of this court. Under given circumstances, that which the court characterizes as corrective legislation might be deemed by Congress appropriate and entirely sufficient. Under other circumstances, primary direct legislation may be required. But it is for Congress, not the judiciary, to say that legislation is appropriate—that is, best adapted to the end to be attained. The judiciary may not, with safety to our institutions, enter the domain of legislative discretion and dictate the means which Congress shall employ in the exercise of its granted powers. That would be sheer usurpation of the functions of a coordinate department, which, if often repeated, and permanently acquiesced in, would work a radical change in our system of government. In *United States v. Fisher,* 2 Cr. 38, the court said that

> "Congress must possess the choice of means, and must be empowered to use any means which are, in fact, conducive to the exercise of a power granted by the Constitution. . . . The sound construction of the Constitution,"

said Chief Justice Marshall,

> "must allow to the national legislature that discretion, with respect to the means by which the powers it confers are to be carried into execution, which will enable that body to perform the high duties assigned to it in the manner most beneficial to the people. Let the end be legitimate, let it be within the scope of the Constitution, and all means which are appropriate, which are plainly adapted to that end, which are not prohibited, but consist with the letter and spirit of the Constitution, are constitutional."

*McCulloch v. Maryland,* 4 Wheat. 421.

Must these rules of construction be now abandoned? Are the powers of the national legislature to be restrained in proportion as the rights and privileges, derived from the nation, are valuable? Are constitutional provisions, enacted to secure the dearest rights of freemen and citizens, to be subjected to that rule of construction, applicable to private instruments, which requires that the words to be interpreted must be taken most strongly against those who employ them? Or shall it be remembered that

> "a constitution of government, founded by the people for themselves and their posterity and for objects of the most momentous nature—for perpetual union, for the establishment of justice, for the general welfare, and for a perpetuation of the blessings of liberty—necessarily requires that every interpretation of its powers should have a constant reference to these objects? No interpretation of the words in which those powers are granted can be a sound one which narrows down their ordinary import so as to defeat those objects."

Story Const. § 422.

The opinion of the court, as I have said, proceeds upon the ground that the power of Congress to legislate for the protection of the rights and privileges secured by the Fourteenth Amendment cannot be brought into activity except with the view, and as it may become necessary, to correct and annul State laws and State proceedings in hostility to such rights and privileges. In the absence of State laws or State action adverse to such rights and privileges, the nation may not actively interfere for their protection and security, even against corporations and individuals exercising public or *quasi*-public functions. Such I understand to be the position of my brethren. If the grant to colored citizens of the United States of citizenship in their respective States imports exemption from race discrimination in their States in respect of such civil rights as belong to citizenship, then to hold that the amendment remits that right to the States for their protection, primarily, and stays the hands of the nation until it is assailed by State laws or State proceedings is to adjudge that the amendment, so far from enlarging the powers of Congress—as we have heretofore said it did—not only curtails them, but reverses the policy which the general government has pursued from its very organization. Such an interpretation of the amendment is a denial to Congress of the power, by appropriate legislation, to enforce one of its provisions. In view of the circumstances under which the recent amendments were

incorporated into the Constitution, and especially in view of the peculiar character of the new rights they created and secured, it ought not to be presumed that the general government has abdicated its authority, by national legislation, direct and primary in its character, to guard and protect privileges and immunities secured by that instrument. Such an interpretation of the Constitution ought not to be accepted if it be possible to avoid it. Its acceptance would lead to this anomalous result: that, whereas, prior to the amendments, Congress, with the sanction of this court, passed the most stringent laws—operating directly and primarily upon States and their officers and agents, as well as upon individuals—in vindication of slavery and the right of the master, it may not now, by legislation of a like primary and direct character, guard, protect, and secure the freedom established, and the most essential right of the citizenship granted, by the constitutional amendments. With all respect for the opinion of others, I insist that the national legislature may, without transcending the limits of the Constitution, do for human liberty and the fundamental rights of American citizenship what it did, with the sanction of this court, for the protection of slavery and the rights of the masters of fugitive slaves. If fugitive slave laws, providing modes and prescribing penalties whereby the master could seize and recover his fugitive slave, were legitimate exercises of an implied power to protect and enforce a right recognized by the Constitution, why shall the hands of Congress be tied so that—under an express power, by appropriate legislation, to enforce a constitutional provision granting citizenship—it may not, by means of direct legislation, bring the whole power of this nation to bear upon States and their officers and upon such individuals and corporations exercising public functions as assume to abridge, impair, or deny rights confessedly secured by the supreme law of the land?

It does not seem to me that the fact that, by the second clause of the first section of the Fourteenth Amendment, the States are expressly prohibited from making or enforcing laws abridging the privileges and immunities of citizens of the United States furnishes any sufficient reason for holding or maintaining that the amendment was intended to deny Congress the power, by general, primary, and direct legislation, of protecting citizens of the several States, being also citizens of the United States, against all discrimination in respect of their rights as citizens which is founded on race, color, or previous condition of servitude.

Such an interpretation of the amendment is plainly repugnant to its fifth section, conferring upon Congress power, by appropriate legislation, to enforce not merely the provisions containing prohibitions upon the States, but all of the provisions of the amendment, including the provisions, express and implied, in the first clause of the first section of the article granting citizenship. This alone is sufficient for holding that Congress is not restricted to the enactment of laws adapted to counteract and redress the operation of State legislation, or the action of State officers, of the character prohibited by the amendment. It was perfectly well known that the great danger to the equal enjoyment by citizens of their rights as citizens was to be apprehended not altogether from unfriendly State legislation, but from the hostile action of corporations and individuals in the States. And it is to be presumed that it was intended by that section to clothe Congress with power and authority to meet that danger. If the rights intended to be secured by the act of 1875 are such as belong to the citizen in common or equally with other citizens in the same State, then it is not to be denied that such legislation is peculiarly appropriate to the end which Congress is authorized to accomplish, *viz.,* to protect the citizen, in respect of such rights, against discrimination on account of his race. Recurring to the specific prohibition in the Fourteenth Amendment upon the making or enforcing of State laws abridging the privileges of citizens of the United States, I remark that if, as held in the *Slaughterhouse Cases,* the privileges here referred to were those which belonged to citizenship of the United States, as distinguished from those belonging to State citizenship, it was impossible for any State prior to the adoption of that amendment to have enforced laws of that character. The judiciary could have annulled all such legislation under the provision that the Constitution shall be the supreme law of the land, anything in the constitution or laws of any State to the contrary notwithstanding. The States were already under an implied prohibition not to abridge any privilege or immunity belonging to citizens of the United States as such. Consequently, the prohibition upon State laws in hostility to rights belonging to citizens of the United States was intended—in view of the introduction into the body of citizens of a race former-

ly denied the essential rights of citizenship—only as an express limitation on the powers of the States, and was not intended to diminish in the slightest degree the authority which the nation has always exercised of protecting, by means of its own direct legislation, rights created or secured by the Constitution. Any purpose to diminish the national authority in respect of privileges derived from the nation is distinctly negatived by the express grant of power by legislation to enforce every provision of the amendment, including that which, by the grant of citizenship in the State, secures exemption from race discrimination in respect of the civil rights of citizens.

It is said that any interpretation of the Fourteenth Amendment different from that adopted by the majority of the court would imply that Congress had authority to enact a municipal code for all the States covering every matter affecting the life, liberty, and property of the citizens of the several States. Not so. Prior to the adoption of that amendment, the constitutions of the several States, without perhaps an exception, secured all *persons* against deprivation of life, liberty, or property otherwise than by due process of law, and, in some form, recognized the right of all *persons* to the equal protection of the laws. Those rights therefore existed before that amendment was proposed or adopted, and were not created by it. If, by reason of that fact, it be assumed that protection in these rights of persons still rests primarily with the States, and that Congress may not interfere except to enforce, by means of corrective legislation, the prohibitions upon State laws or State proceedings inconsistent with those rights, it does not at all follow that privileges which have been *granted by the nation* may not be protected by primary legislation upon the part of Congress. The personal rights and immunities recognized in the prohibitive clauses of the amendment were, prior to its adoption, under the protection, primarily, of the States, while rights, created by or derived from the United States have always been and, in the nature of things, should always be, primarily under the protection of the general government. Exemption from race discrimination in respect of the civil rights which are fundamental in *citizenship* in a republican government, is, as we have seen, a new right, created by the nation, with express power in Congress, by legislation, to enforce the constitutional provision from which it is derived. If, in some sense, such race discrimination is, within the letter of the last clause of the first section, a denial of that equal protection of the laws which is secured against State denial to all persons, whether citizens or not, it cannot be possible that a mere prohibition upon such State denial, or a prohibition upon State laws abridging the privileges and immunities of citizens of the United States, takes from the nation the power which it has uniformly exercised of protecting, by direct primary legislation, those privileges and immunities which existed under the Constitution before the adoption of the Fourteenth Amendment or have been created by that amendment in behalf of those thereby made *citizens* of their respective States.

This construction does not in any degree intrench upon the just rights of the States in the control of their domestic affairs. It simply recognizes the enlarged powers conferred by the recent amendments upon the general government. In the view which I take of those amendments, the States possess the same authority which they have always had to define and regulate the civil rights which their own people, in virtue of State citizenship, may enjoy within their respective limits, except that its exercise is now subject to the expressly granted power of Congress, by legislation, to enforce the provisions of such amendments—a power which necessarily carries with it authority, by national legislation, to protect and secure the privileges and immunities which are created by or are derived from those amendments. That exemption of citizens from discrimination based on race or color, in respect of civil rights, is one of those privileges or immunities can no longer be deemed an open question in this court.

It was said of the case of *Dred Scott v. Sandford* that this court there overruled the action of two generations, virtually inserted a new clause in the Constitution, changed its character, and made a new departure in the workings of the federal government. I may be permitted to say that, if the recent amendments are so construed that Congress may not, in its own discretion and independently of the action or nonaction of the States, provide by legislation of a direct character for the security of rights created by the national Constitution, if it be adjudged that the obligation to protect the fundamental privileges and immunities granted by the Fourteenth Amendment to citizens residing in the several States rests primarily not on the nation, but on the States, if it be further adjudged that individuals and corporations exercising public

functions or wielding power under public authority may, without liability to direct primary legislation on the part of Congress, make the race of citizens the ground for denying them that equality of civil rights which the Constitution ordains as a principle of republican citizenship, then not only the foundations upon which the national supremacy has always securely rested will be materially disturbed, but we shall enter upon an era of constitutional law when the rights of freedom and American citizenship cannot receive from the nation that efficient protection which heretofore was unhesitatingly accorded to slavery and the rights of the master.

But if it were conceded that the power of Congress could not be brought into activity until the rights specified in the act of 1875 had been abridged or denied by some State law or State action, I maintain that the decision of the court is erroneous. There has been adverse State action within the Fourteenth Amendment as heretofore interpreted by this court. I allude to *Ex parte Virginia, supra.* It appears in that case that one Cole, judge of a county court, was charged with the duty by the laws of Virginia of selecting grand and petit jurors. The law of the State did not authorize or permit him, in making such selections, to discriminate against colored citizens because of their race. But he was indicted in the federal court, under the act of 1875, for making such discriminations. The attorney general of Virginia contended before us that the State had done its duty, and had not authorized or directed that county judge to do what he was charged with having done; that the State had not denied to the colored race the equal protection of the laws, and that consequently the act of Cole must be deemed his individual act, in contravention of the will of the State. Plausible as this argument was, it failed to convince this court, and after saying that the Fourteenth Amendment had reference to the political body denominated a State "by whatever instruments or in whatever modes that action may be taken," and that a State acts by its legislative, executive, and judicial authorities, and can act in no other way, we proceeded:

> "The constitutional provision, therefore, must
> mean that no agency of the State or of the offi-
> cers or agents by whom its powers are exerted
> shall deny to any person within its jurisdiction
> the equal protection of the laws. Whoever, by
> virtue of public position under a State govern-

ment, deprives another of property, life, or liberty without due process of law, or denies or takes away the equal protection of the laws, violates the constitutional inhibition; and, as he acts under the name and for the State, and is clothed with the State's power, his act is that of the State. This must be so, or the constitutional prohibition has no meaning. Then the State has clothed one of its agents with power to annul or evade it. But the constitutional amendment was ordained for a purpose. It was to secure equal rights to all persons, and, to insure to all persons the enjoyment of such rights, power was given to Congress to enforce its provisions by appropriate legislation. Such legislation must act upon persons, not upon the abstract thing denominated a State, but upon the persons who are the agents of the State in the denial of the rights which were intended to be secured."

*Ex parte Virginia,* 100 U. S. 346-347.

In every material sense applicable to the practical enforcement of the Fourteenth Amendment, railroad corporations, keepers of inns, and managers of places of public amusement are agents or instrumentalities of the State, because they are charged with duties to the public and are amenable, in respect of their duties and functions, to governmental regulation. It seems to me that, within the principle settled in *Ex parte Virginia,* a denial by these instrumentalities of the State to the citizen, because of his race, of that equality of civil rights secured to him by law is a denial by the State within the meaning of the Fourteenth Amendment. If it be not, then that race is left, in respect of the civil rights in question, practically at the mercy of corporations and individuals wielding power under the States.

But the court says that Congress did not, in the act of 1866, assume, under the authority given by the Thirteenth Amendment, to adjust what may be called the social rights of men and races in the community. I agree that government has nothing to do with social, as distinguished from technically legal, rights of individuals. No government ever has brought, or ever can bring, its people into social intercourse against their wishes. Whether one person will permit or maintain social relations with another is a matter with which government has no concern. I agree that, if one citizen

chooses not to hold social intercourse with another, he is not and cannot be made amenable to the law for his conduct in that regard, for even upon grounds of race, no legal right of a citizen is violated by the refusal of others to maintain merely social relations with him. What I affirm is that no State, nor the officers of any State, nor any corporation or individual wielding power under State authority for the public benefit or the public convenience, can, consistently either with the freedom established by the fundamental law or with that equality of civil rights which now belongs to every citizen, discriminate against freemen or citizens in those rights because of their race, or because they once labored under the disabilities of slavery imposed upon them as a race. The rights which Congress, by the act of 1875, endeavored to secure and protect are legal, not social, rights. The right, for instance, of a colored citizen to use the accommodations of a public highway upon the same terms as are permitted to white citizens is no more a social right than his right under the law to use the public streets of a city or a town, or a turnpike road, or a public market, or a post office, or his right to sit in a public building with others, of whatever race, for the purpose of hearing the political questions of the day discussed. Scarcely a day passes without our seeing in this courtroom citizens of the white and black races sitting side by side, watching the progress of our business. It would never occur to anyone that the presence of a colored citizen in a courthouse, or courtroom, was an invasion of the social rights of white persons who may frequent such places. And yet such a suggestion would be quite as sound in law—I say it with all respect—as is the suggestion that the claim of a colored citizen to use, upon the same terms as is permitted to white citizens, the accommodations of public highways, or public inns, or places of public amusement, established under the license of the law, is an invasion of the social rights of the white race.

The court, in its opinion, reserves the question whether Congress, in the exercise of its power to regulate commerce amongst the several States, might or might not pass a law regulating rights in public conveyances passing from one State to another. I beg to suggest that that precise question was substantially presented here in the only one of these cases relating to railroads— *Robinson and Wife v. Memphis & Charleston Railroad Company.* In that case, it appears that Mrs. Robinson, a citizen of Mississippi, purchased a railroad ticket entitling her to be carried from Grand Junction, Tennessee, to Lynchburg, Virginia. Might not the act of 1875 be maintained in that case as applicable at least to commerce between the States, notwithstanding it does not, upon its face, profess to have been passed in pursuance of the power of Congress to regulate commerce? Has it ever been held that the judiciary should overturn a statute because the legislative department did not accurately recite therein the particular provision of the Constitution authorizing its enactment? We have often enforced municipal bonds in aid of railroad subscriptions where they failed to recite the statute authorizing their issue, but recited one which did not sustain their validity. The inquiry in such cases has been was there, in any statute, authority for the execution of the bonds? Upon this branch of the case, it may be remarked that the State of Louisiana, in 1869, passed a statute giving to passengers, without regard to race or color, equality of right in the accommodations of railroad and street cars, steamboats or other watercrafts, stage coaches, omnibuses, or other vehicles. But in *Hall v. De Cuir,* 95 U. S. 487, that act was pronounced unconstitutional so far as it related to commerce between the States, this court saying that, "if the public good requires such legislation, it must come from Congress, and not from the States." I suggest, that it may become a pertinent inquiry whether Congress may, in the exertion of its power to regulate commerce among the States, enforce among passengers on public conveyances equality of right, without regard to race, color or previous condition of servitude, if it be true—which I do not admit—that such legislation would be an interference by government with the social rights of the people.

My brethren say that, when a man has emerged from slavery, and by the aid of beneficent legislation has shaken off the inseparable concomitants of that state, there must be some stage in the progress of his elevation when he takes the rank of a mere citizen, and ceases to be the special favorite of the laws, and when his rights as a citizen or a man are to be protected in the ordinary modes by which other men's rights are protected. It is, I submit, scarcely just to say that the colored race has been the special favorite of the laws. The statute of 1875, now adjudged to be unconstitutional, is for the benefit of citizens of every race and color. What the nation, through Congress, has sought to accomplish in reference to that race is what had

already been done in every State of the Union for the white race—to secure and protect rights belonging to them as freemen and citizens, nothing more. It was not deemed enough "to help the feeble up, but to support him after." The one underlying purpose of congressional legislation has been to enable the black race to take the rank of mere citizens. The difficulty has been to compel a recognition of the legal right of the black race to take the rank of citizens, and to secure the enjoyment of privileges belonging, under the law, to them as a component part of the people for whose welfare and happiness government is ordained.

At every step in this direction, the nation has been confronted with class tyranny, which a contemporary English historian says is, of all tyrannies, the most intolerable,

> "for it is ubiquitous in its operation and weighs perhaps most heavily on those whose obscurity or distance would withdraw them from the notice of a single despot."

Today it is the colored race which is denied, by corporations and individuals wielding public authority, rights fundamental in their freedom and citizenship. At some future time, it may be that some other race will fall under the ban of race discrimination. If the constitutional amendments be enforced according to the intent with which, as I conceive, they were adopted, there cannot be, in this republic, any class of human beings in practical subjection to another class with power in the latter to dole out to the former just such privileges as they may choose to grant. The supreme law of the land has decreed that no authority shall be exercised in this country upon the basis of discrimination, in respect of civil rights, against freemen and citizens because of their race, color, or previous condition of servitude. To that decree—for the due enforcement of which, by appropriate legislation, Congress has been invested with express power—everyone must bow, whatever may have been, or whatever now are, his individual views as to the wisdom or policy either of the recent changes in the fundamental law or of the legislation which has been enacted to give them effect.

For the reasons stated, I feel constrained to withhold my assent to the opinion of the court.

## Glossary

**beneficent:** kind, producing good

**Black Code:** any state or local law or set of laws intended to limit the rights or liberties of African Americans

***brutum fulmen:*** Latin for "inert thunder," meaning an empty threat or display of force

**concomitants:** things that accompany or are related to something else

***ex directo:*** a Latin expression meaning literally "from the direct"; directly, immediately

***ex parte:*** Latin for "by (or for) one party," used in the law to refer to a legal proceeding brought by one party without the presence of the other being required

**feudal vassalage:** the state of being a serf, owing allegiance to a lord, under the medieval feudal system

**forborne:** refrained

**incidents:** accompaniments

**nugatory:** of no value, trifling, ineffective

***posse comitatus:*** Latin for "power of the county" and referring to a municipality's power to form a temporary police force, commonly called a posse

**previous condition of servitude:** slavery; used to refer to the status of former slaves

**privileges and immunities:** a legal term referring to Article IV of the Constitution, which requires that a citizen in one state be considered equal to a citizen in any other state with regard to U.S. citizenship rights

**self-executing:** a law that takes effect immediately under given conditions, without the need for any intervening court action

**Territories:** the western lands that would later become U.S. states

**writ of error:** a judicial writ from an appellate court ordering the court of record to produce the records of trial; an appeal

# ELK V. WILKINS

| DATE | CITATION |
|------|----------|
| 1884 | 112 U.S. 94 |
| **AUTHOR** | **SIGNIFICANCE** |
| Horace Gray | Held that a Native American born in the United States was not a citizen and could therefore be denied the right to vote |
| **VOTE** | |
| 7–2 | |

## Overview

John Elk was a Winnebago Indian who, in 1880, tried to register to vote in Omaha, Nebraska. The local registrar of voters, Charles Wilkins, denied his application. Elk sued Wilkins, arguing that he was a U.S. citizen under the Fourteenth Amendment to the Constitution, that he had renounced his allegiance to his tribe, and that because he was born in the United States, the Fifteenth Amendment guaranteed him the right to vote. After the circuit court dismissed the case, Elk appealed to the U.S. Supreme Court, which held that Elk was not a citizen of the United States under the Fourteenth Amendment and thus had not been deprived of any right under the Fifteenth Amendment. The Court found that even though Elk was born in the United States and had severed his tribal relationship, he had never been naturalized and had not become a citizen through any statute or treaty.

## Context

The legal status of Native Americans was a thorny issue virtually from the founding of the republic. Initial-ly, the United States entered into treaties with Native tribes as though they were foreign nations, but their status within the country remained unclear. Two decisions rendered by the U.S. Supreme Court under Chief Justice John Marshall during the administration of President Andrew Jackson attempted to clarify the status of the Native tribes. Both cases involved the Cherokee Nation and the state of Georgia. Although the Cherokee had adopted many of the ways and institutions of white culture, many Georgians objected to their very presence in the state. In *Cherokee Nation v. Georgia* (1831), Marshall refused to rule on the Georgia legislature's nullification of Cherokee law. In his decision, he characterized Indian tribes as "domestic dependent nations." In *Worcester v. Georgia* (1832), Marshall held that the Cherokee nation was "a distinct community occupying its own territory . . . in which the laws of Georgia can have no force, and which the citizens of Georgia have no right to enter, but with the assent of the Cherokees themselves, or in conformity with treaties and with the acts of Congress." Despite this holding, Jackson and the state of Georgia soon removed the Cherokee from the state under the terms of the Indian Removal Act of 1830.

The issue of citizenship, central to the Court's later decision in *Elk v. Wilkins,* arose in the famous—or infamous—Supreme Court decision in *Dred Scott v. Sanford* (1857). In his decision, Chief Justice Roger Taney differentiated the legal status of African Americans and Native Americans. He stated that Native Americans, unlike Blacks, could be naturalized by an act of Congress and that individual Native Americans who renounced their tribal affiliations and lived among whites were entitled to the rights and privileges of foreign immigrants; presumably, this would include the right to vote. The issue arose again connection with the Civil Rights Act of 1866, which stated that "all persons born in the United States and not subject to any foreign power, excluding Indians not taxed, are hereby declared to be citizens of the United States." The troublesome phrase "Indians not taxed" was added during the debate over the bill because of concerns that the law would extend the rights of citizenship to *all* Indians, not just "domesticated" ones, although some congressmen argued that all Indians should be naturalized.

The issue arose anew in the 1868 debate over the Fourteenth Amendment. The question was whether Indians were to be included among the citizenry. The belief persisted that Indians, with their ties to tribes, were not amenable to the jurisdiction of the United States. The issue remained murky in 1871 when Congress added to the annual Indian Appropriations Act the statement that "no Indian nation or tribe within the territory of the United States shall be acknowledged or recognized as an independent nation, tribe, or power with whom the United States may contract by treaty." The problem this act created for Native American tribes was that in the post–Civil War era, Congress evinced reluctance to negotiate treaties with the tribes, leaving them unable to protect their rights through treaties, and because they were not citizens, they could not protect their rights either in the court system or by voting. Whatever right to vote the Indians did have tended to depend on the caprice of local registrars and other officials.

The issue of voting rights came to a head in 1880. John Elk was a Winnebago Indian living in Omaha, Nebraska. He had lived in the white community for more than a year. On April 5, 1880, he tried to register to vote. The local registrar, Charles Wilkins, denied his application. A local law firm brought suit on Elk's behalf, arguing that Elk was a U.S. citizen by virtue of the Fourteenth Amendment. Further, according to the Fifteenth Amendment,

**Elk v. Wilkins** *held that a Native American born in the United States was not a citizen and could be denied the right to vote.*
(Henry Hamilton Bennett)

he could not be denied the right to vote because of his race or color. He had been born in the United States, he had renounced his affiliation with the tribe, he was a bona fide resident of Omaha and Nebraska, and he had surrendered himself to U.S. jurisdiction. He sought damages of $6,000. He received help in the case from the so-called Ponca Committee headed by T. H. Tibbles, the editor of the *Omaha Herald*, who had formed the committee to oppose the forced removal of the Ponca Indians from the state. Four years later, on November 3, 1884, the Court finally rendered its decision, upholding the decision of a federal circuit court in denying Elk's petition. The decision, incidentally, did not attract much national attention, for the nation's gaze was fixed on the close presidential contest between Benjamin Harrison and Grover Cleveland; indeed, the Court's decision was handed down on the Monday before Election Day and remained buried in election news.

Meanwhile, while *Elk* was pending, the Supreme Court issued a controversial decision in *Ex Parte Crow Dog* (1883). (An ex parte decision is one decided by a judge without all parties having to be present.) Crow Dog was an Oglala Sioux chief accused of murdering another Sioux chief. He had been tried in a tribal court and in the District Court of Dakota Territory, which was under the authority of the U.S. Circuit Court, and was convicted and sentenced to death. On appeal to the Supreme Court, he argued that because he had violated no U.S. laws, the U.S. courts had no jurisdiction over him. The Court ruled that although the district court had jurisdiction over certain disputes involving Native Americans, only the tribal court had jurisdiction over the murder of one Indian by another. On this basis, Crow Dog was freed. Public outrage over the decision led to the passage by Congress of the Major Crimes Act (1885), which placed all Native Americans, whether they lived on a reservation or not, under the jurisdiction of the federal and territorial courts for major crimes such as murder, manslaughter, rape, assault with intent to kill, arson, burglary, and larceny.

## About the Author

Horace Gray was born on March 24, 1828, to a prominent merchant and shipbuilding family in Boston, Massachusetts. His father, who built and sustained the family fortune, was Horace Gray Sr. His mother, Harriet Upham, the daughter of a U.S. congressman, died when the younger Horace was just six years old. As a child Gray attended private schools in the Boston area. He graduated from Harvard University in 1845 with an undistinguished record, although he showed some facility for modern languages and, under the influence of naturalist Louis Agassiz, developed an interest in insects and birds. He returned to Harvard to attend law school and threw himself into his studies. After graduating in 1849 he continued to read law and clerked for a law firm until he was admitted to the bar in 1851.

Gray established a private law practice, but during this period he discovered an interest in legal history and historical records. He did some work for Luther S. Cushing, the reporter of decisions for the Massachusetts Supreme Court, and when Cushing became ill, Gray took on more and more of the work until he was officially appointed reporter, a prestigious position at the time. He also maintained his legal practice, and from 1854 to 1864 he argued thirty-one cases before the Massachusetts Supreme Court, winning twenty-four of them. But it was his reporting and independent scholarship, in which he discovered obscure legal precedents and historical references that bolstered his positions, that began to win him a reputation.

In 1864, on the strength of that growing reputation, Gray was appointed to the Massachusetts Supreme Court. In 1873 he was elevated to the position of chief justice, where he remained until 1881. Gray disliked divided courts, which he believed weakened the judiciary and public trust in its decisions, so he worked tirelessly to find common ground with the rest of the court. In seventeen years wrote just one dissent among almost 1,400 opinions, and not one of his decisions was ever overturned by a higher court. He continued to rely heavily on precedent: in his first case on the court, he issued a five-page ruling that cited a textbook, eight English cases (some going back to the reign of Henry VIII), twenty-six state cases, one federal case, and twenty-one statutes (some going back to 1641). The case was a suit to recover a lost cow.

On December 19, 1881, Gray was appointed to the U.S. Supreme Court by President Chester A. Arthur, and he was confirmed the following day in the Senate. Although he wrote more than 450 opinions during his twenty years on the Court, constitutional scholars find it difficult to pinpoint any overriding judicial philosophy that animated his opinions, although he tended to support a strong federal government and protect private property rights. Instead, he continued to function as the Court's scholar and historian, consistently governed by history and precedent.

In his personal life, Gray was widely respected for his intellect augmented by an extensive library. He met many of the foremost minds of his time and was even invited to join the famous Saturday Club, a group of Boston intellectuals and writers that included James Russell Lowell, Henry Wadsworth Longfellow, Ralph Waldo Emerson, Oliver Wendell Holmes Sr., Nathaniel Hawthorne, and others. Gray remained a bachelor for over sixty years, but in 1889 he met and married Jane Matthews, the young daughter of fellow Supreme Court Justice Stanley Matthews.

Illness forced Gray to miss a good deal of the 1894 Court term. In 1896 his share of the Court's workload began to drop off, but he persisted until February 3, 1902, when he suffered a stroke. In July that year he submitted his resignation to President Teddy Roosevelt. He died on September 15 in Nahant, Massachusetts.

## Explanation and Analysis of the Document

### The Majority Opinion

In *Elk v. Wilkins* the court ruled that the Fourteenth Amendment did not grant citizenship to Indians. Justice Gray states:

> Though the plaintiff alleges that he "had fully and completely surrendered himself to the jurisdiction of the United States," he does not allege that the United States accepted his surrender, or that he has ever been naturalized, or taxed, or in any way recognized or treated as a citizen by the state or by the United States. Nor is it contended by his counsel that there is any statute or treaty that makes him a citizen.

This was the crux of the issue: Because Elk was an Indian, he could not be a citizen without a positive recognition of his citizenship by the U.S. government. Elk stated that he had surrendered himself to the jurisdiction of the United States, but the federal government had not accepted his surrender, had not taxed him, and had not treated him as a citizen of the United States or the state of Nebraska.

Gray goes on to state the fundamental question raised by the case:

> The question, then, is whether an Indian, born a member of one of the Indian tribes within the United States, is, merely by reason of his birth within the United States and of his afterwards voluntarily separating himself from his tribe and taking up his residence among white citizens, a citizen of the United States within the meaning of the first section of the Fourteenth Amendment of the Constitution.

Justice Gray explains that the Fourteenth Amendment requires that for a person to be considered a citizen, he has to be born in the United States and be subject to its jurisdiction *or* be naturalized. Indians, however, because of their tribal ties, are not naturalized. He goes on to characterize the status of Indian tribes, calling them "alien nations" with whom the United States had dealt through treaties or acts of Congress.

After examining the judicial and legislative history of the issue of Indian citizenship, Gray writes:

The members of those tribes owed immediate allegiance to their several tribes, and were not part of the people of the United States. They were in a dependent condition, a state of pupilage, resembling that of a ward to his guardian. Indians and their property, exempt from taxation by treaty or statute of the United States, could not be taxed by any state.

He further states that "the alien and dependent condition of the members of the Indian tribes" could not be relinquished "at their own will" without "the action or assent of the United States." They were never regarded as citizens of the United States "except under explicit provisions of treaty or statute to that effect." Such a treaty or statute would either declare "a certain tribe, or such members of it as chose to remain behind on the removal of the tribe westward, to be citizens," or it would authorize "individuals of particular tribes to become citizens on application to a court of the United States for naturalization and satisfactory proof of fitness for civilized life."

Gray explains in further detail that

> Indians born within the territorial limits of the United States, members of and owing immediate allegiance to one of the Indiana tribes (an alien though dependent power), although in a geographical sense born in the United States, are no more "born in the United States and subject to the jurisdiction thereof," within the meaning of the first section of the Fourteenth Amendment, than the children of subjects of any foreign government born within the domain of that government, or the children born within the United States of ambassadors or other public ministers of foreign nations.

In other words, the status of Indians was not different from that of, say, the child of a French ambassador that is born in the United States. Grays concludes by quoting Judge Matthew Paul Deady of the U.S. District Court for the District of Oregon, who wrote in a similar case:

> But an Indian cannot make himself a citizen of the United States without the consent and co-operation of the government. The fact that he has abandoned his nomadic life or tribal relations, and adopted the habits and manners of civilized people, may be a good reason

why he should be made a citizen of the United States, but does not of itself make him one. To be a citizen of the United States is a political privilege which no one, not born to, can assume without its consent in some form.

## *The Dissenting Opinion*

Two justices dissented from the majority opinion. The dissent was written by Justice John Marshall Harlan, with Justice William Burnham Woods joining. Harlan insists that Elk was a citizen, that he had the obligations of a citizen, and that he was subject to taxation by Nebraska—in other words, he was an "Indian taxed." Harlan calls attention to the constitutional provision that excluded "Indians not taxed" from the number of citizens used to determine congressional representation. The provision itself implies that some Indians who were taxed were by definition not affected by that provision. As an "Indian taxed," he was entitled to the privileges of the Fourteenth Amendment, including the right to vote.

Harlan concludes by stating: "It seems to us that the Fourteenth Amendment, insofar as it was intended to confer national citizenship upon persons of the Indian race, is robbed of its vital force by a construction which excludes from such citizenship those who, although born in tribal relations, are within the complete jurisdiction of the United States." He goes on to ask: "Is it conceivable that the statesmen who framed, the Congress which submitted, and the people who adopted that amendment intended to confer citizenship, national and state, upon the entire population in this country of African descent" but by the same provision "to exclude from such citizenship Indians who had never been in slavery, and who, by becoming *bona fide* residents of states and territories within the complete jurisdiction of the United States, had evinced a purpose to abandon their former mode of life, and become a part of the people of the United States?" Clearly, he believes the answer is no.

Harlan ends by lamenting the status of Indians as "a despised and rejected class of persons with no nationality whatever."

## Impact

*Elk v. Wilkins* did not put to bed the issues that it raised. In 1886 the Court held in *United States v. Kagama* that

Indian tribes were "wards of the nation" and "communities dependent on the United States." The decision, however, still failed to clarify the citizenship status of Native Americans. The debate grew more heated because many Americans pointed to the inconsistency of enfranchising African Americans after the Civil War but not Native Americans—although many southerners and westerners believed that enfranchising Blacks was a mistake that should not be compounded in the case of Indians.

The status of Native Americans was at issue with the passage of the 1887 General Allotment Act, also called the Dawes Act or the Dawes Severalty Act, named after its sponsor, Senator Henry Dawes of Massachusetts. The goal of the act was to assimilate Native Americans into mainstream society by eradicating their social and cultural traditions and converting them into sedentary farmers. The act authorized the president to confiscate reservation lands and divide them among individual tribal members; these parcels, called allotments, consisted of 80- or 160-acre sections to be used for farming or grazing by individual tribal members. Any Native American who accepted an allotment was allowed to become a U.S. citizen. The act also extended citizenship to any Indian who voluntarily resided away from his or her tribe. John Elk would have become a citizen under the act.

Into the twentieth century, the issue remained in abeyance. World War I distracted the nation from any issue that was not war related. Some 9,000 Native Americans served in the armed forces, many of them dying to defend a nation that continued to deny them the ability to take part in the political process. After the war, Congress passed legislation, the Citizenship Act of 1919, that granted citizenship to Indian veterans. Finally, in 1924, Native Americans were granted federal citizenship when Congress passed the Indian Citizenship Act—the end product of the progressive movement, lobbying by supporters of Indians, recognition of their war service, and agitation by the tribes themselves. But the matter still did not end there. A number of states in the West continued to deny Indians the right to vote, often resorting to the argument that the Constitution excluded "Indians not taxed" and relying on such phrases as "persons under guardianship" and "Indians living in tribal relations"—phrases that reflected the fact that most Indians in the West lived on reservations. It was not until the middle of the twentieth century that Arizona and New Mexico granted the franchise to Native Americans living in their states and the issue was put to rest.

## Questions for Further Study

1. On what basis did the Court deny the citizenship claim of John Elk?

2. How might the decision in *Elk v. Wilkins* have affected Native Americans in ensuing years?

3. To what extent might racism have played a part in the Court's decision in *Elk v. Wilkins*?

4. On what basis did Justices Harlan and Woods base their dissent in this case?

5. Why were Native Americans denied the right to vote while African Americans were granted that right?

## Further Reading

### *Books*

Pommersheim, Frank. "Elk v. Wilkins: Exclusion, Inclusion, and the Ambiguities of Citizenship." In *Broken Landscape: Indians, Indian Tribes, and the Constitution:* 155–82. New York: Oxford University Press, 2012.

Wildenthal, Bryan H. *Native American Sovereignty on Trial: A Handbook with Cases, Laws, and Documents.* Santa Barbara, CA: ABC-CLIO, 2003.

Wunder, John R. *"Retained by the People": A History of American Indians and the Bill of Rights.* New York: Oxford University Press, 1994.

Wunder, John R., and Mark R. Scherer. *Echo of Its Time: The History of the Federal District Court of Nebraska, 1867–1933.* Lincoln: University of Nebraska Press, 2019

### *Articles*

Allen, John H. Allen. "Denial of Voting Rights to Reservation Indians." *Utah Law Review* 5 (1956): 247–56.

Bodayla, Stephen D. "'Can an Indian Vote?': Elk v. Wilkins, a Setback for Indian Citizenship." *Nebraska History* 67 (1986): 372–80. http://www.nebraskahistory.org/publish/publicat/history/full-text/NH1986IndianVote.pdf.

Lee, R. Alton. "Indian Citizenship and the Fourteenth Amendment." *South Dakota History* 4, no. 2 (Spring 1974): 198–221.

Rollings, William Hughes, "Citizenship and Suffrage: The Native American Struggle for Civil Rights in the American West 1830–1965." *Nevada Law Journal* 5 (Fall 2004): 126–40. https://scholars.law.unlv.edu/cgi/viewcontent.cgi?article=1311&context=nlj.

Tennant, Brad. "'Excluding Indians Not Taxed': Dred Scott, Standing Bear, Elk and the Legal Status of Native Americans in the Latter Half of the Nineteenth Century." *International Social Science Review* 86, nos. 1–2 (2011): 24–43. https://www.jstor.org/stable/41887472.

## Further Reading

### Websites

Berger, Bethany. "Birthright Citizenship on Trial: Elk v. Wilkins and United States v. Wong Kim Ark." *Faculty Articles and Papers*, 2016. Accessed March 13, 2023, https://opencommons.uconn.edu/law_papers/378.

Bomboy, Scott. "On This Day: Supreme Court Says Tax-Paying American Indians Can't Vote." *National Constitution Center*, November 3, 2021. Accessed March 13, 2023, https://constitutioncenter.org/blog/on-this-day-supreme-court-says-tax-paying-indians-cant-vote.

—Commentary by Michael J. O'Neal

# ELK V. WILKINS

## Document Text

### MR. JUSTICE GRAY delivered the opinion of the Court

He stated the facts in the foregoing language, and continued:

The plaintiff, in support of his action, relies on the first clause of the first section of the Fourteenth Article of Amendment of the Constitution of the United States, by which

"All persons born or naturalized in the United States, and subject to the jurisdiction thereof, are citizens of the United States and of the state wherein they reside,"

and on the Fifteenth Article of Amendment, which provides that

"The right of citizens of the United States to vote shall not be denied or abridged by the United States or by any state on account of race, color, or previous condition of servitude."

This being a suit at common law in which the matter in dispute exceeds $500, arising under the Constitution of the United States, the circuit court had jurisdiction of it under the Act of March 3, 1875, c. 137, § 1, even if the parties were citizens of the same state. 18 Stat. 470; *Ames v. Kansas,* 111 U. S. 449. The judgment of that court, dismissing the action with costs, must have proceeded upon the merits, for if the dismissal had been for want of jurisdiction, no costs could have been awarded. *Mayor v. Cooper,* 6 Wall. 247; *Mansfield & Coldwater Railway v. Swan,* 111 U. S. 379. And the only point argued by the defendant in this Court is wheth-

er the petition sets forth facts enough to constitute a cause of action.

The decision of this point, as both parties assume in their briefs, depends upon the question whether the legal conclusion that under and by virtue of the Fourteenth Amendment of the Constitution the plaintiff is a citizen of the United States is supported by the facts alleged in the petition and admitted by the demurrer, to-wit, the plaintiff is an Indian and was born in the United States and has severed his tribal relation to the Indian tribes and fully and completely surrendered himself to the jurisdiction of the United States, and still continues to be subject to the jurisdiction of the United States, and is a *bona fide* resident of the State of Nebraska and City of Omaha. The petition, while it does not show of what Indian tribe the plaintiff was a member, yet, by the allegations that he "is an Indian, and was born within the United States," and that "he had severed his tribal relations to the Indian tribes," clearly implies that he was born a member of one of the Indian tribes within the limits of the United States which still exists and is recognized as a tribe by the government of the United States. Though the plaintiff alleges that he "had fully and completely surrendered himself to the jurisdiction of the United States," he does not allege that the United States accepted his surrender, or that he has ever been naturalized, or taxed, or in any way recognized or treated as a citizen by the state or by the United States. Nor is it contended by his counsel that there is any statute or treaty that makes him a citizen.

The question, then, is whether an Indian, born a member of one of the Indian tribes within the United States, is, merely by reason of his birth within the United States and of his afterwards voluntarily separating himself from his tribe and taking up his residence among white citizens, a citizen of the United States within the meaning of the first section of the Fourteenth Amendment of the Constitution. Under the Constitution of the United States as originally established, "Indians not taxed" were excluded from the persons according to whose numbers representatives and direct taxes were apportioned among the several states, and Congress had and exercised the power to regulate commerce with the Indian tribes, and the members thereof, whether within or without the boundaries of one of the states of the Union. The Indian tribes, being within the territorial limits of the United States, were not, strictly speaking, foreign states, but they were alien nations, distinct political communities, with whom the United States might and habitually did deal as they thought fit, either through treaties made by the President and Senate or through acts of Congress in the ordinary forms of legislation. The members of those tribes owed immediate allegiance to their several tribes, and were not part of the people of the United States. They were in a dependent condition, a state of pupilage, resembling that of a ward to his guardian. Indians and their property, exempt from taxation by treaty or statute of the United States, could not be taxed by any state. General acts of Congress did not apply to Indians unless so expressed as to clearly manifest an intention to include them. Constitution, Article I, Sections 2, 8; Article II, Section 2; *Cherokee Nation v. Georgia,* 5 Pet. 1; *Worcester v. Georgia,* 6 Pet. 515; *United States v. Rogers,* 4 How. 567; *United States v. Holliday,* 3 Wall. 407; *Case of the Kansas Indians,* 5 Wall. 737; *Case of the New York Indians,* 5 Wall. 761; *Case of the Cherokee Tobacco,* 11 Wall. 616; *United States v. Whisky,* 93 U. S. 188; *Pennock v. Commissioners,* 103 U. S. 44; *Crow Dog's Case,* 109 U. S. 556; *Goodell v. Jackson,* 20 Johns. 693; *Hastings v. Farmer,* 4 N.Y. 293.

The alien and dependent condition of the members of the Indian tribes could not be put off at their own will without the action or assent of the United States. They were never deemed citizens of the United States except under explicit provisions of treaty or statute to that effect either declaring a certain tribe, or such members of it as chose to remain behind on the removal of the tribe westward, to be citizens or authorizing individuals of particular tribes to become citizens on applica-

tion to a court of the United States for naturalization and satisfactory proof of fitness for civilized life, for examples of which see treaties in 1817 and 1835 with the Cherokees, and in 1820, 1825, and 1830 with the Choctaws, 7 Stat. 159, 211, 236, 335, 483, 488; *Wilson v. Wall,* 6 Wall. 83; Opinion of Attorney General Taney, 2 Opinions of Attorneys General 462; in 1855 with the Wyandotts, 10 Stat. 1159; *Karrahoo v. Adams,* 1 Dillon 344, 346; *Gray v. Coffman,* 3 Dillon 393; *Hicks v. Butrick,* 3 Dillon 413; in 1861 and in March, 1866 with the Pottawatomies, 12 Stat. 1192; 14 Stat. 763; in 1862 with the Ottawas, 12 Stat. 1237; and the Kickapoos, 13 Stat. 624; and Acts of Congress of March 3, 1839, c. 83, § 7, concerning the Brothertown Indians, and of March 3, 1843, c. 101 § 7, August 6, 1846, c. 88, and March 3, 1865, c. 127 § 4, concerning the Stockbridge Indians, 5 Stat. 351, 647; 9 Stat. 55; 13 Stat. 562. *See also* treaties with the Stockbridge Indians in 1848 and 1856, 9 Stat. 955; 11 Stat. 667; 7 Opinions of Attorneys General 746.

Chief Justice Taney, in the passage cited for the plaintiff from his opinion in *Scott v. Sandford,* 19 How. 393, 60 U. S. 404, did not affirm or imply that either the Indian tribes, or individual members of those tribes, had the right, beyond other foreigners, to become citizens of their own will, without being naturalized by the United States. His words were:

"They [the Indian tribes] may without doubt, like the subjects of any foreign government, be naturalized by the authority of Congress and become citizens of a state and of the United States, and if an individual should leave his nation or tribe, and take up his abode among the white population, he would be entitled to all the rights and privileges which would belong to an emigrant from any other foreign people."

But an emigrant from any foreign state cannot become a citizen of the United States without a formal renunciation of his old allegiance, and an acceptance by the United States of that renunciation through such form of naturalization as may be required law.

The distinction between citizenship by birth and citizenship by naturalization is clearly marked in the provisions of the Constitution, by which

"No person, except a natural born citizen or a citizen of the United States at the time of the adoption of this Constitution shall be eligible to the office of President," and "The Congress shall have power to establish an uniform rule of naturalization." Constitution, Article II, Section 1; Article I, Section 8. By the Thirteenth Amendment of the Constitution, slavery was prohibited. The main object of the opening sentence of the Fourteenth Amendment was to settle the question, upon which there had been a difference of opinion throughout the country and in this Court, as to the citizenship of free negroes (*Scott v. Sandford,* 19 How. 393), and to put it beyond doubt that all persons, white or black, and whether formerly slaves or not, born or naturalized in the United States, and owing no allegiance to any alien power, should be citizens of the United States and of the state in which they reside. *Slaughterhouse Cases,* 16 Wall. 36, 83 U. S. 73; *Strauder v. West Virginia,* 100 U. S. 303, 100 U. S. 306.

This section contemplates two sources of citizenship, and two sources only: birth and naturalization. The persons declared to be citizens are "all persons born or naturalized in the United States, and subject to the jurisdiction thereof." The evident meaning of these last words is not merely subject in some respect or degree to the jurisdiction of the United States, but completely subject to their political jurisdiction and owing them direct and immediate allegiance. And the words relate to the time of birth in the one case, as they do to the time of naturalization in the other. Persons not thus subject to the jurisdiction of the United States at the time of birth cannot become so afterwards except by being naturalized, either individually, as by proceedings under the naturalization acts, or collectively, as by the force of a treaty by which foreign territory is acquired.

Indians born within the territorial limits of the United States, members of and owing immediate allegiance to one of the Indiana tribes (an alien though dependent power), although in a geographical sense born in the United States, are no more "born in the United States and subject to the jurisdiction thereof," within the meaning of the first section of the Fourteenth Amendment, than the children of subjects of any foreign government born within the domain of that government, or the children born within the United States of ambassadors or other public ministers of foreign nations.

This view is confirmed by the second section of the Fourteenth Amendment, which provides that

"Representatives shall be apportioned among the several states according to their respective numbers, counting the whole number of persons in each state, excluding Indians not taxed."

Slavery having been abolished, and the persons formerly held as slaves made citizens, this clauses fixing the apportionment of representatives has abrogated so much of the corresponding clause of the original Constitution as counted only three-fifths of such persons. But Indians not taxed are still excluded from the count for the reason that they are not citizens. Their absolute exclusion from the basis of representation in which all other persons are now included is wholly inconsistent with their being considered citizens. So the further provision of the second section for a proportionate reduction of the basis of the representation of any state in which the right to vote for Presidential electors, representatives in Congress, or executive or judicial officers or members of the legislature of a state is denied, except for participation in rebellion or other crime, to "any of the male inhabitants of such state, being twenty-one years of age and citizens of the United States," cannot apply to a denial of the elective franchise to Indians not taxed, who form no part of the people entitled to representation.

It is also worthy of remark that the language used about the same time by the very Congress which framed the Fourteenth Amendment, in the first section of the Civil Rights Act of April 9, 1866, declaring who shall be citizens of the United States, is "all persons born in the United States, and not subject to any foreign power, excluding Indians not taxed." 14 Stat. 27; Rev.Stat. § 1992.

Such Indians, then, not being citizens by birth, can only become citizens in the second way mentioned in the Fourteenth Amendment, by being "naturalized in the United States," by or under some treaty or statute.

The action of the political departments of the government, not only after the proposal of the amendment by Congress to the states in June, 1866, but since the proclamation in July, 1868, of its ratification by the requisite number of states, accords with this construction.

While the amendment was pending before the legislatures of the several states, treaties containing provisions for the naturalization of members of Indian tribes as citizens of the United States were made on July 4, 1866, with the Delawares, in 1867 with various tribes in Kansas, and with the Pottawatomies, and in April, 1868, with the Sioux. 14 Stat. 794, 796; 15 Stat. 513, 532, 533, 637.

The treaty of 1867 with the Kansas Indians strikingly illustrates the principle that no one can become a citizen of a nation without its consent, and directly contradicts the supposition that a member of an Indian tribe can at will be alternately a citizen of the United States and a member of the tribe.

That treaty not only provided for the naturalization of members of the Ottawa, Miami, Peoria, and other tribes, and their families, upon their making declaration before the district court of the United States of their intention to become citizens, 15 Stat. 517, 520, 521; but, after reciting that some of the Wyandotts, who had become citizens under the treaty of 1855, were "unfitted for the responsibilities of citizenship" and enacting that a register of the whole people of this tribe, resident in Kansas or elsewhere, should be taken, under the direction of the Secretary of the Interior, showing the names of "all who declare their desire to be and remain Indians and in a tribal condition," and of incompetents and orphans as described in the treaty of 1855, and that such persons, and those only, should thereafter constitute the tribe, it provided that

"No one who has heretofore consented to become a citizen, nor the wife or children of any such person, shall be allowed to become members of the tribe except by the free consent of the tribe after its new organization and unless the agent shall certify that such party is, through poverty or incapacity, unfit to continue in the exercise of the responsibilities of citizenship of the United States and likely to become a public charge."

15 Stat. 514, 516.

Since the ratification of the Fourteenth Amendment, Congress has passed several acts for naturalizing Indians of certain tribes, which would have been superfluous if they were, or might become without any action of the government, citizens of the United States. By the Act of July 15, 1870, c. 296, § 10, for instance, it was provided that if at any time thereafter any of the Winnebago Indians in the State of Minnesota should desire to become citizens of the United States, they should make application to the District Court of the United States for the District of Minnesota, and in open court

make the same proof, and take the same oath of allegiance as is provided by law for the naturalization of aliens, and should also make proof, to the satisfaction of the court, that they were sufficiently intelligent and prudent to control their affairs and interests, that they had adopted the habits of civilized life, and had for at least five years before been able to support themselves and their families, and thereupon they should be declared by the court to be citizens of the United States, the declaration entered of record, and a certificate thereof given to the applicant, and the Secretary of the Interior, upon presentation of that certificate, might issue to them patents in fee simple, with power of alienation, of the lands already held by them in severalty, and might cause to be paid to them their proportion of the money and effects of the tribe held in trust under any treaty or law of the United States, and thereupon such persons should cease to be members of the tribe, and the lands so patented to them should be subject to levy, taxation, and sale in like manner with the property of other citizens. 16 Stat. 361. By the Act of March 3, 1873, c. 332, § 3, similar provision was made for the naturalization of any adult members of the Miami tribe in Kansas, and of their minor children. 17 Stat. 632. And the Act of March 3, 1865, c. 127, before referred to, making corresponding provision for the naturalization of any of the chiefs, warriors, or heads of families of the Stockbridge Indians, is reenacted in § 2312 of the Revised Statutes.

The Act of January 25, 1871, c. 38, for the relief of the Stockbridge and Munsee Indians in the State of Wisconsin, provided that "for the purpose of determining the persons who are members of said tribes, and the future relation of each to the government of the United States," two rolls should be prepared under the direction of the Commissioner of Indian Affairs, signed by the sachem and councilors of the tribe, certified by the person selected by the commissioner to superintend the same, and returned to the commissioner, the one, to be denominated the citizen roll, of the names of all such persons of full age, and their families, "as signify their desire to separate their relations with said tribe and to become citizens of the United States," and the other to be denominated the Indian roll, of the names of all such "as desire to retain their tribal character and continue under the care and guardianship of the United States," and that those rolls, so made and returned, should be held as a full surrender and relinquishment, on the part of all those of the first class, of all claims to be known or considered as members of the tribe, or to be interested in any provision made or to be made by the United States for its benefit, "and they and their descendants shall thenceforth be admitted to all the rights and privileges of citizens of the United States." 16 Stat. 406.

The Pension Act exempts Indian claimants of pensions for service in the army or navy from the obligation to take the oath to support the Constitution of the United States. Act of March 3, 1873, c. 234, § 28, 17 Stat. 574; Rev.Stat. § 4721.

The recent statutes concerning homesteads are quite inconsistent with the theory that Indians do or can make themselves independent citizens by living apart from their tribe. The Act of March 3, 1875, c. 131, § 15, allowed to "any Indian born in the United States, who is the head of a family, or who has arrived at the age of twenty-one years, and who has abandoned, or may hereafter abandon, his tribal relations" the benefit of the homestead acts, but only upon condition of his "making satisfactory proof of such abandonment, under rules to be prescribed by the Secretary of the Interior," and further provided that his title in the homestead should be absolutely inalienable for five years from the date of the patent, and that he should be entitled to share in all annuities, tribal funds, lands, and other property, as if he had maintained his tribal relations. 18 Stat. 420. And the Act of March 3, 1884, c. 180, § 1, while it allows Indians "located on public lands" to "avail themselves of the homestead laws as fully, and to the same extent, as may now be done by citizens of the United States," provides that the form and the legal effect of the patent shall be that the United States does and will hold the land for twenty-five years in trust for the Indian making the entry, and his widow and heirs, and will then convey it in fee to him or them. 23 Stat. 96.

The national legislation has tended more and more toward the education and civilization of the Indians, and fitting them to be citizens. But the question whether any Indian tribes, or any members thereof, have become so far advanced in civilization that they should be let out of the state of pupilage, and admitted to the privileges and responsibilities of citizenship, is a question to be decided by the nation whose wards they are and whose citizens they seek to become, and not by each Indian for himself. There is nothing in the statutes or decisions referred to by counsel to control the

conclusion to which we have been brought by a consideration of the language of the Fourteenth Amendment and of the condition of the Indians at the time of its proposal and ratification.

The Act of July 27, 1868, c. 249, declaring the right of expatriation to be a natural and inherent right of all people, and reciting that "in the recognition of this principle this government has freely received emigrants from all nations, and invested them with the rights of citizenship," while it affirms the right of every man to expatriate himself from one country, contains nothing to enable him to become a citizen of another without being naturalized under its authority. 15 Stat. 223; Rev.Stat. § 1999.

The provision of the Act of Congress of March 3, 1871, c. 120, that

"Hereafter no Indian nation or tribe within the territory of the United States shall be acknowledged or recognized as an independent nation, tribe, or power with whom the United States may contract by treaty"

is coupled with a provision that the obligation of any treaty already lawfully made is not to be thereby invalidated or impaired, and its utmost possible effect is to require the Indian tribes to be dealt with for the future through the legislative and not through the treatymaking power. 16 Stat. 566; Rev.Stat. § 2079.

In the case of *United States v. Elm*, 23 Int.Rev.Rec. 419, decided by Judge Wallace in the District Court of the United States for the Northern District of New York, the Indian who was held to have a right to vote in 1876 was born in the State of New York, one of the remnants of a tribe which had ceased to exist as a tribe in that state, and by a statute of the state it had been enacted that any native Indian might purchase, take, hold, and convey lands, and whenever he should have become a freeholder to the value of $100 should be liable to taxation and to the civil jurisdiction of the courts in the same manner and to the same extent as a citizen. N.Y. Stat. 1843, c. 87. The condition of the tribe from which he derived his origin, so far as any fragments of it remained within the State of New York, resembled the condition of those Indian nations of which Mr. Justice Johnson said in *Fletcher v. Peck*, 6 Cranch 87, 10 U. S. 146, that they "have totally extinguished their national fire, and submitted themselves to the laws of the states," and which Mr. Justice McLean had in view when he observed in *Worcester v. Georgia,* 6 Pet. 515, 31 U. S. 580, that in some of the old states

"where small remnants of tribes remain, surrounded by white population, and who, by their reduced numbers, had lost the power of self-government, the laws of the state have been extended over them, for the protection of their persons and property."

*See also,* as to the condition of Indians in Massachusetts, remnants of tribes never recognized by the treaties or legislative or executive acts of the United States as distinct political communities, *Danzell v. Webquish,* 108 Mass. 133; *Pells v. Webquish,* 129 Mass. 469; Mass. Stat. 1862, c. 184; 1869, c. 463.

The passages cited as favorable to the plaintiff, from the opinions delivered in *Ex Parte Kenyon,* 5 Dillon 385, 390, in *Ex Parte Reynolds,* 5 Dillon 394, 397, and in *United States v. Crook,* 5 Dillon 453, 464, were *obiter dicta.* The *Case of Reynolds* was an indictment, in the Circuit Court of the United States for the Western District of Arkansas, for a murder in the Indian country, of which that court had jurisdiction if either the accused or the dead man was not an Indian, and was decided by Judge Parker in favor of the jurisdiction, upon the ground that both were white men and that, conceding the one to be an Indian by marriage, the other never was an Indian in any sense. 5 Dillon 397, 404. Each of the other two cases was a writ of habeas corpus, and any person, whether a citizen or not, unlawfully restrained of his liberty, is entitled to that writ. *Case of the Hottentot Venus,* 13 East 195; *Case of Dos Santos,* 2 Brock. 493; *In re Kaine,* 14 How. 103. In *Kenyon's Case,* Judge Parker held that the court in which the prisoner had been convicted had no jurisdiction of the subject matter because the place of the commission of the act was beyond the territorial limits of its jurisdiction, and, as was truly said, "this alone would be conclusive of this case." 5 Dillon 390. In *United States v. Crook,* the Ponca Indians were discharged by Judge Dundy because the military officers who held them were taking them to the Indian Territory by force and without any lawful authority, 5 Dillon 468, and in the case at bar, as the record before us shows, that learned judge concurred in the judgment below for the defendant.

The law upon the question before us has been well stated by Judge Deady in the District Court of the Unit-ed States for the District of Oregon. In giving judgment against the plaintiff in a case resembling the case at bar, he said:

"Being born a member of 'an independent political community'—the Chinook—he was not born subject to the jurisdiction of the United States—not born in its allegiance."

*McKay v. Campbell,* 2 Sawyer 118, 134. And in a later case, he said:

"But an Indian cannot make himself a citizen of the United States without the consent and cooperation of the government. The fact that he has abandoned his nomadic life or tribal relations and adopted the habits and manners of civilized people may be a good reason why he should be made a citizen of the United States, but does not of itself make him one. To be a citizen of the United States is a political privilege which no one not born to can assume without its consent in some form. The Indians in Oregon, not being born subject to the jurisdiction of the United States, were not born citizens thereof, and I am not aware of any law or treaty by which any of them have been made so since."

*United States v. Osborne,* 6 Sawyer 406, 409.

Upon the question whether any action of a state can confer rights of citizenship on Indians of a tribe still recognized by the United States as retaining its tribal existence, we need not and do not express an opinion, because the State of Nebraska is not shown to have taken any action affecting the condition of this plaintiff. *See Chirac v. Chirac,* 2 Wheat. 259; *Fellows v. Blacksmith,* 19 How. 366; *United States v. Holliday,* 3 Wall. 407, 70 U. S. 420; *United States v. Joseph,* 94 U. S. 614, 94 U. S. 618. The plaintiff, not being a citizen of the United States under the Fourteenth Amendment of the Constitution, has been deprived of no right secured by the Fifteenth Amendment, and cannot maintain this action.

*Judgment affirmed.*

## MR. JUSTICE HARLAN, with whom concurred MR. JUSTICE WOODS, dissenting

MR. JUSTICE WOODS and myself feel constrained to express our dissent from the interpretation which our brethren give to that clause of the Fourteenth Amendment which provides that

"All persons born or naturalized in the United States, and subject to the jurisdiction thereof, are citizens of the United States and of the state wherein they reside."

The case, as presented by the record, is this:

John Elk, the plaintiff in error, is a person of the Indian race. He was born within the territorial limits of the United States. His parents were, at the time of his birth, members of one of the Indian tribes in this country. More than a year, however, prior to his application to be registered as a voter in the City of Omaha, he had severed all relations with his tribe and, as he alleges, fully and completely surrendered himself to the jurisdiction of the United States. Such surrender was, of course, involved in his act of becoming, as the demurrer to the petition admits that he did become, a *bona fide* resident of the State of Nebraska. When he applied in 1880 to be registered as a voter, he possessed, as is also admitted, the qualifications of age and residence in state, county, and ward, required for electors by the constitution and laws of that state. It is likewise conceded that he was entitled to be so registered if at the time of his application, he was a citizen of the United States, for, by the Constitution and laws of Nebraska, every citizen of the United States having the necessary qualifications of age and residence in state, county, and ward is entitled to vote. Whether he was such citizen is the question presented by this writ of error.

It is said that the petition contains no averment that Elk was taxed in the state in which he resides, or had ever been treated by her as a citizen. It is evident that the court would not have held him to be a citizen of the United States even if the petition had contained a direct averment that he was taxed, because its judgment, in legal effect, is that, although born within the territorial limits of the United States, he could not, if at his birth a member of an Indian tribe, acquire national citizenship by force of the Fourteenth Amendment, but only in pursuance of some statute or treaty providing for his naturalization. It would therefore seem unnecessary to inquire whether he was taxed at the time of his application to be registered as a voter, for if the words "all persons born . . . in the United States and subject to the jurisdiction thereof" were not intended to embrace Indians born in tribal relations, but who subsequently became *bona fide* residents of the several states, then

manifestly the legal status of such Indians is not altered by the fact that they are taxed in those states.

While denying that national citizenship, as conferred by that amendment, necessarily depends upon the inquiry whether the person claiming it is taxed in the state of his residence or has property therein from which taxes may be derived, we submit that the petition does sufficiently show that the plaintiff was taxed—that is, belongs to the class which, by the laws of Nebraska, are subject to taxation. By the Constitution and laws of Nebraska, all real and personal property in that state are subject to assessment and taxation. Every person of full age and sound mind, being a resident thereof, is required to list his personal property for taxation. Const.Neb. art. 9, § 1; Compiled Stat. of Neb., c. 77, pp. 400, 401. Of these provisions upon the subject of taxation this Court will take judicial notice. Good pleading did not require that they should be set forth at large in the petition. Consequently an averment that the plaintiff is a citizen and *bona fide* resident of Nebraska implies in law that he is subject to taxation, and is taxed, in that state. Further: The plaintiff has become so far incorporated with the mass of the people of Nebraska that being, as the petition avers, a citizen and resident thereof, he constitutes a part of her militia. Compiled Stat. Neb. c. 56. He may, being no longer a member of an Indian tribe, sue and be sued in her courts. And he is counted in every apportionment of representation in the legislature, for the requirement of her Constitution is that

"The legislature shall apportion the Senators and representatives according to the number of inhabitants, excluding Indians not taxed, and soldiers and officers of the United States army."

Const.Neb., art. 3 § 1. At the adoption of the Constitution there were, in many of the states, Indians, not members of any tribe, who constituted a part of the people for whose benefit the state governments were established. This is apparent from that clause of Article I, Section 3, which requires, in the apportionment of representatives and direct taxes among the several states "according to their respective numbers," the exclusion of "Indians not taxed." This implies that there were at that time, in the United States, Indians who were taxed—that is, were subject to taxation by the laws of the State of which they were residents. Indians not taxed were those who held tribal relations, and therefore were not subject to the authority of any state, and were subject only to the authority of the United States, under the power conferred upon Congress in reference to Indian tribes in this country. The same provision is retained in the Fourteenth Amendment; for now, as at the adoption of the Constitution, Indians in the several states, who are taxed by their laws, are counted in establishing the basis of representation in Congress.

By the Act of April 9, 1866, entitled "An act to protect all persons in the United States in their civil rights, and furnish means for their vindication," 14 Stat. 27, it is provided that

"all persons born in the United States, and not subject to any foreign power, excluding Indians not taxed, are hereby declared to be citizens of the United States."

This, so far as we are aware, is the first general enactment making persons of the Indian race citizens of the United States. Numerous statutes and treaties previously provided for all the individual members of particular Indian tribes becoming, in certain contingencies, citizens of the United States. But the act of 1866 reached Indians not in tribal relations. Beyond question, by that act, national citizenship was conferred directly upon all persons in this country, of whatever race (excluding only "Indians not taxed") who were born within the territorial limits of the United States, and were not subject to any foreign power. Surely everyone must admit that an Indian residing in one of the states and subject to taxation there became, by force alone of the act of 1866, a citizen of the United States, although he may have been, when born, a member of a tribe. The exclusion of Indians not taxed evinced a purpose to include those subject to taxation in the state of their residence. Language could not express that purpose with more distinctness than does the act of 1866. Any doubt upon the subject, in respect to persons of the Indian race residing in the United States or territories, and not members of a tribe, will be removed by an examination of the debates, in which many distinguished statesmen and lawyers participated in the Senate of the United States when the act of 1866 was under consideration.

In the bill as originally reported from the Judiciary Committee there were no words excluding "Indians not taxed" from the citizenship proposed to be grant-

ed. Attention being called to this fact, the friends of the measure disclaimed any purpose to make citizens of those who were in tribal relations, with governments of their own. In order to meet that objection, while conforming to the wishes of those desiring to invest with citizenship all Indians permanently separated from their tribes, and who, by reason of their residence away from their tribes, constituted a part of the people under the jurisdiction of the United States, Mr. Trumbull, who reported the bill, modified it by inserting the words "excluding Indians not taxed." What was intended by that modification appears from the following language used by him in debate:

"Of course, we cannot declare the wild Indians who do not recognize the government of the United States, who are not subject to our laws, with whom we make treaties, who have their own laws, who have their own regulations, whom we do not intend to interfere with or punish for the commission of crimes one upon the other, to be the subjects of the United States in the sense of being citizens. They must be excepted. The Constitution of the United States excludes them from the enumeration of the population of the United States when it says that Indians not taxed are to be excluded. It has occurred to me that, perhaps, the amendment would meet the views of all gentlemen, which used these constitutional words, and said that all persons born in the United States, excluding Indians not taxed, and not subject to any foreign power, shall be deemed citizens of the United States."

Cong.Globe, 1st Sess. 39th Congress, p. 527.

In replying to the objections urged by Mr. Hendricks to the bill even as amended, Mr. Trumbull said:

"Does the Senator from Indiana want the wild roaming Indians, not taxed, not subject to our authority, to be citizens of the United States—persons that are not to be counted, in our government? If he does not, let him not object to this amendment that brings in *even* [only] *the Indian when he shall have cast off his wild habits, and submitted to the laws of organized society and become a citizen.*"

*Ibid.*, 528.

The entire debate shows, with singular clearness, indeed, with absolute certainty, that no Senator who participated in it, whether, in favor of or in opposition to the measure, doubted that the bill as passed admitted, and was intended to admit, to national citizenship Indians who abandoned their tribal relations and became residents of one of the states or territories, within the full jurisdiction of the United States. It was so interpreted by President Johnson, who, in his veto message, said:

"By the first section of the bill all persons born in the United States, and not subject to any foreign power, excluding Indians not taxed, are declared to be citizens of the United States. This provision comprehends the Chinese of the Pacific states, *Indians subject to taxation,* the people called gypsies, as well as the entire race designated as blacks, persons of color, negroes, mulattoes, and persons of African blood. Every individual of those races, born in the United States, is, by the bill, made a citizen of the United States."

It would seem manifest, from this brief review of the history of the act of 1866, that one purpose of that legislation was to confer national citizenship upon a part of the Indian race in this country—such of them at least, as resided in one of the states or territories, and were subject to taxation and other public burdens. And it is to be observed that, whoever was included within the terms of the grant contained in that act, became citizens of the United States without any record of their names being made. The citizenship conferred was made to depend wholly upon the existence of the facts which the statute declared to be a condition precedent to the grant taking effect.

At the same session of the Congress which passed the act of 1866, the Fourteenth Amendment was approved and submitted to the states for adoption. Those who sustained the former urged the adoption of the latter. An examination of the debates, pending the consideration of the amendment, will show that there was no purpose on the part of those who framed it, or of those who sustained it by their votes, to abandon the policy inaugurated by the act of 1866, of admitting to national citizenship such Indians as were separated from their tribes and were residents of one of the states or territories outside of any reservation set apart for the exclusive use and occupancy of Indian tribes.

Prior to the adoption of the Fourteenth Amendment, numerous statutes were passed with reference to particular bodies of Indians, under which the individual members of such bodies, upon the dissolution of their tribal relations, or upon the division of their lands derived from the government, became, or were entitled to become, citizens of the United States by force alone of the statute, without observing the forms required by the naturalization laws in the case of a foreigner becoming a citizen of the United States. Such was the statute of March 3, 1839, 5 Stat. 349, relating to the Brothertown Indians in the then Territory of Wisconsin. Congress consented that the lands reserved for their use might be partitioned among the individuals composing the tribe. The act required the petition to be evidenced by a report and map to be filed with the Secretary of the Interior, by whom it should be transmitted to the President; whereupon the act proceeded:

"The said Brothertown Indians, and each and every of them, shall then be deemed to be, and from that time forth are hereby declared to be, citizens of the United States to all intents and purposes, and shall be entitled to all the rights, privileges, and immunities of such citizens,"

etc. Similar legislation was enacted with reference to the Stockbridge Indians. 5 Stat. 646-647. Legislation of this character has an important bearing upon the present question, for it shows that prior to the adoption of the Fourteenth Amendment it had often been the policy of Congress to admit persons of the Indian race to citizenship upon their ceasing to have tribal relations, and without the slightest reference to the fact that they were born in tribal relations. It shows also that the citizenship thus granted was not in every instance required to be evidenced by the record of a court.

If it be said that the statutes prior to 1866, providing for the admission of Indians to citizenship, required in their execution that a record be made of the names of those who thus acquired citizenship, our answer is that it was entirely competent for Congress to dispense, as it did in the act of 1866, with any such record being made in a court or in any department of the government. And certainly it must be conceded that, except in cases of persons "naturalized in the United States," which phrase refers only to those who are embraced by the naturalization laws, and not to Indians, the Fourteenth Amendment does not require the citizenship granted by it to be evidenced by the record of any court, or of any department of the government. Such citizenship passes to the person of whatever race who is embraced by its provisions, leaving the fact of citizenship to be determined, when it shall become necessary to do so in the course of legal inquiry, in the same way that questions as to one's nativity, domicile, or residence are determined.

If it be also said that since the adoption of the Fourteenth Amendment, Congress has enacted statutes providing for the citizenship of Indians, our answer is that those statutes had reference to tribes the members of which could not, while they continued in tribal relations, acquire the citizenship granted by the Fourteenth Amendment. Those statutes did not deal with individual Indians who had severed their tribal connections and were residents within the states of the Union, under the complete jurisdiction of the United States.

There is nothing in the history of the adoption of the Fourteenth Amendment which in our opinion justifies the conclusion that only those Indians are included in its grant of citizenship who were at the time of their birth, subject to the complete jurisdiction of the United States. As already stated, according to the doctrines of the Court in this case—if we do not wholly misapprehend the effect of its decision—the plaintiff, if born while his parents were members of an Indian tribe, would not be embraced by the amendment even had he been at the time it was adopted, a permanent resident of one of the states, subject to taxation and in fact paying property and personal taxes, to the full extent required of the white race in the same state.

When the Fourteenth Amendment was pending in the Senate of the United States, Mr. Doolittle moved to insert after the words "subject to the jurisdiction thereof" the words "excluding Indians not taxed." His avowed object in so amending the measure was to exclude beyond all question from the proposed grant of national citizenship, tribal Indians who—since they were, in a sense, subject to the jurisdiction of the United States—might be regarded as embraced in the grant. The proposition was opposed by Mr. Trumbull and other friends of the proposed constitutional amendment upon the ground that the words "Indians not taxed" might be misconstrued, and also because those words were unnecessary, in that the phrase "subject to the jurisdiction thereof" embraced only those who were subject to the complete jurisdiction of the United States, which could not be properly said of Indians in tribal relations. But it was distinctly announced by the friends of the amendment that they

intended to include in the grant of national citizenship Indians who were within the jurisdiction of the states and subject to their laws, because such Indians would be completely under the jurisdiction of the United States. Said Mr. Trumbull:

"It is only those who come completely within our jurisdiction, who are subject to our laws, that we think of making citizens, and there can be no objection to the proposition that such persons should be citizens."

Cong.Globe, Pt. 4, 1st Sess. 39th Cong., pp. 2890-2893. Alluding to the phrase "Indians not taxed," he remarked that the language of the proposed constitutional amendment was better than that of the act of 1866 passed at the same session. He observed:

"There is a difficulty about the words 'Indians not taxed.' Perhaps one of the reasons why I think so is because of the persistency with which the Senator from Indiana himself insisted that the phrase 'Indians not taxed,' the very words which the Senator from Wisconsin wishes to insert here, would exclude everybody that did not pay a tax; that that was the meaning of it; we must take it literally. The Senator from Maryland did not agree to that, nor did I; but, if the Senator from Indiana was right, it would receive a construction which, I am sure, the Senator from Wisconsin would not be for, for if these Indians come within our limits and within our jurisdiction and are civilized, he would just as soon make a citizen of a poor Indian as of the rich Indian."

*Ibid.*, 2894.

A careful examination of all that was said by Senators and representatives, pending the consideration by Congress of the Fourteenth Amendment, justifies us in saying that everyone who participated in the debates, whether for or against the amendment, believed that, in the form in which it was approved by Congress, it granted, and was intended to grant, national citizenship to every person of the Indian race in this country who was unconnected with any tribe, and who resided, in good faith, outside of Indian reservations and within one of the states or territories of the Union. This fact is, we think, entitled to great weight in determining the meaning and scope of the amendment. *Lithographic Co. v. Sarony*, 111 U. S. 57.

In this connection, we refer to an elaborate report made by Mr. Carpenter, to the Senate of the United

States, in behalf of its Judiciary Committee, on the 14th of December, 1870. The report was made in obedience to an instruction to inquire as to the effect of the Fourteenth Amendment upon the treaties which the United States had with various Indian tribes of the country. The report says:

"For these reasons your committee do not hesitate to say that the Indian tribes within the limits of the United States, and the individuals, members of such tribes, while they adhere to and form a part of the tribes to which they belong, are not, within the meaning of the Fourteenth Amendment, 'subject to the jurisdiction' of the United States, and therefore that *such* Indians have not become citizens of the United States by virtue of that amendment; and, if your committee are correct in this conclusion, it follows that the treaties heretofore made between the United States and the Indian tribes are not annulled by that amendment."

The report closes with this significant language:

"It is pertinent to say, in concluding this report, that treaty relations can properly exist with Indian tribes or nations only, and that, *when the members of any Indian tribe are scattered, they are merged in the mass of our people, and become equally subject to the jurisdiction of the United States.*"

The question before us has been examined by a writer upon constitutional law whose views are entitled to great respect. Judge Cooley, referring to the definition of national citizenship as contained in the Fourteenth Amendment, says:

"By the express terms of the amendment, persons of foreign birth, who have never renounced the allegiance to which they were born, though they may have a residence in this country, more or less permanent, for business, instruction, or pleasure, are not citizens. Neither are the aboriginal inhabitants of the country citizens, so long as they preserve their tribal relations and recognize the headship of their chiefs, notwithstanding that, as against the action of our own people, they are under the protection of the laws, and may be said to owe a qualified allegiance to the government. When living within territory over which the laws, either state or territorial, are extended, they are protected by, and at the same time, held amenable to, those laws in all their intercourse with the body politic, and with the individ-

uals composing it; but they are also, as a *quasi*-foreign people, regarded as being under the direction and tutelage of the general government, and subjected to peculiar regulations as dependent communities. They are 'subject to the jurisdiction' of the United States only in a much qualified sense, and it would be obviously inconsistent with the semi-independent character of such a tribe, and with the obedience they are expected to render to their tribal head, that they should be vested with the complete rights, or, on the other hand, subjected to the full responsibilities of American citizens. It would not for a moment be contended that such was the effect of this amendment."

"When, however, the tribal relations are dissolved, when the headship of the chief or the authority of the tribe is no longer recognized, and the individual Indian, turning his back upon his former mode of life, makes himself a member of the civilized community, the case is wholly altered. He then no longer acknowledges a divided allegiance; he joins himself to the body politic; he gives evidence of his purpose to adopt the habits and customs of civilized life; and, as his case is then within the terms of this amendment, it would seem that his right to protection, in person, property, and privilege, must be as complete as the allegiance to the government to which he must then be held; as complete, in short, as that of any other native-born inhabitant."

2 Story's Const., Cooley's ed., § 1933, p. 654.

To the same effect are *Ex Parte Kenyon,* 5 Dillon 390; *Ex Parte Reynolds, ib.,* 307; *United States v. Crook, ib.,* 454; *United States v. Elm,* Dist.Ct. U.S., N.D.N.Y. 23 Int.Rev.Rec. 419.

It seems to us that the Fourteenth Amendment, insofar as it was intended to confer national citizenship upon persons of the Indian race, is robbed of its vital force by a construction which excludes from such citizenship those who, although born in tribal relations, are within the complete jurisdiction of the United States. There were, in some of our states and territories at the time the amendment was submitted by Congress, many Indians who had finally left their tribes and come within the complete jurisdiction of the United States. They were as fully prepared for citizenship as were or are vast numbers of the white and colored races in the same localities. Is it conceivable that the statesmen who framed, the Congress which submitted, and the people who adopted that amendment intended to confer citizenship, national and state, upon the entire population in this country of African descent (the larger part of which was shortly before held in slavery), and, by the same constitutional provision, to exclude from such citizenship Indians who had never been in slavery and who, by becoming *bona fide* residents of states and territories within the complete jurisdiction of the United States, had evinced a purpose to abandon their former mode of life, and become a part of the people of the United States? If this question be answered in the negative, as we think it must be, then we are justified in withholding our assent to the doctrine which excludes the plaintiff from the body of citizens of the United States upon the ground that his parents were, when he was born, members of an Indian tribe, for, if he can be excluded upon any such ground, it must necessarily follow that the Fourteenth Amendment did not grant citizenship even to Indians who, although born in tribal relations, were at its adoption, severed from their tribes, subject to the complete jurisdiction as well of the United States as of the state or territory in which they resided.

Our brethren, it seems to us, construe the Fourteenth Amendment as if it read:

"All persons *born subject* to the jurisdiction of, or naturalized in, the United States, are citizens of the United States and of the state in which they reside,"

whereas the amendment, as it is, implies in respect of persons born in this country that they may claim the rights of national citizenship from and after the moment they become subject to the complete jurisdiction of the United States. This would not include the children born in this country of a foreign minister, for the reason that, under the fiction of extraterritoriality as recognized by international law, such minister, "though actually in a foreign country, is considered still to remain within the territory of his own state," and, consequently, he continues

"subject to the laws of his own country, both with respect to his personal status and his rights of property, and his children, though born in a foreign country, are considered as natives."

Halleck's International Law, c. 10 § 12. Nor was plaintiff born without the jurisdiction of the United States

in the same sense that the subject of a foreign state, born within the territory of that state, may be said to have been born without the jurisdiction of our government. For, according to the decision in *Cherokee Nation v. Georgia*, 5 Pet. 17, the tribe of which the parents of plaintiff were members was not "a foreign state, in the sense of the Constitution," but a domestic dependent people, "in a state of pupilage," and

"so completely under the sovereignty and dominion of the United States that any attempt to acquire their lands, or to form a political connection with them, would be considered an invasion of our territory and an act of hostility."

They occupied territory which the court, in that case, said composed "a part of the United States," the title to which this nation asserted independent of their will. "In all our intercourse with foreign nations," said Chief Justice Marshall in the same case,

"In our commercial regulations, in any attempt at intercourse between Indians and foreign nations, they are considered as within the jurisdictional limits of the United States, subject to many of those restraints which are imposed upon our citizens. . . . They look to our government for protection; rely upon its kindness and its power; appeal to it for relief to their wants, and address the President as their great father."

And, again, in *United States v. Rogers*, 4 How. 572, this Court, speaking by Chief Justice Taney, said that it was

"too firmly and clearly established to admit of dispute that the Indian tribes, residing within the territorial limits of the United States, are subject to their authority."

*The Cherokee Tobacco*, 11 Wall. 616.

Born, therefore, in the territory, under the dominion and within the jurisdictional limits of the United States, plaintiff has acquired, as was his undoubted right, a residence in one of the states, with her consent, and is subject to taxation and to all other burdens imposed by her upon residents of every race. If he did not acquire national citizenship on abandoning his tribe and becoming, by residence in one of the states, subject to the complete jurisdiction of the United States, then the Fourteenth Amendment has wholly failed to accomplish, in respect of the Indian race, what, we think, was intended by it, and there is still in this country a despised and rejected class of persons with no nationality whatever, who, born in our territory, owing no allegiance to any foreign power, and subject, as residents of the states, to all the burdens of government, are yet not members of any political community, nor entitled to any of the rights, privileges, or immunities of citizens of the United States.

---

### Glossary

**annulled:** invalidated

**domestic dependent nation:** a nation or government within and subservient to the United States

**ex parte decision:** a decision reached by a judge without all parties having to be present

**naturalization:** the admittance of a foreigner to citizenship in the country

**pupilage:** the state of being a pupil; dependent

---

# PLESSY V. FERGUSON

| | |
|---|---|
| **DATE**<br>1896 | **CITATION**<br>163 U.S. 537 |
| **AUTHOR**<br>Henry Billings Brown | **SIGNIFICANCE**<br>Ruled that public facilities could be racially segregated as long as they were equal in quality, an infamous ruling that would lead to restrictive Jim Crow laws |
| **VOTE**<br>7-1 | |

## Overview

*Plessy v. Ferguson*, argued on April 13, 1896, and decided on May 18, 1896, is probably best known for giving the United States the "separate but equal" doctrine. The case probably ranks close to *Dred Scott v. Sandford* (1857) as one of the most influential and thoroughly repudiated cases the Supreme Court has ever decided. The majority opinion was written by Justice Henry Billings Brown of Massachusetts, and it gained the assent of six additional justices. That opinion provided a legal imprimatur to segregation and the Jim Crow system of laws that flourished from the late nineteenth century through much of the twentieth century. *Plessy* held that notwithstanding the Reconstruction amendments (the Thirteenth, Fourteenth, and Fifteenth Amendments), which were passed in the wake of the Civil War to grant equal citizenship to African Americans and promised the equal protection of the laws to all persons, the United States Constitution allowed states to segregate Black and white citizens when traveling on intrastate railroads. The separate but equal doctrine was applied to more than just railroads and supported segregation until it was largely repudiated, though not explicitly overruled, in *Brown v. Board of Education of Topeka* (1954).

Justice John Marshall Harlan of Kentucky wrote the sole dissent in *Plessy*, which provided much of the rhetorical support for the twentieth-century civil rights movement. Justice Harlan argued that the Reconstruction amendments' guarantees of equality were so incompatible with segregation that segregation was unconstitutional. Justice David Brewer did not participate in the case.

## Context

Although the Civil War ended just over thirty years before *Plessy v. Ferguson* was decided, the case was nonetheless a result of the lingering conflict that existed after the war. During the decade following the Civil War, known as the Reconstruction era, America was a place of great change with respect to race relations. During the five years following the end of the war, the Thirteenth, Fourteenth, and Fifteenth Amendments (collectively known as the Civil War or Reconstruction amendments) were passed. The Thirteenth Amendment outlawed slavery. The Fourteenth Amendment was passed after it became clear that the

*The case is known for the "separate but equal" doctrine, demonstrated in this 1939 photograph of a "colored" drinking fountain.*
(Library of Congress)

Thirteenth Amendment could not guarantee that individual states would grant the full equality that many had believed would result from the end of slavery. The Fifteenth Amendment, which stated that voting rights could not be abridged based on race, color, or previous condition of servitude, was ratified to guarantee political equality for African American men. Taken together, these amendments were designed to make African Americans ( formerly enslaved and free Blacks) full and equal participants in American society. In addition, Congress passed a number of laws designed to protect the newly won civil rights of Black citizens and allow the full enjoyment of equal citizenship. For example, Congress passed the Civil Rights Act of 1875, which required that Black citizens be provided the same access to public accommodations, such as railroads, theaters, and inns, as white citizens.

Although race relations were hardly smooth after the Civil War, Congress made clear that equality under the

law was to be the order of the day. However, the presidential election of 1876 changed the course of the country. Rutherford Hayes and Samuel Tilden ran a very close election that had to be decided in the House of Representatives. In exchange for support to become president, Hayes agreed to end the Reconstruction era in the South and withdraw the remaining federal troops there. The withdrawal of troops signaled the psychological end to Reconstruction and the coming of a Jim Crow society based on racial separation and racial caste.

Louisiana's story tracks that of the South, though New Orleans had always enjoyed more racial mixing than other parts of the South. For example, just after the end of the Civil War, Louisiana enacted its Black Code. However, in 1868 Louisiana ratified a state constitution that provided equal rights to African Americans. Around this time, Louisiana also desegregated its schools. As with the rest of the South, however, the end of Reconstruction triggered the arrival of Jim

Crow laws. Both Louisiana and New Orleans slid toward state-mandated segregation.

The segregationists consolidated power through the 1870s and the 1880s. In the 1880s many southern states began to pass laws requiring the segregation of railroad cars. In 1890 Louisiana joined those states in passing the Separate Car Act of 1890. As a result of the legislation, a number of African Americans created the Citizens' Committee to Test the Constitutionality of the Separate Car Act to challenge the law and to attempt to protect the gains won for African Americans during the Reconstruction era. Homer Plessy's case was a test case designed specifically to challenge the Separate Car Act and the coming of the Jim Crow laws. The case had the potential to either stem the tide of racial separatism or drive a nail in the coffin of racial equality and reconciliation.

## About the Author

Justice Henry Billings Brown wrote the majority opinion in *Plessy v. Ferguson*. Brown was born on March 2, 1836, in South Lee, Massachusetts. After graduating from Yale College, he studied law at Yale Law School and Harvard Law School. He served as a U.S. deputy marshal, assistant U.S. attorney, and federal judge of the Eastern District of Michigan for fifteen years before being confirmed to the U.S. Supreme Court in 1890. He retired from the Court in 1906 and died on September 4, 1913.

Justice John Marshall Harlan wrote the sole dissenting opinion in *Plessy v. Ferguson*. Harlan was born on June 1, 1833, in Boyle County, Kentucky. After graduating from Centre College, he studied law at Transylvania University. Although he was a former slaveholder, Harlan fought for the Union Army in the Civil War. Harlan opposed abolition before the war and full equality for Blacks just after the war. However, in the wake of the Civil War, Harlan joined the Republican Party and reversed his view of slavery and many racial equality issues. Harlan was confirmed to the Court on November 29, 1877. In addition to the *Plessy* dissent, he dissented in the Civil Rights Cases (1883), arguing that the Civil Rights Act of 1875 was constitutional and should have been held to legally require equal public accommodations for those of all races. Harlan served on the Court until his death on October 14, 1911.

## Explanation and Analysis of the Document

### Statement of the Case

The case begins with a recitation of the facts of the case and its legal posture. On June 7, 1892, Plessy, the defendant (also known as the plaintiff in error), paid for a first-class train ticket on the East Louisiana Railway headed from New Orleans to Covington, Louisiana, and sat down in an empty seat in the railroad car reserved for whites. He was "of seven-eighths Caucasian and one-eighth African blood" and had such a light complexion that one could not tell that he had any African ancestry. However, Plessy had already decided to challenge the law before boarding the train. Thus, after sitting down, Plessy informed the conductor that he was of mixed blood. He was told he had to move to the section for nonwhites or get off the train. Plessy was "forcibly ejected from said coach" and taken to jail after he refused to move.

Plessy was charged with violating an act of the Louisiana legislature commonly known as the Separate Car Act of 1890. In response to the charge, Plessy asserted that the act violated the U.S. Constitution. The Louisiana trial court disagreed and, according to the statement of the case as noted in the *Plessy* decision, stated that unless "the judge of the said court be enjoined by a writ of prohibition from further proceeding in such case, the court will proceed to fine and sentence petitioner to imprisonment." Plessy sought a writ of prohibition that would stop the court from enforcing the act. The Louisiana Supreme Court determined that the Separate Car Act was constitutional and denied the writ of prohibition. Consequently, Plessy "prayed for a writ of error from this court," and the case came to the United States Supreme Court.

### The Majority Opinion

Justice Henry Billings Brown's opinion for the Court follows the recitation of facts. It begins by noting that the key issue is "the constitutionality of an act of the general assembly of the state of Louisiana, passed in 1890, providing for separate railway carriages for the white and colored races." The opinion then describes the content of the statute. The first section of the statute requires that railway companies other than street railroads provide "equal but separate accommodations for the white, and colored races," either by providing separate train cars or by erecting partitions in a single railcar that separates the races. The second section of the statute requires that the companies segregate their passengers by race. Train conductors and other company employees were required to assign passengers to respective accommodations by race. Passengers who refused to go to their assigned accommodations and train employees who intentionally assigned passengers to the wrong accommodations were liable for a fine of $25 or up to twenty days in jail. A railway company could refuse to carry a passenger who refused to sit in his or her assigned car, and no damages would arise based on the refusal. The third section of the act provides penalties for employees of the railway company who refuse to comply with the act, but it excepts "nurses attending children of the other race." According to Brown, the fourth section of the act is immaterial.

The opinion repeats facts from the statement of the case: that Plessy was of seven-eighths Caucasian and one-eighth African blood, that one could not tell that he was part African by looking at him, that he sat down in a vacant seat in the coach assigned for whites, that he did not move when he was told to move, that he was removed from the train, and that he was taken to the parish jail. Brown notes that Plessy claims that the Separate Car Act is unconstitutional under both the Thirteenth and Fourteenth Amendments. Brown quickly addresses the Thirteenth Amendment claim and then spends the rest of the opinion addressing the Fourteenth Amendment claim.

Brown explains that the Thirteenth Amendment addresses slavery and like conditions such as "Mexican peonage or the Chinese coolie trade." In addition, the amendment applies to attempts to place people into involuntary servitude or to place badges of slavery on former slaves. However, says Brown, the Thirteenth Amendment is not applicable to this case. The statute at issue makes a distinction between the races based on color but does not seek to "destroy the legal equality of the two races, or re-establish a state of involuntary servitude." Brown notes that in cases like this one where a law allows or requires discrimination, if any amendment will apply, it will be the Fourteenth, not the Thirteenth. This is because the Fourteenth Amendment was passed to address race-based distinctions that some believed effectively devalued the freedom given by the Thirteenth Amendment.

Brown begins his explanation of the applicability of the Fourteenth Amendment with an elucidation of its scope and limitations. He notes that the purpose of the amendment is "to establish the citizenship of the negro, to given definitions of citizenship of the United States and of the states, and to protect from the hostile legislation of the states the privileges and immunities of citizens of the United States, as distinguished from those of citizens of the states." Simply, the amendment provides equality of the races before the law. Equality before the law is not necessarily inconsistent with making race-based distinctions or even segregating the races, however. Brown notes that school segregation was allowed even in jurisdictions that scrupulously provided equal political rights between the races, citing Justice Lemuel Shaw's opinion in the 1849 case *Roberts v. City of Boston*. Although that case was decided before the Civil War and the passage of the Fourteenth Amendment and could not be deemed binding on any construction of the Fourteenth Amendment, Brown's point appears to be that there is a distinction between requiring equality before the law and requiring what he believes constituted social equality. In making his point, Brown previews an argument, which he would use later in the opinion, that enforced separation of the races does not suggest the inferiority of either race.

Brown argues that the Fourteenth Amendment is a limitation on states when political or civil equality is at stake, rather than a mandate to allow Congress to grant positive rights to support notions of equality. For example, the Fourteenth Amendment requires that Blacks and whites be treated equally when civil rights such as the ability to serve on a jury are at issue. Conversely, when social equality issues are at stake, such as conditions of travel, the Fourteenth Amendment leaves those matters to the states to regulate so long as no other constitutional provisions are violated. For example, when Louisiana sought to regulate racial aspects of how passengers were to be treated when traveling through the state in interstate travel, it would have been able to do so had the law not been related to interstate commerce, the regulation of which is left to Congress under the Constitution. That the Fourteenth Amendment generally leaves state prerogatives to regulate intact was made clear when the Court passed on the Civil Rights Act of 1875 in the Civil Rights Cases. There, the Court indicated that the Fourteenth Amendment does not give Congress the power to pass legislation that provides positive rights in areas of state prerogative such as the public accommodation of the races with respect to private businesses. Simply, the Fourteenth Amendment does not provide positive rights; it merely limits the kind of legislation states can pass.

Brown then directly addresses the constitutionality of the Separate Car Act. Although the act forced segregation, Brown finds that it does not harm the rights of African Americans because it "neither abridges the privileges or immunities of the colored man, deprives him of his property without due process of law, nor denies him the equal protection of the laws, within the meaning of the fourteenth amendment." The act had the potential to harm the rights of whites, however. If, as Plessy argues in the claim, the reputation of being a white person in a mixed-race community is like property, the act may have gone too far in protecting a conductor who improperly assigns whites to the Black car and therefore damages the property value of the white person. Brown notes that this problem is of no moment to Plessy's claim, because a Black man like Plessy loses no property value in his reputation by being improperly categorized as a white person.

In response to the argument that allowing racial separation opens the door to allowing the state to create other arbitrary distinctions based on race, Brown answers that the exercise of the state's police power itself has to be reasonable. The question is whether the Separate Car Act is reasonable based on "the established usages, customs, and traditions of the people, and with a view to the promotion of their comfort, and the preservation of the public peace and good order." Based on that standard, it is unclear that the segregation here is any worse than school segregation that, according to Brown, most courts appear to agree is constitutional.

After determining that the act is constitutional, Brown attempts to explain why the rule itself treats the races equally. He reprises his argument that forced segregation does not suggest the inferiority of either race and states that any inferiority that Black citizens may feel comes from the spin Blacks give to the act and not from the act itself. Indeed, he suggests that if a majority-Black legislature had passed the act, whites would not feel inferior to Blacks. Oddly, Brown then explains that voluntary mingling between the races is

acceptable, but forced mingling by the state is not required. Given that the statute at issue stops voluntary mingling, Brown's argument is somewhat nonsensical. Brown ends the argument by suggesting that formal civil and political equality is as far as the Constitution does and can go. If the races are social unequals, the Constitution cannot remedy that situation. Brown ends his opinion by noting that it is unclear how much African blood makes one Black for purposes of segregation statutes, but he leaves that issue to the individual states to decide.

## *The Dissenting Opinion*

Justice John Marshall Harlan begins by highlighting a few of the statute's salient points. He notes that the statute requires strict separation of the races with the exception of a nurse caring for a child of a different race. Indeed, a personal attendant could not attend to the needs of her employer if the attendant and employer were of different races unless the attendant wished to be held criminally liable. However, he notes, regardless of the fairness of the statute, the question for the Court is whether the statute's explicit regulation based on race is constitutional.

Harlan provides the general structure of his argument. The civil rights of all citizens are to be protected equally. Consequently, there is no reason for the government to consider the race of any person when regulating civil rights. When a government considers race when legislating regarding civil rights, not only does it improperly provide civil rights, it also improperly affects the liberty of all United States residents.

Harlan then indicates the purpose of the Reconstruction amendments. The Reconstruction amendments provide a broad protection for the rights of all citizens. The Thirteenth Amendment abolishes slavery, "prevents the imposition of any burdens or disabilities that constitute badges of slavery or servitude," and "decreed universal civil freedom in this country." But the Thirteenth Amendment was not strong enough to fully protect the rights of former slaves. Consequently, the Fourteenth Amendment was ratified to ensure that the freedom provided by the Thirteenth Amendment could be fully exercised. By explicitly making African Americans citizens and by stopping states from regulating rights based on race, the Fourteenth Amendment "added greatly to the dignity and glory of

American citizenship, and to the security of personal liberty." In combination, the Thirteenth and Fourteenth Amendments were supposed to guarantee that "all the civil rights that pertain to freedom and citizenship" would be protected. The Fifteenth Amendment, which states that the right to vote is not provided on the basis of race, color, or previous condition of servitude, was added to guarantee that all citizens could participate "in the political control of his country." As a group, the Reconstruction amendments were designed to guarantee that African Americans enjoyed the same rights as whites in the eyes of the law.

The Reconstruction amendments were meant to ensure that Blacks and former slaves were to be equal with whites and would enjoy the same rights. Even though the Fourteenth Amendment does not give positive rights, it does stop state governments from treating Blacks badly merely because of their skin color. Indeed, the Supreme Court has made clear that with respect to civil and political rights, "all citizens are equal before the law." In concrete terms, this means that Blacks cannot, for example, be kept from serving on juries. Harlan notes that the Supreme Court had decided so in *Strauder v. West Virginia* (1880).

Harlan then begins his attack on the majority's opinion by noting that the statute is clearly designed to keep Blacks away from whites and that anyone who claims otherwise is lacking in candor. Then, rather than focusing directly on the equality issue, he suggests that the statute imperils liberty interests. That is, if people of different races want to sit together on a train, they are not allowed to do so under the statute without breaking the law.

Harlan next suggests that allowing the law to stand could lead to ludicrous results, such as requiring that Blacks use one side of the street and whites use the other side or requiring that Blacks use one side of the courtroom and whites use the other side. Harlan's suggestion that Blacks and whites might be segregated in the jury box is particularly biting, given that the Court had made clear in prior cases that Blacks had a right to serve on integrated juries. How an integrated jury in a segregated jury box might work is anyone's guess.

Harlan then challenges the majority's notion that reasonableness is a ground on which to determine the constitutionality of a statute. He suggests that reasonableness is an issue for the legislature when passing a law. Constitutionality is an issue for the Court when reviewing legislation. It may be acceptable to consider reasonableness when determining how a statute will be interpreted consistent with legislative intent, but it is not acceptable to consider it when determining whether the legislature is allowed to pass a certain statute under the Constitution.

Harlan next begins a discussion that, through the years, would overtake the majority opinion in significance. First, he asserts that the Constitution is color-blind. Harlan, making his point in terms that are harsh to twenty-first-century ears, notes that the white race is dominant in America and that it likely would continue to be so. However, he states that the dominance of the white race does not mean that there is a caste system in America. Indeed, he argues that notwithstanding the relative position of the races, individuals must be treated as equals under the law. He states that the most powerful has no greater rights than the least powerful has and that the Court does a disservice when it claims otherwise. Harlan suggests, in fact, that the Court's vision is so troubling and antithetical to equality that the *Plessy* decision would become as nettlesome as the *Dred Scott* decision.

The effect of the *Plessy* decision, suggests Harlan, would be to encourage some to create a caste system that would be antithetical to the Reconstruction amendments. The decision is likely to cause great harm, given that Blacks and whites need to learn to live together. Harlan suggests that laws like Louisiana's, which imply that Blacks are "so inferior and degraded that they cannot be allowed to sit in public coaches occupied by white citizens," would elicit discord, distrust, and hate between the races.

Harlan then attacks the notion that the case is about social equality. The statute at issue relates to allowing people to sit in the same train car. Social equality is no more relevant to that issue than it is to the issue of having citizens of different races share the same street, share the same ballot box, or stand together at a political assembly. Indeed, Harlan notes, it is odd that one would raise the social equality issue in this context, given that the Chinese are considered so different from Americans that they are not allowed to become citizens. Although the Chinese cannot become citizens, they are allowed to ride in the same car as whites.

Given that Blacks are supposed to have equal rights as citizens, that they have fought in wars to preserve the Union, and that they have the right to share political control of the country, it is odd that they would not be allowed to share the same railway car with whites. In fact, Harlan argues, "the arbitrary separation of citizens, on the basis of race, while they are on a public highway, is a badge of servitude wholly inconsistent with the civil freedom and the equality before the law established by the constitution. It cannot be justified upon any legal grounds."

Harlan suggests that any harm that might come from having Blacks and whites share railcars pales in comparison to the problems that will arise from denying civil rights by separating the races. If separation is appropriate, it is unclear why separation would not be appropriate when Blacks are exercising rights that the Court agrees they must be allowed to exercise. He again suggests that, under the reasoning of *Plessy*, there would be nothing unconstitutional in a state forcing jury boxes to be partitioned on the basis of race.

As he moves toward the conclusion of the dissent, Harlan argues that the cases that Brown cites to support segregation are from a bygone, pre–Civil War era during which inequality and slavery ruled. Given the mind-set of those who passed the laws and the absence of the Reconstruction amendments, such cases are inapplicable to this situation and should be ignored. The question is not how to think about rights in an era of admitted inequality, but what to do in an era when free Blacks and former slaves are citizens and must be provided equal rights.

Harlan finishes by arguing that the law at issue is an affront to the liberty of all citizens and is inconsistent with the Constitution. He notes that if similar laws were passed by states and localities, trouble would ensue. Lastly, he indicates that if the right to provide rights unequally to citizens is allowed, Black citizens who are full members in society would be placed "in a condition of legal inferiority." For the aforementioned reasons, Harlan notes, he is required to dissent.

## Impact

The effect of *Plessy v. Ferguson* on the first half of the twentieth century cannot be overstated. Although the *Plessy* Court was not the first Court to provide a cramped reading of the Fourteenth Amendment, the

context in which the reading occurred was important. Before *Plessy*, the Supreme Court decided that the Reconstruction amendments could not be used to allow Congress to provide many positive rights to African Americans, notwithstanding the enforcement power provided to Congress in Section 5 of the amendment. However, *Plessy* limited the use of the Reconstruction amendments by the courts to block state legislation that provided unequal rights to African Americans. Given the Fourteenth Amendment's equal protection clause, the blocking function was arguably the narrowest and most essential function the Reconstruction amendments could have had. Without the Reconstruction amendments being broadly available to stop attempts to limit participation of African Americans in as much of American life as possible, the proponents of Jim Crow laws had a largely open field. *Plessy* simply helped extend and legitimize the Jim Crow era, during which Blacks would lose many of the gains made in the South since the end of the Civil War. It allowed for years of poor treatment of Blacks at the hands of state legislatures rather than merely at the hands of private actors.

The separate but equal doctrine was the *Plessy* Court's lasting legacy. The doctrine was simple and effective. It provided segregationists with a simple tool and a constitutional imprimatur to regulate out of existence many rights thought to be protected by the Fourteenth Amendment. That doctrine provided constitutional protection to those who sought to limit the equality of African Americans. Segregationists were not simply allowed to make Black citizens somewhat invisible through segregation; they were also emboldened to push the envelope of disenfranchisement and inequality as far as possible, knowing that the Supreme Court likely would not act to protect the equality of African Americans. Indeed, a number of southern states, including Louisiana, reworked their constitutions in the late nineteenth century to implicitly or explicitly take rights away from African Americans. Although some of these attempts predated *Plessy*, the results of some of those actions were effectively immunized by *Plessy*. *Plessy* simply made a caste system legally enforceable under a Constitution that guaranteed due process and equal protection.

*Plessy* was not a radical decision that took the country in a shockingly new direction. However, it did confirm a type of legislation that had been of questionable constitutionality in light of the Fourteenth Amendment.

At the time of its passage, *Plessy* was not overly controversial to any of the justices save Harlan and possibly Brewer, who took no part in the decision. Indeed, the decision was not a widely cited constitutional case at its time or for a number of ensuing decades. Until the notion of "separate but equal" was challenged through cases brought by the National Association for the Advancement of Colored People and others, *Plessy* was standard constitutional law fare.

Over time, the majority opinion in *Plessy* fell out of favor, though many held on to the notion that separate but equal was a reasonable goal. The doctrine was the touchstone for segregationists for years. Segregationists, however, tended to adhere to the "separate" part of the doctrine but not the "equal" part. The claims of separate but equal facilities rang hollow when various groups documented the separate and unequal conditions that tended to exist in the South. The arguments eventually became too strong for the doctrine to resist. The doctrine was discarded in a string of Supreme Court cases throughout the middle part of the twentieth century, including *Brown v. Board of Education of Topeka*.

The eventual discarding of the majority opinion means that Harlan's dissent is far more well known and arguably more important than the majority opinion is today. The dissent not only predicted the racial discord that would follow *Plessy*, but it also gave us the notion of a color-blind Constitution. The phrase "color-blind Constitution" was a slogan used to argue for an end to segregation and other racist laws. However, it has been used recently by some to argue that affirmative action and other race-conscious laws and remedies are inconsistent with constitutional doctrine. That battle continues to rage and is unlikely to be resolved any time soon.

---

## Questions for Further Study

1. Compare the majority opinions in *Plessy v. Ferguson* and *Dred Scott v. Sandford*. Many claim that both were riddled with factual and logical errors. However, taking the facts as the authors of the majority opinions claimed them to be, were either, both, or neither consistent with the Constitution as it was then written?

2. Compare *Plessy v. Ferguson* with *Brown v. Board of Education of Topeka*. Is the key distinction between them that the *Brown* Court took the harms of segregation seriously while the *Plessy* Court did not, or are there other distinctions that explain why the cases were decided so differently? How could each opinion have garnered such large majorities of the Court's justices? How could both cases be consistent with the Constitution?

3. Did *Plessy v. Ferguson* effectively gut the Reconstruction amendments in general or the Fourteenth Amendment in particular? How so?

4. Should the legacy of Jim Crow laws be placed at Justice Brown's feet, as he was the writer of the *Plessy v. Ferguson* majority opinion? Why or why not?

5. What would a world governed by Harlan's dissent in *Plessy v. Ferguson* have looked like twenty years after the case was decided?

---

## Further Reading

### Books

Davis, Thomas Joseph. *Plessy v. Ferguson.* Santa Barbara, CA: ABC-CLIO, 2012.

Fireside, Harvey. *Separate and Unequal: Homer Plessy and the Supreme Court Decision That Legalized Racism.* New York: Carroll & Graf, 2004.

Hoffer, Williamjames Hull. *Plessy v. Ferguson: Race and Inequality in Jim Crow America.* Lawrence: University Press of Kansas, 2012.

Kelley, Blair L. M. *Right to Ride: Streetcar Boycotts and African American Citizenship in the Era of Plessy v. Ferguson.* Chapel Hill: University of North Carolina Press, 2010.

Klarman, Michael J. *From Jim Crow to Civil Rights: The Supreme Court and the Struggle for Racial Equality.* New York: Oxford University Press, 2004.

Lofgren, Charles A. *The Plessy Case: A Legal-Historical Interpretation.* New York: Oxford University Press, 1987.

Luxenberg, Steve. *Separate: The Story of Plessy v. Ferguson, and America's Journey from Slavery to Segregation.* New York: Norton, 2019.

Medley, Keith Weldon. *We as Freemen: Plessy v. Ferguson.* Gretna, LA: Pelican, 2003.

Meyer, Howard N. *The Amendment That Refused to Die: Equality and Justice Deferred—A History of the Fourteenth Amendment.* Lanham, MD: Madison Books, 2000.

Patrick, John J. *The Young Oxford Companion to the Supreme Court of the United States.* New York: Oxford University Press, 1998.

Thomas, Brook, ed. *Plessy v. Ferguson: A Brief History with Documents.* Boston: Bedford/St. Martin's, 1996.

Woodward, C. Vann. "The Case of the Louisiana Traveler." In *Quarrels That Have Shaped the Constitution,* edited by John A. Garraty. New York: Harper & Row, 1987.

### Articles

Brockell, Gillian. "Louisiana Board Votes to Pardon Homer Plessy of Plessy v. Ferguson." *Washington Post,* November 12, 2021. https://www.washingtonpost.com/history/2021/11/12/homer-plessy-pardon-ferguson-louisiana/.

Johnson, Maureen. "Separate but (Un)Equal: Why Institutionalized Anti-Racism Is the Answer to the Never-Ending Cycle of Plessy v. Ferguson." *University of Richmond Law Review* 52 (2017): 327–86.

### Websites

"Plessy v. Ferguson." Landmark Supreme Court Cases website. Accessed February 23, 2020. http://www.landmarkcases.org/plessy/home.html.

—Commentary by Henry L. Chambers Jr. and Michael J. O'Neal

# *PLESSY V. FERGUSON*

## Document Text

### *Mr. Justice Brown . . . Delivered the Opinion of the Court*

This case turns upon the constitutionality of an act of the general assembly of the state of Louisiana, passed in 1890, providing for separate railway carriages for the white and colored races. Acts 1890, No. 111, p. 152.

The first section of the statute enacts "that all railway companies carrying passengers in their coaches in this state, shall provide equal but separate accommodations for the white, and colored races, by providing two or more passenger coaches for each passenger train, or by dividing the passenger coaches by a partition so as to secure separate accommodations: provided, that this section shall not be construed to apply to street railroads. No person or persons shall be permitted to occupy seats in coaches, other than the ones assigned to them, on account of the race they belong to."

By the second section it was enacted "that the officers of such passenger trains shall have power and are hereby required to assign each passenger to the coach or compartment used for the race to which such passenger belongs; any passenger insisting on going into a coach or compartment to which by race he does not belong, shall be liable to a fine of twenty-five dollars, or in lieu thereof to imprisonment for a period of not more than twenty days in the parish prison, and any officer of any railroad insisting on assigning a passenger to a coach or compartment other than the one set aside for the race to which said passenger belongs, shall be liable to a fine of twenty-five dollars, or in lieu thereof to imprisonment for a period of not more than twenty days in the parish

prison; and should any passenger refuse to occupy the coach or compartment to which he or she is assigned by the officer of such railway, said officer shall have power to refuse to carry such passenger on his train, and for such refusal neither he nor the railway company which he represents shall be liable for damages in any of the courts of this state."

The third section provides penalties for the refusal or neglect of the officers, directors, conductors, and employees of railway companies to comply with the act, with a proviso that "nothing in this act shall be construed as applying to nurses attending children of the other race." The fourth section is immaterial.

The information filed in the criminal district court charged, in substance, that Plessy, being a passenger between two stations within the state of Louisiana, was assigned by officers of the company to the coach used for the race to which he belonged, but he insisted upon going into a coach used by the race to which he did not belong. Neither in the information nor plea was his particular race or color averred.

The petition for the writ of prohibition averred that petitioner was seven-eights Caucasian and one-eighth African blood; that the mixture of colored blood was not discernible in him; and that he was entitled to every right, privilege, and immunity secured to citizens of the United States of the white race; and that, upon such theory, he took possession of a vacant seat in a coach where passengers of the white race were accommodated, and was ordered by the conductor to vacate said coach, and take a seat in another, assigned to persons of the colored race, and, having refused to comply with such demand, he was forcibly ejected, with the aid of a police officer, and imprisoned in the parish jail to answer a charge of having violated the above act.

The constitutionality of this act is attacked upon the ground that it conflicts both with the thirteenth amendment of the constitution, abolishing slavery, and the fourteenth amendment, which prohibits certain restrictive legislation on the part of the states.

1. That it does not conflict with the thirteenth amendment, which abolished slavery and involuntary servitude, except a punishment for crime, is too clear for argument. Slavery implies involuntary servitude, a state of bondage; the ownership of mankind as a chattel, or, at least, the control of the labor and services of one man for the benefit of another, and the absence of a legal right to the disposal of his own person, property, and services. This amendment was said in the Slaughter-House Cases, 16 Wall. 36, to have been intended primarily to abolish slavery, as it had been previously known in this country, and that it equally forbade Mexican peonage or the Chinese coolie trade, when they amounted to slavery or involuntary servitude, and that the use of the word "servitude" was intended to prohibit the use of all forms of involuntary slavery, of whatever class or name. It was intimated, however, in that case, that this amendment was regarded by the statesmen of that day as insufficient to protect the colored race from certain laws which had been enacted in the Southern states, imposing upon the colored race onerous disabilities and burdens, and curtailing their rights in the pursuit of life, liberty, and property to such an extent that their freedom was of little value; and that the fourteenth amendment was devised to meet this exigency.

So, too, in the Civil Rights Cases, 109 U.S. 3, 3 Sup. Ct. 18, it was said that the act of a mere individual, the owner of an inn, a public conveyance or place of amusement, refusing accommodations to colored people, cannot be justly regarded as imposing any badge of slavery or servitude upon the applicant, but only as involving an ordinary civil injury, properly cognizable by the laws of the state, and presumably subject to redress by those laws until the contrary appears. "It would be running the slavery question into the ground," said Mr. Justice Bradley, "to make it apply to every act of discrimination which a person may see fit to make as to the guests he will entertain, or as to the people he will take into his coach or cab or car, or admit to his concert or theater, or deal with in other matters of intercourse or business."

A statute which implies merely a legal distinction between the white and colored races—a distinction which is founded in the color of the two races, and which must always exist so long as white men are distinguished from the other race by color—has no tendency to destroy the legal equality of the two races, or re-establish a state of involuntary servitude. Indeed, we do not understand that the thirteenth amendment is strenuously relied upon by the plaintiff in error in this connection.

2. By the fourteenth amendment, all persons born or naturalized in the United States, and subject to the jurisdiction thereof, are made citizens of the United States and of the state wherein they reside; and the states are forbidden from making or enforcing any law which shall abridge the privileges or immunities of citizens of the United States, or shall deprive any person of life, liberty, or property without due process of law, or deny to any person within their jurisdiction the equal protection of the laws.

The proper construction of this amendment was first called to the attention of this court in the Slaughter-House Cases, 16 Wall. 36, which involved, however, not a question of race, but one of exclusive privileges. The case did not call for any expression of opinion as to the exact rights it was intended to secure to the colored race, but it was said generally that its main purpose was to establish the citizenship of the negro, to give definitions of citizenship of the United States and of the states, and to protect from the hostile legislation of the states the privileges and immunities of citizens of the United States, as distinguished from those of citizens of the states. The object of the amendment was undoubtedly to enforce the absolute equality of the two races before the law, but, in the nature of things, it could not have been intended to abolish distinctions based upon color, or to enforce social, as distinguished from political, equality, or a commingling of the two races upon terms unsatisfactory to either. Laws permitting, and even requiring, their separation, in places where they are liable to be brought into contact, do not necessarily imply the inferiority of either race to the other, and have been generally, if not universally, recognized as within the competency of the state legislatures in the exercise of their police power. The most common instance of this is connected with the establishment of separate schools for white and colored children, which have been held to be a valid exercise of the legislative power even by courts of states where the political rights of the colored race have been longest and most earnestly enforced.

One of the earliest of these cases is that of *Roberts v. City of Boston*, 5 Cush. 198, in which the supreme judicial court of Massachusetts held that the general school committee of Boston had power to make provision for the instruction of colored children in separate schools established exclusively for them, and to prohibit their attendance upon the other schools. "The great principle," said Chief Justice Shaw, "advanced by the learned and eloquent advocate for the plaintiff [Mr. Charles Sumner], is that, by the constitution and laws of Massachusetts, all persons, without distinction of age or sex, birth or color, origin or condition, are equal before the law.... But, when this great principle comes to be applied to the actual and various conditions of persons in society, it will not warrant the assertion that men and women are legally clothed with the same civil and political powers, and that children and adults are legally to have the same functions and be subject to the same treatment; but only that the rights of all, as they are settled and regulated by law, are equally entitled to the paternal consideration and protection of the law for their maintenance and security." It was held that the powers of the committee extended to the establishment of separate schools for children of different ages, sexes and colors, and that they might also establish special schools for poor and neglected children, who have become too old to attend the primary school, and yet have not acquired the rudiments of learning, to enable them to enter the ordinary schools.

Similar laws have been enacted by congress under its general power of legislation over the District of Columbia (sections 281–283, 310, 319, Rev. St. D. C.), as well as by the legislatures of many of the states, and have been generally, if not uniformly, sustained by the courts. *State v. McCann*, 21 Ohio St. 210; *Lehew v. Brummell* (Mo. Sup.) 15 S. W. 765; *Ward v. Flood*, 48 Cal. 36; *Bertonneau v. Directors of City Schools*, 3 Woods, 177, Fed. Cas. No. 1,361; *People v. Gallagher*, 93 N. Y. 438; *Cory v. Carter*, 48 Ind. 337; *Dawson v. Lee*, 83 Ky. 49.

Laws forbidding the intermarriage of the two races may be said in a technical sense to interfere with the freedom of contract, and yet have been universally recognized as within the police power of the state. *State v. Gibson*, 36 Ind. 389.

The distinction between laws interfering with the political equality of the negro and those requiring the separation of the two races in schools, theaters, and railway carriages has been frequently drawn by this court. Thus, in *Strauder v. West Virginia*, 100 U.S. 303, it was held that a law of West Virginia limiting to white male persons 21 years of age, and citizens of the state, the right to sit upon juries, was a discrimination which implied a legal inferiority in civil society, which lessened the security of the right of the colored race, and was a step towards reducing them to a condition of servility. Indeed, the right of a colored man that, in the selection of jurors to pass upon his life, liberty, and property, there shall be no exclusion of his race, and no discrimination against them because of color, has been asserted in a number of cases. *Virginia v. Rivers*, 100 U.S. 313; *Neal v. Delaware*, 103 U.S. 370; *Bush v. Com.*, 107 U.S. 110, 1 Sup. Ct. 625; *Gibson v. Mississippi*, 162 U.S. 565, 16 Sup. Ct. 904. So, where the laws of a particular locality or the charter of a particular railway corporation has provided that no person shall be excluded from the cars on account of color, we have held that this meant that persons of color should travel in the same car as white ones, and that the enactment was not satisfied by the company providing cars assigned exclusively to people of color, though they were as good as those which they assigned exclusively to white persons. *Railroad Co. v. Brown*, 17 Wall. 445.

Upon the other hand, where a statute of Louisiana required those engaged in the transportation of passengers among the states to give to all persons traveling within that state, upon vessels employed in that business, equal rights and privileges in all parts of the vessel, without distinction on account of race or color, and subjected to an action for damages the owner of such a vessel who excluded colored passengers on account of their color from the cabin set aside by him for the use of whites, it was held to be, so far as it applied to interstate commerce, unconstitutional and void. *Hall v. De Cuir*, 95 U.S. 485. The court in this case, however, expressly disclaimed that it had anything whatever to do with the statute as a regulation of internal commerce, or affecting anything else than commerce among the states.

In the Civil Rights Cases, 109 U.S. 3, 3 Sup. Ct. 18, it was held that an act of congress entitling all persons within the jurisdiction of the United States to the full and equal enjoyment of the accommodations, advantages, facilities, and privileges of inns, public conveyances, on land or water, theaters, and other places of public amusement, and made applicable to citizens of every race and color, regardless of any previous condition of servitude, was unconstitutional and void, upon the ground that the fourteenth amendment was prohibitory upon the states only, and the legislation authorized to be adopted by congress for enforcing it was not direct legislation on matters respecting which the states were prohibited from making or enforcing certain laws, or doing certain acts, but was corrective legislation, such as might be necessary or proper for counter-acting and redressing the effect of such laws or acts. In delivering the opinion of the court, Mr. Justice Bradley observed that the fourteenth amendment "does not invest congress with power to legislate upon subjects that are within the domain of state legislation, but to provide modes of relief against state legislation or state action of the kind referred to. It does not authorize congress to create a code of municipal law for the regulation of private rights, but to provide modes of redress against the operation of state laws, and the action of state officers, executive or judicial, when these are subversive of the fundamental rights specified in the amendment. Positive rights and privileges are undoubtedly secured by the fourteenth amendment; but they are secured by way of prohibition against state laws and state proceedings affecting those rights and privileges, and by power given to congress to legislate for the purpose of carrying such prohibition into effect; and such legislation must necessarily be predicated upon such supposed state laws or state proceedings, and be directed to the correction of their operation and effect."

Much nearer, and, indeed, almost directly in point, is the case of the Louisville, *N. O. & T. Ry. Co. v. State*, 133 U.S. 587, 10 Sup. Ct. 348, wherein the railway company was indicted for a violation of a statute of Mississippi, enacting that all railroads carrying passengers should provide equal, but separate, accommodations for the white and colored races, by providing two or more passenger cars for each passenger train, or by dividing the passenger cars by a partition, so as to secure separate accommodations. The case was presented in a different aspect from the one under consideration, inasmuch as it was an indictment against the railway company for failing to provide the separate accommodations, but the question considered was the constitutionality of the law. In that case, the supreme court of Mississippi (66 Miss. 662, 6 South. 203) had held that the statute applied solely to commerce within the state, and, that being the construction of the state statute by its highest court, was accepted as conclusive. "If it be a matter," said the court (page 591, 133 U. S., and page 348, 10 Sup. Ct.), "respecting commerce wholly within a state, and not interfering with commerce between the states, then, obviously, there is no violation of the commerce clause of the federal constitution. . . . No question arises under this section as to the power of the state to separate in different compartments interstate passengers, or affect, in any manner, the privileges and rights of such passengers. All that we can consider is whether the state has the power to require that railroad trains within her limits shall have separate accommodations for the two races. That affecting only commerce within the state is no invasion of the power given to congress by the commerce clause."

A like course of reasoning applies to the case under consideration, since the supreme court of Louisiana, in the case of *State v. Judge*, 44 La. Ann. 770, 11 South. 74, held that the statute in question did not apply to interstate passengers, but was confined in its application to passengers traveling exclusively within the borders of the state. The case was decided largely upon the authority of Louisville, *N. O. & T. Ry. Co. v. State*, 66 Miss. 662, 6 South, 203, and affirmed by this court in 133 U.S. 587, 10 Sup. Ct. 348. In the present case no question of interference with interstate commerce can possibly arise, since the East Louisiana Railway appears to have been purely a local line, with both its termini within the state of Louisiana. Similar statutes for the separation of the two races upon public conveyances were held to be constitutional in *Railroad v. Miles*, 55 Pa. St. 209; *Day v. Owen* 5 Mich. 520; *Railway Co. v. Williams*, 55 Ill. 185; *Railroad Co. v. Wells*, 85 Tenn. 613; 4 S. W. 5; *Railroad Co. v. Benson*, 85 Tenn. 627, 4 S. W. 5; *The Sue*, 22 Fed. 843; *Logwood v. Railroad Co.*, 23 Fed. 318; *McGuinn v. Forbes*, 37 Fed. 639; *People v. King* (N. Y. App.) 18 N. E. 245; *Houck v. Railway Co.*, 38 Fed. 226; *Heard v. Railroad Co.*, 3 Inter St. Commerce Com. R. 111, 1 Inter St. Commerce Com. R. 428.

While we think the enforced separation of the races, as applied to the internal commerce of the state, neither abridges the privileges or immunities of the colored man, deprives him of his property without due process of law, nor denies him the equal protection of the laws, within the meaning of the fourteenth amendment, we are not prepared to say that the conductor, in assigning passengers to the coaches according to their race, does not act at his peril, or that the provision of the second section of the act that denies to the passenger compensation in damages for a refusal to receive him into the coach in which he properly belongs is a valid exercise of the legislative power. Indeed, we understand it to be conceded by the state's attorney that such part of the act as exempts from liability the railway company and its officers is unconstitutional. The power to assign to a particular coach obviously implies the power to determine to which race the passenger belongs, as well as the power to determine who, under the laws of the particular state, is to be deemed a white, and who a colored, person. This question, though indicated in the brief of the plaintiff in error, does not properly arise upon the record in this case, since the only issue made is as to the unconstitutionality of the act, so far as it requires the railway to provide separate accommodations, and the conductor to assign passengers according to their race.

It is claimed by the plaintiff in error that, in an mixed community, the reputation of belonging to the dominant race, in this instance the white race, is "property," in the same sense that a right of action or of inheritance is property. Conceding this to be so, for the purposes of this case, we are unable to see how this statute deprives him of, or in any way affects his right to, such property. If he be a white man, and assigned to a colored coach, he may have his action for damages against the company for being deprived of his so-called "property." Upon the other hand, if he be a colored man, and be so assigned, he has been deprived of no property, since he is not lawfully entitled to the reputation of being a white man.

In this connection, it is also suggested by the learned counsel for the plaintiff in error that the same argument that will justify the state legislature in requiring railways to provide separate accommodations for the two races will also authorize them to require separate cars to be provided for people whose hair is of a certain color, or who are aliens, or who belong to certain nationalities, or to enact laws requiring colored people to walk upon one side of the street, and white people upon the other, or requiring white men's houses to be painted white, and colored men's black, or their vehicles or business signs to be of different colors, upon the theory that one side of the street is as good as the other, or that a house or vehicle of one color is as good as one of another color. The reply to all this is that every exercise of the police power must be reasonable, and extend only to such laws as are enacted in good faith for the promotion of the public good, and not for the annoyance or oppression of a particular class. Thus, in *Yick Wo v. Hopkins*, 118 U.S. 356, 6 Sup. Ct. 1064, it was held by this court that a municipal ordinance of the city of San Francisco, to regulate the carrying on of public laundries within the limits of the municipality, violated the provisions of the constitution of the United States, if it conferred upon the municipal authorities arbitrary power, at their own will, and without regard to discretion, in the legal sense of the term, to give or withhold consent as to persons or places, without regard to the competency of the persons applying or the propriety of the places selected for the carrying on of the business. It was held to be a covert attempt on the part of the municipality to make an arbitrary and unjust discrimination against the Chinese race. While this was the case of a municipal ordinance, a like principle has been held to apply to acts of a state legislature passed in the exercise of the police power. *Railroad Co. v. Husen*, 95 U.S. 465; *Louisville & N. R. Co. v. Kentucky*, 161 U.S. 677, 16 Sup. Ct. 714, and cases cited on page 700, 161 U. S., and page 714, 16 Sup. Ct.; *Daggett v. Hudson*, 43 Ohio St. 548, 3 N. E. 538; *Capen v. Foster*, 12 Pick. 485; *State v. Baker*, 38 Wis. 71; *Monroe v. Collins*, 17 Ohio St. 665; *Hulseman v. Rems*, 41 Pa. St. 396; *Osman v. Riley*, 15 Cal. 48.

So far, then, as a conflict with the fourteenth amendment is concerned, the case reduces itself to the question whether the statute of Louisiana is a reasonable regulation, and with respect to this there must necessarily be a large discretion on the part of the legislature. In determining the question of reasonableness, it is at liberty to act with reference to the established usages, customs, and traditions of the people, and with a view to the promotion of their comfort, and the preservation of the public peace and good order. Gauged by this standard, we cannot say that a law which authorizes or even requires the separation of the two races in public conveyances is unreasonable, or more obnoxious to the fourteenth amendment than the acts of congress requiring separate schools for colored children in the District of Columbia, the constitutionality of which does not seem to have been questioned, or the corresponding acts of state legislatures.

We consider the underlying fallacy of the plaintiff's argument to consist in the assumption that the enforced separation of the two races stamps the colored race with a badge of inferiority. If this be so, it is not by reason of anything found in the act, but solely because the colored race chooses to put that construction upon it. The argument necessarily assumes that if, as has been more than once the case, and is not unlikely to be so again, the colored race should become the dominant power in the state legislature, and should enact a law in precisely similar terms, it would thereby relegate the white race to an inferior position. We imagine that the white race, at least, would not acquiesce in this assumption. The argument also assumes that social prejudices may be overcome by legislation, and that equal rights cannot be secured to the negro except by an enforced commingling of the two races. We cannot accept this proposition. If the two races are to meet upon terms of social equality, it must be the result of natural affinities, a mutual appreciation of each other's merits, and a voluntary consent of individuals. As was said by the court of appeals of New York in *People v. Gallagher*, 93 N. Y. 438, 448: "This end can neither be accomplished nor promoted by laws which conflict with the general sentiment of the community upon whom they are designed to operate. When the government, therefore, has secured to each of its citizens equal rights before the law, and equal opportunities for improvement and progress, it has accomplished the end for which it was organized, and performed all of the functions respecting social advantages with which it is endowed." Legislation is powerless to eradicate racial instincts, or to abolish distinctions based upon physical differences, and the attempt to do so can only result in accentuating the difficulties of the present situation. If the civil and political rights of both races be equal, one cannot be inferior to the other civilly or politically. If one race be inferior to the other socially, the constitution of the United States cannot put them upon the same plane.

It is true that the question of the proportion of colored blood necessary to constitute a colored person, as distinguished from a white person, is one upon which there is a difference of opinion in the different states; some holding that any visible admixture of black blood stamps the person as belonging to the colored race (*State v. Chavers*, 5 Jones [N. C.] 1); others, that it depends upon the preponderance of blood (*Gray v. State*, 4 Ohio, 354; *Monroe v. Collins*, 17 Ohio St. 665); and still others, that the predominance of white blood must only be in the proportion of three-fourths (*People v. Dean*, 14 Mich. 406; *Jones v. Com.*, 80 Va. 544). But these are questions to be determined under the laws of each state, and are not properly put in issue in this case. Under the allegations of his petition, it may undoubtedly become a question of importance whether, under the laws of Louisiana, the petitioner belongs to the white or colored race.

The judgment of the court below is therefore affirmed.

Mr. Justice BREWER did not hear the argument or participate in the decision of this case.

### Mr. Justice Harlan Dissenting

By the Louisiana statute the validity of which is here involved, all railway companies (other than street-railroad companies) carry passengers in that state are required to have separate but equal accommodations for white and colored persons, "by providing two or more passenger coaches for each passenger train, or by dividing the passenger coaches by a partition so as to secure separate accommodations." Under this statute, no colored person is permitted to occupy a seat in a coach assigned to white persons; nor any white person to occupy a seat in a coach assigned to colored persons. The managers of the railroad are not allowed to exercise any discretion in the premises, but are required to assign each passenger to some coach or compartment set apart for the exclusive use of is race. If a passenger insists upon going into a coach or compartment not set apart for persons of his race, he is subject to be fined, or to be imprisoned in the parish jail. Penalties are prescribed for the refusal or neglect of the officers, directors, conductors, and employees of railroad companies to comply with the provisions of the act.

Only "nurses attending children of the other race" are excepted from the operation of the statute. No exception is made of colored attendants traveling with adults. A white man is not permitted to have his colored servant with him in the same coach, even if his condition of health requires the constant personal assistance of such servant. If a colored maid insists upon riding in the same coach with a white woman whom she has been employed to serve, and who may need her personal attention while traveling, she is subject to be fined or imprisoned for such an exhibition of zeal in the discharge of duty.

While there may be in Louisiana persons of different races who are not citizens of the United States, the words in the act "white and colored races" necessarily include all citizens of the United States of both races residing in that state. So that we have before us a state enactment that compels, under penalties, the separation of the two races in railroad passenger coaches, and makes it a crime for a citizen of either race to enter a coach that has been assigned to citizens of the other race.

Thus, the state regulates the use of a public highway by citizens of the United States solely upon the basis of race.

However apparent the injustice of such legislation may be, we have only to consider whether it is consistent with the constitution of the United States.

That a railroad is a public highway, and that the corporation which owns or operates it is in the exercise of public functions, is not, at this day, to be disputed. Mr. Justice Nelson, speaking for this court in *New Jersey Steam Nav. Co. v. Merchants' Bank*, 6 How. 344, 382, said that a common carrier was in the exercise "of a sort of public office, and has public duties to perform, from which he should not be permitted to exonerate himself without the assent of the parties concerned." Mr. Justice Strong, delivering the judgment of this court in *Olcott v. Supervisors*, 16 Wall. 678, 694, said: "That railroads, though constructed by private corporations, and owned by them, are public highways, has been the doctrine of nearly all the courts ever since such conveniences for passage and transportation have had any existence. Very early the question arose whether a state's right of eminent domain could be exercised by a private corporation created for the purpose of constructing a railroad. Clearly, it could not, unless taking land for such a purpose by such an agency is taking land for public use. The right of eminent domain nowhere justifies taking property for a private use. Yet it is a doctrine universally accepted that a state legislature may authorize a private corporation to take land for the construction of such a road, making compensation to the owner. What else does this doctrine mean if not that building a railroad, though it be built by a private corporation, is an act done for a public use?" So, in *Township of Pine Grove v. Talcott*, 19 Wall. 666, 676: "Though the corporation [a railroad company] was private, its work was public, as much so as if it were to be constructed by the state." So, in *Inhabitants of Worcester v. Western R. Corp.*, 4 Metc. (Mass.) 564: "The establishment of that great thoroughfare is regarded as a public work, established by public authority, intended for the public use and benefit, the use of which is secured to the whole community, and constitutes, therefore, like a canal, turnpike, or highway, a public easement." "It is true that the real and personal property, necessary to the establishment and management of the railroad, is vested in the corporation; but it is in trust for the public."

In respect of civil rghts, common to all citizens, the constitution of the United States does not, I think, permit any public authority to know the race of those entitled to be protected in the enjoyment of such rights. Every true man has pride of race, and under appropriate circumstances, when the rights of others, his equals before the law, are not to be affected, it is his privilege to express such pride and to take such action based upon it as to him seems proper. But I deny that any legislative body or judicial tribunal may have regard to the race of citizens when the civil rights of those citizens are involved. Indeed, such legislation as that here in question is inconsistent not only with that equality of rights which pertains to citizenship, national and state, but with the personal liberty enjoyed by every one within the United States.

The thirteenth amendment does not permit the withholding or the deprivation of any right necessarily inhering in freedom. It not only struck down the institution of slavery as previously existing in the United States, but it prevents the imposition of any burdens or disabilities that constitute badges of slavery or servitude. It decreed universal civil freedom in this country. This court has so adjudged. But, that amendment having been found inadequate to the protection of the rights of those who had been in slavery, it was followed by the fourteenth amendment, which added greatly to the dignity and glory of American citizenship, and to the security of personal liberty, by declaring that "all persons born or naturalized in the United States, and subject to the jurisdiction thereof, are citizens of the United States and of the state wherein they reside," and that "no state shall make or enforce any law which shall abridge the privileges or immunities of citizens of the United States; nor shall any state deprive any person of life, liberty or property without due process of law, nor deny to any person within its jurisdiction the equal protection of the laws." These two amendments, if enforced according to their true intent and meaning, will protect all the civil rights that pertain to freedom and citizenship. Finally, and to the end that no citizen should be denied, on account of his race, the privilege of participating in the political control of his country, it was declared by the fifteenth amendment that "the right of citizens of the United States to vote shall not be denied or abridged by the United States or by any state on account of race, color or previous condition of servitude."

These notable additions to the fundamental law were welcomed by the friends of liberty throughout the world. They removed the race line from our governmental systems. They had, as this court has said, a common purpose, namely, to secure "to a race recently emancipated, a race that through many generations have been held in slavery, all the civil rights that the superior race enjoy." They declared, in legal effect, this court has further said, "that the law in the states shall be the same for the black as for the white; that all persons, whether colored or white, shall stand equal before the laws of the states; and in regard to the colored race, for whose protection the amendment was primarily designed, that no discrimination shall be made against them by law because of their color." We also said: "The words of the amendment, it is true, are prohibitory, but they contain a necessary implication of a positive immunity or right, most valuable to the colored race, the right to exemption from unfriendly legislation against them distinctively as colored; exemption from legal discriminations, implying inferiority in civil society, lessening the security of their enjoyment of the rights which others enjoy; and discriminations which are steps towards reducing them to the condition of a subject race." It was, consequently, adjudged that a state law that excluded citizens of the colored race from juries, because of their race, however well qualified in other respects to dischar e the duties of jurymen, was repugnant to the fourteenth amendment.

*Strauder v. West Virginia*, 100 U.S. 303, 306, 307 S.; *Virginia v. Rives*, Id. 313; *Ex parte Virginia*, Id. 339; *Neal v. Delaware*, 103 U.S. 370, 386; *Bush v. Com.*, 107 U.S.

110, 116, 1 S. Sup. Ct. 625. At the present term, referring to the previous adjudications, this court declared that "underlying all of those decisions is the principle that the constitution of the United States, in its present form, forbids, so far as civil and political rights are concerned, discrimination by the general government or the states against any citizen because of his race. All citizens are equal before the law." *Gibson v. State*, 162 U.S. 565, 16 Sup. Ct. 904.

The decisions referred to show the scope of the recent amendments of the constitution. They also show that it is not within the power of a state to prohibit colored citizens, because of their race, from participating as jurors in the administration of justice.

It was said in argument that the statute of Louisiana does not discriminate against either race, but prescribes a rule applicable alike to white and colored citizens. But this argument does not meet the difficulty. Every one knows that the statute in question had its origin in the purpose, not so much to exclude white persons from railroad cars occupied by blacks, as to exclude colored people from coaches occupied by or assigned to white persons. Railroad corporations of Louisiana did not make discrimination among whites in the matter of commodation for travelers. The thing to accomplish was, under the guise of giving equal accommodation for whites and blacks, to compel the latter to keep to themselves while traveling in railroad passenger coaches. No one would be so wanting in candor as to assert the contrary. The fundamental objection, therefore, to the statute, is that it interferes with the personal freedom of citizens. "Personal liberty," it has been well said, "consists in the power of locomotion, of changing situation, or removing one's person to whatsoever places one's own inclination may direct, without imprisonment or restraint, unless by due course of law." 1 Bl. Comm. 134. If a white man and a black man choose to occupy the same public conveyance on a public highway, it is their right to do so; and no government, proceeding alone on grounds of race, can prevent it without infringing the personal liberty of each.

It is one thing for railroad carriers to furnish, or to be required by law to furnish, equal accommodations for all whom they are under a legal duty to carry. It is quite another thing for government to forbid citizens of the white and black races from traveling in the same public conveyance, and to punish officers of railroad companies for permitting persons of the two races to occupy the same passenger coach. If a state can prescribe, as a rule of civil conduct, that whites and blacks shall not travel as passengers in the same railroad coach, why may it not so regulate the use of the streets of its cities and towns as to compel white citizens to keep on one side of a street, and black citizens to keep on the other? Why may it not, upon like grounds, punish whites and blacks who ride together in street cars or in open vehicles on a public road or street? Why may it not require sheriffs to assign whites to one side of a court room, and blacks to the other? And why may it not also prohibit the commingling of the two races in the galleries of legislative halls or in public assemblages convened for the consideration of the political questions of the day? Further, if this statute of Louisiana is consistent with the personal liberty of citizens, why may not the state require the separation in railroad coaches of native and naturalized citizens of the United States, or of Protestants and Roman Catholics?

The answer given at the argument to these questions was that regulations of the kind they suggest would be unreasonable, and could not, therefore, stand before the law. Is it meant that the determination of questions of legislative power depends upon the inquiry whether the statute whose validity is questioned is, in the judgment of the courts, a reasonable one, taking all the circumstances into consideration? A statute may be unreasonable merely because a sound public policy forbade its enactment. But I do not understand that the courts have anything to do with the policy or expediency of legislation. A statute may be valid, and yet, upon grounds of public policy, may well be characterized as unreasonable. Mr. Sedgwick correctly states the rule when he says that, the legislative intention being clearly ascertained, "the courts have no other duty to perform than to execute the legislative will, without any regard to their views as to the wisdom or justice of the particular enactment." Sedg. St. & Const. Law, 324. There is a dangerous tendency in these latter days to enlarge the functions of the courts, by means of judicial interference with the will of the people as expressed by the legislature. Our institutions have the distinguishing characteristic that the three departments of government are co-ordinate and separate. Each much keep within the limits defined by the constitution. And the courts best discharge their duty by executing the will of the law-making power, constitutionally expressed, leaving the results of legislation to be dealt with by the people through their representatives. Statutes must always have a reasonable construction. Sometimes they are to be construed strictly, sometimes literally, in order to carry out the legislative will. But, however construed, the intent of the legislature is to be respected if the particular statute in question is valid, although the courts, looking at the public interests, may conceive the statute to be both unreasonable and impolitic. If the power exists to enact a statute, that ends the matter so far as the courts are concerned. The adjudged cases in which statutes have been held to be void, because unreasonable, are those in which the means employed by the legislature were not at all germane to the end to which the legislature was competent.

The white race deems itself to be the dominant race in this country. And so it is, in prestige, in achievements, in education, in wealth, and in power. So, I doubt not, it will continue to be for all time, if it remains true to its great heritage, and holds fast to the principles of constitutional liberty. But in view of the constitution, in the eye of the law, there is in this country no superior, dominant, ruling class of citizens. There is no caste here. Our constitution is color-blind, and neither knows nor tolerates classes among citizens. In respect of civil rights, all citizens are equal before the law. The humblest is the peer of the most powerful. The law regards man as man, and takes no account of his surroundings or of his color when his civil rights as guarantied by the supreme law of the land are involved. It is therefore to be regretted that this high tribunal, the final expositor of the fundamental law of the land, has reached the conclusion that it is competent for a state to regulate the enjoyment by citizens of their civil rights solely upon the basis of race.

In my opinion, the judgment this day rendered will, in time, prove to be quite as pernicious as the decision made by this tribunal in the Dred Scott Case.

It was adjudged in that case that the descendants of Africans who were imported into this country, and sold as slaves, were not included nor intended to be included under the word "citizens" in the constitution, and could not claim any of the rights and privileges which that instrument provided for and secured to citizens of the United States; that, at time of the adoption of the constitution, they were "considered as a subordinate and inferior class of beings, who had been subjugated by the dominant race, and, whether emancipated or not, yet remained subject to their authority, and had no rights or privileges but such as those who held the power and the government might choose to grant them." 17 How. 393, 404. The recent amendments of the constitution, it was supposed, had eradicated these principles from our institutions. But it seems that we have yet, in some of the states, a dominant race—a superior class of citizens—which assumes to regulate the enjoyment of civil rights, common to all citizens, upon the basis of race. The present decision, it may well be apprehended, will not only stimulate aggressions, more or less brutal and irritating, upon the admitted rights of colored citizens, but will encourage the belief that it is possible, by means of state enactments, to defeat the beneficent purposes which the people of the United States had in view when they adopted the recent amendments of the constitution, by one of which the blacks of this country were made citizens of the United States and of the states in which they respectively reside, and whose privileges and immunities, as citizens, the states are forbidden to abridge. Sixty millions of whites are in no danger from the presence here of eight millions of blacks. The destinies of the two races, in this country, are indissolubly linked together, and the interests of both require that the common government of all shall not permit the seeds of race hate to be planted under the sanction of law. What can more certainly arouse race hate, what more certainly create and perpetuate a feeling of distrust between these races, than state enactments which, in fact, proceed on the ground that colored citizens are so inferior and degraded that they cannot be allowed to sit in public coaches occupied by white citizens? That, as all will admit, is the real meaning of such legislation as was enacted in Louisiana.

The sure guaranty of the peace and security of each race is the clear, distinct, unconditional recognition by our governments, national and state, of every right that inheres in civil freedom, and of the equality before the law of all citizens of the United States, without regard to race. State enactments regulating the enjoyment of civil rights upon the basis of race, and cunningly devised to defeat legitimate results of the war, under the pretense of recognizing equality of rights, can have no other result than to render permanent

peace impossible, and to keep alive a conflict of races, the continuance of which must do harm to all concerned. This question is not met by the suggestion that social equality cannot exist between the white and black races in this country. That argument, if it can be properly regarded as one, is scarcely worthy of consideration; for social equality no more exists between two races when traveling in a passenger coach or a public highway than when members of the same races sit by each other in a street car or in the jury box, or stand or sit with each other in a political assembly, or when they use in common the streets of a city or town, or when they are in the same room for the purpose of having their names placed on the registry of voters, or when they approach the ballot box in order to exercise the high privilege of voting.

There is a race so different from our own that we do not permit those belonging to it to become citizens of the United States. Persons belonging to it are, with few exceptions, absolutely excluded from our country. I allude to the Chinese race. But, by the statute in question, a Chinaman can ride in the same passenger coach with white citizens of the United States, while citizens of the black race in Louisiana, many of whom, perhaps, risked their lives for the preservation of the Union, who are entitled, by law, to participate in the political control of the state and nation, who are not excluded, by law or by reason of their race, from public stations of any kind, and who have all the legal rights that belong to white citizens, are yet declared to be criminals, liable to imprisonment, if they ride in a public coach occupied by citizens of the white race. It is scarcely just to say that a colored citizen should not object to occupying a public coach assigned to his own race. He does not object, nor, perhaps, would he object to separate coaches for his race if his rights under the law were recognized. But he does object, and he ought never to cease objecting, that citizens of the white and black races can be adjudged criminals because they sit, or claim the right to sit, in the same public coach on a public highway. The arbitrary separation of citizens, on the basis of race, while they are on a public highway, is a badge of servitude wholly inconsistent with the civil freedom and the equality before the law established by the constitution. It cannot be justified upon any legal grounds.

If evils will result from the commingling of the two races upon public highways established for the benefit of all, they will be infinitely less than those that will surely come from state legislation regulating the enjoyment of civil rights upon the basis of race. We boast of the freedom enjoyed by our people above all other peoples. But it is difficult to reconcile that boast with a state of the law which, practically, puts the brand of servitude and degradation upon a large class of our fellow citizens, our equals before the law. The thin disguise of "equal" accommodations for passengers in railroad coaches will not mislead any one, nor atone for the wrong this day done.

The result of the whole matter is that while this court has frequently adjudged, and at the present term has recognized the doctrine, that a state cannot, consistently with the constitution of the United States, prevent white and black citizens, having the required qualifications for jury service, from sitting in the same jury box, it is now solemnly held that a state may prohibit white and black citizens from sitting in the same passenger coach on a public highway, or may require that they be separated by a "partition" when in the same passenger coach. May it not now be reasonably expected that astute men of the dominant race, who affect to be disturbed at the possibility that the integrity of the white race may be corrupted, or that its supremacy will be imperiled, by contact on public highways with black people, will endeavor to procure statutes requiring white and black jurors to be separated in the jury box by a "partition," and that, upon retiring from the court room to consult as to their verdict, such partition, if it be a movable one, shall be taken to their consultation room, and set up in such way as to prevent black jurors from coming too close to their brother jurors of the white race. If the "partition" used in the court room happens to be stationary, provision could be made for screens with openings through which jurors of the two races could confer as to their verdict without coming into personal contact with each other. I cannot see but that, according to the principles this day announced, such state legislation, although conceived in hostility to, and enacted for the purpose of humiliating, citizens of the United States of a particular race, would be held to be consistent with the constitution.

I do not deem it necessary to review the decisions of state courts to which reference was made in argument.

Some, and the most important, of them, are wholly inapplicable, because rendered prior to the adoption of the last amendments of the constitution, when colored people had very few rights which the dominant race felt obliged to respect. Others were made at a time when public opinion, in many localities, was dominated by the institution of slavery; when it would not have been safe to do justice to the black man; and when, so far as the rights of blacks were concerned, race prejudice was, practically, the supreme law of the land. Those decisions cannot be guides in the era introduced by the recent amendments of the supreme law, which established universal civil freedom, gave citizenship to all born or naturalized in the United States, and residing ere, obliterated the race line from our systems of governments, national and state, and placed our free institutions upon the broad and sure foundation of the equality of all men before the law.

I am of opinion that the state of Louisiana is inconsistent with the personal liberty of citizens, white and black, in that state, and hostile to both the spirit and letter of the constitution of the United States. If laws of like character should be enacted in the several states of the Union, the effect would be in the highest degree mischievous. Slavery, as an institution tolerated by law, would, it is true, have disappeared from our country; but there would remain a power in the states, by sinister legislation, to interfere with the full enjoyment of the blessings of freedom, to regulate civil rights, common to all citizens, upon the basis of race, and to place in a condition of legal inferiority a large body of American citizens, now constituting a part of the political community, called the "People of the United States," for whom, and by whom through representatives, our government is administered. Such a system is inconsistent with the guaranty given by the constitution to each state of a republican form of government, and may be stricken down by congressional action, or by the courts in the discharge of their solemn duty to maintain the supreme law of the land, anything in the constitution or laws of any state to the contrary notwithstanding.

For the reason stated, I am constrained to withhold my assent from the opinion and judgment of the majority.

## Glossary

**averring:** asserting

**chattel:** property

**coolie:** manual laborer, usually of Chinese descent, who was brought to the United States to help build railroads (now considered a racial slur)

**damages:** monies paid for harm caused

**defendant in error:** the party that is defending the lower court's ruling

**demurrer:** contention by the defendant that although the facts put forward by the plaintiff may be true, they do not entitle the plaintiff to prevail in the lawsuit.

**due process:** the appropriate procedures that are necessary to affect a person's right to life, liberty, or property

**eminent domain:** the right of a jurisdiction to take property for a public purpose if adequate compensation is paid

**equal protection of the laws:** the requirement that all persons be provided the same rights under the law and be granted equal treatment by the laws

**immunity:** exemption

**information:** a substitute for a grand jury indictment issued directly by a prosecutor

**intermarriage:** interracial marriage

**liability:** responsibility for causing harm

**naturalized:** made a citizen without being born a citizen

**parish:** in some regions, a political subdivision or county

**peonage:** a style of forced labor generally associated with Mexico

**petitioner:** the party filing for relief in court

**plaintiff in error:** the party that has appealed a lower court's ruling

**prayed:** asked

**respondent:** party defending against a suit

**writ of error:** an order of an appellate court requesting the records of a lower court so the appellate court can examine the record for mistakes that may affect the lower court's judgment

**writ of prohibition:** an order from a court directing a lower court to refrain from prosecuting a case

# UNITED STATES V. WONG KIM ARK

| DATE | CITATION |
|------|----------|
| 1898 | 169 U.S. 649 |

| AUTHOR | SIGNIFICANCE |
|--------|--------------|
| Horace Gray | Held that a child born in the United States to parents who are subjects of China and of Chinese descent automatically becomes a U.S. citizen at birth |

| VOTE | |
|------|---|
| 6–2 | |

## Overview

*United States v. Wong Kim Ark* was an 1898 U.S. Supreme Court case that dealt with the issue of birthright citizenship as it applied, in this case, to a person of Chinese descent born in the United States. Wong was born in San Francisco in 1873 to immigrant parents. His father was a merchant and was affiliated with the firm Quong Sing & Co. in San Francisco. Under the Naturalization Act of 1790, Wong's parents were not eligible to become citizens of the United States, which the act extended only to "free white persons." Nothing changed after the passage of the Naturalization Act of 1870, which extended citizenship to "aliens of African nativity and persons of African descent." Wong, however, was born in the United States, so he was presumably entitled to U.S. citizenship under the citizenship clause of the Fourteenth Amendment to the Constitution, which states: "All persons born or naturalized in the United States, and subject to the jurisdiction thereof, are citizens of the United States and of the state wherein they reside." That is to say, under the doctrine of birthright citizenship, he was in fact a U.S. citizen.

After Wong's parents moved to China, Wong remained in the United States. On two occasions, he visited his parents in China. After the first trip, his return to the United States in 1890 was uneventful, but in 1895 he was denied reentry by the collector of customs, who asserted that Wong was not a citizen under the terms of the Chinese Exclusion Act of 1882—the first and only U.S. immigration law that specifically targeted a racial group. For help, Wong turned to the "Chinese Six Companies," more formally, the Chinese Consolidated Benevolent Society, an amalgamation of six district associations that had been formed in California to support Chinese immigrants and that united into a single organization in 1882. The Supreme Court case was an appeal from the ruling of the District Court of the Northern District of California, which issued a writ of habeas corpus on behalf of Wong, who was under detention by U.S. officials.

The issue presented to the Court was whether Wong, by virtue of having been born in the United States, was a citizen. Lawyers for the United States argued that because Wong's parents were still subjects of China and the Chinese emperor, their son, too, was a subject of China and therefore not "subject to the jurisdiction" of the Unit-

***Wong Kim Ark***
(Wikimedia Commons)

ed States. The basis for the distinction was that China granted citizenship by bloodline; China regarded any person born of Chinese parents anywhere in the world as a Chinese citizen. In a 6–2 decision, the Supreme Court rejected the government's arguments, noting that in the United States, citizenship is based on the legal doctrine of jus soli, or citizenship by soil. A person born on the soil of the United States is, according to the Fourteenth Amendment, a U.S. citizen, although there are narrow exceptions to this doctrine (the children of U.S. enemies currently occupying any U.S. territory and the children of diplomats and foreign sovereigns). The Court concluded that to exclude from citizenship children born in the United States to citizens of other countries would be to deny citizenship to a great many persons of European descent who had always been regarded as citizens of the United States. Melville Fuller wrote a dissenting opinion, joined by John Marshall Harlan.

## Context

The Naturalization Act of 1790, sometimes called the Nationality Act, was the first effort to codify U.S. naturalization law. The act restricted citizenship to "any alien, being a free white person" who had been in the United States for two years. The act's effect was to exclude indentured servants, slaves, and even most

women and to render blacks and, in time, Asian immigrants ineligible for citizenship. The act, however, was silent on the issue of nonwhite persons born on American soil. Legislation pertaining to citizenship was superseded by the Naturalization Law of 1802, the relevant provision of which stated that resident children of naturalized citizens were to be considered citizens.

During the nineteenth century, waves of immigrants arrived on the shores of the United States. From 1815 to the start of the Civil War, some five million immigrants arrived, most from England and Ireland. From the end of the war until 1890, another ten million arrived, mostly from England, Wales, Ireland, Germany, and the Scandinavian countries. In 1868, the United States entered into the Burlingame-Seward Treaty, normalizing relations with China and allowing unrestricted immigration of Chinese to the United States. The Naturalization Act of 1870 went a step further, extending citizenship to "aliens of African nativity and persons of African descent." Meanwhile, the issue of citizenship for newly freed slaves was settled by the Fourteenth Amendment to the Constitution, adopted in 1868.

In the late nineteenth century, Chinese immigrants made up just a tiny percentage of the nation's population—a fraction of 1 percent—but Chinese immigrants were heavily concentrated in the West, and white workers in that region attributed falling wages and other economic ills to competition from low-paid Chinese workers. This animosity dated back to the gold rush of the 1850s, when gold was becoming increasingly hard to find and prospectors were facing competition from a growing number of Chinese immigrants. Indeed, in 1850, a mere four thousand persons of Chinese descent lived in the United States, but the 1860 census showed that that number had swelled to nearly thirty-five thousand. These immigrants would then go on to play a major role as laborers in the construction of the first transcontinental railroad lines.

U.S. nativists were concerned about racial purity. To placate them, Congress passed the Page Act of 1875, which prohibited the immigration of Chinese women. The purpose of the act, according to the bill's sponsors, was to end "the danger of cheap Chinese labor and immoral Chinese women." A persistent complaint lodged against Chinese women immigrants was that they were engaged in prostitution, often as virtual slaves, while other objections focused on the prevalence of opium usage among the Chinese. In fact, during the mid-1800s a secret society (a "tong," or gang) called Hip Yee imported more than six thousand Chinese women to serve as prostitutes. In 1880 the Burlingame Treaty was renegotiated as the Treaty Regulating Immigration from China, which suspended, but did not prohibit, immigration from China.

In this environment, Congress passed the Chinese Exclusion Act on May 6, 1882. The legislation was signed into law by President Chester A. Arthur. The act suggested that "the coming of Chinese laborers to this country endangers the good order of certain localities" and, for this reason, suspended the entry of Chinese laborers into the United States for ten years. Strictly speaking, not all Chinese were excluded. Those who were not laborers could be admitted if they had certification from the Chinese government that they were "nonlaborers," but this certification was exceedingly difficult to obtain. The act also excluded Chinese from U.S. citizenship.

In the wake of the act, animosity toward the Chinese sometimes erupted in violence against them, notably the Rock Springs massacre in Wyoming in 1885 and the Hells Canyon massacre in 1887. It led to further legislation, such as the Scott Act of 1888, which expanded the Chinese Exclusion Act to prevent Chinese laborers who traveled abroad from returning to the United States. In 1889, the Supreme Court issued its decision in *Chae Chan Ping v. United States,* a case commonly known as the Chinese Exclusion Case. The case was a challenge to the Scott Act, based on the ground that the act was inconsistent with the Burlingame Treaty. The Supreme Court rejected the challenge, holding that the federal government has the authority to determine immigration policy and pass legislation that would override an earlier treaty. The effect of the Scott Act was to leave twenty thousand to thirty thousand Chinese stranded.

In 1892, the Act to Prohibit the Coming of Chinese Persons into the United States, commonly called the Geary Act, extended the term of the Chinese Exclusion Act for another ten years but introduced additional restraints: Chinese residents had to carry a residence permit at all times, and they were prohibited from testifying in court or from receiving bail in habeas corpus proceedings. The constitutionality of the Geary Act was upheld in 1893 by the U.S. Supreme Court in *Fong Yue Ting v. United States,* a decision written by Justice Horace Gray, the author of the decision in *Wong Kim Ark.*

In 1902, the Chinese Exclusion Act was made permanent. The act was not repealed until the Magnuson Act of 1943, more formally, the Chinese Exclusion Repeal Act of 1943. Although Chinese could now immigrate to the United States and those already residing in the United States could become naturalized citizens, Chinese still could not own property or businesses. The Magnuson Act was repealed in 1965.

## About the Author

George Hoar, in "Memoir of Horace Gray," published in the 1904 *Massachusetts Historical Society Proceedings,* wrote of Gray, the author of the Court›s opinion in *Wong Kim Ark v. United States:* "His wonderful capacity for research, the instinct which, when some interesting question of law was up, would direct his thumb and finger to some obscure volume of English reports of law or equity, was almost like the scent of a wide animal or bird of prey." Gray's penchant for exhaustive historical legal research is apparent in *Wong Kim Ark,* which runs to nearly twenty-two thousand words and includes scores of references to statutes from the world over, legal treatises, and British and American common law precedents.

Gray was born in Boston on March 24, 1828. He graduated from Harvard in 1845, but ironically his record was undistinguished. After his father's business collapsed, financial considerations led him to return to Harvard to attend law school, graduating in 1849. After he was admitted to the Massachusetts bar in 1851, he established a private law practice, but he discovered that his real niche was legal history and historical records. With this expertise, he served as the reporter for the Supreme Judicial Court of Massachusetts. His pamphlet *Abolition of Slavery in Massachusetts* examined the history of slavery in the state. He also wrote a lengthy article for the *Monthly Law Reporter* scrutinizing the infamous *Dred Scott v. Sandford* case of 1857, which essentially barred blacks from citizenship and refused them the rights and privileges conferred on American citizens. In these and other writings, he relied extensively on obscure legal precedents and historical references to buttress his positions.

In 1864, Gray was appointed to the Supreme Judicial Court of Massachusetts; in 1873, he was elevated to

## Explanation and Analysis of the Document

Gray begins by outlining the facts of the case as they pertained to Wong, emphasizing that he had lived in California since his birth and that he had never renounced his allegiance to the United States. He goes on to state the fundamental question raised by the case: Can a child born in the United States to parents who live in the country but who are not citizens of it and instead are "subjects of the Emperor of China" be considered a U.S. citizen under the Fourteenth Amendment?

Gray goes on to examine what is meant by the term *citizen* according to the Constitution and subsequent law. He notes, however, that the word *citizen* is defined by neither the Constitution nor statute, so he turns to common law for an answer. He examines legislation passed in the late eighteenth century, particularly the Naturalization Act of 1790 and the Naturalization Law of 1802, which states that the "children of persons duly naturalized under any of the laws of the United States . . . shall, if dwelling in the United States, be considered as citizens of the United States." Gray concludes his examination of the legislative history of the issue of naturalization during the first half of the century by stating: "Here is nothing to countenance the theory that a general rule of citizenship by blood or descent has displaced in this country the fundamental rule of citizenship by birth within its sovereignty." The implication is that Wong is a U.S. citizen by virtue of having been born on U.S. soil and that he is not a Chinese subject as a result of his bloodline.

This position was buttressed by the Civil Rights Act of 1866, which states that all those born in the United States and who do not answer to a "foreign power" are considered to be citizens of the United States, with all the benefits that come with citizenship. It was this act that prompted passage of the Fourteenth Amendment, which begins: "All persons born or naturalized in the United States, and subject to the jurisdiction thereof, are citizens of the United States and of the State wherein they reside." Gray goes on to parse the meaning of "jurisdiction" and "not subject to any foreign power" as used in legislation and in the Fourteenth Amendment to demonstrate that Wong was under U.S. jurisdiction and that he was not "subject to a foreign power."

Based on his examination of the history of legislation pertaining to naturalization and on the Fourteenth Amend-

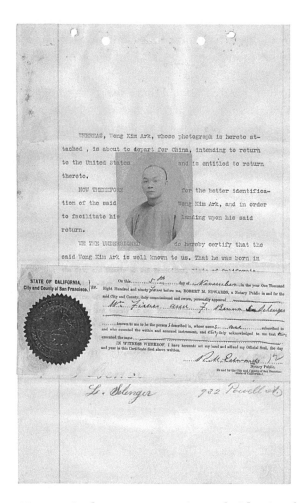

***1894 notarized statement attesting to the identity of Wong Kim Ark***
(Wikimedia Commons)

the position of chief justice. He disliked divided courts, believing that they undermined public faith in the integrity of the court's decisions. Accordingly, in the course of seventeen years, he wrote just *one* dissent in nearly fourteen hundred cases. He became widely known, and feared, for his irascibility and intimidating manner to lawyers and witnesses.

On December 19, 1881, President Chester A. Arthur nominated Gray to the U.S. Supreme Court. His nomination was confirmed by the Senate the following day. During twenty years on the Court, he wrote more than 450 opinions. His judicial opinions were marked by deference to the legislature, and legal historians believe that through his decisions he expanded the powers of Congress. On February 3, 1902, he suffered a stroke. He resigned from the Court and died on September 15 in Nahant, Massachusetts.

ment, Gray concludes that "the Fourteenth Amendment affirms the ancient and fundamental rule of citizenship by birth within the territory." He further concludes that children born in the United States to parents residing in the country are likewise citizens. He then states that "to hold that the Fourteenth Amendment of the Constitution excludes from citizenship the children, born in the United States, of citizens or subjects of other countries would be to deny citizenship to thousands of persons of English, Scotch, Irish, German, or other European parentage who have always been considered and treated as citizens of the United States." Race, Gray asserts, cannot be the basis for denying anyone his or her rights.

Gray turns to the specific issue of Chinese persons and the reach and extent of the Chinese Exclusion Acts (which included the original act, plus the Scott Act and the Geary Act). He notes and accepts that under the law as then existing, persons born in China cannot be naturalized in the United States. Even so, the fact that U.S. law does not permit persons born in China to be naturalized does not mean that their children born in the United States cannot be naturalized. Gray concludes that Wong is a citizen, possessed of all the rights of U.S. citizenship, including those extended by the Fourteenth Amendment. On this basis, Gray affirms the ruling of the circuit court ordering the release of Wong from custody.

## Impact

The specific impact of the Court's decision in *Wong Kim Ark* would be difficult to trace. The immediate impact was that Wong›s rights as a citizen were recognized and that he was released from immigration custody. Still, the provisions of the Chinese Exclusion Act retained the force of law. In 1900, the Office of the Superintendent of Immigration, which had been established as part of the Department of the Treasury in 1891, became the principal agency responsible for implementing the Chinese Exclusion Act. This agency evolved into the present Immigration and Naturalization Service. The agency employed Chinese inspectors who were specifically assigned the task of enforcing the Chinese Exclusion Acts, but their decisions were often challenged in federal courts.

In 1900, two years after the Court's decision in *Wong Kim Ark*, about 119,000 persons of Chinese descent resided in the United States, about 0.16 percent of the population. That number would decline in subsequent years—to 94,000 in 1910 and 85,000 in 1920. These figures include persons of mixed ethnic origin. While Chinese immigration had been curtailed, the citizenship rights of most of these persons were protected. The number of Chinese citizens in the United States did not show an increase until the 1930 census, when the number was up to 102,00v0. A marked increase in the number of Chinese Americans came about after the passage of the Chinese Exclusion Repeal Act of 1943. In the 1950 census, the number had increased to 150,000. The U.S. Census of 2010 reported that nearly 3.8 million persons of Chinese descent lived in the United States, and the Census Bureau estimated the number in 2019 to be five million.

---

### Questions for Further Study

1. Why was Wong Kim Ark detained when he attempted to reenter the United States in 1895?

2. What was the fundamental issue presented to the Supreme Court in *Wong Kim Ark*?

3. What was the significance of the Fourteenth Amendment to the Constitution in the Court's decision?

4. What social and economic factors led to the passage of the Chinese Exclusion Act?

5. What was the relevance, if any, to Gray's analysis of the fact that Wong's parents were still Chinese citizens, subjects of the emperor of China?

---

## Further Reading

### Books

Ahmad, Diana L. *The Opium Debate and Chinese Exclusion Laws in the Nineteenth Century American West.* Reno: University of Nevada Press, 2011.

Ho, James, Margaret D. Stock, Eric K. Ward, and Elizabeth Wydra. *Made in America: Myths and Facts about Birthright Citizenship.* Immigration Policy Center, September 2009.

Lee, Erika. *At America's Gates: Chinese Immigration during the Exclusion Era, 1882–1943.* Chapel Hill: University of North Carolina Press, 2003.

Lew-Williams, Beth. *The Chinese Must Go: Violence, Exclusion, and the Making of the Alien in America.* Cambridge, MA: Harvard University Press, 2018.

McClain, Charles J. *In Search of Equality: The Chinese Struggle against Discrimination in Nineteenth-Century America.* Berkeley: University of California Press, 1994.

Motomura, Hiroshi. *Americans in Waiting: The Lost Story of Immigration in the United States.* New York: Oxford University Press, 2006.

Salyer, Lucy E. "Wong Kim Ark: The Contest over Birthright Citizenship." In *Immigration Stories,* edited by David Martin and Peter Schuck, 51–85. New York: Foundation Press, 2005.

### Articles

Berger, Bethany. "Birthright Citizenship on Trial: Elk v. Wilkins and United States v. Wong Kim Ark." *Cardozo Law Review* 37, no. 4 (2016): 1185–1258.

Davis, Elbridge B., and Harold A. Davis. "Mr. Justice Horace Gray: Some Aspects of His Judicial Career." *American Bar Association Journal* 41, no. 5 (May 1955): 421–424, 468–471.

Eastman, John C. "The Significance of 'Domicile' in Wong Kim Ark." *Chapman Law Review* 22 (2019): 301–317.

Epps, Garrett. "The Citizenship Clause: A 'Legislative History.'" *American University Law Review* 60, no. 2 (2010): 331–388.

Hoar, George F. "Memoir of Horace Gray, LLD." *Proceedings of the Massachusetts Historical Society* 18 (1903–1904): 155–187.

Lollman, Justin. "The Significance of Parental Domicile under the Citizenship Clause." *Virginia Law Review* 101, no. 2 (2015): 455–500.

Thomas, Brook. "China Men, United States v. Wong Kim Ark, and the Question of Citizenship." *American Quarterly* 50, no. 4 (December 1998): 689–717.

—Commentary by Michael J. O'Neal

# UNITED STATES V. WONG KIM ARK

## Document Text

### MR. JUSTICE GRAY, after stating the case, delivered the opinion of the Court

The facts of this case, as agreed by the parties, are as follows: Wong Kim Ark was born in 1873 in the city of San Francisco, in the State of California and United States of America, and was and is a laborer. His father and mother were persons of Chinese descent, and subjects of the Emperor of China; they were at the time of his birth domiciled residents of the United States, having previously established and still enjoying a permanent domicil and residence therein at San Francisco; they continued to reside and remain in the United States until 1890, when they departed for China, and during all the time of their residence in the United States, they were engaged in business, and were never employed in any diplomatic or official capacity under the Emperor of China. Wong Kim Ark, ever since his birth, has had but one residence, to-wit, in California, within the United States, and has there resided, claiming to be a citizen of the United States, and has never lost or changed that residence, or gained or acquired another residence, and neither he nor his parents acting for him ever renounced his allegiance to the United States, or did or committed any act or thing to exclude him therefrom. In 1890 (when he must have been about seventeen years of age), he departed for China on a temporary visit and with the intention of returning to the United States, and did return thereto by sea in the same year, and was permitted by the collector of customs to enter the United States upon the sole ground that he was a native-born citizen of the United States. After such return, he remained in the United States, claiming to be a citizen thereof, until

1894, when he (being about twenty-one years of age, but whether a little above or a little under that age does not appear) again departed for China on a temporary visit and with the intention of returning to the United States, and he did return thereto by sea in August, 1895, and applied to the collector of customs for permission to land, and was denied such permission upon the sole ground that he was not a citizen of the United States.

It is conceded that, if he is a citizen of the United States, the acts of Congress, known as the Chinese Exclusion Acts, prohibiting persons of the Chinese race, and especially Chinese laborers, from coming into the United States, do not and cannot apply to him.

The question presented by the record is whether a child born in the United States, of parents of Chinese descent, who, at the time of his birth, are subjects of the Emperor of China, but have a permanent domicil and residence in the United States, and are there carrying on business, and are not employed in any diplomatic or official capacity under the Emperor of China, becomes at the time of his birth a citizen of the United States by virtue of the first clause of the Fourteenth Amendment of the Constitution,

"All persons born or naturalized in the United States, and subject to the jurisdiction thereof, are citizens of the United States and of the State wherein they reside."

I. In construing any act of legislation, whether a statute enacted by the legislature or a constitution established by the people as the supreme law of the land, regard is to be had not only to all parts of the act itself, and of any former act of the same lawmaking power of which the act in question is an amendment, but also to the condition and to the history of the law as previously existing, and in the light of which the new act must be read and interpreted.

The Constitution of the United States, as originally adopted, uses the words "citizen of the United States," and "natural-born citizen of the United States." By the original Constitution, every representative in Congress is required to have been "seven years a citizen of the United States," and every Senator to have been "nine years a citizen of the United States." and "no person except a natural-born citizen, or a citizen of the United States at the time of the adoption of this Constitution, shall be eligible to the office of President." The Fourteenth Article of Amendment, besides declaring that

"all persons born or naturalized in the United States, and subject to the jurisdiction thereof, are citizens of the United States and of the State wherein they reside,"

also declares that

"no State shall make or enforce any law which shall abridge the privileges or immunities of citizens of the United States; nor shall any State deprive any person of life, liberty or property, without due process of law; nor deny to any person within its jurisdiction the equal protection of the laws."

And the Fifteenth Article of Amendment declares that

"the right of citizens of the United States to vote shall not be denied or abridged by the United States, or by any State, on account of race, color or previous condition of servitude."

The Constitution nowhere defines the meaning of these words, either by way of inclusion or of exclusion, except insofar as this is done by the affirmative declaration that "all persons born or naturalized in the United States, and subject to the jurisdiction thereof, are citizens of the United States." In this as in other respects, it must be interpreted in the light of the common law. . . .

It thus clearly appears that, by the law of England for the last three centuries, beginning before the settlement of this country and continuing to the present day, aliens, while residing in the dominions possessed by the Crown of England, were within the allegiance,

the obedience, the faith or loyalty, the protection, the power, the jurisdiction of the English Sovereign, and therefore every child born in England of alien parents was a natural-born subject unless the child of an ambassador or other diplomatic agent of a foreign State or of an alien enemy in hostile occupation of the place where the child was born. . . .

There is, therefore, little ground for the theory that, at the time of the adoption of the Fourteenth Amendment of the Constitution of the United States, there was any settled and definite rule of international law, generally recognized by civilized nations, inconsistent with the ancient rule of citizenship by birth within the dominion.

Nor can it be doubted that it is the inherent right of every independent nation to determine for itself, and according to its own constitution and laws, what classes of persons shall be entitled to its citizenship.

Both in England and in the United States, indeed, statutes have been passed at various times enacting that certain issue born abroad of English subjects or of American citizens, respectively, should inherit, to some extent at least, the rights of their parents. But those statutes applied only to cases coming within their purport, and they have never been considered in either country as affecting the citizenship of persons born within its dominion. . . .

By the Constitution of the United States, Congress was empowered "to establish an uniform rule of naturalization." In the exercise of this power, Congress, by successive acts, beginning with the act entitled "An act to establish an uniform rule of naturalization," passed at the second session of the First Congress under the Constitution, has made provision for the admission to citizenship of three principal classes of persons: First. Aliens, having resided for a certain time "within the limits and under the jurisdiction of the United States," and naturalized individually by proceedings in a court of record. Second. Children of persons so naturalized, "dwelling within the United States, and being under the age of twenty-one years at the time of such naturalization." Third. Foreign-born children of American citizens, coming within the definitions prescribed by Congress. . . .

In the act of 1790, the provision as to foreign-born children of American citizens was as follows:

"The children of citizens of the United States, that may be born beyond sea, or out of the limits of the United States, shall be considered as natural-born citizens: Provided, that the right of citizenship shall not descend to persons whose fathers have never been resident in the United States." . . .

In 1795, this was reenacted in the same words, except in substituting for the words "beyond sea, or out of the limits of the United States" the words "out of the limits and jurisdiction of the United States." . . .

In 1802, all former acts were repealed, and the provisions concerning children of citizens were reenacted in this form:

"The children of persons duly naturalized under any of the laws of the United States, or who, previous to the passing of any law on that subject by the Government of the United States, may have become citizens of any one of the said States under the laws thereof, being under the age of twenty-one years at the time of their parents' being so naturalized or admitted to the rights of citizenship, shall, if dwelling in the United States, be considered as citizens of the United States, and the children of persons who now are, or have been citizens of the United States shall, though born out of the limits and jurisdiction of the United States, be considered as citizens of the United States: Provided, that the right of citizenship shall not descend to persons whose fathers have never resided within the United States." . . .

The provision of that act concerning "the children of persons duly naturalized under any of the laws of the United States," not being restricted to the children of persons already naturalized, might well be held to include children of persons thereafter to be naturalized. . . .

But the provision concerning foreign-born children, being expressly limited to the children of persons who then were or had been citizens, clearly did not include foreign-born children of any person who became a citizen since its enactment. 2 Kent.Com. 52, 53; Binney on Alienigenae 20, 25; 2 Amer.Law Reg. 203, 205. Mr. Binney's paper, as he states in his preface, was printed by him in the hope that Congress might supply this defect in our law.

In accordance with his suggestions, it was enacted by the statute of February 10, 1855, c. 71, that

"persons heretofore born, or hereafter to be born, out of the limits and jurisdiction of the United States, whose fathers were or shall be at the time of their birth citizens of the United States, shall be deemed and considered and are hereby declared to be citizens of the United States: Provided, however, that the rights of citizenship shall not descend to persons whose fathers never resided in the United States." . . .

It thus clearly appears that, during the half century intervening between 1802 and 1855, there was no legislation whatever for the citizenship of children born abroad, during that period, of American parents who had not become citizens of the United States before the act of 1802, and that the act of 1855, like every other act of Congress upon the subject, has, by express proviso, restricted the right of citizenship, thereby conferred upon foreign-born children of American citizens, to those children themselves, unless they became residents of the United States. Here is nothing to countenance the theory that a general rule of citizenship by blood or descent has displaced in this country the fundamental rule of citizenship by birth within its sovereignty.

So far as we are informed, there is no authority, legislative, executive or judicial, in England or America, which maintains or intimates that the statutes (whether considered as declaratory or as merely prospective) conferring citizenship on foreign-born children of citizens have superseded or restricted, in any respect, the established rule of citizenship by birth within the dominion. Even those authorities in this country, which have gone the farthest towards holding such statutes to be but declaratory of the common law have distinctly recognized and emphatically asserted the citizenship of native-born children of foreign parents. . . .

Passing by questions once earnestly controverted, but finally put at rest by the Fourteenth Amendment of the Constitution, it is beyond doubt that, before the enactment of the Civil Rights Act of 1866 or the adoption of the Constitutional Amendment, all white persons, at least, born within the sovereignty of the United States, whether children of citizens or of foreigners, excepting only children of ambassadors or public ministers of a foreign government, were native-born citizens of the United States.

V. In the forefront both of the Fourteenth Amendment of the Constitution and of the Civil Rights Act of 1866, the fundamental principle of citizenship by birth within the dominion was reaffirmed in the most explicit and comprehensive terms.

The Civil Rights Act, passed at the first session of the Thirty-ninth Congress, began by enacting that

"all persons born in the United States, and not subject to any foreign power, excluding Indians not taxed, are hereby declared to be citizens of the United States, and such citizens, of every race and color, without regard to any previous condition of slavery or involuntary servitude, except as a punishment for crime whereof the party shall have been duly convicted, shall have the same right, in every State and Territory in the United States, to make and enforce contracts, to sue, be parties and give evidence, to inherit, purchase, lease, sell, hold and convey real and personal property, and to full and equal benefit of all laws and proceedings for the security of person and property as is enjoyed by white citizens, and shall be subject to like punishment, pains and penalties, and to none other, any law, statute, ordinance, regulation or custom to the contrary notwithstanding." . . .

The same Congress, shortly afterwards, evidently thinking it unwise, and perhaps unsafe, to leave so important a declaration of rights to depend upon an ordinary act of legislation, which might be repealed by any subsequent Congress, framed the Fourteenth Amendment of the Constitution, and, on June 16, 1866, by joint resolution, proposed it to the legislatures of the several States, and on July 28, 1868, the Secretary of State issued a proclamation showing it to have been ratified by the legislatures of the requisite number of States. 14 Stat. 358; 1 Stat. 708.

The first section of the Fourteenth Amendment of the Constitution begins with the words,

"All persons born or naturalized in the United States, and subject to the jurisdiction thereof, are citizens of the United States and of the State wherein they reside."

As appears upon the face of the amendment, as well as from the history of the times, this was not intended to impose any new restrictions upon citizenship, or to prevent any persons from becoming citizens by the fact of birth within the United States who would thereby have become citizens according to the law existing before its adoption. It is declaratory in form, and enabling and extending in effect. Its main purpose doubtless was, as has been often recognized by this court, to establish the citizenship of free negroes, which had been denied in the opinion delivered by Chief Justice Taney in *Dred Scott v. Sandford,* (1857) 19 How. 393, and to put it beyond doubt that all blacks, as well as whites, born or naturalized within the jurisdiction of the United States are citizens of the United States. . . .

From the first organization of the National Government under the Constitution, the naturalization acts of the United States, in providing for the admission of aliens to citizenship by judicial proceedings, uniformly required every applicant to have resided for a certain time "within the limits and under the jurisdiction of the United States," and thus applied the words "under the jurisdiction of the United States" to aliens residing here before they had taken an oath to support the Constitution of the United States, or had renounced allegiance to a foreign government. . . . And, from 1795, the provisions of those acts which granted citizenship to foreign-born children of American parents described such children as "born out of the limits and jurisdiction of the United States." . . . Thus, Congress, when dealing with the question of citizenship in that aspect, treated aliens residing in this country as "under the jurisdiction of the United States," and American parents residing abroad as "out of the jurisdiction of the United States."

The words "in the United States, and subject to the jurisdiction thereof" in the first sentence of the Fourteenth Amendment of the Constitution must be presumed to have been understood and intended by the Congress which proposed the Amendment, and by the legislatures which adopted it, in the same sense in which the like words had been used by Chief Justice Marshall in the well known case of *The Exchange* and as the equivalent of the words "within the limits and under the jurisdiction of the United States," and the converse of the words "out of the limits and jurisdiction of the United States" as habitually used in the naturalization acts. This presumption is confirmed by the use of the word "jurisdiction" in the last clause of the same section of the Fourteenth Amendment, which forbids any State to "deny to any person within its jurisdiction the equal protection of the laws." It is impossible to construe the words "subject to the jurisdiction thereof" in the opening sentence, as less comprehensive than the words "within its jurisdiction" in the concluding sentence of the same section; or to hold that persons "within the jurisdiction" of one of the States of the Union are not "subject to the jurisdiction of the United States."

These considerations confirm the view, already expressed in this opinion, that the opening sentence of the Fourteenth Amendment is throughout affirmative and declaratory, intended to allay doubts and to settle controversies which had arisen, and not to impose any new restrictions upon citizenship.

By the Civil Rights Act of 1866, "all persons born in the United States, and not subject to any foreign power, excluding Indians not taxed," were declared to be citizens of the United States. In the light of the law as previously established, and of the history of the times, it can hardly be doubted that the words of that act, "not subject to any foreign power," were not intended to exclude any children born in this country from the citizenship which would theretofore have been their birthright, or, for instance, for the first time in our history, to deny the right of citizenship to native-born children of foreign white parents not in the diplomatic service of their own country nor in hostile occupation of part of our territory. But any possible doubt in this regard was removed when the negative words of the Civil Rights Act, "not subject to any foreign power," gave way, in the Fourteenth Amendment of the Constitution, to the affirmative words, "subject to the jurisdiction of the United States."

This sentence of the Fourteenth Amendment is declaratory of existing rights and affirmative of existing law as to each of the qualifications therein expressed—"born in the United States," "naturalized in the United States," and "subject to the jurisdiction thereof"—in short, as to everything relating to the acquisition of citizenship by facts occurring within the limits of the United States. But it has not touched the acquisition of citizenship by being born abroad of American parents, and has left that subject to be regulated, as it had always been, by Congress in the exercise of the power conferred by the Constitution to establish an uniform rule of naturalization.

The effect of the enactments conferring citizenship on foreign-born children of American parents has been defined, and the fundamental rule of citizenship by birth within the dominion of the United States, notwithstanding alienage of parents, has been affirmed, in well considered opinions of the executive depart-

ments of the Government since the adoption of the Fourteenth Amendment of the Constitution....

The foregoing considerations and authorities irresistibly lead us to these conclusions: the Fourteenth Amendment affirms the ancient and fundamental rule of citizenship by birth within the territory, in the allegiance and under the protection of the country, including all children here born of resident aliens, with the exceptions or qualifications (as old as the rule itself) of children of foreign sovereigns or their ministers, or born on foreign public ships, or of enemies within and during a hostile occupation of part of our territory, and with the single additional exception of children of members of the Indian tribes owing direct allegiance to their several tribes. The Amendment, in clear words and in manifest intent, includes the children born, within the territory of the United States, of all other persons, of whatever race or color, domiciled within the United States. Every citizen or subject of another country, while domiciled here, is within the allegiance and the protection, and consequently subject to the jurisdiction, of the United States. His allegiance to the United States is direct and immediate, and, although but local and temporary, continuing only so long as he remains within our territory, is yet, in the words of Lord Coke in *Calvin's Case,* 7 Rep. 6a, "strong enough to make a natural subject, for if he hath issue here, that issue is a natural-born subject;" and his child, as said by Mr. Binney in his essay before quoted, "if born in the country, is as much a citizen as the natural-born child of a citizen, and by operation of the same principle." It can hardly be denied that an alien is completely subject to the political jurisdiction of the country in which he resides—seeing that, as said by Mr. Webster, when Secretary of State, in his Report to the President on *Thrasher's Case* in 1851, and since repeated by this court,

"independently of a residence with intention to continue such residence; independently of any domiciliation; independently of the taking of any oath of allegiance or of renouncing any former allegiance, it is well known that, by the public law, an alien, or a stranger born, for so long a time as he continues within the dominions of a foreign government, owes obedience to the laws of that government, and may be punished for treason, or other crimes, as a native-born subject might be, unless his case is varied by some treaty stipulations." ...

To hold that the Fourteenth Amendment of the Constitution excludes from citizenship the children, born in the United States, of citizens or subjects of other countries would be to deny citizenship to thousands of persons of English, Scotch, Irish, German, or other European parentage who have always been considered and treated as citizens of the United States.

VI. Whatever considerations, in the absence of a controlling provision of the Constitution, might influence the legislative or the executive branch of the Government to decline to admit persons of the Chinese race to the status of citizens of the United States, there are none that can constrain or permit the judiciary to refuse to give full effect to the peremptory and explicit language of the Fourteenth Amendment, which declares and ordains that "All persons born or naturalized in the United States, and subject to the jurisdiction thereof, are citizens of the United States."

Chinese persons, born out of the United States, remaining subjects of the Emperor of China, and not having become citizens of the United States, are entitled to the protection of, and owe allegiance to, the United States so long as they are permitted by the United States to reside here, and are " subject to the jurisdiction thereof" in the same sense as all other aliens residing in the United States....

It necessarily follows that persons born in China, subjects of the Emperor of China but domiciled in the United States, having been adjudged, in *Yick Wo v. Hopkins* to be within the jurisdiction of the State within the meaning of the concluding sentence, must be held to be subject to the jurisdiction of the United States within the meaning of the first sentence of this section of the Constitution, and their children "born in the United States" cannot be less "subject to the jurisdiction thereof."...

The acts of Congress known as the Chinese Exclusion Acts, the earliest of which was passed some fourteen years after the adoption of the Constitutional Amendment, cannot control its meaning or impair its effect, but must be construed and executed in subordination to its provisions. And the right of the United States, as exercised by and under those acts, to exclude or to expel from the country persons of the Chinese race born in China and continuing to be subjects of the Emperor of China, though having acquired a commercial dom-

icil in the United States, has been upheld by this court for reasons applicable to all aliens alike, and inapplicable to citizens of whatever race or color....

It is true that Chinese persons born in China cannot be naturalized, like other aliens, by proceedings under the naturalization laws. But this is for want of any statute or treaty authorizing or permitting such naturalization, as will appear by tracing the history of the statutes, treaties and decisions upon that subject—always bearing in mind that statutes enacted by Congress, as well as treaties made by the President and Senate, must yield to the paramount and supreme law of the Constitution....

The fact, therefore, that acts of Congress or treaties have not permitted Chinese persons born out of this country to become citizens by naturalization, cannot exclude Chinese persons born in this country from the operation of the broad and clear words of the Constitution, "All persons born in the United States, and subject to the jurisdiction thereof, are citizens of the United States."

VII. Upon the facts agreed in this case, the American citizenship which Wong Kim Ark acquired by birth within the United States has not been lost or taken away by anything happening since his birth. No doubt he might himself, after coming of age, renounce this citizenship and become a citizen of the country of his parents, or of any other country; for, by our law, as solemnly declared by Congress, "the right of expatriation is a natural and inherent right of all people," and

"any declaration, instruction, opinion, order or direction of any officer of the United States which denies, restricts, impairs or questions the right of expatriation, is declared inconsistent with the fundamental principles of the Republic."...

Whether any act of himself or of his parents during his minority could have the same effect is at least doubtful. But it would be out of place to pursue that inquiry, inasmuch as it is expressly agreed that his residence has always been in the United States, and not elsewhere; that each of his temporary visits to China, the one for some months when he was about seventeen years old, and the other for something like a year about the time of his coming of age, was made with the intention of returning, and was followed by his actual return, to the United States, and "that said Wong Kim Ark has not, either by himself or his parents acting for him, ever renounced his allegiance to the United States, and that he has never done or committed any act or thing to exclude him therefrom."

The evident intention, and the necessary effect, of the submission of this case to the decision of the court upon the facts agreed by the parties were to present for determination the single question stated at the beginning of this opinion, namely, whether a child born in the United States, of parent of Chinese descent, who, at the time of his birth, are subjects of the Emperor of China, but have a permanent domicil and residence in the United States, and are there carrying on business, and are not employed in any diplomatic or official capacity under the Emperor of China, becomes at the time of his birth a citizen of the United States. For the reasons above stated, this court is of opinion that the question must be answered in the affirmative.

*Order affirmed.*

---

## Glossary

**act of 1790:** reference to the Naturalization Act of 1790

**alienage:** legal status of an alien

**common law:** body of law developed over time through judicial precedents rather than through legislation

**domicil:** country that a person treats as his or her permanent home or lives in; to be distinguished from *domicile,* which refers to a home or dwelling

**1802:** reference to the Naturalization Law of 1802

**expatriation:** act of renouncing allegiance to one's country or of leaving one's country to live elsewhere

**issue:** children; descendants

**naturalization:** legal process by which a foreign citizen applies for and is granted citizenship in the United States

**privileges and immunities:** phrase used in Article IV, section 2, of the Constitution that protects the fundamental rights of individual citizens and prevents discrimination against out-of-state citizens

**writ of habeas corpus:** order from a court requiring the person detaining another to produce the person to test the legality of the detention

---

# *LOCHNER V. NEW YORK*

<table>
<tr><td>

**DATE**
1905

**AUTHOR**
Rufus W. Peckham

**VOTE**
5–4

</td><td>

**CITATION**
198 U.S. 45

**SIGNIFICANCE**
Ruled that a New York State law limiting maximum hours for bakers violated employers' and employees' right to freedom of contract under the Fourteenth Amendment

</td></tr>
</table>

## Overview

In 1895, the state of New York enacted a law, the Bakeshop Act, that regulated conditions in the state's many small bakeries and limited the workweek to sixty hours. When Joseph Lochner, the owner of a bakeshop in Utica, was convicted and fined for allowing an employee to work more than sixty hours, he appealed his conviction to the New York appeals courts, which upheld the constitutionality of the law and Lochner's conviction. He then appealed to the U.S. Supreme Court, where he argued that the Fourteenth Amendment guaranteed that he could not be deprived of his liberty of contract without due process. The Court ruled in Lochner's favor by a 5–4 vote. Justice Rufus W. Peckham wrote the majority opinion, ruling that the right to buy and sell labor without government interference was protected by the Fourteenth Amendment.

## Context

The late nineteenth and early twentieth centuries were a time of rapid industrialization and urbanization. Large numbers of penniless immigrants were arriving on U.S. shores. Wealth was concentrated in the hands of elites, many of them characterized as "robber barons," among them J. P. Morgan, Cornelius Vanderbilt, John D. Rockefeller, and Andrew Carnegie. It was the Gilded Age, although the prevalence of urban slums, the exploitation of workers, unsafe and unhygienic working conditions, child labor, Jim Crow laws, and crushing poverty provided evidence that the age was "gilded" for only the few.

The *Lochner* decision was rendered during the Progressive Era in U.S. history, which spanned roughly the 1890s to the late 1910s. The era was one of widespread social activism and political reform. Progressive activists were bent on combating corruption in government, business monopolies and trusts, waste, and inefficiency, as well as on ameliorating the condition of the laboring poor. Many of the abuses of business and government were exposed in mass-circulation newspapers and magazines, which published the work of investigative journalists known as muckrakers. One target of progressives was the corrupt and undemocratic political machines and their bosses in the big cities; Peckham's brother, Wheeler Hazard Peckham, played a prominent role in busting up the infamous Boss Tweed political machine, Tammany Hall, that bilked New York City taxpayers out of millions of dollars. Another major goal of progressives during this era was gaining the right to vote for women.

One of the chief ways progressives sought to curb the abuses of big business was through regulation. A major achievement during the era was the passage of the Sherman Antitrust Act of 1890, which went a long way toward trustbusting, or busting up business trusts—that is, organizations of several businesses in the same industry to control production and distribution of goods at the expense of the consumer. The Sherman Act was given more teeth with the passage of the Clayton Act in 1914. Progressive also called for government to adopt new roles and for the creation of agencies to enforce increased regulation of business.

*Lochner v. New York* had its origins in 1899, in the midst of the Progressive Era. Joseph Lochner was a German immigrant who owned a bakery in Utica, New York. At the time, small bakeshops were often owned and operated by Jewish, German, and other immigrants. These bakers tended to fiercely resist unionization and any laws that would limit the number of hours their employees could work. Generally, they needed only a few workers to operate the ovens over a twenty-four-hour period. It was commonplace for workers to sleep on the premises while dough was rising overnight, then resume work in the morning to bake the bread. This was the case with Lochner's bakeshop. Rather than having a morning and an evening shift, like large, corporate bakers employed, he employed a single crew. They arrived in the evening, prepared the dough, slept for several hours in an on-site dormitory, then rose in the morning to bake the bread. Lochner paid the employees for the time they were sleeping.

At the time, most of the bakeries that operated in New York City did so in tenement house cellars, largely because the rent was low and the cellar floors were sturdy enough to support the weight of ovens. The spaces—never designed for commercial use—were cramped, however, and sometimes posed serious sanitation issues. To address these problems, the state enacted the Bakeshop Act of 1895, which established a detailed sanitation code. At the request of the bakeshop union, however, the legislature added another provision to the act: it would be illegal for bakery employees to work more than ten hours a day or sixty hours per week. This provision had the effect—which may

*Oliver Wendell Holmes gave a famous dissent in* **Lochner v. New York.**
(Wikimedia Commons)

have been intended—of benefitting corporate-owned, unionized bakeshops at the expense of their smaller, immigrant-owned competitors. The large bakeries, in contrast to their small competitors, could employ shift workers to comply with maximum-hour laws.

Lochner was indicted on the charge of violating the Bakeshop Act by allowing employees to work more than sixty hours a week. His lawyers argued that as a matter of substantive due process, he had a right to contract freely with his employees, and they with him. ("Substantive due process" is the principle that the Fifth and Fourteenth Amendments protect fundamental rights from government interference; it is distinguished from "procedural due process," or simply "due process," which refers to the process of trying and convicting criminal defendants.) Perhaps oddly, Lochner's case was argued by the same attorney who had been a prominent advocate of the Bakeshop Act when he was secretary of the Journeymen Bakers' Union. In his brief for Lochner, he deprecated the notion that "the treasured freedom of the individual . . . should be swept away under the guise of the police power of the State." He disputed the state's argument that the Bakeshop Act was a necessary health measure and even provided statistical data showing that the mortality rate of bakers was similar to that of white-collar workers.

Lochner was convicted in the county court and fined $50 (nearly $1,700 in 2021 inflation-adjusted dollars). He appealed to the New York Supreme Court, then to the New York Court of Appeals, but in each court his conviction was affirmed. Accordingly, he appealed to the U.S. Supreme Court, which ruled that the New York law violated the Constitution's principle of substantive due process, stating that the law was an "unreasonable, unnecessary and arbitrary interference with the right and liberty of the individual to contract." The ruling, though, was narrow, for four justices dissented from the Court majority.

The Court's decision in *Lochner* was one of the most controversial ones in the history of the Supreme Court. It even provided the name "Lochner era" to the period, when the Court reached a number of decisions that invalidated state and federal laws that sought to regulate working conditions. It is thought that the Lochner era ended in 1937 when the Court upheld the constitutionality of minimum wage laws enacted in Washington State in *West Coast Hotel Co. v. Parrish*.

## About the Author

Rufus W. Peckham was born on November 8, 1838, to a family distinguished in New York politics and the legal community. His father, Rufus Wheeler Peckham Sr., served on the New York Supreme Court and on the state's Court of Appeals. His brother, Wheeler Hazard Peckham, was a distinguished attorney in his own right.

Peckham was educated at the Albany Boys Academy and later studied privately in Philadelphia. In 1856 he and his brother took a yearlong tour of Europe, a common practice among privileged young Americans at the time. When he returned to the United States, he studied law for two years at his father's firm, Peckham & Tremain, where he practiced with his brother after passing the bar examination at age twenty-one. Peckham proved to be a successful attorney. Among his clients was the Albany and Susquehanna Railroad, which he defended against the Erie Railroad and its owners, the notorious financiers Jim Fiske and Jay Gould. He was also active in politics, allying himself with the upstate wing of the Democratic Party, which led to his election in 1869 as district attorney for Albany County. In this capacity he became friends with Grover Cleveland, who later became governor of New York and president of the United States.

After three years, Peckham returned to private practice, but he entered public life again in 1881 when he became counsel to the city of Albany. Promotion came rapidly: in 1883 he was appointed to the New York Supreme Court, and in 1886 he was elected to the New York Court of Appeals, where he served until 1895. Although he was a partisan Democrat, he successfully kept his political opinions out of the courtroom—so much so that in 1891 he upheld the election of Republican candidates in contested election cases. It was this nonpartisanship in the courtroom that made him a suitable candidate for elevation to the U.S. Supreme Court to replace Justice Howell Jackson when he died in 1895. Peckham was nominated by his old friend, Grover Cleveland, and he was confirmed by the Senate later that year. He took his seat in January 1896.

Peckham devoted the rest of his life to his work as a Supreme Court justice and to staying out of politics, though his name was mentioned as a possible candidate for New York governor in 1907. His tenure coincided with a period of extraordinarily rapid business expansion, years during which the Court struggled with new and evolving concepts of the proper role of government in regulating the affairs of business. The Court often stood in opposition to the progressive and populist movements, which wanted government to restrain what they saw as the excesses of corporations and business trusts. As a justice, Peckham believed that his primary duty was to draw—and to police—sharp lines between the powers of the state governments, those of the federal government, and the rights of individuals. Thus, for example, he believed that government had the power to regulate business, but only when interstate commerce was directly and significantly affected. He also believed in the right of the individual to enter freely into contracts and to be free from government interference in the process.

These views led to what may have been Peckham's most significant decision, in *Lochner v. New York* (1905). In the view of many constitutional scholars, the *Lochner* decision represented the high-water mark of the Court's tendency to judge cases on the basis of abstract principles and precedents rather than social and economic changes that may have left those principles and precedents outdated.

Rufus W. Peckham died while still on the bench on October 24, 1909, in Altamont, New York.

## Explanation and Analysis of the Document

After summarizing the facts of the case, Justice Peckham examines the use of the word "required" in the New York statute, noting that the lower courts did not interpret "required" to suggest any kind of force used to obtain labor from an employee. He notes that "the word means nothing more than the requirement arising from voluntary contract for such labor in excess of the number of hours specified in the statute." He adds that "there is no pretense in any of the opinions that the statute was intended to meet a case of involuntary labor in any form. All the opinions assume that there is no real distinction, so far as this question is concerned, between the words 'required' and 'permitted.'" He notes, then, that an employee may want to earn extra money by working more hours than the law allows, "but this statute forbids the employer from permitting the employee to earn it."

Peckham then observes that "the statute necessarily interferes with the right of contract between the employer and employes [*sic*] concerning the number of hours in which the latter may labor in the bakery of the employer." He goes on to examine the matter in light of the Fourteenth Amendment, stating that the right to purchase or sell labor is part of the liberty protected by the amendment under the principle of substantive due process.

### *Police Powers*

Peckham takes up the issue of the police powers of the state:

> When the State, by its legislature, in the assumed exercise of its police powers, has passed an act which seriously limits the right to labor or the right of contract in regard to their means of livelihood between persons who are *sui juris* (both employer and employee), it becomes of great importance to determine which shall prevail—the right of the individual to labor for such time as he may choose or the right of the State to prevent the individual from laboring or from entering into any contract to labor beyond a certain time prescribed by the State.

(*Sui juris* means "of age" or "independent.") He concedes that the state sometimes can exercise police powers, citing a Utah statute that limits the hours of underground mine workers and smelters to eight, based on the nature of the work. He also cites a case involving the state's police power in the matter of compulsory vaccination, noting that public health was at issue. He maintains, though, that the case before the Court is very different from these. He insists that "it must, of course, be conceded that there is a limit to the valid exercise of the police power by the State." Otherwise, the "legislatures of the States would have unbounded power," and the claim of police power would too often be a "mere pretext." With regard to the case before the Court, he asks:

> Is this a fair, reasonable and appropriate exercise of the police power of the State, or is it an unreasonable, unnecessary and arbitrary interference with the right of the individual to his personal liberty or to enter into those contracts in relation to labor which may seem to him appropriate or necessary for the support of himself and his family?

It is clear that the Court majority believes the latter proposition to be the case. Peckham goes on to state that "there is no reasonable ground for interfering with the liberty of the person or the right of free contract by determining the hours of labor in the occupation of a baker." Bakers, he says, "are in no sense wards of the State." He adds that the law in question involves neither the safety, the morals, nor the welfare of the public and that "clean and wholesome bread does not depend upon whether the baker works but ten hours per day or only sixty hours a week."

Peckham continues to make the majority's opinion clear when he writes that "we think the limit of the police power has been reached and passed in this case." He continues: "There is, in our judgment, no reasonable foundation for holding this to be necessary or appropriate as a health law to safeguard the public health or the health of the individuals who are following the trade of a baker." He adds that the trade of a baker is not an unhealthy one "to that degree which would authorize the legislature to interfere with the right to labor, and with the right of free contract on the part of the individual." He draws comparisons with other trades, wondering whether printers, tinsmiths, locksmiths, carpenters, clerks, and other are "at the mercy of legislative majorities" and their "all-pervading power." Put simply, Peckham simply does not see the matter as a health issue for workers.

As if the position of the majority were not clear enough by this point, Peckham turns to the issue of public health to oppose the notion that any measure that conduces to the public health is "justified as a valid exercise of the police power." He states that the Bakeshop Act "is not, within any fair meaning of the term, a health law, but is an illegal interference with the rights of individuals, both employers and employees, to make contracts regarding labor upon such terms as they may think best." He refutes the notion that restricting the hours of bakers would lead to greater cleanliness among them, resulting in cleaner bread. For the Court majority, "The State in that case would assume the position of a supervisor, or *pater familias*, over every act of the individual."

Peckham wonders whether there was a shadowy ulterior motive behind the passage of the Bakeshop Act. He states:

> When assertions such as we have adverted to become necessary in order to give, if possible, a plausible foundation for the contention that the law is a "health law," it gives rise to at least a suspicion that there was some other motive dominating the legislature than the purpose to subserve the public health or welfare.

Peckham, however, does not speculate about what that "other motive" might have been other than the desire to regulate hours.

Peckham turns his attention to other cases, including a New York case bearing on a statute regulating the trade of horseshoeing. The requirement that a horseshoer had to obtain and file a certificate with the county was held by the New York court to be invalid "as an arbitrary interference with personal liberty and private property without due process of law." A similar statute enacted in Illinois was deemed by the court to be "an illegal interference with the liberty of the individual in adopting and pursuing such calling as he may choose."

Peckham concludes by stating that the Bakeshop Act was not a health law: "It seems to us that the real object and purpose were simply to regulate the hours of labor between the master and his employees (all being men *sui juris*) in a private business, not dangerous

in any degree to morals or in any real and substantial degree to the health of the employees." Given all these arguments, the judgment of the New York Court of Appeals was reversed.

## Dissents

Justice John M. Harlan, joined by Justices Edward D. White and William R. Day, dissented from the majority. After citing a number of similar cases, Justice Harlan states: "All the cases agree that this power [i.e., police power] extends at least to the protection of the lives, the health, and the safety of the public against the injurious exercise by any citizen of his own rights." A separate dissent issued by Justice Oliver Wendell Holmes Jr. survives as perhaps one of the most forceful and eloquent dissents in Court history. Holmes begins by stating that he takes it "to be firmly established that what is called the liberty of contract may, within certain limits, be subjected to regulations designed and calculated to promote the general welfare or to guard the public health, the public morals or the public safety."

Holmes then outlines his argument. He states that his personal agreement or disagreement with the right of the majority to "embody their opinion in law" has no bearing on this or any other case. The Court, state constitutions, and state laws "regulate life in many ways which we, as legislators, might think as injudicious, or . . . tyrannical" and "interfere with the liberty of contract." He points out a number of ways in which this liberty is circumscribed: Sunday laws, usury laws, prohibitions of lotteries, school laws, the post office, and any "state or municipal institution which takes [a person's] money for purposes thought desirable, whether he likes it or not." He characterizes the view that "the liberty of the citizen to do as he likes so long as he does not interfere with the liberty of others" as a "shibboleth for some well-known writers." (A shibboleth is a saying used by adherents of a party, sect, or belief regarded by others as empty of real meaning.) He concludes his argument by stating, "The Fourteenth Amendment does not enact Mr. Herbert Spencer's Social Statics." Spencer was a nineteenth-century philosopher who wrote in his 1851 book *Social Statics*:

> As a corollary to the proposition that all institutions must be subordinated to the law of equal freedom, we cannot choose but admit the right of the citizen to adopt a condition of voluntary outlawry. If every man has freedom

to do all that he wills, provided he infringes not the equal freedom of any other man, then he is free to drop connection with the state—to relinquish its protection, and to refuse paying towards its support.

Holmes concludes: "I think that the word 'liberty,' in the Fourteenth Amendment, is perverted when it is held to prevent the natural outcome of a dominant opinion."

## Questions for Further Study

1. On what basis did the Supreme Court overturn the ruling of the lower courts in this case?

2. How fair or unfair was the decision of the lower courts in convicting Lochner?

3. To what extent might evolving social standards have contributed to the Bakeshop Law of 1895?

4. Why did some legal observers believe that the Bakeshop Law was deliberately intended to place small, non-unionized bakeshops operated by immigrants at a disadvantage compared to large corporate bakeries?

## Further Reading

### Books

Bernstein, David E. *Rehabilitating Lochner: Defending Individual Rights against Progressive Reform.* Chicago: University of Chicago Press, 2012.

Chemerinsky, Erwin. *Constitutional Law: Principles and Policies,* 6th ed. New York: Wolters Kluwer, 2019.

Epstein, Richard A. *The Classical Liberal Constitution: The Uncertain Quest for Limited Government.* Cambridge, MA: Harvard University Press, 2014.

Kens, Paul. *Lochner v. New York: Economic Regulation on Trial.* Lawrence: University Press of Kansas, 1998.

Sandefur, Timothy. *The Right to Earn a Living: Economic Freedom and the Law.* Washington, D.C.: Cato Institute, 2010.

Tushnet, Mark. *I Dissent: Great Opposing Opinions in Landmark Supreme Court Cases.* Boston: Beacon Press, 2008.

### Articles

Barnett, Randy E. "Foreword: What's So Wicked about Lochner?" *NYU Journal of Law and Liberty* 1, no. 1 (2005): 1–9. https://www.law.nyu.edu/sites/default/files/ECM_PRO_060899.pdf.

Bernstein, David E. "Lochner v. New York: A Centennial Retrospective." *Washington University Law Review* 83, no. 5 (2005): 1469–1527. https://openscholarship.wustl.edu/cgi/viewcontent.cgi?article=1259&context=law_law-review.

## Further Reading

### Articles

Bewig, Matthew S. "Lochner v. the Journeymen Bakers of New York: The Journeymen Bakers, Their Hours of Labor, and the Constitution: A Case Study in the Social History of Legal Thought." *American Journal of Legal History* 38, No. 4 (October 1994): 413–51. https://www.jstor.org/stable/845444.

Calabresi, Steven G., and Sarah Agudo. "Individual Rights under State Constitutions When the Fourteenth Amendment Was Ratified in 1868: What Rights Are Deeply Rooted in American History and Tradition?" *Texas Law Review* 87, no. 7 (2008): 11–120.

Sunstein, Cass R. "Lochner's Legacy." *Columbia Law Review* 87, no. 5 (1987): 873–919. https://www.jstor.org/stable/1122721.

White, G. Edward. "Revisiting Substantive Due Process and Holmes's Lochner Dissent." *Brooklyn Law Review* 63, no. 1 (1997): 87–128.

—Commentary by Michael J. O'Neal

# LOCHNER V. NEW YORK

## Document Text

### MR. JUSTICE PECKHAM . . . delivered the opinion of the Court

The indictment, it will be seen, charges that the plaintiff in error violated the one hundred and tenth section of article 8, chapter 415, of the Laws of 1897, known as the labor law of the State of New York, in that he wrongfully and unlawfully required and permitted an employee working for him to work more than sixty hours in one week. There is nothing in any of the opinions delivered in this case, either in the Supreme Court or the Court of Appeals of the State, which construes the section, in using the word "required," as referring to any physical force being used to obtain the labor of an employee. It is assumed that the word means nothing more than the requirement arising from voluntary contract for such labor in excess of the number of hours specified in the statute. There is no pretense in any of the opinions that the statute was intended to meet a case of involuntary labor in any form. All the opinions assume that there is no real distinction, so far as this question is concerned, between the words "required" and "permitted." The mandate of the statute that "no employee shall be required or permitted to work," is the substantial equivalent of an enactment that "no employee shall contract or agree to work," more than ten hours per day, and, as there is no provision for special emergencies, the statute is mandatory in all cases. It is not an act merely fixing the number of hours which shall constitute a legal day's work, but an absolute prohibition upon the employer's permitting, under any circumstances, more than ten hours' work to be done in his establishment. The employee may desire to earn the extra money which would arise from his working more than the prescribed time, but this statute forbids the employer from permitting the employee to earn it.

The statute necessarily interferes with the right of contract between the employer and employes concerning the number of hours in which the latter may labor in the bakery of the employer. The general right to make a contract in relation to his business is part of the liberty of the individual protected by the Fourteenth Amendment of the Federal Constitution. *Allgeyer v. Louisiana,* 165 U. S. 578. Under that provision, no State can deprive any person of life, liberty or property without due process of law. The right to purchase or to sell labor is part of the liberty protected by this amendment unless there are circumstances which exclude the right. There are, however, certain powers, existing in the sovereignty of each State in the Union, somewhat vaguely termed police powers, the exact description and limitation of which have not been attempted by the courts. Those powers, broadly stated and without, at present, any attempt at a more specific limitation, relate to the safety, health, morals and general welfare of the public. Both property and liberty are held on such reasonable conditions as may be imposed by the governing power of the State in the exercise of those powers, and with such conditions the Fourteenth Amendment was not designed to interfere. *Mugler v. Kansas,* 123 U. S. 623; *In re Kemmler,* 136 U. S. 436; *Crowley v. Christensen,* 137 U. S. 86; *In re Converse,* 137 U. S. 624.

The State therefore has power to prevent the individual from making certain kinds of contracts, and, in regard to them, the Federal Constitution offers no protection. If the contract be one which the State, in the legitimate exercise of its police power, has the right to prohibit, it is not prevented from prohibiting it by the Fourteenth Amendment. Contracts in violation of a statute, either of the Federal or state government, or a contract to let one's property for immoral purposes, or to do any other unlawful act, could obtain no protection from the Federal Constitution as coming under the liberty of person or of free contract. Therefore, when the State, by its legislature, in the assumed exercise of its police powers, has passed an act which seriously limits the right to labor or the right of contract in regard to their means of livelihood between persons who are *sui juris* (both employer and employee), it becomes of great importance to determine which shall prevail—the right of the individual to labor for such time as he may choose or the right of the State to prevent the individual from laboring or from entering into any contract to labor beyond a certain time prescribed by the State.

This court has recognized the existence and upheld the exercise of the police powers of the States in many cases which might fairly be considered as border ones, and it has, in the course of its determination of questions regarding the asserted invalidity of such statutes on the ground of their violation of the rights secured by the Federal Constitution, been guided by rules of a very liberal nature, the application of which has resulted, in numerous instances, in upholding the validity of state statutes thus assailed. Among the later cases where the state law has been upheld by this court is that of *Holden v. Hardy,* 169 U. S. 366. A provision in the act of the legislature of Utah was there under consideration, the act limiting the employment of workmen in all underground mines or workings to eight hours per day "except in cases of emergency, where life or property is in imminent danger." It also limited the hours of labor in smelting and other institutions for the reduction or refining of ores or metals to eight hours per day except in like cases of emergency. The act was held to be a valid exercise of the police powers of the State. A review of many of the cases on the subject, decided by this and other courts, is given in the opinion. It was held that the kind of employment, mining, smelting, etc., and the character of the employes in such kinds of labor, were such as to make it reasonable and proper for the State to interfere to prevent the employees

from being constrained by the rules laid down by the proprietors in regard to labor. The following citation from the observations of the Supreme Court of Utah in that case was made by the judge writing the opinion of this court, and approved:

"The law in question is confined to the protection of that class of people engaged in labor in underground mines and in smelters and other works wherein ores are reduced and refined. This law applies only to the classes subjected by their employment to the peculiar conditions and effects attending underground mining and work in smelters and other works for the reduction and refining of ores. Therefore it is not necessary to discuss or decide whether the legislature can fix the hours of labor in other employments."

It will be observed that, even with regard to that class of labor, the Utah statute provided for cases of emergency wherein the provisions of the statute would not apply. The statute now before this court has no emergency clause in it, and, if the statute is valid, there are no circumstances and no emergencies under which the slightest violation of the provisions of the act would be innocent. There is nothing in *Holden v. Hardy* which covers the case now before us. Nor does *Atkin v. Kansas,* 191 U. S. 207, touch the case at bar. The *Atkin* case was decided upon the right of the State to control its municipal corporations and to prescribe the condition upon which it will permit work of a public character to be done for a municipality. *Knoxville Iron Co. v. Harbison,* 183 U. S. 13, is equally far from an authority for this legislation. The employees in that case were held to be at a disadvantage with the employer in matters of wages, they being miners and coal workers, and the act simply provided for the cashing of coal orders when presented by the miner to the employer.

The latest case decided by this court involving the police power is that of *Jacobson v. Massachusetts,* decided at this term and reported in 197 U. S. 197 U.S. 11. It related to compulsory vaccination, and the law was held valid as a proper exercise of the police powers with reference to the public health. It was stated in the opinion that it was a case

"of an adult who, for aught that appears, was himself in perfect health and a fit subject for vaccination, and yet, while remaining in the community, refused to obey the statute and the regulation adopted in execution of its provisions for the protection of the public health and the public safety, confessedly endangered by the presence of a dangerous disease."

That case is also far from covering the one now before the court.

*Petit v. Minnesota,* 177 U. S. 164, was upheld as a proper exercise of the police power relating to the observance of Sunday, and the case held that the legislature had the right to declare that, as matter of law, keeping barber shops open on Sunday was not a work of necessity or charity.

It must, of course, be conceded that there is a limit to the valid exercise of the police power by the State. There is no dispute concerning this general proposition. Otherwise the Fourteenth Amendment would have no efficacy, and the legislatures of the States would have unbounded power, and it would be enough to say that any piece of legislation was enacted to conserve the morals, the health or the safety of the people; such legislation would be valid no matter how absolutely without foundation the claim might be. The claim of the police power would be a mere pretext— become another and delusive name for the supreme sovereignty of the State to be exercised free from constitutional restraint. This is not contended for. In every case that comes before this court, therefore, where legislation of this character is concerned and where the protection of the Federal Constitution is sought, the question necessarily arises: is this a fair, reasonable and appropriate exercise of the police power of the State, or is it an unreasonable, unnecessary and arbitrary interference with the right of the individual to his personal liberty or to enter into those contracts in relation to labor which may seem to him appropriate or necessary for the support of himself and his family? Of course, the liberty of contract relating to labor includes both parties to it. The one has as much right to purchase as the other to sell labor.

This is not a question of substituting the judgment of the court for that of the legislature. If the act be within the power of the State, it is valid although the judgment of the court might be totally opposed to the enactment of such a law. But the question would still remain: is it within the police power of the State?, and that question must be answered by the court.

The question whether this act is valid as a labor law, pure and simple, may be dismissed in a few words. There is no reasonable ground for interfering with the liberty of person or the right of free contract by determining the hours of labor in the occupation of a baker. There is no contention that bakers as a class are not equal in intelligence and capacity to men in other trades or manual occupations, or that they are not able to assert their rights and care for themselves without the protecting arm of the State, interfering with their independence of judgment and of action. They are in no sense wards of the State. Viewed in the light of a purely labor law, with no reference whatever to the question of health, we think that a law like the one before us involves neither the safety, the morals, nor the welfare of the public, and that the interest of the public is not in the slightest degree affected by such an act. The law must be upheld, if at all, as a law pertaining to the health of the individual engaged in the occupation of a baker. It does not affect any other portion of the public than those who are engaged in that occupation. Clean and wholesome bread does not depend upon whether the baker works but ten hours per day or only sixty hours a week. The limitation of the hours of labor does not come within the police power on that ground.

It is a question of which of two powers or rights shall prevail—the power of the State to legislate or the right of the individual to liberty of person and freedom of contract. The mere assertion that the subject relates though but in a remote degree to the public health does not necessarily render the enactment valid. The act must have a more direct relation, as a means to an end, and the end itself must be appropriate and legitimate, before an act can be held to be valid which interferes with the general right of an individual to be free in his person and in his power to contract in relation to his own labor.

This case has caused much diversity of opinion in the state courts. In the Supreme Court, two of the five judges composing the Appellate Division dissented from the judgment affirming the validity of the act. In the Court of Appeals, three of the seven judges also dissented from the judgment upholding the statute. Although found in what is called a labor law of the State, the Court of Appeals has upheld the act as one relating to the public health—in other words, as a health law. One of the judges of the Court of Appeals, in upholding the law, stated that, in his opinion, the regulation in question could not be sustained unless they were able to say, from common knowledge, that working in a bakery and candy factory was an unhealthy employment. The judge held that, while the evidence was not uniform, it still led him to the conclusion that the occupation of a baker or confectioner was unhealthy, and tended to result in diseases of the respiratory organs. Three of the judges dissented from that view, and they thought the occupation of a baker was not to such an extent unhealthy as to warrant the interference of the legislature with the liberty of the individual.

We think the limit of the police power has been reached and passed in this case. There is, in our judgment, no reasonable foundation for holding this to be necessary or appropriate as a health law to safeguard the public health or the health of the individuals who are following the trade of a baker. If this statute be valid, and if, therefore, a proper case is made out in which to deny the right of an individual, *sui juris,* as employer or employee, to make contracts for the labor of the latter under the protection of the provisions of the Federal Constitution, there would seem to be no length to which legislation of this nature might not go. The case differs widely, as we have already stated, from the expressions of this court in regard to laws of this nature, as stated in *Holden v. Hardy* and *Jacobson v. Massachusetts, supra.*

We think that there can be no fair doubt that the trade of a baker, in and of itself, is not an unhealthy one to that degree which would authorize the legislature to interfere with the right to labor, and with the right of free contract on the part of the individual, either as employer or employee. In looking through statistics regarding all trades and occupations, it may be true that the trade of a baker does not appear to be as healthy as some other trades, and is also vastly more healthy than still others. To the common understanding, the trade of a baker has never been regarded as an unhealthy one. Very likely, physicians would not recommend the exercise of that or of any other trade as a remedy for ill health. Some occupations are more healthy than others, but we think there are none which might not come under the power of the legislature to supervise and control the hours of working therein if the mere fact that the occupation is not absolutely and perfectly healthy is to confer that right upon the legislative department of the Government. It might be safely affirmed that almost all occupations more or less affect the health. There must be more than the mere fact of the possible existence of some small amount of unhealthiness to warrant legislative interference with liberty. It is unfortunately true that labor, even in any department, may possibly carry with it the seeds of unhealthiness. But are we all, on that account, at the mercy of legislative majorities? A printer, a tinsmith, a locksmith, a carpenter, a cabinetmaker, a dry goods clerk, a bank's, a lawyer's or a physician's clerk, or a clerk in almost any kind of business, would all come under the power of the legislature on this assumption. No trade, no occupation, no mode of earning one's living could escape this all-pervading power, and the acts of the legislature in limiting the hours of labor in all employments would be valid although such limitation might seriously cripple the ability of the laborer to support himself and his family. In our large cities there are many buildings into which the sun penetrates for but a short time in each day, and these buildings are occupied by people carrying on the business of bankers, brokers, lawyers, real estate, and many other kinds of business, aided by many clerks, messengers, and other employs. Upon the assumption of the validity of this act under review, it is not possible to say that an act prohibiting lawyers' or bank clerks, or others from contracting to labor for their employers more than eight hours a day would be invalid. It might be said that it is unhealthy to work more than that number of hours in an apartment lighted by artificial light during the working hours of the day; that the occupation of the bank clerk, the lawyer's clerk, the real estate clerk, or the broker's clerk in such offices is therefore unhealthy, and the legislature, in its paternal wisdom, must therefore have the right to legislate on the subject of, and to limit the hours for, such labor, and, if it exercises that power and its validity be questioned, it is sufficient to say it has reference to the public health; it has reference to the health of the employees condemned to labor day after day in buildings where the sun never shines; it is a health law, and therefore it is valid, and cannot be questioned by the courts.

It is also urged, pursuing the same line of argument, that it is to the interest of the State that its population should be strong and robust, and therefore any legislation which may be said to tend to make people healthy must be valid as health laws, enacted under the police power. If this be a valid argument and a justification for this kind of legislation, it follows that the protection of the Federal Constitution from undue interference with liberty of person and freedom of contract is visionary wherever the law is sought to be justified as a valid exercise of the police power. Scarcely any law but might find shelter under such assumptions, and conduct, properly so called, as well as contract, would come under the restrictive sway of the legislature. Not only the hours of employees, but the hours of employers, could be regulated, and doctors, lawyers, scientists, all professional men, as well as athletes and artisans, could be forbidden to fatigue their brains and bodies by prolonged hours of exercise, lest the fighting strength of the State be impaired. We mention these extreme cases because the contention is extreme. We do not believe in the soundness of the views which uphold this law. On the contrary, we think that such a law as this, although passed in the assumed exercise of the police power, and as relating to the public health, or the health of the employees named, is not within that power, and is invalid. The act is not, within any fair meaning of the term, a health law, but is an illegal interference with the rights of individuals, both employers and employees, to make contracts regarding labor upon such terms as they may think best, or which they may agree upon with the other parties to such contracts. Statutes of the nature of that under review, limiting the hours in which grown and intelligent men may labor to earn their living, are mere meddlesome interferences with the rights of the individual, and they are not saved from condemnation by the claim that they are passed in the exercise of the police power and upon the subject of the health of the individual whose rights are interfered with, unless there be some fair ground, reasonable in and of itself, to say that there is material danger to the public health or to the health of the employees if the hours of labor are not curtailed. If this be not clearly the case, the individuals whose rights are thus made the subject of legislative interference are under the protection of the Federal Constitution regarding their liberty of contract as well as of person, and the legislature of the State has no power to limit their right as proposed in this statute. All that it could properly do has been done by it with regard to the conduct of bakeries, as provided for in the other sections of the act above set forth. These several sections provide for the inspection of the premises where the bakery is carried on, with regard to furnishing proper wash-rooms and water-closets, apart from the bake-room, also with regard to providing proper drainage, plumbing and painting; the sections, in addi-

tion, provide for the height of the ceiling, the cementing or tiling of floors, where necessary in the opinion of the factory inspector, and for other things of that nature; alterations are also provided for and are to be made where necessary in the opinion of the inspector, in order to comply with the provisions of the statute. These various sections may be wise and valid regulations, and they certainly go to the full extent of providing for the cleanliness and the healthiness, so far as possible, of the quarters in which bakeries are to be conducted. Adding to all these requirements a prohibition to enter into any contract of labor in a bakery for more than a certain number of hours a week is, in our judgment, so wholly beside the matter of a proper, reasonable and fair provision as to run counter to that liberty of person and of free contract provided for in the Federal Constitution.

It was further urged on the argument that restricting the hours of labor in the case of bakers was valid because it tended to cleanliness on the part of the workers, as a man was more apt to be cleanly when not overworked, and, if cleanly, then his "output" was also more likely to be so. What has already been said applies with equal force to this contention. We do not admit the reasoning to be sufficient to justify the claimed right of such interference. The State in that case would assume the position of a supervisor, or *pater familias*, over every act of the individual, and its right of governmental interference with his hours of labor, his hours of exercise, the character thereof, and the extent to which it shall be carried would be recognized and upheld. In our judgment, it is not possible, in fact, to discover the connection between the number of hours a baker may work in the bakery and the healthful quality of the bread made by the workman. The connection, if any exists, is too shadowy and thin to build any argument for the interference of the legislature. If the man works ten hours a day, it is all right, but if ten and a half or eleven, his health is in danger and his bread may be unhealthful, and, therefore, he shall not be permitted to do it. This, we think, is unreasonable, and entirely arbitrary. When assertions such as we have adverted to become necessary in order to give, if possible, a plausible foundation for the contention that the law is a "health law," it gives rise to at least a suspicion that there was some other motive dominating the legislature than the purpose to subserve the public health or welfare.

This interference on the part of the legislatures of the several States with the ordinary trades and occupations of the people seems to be on the increase. In the Supreme Court of New York, in the case of *People v. Beattie,* Appellate Division, First Department, decided in 1904, 89 N.Y.Supp. 193, a statute regulating the trade of horseshoeing, and requiring the person practicing such trade to be examined and to obtain a certificate from a board of examiners and file the same with the clerk of the county wherein the person proposes to practice his trade, was held invalid as an arbitrary interference with personal liberty and private property without due process of law. The attempt was made, unsuccessfully, to justify it as a health law.

The same kind of a statute was held invalid (*In re Aubry*) by the Supreme Court of Washington in December, 1904. 78 Pac.Rep. 900. The court held that the act deprived citizens of their liberty and property without due process of law and denied to them the equal protection of the laws. It also held that the trade of a horseshoer is not a subject of regulation under the police power of the State as a business concerning and directly affecting the health, welfare or comfort of its inhabitants, and that, therefore, a law which provided for the examination and registration of horseshoers in certain cities was unconstitutional as an illegitimate exercise of the police power.

The Supreme Court of Illinois in *Bessette v. People,* 193 Illinois 334, also held that a law of the same nature, providing for the regulation and licensing of horseshoers, was unconstitutional as an illegal interference with the liberty of the individual in adopting and pursuing such calling as he may choose, subject only to the restraint necessary secure the common welfare. *See also Godcharles v. Wigeman,* 113 Pa. St. 431, 437; *Low v. Rees Printing Co.,* 41 Nebraska 127, 145. In these cases, the courts upheld the right of free contract and the right to purchase and sell labor upon such terms as the parties may agree to.

It is impossible for us to shut our eyes to the fact that many of the laws of this character, while passed under what is claimed to be the police power for the purpose of protecting the public health or welfare, are, in reality, passed from other motives. We are justified in saying so when, from the character of the law and the subject upon which it legislates, it is apparent that the public health or welfare bears but the most remote relation to the law. The purpose of a statute must be determined from the natural and legal effect of the language employed, and whether it is or is not repugnant to the Constitution of the United States must be determined from the natural effect of such statutes when put into operation, and not from their proclaimed purpose. *Minnesota v. Barber,* 136 U. S. 313; *Brimmer v. Rebman,* 138 U. S. 78. The court looks beyond the mere letter of the law in such cases. *Yick Wo v. Hopkins,* 118 U. S. 356.

It is manifest to us that the limitation of the hours of labor as provided for in this section of the statute under which the indictment was found, and the plaintiff in error convicted, has no such direct relation to, and no such substantial effect upon, the health of the employee as to justify us in regarding the section as really a health law. It seems to us that the real object and purpose were simply to regulate the hours of labor between the master and his employees (all being men *sui juris*) in a private business, not dangerous in any degree to morals or in any real and substantial degree to the health of the employees. Under such circumstances, the freedom of master and employee to contract with each other in relation to their employment, and in defining the same, cannot be prohibited or interfered with without violating the Federal Constitution.

The judgment of the Court of Appeals of New York, as well as that of the Supreme Court and of the County Court of Oneida County, must be reversed, and the case remanded to the County Court for further proceedings not inconsistent with this opinion.

*Reversed.*

## MR. JUSTICE HOLMES dissenting

I regret sincerely that I am unable to agree with the judgment in this case, and that I think it my duty to express my dissent.

This case is decided upon an economic theory which a large part of the country does not entertain. If it were a question whether I agreed with that theory, I should desire to study it further and long before making up my mind. But I do not conceive that to be my duty, because I strongly believe that my agreement or disagreement has nothing to do with the right of a majority to embody their opinions in law. It is settled by various decisions of this court that state constitutions and state laws may regulate life in many ways which we, as legislators, might think as injudicious, or, if you like, as tyrannical, as this, and which, equally with this, interfere with the liberty to contract. Sunday laws and usury laws are ancient examples. A more modern one is the prohibition of lotteries. The liberty of the citizen to do as he likes so long as he does not interfere with the liberty of others to do the same, which has been a shibboleth for some well known writers, is interfered with by school laws, by the Post Office, by every state or municipal institution which takes his money for purposes thought desirable, whether he likes it or not. The Fourteenth Amendment does not enact Mr. Herbert Spencer's Social Statics. The other day, we sustained the Massachusetts vaccination law. *Jacobson v. Massachusetts,* 197 U. S. 11. United States and state statutes and decisions cutting down the liberty to contract by way of combination are familiar to this court. *Northern Securities Co. v. United States,* 193 U. S. 197. Two years ago, we upheld the prohibition of sales of stock on margins or for future delivery in the constitution of California. *Otis v. Parker,* 187 U. S. 606. The decision sustaining an eight hour law for miners is still recent. *Holden v. Hardy,* 169 U. S. 366. Some of these laws embody convictions or prejudices which judges are likely to share. Some may not. But a constitution is not intended to embody a particular economic theory, whether of paternalism and the organic relation of the citizen to the State or of *laissez faire.*

It is made for people of fundamentally differing views, and the accident of our finding certain opinions natural and familiar or novel and even shocking ought not to conclude our judgment upon the question whether statutes embodying them conflict with the Constitution of the United States.

General propositions do not decide concrete cases. The decision will depend on a judgment or intuition more subtle than any articulate major premise. But I think that the proposition just stated, if it is accepted, will carry us far toward the end. Every opinion tends to become a law. I think that the word liberty in the Fourteenth Amendment is perverted when it is held to prevent the natural outcome of a dominant opinion, unless it can be said that a rational and fair man necessarily would admit that the statute proposed would infringe fundamental principles as they have been understood by the traditions of our people and our law. It does not need research to show that no such sweeping condemnation can be passed upon the statute before us. A reasonable man might think it a proper measure on the score of health. Men whom I certainly could not pronounce unreasonable would uphold it as a first instalment of a general regulation of the hours of work. Whether in the latter aspect it would be open to the charge of inequality I think it unnecessary to discuss.

---

## Glossary

**due process:** the constitutional requirement that when the federal government acts in such a way that denies a citizen of a life, liberty, or property interest, the person must be given notice, the opportunity to be heard, and a decision by a neutral decision-maker

***pater familias*:** Latin for the male head of a household; implies paternalistic oversight

**police power:** the right and the duty of a government or legislative body to define proper areas to conduct lawful business

**shibboleth:** a saying used by adherents of a party, sect, or belief regarded by others as empty of real meaning

**substantive due process:** the principle that the Fifth and Fourteenth Amendments protect fundamental rights from government interference

***sui juris*:** Latin for "of age" or "independent"

# MULLER V. OREGON

| | |
|---|---|
| **DATE**<br>1908 | **CITATION**<br>208 U.S. 41 |
| **AUTHOR**<br>David J. Brewer | **SIGNIFICANCE**<br>Upheld a state law that regulated the employment of women, legitimating a view of women that supported sex discrimination and hindering the campaign for gender equality far into the twentieth century |
| **VOTE**<br>9-0 | |

## Overview

 In the late 1800s and early 1900s, political progressives pursued economic and political reforms. Many pushed hard to improve working conditions for men, women, and children laboring in shops and factories. The women's movement was pressing for the right to vote and the right to exercise autonomy in legal and economic affairs. In 1908, in *Muller v. Oregon*, the U.S. Supreme Court heard a case challenging a state law that regulated the employment of women. The Court's decision gave rise to many questions about the progressive agenda and how its goals might be best achieved.

The case arose when the owner of a laundry in Portland, Oregon, violated a state law limiting the number of hours a woman could work in his shop. The man challenged the constitutionality of this protective legislation; the direction the Supreme Court was taking in cases of this sort at the time portended a victory for the laundry owner. However, the Court, presented with a mountain of evidence demonstrating the danger to women workers of industrial practices left unregulated, unanimously upheld Oregon's law. This vic-

tory for progressives supporting worker protections thus came at a cost, as the Court's decision upholding protective legislation undermined women's rights.

## Context

Rapid industrialization and increased urbanization in the United States in the late nineteenth century inspired reform campaigns associated with the progressive movement. In the early 1900s, progressives worked to secure the health of citizens, to address the plights of workers, and to win rights for women. While many tactics were employed and many roads taken, an especially successful, if often arduous, route lay in persuading legislatures to pass laws supporting the progressive agenda. Even after legislative victory, however, a formidable obstacle remained—the U.S. Supreme Court.

A conservative majority sat on the Court during the time of this progressive movement. When called on to determine the constitutionality of laws intended to alter social conditions and economic relations, this bloc of justices consistently struck down government regulation. The Court protected the private sector and enforced its own preferred system of economic relations, the laissez-faire doctrine. The prime case in which government regulation was defeated and individual economic liberty supported was *Lochner v. New York*, decided in 1905.

In *Lochner*, the Supreme Court considered New York's law restricting bakery employees to a sixty-hour workweek. The state argued that its law was a legitimate exercise of its police power, which included the authority to protect the health, safety, and welfare of its citizens. The Court thought otherwise, however, asserting that no reasonable foundation existed for the contention that the maximum-hours regulation was necessary or appropriate for the safeguarding of the health of the bakery employees or the public. The regulation was held to interfere with the right of individuals to contract in the labor market, which the Court identified as a liberty interest protected by the Fourteenth Amendment. The Court declared New York's law unconstitutional.

In cases that followed, the Court employed the principles put forth in *Lochner* to strike down state and federal legislation that regulated economic activity. Critics of these results argued that the Supreme Court was prioritizing abstract principles and was taking no account at all of the real-world conditions, social and economic, to which regulatory legislation was responding. The Court was failing, the critics contended, to consider the impact its decisions had on society. These arguments informed the supporters of government regulation who participated in the 1908 constitutional challenge to Oregon's law restricting the number of hours women could work in a laundry.

## About the Author

The decision in *Muller v. Oregon* was unanimous, with Justice David J. Brewer writing the opinion for the Court. Born in 1837 in what is now the nation of Turkey to missionary parents, Brewer was a member of a family prominent in U.S. legal history. His uncle Stephen J. Field served on the Court from 1863 to 1897; Field's final years on the bench overlapped with Brewer's early years there. David Dudley Field, another uncle, was the

***Justice David Josiah Brewer wrote the unanimous opinion in* Muller v. Oregon.**
(Library of Congress)

driving force behind the development of the code of civil procedure, a major contribution to U.S. law. In 1890, President Benjamin Harrison appointed Brewer to the Supreme Court, where he served for 20 years. His votes consistently supported a free-market economy.

Louis D. Brandeis was not an author of the decision, but on behalf of the defendant he contributed the "Brandeis brief," for which the *Muller* case is known. Brandeis was a prominent attorney in Boston and was deeply involved in progressive and public-interest causes. When *Muller* was appealed to the Supreme Court, the National Consumers League, a pro-worker group advocating protective regulation, asked Brandeis to prepare a brief supporting Oregon's limit on working hours. Brandeis agreed on the condition that he would be the lead attorney for the Supreme Court appeal. Working closely with officials from the National Consumers League, Brandeis prepared the brief submitted to support Oregon's case. In its decision, the Court famously refers to the Brandeis brief. In 1916, President Woodrow Wilson appointed Brandeis to the Supreme Court; he served there until 1939.

## Explanation and Analysis of the Document

The first party, Curt Muller, is the "plaintiff in error"; the Oregon Supreme Court decided against Muller, and in this case he appealed that decision to the U.S. Supreme Court. The second party is the State of Oregon, which convicted and fined Muller for violating the state law that set a limit on work hours. William D. Fenton, the lead attorney for Muller, was a member of a prominent Portland law firm. His regular clients included large corporate interests. For the State of Oregon, Louis Brandeis took charge of the case upon its appeal to the U.S. Supreme Court.

The Court begins by citing the Oregon law that Muller violated. An example of protective legislation, it is quite focused. It applies only to females and only to females working in particular places of employment. It sets maximum hours for any one day but does not restrict the number of days per week a woman might work. Moreover, this law does not limit the particular time during the day when a woman may work. Some protective laws, by contrast, set maximum working hours per week and prohibited women from working at nighttime.

The Court proceeds in paragraphs 2 and 3 to cite the enforcement mechanism contained in the law. This case arose from a complaint lodged by an employee of the Portland Grand Laundry, Emma Gotcher, who stated that her supervisor had forced her to work past the ten-hour daily limit. The laundry owner, Muller, was charged, found guilty by the circuit-court judge, and fined $10, the minimum penalty. Upon appeal, the Oregon Supreme Court upheld the conviction.

Much is implied by the Court in the first sentence of paragraph 4, which begins, "The single question." The issue in this case is whether Oregon's law is consistent with the U.S. Constitution, "so far as it affects the work of a female in a laundry." The Court signals that it will construct a holding that applies only to women workers engaged in a particular kind of labor. The ruling will not go beyond the facts of the case. In the next sentence, the Court, as is customary, accepts as authority the state supreme court's ruling that the law in question is consistent with the state's constitution. In the third sentence, the Court lists the arguments underlying the appeal by Muller. His "brief" consists of the written arguments prepared by his attorneys, setting out the facts and the legal issues as perceived by them in support of their side.

The Court lists three arguments brought by Muller, each grounded in the U.S. Constitution: First, Muller argues that Oregon's statute violates the Constitution by preventing persons (women working in laundries) who are sui juris (of age and of capacity to exercise their rights) from making their own contracts (deciding on their own how many hours in a day they wish to work). The right to contract, Muller argues, is protected by the Fourteenth Amendment. The text of the Fourteenth Amendment, quoted here, does not specifically mention a "right to contract," but the Court states that the amendment's due process clause included that right in 1905 in *Lochner v. New York*. (The "right to contract" established in *Lochner* is an example of a substantive due process right.)

Second, Muller argues that Oregon's statute violates the Fourteenth Amendment's equal protection clause: "No state shall . . . deny to any person within its jurisdiction the equal protection of the laws." The class of people treated differently by the state's legislation is women, in that it restricts their right to contract.

Third, Muller argues that "the statute is not a valid exercise of the police power" retained by the states under the Constitution, permitting them to protect the health, safety, morals, and general welfare of their citizens. *Lochner* set this standard: The state may use its police powers to restrict the right to contract, but the restriction must be fair, reasonable, and appropriate; it may not be unreasonable, unnecessary, or arbitrary. Muller argues that the legitimate goals of public health, safety, and welfare are not advanced by Oregon's restriction. The state's use of its police powers, Muller posits, is unconstitutional.

The Court proceeds to recognize that Oregon law establishes legal status for women equal to men's. Common law tradition merged a woman's legal status with her husband's, effectively making her a dependent in the eyes of the law. Statutes passed by Oregon in the late 1800s extended to women legal rights denied them under common law, including, as held by the state supreme court, the right to make binding contracts.

At issue in *Muller* was whether Oregon's law limiting daily work hours for a woman employed by a laundry was consistent with the U.S. Constitution; therefore, a woman's legal equality under Oregon law did not determine the decision in this case. (Even so, the state's supreme court, which recognized that a state law insured a woman's equal right to make a binding contract, had also ruled that the maximum-hours law for women under review in this case did not violate the state's constitution.)

Paragraph 6 contains the point upon which the case turned. In Oregon, the Court writes, women are equal to men regarding the right to contract, "putting to one side the elective franchise." (The state's woman suffrage proclamation would not be signed until 1912.) In *Lochner*, a law for maximum work hours applied to men was unconstitutional. Muller urges the Court to reach the same finding here. "But this," writes the Court, "assumes that the difference between the sexes does not justify a different rule respecting a restriction of the hours of labor." The direction the Court is taking is clear: Women in Oregon have an equal right to contract, but a state's police powers may apply different protections to women than to men.

In paragraph 7 the Court states that it will note "the course of legislation, as well as expressions of opinion from other than judicial sources." The nonjudicial information taken note of by the Court is abridged in the first footnote and famously includes over one hundred pages of "facts"—including laws passed in other jurisdictions protecting women employees and the opinions of government, medical, and social work experts who, based on their observations of modern industry, concluded that long hours of labor are dangerous for women.

This "very copious collection" of facts was compiled by Louis Brandeis, attorney for Oregon, and his collaborator, Josephine Goldmark, an official with the National Consumers League. That organization was lobbying hard around the nation for protective legislation advancing the cause of workers. The regulatory laws and expert opinions that Brandeis and Goldmark assembled and submitted as a brief, intending to overwhelm the Court with facts supporting a law protecting women workers, became known as the "Brandeis brief." It won acclaim as an early and auspicious demonstration of a realist style of argument bringing to bear on judicial reasoning the real-world causes and consequences of laws and of decisions made by courts.

In paragraph 8 the Court acknowledges and tries to explain its reliance on the nontraditional sources contained in the Brandeis brief, which "may not be, technically speaking, authorities." Here, the term *authorities* refers to the established sources relied on by the Court to arrive at decisions, a venerable example being precedent established in prior cases. Though technically not authorities, says the Court, the state laws and opinions contained in the Brandeis brief "are significant of a widespread belief" that a woman's physical structure and the functions she performs justify protective legislation that restricts "the conditions under which she should be permitted to toil." The Constitution places limits on legislative action "in unchanging form"; nevertheless, a "widespread and long continued belief"—here, regarding how a woman's physical nature affects her ability to work—may influence the extent to which a constitutional limitation is applied.

The Court next states the principles of *Lochner*: The right to contract is protected by the Fourteenth Amendment, but, consistent with the Constitution, a state may restrict that right, to an extent. The question begged is, of course, to what extent may that right be restricted? The answer, the Court asserts, can be found in three prior cases: *Allgeyer v. Louisiana* (1897), in which the Court struck down a state law prohibiting the purchase of insurance from companies outside the state because the law violated the Fourteenth Amendment rights of individuals; *Holden v. Hardy* (1898), in which the Court upheld a state law setting maximum work hours for coal miners owing to the dangers of exposure to coal dust; and *Lochner v. New York* (1905), in which the Court struck down a state law setting maximum work hours for bakery employees because the restriction was unreasonable and arbitrary.

In paragraphs 10 and 11 the Court states two findings that, as of 1908, added shape to the body of constitutional law then developing around the issues of right to contract and the government's power to regulate economic activity: Equal protection is not violated by Oregon's laws treating women differently than men, and women's physical nature and maternal functions permit states to restrict their right to contract in the way Oregon has done here. The Court surrounds these holdings with extensive commentary on the limitations placed on women by their physical nature and societal role.

Women, the Court states, have a particular physical structure, and they also perform maternal functions. Up to this point, nothing about Oregon's law or its application has been associated with "maternal functions." In fact, the generalization drawn by the Court ignores the truths that all women do not have the same "physical structure" and that not all women are mothers. Nonetheless, the opinion holds that these characteristics "place her at a disadvantage in the struggle for subsistence." The Court knows that, at this time in history, most women who work are paid low wages; but the law under review is not about pay—it is about maximum-hour regulations.

The Court sharpens its portrait of women by drawing comparisons to men. Women are held to be dependent on men, who are stronger. As such, courts have always made compensations for women. Although they have gained equal rights, their dispositions and habits of life keep them from asserting those rights. The opinion reads, "She is properly placed in a class by herself, and legislation designed for her protection may be sustained, even when like legislation is not necessary for men, and could not be sustained." The Court is rejecting Muller's second argument, that Oregon's maximum-hours law for women workers denies women the equal protection of the law. A woman may be singled out by legislation, the Court holds, for the sake of her own health and for the sake of the race, which depends on the "proper discharge of her maternal functions." The Court thus cements the connection it requires between the state's power to protect the health and safety of its citizens and its restriction on the number of hours women may work.

In paragraph 12 the Court notes for the second time that women are not able to vote in Oregon. Women's suffrage was a hotly debated issue throughout the country and would result four years later in the establishment of woman's right to vote in Oregon and a dozen years later in the Nineteenth Amendment to the U.S. Constitution, which nationalized suffrage for women. The Court states that its decision that Oregon may restrict working hours for women, even when a restriction on men would not stand, does not depend on Oregon's denial to women of the right to vote. "The reason runs deeper," the Court states, "and rests in the inherent difference between the two sexes."

In closing, the Court confirms that its decision in *Muller* is not to be extended past the facts of the case:

Oregon's protective legislation does not violate the Constitution "so far as it respects the work of a female in a laundry." The decision in *Muller* does not challenge "in any respect" the decision in *Lochner*.

## Impact

The Court cabined, or kept narrow, its holding in *Muller*, but the long-term impacts of the decision were profound and far reaching. These effects traveled in two distinct directions. Along one path, *Muller* legitimated consideration by the Supreme Court of real-world conditions, as demonstrated in facts supplied by experts and scientists, when giving shape to the law. Along another path, *Muller* legitimated a view of women that supported sex discrimination, thus blocking or hindering the campaign for gender equality far into the twentieth century.

Predictably, the persuasive power of the Brandeis brief in *Muller* generated reliance on the same strategy in later cases. In state and federal courts alike, lawyers defending protective restrictions on economic activity compiled studies and statistics to bolster their cases. A high mark for sheer volume was achieved with the brief of over 1,000 pages prepared, again by Brandeis and Goldmark, to support a maximum-working-hours law for manufacturing employees, which was passed by the Oregon legislature in 1913 and promptly challenged in court. By 1917, when *Bunting v. Oregon* reached the Supreme Court, Brandeis had been appointed to a seat there. He recused himself from the case, which resulted in a 5–3 decision to uphold Oregon's restriction on the right to contract. Brandeis's selection to the Court signaled the respect given to the idea that factual studies of real-world conditions merited consideration by courts. The approach has played a role in many cases since, including the landmark decision in *Brown v. Board of Education* (1954). There, the Court struck down separate-but-equal educational facilities for different racial groups, stating its reliance on "modern authority," including psychological and sociological studies (*Brown v. Board of Education*, 47 U.S. 483 [1954]).

In *Muller*, the Court justified Oregon's restriction on the right to contract by linking the state's protective regulation to cited characteristics of women workers emphasizing their relative weakness and their difference from men workers. Much of the Court's description of women in this vein was gratuitous. Observations on the weakness of women were iterated and then reiterated. A woman's "physical structure" and her "maternal functions," it was argued, justify the diminishing of her rights. The Court's view of women in the workplace did not arise solely from the Brandeis brief. The historian Nancy Woloch remarks, "Leaving the 'facts' of the Brandeis brief behind, [Justice] Brewer presented a timeless portrait of the 'dependent women' " (p. 38). One might easily imagine that the Brandeis brief supplied the Court (particularly Brewer, who wrote for the Court) with facts used to support opinions about women already held.

The decision in *Muller* marked an important step in the evolution of the law during the first four decades of the twentieth century regarding when government regulation may interfere with the right to contract. The case also stitched into the law a retro-view of women, as embodied in prior legal discourse, that equal rights advocates were fighting to change at the time the decision was announced. With respect to the decision in *Muller*, Kirp, Yudof, and Franks write, "This description of 'dependent' woman has its obvious antecedents in rationales for earlier common law paternalism. Women won their maximum-hours laws, but only because they could be described in a way which rendered such special treatment permissible, even laudable" (p. 38). Thus, the *Muller* decision and the Court's recognition of the Brandeis brief—victories for progressives campaigning for protective workplace measures—were at the same time defeats for progressives campaigning for women's equal rights. The view adopted in *Muller* that a particular characterization of women could form the basis for laws treating them unequally survived a long time. "For more than sixty years," writes political scientist Judith Baer, "courts upheld nearly all cases of sex discrimination, citing this case as binding precedent, following its lead in emphasizing permanent rather than temporary, physical rather than economic or social, aspects of women's condition" (pp. 66–67).

## Questions for Further Study

1. In paragraph 9, the Court discusses how it is using legislation and opinions supplied in the Brandeis brief. These are not authorities typically relied on, and they do not address the case's constitutional question. Rather, they are "significant of a widespread belief" about a woman's structure and function. Untangle the rest of what the Court says in this paragraph and answer these questions: Is the Court relying on the facts presented in the Brandeis brief or on widespread belief derived from those facts? Is there a difference? Why?

2. Progressive organizations like the National Consumers League, whose official Josephine Goldmark played a key role in constructing the Brandeis brief, supported Oregon's 1903 law setting maximum workday hours for women in laundries and like establishments as a beginning step toward the larger goal of legislation protecting all workers in all industries. Use what the Court wrote to answer these questions: In what ways did the opinion in Muller support this agenda? In what ways did the opinion undermine this agenda? Overall, did the opinion support or undermine this agenda?

3. In paragraphs 11 and 12, the Court explains how Oregon's restriction on the right to contract legitimately relates to its power to protect the health, safety, and welfare of its citizens. Could the Court have written these passages in a way that would not have limited, or would have put fewer limits on, a woman's rights? Can you rewrite these passages to achieve those aims?

4. Consider *Muller v. Oregon* (upholding a maximum-hours law) in light of *Lochner v. New York* (striking down a maximum-hours law). Was the connection between a state's police powers and its regulation of workers better established in *Muller* than in *Lochner*? (Look especially at Justice John Marshall Harlan's dissent in Lochner.) Was the restriction placed on the right to contract by New York's law different than the restriction created by Oregon's law?

## Further Reading

### Books

Baer, Judith A. *The Chains of Protection: The Judicial Response to Women's Labor Legislation.* Westport, CT: Greenwood Press, 1978.

Bartlett, Katharine T., Deborah L. Rhode, and Joanna L. Grossman. *Gender and Law: Theory, Doctrine, Commentary.* Alphen aan den Rijn, Netherlands: Wolters Kluwer Law & Business, 2016.

Kirp, David L., Mark G. Yudof, and Marlene Strong Franks. *Gender Justice.* Chicago: University of Chicago Press, 1986.

Mason, Alpheus Thomas. "The Case of the Overworked Laundress." In *Quarrels That Have Shaped the Constitution,* ed. John A. Garraty. New York: Harper & Row, 1964.

Rhode, Deborah L. *Justice and Gender: Sex Discrimination and the Law.* Cambridge, MA: Harvard University Press, 1989.

Sklar, Kathryn Kish. "Why Were Most Politically Active Women Opposed to the ERA in the 1920s?" In *Rights of Passage: The Past and Future of the ERA,* ed. Joan Hoff-Wilson. Bloomington: Indiana University Press, 1986.

Urofsky, Melvin I. *Louis D. Brandeis and the Progressive Tradition.* Boston: Little, Brown, 1981.

Woloch, Nancy. *Muller v. Oregon: A Brief History with Documents.* Boston: Bedford/St. Martin's, 1996.

### Articles

Calabresi, Steven G., and Julia T. Rickert. "Originalism and Sex Discrimination." *Texas Law Review* 90, no. 1 (2011): 1–101.

Erickson, Nancy S. "Muller v. Oregon Reconsidered: The Origins of a Sex-Based Doctrine of Liberty of Contract." *Labor History* 30, no. 2 (1989): 228–250.

Zimmerman, Joan G. "The Jurisprudence of Equality: The Women's Minimum Wage, the First Equal Rights Amendment, and Adkins v. Children's Hospital, 1905–1923." *Journal of American History* 78, no. 1 (1991): 188–225.

### Websites

"Muller v. Oregon (Supreme Court upholds maximum hour law), February 24, 1908." Women Working, 1800–1930, Harvard University Library website. Accessed April 12, 2023. http://ocp.hul.harvard.edu/ww/events_muller.html.

—Commentary by Randy Wagner

# MULLER V. OREGON

## Document Text

### Mr. Justice Brewer Delivered the Opinion of the Court

On February 19, 1903, the legislature of the state of Oregon passed an act (Session Laws 1903, p. 148) the first section of which is in these words:

> Sec. 1. That no female (shall) be employed in any mechanical establishment, or factory, or laundry in this state more than ten hours during any one day. The hours of work may be so arranged as to permit the employment of females at any time so that they shall not work more than ten hours during the twenty-four hours of any one day.

Sec. 3 made a violation of the provisions of the prior sections a misdemeanor subject to a fine of not less than $10 nor more than $25. On September 18, 1905, an information was filed in the circuit court of the state for the county of Multnomah, charging that the defendant "on the 4th day of September, A. D. 1905, in the county of Multnomah and state of Oregon, then and there being the owner of a laundry, known as the Grand Laundry, in the city of Portland, and the employer of females therein, did then and there unlawfully permit and suffer one Joe Haselbock, he, the said Joe Haselbock, then and there being an overseer, superintendent, and agent of said Curt Muller, in the said Grand Laundry, to require a female, to wit, one Mrs. E. Gotcher, to work more than ten hours in said laundry on said 4th day of September, A. D. 1905, contrary to the statutes in such cases made and provided, and against the peace and dignity of the state of Oregon."

A trial resulted in a verdict against the defendant, who was sentenced to pay a fine of $10. The supreme court of the state affirmed the conviction (48 Or. 252, 85 Pac. 855), whereupon the case was brought here on writ of error.

The single question is the constitutionality of the statute under which the defendant was convicted, so far as it affects the work of a female in a laundry. That it does not conflict with any provisions of the state Constitution is settled by the decision of the supreme court of the state. The contentions of the defendant, now plaintiff in error, are thus stated in his brief:

> (1) Because the statute attempts to prevent persons sui juris from making their own contracts, and thus violates the provisions of the 14th Amendment, as follows:

No state shall make or enforce any law which shall abridge the privileges or immunities of citizens of the United States; nor shall any state deprive any person of life, liberty, or property, without due process of law; nor deny to any person within its jurisdiction the equal protection of the laws.

(2) Because the statute does not apply equally to all persons similarly situated, and is class legislation.

(3) The statute is not a valid exercise of the police power. The kinds of work prescribed are not unlawful, nor are they declared to be immoral or dangerous to the public health; nor can such a law be sustained on the ground that it is designed to protect women on account of their sex. There is no necessary or reasonable

connection between the limitation prescribed by the act and the public health, safety, or welfare.

It is the law of Oregon that women, whether married or single, have equal contractual and personal rights with men. As said by Chief Justice Wolverton, in *First Nat. Bank v. Leonard*, 36 Or. 390, 396, 59 Pac. 873, 874, after a review of the various statutes of the state upon the subject:

> We may therefore say with perfect confidence that, with these three sections upon the statute book, the wife can deal, not only with her separate property, acquired from whatever source, in the same manner as her husband can with property belonging to him, but that she may make contracts and incur liabilities, and the same may be enforced against her, the same as if she were a feme sole. There is now no residuum of civil disability resting upon her which is not recognized as existing against the husband. The current runs steadily and strongly in the direction of the emancipation of the wife, and the policy, as disclosed by all recent legislation upon the subject in this state, is to place her upon the same footing as if she were a feme sole, not only with respect to her separate property, but as it affects her right to make binding contracts; and the most natural corollary to the situation is that the remedies for the enforcement of liabilities incurred are made coextensive and coequal with such enlarged conditions.

It thus appears that, putting to one side the elective franchise, in the matter of personal and contractual rights they stand on the same plane as the other sex. Their rights in these respects can no more be infringed than the equal rights of their brothers. We held in *Lochner v. New York*, 198 U.S. 45 , 49 L. ed. 937, 25 Sup. Ct. Rep. 539, that a law providing that no laborer shall be required or permitted to work in bakeries more than sixty hours in a week or ten hours in a day was not as to men a legitimate exercise of the police power of the state, but an unreasonable, unnecessary, and arbitrary interference with the right and liberty of the individual to contract in relation to his labor, and as such was in conflict with, and void under, the Federal Constitution. That decision is invoked by plaintiff in error as decisive of the question before us. But this assumes that the dif-

ference between the sexes does not justify a different rule respecting a restriction of the hours of labor.

In patent cases counsel are apt to open the argument with a discussion of the state of the art. It may not be amiss, in the present case, before examining the constitutional question, to notice the course of legislation, as well as expressions of opinion from other than judicial sources. In the brief filed by Mr. Louis D. Brandeis for the defendant in error is a very copious collection of all these matters, an epitome of which is found in the margin. While there have been but few decisions bearing directly upon the question, the following sustain the constitutionality of such legislation: *Com. v. Hamilton Mfg. Co.* 120 Mass. 383; *Wenham v. State*, 65 Neb. 394, 400, 406, 58 L.R.A. 825, 91 N. W. 421; *State v. Buchanan*, 29 Wash. 602, 59 L.R. A. 342, 92 Am. St. Rep. 930, 70 Pac. 52; *Com. v. Beatty*, 15 Pa. Super. Ct. 5, 17; against them is the case of *Ritchie v. People*, 155 Ill. 98, 29 L.R. A. 79, 46 Am. St. Rep. 315, 40 N. E. 454.

The legislation and opinions referred to in the margin may not be, technically speaking, authorities, and in them is little or no discussion of the constitutional question presented to us for determination, yet they are significant of a widespread belief that woman's physical structure, and the functions she performs in consequence thereof, justify special legislation restricting or qualifying the conditions under which she should be permitted to toil. Constitutional questions, it is true, are not settled by even a consensus of present public opinion, for it is the peculiar value of a written constitution that it places in unchanging form limitations upon legislative action, and thus gives a permanence and stability to popular government which otherwise would be lacking. At the same time, when a question of fact is debated and debatable, and the extent to which a special constitutional limitation goes is affected by the truth in respect to that fact, a widespread and long continued belief concerning it is worthy of consideration. We take judicial cognizance of all matters of general knowledge.

It is undoubtedly true, as more than once declared by this court, that the general right to contract in relation to one's business is part of the liberty of the individual, protected by the 14th Amendment to the Federal Constitution; yet it is equally well settled that this liberty is not absolute and extending to all contracts, and that a state may, without conflicting with the provisions of the 14th Amendment, restrict in many respects the individual's power of contract. Without stopping to discuss at length the extent to which a state may act in this respect, we refer to the following cases in which the question has been considered: *Allgeyer v. Louisiana*, 165 U.S. 578 , 41 L. ed. 832, 17 Sup. Ct. Rep. 427; *Holden v. Hardy*, 169 U.S. 366 , 42 L. ed. 780, 18 Sup. Ct. Rep. 383; *Lochner v. New York*, supra.

That woman's physical structure and the performance of maternal functions place her at a disadvantage in the struggle for subsistence is obvious. This is especially true when the burdens of motherhood are upon her. Even when they are not, by abundant testimony of the medical fraternity continuance for a long time on her feet at work, repeating this from day to day, tends to injurious effects upon the body, and, as healthy mothers are essential to vigorous offspring, the physical well-being of woman becomes an object of public interest and care in order to preserve the strength and vigor of the race.

Still again, history discloses the fact that woman has always been dependent upon man. He established his control at the outset by superior physical strength, may, without conflicting with the provisions and this control in various forms, with diminishing intensity, has continued to the present. As minors, thought not to the same extent, she has been looked upon in the courts as needing especial care that her rights may be preserved. Education was long denied her, and while now the doors of the schoolroom are opened and her opportunities for acquiring knowledge are great, yet even with that and the consequent increase of capacity for business affairs it is still true that in the struggle for subsistence she is not an equal competitor with her brother. Though limitations upon personal and contractual rights may be removed by legislation, there is that in her disposition and habits of life which will operate against a full assertion of those rights. She will still be where some legislation to protect her seems necessary to secure a real equality of right. Doubtless there are individual exceptions, and there are many respects in which she has an advantage over him; but looking at it from the viewpoint of the effort to maintain an independent position in life, she is not upon an equality. Differentiated by these matters from the other sex, she is properly placed in a class by herself, and legislation designed for her protection may be sustained, even when like legislation is not necessary for men, and could not be sustained. It is impossible to close one's eyes to the fact that she still looks to her brother and depends upon him. Even though all restrictions on political, personal, and contractual rights were taken away, and she stood, so far as statutes are concerned, upon an absolutely equal plane with him, it would still be true that she is so constituted that she will rest upon and look to him for protection; that her physical structure and a proper discharge of her maternal functions—having in view not merely her own health, but the well-being of the race—justify legislation to protect her from the greed as well as the passion of man. The limitations which this statute places upon her contractual powers, upon her right to agree with her employer as to the time she shall labor, are not imposed solely for her benefit, but also largely for the benefit of all. Many words cannot make this plainer. The two sexes differ in structure of body, in the functions to be performed by each, in the amount of physical strength, in the capacity for long continued labor, particularly when done standing, the influence of vigorous health upon the future well-being of the race, the self-reliance which enables one to assert full rights, and in the capacity to maintain the struggle for subsistence. This difference justifies a difference in legislation, and upholds that which is designed to compensate for some of the burdens which rest upon her.

We have not referred in this discussion to the denial of the elective franchise in the state of Oregon, for while that may disclose a lack of political equality in all things with her brother, that is not of itself decisive. The reason runs deeper, and rests in the inherent difference between the two sexes, and in the different functions in life which they perform.

For these reasons, and without questioning in any respect the decision in *Lochner v. New York*, we are of the opinion that it cannot be adjudged that the act in question is in conflict with the Federal Constitution, so far as it respects the work of a female in a laundry, and the judgment of the Supreme Court of Oregon is affirmed.

## Glossary

*feme sole*: in the English-American common law tradition, an unmarried woman in charge of her separate estate and against whom legal obligations are enforceable; the term is of French origin

**epitome:** an abstract account of a longer text

**sui juris:** of age and capacity to take full possession of one's rights